PERSPECTIVES ON FAMILY COMMUNICATION

Fourth Edition

Lynn H. Turner

Marquette University

Richard West

Emerson College

Connect
Learn
Succeed™

Connect
Learn
Succeed™

PERSPECTIVES ON FAMILY COMMUNICATION, FOURTH EDITION

Published by McGraw-Hill, a business unit of The McGraw-Hill Companies, Inc., 1221 Avenue of the Americas, New York, NY, 10020. Copyright © 2013 by The McGraw-Hill Companies, Inc. All rights reserved. Printed in the United States of America. Previous editions © 2006. No part of this publication may be reproduced or distributed in any form or by any means, or stored in a database or retrieval system, without the prior written consent of The McGraw-Hill Companies, Inc., including, but not limited to, in any network or other electronic storage or transmission, or broadcast for distance learning.

Some ancillaries, including electronic and print components, may not be available to customers outside the United States.

This book is printed on acid-free paper.

1 2 3 4 5 6 7 8 9 0 DOC/DOC 1 0 9 8 7 6 5 4 3 2

ISBN 978-0-07-3406824
MHID 0-07-3406821

Vice President & General Manager: *Michael Ryan*
Managing Director: *David Patterson*
Executive Director of Development: *Lisa Pinto*
Brand Manager: *Susan Gouijnstook*
Developmental Editor: *Penina Braffman*
Marketing Specialist: *Alexandra Schultz*
Editorial Coordinator: *Adina Lonn*
Project Manager: *Judi David*
Buyer: *Laura Fuller*
Media Project Manager: *Sridevi Palani*
Cover Designer: *Studio Montage, St. Louis, MO*
Typeface: *10/12 Sabon*
Compositor: *Cenveo Publisher Services*
Printer: *R. R. Donnelley*

Credits: The credits section for this book begins on page C–1 and is considered an extension of the copyright page.

Library of Congress Cataloging-in-Publication Data

Turner, Lynn H.
   Perspectives on family communication / Lynn H. Turner, Richard West.—4th ed.
      p. cm.
   ISBN 978-0-07-340682-4 (alk. paper)
   1. Communication in families.   2. Families.   I. West, Richard L.   II. Title.

HQ734.T915   2013
306.85—dc23   2012027840

The Internet addresses listed in the text were accurate at the time of publication. The inclusion of a Web site does not indicate an endorsement by the authors or McGraw-Hill, and McGraw-Hill does not guarantee the accuracy of the information presented at these sites.

www.mhhe.com

To those who teach us about family communication:
Our families, our mentors, our friends,
and our students—your lessons endure.
. . . And especially for my parents—whose memory I cherish.
They mean family to me. (Lynn)
. . . And especially for my mother—my best friend. (Richard)

Contents

Preface

The fourth edition of *Perspectives of Family Communication* represents our ongoing commitment to a quickly evolving field of study and an area that is of more than professional interest to us both. Everyone has extensive personal experience with family interactions of some sort. At times our encounters with our families bring us painful challenges; other times they bring us intense joy. Because of these powerful experiences, we are motivated to understand the communication dynamics within our families. For over 30 years, family communication research has flourished, and classes on family communication have proliferated. The area of family communication has a journal devoted to academic studies on the topic, *Journal of Family Communication* (Routledge), and a thriving presence at national and regional conventions.

Our purpose in writing this book is to celebrate the breadth and depth of scholarship on the family within the field of communication. In the past, communication students and researchers had to depend on research from our colleagues in psychology, sociology, and family studies. Although we still find that some of this research informs our understanding of the family, growth in our own field now allows us to place communication at the center of our investigation of families. Thus this edition of *Perspectives on Family Communication* reflects the most current scholarship in the communication discipline. We were gratified and excited in preparing the fourth edition to review the large body of research on the topic of family communication. In the relatively short time since beginning the first edition and completing this one, we have been impressed with the explosion of research in this area.

In this text, we have never prescribed antidotes for family ills, nor do we believe this is appropriate. Although an understanding of family communication dynamics can promote improved family relations, we do not believe it does so in the simple formulation some popular self-help books advocate. The complexities of family communication defy such prescriptions. We suggest that the material in this book should be read with a questioning attitude. While we do not necessarily have all the answers, exploring vital questions helps us move toward conclusions.

GOALS OF THIS BOOK

When we originally wrote this text, we had three major goals: (1) to provide a consistent communication focus in viewing family life, (2) to demonstrate the utility of applying theoretical frameworks to questions about family communication, and (3) to broaden the definition of family. In the second edition, we added a fourth goal: to examine the impacts of technology on family communication. In the third edition, we tried to keep all these goals in mind while working even harder to make our writing accessible and encouraging students to engage in critical thinking while reading the material. For this edition, all these goals remain, with a renewed dedication to making our perspectives as current as possible, drawing on recent family communication research as well as the popular press, where appropriate. In fulfilling our first goal, to provide a consistent communication focus in viewing family life, we worked to help students understand how this perspective differs from the way other disciplines approach the family. Students will find the communication perspective embedded within each chapter. Everything we discuss, from our consideration of types of families in Chapter 1 to our conclusions in Chapter 10, is related to communication behavior. Further, interaction and language are primary concerns throughout the book.

We worked toward our second goal, to illustrate how theoretical frameworks enrich our understanding of family communication, by devoting an entire chapter to theoretical thinking about the family. In Chapter 2 we lay out several theoretical structures—systems theory, social construction, developmental theory, and dialectics—that often inform family communication research. Further, throughout the book we emphasize how theoretical thinking maximizes our ability to capture the complexities of family interactions. For example, in Chapter 5 we discuss how dialectics, social exchange, attachment theory, and the Circumplex Model help us understand the expression of intimacy among family members.

In our efforts to broaden the definition of family, our third goal, we spend a great deal of time in Chapter 1 discussing some of the variety that can come under the umbrella of family. We craft a definition that includes multiple family types. We do this because we recognize that, while students bring a wealth of family communication experience to this class, their experiences necessarily are drawn from a limited number of family types. Few people have intimate knowledge of families other than those in which they have lived. We provide examples and research pertaining to a wide range of family types in an effort to help students expand their understanding of family interactions. Additionally, we are mindful that families exist in myriad cultures. We therefore include examples from a wide variety of cultures and co-cultures. Our goal is to illustrate the effects that culture may have on communication practices within the family. When we speak about cultural variety in the text, we necessarily generalize about cultural customs and behaviors. These generalizations have to be read with the acknowledgment that they do not apply to every member of the group. We try to balance sensitivity to differences with a desire to draw conclusions.

In working toward our fourth goal, we draw students' attention to the fascinating ways that technology interfaces with family communication.

We want students to reflect on the potential strengths and connections technology may bring to family life, as well as some of the dangers technology may pose for family interaction. Wherever possible, we included research examining technology's interface with family communication. Finally, we tested our new material and examples in our own classes to get feedback on our writing, making changes where necessary. We revised the questions at the end of each chapter with an eye toward developing critical thinking about the material.

FEATURES

To accomplish our goals we have incorporated the following features that make this book especially appealing to students:

- Examination of the family from a communication perspective. Toward this end, we have drawn our research examples extensively from communication scholars.
- Inclusive definition of family and examples drawn from a wide range of cultures and co-cultures.
- Chapter opening vignettes. Each chapter begins with three short scenarios featuring a diverse range of family types. We refer to these three family scenarios to illustrate points we make in the chapter.
- Student perspectives. Students' personal experiences and comments about family communication issues are presented in boxes throughout the chapters. We changed students' names to preserve their privacy. We invite students to use these commentaries to reflect on both the subject matter and their own experiences. In this revised edition, we have incorporated a number of new student voices.
- Attention to co-cultures. We have made a significant effort to address the myriad co-cultures in the United States. We therefore include a number of research conclusions and examples pertaining to families of a variety of races, ethnicities, religions, and sexual identities. We also address homeless families in our discussions.
- Questions for reflection. At the end of each chapter we provide a series of questions geared to stimulate student thinking about the material presented. The questions may also be used as class discussion starters and guides. We have included many new discussion questions throughout the new edition.
- Glossary. Each chapter includes a list of key terms. When we first mention these key terms in the text, they appear in boldface. At the end of the book, they are all listed and defined in the glossary.

New to this Edition

- A comprehensive reorganization of the overall chapter structure of the book to reflect the way teachers and students approach the course.
- New insights and coverage into the relationship between family communication and the media.
- Additional coverage of how culture and diversity influence families.
- The latest information on social, health, and demographic trends affecting family communication, including divorce, breast cancer, spirituality, and homelessness.
- New material on the family–work interface, immigration, and same-sex marriage.
- Integration of popular press perspectives related to family life.

ACKNOWLEDGMENTS

Any book owes its existence to efforts made by others in addition to the listed authors, and some people who have helped with this book may not even realize the debt we acknowledge here. We would like to thank all those who have helped us as we worked on this project. First, our own families contributed in ways both large and small to the book's creation. For providing us with daily object lessons and a variety of examples of communication and family life, we cannot thank them enough.

Additionally, we owe a great deal to the students who have enrolled in our family communication classes over the years, providing us with their insights and expanding our own knowledge about this topic. Our students have contributed greatly to our thinking about family communication. First, we have quoted many of their specific comments. We chose comments reflecting how the communication principles we discuss related to students' life experiences. Second, we have drawn on our past interactions with students to inspire us to write with clarity and purpose.

Further, our chosen family of friends and colleagues have helped with this project in many ways. We wish to acknowledge Marquette University and Emerson College. Both provided support and funding, which allowed us to finish the fourth edition. We are grateful for the secretarial help, the research assistance, and the general climate of support for our endeavors at both our institutions.

We thank the team at McGraw-Hill for working with us so well to produce a high-quality book. McGraw-Hill's attention to detail and concern for the quality of the product has sustained us throughout and has been a joy to us. We thank our book team: Penina Braffman, developmental editor, whose help has been invaluable; Leslie Oberhuber, marketing manager; Judi David, project manager; designer, production supervisor, and photo researcher. Of course, we owe our greatest thanks to our editor. Finally, we thank the reviewers who gave their time and expertise to improve our efforts. Their careful reading and insightful suggestions expanded and clarified our thinking in many significant ways. We benefited from the comments they shared, often based on their use of the book in their classes. The flaws in the book are our own, but the strengths were greatly enhanced by the following reviewers:

Alicia Alexander,
Southern Illinois University Edwardsville

Trish Amason,
University of Arkansas

Gerald Driskill,
University of Arkansas at Little Rock

Vickie Ellis,
Oklahoma Baptist University

Jacki Fitzpatrick,
Texas Tech University

Paulette Grotrian,
Washtenaw Community College

Meredith Harrigan,
SUNY Geneseo

Marceline Thompson-Hayes,
Arkansas State University

Theresa Hest,
Minnesota State University Moorhead

Jennifer Heisler,
Oakland University

Brian Heisterkamp,
CSU San Bernardino

Diane Tobin Johnson,
Truman State University

Emily Langan,
Wheaton College

Kristin Lindholm,
Trinity International University

Diana Karol-Nagy,
University of Florida

Lori Roscoe,
University of South Florida

Erin Sahlstein,
University of Nevada-Las Vegas

Deborah Shelley,
University of Houston-Downtown

Jerry Thomas,
Lindsey Wilson College

Lindsay Timmerman,
University of Wisconsin-Milwaukee

Kandi Walker,
University of Louisville

To the Student

Our society is rapidly redefining what it means to be a family. As you take this course and listen to classmates' contributions, you may hear from people who come from large families, small families, families that include grandparents, adopted children, and special friends. You may hear individuals speak about their stay-at-home fathers, their two mothers, or their aunts who raised them. Some may speak of divorces and reconfigured families. As you will learn in this class, families are rich in their diversity, and family communication may vary in different types of families.

We encourage you to keep an open mind as you read this text. Some of what you encounter will sound familiar. Other material may not apply to your own family at all. As you read about different families, keep in mind that there really is no such thing as a typical family in the United States, in any meaningful way. Yet while families differ greatly, some communication practices and processes do resonate across diverse families, giving us insight into what unites many families. As you take this course, we ask that you cultivate a healthy tension between what sets families apart from one another and what ties them together.

Although we realize we will not meet most of you in person, we tried to imagine you reading this text as we were writing it, and we thought you might wish to know something about us as people and as family members while you read what we have written. Our stories are different from one another's (and, no doubt, from your own). As such, they provide a beginning look at the diversity of family experience that we try to introduce throughout the text.

One of the authors, Lynn Turner, grew up in a white, middle-class nuclear family in suburban Chicago. Her family consisted of two parents, Jerry and Roberta, and one younger brother, Scott. Her father worked full-time, and her mom stayed at home to care for the children. Her parents were each the elder of two children, and Lynn's aunts, uncles, and cousins all lived nearby as she was growing up. In fact, one of her aunts and her family lived next door to Lynn's family for most of her growing-up years. Lynn met and married Ted while they were both in college at the University of Iowa.

Ted's family-of-origin was much different from Lynn's. He grew up in rural Iowa and had four younger sisters. His mother was employed for most of her life, and his father managed the family farmland. Ted had aunts and uncles spread out from New Zealand to New York. He also had been married before and had two children. Together, Lynn and Ted had one more child.

Their blended family, which provides so much of what interests Lynn in family communication issues, keeps expanding. Lynn and Ted now have six grandchildren.

The other author, Rich West, is also from the Midwest. His background in a small town in central Illinois was rather traditional. He is the fourth of five children, and for many years before going to work full-time, his mother worked at home while his father was employed as a steel factory customer service representative. Rich's influences regarding family life come from his mother, Beverly, and his grandmothers, Lucille and Helen. The three women provided a network of love, support, and unconditional acceptance.

Rich also shares his private life with Chris, who provides him with an important nurturance found in special families.

The authors met each other at a communication conference over 30 years ago. We were drawn to each other because of our common interests in family communication and gender and communication, and because of our common senses of humor. Our collaborations on this book and on other work have intensified our personal and professional bond. We continue to learn from each other as we write together and evolve as students and teachers of family communication. We both believe that much of the enduring charm of this discipline rests in continued discoveries and ever developing understandings of communication. We hope that as you read this book, you participate with us in creating your own insights about family communication.

Chapter
1

PROVIDING DEFINITIONS

Family Culture

Defining the Family

Self-Definitions of Family • Definition Through Interaction
Voluntary and Involuntary Ties • Creation of Boundaries
Evolving Time

Family Communication Perspective

Defining Communication • Axioms of Communication

Cultural and Demographic Trends Affecting the Family

From Tradition to Transition: Family Types in the United States

Family-of-Origin, Intergenerationality, and Family Genograms
Nuclear Families • Gay and Lesbian Families • Extended Families
Stepfamilies • Single-Parent Families • Couples
Marital and Family Typologies

Summary

Key Terms

Questions for Reflection

THE BARKER FAMILY

Paula and Evan Barker live in a small suburban neighborhood near Omaha, Nebraska. They have one child, Alex, whom they adopted from an orphanage in Cambodia. They saved for years to pay for the trip and to pay the orphanage. Paula Barker is a substitute teacher who took a professional leave after Alex arrived in the United States. Evan is a freelance journalist who writes for a number of publications in the Omaha area. The Barkers are neither wealthy nor impoverished. Although Paula and Evan have little conflict, lately, because of the adoption, they have been going through a tough time making ends meet. Their financial situation has caused quite a bit of friction in the family. Evan has told Paula that she needs to go back to work, and Paula is insistent on staying at home until Alex can go to school. Evan's pay is insufficient to pay the rent and utilities, buy groceries, keep the car functioning, and have enough left for unforeseen expenses brought on by adopting Alex. Both are very careful not to argue in front of their son. When they do sense an argument coming, Paula stares intently at Evan, and the two go to another room. They try their best to keep things moving along despite their financial problems.

THE ROBINSON FAMILY

Willard Robinson and his wife, Rachel, live with their two children, Taylor and Lindsay, in a two-bedroom apartment in Dallas. Both Taylor, age 12, and Lindsay, age 7, are from Willard's and Rachel's previous marriages. The four generally get along with one another, although there are frequent blow-ups over using the one bathroom in the apartment. Because both parents work, the kids are often left by themselves after school for a few hours. Although neither Willard nor Rachel like having the girls in the apartment by themselves, they know that it is the only way they can both work. Willard's parents are both deceased, and Rachel's mom lives over 100 miles away. A babysitter is out of the question because of the cost. So, each day after school, the girls come home, grab a snack from the refrigerator, and sit and watch either a movie or one of the "kids' stations" found on television. Once Willard and Rachel get home, the family tries to have dinner together each night. Privately, the parents wish that another arrangement could be financially possible.

THE ORTIZ-DELGADO FAMILY

Five-year-old Luisa is the child of Karen Ortiz and Julien Delgado. The family lives in Miami. Karen and Julien are lesbians in a committed relationship with each other, and they are each mothers for Luisa. Both women desired children. After six years together, the couple decided that they wanted

Chapter
1

PROVIDING DEFINITIONS

Family Culture

Defining the Family

Self-Definitions of Family • Definition Through Interaction

Voluntary and Involuntary Ties • Creation of Boundaries

Evolving Time

Family Communication Perspective

Defining Communication • Axioms of Communication

Cultural and Demographic Trends Affecting the Family

From Tradition to Transition: Family Types in the United States

Family-of-Origin, Intergenerationality, and Family Genograms

Nuclear Families • Gay and Lesbian Families • Extended Families

Stepfamilies • Single-Parent Families • Couples

Marital and Family Typologies

Summary

Key Terms

Questions for Reflection

THE BARKER FAMILY

Paula and Evan Barker live in a small suburban neighborhood near Omaha, Nebraska. They have one child, Alex, whom they adopted from an orphanage in Cambodia. They saved for years to pay for the trip and to pay the orphanage. Paula Barker is a substitute teacher who took a professional leave after Alex arrived in the United States. Evan is a freelance journalist who writes for a number of publications in the Omaha area. The Barkers are neither wealthy nor impoverished. Although Paula and Evan have little conflict, lately, because of the adoption, they have been going through a tough time making ends meet. Their financial situation has caused quite a bit of friction in the family. Evan has told Paula that she needs to go back to work, and Paula is insistent on staying at home until Alex can go to school. Evan's pay is insufficient to pay the rent and utilities, buy groceries, keep the car functioning, and have enough left for unforeseen expenses brought on by adopting Alex. Both are very careful not to argue in front of their son. When they do sense an argument coming, Paula stares intently at Evan, and the two go to another room. They try their best to keep things moving along despite their financial problems.

THE ROBINSON FAMILY

Willard Robinson and his wife, Rachel, live with their two children, Taylor and Lindsay, in a two-bedroom apartment in Dallas. Both Taylor, age 12, and Lindsay, age 7, are from Willard's and Rachel's previous marriages. The four generally get along with one another, although there are frequent blow-ups over using the one bathroom in the apartment. Because both parents work, the kids are often left by themselves after school for a few hours. Although neither Willard nor Rachel like having the girls in the apartment by themselves, they know that it is the only way they can both work. Willard's parents are both deceased, and Rachel's mom lives over 100 miles away. A babysitter is out of the question because of the cost. So, each day after school, the girls come home, grab a snack from the refrigerator, and sit and watch either a movie or one of the "kids' stations" found on television. Once Willard and Rachel get home, the family tries to have dinner together each night. Privately, the parents wish that another arrangement could be financially possible.

THE ORTIZ-DELGADO FAMILY

Five-year-old Luisa is the child of Karen Ortiz and Julien Delgado. The family lives in Miami. Karen and Julien are lesbians in a committed relationship with each other, and they are each mothers for Luisa. Both women desired children. After six years together, the couple decided that they wanted

Chapter

1

PROVIDING DEFINITIONS

Family Culture

Defining the Family

Self-Definitions of Family • Definition Through Interaction
Voluntary and Involuntary Ties • Creation of Boundaries
Evolving Time

Family Communication Perspective

Defining Communication • Axioms of Communication

Cultural and Demographic Trends Affecting the Family

From Tradition to Transition: Family Types in the United States

Family-of-Origin, Intergenerationality, and Family Genograms
Nuclear Families • Gay and Lesbian Families • Extended Families
Stepfamilies • Single-Parent Families • Couples
Marital and Family Typologies

Summary

Key Terms

Questions for Reflection

THE BARKER FAMILY

Paula and Evan Barker live in a small suburban neighborhood near Omaha, Nebraska. They have one child, Alex, whom they adopted from an orphanage in Cambodia. They saved for years to pay for the trip and to pay the orphanage. Paula Barker is a substitute teacher who took a professional leave after Alex arrived in the United States. Evan is a freelance journalist who writes for a number of publications in the Omaha area. The Barkers are neither wealthy nor impoverished. Although Paula and Evan have little conflict, lately, because of the adoption, they have been going through a tough time making ends meet. Their financial situation has caused quite a bit of friction in the family. Evan has told Paula that she needs to go back to work, and Paula is insistent on staying at home until Alex can go to school. Evan's pay is insufficient to pay the rent and utilities, buy groceries, keep the car functioning, and have enough left for unforeseen expenses brought on by adopting Alex. Both are very careful not to argue in front of their son. When they do sense an argument coming, Paula stares intently at Evan, and the two go to another room. They try their best to keep things moving along despite their financial problems.

THE ROBINSON FAMILY

Willard Robinson and his wife, Rachel, live with their two children, Taylor and Lindsay, in a two-bedroom apartment in Dallas. Both Taylor, age 12, and Lindsay, age 7, are from Willard's and Rachel's previous marriages. The four generally get along with one another, although there are frequent blow-ups over using the one bathroom in the apartment. Because both parents work, the kids are often left by themselves after school for a few hours. Although neither Willard nor Rachel like having the girls in the apartment by themselves, they know that it is the only way they can both work. Willard's parents are both deceased, and Rachel's mom lives over 100 miles away. A babysitter is out of the question because of the cost. So, each day after school, the girls come home, grab a snack from the refrigerator, and sit and watch either a movie or one of the "kids' stations" found on television. Once Willard and Rachel get home, the family tries to have dinner together each night. Privately, the parents wish that another arrangement could be financially possible.

THE ORTIZ-DELGADO FAMILY

Five-year-old Luisa is the child of Karen Ortiz and Julien Delgado. The family lives in Miami. Karen and Julien are lesbians in a committed relationship with each other, and they are each mothers for Luisa. Both women desired children. After six years together, the couple decided that they wanted

a child. Their own parents were not too keen on the idea of bringing a child into a household with lesbian parents. Still, Karen and Julien view themselves as co-parents and think of Luisa as their treasure in life. The women experience prejudice from both their families and the community at large, causing them to struggle with stereotypes, bias, and hatred every day of their lives. So far, Karen and Julien believe that these problems have not affected Luisa. They hope that Luisa will grow up in a more tolerant world.

Family is one of the most provocative of all groups in a person's life. The 2010 Pew Research Center (*http://pewresearch.org/pubs/1802/decline-marriage-rise-new-families*) notes that families are becoming increasingly complex. Over 75 percent of people surveyed in the United States believe that family is the most important part of their lives; nearly the same percentage indicates that they are "very satisfied" with their family life. These numbers suggest that family members (and family communication) remain an essential ingredient of an individual's daily experiences and activities.

The Barkers, the Robinsons, and the Ortiz-Delgados are very different families with different resources, goals, and life events. Now, more than ever before, as we move further into the 21st century, the concept of what it means to be "a family" is neither universally understood nor accepted. We have seen an unprecedented evolution of what it means to be a family in the United States. Underscoring the variability and fluid nature of family, Sharon Jayson (2010), in *USA Today*, quotes researcher Brian Powell: "Think about what families do. Families take care of each other. Families help each other out. They love each other. As long as Americans have a signal out there that a living arrangement is doing those types of tasks, then they're willing to accept the idea that these are families" (p. 4D). In other words, people in America seem more concerned about what a family can *do*, rather than what comprises a family.

In this book, we approach these and other issues with a communication perspective, meaning that we focus on conversations and interactions within the family and messages within and about the family. We chose this approach because we honor the notion that family communication can help bridge some of the differences we find in and across families in the United States. We acknowledge upfront that not everyone reading this book has had, nor, perhaps, will ever have, some of the sorts of families we describe. Further, we are well aware that some of what we present in this text will resonate much more for some than for others. Still, we believe that the information will provide a necessary foundation related to the interplay between family and communication.

Although diverse family structures and ethnicities affect family communication (e.g., Gagotena, 2012; Hendrix, 2012; McAdoo, 2007), interaction constructs the life of all families. Families use communication—verbal, non-verbal, American Sign Language—in some way to deal with issues of close-ness and distance, to maintain (or reject) traditions, make decisions, deal with problems, and so forth. Before we can see some of our commonalities, however, it is important to be aware of our diversity since our cultural makeup necessarily influences how we view the world around us. Thus, we begin our investigation of family communication by examining the notion of family in a multifaceted way.

Diversity in family demographics can be seen by examining the U.S. Census undertaken in 2010. With over 310 million citizens, the United States is a heterogeneous mix of various cultural backgrounds. This diver-sity has far-reaching implications. Alberto González, Marsha Houston, and Victoria Chen (2012), for instance, observed: "Race, culture, gender, class, and ethnicity are not 'external' variables but rather inherent to the ongoing process of constructing how collectively we understand and par-ticipate in social, cultural, and political discourse" (p. xii). But concurrent with growing attention to diversity is the potential for volatility. Several years ago, Ruben Martinez, a writer for the *New York Times Magazine's* (2000) special issue on race relations, observed that "all across the coun-try, people of different races, ethnicities, and nationalities are being thrown together and torn apart. . . . It is a terrifying experience, this coming together, one for which we have as of yet only the most awkward vocabulary" (pp. 11–12). Today, over a decade since Martinez wrote those words, many people continue to struggle with the diverse makeup of our families.

The 2003 Statistical Abstract of the United States, an arm of the Census Bureau, indicates the racial makeup of the country's population since 1790 (see Table 1-1). Note particularly the increase in citizens who are African American, American Indian, Asian and Pacific Islander, and those with Hispanic origin. Accompanying these racial changes are family changes. That is, families differ in form and type, thereby rendering a monolithic family image as unrepresentative and unfair.

The mosaic of diversity in families is apparent if we examine the basic changes in our country's multicultural profile as reflected in the U.S. Census. Years ago, we referred to this diversity as a *melting pot,* meaning that our country had a unified national identity. Today, this view is out-dated and inaccurate. Communication scholars now refer to the United States as a symphony, a stew, or a salad (Lustig & Koester, 2010). This more contemporary imagery (symphony, stew, salad) suggests that each family is unique, with a variety of "tints, textures, and tastes" (p. 16). Beatriz Lopez-Flores (2001) observes, "the more mixed we are, the more likely it is that we will be sensitive to each other" (cited in Kasindorf & El Nasser, 2001).

This change in the cultural dynamic has been welcomed by millions of people. For example, the 2010 U.S. Census allowed people to mark

TABLE 1-1 Resident Population: Selected Characteristics and Projections (in thousands)

			RACE		
YEAR	White	Black	American Indian, Eskimo, Aleut	Asian and Pacific Islanders	Hispanic Origin[a]
1790	3,172	757	(NA)	(NA)	(NA)
1800	4,306	1,002	(NA)	(NA)	(NA)
1850	19,553	3,639	(NA)	(NA)	(NA)
1860	26,923	4,442	(NA)	(NA)	(NA)
1870	33,589	4,880	(NA)	(NA)	(NA)
1880	43,403	6,581	(NA)	(NA)	(NA)
1890	55,101	7,489	(NA)	(NA)	(NA)
1900	66,809	8,834	(NA)	(NA)	(NA)
1910	81,732	9,828	(NA)	(NA)	(NA)
1920	94,821	10,463	(NA)	(NA)	(NA)
1930	110,287	11,891	(NA)	(NA)	(NA)
1940	118,215	12,866	(NA)	(NA)	(NA)
1950	134,942	15,042	(NA)	(NA)	(NA)
1950	135,150	15,045	(NA)	(NA)	(NA)
1960	158,832	18,872	(NA)	(NA)	(NA)
1970	178,098	22,581	(NA)	(NA)	(NA)
1980	194,713	26,683	1,420	3,729	14,609
1990	208,727	30,511	2,065	7,462	22,372
1990	209,182	30,623	2,074	7,560	22,565
1991	210,961	31,131	2,110	7,925	23,384
1992	212,860	31,667	2,148	8,319	24,275
1993	214,677	32,179	2,185	8,705	25,214
1994	216,365	32,654	2,221	9,050	26,152
1995	218,010	33,098	2,254	9,403	27,099
1996	219,623	33,518	2,289	9,761	28,092
1997	221,317	33,973	2,324	10,130	29,160
1998	223,001	34,431	2,360	10,507	30,250
1999	224,103	34,997	2,369	10,861	30,461
2000	225,532	35,454	2,402	11,245	31,366
2005	232,463	37,734	2,572	13,212	36,057
2010	239,588	40,109	2,754	15,265	41,139
2015	247,193	42,586	2,941	17,413	46,705
2020	254,887	45,075	3,129	19,651	52,652
2025	262,227	47,539	3,319	21,965	58,930
2050	294,615	60,592	4,371	34,352	96,508

NA = not available. [a]Persons of Hispanic origin may be of any race.
Source: U.S. Census Bureau (2003a).

one or more races as a way to accommodate people of mixed race. This opportunity legitimized the nearly 9 million citizens, or 2.9 percent of the population, who chose to identify with more than one race (U.S. Census Bureau, 2010). In fact, according to the Census, as a result of record immigration rates and interracial marriages, by 2050 the United States will have no racial or ethnic majority (El Nasser, 2010). Many celebrities, political leaders, sports heroes, and dignitaries have mixed ancestry, including singer Christina Aguilera (white, Hispanic), astronaut Franklin Chang-Diaz (Chinese, Costa Rican), news anchor Ann Curry (Japanese, white, American Indian), shortstop Derek Jeter (African American, white), wrestler/actor The Rock (Samoan, African American), and actor Keanu Reeves (white, Hawaiian, Portuguese, Irish, Chinese). These are the "visible" images of a multiracial society. The challenge for individuals to reclaim their cultural identity, however, will continue to face the family and affect other societal institutions as well (see Figure 1-1).

Because we are interested in the diversity of the family, we include in this book families of multiple cultures, sexual identities, and compositions. These families typically do not fit the traditional images exemplified in the media. Although traditional views of the family are not necessarily problematic, we wish to expand these perceptions. Moreover, we will also discuss those families who can be considered at risk. **At-risk families** are families whose members, for a variety of reasons, face a high probability of not attaining the basic diet, skills, health, and credentials that society considers to be necessary for survival. Homeless families constitute the greatest number of at-risk families (Koblinsky & Anderson, 1999; National Coalition for the Homeless, 2002), and so our discussion of these families will necessarily include this vulnerable population. Many within this homeless group have found themselves in this situation as a result of job loss, divorce/separation, personal catastrophe (for example, fire, flood), or cutbacks in social support services such as Medicaid or welfare. Further, given that nearly 3.5 million people are homeless on any given night, affecting nearly 1.5 million children (National Coalition for the Homeless, 2002), we cannot ignore the importance of addressing at-risk families.

One thing is certain: Our diversity and our desire for inclusiveness make defining the family a challenge. The family is as diverse as our population. Although we believe that some communication behaviors are similar across many families, race, status, and family form, among other things, have a profound influence on how families communicate. Throughout this book we point out how variability affects family communication behaviors.

Student Perspective: Vladimir

What a great country America is! I see people from across the world walking the streets. They're Irish, Italian, Jewish, in wheelchairs, and some are even Russian like me. My dad wouldn't like it so much here. He thinks that people in this country are not all that tolerant of people who aren't born here. I haven't found that. In school, I have friends from the United States and from some places in Europe. I wish my dad could see me today. But he'll stay in Russia waiting for me to finish my studies here.

FIGURE 1.1 A County-by-County Look at Diversity

Racial and ethnic diversity have increased significantly since 2000, new Census data show. The probability that two people chosen at random in each of the USA's 3,143 counties would be of a different race or ethnicity (on a 0–100 scale):

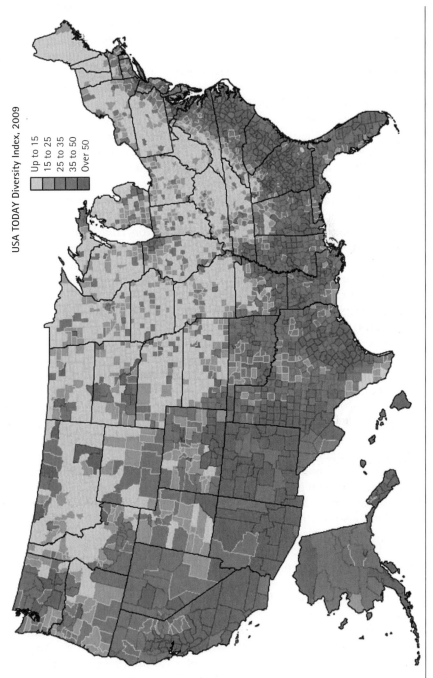

USA TODAY Diversity Index, 2009

- Up to 15
- 15 to 25
- 25 to 35
- 35 to 50
- Over 50

Source: Analysis of 2009 Census Bureau estimates by Paul Overberg, USA TODAY.

FAMILY CULTURE

Family and culture are recurrent themes of this book. Part of the diversity in families comes from the fact that the United States is a multicultural nation. As Michael Hecht, Mary Jane Collier, and Sidney Ribeau (1993) note, the relationship between culture and communication is an inherent one: "All communication exists in a cultural context and all culture is communicated" (p. 1). We hope that this book will serve as an important beginning in understanding that families come in many forms and are rooted in various cultures. Further, we hope you will agree that each of these forms and cultures contains some families that are rich in heritage and others that are now writing their own history for the first time.

The word *culture* has been defined in hundreds of ways, and frequently these definitions conflict with one another. For purposes of our discussion, we refer to **culture** as a "historical shared system of symbolic resources through which we make our world meaningful" (Hall, 2005, p. 4). We agree with Alberto González, Marsha Houston, and Victoria Chen (2012) who purport that personal experience and the cultural backgrounds of communicators are essential when discussing communication and that "cultural participants engage in communication that constantly defines and redefines the community" (p. xv). Culture is an organizing concept that helps us understand how groups come together and create communities around common languages, symbols, foods, religions, belief systems, and so forth. When families from different cultures come together (as in the United States), they often realize more about their own cultural patterns by seeing them in contrast to another's. For instance, Azim Nanji (2008) points out that in some Muslim families living in the United States there is a "Friday problem." The Friday problem refers to Muslim teenagers being restricted from socializing with their friends on Friday evenings. Instead they must go with their families to the mosque and observe the day of congregational prayer in Islam.

In an example of language differences engendered by culture, MaryAnn Eklund (1996) reports that Mexican American women living in the Southwestern United States often have difficulties with organized health care. Eklund provides one example in which a pregnant woman responded "no" when her doctor asked if she was sexually active. When her pregnancy was discovered later and the woman was asked why she had said no in response to the doctor, she replied, "He asked if I was sexually active. I am not. I just lay there." Culture, then, provides connections for those who share it and barriers to those who do not.

The approach we take in this book is primarily cultural, and we broaden the cultural view to include three levels of culture: (1) **relational culture** (family members' shared understandings of the function and value of their relationships with one another); (2) **popular culture** (messages about the family sent through television, the Internet, film, and other mass media); and

(3) **co-culture** (groups of individuals who are part of the larger culture, but who, through unity and individual identification around attributes such as race and sexual identity, create unique experiences of their own). We embrace this cultural model of family communication in our discussions of family life throughout the book.

In addition to culture, we take a contextual approach to family communication in this book. Popular culture and co-cultures are parts of the external context surrounding the relational culture the family constructs. Additional elements of this context include the influence of governmental policies, social movements, and the economic conditions on the family and its patterns of communication. We examine each of these in this text.

Looking at family communication through a cultural and contextual lens reveals the complexities of families in the United States. The Barkers, the Robinsons, and the Ortiz-Delgados, for example, create their family culture contextualized by their heritage, their family type, and the entire spectrum of popular culture and external context surrounding the three different families. Yet, they may differ in many other respects—for instance, religion, family type, and ethnicity. These differences affect their family communication and, in turn, the lens by which they view family life.

DEFINING THE FAMILY

As you can see, defining the family involves attention to a number of issues, including diversity, culture, and communication. So, how do we go about this process of interpreting family? We have proposed elsewhere (Turner & West, 2003, 2012) that the study of family communication must necessarily be as inclusive as possible. Thus, we define *family* as follows:

> *A family is a self-defined group of intimates who create and maintain themselves through their own interactions and their interactions with others; a family may include both voluntary and involuntary relationships; it creates both literal and symbolic internal and external boundaries; and it evolves through time: It has a history, a present, and a future.*

Our definition is broad, inclusive, and a bit abstract. You may not have viewed family in this way before. Other definitions specify an intergenerational tie of some kind, but we do not because that would mean that married couples, groups of same-generation close friends, or siblings living together without parents could not be called a family. Also, whereas other definitions specify that families have to live (or have lived) in the same house, that interpretation would exclude intimate friendships from the definition. In our opinion, the definition of family must be all-encompassing to account for those families who—for years—have remained invisible because of restrictive perceptions of what or who constitutes a family. We favor our definition, although it is complex, because, like Mary Anne Fitzpatrick and Diane Badzinski (1994), we believe that the definition of family should emphasize the value of communication in family life and encompass the diversity of contemporary families. To give you a better understanding of why we have chosen to define family in this fashion, let's consider each of our definition's central themes: (1) self-definition, (2) interaction, (3) voluntary and involuntary ties, (4) creation of literal (physical) and symbolic (psychological) boundaries internally and externally, and (5) evolving time.

Self-Definitions of Family

When family members identify other individuals as family, their self-definition is their reality. In other words, some individuals identify close friends, long-term roommates, and even work colleagues as family. For some of you, this may make perfect sense. For others, this may seem challenging. After all, if we begin to define family outside of a biological framework, then what would *not* be considered family?

Yet, we are not talking about *everyone* as family, but rather those with whom we have an intimate and trusting relationship. Hollywood has already depicted "families" that are not blood-related and many of these shows have been some of the most watched in television history: *Cheers* (Norm, Sam, Cliff, Carla, Woody, Rebecca, Diane), *Seinfeld* (Jerry, George, Elaine, and Kramer), *The Golden Girls* (Dorothy, Sophia, Blanche, and Rose), *Friends* (Monica, Rachel, Joey, Phoebe, Ross, and Chandler), and even the expansive high school kids on *Glee* (Rachel, Finn, Quinn, Brittany, Noah, Sam, Tina, Santana, Mercedes, Artie, Mike, and Mr. Schuester). Most viewers of these programs would contend that each show featured a group of individuals who, because of their closeness and life experiences, could be defined as family. We will return to the media and family images again in Chapter 4.

It is not only Hollywood, however, where we find self-definitions of family. Our society is replete with examples of self-definitions of family. In retirement villages, for instance, because some biological family members rarely visit, residents often refer to their neighbors and roommates as family. Some college students identify close friends or roommates as family. And there are numerous examples of individuals who, after being transferred to different parts of the country with no familial ties, define close work colleagues as family.

An additional example of a self-defined family can be found by considering Ana, a 31-year-old student majoring in environmental science. Ana's father died during her adolescence, and her mother has not corresponded with her in more than 11 years. She has a brother, Raphael, but he lives in Mexico, and she has not seen him in almost 6 years. When Ana's friends ask about her family, Ana says that she has two siblings, Mark and Jen. Mark and Jen are her two best friends, who go to school with her, but she describes their relationship as a family relationship. Ana has thus defined Mark and Jen into her family portrait.

Definition Through Interaction

Families create and maintain themselves through their own interactions and their interactions with others outside of the family unit. This assumption, persuasively argued by Gerald Handel and Gail Whitchurch (1994), is based on the belief that conversation is the foundation of family life. Conversation serves several purposes: (1) to inform others about the kinds of relationships you have with members of your family, (2) to explain to others how your family fits within the larger culture, and (3) to define family relationships with individual family members.

An example will help explain these three purposes. Julia is a single parent of three teenagers. She is very proud of the fact that she holds down a full-time job, is paying a mortgage on a home, and has enough time to spend with her children. Although the kids may not always want to be around their mom, they know that she is available if they need her. She has, in fact, helped them out considerably over the past few years. When asked at work about her family, Julia is quick to point out the preceding information. She enjoys talking about her two daughters and son and frequently discusses several of the family's vacations to Canada.

Julia's conversations with others are important for a few reasons. First, she informs the community around her about her pride in being successful as a single parent. Second, she provides others some indication of the quality of her relationships with her children. Third, she communicates one of the values inherent in her family: Time together is essential. Julia's conversations give others some indication of her family life; she creates an image of her family through her discourse.

Families also create and maintain themselves by explaining how they fit within the larger culture. For instance, how many times have you heard someone say, "We have a really strange family." This strangeness can include speech (accents or dialects), way of dress, family hierarchy, or eccentric family members. What's important here is that implicit in such a claim is a cultural comparison; people like to compare their families to what their culture prescribes as normal. Yet some writers argue there is no such thing as a normal or typical family in our culture. Researchers suggest that normalcy is a myth, and any family, regardless of structure or culture, can be functional (McKenry, Everett, Ramseur, & Carter, 1989).

Stephanie Coontz (1988) has identified this cultural comparison process as a **terrain of struggle.** In this process, families and other groups (such as politicians, filmmakers, and so on) struggle over the definition of family. The struggle may have negative implications for families, however. For example, families of African American or other co-cultural groups may use idealized European American middle-class families for their comparison group, finding their own families lacking as a result (Adams, 1988). And European American middle-class families may see themselves as deficient when measured against the idealized, optimal family presented in media images. In sum, although researchers argue that no one family is the standard, people continue to use "prevailing cultural ideologies in evaluating

ᴍᴍ POPULAR PRESS PERSPECTIVES ᴍᴍ

The New York Times online (2011) examined the definition of family, stating "a family tree today is beginning to look more like a tangled forest." First, the author of this article, Laura Holson, discussed the case of a woman who was unable to conceive a child with her husband. Her sister volunteered to become pregnant with a donor's sperm. The sister gave birth to a daughter who was adopted by the childless couple. Holson notes that the family relationships are confusing because for medical purposes, the birth mother was the mother, but relationally, she is the child's aunt.

Holson also reviews the case of Rob Okun (see "A Tangled Family Tree"). In Okun's case, he donated his sperm to a lesbian couple 16 years ago with no expectations of being a part of their family. He already had two biological children and two stepchildren. More recently, he has reconsidered and now includes the daughter and son of the lesbian couple as a part of his family as well. Holson observes that "some families now organize their family tree into two separate histories: genetic and emotional." She quotes Ms. Kogut, the biological mother of the two children for which Mr. Okun donated sperm, as saying: "There is the family tree and there is the day-to-day structure of the family."

While most of the stories Holson recounts show that families are adjusting well to complex relationships, she also notes that tangled family trees can cause problems for school teachers, many of whom are now staying away from family tree projects at school. Holson also cites Peggy Gillespie, a founder of Family Diversity Projects, a family education advisory group as noting that having to explain their family's complicated interconnections can cause kids pain, sometimes in unexpected ways.

A Tangled Family Tree

Rob Okun, a 61-year-old magazine editor from Massachusetts, has four biological children. He has a daughter, 26, and a son, 23, by a woman with whom he had a long-term relationship. He gave up parental rights to two other children, a 12-year-old boy and 15-year-old girl, both the result of sperm donated to a lesbian couple. He has two stepdaughters with his current wife, Adi Bemak.

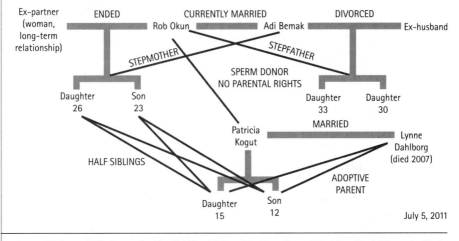

Laura Holson, "Who's on the Family Tree? Now It's Complicated." *New York Times* (online). July 4, 2011. Retrieved August 10, 2011.

their own families" (Stafford & Dainton, 1994, p. 261). And this process may discourage real families who see themselves as deviant or deficient in comparison with the ideal.

Finally, through discussion between and among themselves, family members also create and maintain a sense of themselves. We tend to understand and create our sense of family through our perception of our family's interaction patterns. Thus, we characterize our family as quiet, extroverted, weird, and so forth, based on how we think we talk to one another. Further, we tell stories in our families about our past, our experiences, and our expectations. This communication practice is based on our sense of what our family is like and simultaneously helps create family identity. We discuss this practice further in Chapter 3. For instance, one of the authors' brothers, Lucas, owns several travel agencies. His job takes him to exotic ports of call across the world. Yet he enjoys coming home to the United States for extended periods of time because his birth family lives here. When in this country, Lucas tries to stay connected to his parents and siblings by discussing his sojourns, as well as by listening to stories of what each family member is doing in his or her life. This sort of conversation is intended to ensure Lucas's family connection and also allows the whole family to create a sense of their identity.

Voluntary and Involuntary Ties

Families can be biologically, legally, or socially derived, although these categories overlap. For most couples who marry, the family bond between them is voluntary; for each of the couple's relationship with in-laws, the bond is involuntary. For any children the couple brings into the family, the connection is involuntary. The **involuntary family** is normally a group of people who are bound by birth or law. Marriage laws generally refer to a voluntary relationship, except in those cultures, such as Asian Indian, that often practice arranged marriages. A biological connection creates an involuntary family, as no one asks to be born (something children may remind their parents of periodically). Adoption laws also govern involuntary relationships. **Voluntary family** relationships are entered into intentionally, although that may not necessarily mean they are more satisfying than involuntary ones. A relatively high divorce rate attests to problems even in voluntary relations.

Creation of Boundaries

Boundaries mark limits in the family. Boundaries within families are primarily metaphorical, or symbolic (Steinglass, 1987), although it is true that some families construct concrete, or literal, boundaries. Boundaries can be either external or internal as well as literal or symbolic. **External boundaries** essentially decide family membership, delineating who is part, and who is not part, of a family. When Lucas, in our earlier example, tells his family stories about his travels, he is affirming that no external boundary symbolically excludes him. His stories serve to bridge the physical distance between him and other family members. As he often claims, "I'm gone in person, but not in spirit!"

In another example, when Eric disclosed his homosexuality to his French Canadian Catholic family, he was immediately rejected and disowned by several members of his biological family. This behavior had two results. First, Eric developed a voluntary family later on with close friends. Second, he soon realized that several of his six siblings created an external, symbolic boundary and decided that he was not part of their family anymore. In fact, Eric's family members actively prevented others from learning about Eric by constructing a shroud of secrecy surrounding his homosexuality. The external boundary enacted by these family members labeled Eric as an outsider. Although Eric's family did not erect literal external boundaries such as fences or bushes to exclude him, the symbolic boundary constructed of disapproval, shame, and silence worked effectively to exclude him from the family circle.

Internal boundaries govern the way family members communicate within their family. In other words, internal boundaries determine how informed a voice a family member has. Often, **family secrets** fall within internal family boundaries. Further, some family members keep their internal boundaries so tight that they exert a great deal of energy in preserving the secrets in their families. In fact, family secrets may require some sort of internal cognitive struggle between sharing something painful and the need to keep communication honest and open (Imber-Black, 2010). Tamara Affifi and Keli Steuber (2008) discovered that the boundaries related with maintaining secrets involve many "strategies" for revealing the secrets. Further, perceptions of coercive power within the family from whom the secrets are kept will likely influence concealment (Affifi & Olson, 2005). John Caughlin and Sandra Petronio (2004) observe the difficulty of maintaining this family boundary: "Family members need to be connected to each other through shared confidences, but they also need to keep some information from others to build or maintain their own distinct identities" (p. 380). In fact, they note that both revealing and concealing can benefit family members.

In addition, Anita Vangelisti (1994) discovered that people expect a certain amount of secrecy in their family. In fact, some family members keep their internal boundaries so restricted that they exert much energy in preserving the secrets in their families. When the daughter of one of the authors got a tattoo, she and her parents decided not to tell the grandparents, thus creating an internal symbolic boundary excluding the older generation. Internal literal boundaries are closed doors, separate rooms, name tags on towel racks, and so forth, all of which exclude some family members and include others.

Boundary ambiguity may also occur in families. **Boundary ambiguity** refers to the uncertainty of family members regarding who is and who is not a family member (Pasley & Ihinger-Tallman, 1989). For instance, in the previous example, boundary ambiguity occurs with respect to Eric's family membership. Some of his siblings believe he is still part of the biological family since they consider his homosexuality irrelevant. Others, however, believe that he is not part of their family because of his sexual orientation. Parents who have had a child die often express difficulty answering the (seemingly straightforward) question, "How many children do you have?"

Student Perspective: Ned

The biggest family secret I can think of is that I've been seeing a woman who is 17 years older than I am. She is a great person who really treats me well. My parents would flip out if they ever found out about this! I mean, they think that because I am young I only want to date young women. Yeah, right. I won't tell anyone about this for now, but they're going to have to find out eventually. Won't that be a great family scene!

Pauline Boss (1988) suggests that ambiguity, which results from situations such as divorce or death, may be stressful for a family. We discuss stress in family life further in Chapter 7.

Evolving Time

We say that a definition of family is dependent on the notion of evolving time because critical components of family life are the family's history and the expectation of a future together. This differentiates families from other small groups or interpersonal communication contexts (Whitchurch, 1992). To explain the concept of time and its impact on the definition of family further, we turn to the Abraham family. In 1985, Sophie and Sam Abraham were married. The two were in their mid-30s at the time. Despite this relatively happy event in their lives, the Abrahams were very distressed over the impending health problems of Sam's mother, Mary. Mary had been diagnosed with Alzheimer's disease, and her condition was getting worse. Both Sophie and Sam knew that they wouldn't be able to allow Mary to live with them; a long-term care facility was their only alternative.

As the years went on, Mary became worse. In November 2010, she was found wandering about the grounds at a local county fair. She was also belligerent to the staff at the facility, spitting more than once in their faces. She refused to take her medication regularly, which only exacerbated her problems. In July 2011, it was obvious that Mary's health was taking an emotional and financial toll on Sophie and Sam, but through it all they remained loyal to Mary. Sophie visited her mother-in-law every day, sometimes simply to watch her sleep or to brush her hair as they both looked out the window. Sam did his best to get to the care center but had a difficult time witnessing his mother become more fragile each day. He couldn't help but think about the times when this very sweet woman would take him and his sister to a local diner for hamburgers and cherry Cokes. It was difficult to face his mother these days. Although their pain was evident, Sophie and Sam continued to put Mary first. They even sent thank-you cards to the staff and helped out at the staff's annual picnic in August. In April 2012, Mary died peacefully in her sleep, an end to a difficult and emotional time in Sophie and Sam's lives.

This story of the Abrahams underscores the element of time and process in family life. The family evolved through the past, present, and future. It's clear that Sophie and Sam were concerned with preserving the future of their family while day-to-day events were contextualized by their history with Mary. Thus the Abraham family illustrates the importance of time to our definition. Another small group in our society might not have so rich a history or be concerned about their future together.

FAMILY COMMUNICATION PERSPECTIVE

There are many ways to examine family life. We could focus on how family roles differed before and after the changes brought about by the feminist movement of the late 1960s and early 1970s. We could ask about the effects of birth order on children's personalities. If we asked the first question, our perspective would be sociological; the second question would lead to a psychological perspective. In this book we ask questions about how family conversation shapes family life. We contextualize our questions with historical, sociological, and psychological data, but our primary interest is in the interaction processes and topics that make up the fabric of family life, and thus our perspective is communicative.

In one of the first surveys in the family literature, Art Bochner (1976) stated that communication is the foundation of family life. Although he stated this conclusion over 30 years ago, his words remain true today. Communication shapes family life, reflects family relations, and is instrumental in family functioning. Communication is vital to establishing relational cultures. In our families, many of us have given meanings to the many activities and interactions that compose our relationships. Julia Wood (1995) comments that these experiences "are realized in communication, which is the genesis of relational culture" (p. 150).

Communication is the foundation of popular culture, grounded as it is in telecommunications and other communication technologies. Further, communication allows us to understand the values of our ethnic or racial cultures. For example, different cultural groups vary in the value they place on different life passages (McGoldrick, 2011). And, despite some cultural variability, various ethnic groups place emphases on different life experiences, including funerals and wakes (e.g., Irish), weddings (e.g., Italians), and bar mitzvahs (Jews). Mahboub Hashem (2012) reports that *wastah,* commonly known in the United States as "clout," is viewed as a very important characteristic in Lebanon and other Middle Eastern countries and is necessary "to get a job, a wife, a date, a passport, a visa, a car, or any other commodity" (p. 176). Clearly, clout, or networking, is a highly valued communication pattern in Lebanese culture.

In addition to life passages, many symbols of cultural groups are passed from one generation to another, thereby allowing for traditions, values, and customs to be better understood. Lynda Dee Dixon (2004) relates the following story about her Oklahoma Cherokee family:

> *In her youth, mamaw's [the tribal mother] first home was Indian allotment land that was stolen by a local physician when her mother was very ill. Mamaw long mourned the loss of what should have been her children's land. She and our family sometimes drove by the rural acreage where mamaw described the tent they had lived in and shared with us her childhood memories. (p. 146)*

These types of cultural differences are accompanied by different communication patterns and rituals to socialize other members of the co-culture to their importance.

Defining Communication

Given that communication forms the prism through which we wish to examine family life, and given the centrality of communication to our definition of family itself, we need to define communication. Simply put, **communication** is the process of meaning-making. The question of intentionality is important to our definition. Scholars have debated whether messages that are sent unintentionally, or "mistaken" meanings that people make ("I didn't mean *that*— you misunderstood me"), fit the definition of communication. Those who say no argue that only intentionally sent and accurately received messages can be called communication. However, more researchers believe the latter approach narrows the definition too much; because so much of what happens when people interact is mistaken or unintentional, the definition of communication must include those messages and meanings. We agree. Thus, when Paula Barker (from the beginning of the chapter) gets a faraway look on her face and her husband responds by reassuring her that their family will be fine, we call that a communication transaction even if Paula had no intention of getting Evan's attention and wasn't aware of the look on her face.

Paul Watzlawick, Janet Beavin, and Don Jackson (1967) coined the phrase "you cannot *not* communicate," reflecting the idea that unintentional messages constitute communication. Their phrase means that anything we do, including ignoring or refusing to speak to another, can serve as a stimulus for someone else to make meaning. This broadens the definition of communication a great deal, making it virtually synonymous with behavior, which is troublesome to some researchers. But for our purposes, it is important to be aware that any behavior can be interpreted as communication. However, we should check to find out whether people are behaving intentionally before we act on our interpretations.

Glen Stamp and Mark Knapp's (1990) conception of an interactional perspective is relevant here. Stamp and Knapp argue that intent is best understood within a relational context. They advocate examining how "participants within the context of a particular relationship structure intent" (p. 291). In our opening vignette, the feedback exchanged between Karen and Julien Ortiz-Delgado about parenting will determine its intentionality.

Axioms of Communication

Proceeding from our definition of communication, we need to explore some axioms (or assertions) about the nature of communication. We will discuss each of the following in turn: (1) communication is a process, (2) communication involves co-construction of definitions, (3) communication is a process involving codes, (4) communication occurs in a context, (5) communication is a transaction, and (6) communication takes place on two levels.

Communication Is a Process　This assertion about the nature of communication allows us to view it as dynamic, complex, and continually changing. By viewing communication in this way, we place more emphasis on the dynamics of meaning-making than on the result of the process. For example, the Robinson and Barker families from our beginning illustrations may have their children say their prayers before going to sleep each night in the apartment. Yet, in the Barker family, the parents have to continually remind Alex to do this, and sometimes he may try to trick his parents, saying he has said his prayers when he hasn't. Willard and Rachel Robinson's children say their prayers automatically each night as Willard walks from Taylor and Lindsay's beds after tucking them in. In each family, the communication outcome (saying nightly prayers) is the same, but the process differs greatly. This underscores the variability in the communication, and although the Barkers and Robinsons are both families with children, each undertakes the process differently.

Communication Involves Co-Construction of Definitions　We could argue that each person speaks a unique language, and the process of communication consists of discussing the meaning of things (will you learn my language, or I learn yours, or will we create a compromise in some way?). When Karen Ortiz from one of our beginning examples tells her partner, Julien Delgado, that she doesn't think their daughter, Luisa, should watch violent television programs, she may become angry when she sees Julien and Luisa watching Saturday morning cartoons together. Julien may have expressed agreement with Karen, but what is at issue is differing definitions of violent programs. The two women have to come to a common definition of what constitutes violence, or they will continue to have conflict when they act on different meanings.

Communication Is a Process Involving Codes　The reason we need to discuss meaning mainly rests on this axiom of communication. To co-construct meaning, people are dependent on using codes for what they are thinking. Karen Ortiz has an idea in her mind about what she wants to keep her daughter from watching on TV. To share that idea with Julien, Karen uses the word (symbol) *violent*. Julien hears the word, but she responds to it differently than Karen.

The codes that we have for communication are verbal and nonverbal. **Verbal codes** are the words we use and their grammatical arrangement, whereas **nonverbal codes** consist of facial expressions, body positions, inflections, gestures, and a host of other communication behaviors. We often send messages using both codes—saying "I love you" and hugging someone, for example—but nonverbal codes can be used alone, without words—sending someone a dirty look. When you contradict your words with your nonverbal behavior—telling your dad you love him in a dull tone of voice with a frown on your face—your nonverbal codes are more believable. In the example, your dad would probably hear that you don't feel too loving toward him. Because communication relies on codes, it is extremely complex. Some researchers (for example, Motley, 1990) distinguish between nonverbal and verbal codes by pointing out that verbal codes are symbolic whereas nonverbal codes are not always symbolic. Using this distinction, most nonverbal behavior would be seen as expressive but nonsymbolic, because while a smile, for example, has communicative potential, it does not symbolize something specific in the way the word *chair* does. The issue rests on communication as an indirect process dependent on codes, symbolic and expressive, for meaning-making and sharing.

Communication Occurs in a Context   The meaning-making process is heavily influenced by the context in which it occurs. Context includes place, culture, historical period, and relational history. You can easily see how an argument between partners would be different if it broke out in the supermarket or in their kitchen. The partners would probably choose different words, speak at a different volume, and alter the length and intensity of the conflict depending on whether it took place in public or private. Further, the communication process is affected by the relational history of the participants. If the Barkers, from our beginning example, have had a good marriage, unmarked by much verbal conflict, they might react very strongly to the first real overt disagreement they have. It might shock and scare them, and they might even wonder whether it threatened their marriage. Another couple who fought regularly would probably not even notice the same level of conflict that so disturbed the Barkers.

Communication Is a Transaction   Communication is a transactional process in which each person exerts influence while acting simultaneously as a sender and a receiver. The transactional process of communication suggests that communication is ongoing. For example, in our opening story, suppose Willard Robinson starts to send a message to Taylor, his oldest daughter, that he doesn't think the family can afford to let Taylor play on the school's lacrosse team because of the cost of uniforms and travel expenses; while speaking, he observes the disappointed look on Taylor's face. Willard both sends and receives messages. As a receiver, Willard may try to modify his message to relieve his daughter's response. Yet, his daughter, as a receiver, may also realize that her dad is doing his best to find the money and may try to change her message, as a sender, to make him feel better. She may tell Willard that it's okay and she doesn't mind skipping it. Or, the two of them (with Rachel) may try to brainstorm ways they could find the extra money, changing the focus of the conversation. In the transactional process, one person's response is the stimulus for another's action. In this way, communication is not linear but evolving.

Communication Takes Place on Two Levels   All messages, verbal and nonverbal, can be understood on a content level (or literally) and on a relational level (or for what they communicate about the participants' relationship; Watzlawick et al., 1967). For example, when teenagers ask a parent if they can use the car, they are asking a literal question for which they want an answer, and they are also communicating their relationship with their parent. They indicate respect for their parent's authority and a realization that it is the parent's car and the parent decides who drives it. A teenager who says "I'm taking the car" communicates a different type of relationship with his or her parent. Nonverbal communication can further affect these levels of communication. A teenager who says "I'm taking the car" in a questioning, humble tone of voice with a smiling face conveys a different relational message than one who says the same words curtly with a frown. Communication among family members creates and re-creates relationships as well as accomplishing literal tasks.

As we said in the beginning of this section, communication is critical to family life. It constructs family meaning in an ongoing transactional process affected by context. Further, given the various needs and resources of the United States, our ability to communicate with a population of diverse families will be critical. Now, more than ever, we need to be able to expand our repertoire of communication skills. Whether we are listening to a Chinese American grand-mother relate her story of warrior women, or whether we are trying to understand the nuances of European American parents' approaches to disciplining their children, our ability to be patient, thoughtful, and sensitive remains crucial to our communication competency within and outside of our family.

CULTURAL AND DEMOGRAPHIC TRENDS AFFECTING THE FAMILY

Dramatic changes have characterized families in the United States. These changes, or trends, influence the configurations of families today. In order to understand why various family forms exist and how they came about, let's explore a number of cultural and demographic trends of family life. We hope that by presenting these six trends, you will better understand how family communication has been transformed and the extent to which society has evolved.

Marriage Rates Are Declining   The numbers are clear: In 1963, nearly 75 percent of all households were comprised of married couples. In 1983, the number dropped to 59 percent. In 2003, Peter Francese of *American Demographics Magazine* (2004) reported that married couples account for just over 51 percent of U.S. households. And in 2010, the Census reported that the figure had dropped to 48 percent (cited in Baker, 2011). This trend toward declining marriage rates demonstrates that marriage is now a less critical feature of what it means to be an adult. Haya El Nasser and Paul Overberg (2011) put it this way: "Marriage is losing ground to a grinding economic slowdown . . . couples at both ends of the economic spectrum are opting to live together rather than marry, largely because women increasingly rely less on men to take care of them financially" (p. 1A). That said, we may be seeing a bit of a spike in marriages with the recognition of same-sex marriages in the United States (more on this later).

Single Parenting Is Increasing   We are witnessing a significant increase in single parents in society. More and more single people are choosing to have or adopt children. Divorce rates have prompted increases in primary-parent arrangements. Important, too, is the fact that single parents are no longer exclusively women. Fathers have gained custody of children and are granted equal access to their children, with the help of such organizations as the Fatherhood Project, the National Fatherhood Initiative, and the National Father's Resource Center.

Same-Sex Relationships Continue to Grow   Perhaps no cultural trend has gained more attention over the past several years than the emergence of same-sex relationships. Although gay men and lesbians have formed partnerships for years, it's only recently that the media have begun to talk about same-sex relationships, and, in general, there is a greater tolerance for same-sex partnerships. Many of these same-sex partners have children, thus increasing attention to this family form. What was once invisible, ridiculed, or dismissed is now a relationship/family type, increasing both in numbers and in visibility.

Stepfamilies Are Increasing   Researchers have discovered that over one-third of the country is, or will be, a member of a stepfamily by adulthood. This family arrangement is generally formed by the death of a parent, the divorce of a parent, and the subsequent remarriage of a parent. In the past, society viewed stepfamilies rather negatively (for example, "the wicked stepmother"). Today, however, with the stepfamily configuration growing, these outdated perceptions are changing.

Childhood Poverty Is Increasing   Despite the fanfare by politicians of all stripes, our society has not begun to sincerely wrestle with the disproportional increases in childhood poverty. The National Center for Children in Poverty (*www.nccp.org*) reports that in 2009 (the most recent available year for statistics), of the 74 million children living in the United States, 42 percent lived in low-income families. And 21 percent (15.3 million) lived in poor families. As a reference marker, in 2010 the federal government defined "poverty level" for a family of four at $22,050 and for a family of two at $14,570. Poverty in childhood increases the likelihood that a child will grow up homeless, and homelessness tends to lead to a lack of education and recurrent illness (National Coalition for the Homeless, 2012). Poverty is a legal, social, and political issue that will seriously challenge all families and all of society.

People Are Living Longer   Thanks to medical advances, technological improvements, and awareness of physical well-being, we are living longer in the United States. Currently, the average U.S. life expectancy is 78.2 years, compared with 68 years in 1950 and 49 in 1900 (*http://www.cdc.gov/nchs/faststats/lifeexpect.htm*). This longevity has prompted a number of cultural scenarios, including (a) grandparents serving as custodial parents, (b) children serving as caregivers of aging parents, and (c) seniors marrying later in life.

FROM TRADITION TO TRANSITION: FAMILY TYPES IN THE UNITED STATES

There are dozens of family types in the United States, for a variety of reasons. In her now classic essay, Helen Wilkinson (2000) provides some explanation:

> *Since the 1960s, the divorce rate has increased sixfold; nearly a quarter of our children see their parents divorce before their 16th birthday. More and more children are growing up in single-parent households. The first-time marriage rate is at an all time low, but cohabitation continues to grow. The birth rate is in decline—almost a fifth of women born since the 1960s are predicted to remain child-free all their lives. (p. 21)*

Wilkinson does not criticize the evolution of family life in the United States; rather, she notes that the family "is not so much dying as being reborn" (p. 22). We agree. We believe it is important to study the communication in diverse family types because these family types do exist in large numbers and will continue to do so.

Finally, we need to be cautious in clinging to past impressions of the family. There is no "average" or "normal" family in the United States. The consequences of this claim are numerous. First, the media and the public frequently struggle with the lack of a common base from which to talk about family life. Second, family communication researchers are willing to explore multiple avenues to understand communication in diverse family forms. Finally, and most importantly, individuals who do not belong to the "average" family can now feel included in conversations about families.

Family-of-Origin, Intergenerationality, and Family Genograms

Before we delve into a discussion of family types, we need to provide a foundation for our discussion. First, our **family-of-origin,** or the family in which we have been raised, is critical in establishing our perceptions, values, and communication style. Our family-of-origin is instrumental in how family communication patterns are passed down from generation to generation. These patterns allow families to form a legacy, which affects the development of individual family members. Establishing a legacy that affects the development of individual family members and the patterns of adjustment found in subsequent family generations is known as **intergenerationality** (Tarrant, 2010).

Imagine growing up in a family in which males make the decisions regarding finances and females make the decisions pertaining to rules. For instance, your father took care of all the bills and your mother took control of the curfews and the assignment of job responsibilities. If, as an adult, you marry, have children, and raise them with a similar division of parental responsibilities, then you have adopted an intergenerational approach to family tasks. This perpetuation of behaviors across generations very often goes on without conscious thought, and sometimes people are surprised to discover themselves behaving in ways modeled by their parents.

One way that family communication scholars and family therapists understand family patterns of communication and family relationships is through a family genogram. A genogram (coined from looking at family genealogy and diagramming it) is a family diagram that visually depicts family communication patterns and relationships across at least three generations (McGoldrick, 2011). Family genograms are useful ways to demonstrate how family communication patterns are learned. Further, genograms can help family members understand how their functional and dysfunctional communication behaviors came about. Finally, genograms help us understand the closeness and distance embedded in family relationships. Some common symbols and abbreviations used in family genograms are noted in Table 1-2. In addition to relationships, a genogram allows family members to depict various levels of emotional attachments of their

TABLE 1-2 Common Symbols and Abbreviations in Family Genograms

☐ Male (always to left of genogram)

○ Female

☐———○ Marriage

☐——/——○ Separation

☐——//——○ Divorce

☐——✕——○ Widowed

☐- - - - - - ○ Engaged

☐-··—··—··-○ Cohabitation

☐-··—··-☐
○-··—··-○ (Same Sex)

Other Symbols:

Pet	Pregnancy	Miscarriage	Abortion	Unknown Sex
◇	△	⧄	⧄	**?**

TABLE 1-3 Examples of Emotional Attachments in Family Genograms

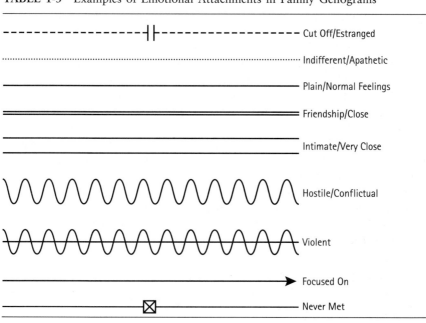

Source: Adapted from *www.genopro.com.*

relationships (see Table 1-3). Let's detail how a family genogram works to give you a better understanding of the relationship between a family-of-origin and intergenerationality.

Let's examine the Cushman family. Bob Cushman has married two times. He had three children with his first wife, Mitsy, then divorced her. Bob then married his second wife, Ardis, had one child, and separated from her. He currently lives with another woman, Wanda. The genogram would look like this:

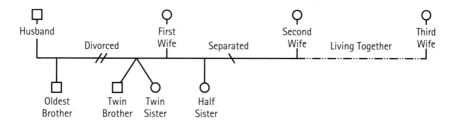

Family genograms depicted by various family members are useful visual ways to represent family relationships and the communication between and among family members. We should point out that not everyone in a family may agree with another's genogram. You, for instance, may think you and your mom have a great relationship; your brother, however, may diagram your relationship with your mother as conflicted after he heard an argument between the two of you. As Monica McGoldrick, Randy Gerson, and Sylvia Shellenberger (1999) observe, different family members may perceive things differently and, consequently, may construct genograms differently.

We hope that as you read this book, you will be able to identify how your family-of-origin, intergenerationality, and genograms may have been pivotal in your current thinking about how a family should function. Perhaps you are comfortable with the ideologies and belief systems learned in your family-of-origin. Or it could be that you will begin to challenge some of the attitudes and values you have held based on how they have been transmitted through the generations.

We all experience family first, in our families-of-origin, making our understanding of family life narrow, but deep. That is, we have a great deal of knowledge about only one family. Reading about families very different from our own helps us widen our understanding of the family. Therefore, let's begin our discussion of various family types.

Before we begin our discussion of the primary family types, we should point out that this category system is not meant to be exhaustive. That is, what we present here is a system rooted in the research. In addition, these categories are often used for legalistic, political, and/or demographic purposes, providing us with a common understanding as we read about the types outside of this text. Finally, governmental organizations such as the Centers for Disease Control and the Department of the Treasury include most of these family types as they gather data.

As you read about the different types, many of you may ask: "Hey, where's my family?" Again, you should interpret the following as if it is a foundation for further discussion. You will likely see some variation of your family structure in the following. Or, it may be that your family is "on the horizon," meaning that scholars have yet to fully investigate this family form. Regardless of impression or life experience, we encourage each of you to think about family life through the various categorical prisms we identify below.

Student Perspective: Jean

Marrying Jason is the best thing that has happened in my life. I don't mind staying at home to take care of the two kids. What's hard is the housekeeping and the meals! It gets pretty tough at times, but I love Jason and he loves me. I'm blessed in that he has a great job that doesn't require him to travel. We get to see him every night.

▶ Nuclear Families

Description   The nuclear family was named, in part, because the "nucleus," or center, was the core where others would gravitate. In a larger context, then, society coalesced this family form, making the nuclear family the foundation of American families for centuries. We categorize the nuclear family in two ways: traditional nuclear and contemporary nuclear. The **traditional nuclear family** is composed of a married couple living with their biological children, with the husband/father working outside the home and the wife/mother working in the home as mother and full-time homemaker. Traditional nuclear families are also called **families of procreation.** The **contemporary nuclear family** is a modernized version of the nuclear family; it may include a stay-at-home dad with a mom working outside the home as the primary financial provider or a **dual-career family** (also called *two-income family*), which is a husband/father and wife/mother working outside the home who are also primary caregivers of children at home.

Demographics For decades, the traditional family was the norm in the United States, thus its reference as "traditional." The U.S. Census Bureau (2011a) found that 21.6 percent of households are defined as nuclear. That figure, according to the Census Bureau, is aligned with Japan, Denmark, and the United Kingdom. However, it is interesting to note that Sweden has approximately 18 percent of households who define as nuclear, and Ireland's nuclear family households total approximately 30 percent. Further, while some may believe in an inevitable demise of the traditional nuclear family, the Census Bureau (*http://www.census.gov/newsroom/releases/archives/families_households/cb10-174.html*) reports that because of likely economic challenges, in 2010, 23 percent of married couples had a stay-at-home mother, up from 21 percent in 2000.

While the traditional nuclear family decreases in size, the contemporary nuclear family is growing in the United States. Stay-at-home dads (married fathers with children under 15 years who are not in the labor force), for instance, number 158,000, up from 143,000 in 2005 (think of movies such as *Mr. Mom* or *Daddy Day Care*). Dual-career families (where both husband and wife simultaneously pursue active careers and family lives), too, have increased substantially over the years, attributed to the nearly 50 percent increase of women currently in the workforce (U.S. Department of Labor, 2011). Contemporary nuclear families will continue to proliferate due to the changing nature of how women and men see themselves and their roles in the family.

What can we expect in the coming years with respect to nuclear families? First, the traditional nuclear family will likely continue to decline because of increased mobility, modern technology, increase in single-parent families, and society's general tolerance for a variety of family types. Second, binuclear families will become more prevalent. **Binuclear families** span two households, each headed by one partner (Ahrons, 1994, 2004; White, 2011). Following divorce and remarriage of the original marital partners and parents, a newly configured (and stable) family context across two homes emerges. Constance Ahrons believes that this binuclear agreement is often considered as a child-supportive arrangement. Finally, the Families and Work Institute estimates that the contemporary nuclear family consisting of dual-wage earners with children will constitute the largest number of nuclear families in the future (*www.familiesandwork.org*). Economic necessity will dictate this family arrangement.

Current Controversies   Today, some "pro-family" individuals and organizations have initiated an effort to reinstate the traditional nuclear family. The National Marriage Project and the Institute for American Values are two such institutions advocating for a return to "family normalcy." Some individuals, such as Phyllis Schlafly of the Eagle Forum (*www.eagleforum.org*), argue that society's very foundation rests upon two-parent families with a stay-at-home mom as the children's primary caregiver. She and others advance that society's willingness to accept alternatives to the traditional family is problematic. Too many options available to families often result in the breakdown of families in society. Returning to more "normal" and "comfortable" images of the family is lauded by many who have been bothered by the diversity of families (Schlafly, 2003).

Stephanie Coontz (2000b) in *The Way We Never Were: American Families and the Nostalgia Trap* warns, however, that Schlafly and others with similar thinking are likely clinging to antiquated perceptions of family life. She notes that many past visions of family life "bear a suspicious resemblance to reruns of old television series" (p. 8). Coontz also notes that many people have been caught up in romantic notions of traditional families, yet these same people often forget that during these more "normal and comfortable" times, abuse, incest, and economic hardship characterized millions of "traditional" households. Coontz (2000a) advises that we should accept the fact that change is here: "It is time to admit that there is no way to reverse the past 200 years of social change" (p. 16).

Communication in Nuclear Families   Members of the traditional nuclear family face some problems while communicating outside of the family, especially given the significant decreases in this family form. Some research shows that men and women in this traditional family form display stereotypical sex role behaviors (Kimmel, 2000). For instance, Theresa Mariani, the 10-year-old daughter of Carlo and Ursala Mariani, may not understand why her best friend's mom works at the local hardware store. Theresa's mom doesn't work outside the home and is around for Theresa when she gets home from school. Or, consider the challenge of Isa Richmond whose father is the sole breadwinner in her family and who makes most of the decisions regarding vacations, major purchases, and other financial matters. Isa's mother, on the other hand, is "in charge" of taking care of her daughter and being the homemaker.

What about the contemporary nuclear family? With respect to one type–the dual-career family–the Work and Families Institute (*http://www.familiesandwork.org/site/newsroom/releases/pr_malemystique_110630.html*) notes that fathers, in particular, have increased the amount of time that they do household tasks, although mothers still do more than fathers around the house. It is clear that family life can affect work life, called the *spillover effect*. John Duckworth and Patrice Buzzanell (2009) found that when specifically examining family life, men tend to link family to their work life. That is, men tended to frame their family responsibilities with their work responsibilities. For some men, then, the spillover entails being committed to and responsible for both family and a community that includes religious institutions and extended family members. In light of all the findings associated with the nuclear family, no family communication research concludes that either a traditional or a contemporary nuclear family has more effective communication between and among family members.

▶ Gay and Lesbian Families

Description **Gay and lesbian families** include two people of the same sex who maintain an intimate relationship and who serve as parents for at least one child. This family form has gained attention over the past several years, particularly given the 2004 Massachusetts Supreme Judicial Court decision effectively declaring that it is unconstitutional (in Massachusetts) to deny gays and lesbians the right to marry. Since then, gay and lesbian families have been front and center in the media.

It hasn't always been this way. In fact, for years family communication scholars did not investigate this family form. One explanation for the lack of research attention may pertain to **homophobia**, which is an irrational fear of homosexuals or homosexuality (much of it unconscious). Another reason surrounding the lack of communication research on this family form is a notion called **heterosexism**, which is the assumption that heterosexuality is universal. In other words, our society tends to support the promotion of heterosexual ways of thinking and relating, thereby inhibiting attention to gay and lesbian families. Contemporary family communication scholars, however, now study gay and lesbian families and our knowledge about this family type is growing.

Student Perspective: Juan

When we first adopted Rachel, our hearts were filled with joy. My partner, David, and I knew from the start that this was exactly what we wanted. The fact that she was HIV-positive was not really all that important. What was important was that we had enough love for her and for each other that we knew we would make it through any hard times. As gay men, we know what hard times are. As gay fathers, we're not so sure what the future holds.

Demographics   Reporting numbers related to sexuality and families is a difficult undertaking. First, there are confusing statistics related to the percentage of gay and lesbian individuals in the United States. Additionally, some surveys report on gay and lesbian families with no information on whether the family is comprised of a single parent or two parents. Third, the percentage of children living with gay- and lesbian-headed households is not fully understood since, like those in heterosexual-headed households, some children may be temporarily living with their parent(s). Despite growing awareness and increased levels of comfort disclosing sexual identity, the number of gay fathers and lesbian mothers (and their children) is not accurately known for several reasons. Continued bigotry and misperception of this family type continues in some parts of the United States. Also, the government has been inconsistent and inaccurate in its surveying of this family type. Over the years, even when same-sex household members identified themselves as "couples," the Census Bureau simply went ahead and changed the sex of one of the partners, rendering this household type as a heterosexual-headed family (Smith & Gates, 2001). Today, the Census Bureau has become more thoughtful and sensitive to this family form. For instance, data from the 2008 American Community Survey show that there are approximately 415,000 reported same-sex unmarried partner households and 150,000 reported same-sex spousal households, representing 27 percent of all same-sex couple households. Finally, the 2010 Census reports that there are 901,997 same-sex couple households in the United States.

Current Controversies   The gay and lesbian family–indeed, the "gayby boom"–does not enjoy complete acceptance in the United States. Although several states and the District of Columbia provide legal recognition and protection of same-sex marriage (e.g., Massachusetts, Vermont, Connecticut, Iowa, New Hampshire), there are movements underway to dismantle such protection. In Iowa, where three of the state Supreme Court justices were ousted as a result of voting in support of gay men and lesbians to marry, life for gay and lesbian families has been, well, normal. Some report that while there has been some stigma, the lives of many gay and lesbian families are rather "boring" (Bulmer, 2011). From a scholarly vantage point, there are no negative repercussions associated with a child being raised by a gay father or lesbian mother. Some organizations, such as the Family Research Council, remain adamantly opposed to the legal recognition of same-sex relationships (*www.frc.org*). In fact, the council notes that "children hunger for their biological parents" (*www.frc.org*). And, in 1996, President Clinton signed the Defense of Marriage Act (DOMA), which, among other things, explicitly defined marriage as occurring between one man and one woman. With this law at the federal level, over 40 states adopted some version of DOMA as state law, making the legality of gay and lesbian relationships that much more difficult. We explore the intersection between government and family life in Chapter 4.

In what was then a very provocative move, in May 2012, President Obama declared his support for the rights of same-sex couples to get married. While some viewed the statement to be political, it was met with a great deal of response. Some felt that he was simply trying to solidify his liberal base of voters for the 2012 election; others felt that he had lost his integrity. Still others were not sure what impact this support would have on gay- and lesbian-headed households. Regardless of perspective, only time will tell just how much impact the words of President Obama had upon the same-sex marriage debate.

These perceptions and political activities, however, are not endorsed by everyone. Not everyone is convinced that the sky is falling. First, after reviewing over 20 studies on gay and lesbian parenting, researchers conclude that a parent's sexuality has no negative effect on the behavior of children (Stacey & Biblarz, 2001). Letitia Anne Peplau and Kristin Beals (2004) also posit that no evidence exists "that the children of gay and lesbian parents differ systematically from children of heterosexual parents . . . in psychological well-being, self-esteem, behavioral problems, intelligence, cognitive abilities, or peer relations" (p. 242). Second, in 2005, the American Psychological Association (APA) voted to support the right of gays and lesbians to marry. In doing this, the organization legitimized gay and lesbian families everywhere. Third, the pervasiveness of gay and lesbian families cannot be ignored: Dan Gilgoff in *U.S. News & World Report* (2004) notes that "gay families have arrived in suburban America, in small-town America, in Bible Belt America—in all corners of the country" (p. 41). In other words, gay and lesbian families live next door, down the block, and around the corner.

Communication in Gay and Lesbian Families   What do we know about communication in this family configuration? We undertook one of the first studies in family communication looking at this family type (West & Turner, 1995). We discovered the following: Gay fathers receive messages of support from their families-of-origin, include their partners in their decision making, and feel that they are flexible with respect to communicating with their children. Lesbian mothers varied in their experiences with their families-of-origin and report open communication with their current families. Both gay fathers and lesbian mothers feel they are the targets of homophobia. Peplau and Beals (2004), in their review, contend that self-disclosure of sexual identity is a difficult issue for gay men and lesbians. The researchers also observed a number of other conclusions relevant to family communication, namely that same-sex couples seek out power equality, gay men and lesbians desire a loving and committed relationship, and when a decision is made to become a parent, "children are strongly desired and planned" (p. 241).

The communication demands on a gay father or lesbian mother are complex and numerous. First, these parents must come to terms with their own homosexuality. Next, these parents must decide whether they wish others, such as their children, to know about their homosexuality, a disclosure with far-reaching implications for most parents. Finally, gay and lesbian parents struggle with parenting issues similar to those of their heterosexual parent peers—from child care to child discipline (Peplau & Beals, 2004; Hicks, 2011). In light of all this, the communication patterns in gay- and lesbian-headed households are both unique and consistent with heterosexual families.

▶ Extended Families

Description Many people belong to family groups that expand beyond the family-of-origin. Unlike other family types, **biological extended families**, sometimes called **multigenerational families**, include parents and children living together, as well as other relatives such as aunts, uncles, and grandparents. Historically, people maintained their extended families because the country was an agricultural economy, and family members worked the land and kept it in the family; therefore, they chose to stay together. Although this description typifies most extended families, it's important to point out that some extended family members often serve as immediate family members as well. Grandparents, for instance, are fast becoming primary caregivers for their grandchildren, with over 2.5 million grandparents providing primary care to nearly 3 million grandchildren (U.S. Census Bureau, 2011), resulting in a more fluid interpretation of the extended family unit. With increases in longevity, what was once a family type typical in many cultural groups now, literally, will extend to millions of families. A variation of this family type is the communal extended family, which includes the voluntary families of friends discussed earlier in the chapter.

Demographics The economic recession a few years back forever influenced the presence of multiple generations under one roof. The loss of jobs, home foreclosures, and the return of children to the home resulted in an increase in extended families in the United States. In addition, historical shifts have prompted major changes in the numbers of extended families. As Donna St. George of the *Washington Post* (March 18, 2010) put it, the number of multigenerational households is at its highest point in 50 years.

The Pew Research Center (*http://pewsocialtrends.org/ 2010/03/18/the-return-of-the-multi-generational-family-household*) reports that 49 million, or about 16 percent of the population,

Student Perspective: Franklin

When I think of my grandmother, I think of someone who helped me with my geography in fifth grade, who always made me carrot cake, who told great stories, who went to church with our family every Sunday morning at 10:30, and who always had time to listen to me. She had lived with us since I was a little boy. In a way, she was my second mom. She's gone now and I really miss her.

live in a multigenerational household. By the year 2050, about 100 million people in the United States will be over the age of 65 (U.S. Census Bureau, 2011), resulting in an obvious uptick in the extended family form. Kenneth Corbin (2011) reports that among those in the 25–34 age bracket, 16.4 percent of men and 10.5 percent of women are currently living with at least one parent. Corbin provides data to conclude that this is the highest level since World War II. And, as we noted earlier, with life expectancy increasing, many families will be asked to care for aging family members, thus increasing the number of extended families.

In addition, a report from the U.S. Department of Health and Human Services (HHS) (*http://www.acf.hhs.gov/healthymarriage/pdf/Gender_Norms .pdf*) reports that in many Hispanic communities, extended family members serve as social support networks when there are economic or personal challenges in a family unit. Interestingly, as a result of migration, some members of the Hispanic population may feel isolated and not have extended family members available for support. Consequently, according to the HHS report, *compadres* (a very close member of the family unit not related to the member) become instrumental.

Extended families are commonplace in many cultural groups. A significant number of Italian American families, for example, include extended family households with close ties to each other (Romeo, 2011). In fact, extended families date back many years. Junious Ricardo Stanton (1999) relates that in Africa, "the extended family was the root and source of strength for the village, tribe, and nation. Not only were there no orphans, but there were also no jails or prisons" (p. 2). Oscar Barbarin (2002) notes that the extended family is also common to many African American households. Extended family members in African American families often provide support in the upward mobility (such as attending college, getting an apartment or house) and self-esteem of family members. Finally, Maria Schmeeckle and Susan Sprecher (2004) report research that explains the cultural variations associated with extended family networks: 1 in 7 whites, 1 in 3 African Americans, 4 in 5 Asian Americans, and over 19 in 20 Native Americans are identified as part of extended families.

Current Controversies At first glance, it may appear that extended family arrangements would elicit little controversy. Yet, there are those who believe that this family configuration can jeopardize children. In extended families, often family members act as foster parents for those children who are abused or neglected. This sort of parenting usually takes place without the knowledge of policy officials. According to a report by the U.S. Department of Health and Human Services (2000), "it has been difficult for Federal and State policy makers, as well as advocates and practitioners, to evaluate how well kinship care ensures children's safety, promotes permanency in their living situations, and enhances their well-being" (p. iv). Further, with so many different family members living under the same roof, some children may also be unclear about the roles and rules in a home (Beaton, Norris, & Pratt, 2003). Some scholars, however, are encouraged by the extended family type. First, Schmeeckle and Sprecher (2012) note that grandparents, aunts, and uncles may play important and useful roles in the raising of a child. For example, this extended family network may be a source of nurturance, a help with economic resources, a connection to those who may be able to provide educational or work opportunities, and a provider of important child care. Despite divergent views of the effects of the extended family on children, we will continue to see increases in extended families due to a number of issues, including unemployment, health care costs, and cultural traditions.

Communication in Extended Families   Older generation family members do play a significant role in family life. The concept of multigenerational transmission of rules, roles, and other patterns of relating under one roof is especially true in extended families. Older family members—specifically grandparents—serve as confidants and, in some cases, as friends of younger family members. Jake Harwood (2004), for example, notes that the grandparent–grandchild relationship "can be a place in which confidences are shared and family histories are learned, in an environment perceived as more 'free' than in conversations with parents" (p. 301). Yet, too much reliance on older family members may cause communication problems in the extended family. For instance, with a grandmother at home virtually 24 hours a day, some family members may make repeated requests for her to do household tasks (laundry, dishes, babysitting). A problem may emerge if the grandmother is reluctant to disclose that she is uncomfortable with the requests. In addition, to refer back to our definition of communication, the grandmother may interpret the request on a relational level and dislike the relationship that she infers. Both these communication issues may result in conflict in the family.

Decisions regarding parenthood, divorce, and remarriage within the extended family are influenced by the social network of friends, neighbors, and other family members (Schmeeckle & Sprecher, 2004). These networks, or kinship systems, can affect decisions in an extended family if the boundaries are permeable. With respect to parenting and the decision to have a child, for instance, the researchers conclude, "For both women and men, interactive networks tended to be primarily composed of extended family members during their children's first few years of life" (p. 363). Kinship systems also affect decisions regarding whether or not a distressed couple should terminate or repair their relationship. If a couple breaks up, the social network is likely to be disrupted. And, with remarriage, there are shared responsibilities with other adults (and children) present.

Rules are especially important in a unique component of the extended family, a variation called **boomerang kids** (Odun, 2003; Okimoto & Stegall, 1987; Pickhardt, 2011). These are children who return home after a period of time away. Other writers have termed this phenomenon **nesting**—an unexpected return of young adults who family members thought had left permanently. Nan Mead of the National Endowment for Financial Education (*www.nefe.org*) reports that more than 25 percent of young adults between the ages of 25 and 34 are living with their parents.

Communication skills can be seriously affected in a family with boomerang kids. Foremost, stressful relationships with a parent may occur because the rules that were intact years ago are now in flux. It's difficult to tell a 30-year-old, for instance, that a curfew exists or that the telephone is off-limits. Different interpretations of household duties can cause conflict between parent and child (Odun, 2003). There's a loss of privacy in physical surroundings; the private has now turned public. Also, parents may feel guilty if their needs are in competition with what their child needs. Finally, the presence of adult children in the family nest may begin to drain the finances of the parent(s), since many children begin to drive the family car, eat food, and utilize home resources such as water and electricity (Pickhardt, 2011).

Not all families experience difficulties with the return of a child. Some parents in particular may be elated to have the company, especially in some Middle Eastern cultures. Others may be excited about having help around the house. Still other parents may be proud that their home continues to be viewed as a place to return.

▶ Stepfamilies

Description   A **stepfamily** is defined as a family with a married couple who provides continued care for at least one child who is not the biological offspring of both the adults. In fact, this family form can be described as "the second time around" insofar as a reconstituted family has evolved from two different families. The stepfamily has frequently been called the blended family; however, the National Stepfamily Resource Center (NSRC) (2011) indicates that the term *blended* is a catchy media phrase that many stepfamilies find troublesome. They note that *stepfamily* is a "preferred" way of looking at this family configuration because it is in line with how many other family types define themselves (vis-à-vis the parent-child relationship). On its website, the NSRC states: "Stepfamilies do not 'blend.' If one is determined to use a cooking phrase, try 'combine' or 'fold gently.' " Children in stepfamilies do not lose their individuality or

Student Perspective: Cassandra

We're no Brady Bunch, that's for sure. My two brothers and I constantly manipulate our mom to get what we want. Sometimes we play our mom off against our stepdad, Brian. And there can be a lot of arguing between our family and Brian's kids. It's strange. First, we had sadness because of our parents' divorce. Then, we had happiness because my mom got remarried to Brian. Now, we have confusion because two adults and seven children are living together.

Children in Stepfamilies Are Referred to as:

- Siblings—biologically related; from the same parents.
- Step-siblings—not biologically related; parents are married to each other.
- Half-siblings—partially related biologically (i.e., share one parent).
- Mutual child—a child born to the remarried couple.
- Residential stepchildren—live in the household with the remarried couple the majority of the time.
- Nonresidential stepchildren—live in the household less than half of the time.

---

their connection and active attachment to the parent who is not part of the remarriage of mother or father." The different labeling of a stepfamily is, in part, because of the reorganization needed following death or divorce of a spouse. The labels and descriptions may vary in connotations, and many who are a part of this family type remain unhappy with the terms available to name themselves.

Demographics   More and more people are now members of stepfamilies. Earlier in the chapter we noted that stepfamilies are increasing. Current estimates show that nearly 50 percent of all first marriages end in divorce (*www.divorcerate .org*). Of those who divorce, the NSRC reports that 75 percent will remarry, and of those who remarry, the Forest Institute of Professional Psychology (2011) reports that 67 percent of all second marriages will end in divorce. In addition, the U.S. Census Current Population Reports (*http://www.census.gov/ prod/2011pubs/p70-126.pdf*) notes that 5.6 million children, or 7.5 percent, live with at least one stepparent. Finally, Marilyn Coleman, Lawrence Ganong, and Mark Fine (2004) point out that stepfamilies are not only formed while children are young. They note that about half a million people over the age of 65 remarry each year, creating stepfamilies with older adults.

Current Controversies   Because millions of stepfamilies occur as a result of divorce and subsequent remarriage, some organizations have engaged in a spirited conversation regarding divorce overall. For instance, Bridget Maher (2001) of the Family Research Council believes that divorce should be more difficult to attain in the United States. She emphatically notes that spouses with children should not be able to walk away from their marriages and remarry. She has received support from an organization called Marriage Savers (2004). This group's mission is "saving" troubled marriages and, therefore, preventing the proliferation of stepfamilies. Marriage Savers (2011) (*www.marriagesavers.com*) issues Congregational Awards to those churches who make the following pledge:

> *We can offer you Marriage Insurance. Your marriage will not only go the distance; it will prosper and be a joy to you and your children and your children's children.*

Age at Marriage for Those Who Divorce in America

Age	Women	Men
Under 20 years old	27.6%	11.7%
20 to 24 years old	36.6%	38.8%
25 to 29 years old	16.4%	22.3%
30 to 34 years old	8.5%	11.6%
35 to 39 years old	5.1%	6.5%

This "covenant" pledge asks clergy to require at least four months of marriage preparation for any couple wishing to get married.

Constance Ahrons (1994) believes such a view is not fair. She notes that there are millions of marriages that end amicably and in which children are not negatively affected. She asserts: "Good divorces don't make headlines" (p. x). The Stepfamily Association of America tends to agree. The organization (*www.saafamilies.org*) explains that among the common myths associated with stepfamilies is the belief that divorce (and remarriage) will forever damage children. The association reports that most children "recover their emotional equilibrium" following a divorce, and after some years together, most children are found "to be no different, in many important ways, from kids in first marriage families."

Communication in Stepfamilies Within the stepfamily, as in all families, there are tensions that exist with both the adults and children. Coleman et al. (2004) note that while many stepfamilies try to re-create nuclear families, their efforts generally fail. Trying to negotiate new relationships within the family is simply too difficult. There are many emotional challenges dealing with feelings of betrayal associated with the absent parent. Further, children are often angry about not being able to talk about past events and grow weary of having to pretend with feelings that do not exist.

Additional research by Dawn Braithwaite and her associates verifies other communication-related issues associated with the stepfamily. For example, Braithwaite, Loreen Olson, Tamara Golish, Charles Soukup, and Paul Turman (2001) looked at the first four years of a stepfamily's existence to get a deeper understanding of the coming-together process. They discovered that family members who were patient, who tried to understand and accept the inevitable changes that will take place, and who understood that it will take time to coalesce as a family tended to see the family get closer as the new stepfamily formed. Those who challenged the process or who fought changes in roles or norms were more inclined to experience conflict.

Finally, Braithwaite, M. Chad McBride, and Paul Schrodt (2003) found that co-parenting is an important factor associated with the communication in stepfamilies. Co-parenting occurs when both parents remain responsible for raising their child(ren). Braithwaite and her colleagues found that co-parents reported moderate levels of satisfaction with how they interacted with each other. Further, these interactions were short episodes rather than long, extended periods of time. What was discussed? Not surprisingly, children accounted for the most number of topics discussed. What did surprise the researchers is that there were relatively few complaints about the "other" adult. Braithwaite and colleagues explain the results this way: "These parent teams had achieved a system of equilibrium and communication that worked at least reasonably well most of the time for the different parties involved" (p. 107).

▶ Single-Parent Families

Description   As recently as 20 years ago, single-parent families were thought of with little respect, particularly those who were single because of divorce. Today, however, images of single parents have evolved. **Single-parent households,** which include one adult and at least one child, have also been referred to as *primary-parent households.* Whether in the mediated, political, or spiritual context, negative impressions of single parents are quickly disappearing.

Although a very small number of single parents are men, many in our culture admire these fathers. One reason for this admiration pertains to our impressions and expectations of men in general. Many people are simply unaccustomed to thinking about men acting out effective parenting roles, a norm frequently associated with how our society views men. That is, our stereotypical sex-role scripts for men suggest that men are not usually perceived as nurturing, loving, and oriented toward child rearing (Ivy, 2012). As a result, single fathers are often admired more than single mothers.

Student Perspective: Maria

When my husband left, I wasn't sure where I was going to turn. With three kids and a part-time job, I was destined for disaster. Yet, for some strange reason, I continue to make it. I think it's because I have pretty good support from friends. I don't know how I'd make it without them. Everybody needs friends, but for a single mom they're essential!

Because mothers are expected to provide child care in families, they do not receive much praise for carrying out this role expectation within the single-parent household. Further, because women are usually designated as the relational experts (Ivy, 2012), society tends to blame them for their single-parent status.

Demographics   During the 1990s, a decade when research on single parents flourished, demographers noted that the number of single-parent households was growing. Available estimates at the time showed that between 1970–1990, occurrences of this family type tripled. Currently, according to the

2011 Statistical Abstract of the United States (*http://www.census.gov/compendia/statab/cats/international statistics.html*), there are over 10 million single-parent households in the United States, comprising 29.5 percent of all households in the country. This figure is similar to the percentage of single-parent households in Canada (24.6) and the United Kingdom (25.0), but is very dissimilar to Japan (10.2). With respect to single mothers, the Census Bureau (*http://www.census.gov/newsroom/releases/archives/children/cb09–170.html*) also reports that there are approximately 13.7 million single parents of all races, responsible for 21.8 million children under the age of 21. Of those, 18 million children live with single mothers (Mather, 2010), meaning that 24 percent of all children in the United States live in homes with single mothers. Overall, Rose Krieder (2010) of the U.S. Census Bureau discovered that there are about 17.3 million single mothers and 2.5 million single fathers in the United States. In sum, single-parent households represent nearly 27 percent of all U.S. households with children.

Current Controversies   One primary argument associated with single-parent families is the belief—held by some—that their existence actually contributes to crime in the United States. Ann Coulter (2009) has remarked that much of the crime in the United States can be attributed to single mothers. In fact, she goes on to say that most social ills can be attributed to the single-parent (mother) family. Patrick Fagan is rather clear in his assessment: "It is now a widely accepted premise that children born into single-parent families are much more likely than children born into intact families to fall into poverty and welfare dependency" (cited in *http://goodnewstucson.wordpress.com/2010/05/05/the-real-root-cause-of-violent-crime-the-breakdown-of-the-family/*). In addition, David Kopel (2000) states that because two-parent households are better for society in general, they are less prone to have family members who break the law.

   As you might guess, others disagree with these claims. First, Stephen Sugarman (1998) reminds us that correlations between family structure and child outcomes do not establish causality. That is, we should not assume that a person's family configuration necessarily leads to crime. Sugarman also questions the value of holding parents accountable for the actions of their children. Second, Carole Baldock (1999) notes that perhaps society's focus should be on the difficulty single parents face with respect to the dual challenge of finding a decent job and staying at home to raise their children. Randy Albelda, Susan Himmelweit, and Jane Humphries (2004) underscore this thinking by noting that single mothers in particular are "caught on the horns of a dilemma: if they work the long hours necessary to provide an acceptable standard of living from a poorly paid job, they condemn their children (and themselves) to insufficient time together as a family" (p. 2). Further, Baldock believes a single-parent family configuration may actually be beneficial to both parent and child. She argues that rather than a hostile home environment where a husband and wife argue, children will fare better under a more peaceful arrangement with only one parent.

Family support for the single parent varies greatly from family to family. Some writers have pointed out that there can be ongoing involvement with the "other" parent (Frisby & Sidelinger, 2009; Graham, 1997; Soliz, 2008). Further, although research has demonstrated that the parent's family-of-origin may be somewhat supportive (Kitson & Morgan, 1990), other researchers conclude that the meta-messages from the family-of-origin may actually communicate blame, betrayal, and abandonment (Lewis, Wallerstein, & Johnson-Reitz, 2004; Spanier & Thompson, 1984). This blame only exacerbates the difficulties of being in a single-parent situation. However, these generalizations must be tempered by understanding the influence of culture. For instance, African American families are generally rooted in the values of collectivism, which, as Doris Wilkinson (1997) notes, has allowed the African American family to thrive "as an essential communal network of sharing, support, protection, emotional reinforcement, and adaptation to the regularity of change" (p. 41). Further, African American families headed by single mothers engage in what has been called "no-nonsense parenting" (Warren, Allen, Hopfer, & Okuyemi, 2010, p. 30), which is a combination of warmth and a deep concern for monitoring and vigilance. Finally, Yolanda Sanchez (1997) and Ana Baumann, Jill Kuhlberg, and Luis Zayas (2010) observe that some Latino cultures value a concept known as familism, which is a focus on the extended family. In sum, then, many single parents receive a great deal of support from family members in many co-cultures.

▶ Couples

Description   We distinguish between two types of couples: **cohabiting couples** and **married couples.** In both cases, two adults live together without the presence of children. Cohabiting and married couples are either child-free (choose not to have children) or childless (not able to have children).

For purposes of our discussion, cohabiting couples are characterized by romantic interest. Married couples, too, are romantically involved, and they have declared that love by a matrimonial bond. We do not include in our definition roommates who live together because of financial advantages or simply because they like each other, nor do we

Student Perspective: Loran

Why is it that our country pressures straight people to get married? I have been living with my girlfriend for over six years now, and we have no intention of getting married. We love our privacy, we want no children, and we learned to love each other without that marriage contract. In fact, we believe that legalizing our relationship by marrying might mess it up and spoil what we have.

consider children living in a cohabiting household. We also focus our discussion on heterosexual couples, since most of the demographic information derived from the government has historically ignored same-sex cohabitation configurations. Nonetheless, we include same-sex couples in our discussion when appropriate.

Some people believe that cohabitation is a relatively recent phenomenon. There is evidence, however, to suggest that this family form was discussed as early as the 1920s (Russell, 1929). Sometimes referred to as **paperless marriage,** cohabitation is often sought out as an alternative to marriage. In some states, **common-law marriage** is a variation of cohabitation. This type of marriage exists without the formality of a ceremony, and some states, such as Texas, recognize common-law marriage as legal when both partners publicly identify themselves as married.

For some, cohabitation is a part of the courtship process, whereby two adults decide to engage in a romantic relationship, and living together solidifies the relationship bond. Some cohabiting partners may have been previously married, and now they prefer to cohabit to assess the future of their relationship. Other cohabitors simply desire to avoid any legal or religious sanctions for their relationship. Some people, especially the elderly, cohabit for financial reasons.

Couples choosing to get married are unlike cohabitors in that in the United States these couples are legally recognized. Although many people consider marriage to be a private affair, the married couple relinquishes considerable control to the government. Public policy often determines what a couple can and cannot do. In many states, for example, there are legal consequences to selling joint property without the consent of one's spouse. Still, married couples are given an abundance of rights and privileges denied to unmarried couples: inheritance rights, medical decisions, transferring property, overseeing burials, and others.

Demographics There are over 100 million unmarried people in the United States, representing approximately 30 percent of the population (*http://www.unmarried.org/statistics.html*). The number of cohabiting couples in the United States has soared over the years. The 2000 Census found 4.9 million households that were comprised of unmarried couples with opposite-sex partners (U.S. Census Bureau, 2004). There were approximately 595,000 unmarried couples with same-sex partners. Today, the numbers have increased substantially. The 2010 Census discovered 7.5 million opposite-sex cohabiting couples living together and over 700,000 same-sex cohabiting partners (*http://californiawatch.org/dailyreport/tracking-unmarried-same-sex-couples-using-social-maps-4233*). Most demographers pointed to the economic recession that gripped the United States in the first decade of the 21st century as a primary reason for the uptick in unmarried couples. It's also important to point out that because of the advent of same-sex marriage (first in 2004 in the state of Massachusetts), the number of same-sex cohabitors remained lower than if same-sex marriage was not legal in various states. Further, demographic characteristics show that women cohabitate at about the same rates as men do (approximately 3.7 percent overall and 9 percent for those between ages 15–44) (*http://.cdc.gov/nchs/data/series/sr_23/sr_23028.pdf*). Further, among various co-cultures, there is some variation among white (3.4 percent), African American (5.3 percent), and Latino (3.9 percent) (*http://www.cdc.gov/nchs/data/series/sr_23/sr23_028.pdf*) couples.

For the first time in U.S. history the number of households with married couples is not the majority household type. And, yet, the number of households headed by married couples in the United States is extremely high. In 2000, nearly 6 in 10 adults (59 percent) were married. In 2010, just 48 percent of households were comprised of married couples (Tavernise, 2011). This number is clearly a steep decline from 1970, when 72 percent of adults in the United States were married. The median age for first marriages in 2010 was 28.2 (for men) and 26.7 (for women), compared to 1950 when the median age for men was 22.8 and for women 20.3 (see Table 1-4).

TABLE 1-4   Median Age at First Marriage, 1890–2010

Year	Males	Females
1890	26.1	22.0
1900	25.9	21.9
1910	25.1	21.6
1920	24.6	21.2
1930	24.3	21.3
1940	24.3	21.5
1950	22.8	20.3
1960	22.8	20.3
1970	23.2	20.8
1980	24.7	22.0
1990	26.1	23.9
1993	26.5	24.5
1994	26.7	24.5
1995	26.9	24.5
1996	27.1	24.8
1997	26.8	25.0
1998	26.7	25.0
1999	26.9	25.1
2000	26.8	25.1
2001	26.9	25.1
2002	26.9	25.3
2003	27.1	25.3
2005	27.0	25.5
2006	27.5	25.9
2007	27.71	26.0
2008	27.6	25.9
2009	28.1	25.9
2010	28.2	26.1

Current Controversies   Despite the decline in people getting married, the institution of marriage enjoys widespread acceptance in society. As Michelle Conlin (2003) notes, "Even as marriage is on the wane, infatuation with the institution has never seemed so fierce" (p. 107). She argues that our society is "marriage-crazed," if not for anything else, for the "bonanza of perks" that are offered to a newly married couple (for example, inheritance rights, unequal taxation, health plan coverage, and so on).

Unlike married couples, cohabiting couples have stirred criticism in the United States. Many conservative religious and secular organizations claim that romantic cohabitation should not be sanctioned in our society because living together without a marriage bond only shatters a "solid" family foundation. Carin Gorrell (2000) in *Psychology Today* also points out that cohabiting couples may be prone to display more negative and fewer positive support behaviors than those who did not cohabit before marriage. Karen Peterson (2003) identifies a child psychologist with Focus on the Family, a conservative organization, as saying, "As a Christian organization, we have a strong view that sexuality is a gift from God, and the Bible clearly tells us it is expressed correctly in marriage" (p. 8A).

Kevin Jones (2011) calls cohabitation a very unstable family choice and reviews research that he believes demonstrates that this family configuration harms children, hurts poor and working-class communities, and is a threat to the future of the family. Kammi Schmeer (2011) also investigated cohabitation and child well-being and discovered that children who are in families with cohabiting parents have worse health than those with "stably" married parents (p. 181). Finally, Kate Choi and Judith Selfzer (2011) posit that when discussing cohabitation, it's important to recognize that there are a multiplicity of issues, themes, and variables to consider. The researchers contend that for some cultural groups, there are numerous reasons (e.g., economic, family, etc.) why people cohabit, resulting in diverse and complex family arrangements. Regardless, the substantive increase in cohabitation since the U.S. Census Bureau began counting this family form in 1990 will likely continue as family options expand in the United States.

Simply because some do not support cohabitation, however, does not mean that this family type is doomed. Many report that this family configuration has been negatively stereotyped. Karen Peterson (2004) reports on one cohabitor who says: "It is important for people to know out there that there are misconceptions about unmarried couples. . . . We are just like any other family" (p. 8A). Further, the increase in cohabiting arrangements suggests that this family type will continue to be a viable option for future families.

Communication and Couples   To understand communication in the cohabiting household, reflect on the experiences of Marsha and Cliff. The two are in their late 60s, both widowed. Since the death of their spouses, the two have spent a great deal of personal time together. After four years, their once distant relationship became romantic. Because the two found themselves attracted to each other and because they lived next to each other in a retirement village, they felt that cohabitation made more sense than living apart. This marital alternative has met with a resounding voice of disapproval from other retirees in their complex. Although Marsha and Cliff haven't sorted out the legal and financial challenges ahead, they still believe that living together has enhanced their romance, cut down on costs, and helped them appreciate each other.

According to Paul Yelsma (1986), couples like Marsha and Cliff may not experience much overt conflict. Yelsma found that older couples (both married and cohabiting) discussed little in terms of personal problems or interpersonal disagreements. So, although they may appear to be getting along just fine, the reality may be that they have bottled up some frustration, and it may be released at an inappropriate time.

As Marsha and Cliff assess their future family configuration, we believe that they may first have to thoroughly examine various consequences of their cohabitation (community property, social support from friends, and so forth). Cohabiting couples do not have many role models, nor has the media attempted to portray such families in the most favorable light. As a result, communication in this type of family can be both freer and more challenging than that of married couples.

The communication of married couples has been researched quite extensively. Research has shown that to maintain a marriage, both the husband and wife need to be involved in the maintenance. Daniel Weigel and Deborah Ballard-Reisch (2001) contend that both spouses need to actively contribute to the marriage and that a "systemic connection between feelings and behaviors" (p. 277) will aid in the maintenance of the marriage. Further, Weigel (2003) looked at how couples regard their commitment to their marriage in the first few years together. His findings show that the couple's interpretation of commitment seems to influence their daily conversations, the way personal time is spent, and the couple's goals for the future together. In addition to these conclusions, David Olson and Amy Olson (2000) indicate that today, although more couples desire shared leadership and decisions in a marriage, achieving those desires is difficult. To get to this egalitarian relationship, Olson and Olson believe that couples should try to be more creative in problem solving (brainstorming, praise, and so forth), which may, in turn, lead to more marital equality. Other scholars (Noller, Feeney, Bonnell, & Callan, 1994) have found that conflict resolution is related to the level of satisfaction that a spouse feels in the marriage. Those who reported high levels of marital satisfaction also reported more involvement in discussions; those with low levels of communication were reported to become destructive in the way they handled a conflict situation. Finally, Jennifer Theiss (2011) investigated the relationship between (in)direct communication and sexual satisfaction between husbands and wives. She found that wives have decreased satisfaction when their husbands communicate indirectly about sexual intimacy. That is, while women tend to want communication about "feelings about emotional and relational closeness that emerge in the context of sexual intimacy" (p. 579), husbands usually don't communicate in such a manner. In fact, Theiss asserts that caution should be exercised in assuming that open and direct communication by husbands about sex will be viewed favorably by wives. For instance, some husbands desiring wives who adhere to traditional gendered norms may be very dissatisfied in their wives taking more proactive and assertive stances on sexual intimacy. And Theiss notes that while a wife typically engages in open communication to facilitate relational closeness, this same wife may be dissatisfied if her husband used open communication to express frustration or criticism of the sexual intimacy in their marriage. In sum, the way married couples communicate depends greatly on the willingness of both spouses to be flexible and tolerant.

Marital and Family Typologies

In addition to the family types we just reviewed (see Table 1-5), some researchers also have been interested in classifying families based on how they organize themselves internally. The relationship between husbands and wives is a significant family relationship that can influence the family in lasting ways (Alberts, Tracy, & Tretheway, 2011; Fincham, 2004). A number of typologies, or category systems, have been advanced to understand marital interaction, but we limit our brief discussion to two that are particularly germane to the study of family communication.

Mary Anne Fitzpatrick's (1977, 1988) pioneering model of couple types (Table 1-6) focuses on how people perceive the marital relationship, that is, their ideology of marriage. Fitzpatrick found that three basic dimensions underlie marital ideologies. The first dimension is conventionality, or how much a person subscribes to traditional sex roles, regular routines, and traditional meanings and functions for marriage. Second, Fitzpatrick found a dimension of interdependence relating to how much space, physical and psychological, partners felt was appropriate in marriage. Last, Fitzpatrick discovered a dimension of communication that measured how much conflictual interaction defined marriage for people. Specifically, this dimension tapped into whether people believed conflict was important or should be avoided in marriage.

Using these dimensions, Fitzpatrick created a questionnaire that she called the Relational Dimensions Instrument (RDI). Couples' scores on this instrument allowed Fitzpatrick to discover three basic marital types: traditionals, independents, and separates. Pure couple types result when both partners' questionnaire responses reveal the same ideology. Mixed couple types are those in which the husband and wife report differing ideologies.

TABLE 1-5   Six Family Configurations and Their Communication

FAMILY TYPE	DESCRIPTION	COMMUNICATION
1. Nuclear family	Wife, husband, and their biological children.	Communication may be facilitated by their culturally sanctioned form.
2. Gay and lesbian family	Two people of the same sex in intimate relationship.	Complex communicative demands. Parental communication similar to that in heterosexual families. Lesbians report maintaining an open communication climate.
3. Extended family	Biological includes relatives such as grandparents, aunts, uncles, and cousins, as well as parent(s) and children. Communal includes intentional family of friends.	May have the potential for conflict if issues such as growth and change are not addressed.
4. Stepfamily	Two adults and child(ren) who are not the biological offspring of both.	Conflict may arise around subsystems, rules, roles, and time management.
5. Single-parent family	One adult with child(ren).	Challenging communication demands. Can be helped in co-cultures that stress the group over the individual.
6. Couples	Two adults living together in romantic relationship. No children.	Cohabitors: Lack of communication role models. Marrieds: Much communication is rooted in daily routines and problem solving.

For example, if a wife held a traditional ideology and her husband adhered to a separate ideology of marriage, Fitzpatrick would label them as a mixed type. Approximately 40 percent of Fitzpatrick's respondents were mixed. The wife as a traditional and the husband as a separate was the most common mixed combination.

TABLE 1-6 Fitzpatrick's Marital Types

COUPLE TYPE	RELATIONAL CHARACTERISTICS
Traditionals	Interdependent High degree of sharing Endorse community customs associated with marriage High marital satisfaction Conventional sex roles Routinized behaviors in marriage
Independents	High degree of sharing Embrace autonomy Assertive when necessary Nonconventional sex roles Low marital satisfaction
Separates	Focus on individual freedom Conflict avoidant Low marital satisfaction Conventional sex roles

Traditional Couples An emphasis on stability more than spontaneity characterizes **traditional couples.** Thus, they maintain regular routines for organizing their lives. They exhibit interdependence and sharing to a high degree. Although they are not particularly assertive, they do not avoid conflict when it comes up in their relationship. They endorse community customs relating to marriage such as the wife taking the husband's name and traditional gendered divisions of labor. Although Fitzpatrick argues that all three of the couple types can be satisfactory for the partners, her research indicates that traditionals report being the most satisfied of the three types (Fitzpatrick, 1988).

Independent Couples The belief that individual freedom should not be constrained by marriage characterizes **independent couples.** These couples believe in less conventional sex roles. Although these couples believe in a high level of sharing and companionship between partners, they also believe sharing should not threaten an individual's autonomy. Therefore, independents try to stay psychologically close while maintaining some physical space between themselves and their spouse. These couples report assertiveness and do not avoid conflicts. Although Fitzpatrick did not include gay and lesbian couples in her sample, Karen Ortiz and Julien Delgado from the beginning of this chapter might illustrate an independent couple.

Separate Couples Although conventional in some gendered aspects of marriage, such as the wife taking the husband's name and keeping a regular schedule, **separate couples** also stress individual freedom over relationship maintenance. These couples opt for both psychological and physical distance in marriage. Separates also report being conflict avoidant in their marriages.

More contemporary applications of the marital types model have been undertaken by a number of family communication scholars. Let's explore a few studies to demonstrate the breadth of study associated with marital types.

Looking specifically at Fitzpatrick's relational dimension called "sharing," Bill Strom (2003) looked at the notion of virtue and the extent to which a spouse displays positive emotional sharing. Strom predicted that the more virtuous (defined as the emotional intention to act and be good) spouses perceive themselves to be, the more their spouse will report the marriage to display such sharing properties as verbal affection, sense of humor, and emotional support. Results showed that spouses tended to report similar degrees of emotional support. In particular, wives reported more emotional sharing from their husbands when the men viewed themselves as virtuous. Husbands, on the other hand, did not tend to report emotional sharing from their wives when the women viewed themselves as virtuous.

Examining humor orientation, James Honeycutt and Renee Brown (1998) explored the application of the RDI to differences in humor. Orientation to humor was defined as an individual's perception of his or her own sense of humor. The researchers discovered that traditional couples used more humor in their conversations than other marital types. Honeycutt and Brown explain that traditionals tend to follow traditional gender roles, and therefore the jokes of one spouse (husband) are laughed at by the other spouse (wife), encouraging a sense of interdependence that is characteristic of traditional couples.

Weigel and Ballard-Reisch (1999) specifically examined how couples maintained their relationship with each other. They compared a number of maintenance behaviors and that relationship to couple type. Their findings showed that traditional and independent couples reported greater use of openness than did separate couples. Further, traditional couples reported greater use of sharing tasks than did either independents or separates. Finally, traditionals believed that they had a more extended and overlapping network than separates.

Family scholars will continue to study Fitzpatrick's typology for years to come. Her work illustrates the complexity of marriage and also shows us that couples can be happy in a variety of marriages, depending on their marital ideology, a subject we will return to in Chapter 2 as we discuss systems theory. Through Fitzpatrick's work, we are able to see that communication operates differently in different types of relationships.

Family Types   David Kantor and William Lehr (1975/1985) observed families in an ethnographic study. Their observations led them to assert that a family's main task is distance regulation. In negotiating closeness and distance, families use the resources of time, space, and energy to get to goals of power (a sense of autonomy and freedom), meaning (a sense of family identity), and affect (a sense of family closeness and caring). Kantor and Lehr mapped families' use of their resources, which the researchers called access dimensions, across their goals, or target dimensions, and discovered three family types: closed families, open families, and random families.

Closed Families In the **closed family** type, goals are reached using fixed space, regular time, and steady energy. When space is fixed, families may establish strict rules for using rooms in the house. Perhaps no one can study in the living room, or take food upstairs, or go into the study when Dad is in there. Regular time suggests that families eat meals at the same time daily and have fixed bedtimes. Steady energy suggests that the family does not exhaust itself at some times, such as during the holiday season, and then rest, restoring energy, at other times. Instead the family expends energy consistently over time.

Open Families The **open family** works toward their goals using movable space, variable time, and flexible energy. Open families are less rigid about their territory than closed families. Spaces can be used for multiple functions, and permission is less likely to be required before entering spaces than in the closed family. People outside the family are allowed into the family fairly easily without a lot of spatial barriers such as fences or large entry halls. Meals and activities are not held to as fixed a time schedule as in the closed family, and individual needs can modify time schedules easily. Energy in the open family is flexible, allowing the family to cope with minor crises necessitating energy investments.

Random Families As the **random family** works toward its goals, family members exhibit dispersed space, irregular time, and fluctuating energy. Some writers have likened this family to a madhouse with lots of unregulated activity occurring in rather unpredictable fashion. Family members may sleep in the living room, and guests may wander in and out of the household. The family does not operate on a time schedule, and meals may take place at different times each day. This type of family seldom plans for the future; they merely react to events as they occur. Sometimes the energy level in the family is very high, at other times, quite low. Some poor, urban families fall into this type because of the chaotic circumstances in which they live. However, other poor, urban families create a closed type in order to combat the chaos outside the family system.

Kantor and Lehr, like Fitzpatrick, show us the variety and complexity of family life. It should be clear that closed, open, and random families use different kinds of communication and evaluate the same communication behavior differently. For example, in random families, difference of opinion and individuality would be more valued than they would be in closed families. Dinners with lots of talk and interruptions would be commonplace in open families, whereas they would be rarer in closed families.

SUMMARY

In this chapter, we have provided you with an overview of our definition for family and discussed its critical elements. We noted that the U.S. culture is a diverse one, and as members of unique families, we must understand that diversity. Failing to realize that there are families different from ours provides us with an incomplete notion of the complexity of family life. The definition of family we have put forth is intended to reflect our desire for an inclusive viewpoint. Further, we have stressed the importance of the communication perspective as a salient lens for understanding the family. Although sociological trends and psychological elements affect the family unit, the family lives in and through talk. We presented several cultural and demographic trends pertaining to family life in the United States. To demonstrate the notion of intergenerationality, we presented information on family genograms. We discussed the six prominent types of families in our larger culture: nuclear families, gay and lesbian families, extended families, stepfamilies, single-parent families, and couples. Finally, we provided two typological systems for classifying relationships that can work in tandem with the family configurations to help us understand how diverse families communicate.

Without doubt, we will all continue to see more changes in family life. How we cope with these changes will be of paramount importance to both researchers and family members alike. Our communication is clearly affected by family type, as evidenced by the discussion and examples presented. If we are all to be effective and efficient in our interactions with people in our larger culture, as well as within our own families, we have to understand the complexities and challenges inherent in the concept of family.

KEY TERMS

at-risk families	external boundaries
binuclear family	families of procreation
biological extended families	family-of-origin
boomerang kids	family secrets
boundary ambiguity	gay and lesbian families
closed family	genogram
co-culture	heterosexism
cohabiting couples	homophobia
common-law marriage	independent couples
communication	intergenerationality
contemporary nuclear family	internal boundaries
culture	involuntary family
dual-career family	married couples

nesting

nonverbal codes

open family

paperless marriage

popular culture

random family

relational culture

separate couples

single-parent households

stepfamily

terrain of struggle

traditional couples

traditional nuclear family

verbal codes

voluntary family

QUESTIONS FOR REFLECTION

1. Agree or disagree with the proposition that the larger culture in which we live is as diverse as it was 50 years ago.

2. Imagine that you have been asked to define family. How would you go about providing an explanation of what family is? Use examples if necessary.

3. What might you say to someone who claims that our families are pretty much the same across all cultures? How could you defend or refute this statement?

4. Do you agree that a communication perspective is significantly different from a psychological or sociological approach? Suggest some questions that are rooted in a communication approach to families. How are these questions different from ones you would ask if you took another approach?

5. Describe other types of families that were not discussed in this chapter. Be sure to define each family type and identify how you envision the communication to be in each family type.

6. Do problems come from having so many family types in our country? What strengths are associated with having numerous family types?

7. Discuss the cultural pressures on people to get married in the United States.

8. Develop a genogram. How might it change based upon significant life events?

9. Discuss how technology has influenced our perceptions of the family.

10. Identify several nonverbal codes for your family-of-origin.

Chapter

2

PROVIDING THEORETICAL FRAMEWORKS

The Definition of Theory
The Goals of Theory
Theories as Tools for Studying Family Communication

Intellectual Traditions
The Positivistic/Empirical Approach
The Interpretive/Hermeneutic Approach • The Critical Approach

The Theoretical Assumptions Underlying this Text
The Centrality of Communication • Change Through
Multidimensional Time • Influences of Social and Cultural
Contexts • The Family as a Meaning-Making System

Family Theories
Systems Theory • Social Construction Theory
Dialectics • Developmental Theory

Methods of Inquiry
Surveys • Experiments • Depth Interviews • Textual Analysis

Summary

Key Terms

Questions for Reflection

THE JOHNSON FAMILY

LaTasha Johnson, 20, gets up at 7 a.m. and heats milk for Jason, her sister Sonia's three-year-old son. LaTasha, Sonia, and Jason have been living together for the past two years. Sonia and LaTasha share much of the responsibility and work involved in raising Jason. This morning, LaTasha has to hurry because she has to do a little overtime and she must be at work by 9 a.m., instead of 10 a.m. as usual. Jason is fussy and LaTasha wakes up Sonia, yelling that she does not have time to deal with Jason today because of her work schedule, and Sonia will have to take care of him herself. Sonia sleepily replies that she will, and Jason crawls into bed with her. LaTasha quickly jumps in the shower, humming to herself.

THE LEMOYNE FAMILY

Mark LeMoyne, 55, makes breakfast while his wife, Jean, 50, sleeps because she had to work the night shift last night—she is a cancer nurse. Mark has to hurry to get to the construction business he owns. Their son, Joel, 26, works for Mark, and he comes by to pick up his father and drive him to their office. Joel arrives just as Mark drops a pan of eggs on the floor. Joel helps Mark clean up the mess while Jean continues to sleep. The two men leave for work with Joel teasing his dad about being all thumbs. Mark jokingly responds that Joel had better watch his remarks when he is talking to his boss. They laugh together as they drive in to work. Then they become serious, as Mark wants to talk to Joel about laying off two employees because their business is down in this bad economy.

THE MURPHY-RODRIGUEZ FAMILY

Tim Murphy walks distractedly around his living room. He is waiting for his wife, Amelia, and her son, Nolan, to arrive home from having dinner with Amelia's former husband, Ray Rodriguez. Amelia, Ray, and Nolan are supposed to be deciding some financial and practical matters about where Nolan will be going to college next year. Tim wasn't able to go to the dinner because he had a work commitment. Tim and Amelia have been married for four years, and they have a good relationship, but Tim still doesn't like it when Amelia spends a lot of time with Ray. He isn't exactly jealous, and he actually likes Ray. The three adults have spent time together to support Nolan—attending sports activities and Nolan's guitar recitals and eating together on Nolan's birthdays. But sometimes Tim thinks that Ray doesn't like the fact that his Mexican American son is living in a household with an Irish American stepfather. Tim suspects that Ray takes advantage of Tim's absence to try to plant little seeds of conflict—like the time Ray mentioned to Amelia that she had forgotten how to cook good Mexican dishes and when he observed that Nolan needed to know more about Mexico. Later Tim and Amelia had argued about whether she'd forgotten her own heritage because they spent so much time with his Irish family.

T he three families in the opening vignettes, like all families, continually experience complex communication interactions such as those described, and often the members wonder to themselves (or even ask one another), "Why do we act the way we do?" One of the goals you probably have in taking this class is to gain an understanding of your own family's communication behaviors. You most likely have also wondered why your family communicates the way it does, what makes you argue over the things you fight about, and even why you tease and express love to one another in certain ways. You probably also have wondered how you can improve the parts of your family's interactions that are bothersome to you. Researchers believe we can answer these kinds of questions with theory, or a type of framework that helps us sort out the separate bits of our behavior and quilt them together in some meaningful way. For example, a theory might offer a general pattern that would explain elements of the communication in the Johnson, LeMoyne, and Murphy-Rodriguez families. Although these families differ in many ways, theoretical links may be found in issues such as stress, autonomy, and intimacy that would generalize across their different demographics and circumstances. Some researchers want to explain many families' behavior, and theories can help them do this. Other researchers, who do not believe we can generalize so widely, still need theories to help them understand what they observe in case studies or in small numbers of families.

Student Perspective: Lucas

When we discussed the implicit theorist idea, I understood that right away. I am not sure I do that so much, but I can see my sister, Rose, in that role completely. She is always asking questions about our family—she thinks we are borderline dysfunctional, so she's always trying to figure out why we act the way we do. Rose always has an opinion about our family. You can expect to hear her holding forth at family gatherings explaining her reasons for our problems. Last Thanksgiving she spent almost an hour talking about her theory that we are organized in a strict hierarchy in the family. She explained that younger children don't have a chance to exert any power until the older siblings leave for college or a job. Sometimes she even proposes little experiments. Once she asked me to ignore our brother, Dylan, for a week to see if he would talk more to her if I didn't talk to him at all. I wouldn't really do it, so I guess I sabotaged her career as a theorist!

In this book we are discussing theory as professional researchers use it in their work; yet all of us in daily life think like researchers, using **implicit theories** (or explanations we carry in our head) to help us understand questions like those we mentioned previously.

When Josie predicts that her brother, Cal, will interrupt her story about planning their family vacation, she's using knowledge from her past experience with Cal to make that prediction. But, in addition, she's operating under, and further refining, her implicit theory about what men are interested in talking about, and how they use interruptions to bring the conversational topic back under their control. Autumn Edwards and Elizabeth Graham (2009) argued that people also have implicit theories about communication (some see it as a game to be played while others see it as a way to negotiate socially constructed meaning, for instance). Edwards and Graham found that these implicit theories impacted the way that people defined family.

Whenever we pose an answer to one of our questions (such as maybe what we are really fighting over is control and not whether to move to New Jersey), we are engaging in theoretical thinking. In this way, we might say that theory and research are intuitive to us. It's natural to ask *why* about things that happen in our families and then proceed to form answers. Then we usually test the answers we've come up with for how well they fit the situation and finally choose the one that seems best to us. Although we're not as rigorous as social scientists—for instance, we often choose the first answer that seems to fit without really examining all of them—we still follow a process that resembles creating a theory and testing it. Learning about theory is challenging, yet it helps to remember that we are already implicit theorists trying to find explanations for our family interactions.

THE DEFINITION OF THEORY

Generally speaking, a **theory** is an abstract system of concepts with indications of the relationships among these concepts that help us understand a phenomenon such as family communication. And that provides a working definition of the term theory for us. But theory is a complicated concept, so we wish to explore it further. Stephen Littlejohn and Karen Foss (2011) suggest that theories are derived through systematic observation. Another group of researchers (Doherty, Boss, LaRossa, Schumm, & Steinmetz, 1993) convey the notion that theories are both process and product. Their definition is as follows: "Theorizing is the process of systematically formulating and organizing ideas to understand a particular phenomenon. A theory is the set of interconnected ideas that emerge from this process" (p. 20). James White and David Klein (2002) comment that theories exist in the "realm of ideas" (p. 3) and in so doing provide reasonable explanations about family functioning.

We can see that several researchers have approached the task of defining theory and have come up with slightly differing statements. James White (2005) observes that although definitions may vary, there are several elements that all scholars would agree capture the definition of theory:

1. Statements about the relevant context(s) (i.e., the theory is about newlywed couples' communication).

2. A set of general propositions (i.e., assertions about the context, such as, newlyweds will express agreement with one another, their communication will be more positive than negative, they depend on social support from their extended networks, etc.).

3. Statements that connect the propositions (i.e., if their extended network shows disapproval, their communication will change from mostly agreement to more disagreement, etc.).

4. The theory must have the capability to be tested or applied in a way that will allow a researcher to see if it is useful.

The Goals of Theory

In a broad, inclusive sense, the goals of theory include explanation, understanding, prediction, and social change. We are able to *explain* something (Mark and Joel LeMoyne's joking behaviors, for example) because of the concepts and relationships specified in a theory. We may be able to *understand* something (LaTasha Johnson's willingness to "mother" her sister's son, for example) because of theoretical thinking. We are also able to *predict* something (how well Tim Murphy and Amelia Rodriguez are able to communicate, for example) based on the patterns suggested by a theory. Finally, we may be able to influence *social change* or empowerment (for example, providing new names for new family relationships such as the relationships among stepparents' extended families and their stepchildren) through theoretical inquiry. Theories, then, help us answer the why and how questions that all of us have about our family experiences. From this, you can see that theory and experience are related, although one (experience) is concrete and the other (theory) is abstract. The traditional social scientific approach suggests that theories are general enough to explain many different specific observations or experiences, although it is always possible to find individual families that do not fit the theory's description.

Theories as Tools for Studying Family Communication

James White (2005) uses the metaphor of a tool to help us understand the ways that researchers can employ theory to study families. White notes that tools have specific purposes ("the purpose of a screwdriver is clearly to drive screws" p. 170), but that people who use tools can innovate and use them for other purposes as well ("opening a paint can, as a pry bar, and as a stir stick. The only limitation on the ways we can use the tool is our imagination and the actual physical construction of the tool" pp. 170–171). White goes on to explain that thinking of theories as tools allows us to see that theories do not contain *truth*, they are simply ways to help researchers accomplish a task (i.e., to explain, understand, predict, or change family communication). In keeping with this line of thought, it is also the case according to White that theories wear out or cease to be useful for some reason or another, just as tools do. White argues that when this happens, researchers seek new theories or elaborate and modify the old ones so that they "work" better.

When thinking of theories as tools for the student/researcher of family communication, it is important to realize that just as theories help us to make sense of family life, they also may prevent us from seeing issues that are critical to family experience. So, if we are used to seeing a hammer as a tool to drive nails, we may have trouble envisioning other uses for it, and we may be inclined to see the world as a place that needs things nailed together (Knapp, 2009). Kerry Daly (2003) observes that families live by implicit theories (as we mentioned in the beginning of the chapter) and that there may be a poor match between those theories and the ones that scholars use to research families. Daly calls what theories lead us to see the "positive spaces" and what they obscure the "negative spaces" in our theorizing.

Specifically, Daly warns us that our theories help us "to understand family experiences like divorce, violence, gender, and fatherhood because they are established parts of our research tradition" (p. 772). But these same theories may not point us to issues like the realm of belief, feeling, intuition, myths, consumption, and the organization of time and space.

This may be the case, in part, because theories are slow to explain some fast-moving aspects of our culture, such as technology and social media. The boundaries of time and space are being transcended by new technologies. Today, people don't have to communicate in real time and space to stay in touch. Increasingly, family members are able to communicate on their own time and over different spaces.

Daly concludes that while we needn't throw out our old theories, we need to look more closely at the issues that engross and perplex real families. Then we must ask if our existing theories are capable of addressing the questions and explanations families are posing. As Daly states, "By examining the shared edge between positive forms and negative spaces, it is possible to see different research agendas—ones that deepen our understanding of the everyday practices in which families are engaged" (p. 781).

These observations could lead us to another metaphor for theory: a lens. Thinking of theory as a lens enables us to see, as James White and David Klein (2002) note, "different theories can be used to make sense of the same set of facts" (p. 1).

Thus, if we applied a theory called uncertainty reduction theory (Berger & Calabrese, 1975) to an analysis of the LeMoyne family we described at the beginning of the chapter, we might explain Mark and Joel's banter about the spilled breakfast and who is boss by positing a high degree of certainty in their relationship. We would reach this conclusion because the theory suggests that certainty and affectionate talk are positively related. Yet, if we applied a dialectic approach (Baxter, 1988, 2011; Baxter & Montgomery, 1996; Rawlins, 1992; Yerby, 1995), an approach we will discuss further throughout this book, we might interpret the teasing differently. It could be seen instead as a strategic means of negotiating tensions between simultaneous desires for closeness and individuality. Dialectics suggests that family life is defined by tensions created by oppositions. Janet Yerby (1995) provides another metaphor by referring to theories as "the stories we have developed to explain our view of reality" (p. 362). Still, we have to be aware, as Yerby suggests, that theories, like stories, change and evolve over time as new information modifies and refines them.

INTELLECTUAL TRADITIONS

Individual theories are grounded in intellectual traditions, which carry with them certain assumptions. By **intellectual traditions**, we mean a general way of thinking, representing a way to approach and learn about the world. Intellectual traditions affect the values, goals, and scholarly style of a researcher, so it is important to understand the intellectual traditions that ground the theories we read and use. White and Klein (2002) discuss three different philosophies of science that are part of separate intellectual traditions and that influence the way we approach our study of family communication. They label these three philosophies the **positivistic approach**, the **interpretive approach**, and the **critical approach.** These three philosophies relate to the three perspectives (empiricism, hermeneutics, and critical theory) that Arthur Bochner (1985) reviewed while discussing the study of interpersonal communication.

The Positivistic/Empirical Approach

The positivistic, or empirical, approach assumes that there are objective truths that can be uncovered about family interaction, and the process of inquiry that discovers these truths can be at least somewhat value neutral. This tradition advocates the methods of the natural sciences, with the goal of constructing general laws governing human interactions. The researcher in this intellectual tradition strives to be objective and works for control over the important concepts in the theory. In other words, when the researcher makes observation, he or she carefully structures the situation so that only one element varies, enabling the researcher to make relatively definitive statements about that element. For instance, if a researcher in the positivistic tradition believed that the communication in a divorced family was affected by the quality of the relationship between the current wife and the ex-wife, then that researcher would study children and adults whose situation was the same in all relevant ways except for the relationship between the two adult women (the biological mother and the woman married to the biological father).

The Interpretive/Hermeneutic Approach

The interpretive, or hermeneutic, tradition views truth as subjective and co-created by the participants. And the researcher herself or himself is clearly one of the participants. No effort is made to remain objective because this is seen as impossible. In this tradition, the researcher believes that the study of families is value relevant, and it is important for researchers to be aware of their own values and clearly state them for a reader, because their values will naturally permeate their research. These researchers are not concerned with control and the ability to generalize across many families as much as they are interested in rich descriptions about the families they study. For example, a researcher operating from this tradition might visit the Johnsons and collect stories from each of the three family members about some of their daily routines. The analysis might clarify themes of family life over which LaTasha, Sonia, and Jason agree and disagree. For researchers in this tradition, theory is best induced from the observations and experiences the researcher shares with the family.

The Critical Approach

The critical approach argues that theories exist to bring values to the surface where they can be challenged and changed. In this tradition, researchers believe that those in power shape knowledge in ways that work to perpetuate the status quo. Thus, powerful people work at keeping themselves in power, which requires silencing minority voices questioning the distribution of power and the powerful's version of truth. Patricia Hill Collins (1990) speaks from this tradition when she says, "The tension between the suppression of Black women's ideas and our intellectual activism in the face of that suppression, comprises the politics of Black feminist thought" (pp. 5–6). Further, Collins links activism to black extended family networks like the Johnsons' (the family we described at the beginning of this chapter). Collins writes:

> *Black women's experiences, as othermothers, provide a foundation for Black women's political activism. Nurturing children in Black extended family networks stimulates a more generalized ethic of caring and personal accountability among African American females who often feel accountable to all the Black community's children. (p. 129)*

Using the critical approach, a researcher might come to the Johnsons with some of the following questions: How is the relationship between

LaTasha and Jason communicatively constructed? Does her experience as "othermother" prepare LaTasha for political activism, as black feminist theory suggests it would? Do LaTasha and Sonia express a general nurturing ethic that extends to other black children in their neighborhood and extended family? Black feminists are not the only researchers who are comfortably rooted in the critical tradition; Marxists, postmodernists, and feminists of all types, among others, also work from this intellectual tradition.

Leslie Baxter and Dawn Braithwaite (2006) collected 289 research articles on the topic of family communication published from 1990 through 2003. They were interested to find which intellectual traditions supported these articles. They found that the vast majority of studies were undertaken from a positivistic-empirical tradition (220 articles or 76.1 percent of the total). Fifty-nine articles, representing 20.4 percent of the total, were grounded in the interpretive-hermeneutic tradition. Only 10 articles, or 3.5 percent, employed the critical tradition.

We can see that each of these traditions suggests something different about the definition of truth and the best method for searching for truth. Additionally, there are other intellectual traditions we have not reviewed that also carry with them different values, goals, and methods. Intellectual traditions contribute to the ways researchers try to understand, explain, predict, and change family communication. When researchers pick a theory to guide them that is rooted in one of these traditions, they also get all the intellectual trappings, assumptions, and beliefs that come along with the tradition. Sometimes people call this a **worldview** because it provides people with a lens for seeing and making sense of the world they inhabit.

Researchers using theories may talk explicitly about these intellectual traditions and their assumptions, but often they do not, and a reader has to infer what tradition underlies a given study. But in all cases you can see that intellectual traditions affect the researcher's thought and approach to questions of family communication just as individual theories do.

In the rest of this chapter we acknowledge our own intellectual traditions and assumptions. Then we explain a variety of theories used to study family communication. Finally, we discuss the relationship between theory and research.

THE THEORETICAL ASSUMPTIONS UNDERLYING THIS TEXT

Now that we have discussed the meaning of theory, it is time to clarify how we will approach the study of family communication in this book. In other words, we need to lay out our intellectual traditions and assumptions about family life. First, we were both trained in the positivist intellectual tradition. Coming from this tradition, we are primed to look for regularities across large numbers of families in an effort to explain and predict family communication behavior. Additionally, we carry the baggage of beliefs in objectivity, value-neutral research, and a desire for experimental control. However, as we have continued to study families, we have been inspired to incorporate some elements from the interpretive and critical traditions in our work. This approach facilitates examination of the family's communication within the context of its own relational culture as well as a recognition of the need for social change.

Given the mix of traditions in which we ground ourselves, we approach the study of family communication (and the writing of this book) with the following assumptions about our subject: (1) communication is central to the lives of families, (2) the family undergoes changes through multidimensional time, (3) families are influenced by social and cultural contexts, and (4) the family is a meaning-making system. We will consider each of these assumptions briefly.

The Centrality of Communication

As we mentioned in Chapter 1, communication constructs family identity. It is the vehicle families use for negotiating meaning, selfhood, and relationships. In many ways (according to the beliefs of the interpretive tradition), families are the creations of communication engaged in by their members. Communication creates the relational culture that we discussed in Chapter 1. Kristin Langellier and Eric Peterson (2004) comment on the importance of communication when they examine the practice of family storytelling. They assert that American families "get a life" through performing family stories. And, further, they note that "a person gets a family life through performing narrative" (p. 112). Thus, family and personal identity are created in these communication interactions. Haley Kranstuber and Jody Koenig Kellas (2011) note that family story telling creates both family and personal identities. Thus, communication establishes a sense of what it means to belong to a particular family. We understand the Sanders or Hebert family identities, for example, by the talk in these families. We are reminded about the Sanders's stubbornness, for instance, by stories of Grandpa Sanders, who clung to his way of doing things although it caused him to lose his position as minister of the church in his town. We know about what it means to be a Hebert by listening to Grandma Lucy tell how she picked strawberries for three cents a quart to get money for food during the Depression. We discuss family storytelling more fully in Chapter 6.

Communication is also central, because, in a paradoxical way, it both creates family conflicts and stress and provides the means for resolving them. Further, communication processes relate to the other assumptions we make about our subject: Families communicate about their changes and manage their pleasures and discomforts about change through communication.

Families negotiate their social and cultural contexts communicatively. Finally, families make meaning through their communication practices.

You might be thinking that this is a very self-evident assumption and that everyone would make the same observation about family life: Communication is a central, defining process. Yet other disciplines, such as psychology or sociology, might be less likely to claim so much importance for communication behavior. Psychologists would see cognitive processes as central, causing communication. Sociologists would be more interested in social change and context, arguing that communication might simply reflect changing social values. Although communication researchers would not disagree that people's thoughts and social change are important, what is primary for us is the communication behavior within families.

Change Through Multidimensional Time

Our second assumption has two parts. First is the notion that many aspects of family life—the relationships and communication among members, the individual members themselves, the structure of the family, the norms, the roles, and so forth—all change with the passage of time. This assumption speaks to our belief that family life is a process. Families are never really settled; they constantly change and evolve. Further, changes over time have implications for families. The past experiences of families affect their present situations, which, in turn, influence the future interactions of family members. Some researchers have commented that one of the elements that distinguishes marriage and family life from other, less enduring relationships is the element of time—possession of a shared history and expectation of a shared future (Mikkelson, Myers, & Hannawa, 2011). Within the family, our reflections on our history and our expectations for our future affect our sense of family identity and our communication behaviors. Joel LeMoyne's ability to tease and joke with his father is grounded in four years of working in the construction business together and forging a different relationship than they had when Joel was growing up.

Student Perspective: Donette

It's interesting to think about how past experiences affect present situations in the family. In my family, we're almost defined by the past. My twin brother, Diego, died when we were 12. We were in a car accident, and my cousin was driving. The loss of my brother was just so hard—my parents were almost destroyed by it. I think my mom stayed in bed for a month. And, for me, it was really tough. Being twins we were together all the time. It was like losing an arm or a leg. It's been hard to see my cousin and his family afterwards. The accident really wasn't his fault, but it has had such a devastating impact on us. It's like we have two families—the old one when Diego was alive and the one in the present without him.

A second aspect of this assumption revolves around the understanding that the flow and change in families is mapped across two types of time. Most of us understand that "time is a monotonic process—once a moment in time is gone, it doesn't come back" (White & Klein, 2002, p. 94). And we know that in our society, time units are equal—all days have 24 hours, all hours consist of 60 minutes, every week has 7 days. This type of time—**calendar or clock time**—allows us to measure and is very well suited to our cultural need for planning and allotting time for activities. Maybe you use your calendar in a smartphone to schedule due dates for your class work and your social obligations. Perhaps you have experienced having to schedule time to talk to a busy parent, or your family may have a large family calendar where you keep track of each member's activities and even record plans for family times.

Social process time (Rodgers, 1973) is another dimension of time that refers to using our family experiences as a way to divide time. Thus, after Dad had his first heart attack, just before Alison and J. C. got married, or before Zöe was born may be more salient markers of time for a family than 1990 or 2011. Although the two dimensions are separate, social process time can be overlaid on calendar or clock time. By combining these two types of time, we can trace the time lines of both the calendar and social process to help us understand a family's interaction. For example, Amelia Rodriguez can think about before and after she and Ray divorced in 2008, as two rather separate family times. Her family communicated differently and was composed differently in these two different eras.

Student Perspective: Joseph

I had a little bit of trouble paying attention to my family after I lost my job. I had so many worries myself that I couldn't concentrate on them. Time goes by so quickly. It is hard to believe that it has been 13 weeks—3 months— that I have been out of work. I think the strain started to show a lot in the last three to four weeks because I started to feel that I was running out of time. The family had a lot of very emotional swings just in the last week or so before I finally got a new job. Now things are complicated because the new job means we have to move. The kids have been very positive about the potential move, and I think that has helped me a lot. But there was one funny thing. The one that I thought wouldn't want to move seems okay with the move, and the boy, who I thought wouldn't care, wants to stay here. I was confused by my own children. I had them just backward.

Influences of Social and Cultural Contexts

We mentioned previously that through communication families create a relational culture. Yet, they do not do this within a vacuum or completely of their own free will and volition. Families live in an external context as well as within the internal context they create (Boss, 2001). Although families have no control in

---

~~~~ POPULAR PRESS PERSPECTIVES ~~~~

</div>

Damien Cave (2011) reports a story in *The New York Times* online that illustrates the influence of social and cultural contexts on family interactions. Cave tells the story of *familias anclada* or families anchored to Ciudad Juárez, Mexico. Cave states that *familias anclada* is a phrase that hardly existed in the city a few years ago, "but over the past several years, the forces of drug violence and recession have reshaped both the city's character—from loose and busy to tight-knit and cautious—and its demographics." He tells the story of Telma Pedro Córdoba, whose husband died in a drive-by shooting in 2009, and who has stayed in Ciudad Juárez living in a small one-bedroom house with her mother, grandmother, sister, brother, and her two children.

The Pedro family represents what is becoming a typical demographic: "multigenerational, led by women and with several children under 14." Cave cites Carlos Galindo, who is a demographer and advises Mexico's National Population Council. Galindo says that the preponderance of women is due to a combination of three things: "It's harder to find a job, migration across the desert is traditionally a thing that men do, and then there's the violence driving many men to leave."

Cave notes that the global recession has "pummeled" the town, and the resulting change in family demographics can be attributed to economic conditions as much as to violence.

Damien Cave, "A Mexican City's Troubles Reshape Its Families." *The New York Times* (online). February 9, 2011. Retrieved August 15, 2011.

---

shaping this external environment, this environment exerts a lot of influence on how families interact. For example, U.S. families from 2008 onward may not have been able to escape the economic impacts of job loss due to downsizing and the collapse of the housing market. In 2000, families who had invested heavily in Internet stocks may have seen financial reversals as the value of many of these stocks fell close to 50 percent over the year.

After September 11, 2001, families in the United States lived with a realization of terrorism that wasn't known to families living in the 1960s, for example. Further, as technological advances continue to shape our world, families live with different communication challenges and opportunities. Families in the United States in the 1950s, for instance, operated differently based on telephone technology than families do currently, when each member of the family may have his or her own cell phone. Families in the '50s spent more face-to-face time interacting with one another while contemporary families spend more time communicating over the phone.

In addition to these external conditions, families are affected by culture, as we discussed in Chapter 1. However, our emphasis on culture and diversity is informed by the recognition that while members of a particular co-culture do share core values and beliefs as well as rules and rituals that guide interaction, it is a mistake to assume that all members of a co-culture are the same. With reference to African Americans, for example, "there is no monolithic Black experience. There is no singular socialization pathway. Indeed, there is a tapestry of variegated socialization possibilities" (Boykin & Toms, 1985, p. 47). Although culture and co-culture are important aspects affecting family life, individual families may be affected somewhat differently, and other issues such as class and socioeconomic status also play an important role.

Culture has implications for theory as well. Three researchers (Dilworth-Anderson, Burton, & Johnson, 1993) explain how two different scholars, operating with different cultural worldviews, used the same data to arrive at different theoretical conclusions about African American families. Daniel Moynihan, a European American scientist, and Robert Hill, an African American scientist, both analyzed the same U.S. census data with similar methods but diverged in their conclusions:

Student Perspective: Damien

My sister and I are having some conflict now because she has entered into a big Afro-centric phase, and she is criticizing me for not acting black enough. I have almost always dated white girls, and I am a Republican, and people do sometimes ask me, "Are you sure you're black?" I laugh it off, but with my sister it has begun to be a major source of conflict between us. I just think there are a lot of ways to be black.

> *Moynihan noted the deterioration of the black family and recom-mended social policies that would encourage changes in their "infe-rior" values and structure. Hill observed resilience and recommended social policies that would build on the strengths of black families. An analysis of their subjective frame of reference shows that Moynihan assumed the underlying values inherent in [the mainstream paradigm] while Hill's assumptions were drawn from [a different paradigm, stressing cultural relativity]. (p. 629)*

If we continue to think about all families through theories that feature only one set of values, we run the risk of misunderstanding the family inter-actions we observe.

The Family as a Meaning-Making System

Our final assumption holds that the family's relational culture is a result of the meanings that family members create among themselves, as well as an influence on the meaning that is made. Thus, meaning-making is a fundamental process within the family. This assumption is based on a constructionist view of the family, which argues that the family constructs its own social reality. Further, this assumption is related to our first assumption, concerning the centrality of communication, because conversation provides the means for creating social reality for families (Burns & Pearson, 2011).

FAMILY THEORIES

As we have discussed, family communication's complexities can be explained by the concepts and principles set forth in theories. There are any number of theories that researchers have developed to do this. Some of them have been created or modified by family communication scholars specifically for untangling communication behaviors. Others have been devised by other scholars in different disciplines, like psychology or sociology, but family communication researchers have applied their thinking to communication questions. In this section, we review four theories that have been used in many family communication studies: systems theory, social construction theory, dialectics, and developmental theory. These four theories are different in many respects: they come from different intellectual traditions; they have differing boundary conditions, that is, some attempt to explain family interaction in its entirety while others are more narrowly focused; and, in some cases, they assume different definitions of family. But each theory has generated a substantial amount of research aimed at understanding family communication practices. As you read about each theory, think about how you might use it to probe questions of family communication.

Systems Theory

Systems theory has been the dominant perspective used in analyzing family communication for over 30 years (Galvin, Dickson, & Marrow, 2006). Systems theory has its roots in the positivistic-empirical intellectual tradition because of three aspects of the theory: (1) it assumes that all systems share certain characteristics; (2) it focuses on recurring patterns that allow us to predict family behaviors; and (3) in examining the components of systems, it seeks to provide explanations for family behaviors. It is also the case, however, that due to systems theory's descriptive nature, it has also been applied in research grounded in the interpretive-hermeneutic tradition (Braithwaite & Baxter, 2006). Family systems thinking is derived from general systems theory (GST), which is both a theory of systems in general— "from thermostats to missile guidance computers, from amoebas to families" (Whitchurch & Constantine, 1993, p. 325)—and "a way of knowing" (White & Klein, 2002, p. 123). Systems thinking captured the attention of family communication researchers because it changed the focus from the individual to the family as a whole. This shift reconceptualized family life for scholars

TABLE 2-1   Properties of Systems Theory as Applied to Families

PROPERTY	DESCRIPTION
Wholeness	The family is not simply all of its members added together. The family unit has a personality that is different from the combination of each of its members.
Interdependence	Family members are tied together, and what happens to one member affects the others.
Hierarchy	Families are complex, hierarchical organizations composed of individuals and combinations of individuals. Additionally, families are embedded in larger hierarchical structures such as communities, cultures, etc.
Boundaries/openness	Families are open systems that receive information from systems outside themselves such as schools, the media, and religious organizations. Families create boundaries to restrict this flow of information from the outside and to delineate relationships on the inside.
Calibration/feedback	Families are organized or calibrated by rules, and they change their organization through positive feedback, which recalibrates the system. They maintain their organization through negative feedback.
Equifinality	Families may reach the same goal in many different ways.

and helped them to think in innovative ways about family experience and interaction. This new conceptualization rests on several central properties: (1) wholeness, (2) interdependence, (3) hierarchy, (4) boundaries/openness, (5) calibration/ feedback, and (6) equifinality. We will explain each of these properties briefly, noting how each one applies to the family. Table 2-1 presents a summary of the properties.

Wholeness   The most fundamental concept of the systems approach, **wholeness** refers to the idea that a system cannot be fully comprehended by a study of its individual parts in isolation from one another. In order to understand the system, it must be seen as a whole:

> *To make a cake, you add butter, sugar, flour, eggs, baking soda and other ingredients, and perhaps chocolate flavoring. When you bake the cake, it changes into something that is more than the individual characteristics of the ingredients. . . . Even though you added just a bit of chocolate, the flavor changed the entire cake. . . . A cake is more than just the individual parts added together, as you might add layers to a sandwich. (Infante, Rancer, & Womack, 1997, p. 91)*

With regard to a family system, wholeness suggests that we learn more about the family by seeing all the members interacting together than we would by simply observing one or two alone. This principle asserts that families have a personality that is different from the personality of any one member and that cannot be understood by adding each family member's individual personality together. Families undergo a synergistic process when they are together that creates this wholeness. For example, you might know a family that seems to be outgoing and extroverted, yet any one member himself or herself may not fit that personality profile. When we think of a famous family such as the Kardashians, for instance, we may think of adjectives such as flamboyant, hard-partying, and outspoken, even though these qualities may not fit every single member of the family.

Interdependence   Ludwig von Bertalanffy (1975), who is generally credited with the foundational work in GST, defined a system as a "set or sets of elements standing in interrelation among themselves and with the environment" (p. 159). Because the elements of a system are interrelated, they exhibit **interdependence**. This means that the behaviors of system members co-construct the system, and all members are affected by shifts and changes in the system. Virginia Satir (1972) compares the family to a mobile to illustrate how this principle applies to families. In her analogy, the family members are seen as connected by the strings of the mobile, and a disturbance to one of the members (or ornaments on the mobile) will reverberate through the entire family (mobile). If you have experienced the illness of a family member, a job change for a family member, or the birth of a new family member, for instance, you have undoubtedly felt the ripples of these changes touching you, even though you were not the one who was ill, changing jobs, or having a baby. In another example, LaTasha Johnson's early work schedule affects both her nephew, Jason, and her sister, Sonia, that morning. Interdependence also implies that within a cycle of behavior, patterns emerge that take on a life of their own, as each behavior acts both as a trigger for another behavior and a response to previous behaviors. Some research (Prescott & LePoire, 2002) focused on the notions of interdependence and wholeness to investigate how mother–daughter communication relates to eating disorders. The researchers found that a systems framework helped them uncover how eating disorders became a family issue that family members maintained through communication.

Hierarchy   The third property of systems, **hierarchy,** is seen in the fact that all systems have levels, or **subsystems,** and all systems are embedded in other systems, or **suprasystems.** Thus, systems are hierarchical, complex organizations. Within the family, two subsystems operate: (1) interpersonal subsystems and (2) personal or psychobiological subsystems. The interpersonal subsystems are the relationships between a small subunit of the family members. For example, in the Murphy-Rodriguez family that we profiled at the beginning of this chapter, 10 interpersonal

Student Perspective: Lisa

The systems approach makes a lot of sense to me because I can never do what I had planned to do in a conversation with anyone in my family. Like if I want to ask my dad for something, I might think a lot about what I'll say before I talk with him, but when we are actually talking, whatever he says will get me thinking about something I never planned to talk about. Like we discussed, we are linked together in the system, and that system is different from what I could think of just on my own.

subsystems could form around the four members: (1) Tim and Amelia; (2) Tim and Nolan; (3) Tim, Amelia, and Nolan; (4) Tim and Ray; (5) Tim, Amelia, and Ray; (6) Amelia and Ray; (7) Nolan and Amelia; (8) Ray, Amelia, and Nolan; (9) Ray and Nolan; (10) Tim, Nolan, and Ray. You can easily see how the complexity can increase as the number of family members increases. Each of the subsystems can function independently of the whole system, but each is an integral part of the whole family. Subsystems generally shift and change over time, but they have the possibility of becoming extremely close and turning into alliances or coalitions that operate to exclude or overpower the members not included. For example, if Amelia confides a great deal in her son and talks negatively about his father to him, the two of them may form a coalition against Ray, making the subsystems that contain Ray more strained and troubled.

The personal or psychobiological subsystem refers to the fact that each individual represents his or her own separate system. Each family member is her or his own person, separate from and yet interdependent with the whole. This idea suggests that if a friend talked to Mark and Joel LeMoyne at the office, she or he might be greeted with lots of joking and teasing upon entering the interpersonal subsystem, yet if this same friend encountered only Joel (the personal subsystem), the friend might receive a more subdued or serious welcome.

In addition to the subsystems within the family, the family itself acts as a subsystem when it confronts outsiders such as neighbors, extended family members, community or school officials, and so forth. The example of a family moving into a new neighborhood highlights the concept that the family itself is a subsystem in a larger suprasystem. This notion is often called the ecosystem approach. Kantor and Lehr (1975/1985) suggest that a major task for families is negotiating the interfaces between subsystems. Thus, when the interpersonal subsystem of Tim and Amelia come in contact with the personal subsystem of Ray, they need strategies to communicate across the space between their subsystems. When visitors come into the family's home, strategies are required to make the interface between systems.

Boundaries/Openness   Implicit in the preceding discussion about hierarchy and complexity is the notion that families develop **boundaries** around themselves and the subsystems they contain. Because human systems are open systems (it is not possible to completely control everything that comes into or goes out of a family), these boundaries are relatively permeable. Thus, although Tim may not be happy about the situation, his wife, Amelia, is receiving information and communication from Ray that passes through the boundary Tim and Amelia have created around their subsystem. All families are open systems, but some may be more or less open, and there are measures that families can take to fortify their boundaries. For example, families that build houses set back from the street and erect fences between their homes and the public sidewalk use physical means to reinforce the boundary between the family and the community. Children who post "Keep Out" signs on their bedroom doors create strong boundaries between their personal subsystem and the rest of the family. Families can create boundaries without physically putting up fences or signs. When parents carefully monitor their children's friends, television viewing, Internet sites, book reading, and so forth, they are creating invisible, but powerful, boundaries around their family. These boundaries attempt to keep out unpopular ideas as well as other people.

> ## Student Perspective: Jewel
>
> *The discussion on boundaries made me think about some of the child-rearing practices my husband and I have. We are very careful about who our children play with—we want to know their families. We restrict the amount and type of television shows the children can watch as well as the movies they see. We also send them to Catholic schools. In all of this I see we are strengthening our boundaries to make sure that information we do not approve of can't pass through, and things that fit with our values do make it through. We are kind of like gatekeepers for our kids.*

Family members can disagree about known boundaries, and they can also be confused when boundaries are ambiguous. Ambiguous boundaries (Boss, 2000) occur when family members are unsure of who is in and who is out of the family system. For example, when divorced partners do not share custody as Amelia and Ray do and one parent is absent, members may be unclear as to where the boundary lies. Nolan may not be completely sure if Tim's sister is a member of his family or not. The lack of a kinship term for this relationship as well as cultural considerations encouraging or discouraging extended family relationships may compound this ambiguity. Military families who experience a family member leaving for long periods of time during deployment may suffer from boundary ambiguity (Wilson, Wilkum, Chernichky, Wadsworth, & Broniarczyk, 2011).

Calibration/Feedback   All systems need stability and constancy within a defined range (Watzlawick, Beavin, & Jackson, 1967). **Calibration,** or checking the scale, and subsequent **feedback** to change or stabilize the system allow for control of the range. The thermostat provides a common example illustrating this process. Home heating is usually set at a certain temperature, say 65 degrees. The thermostat will allow a range around 65 before changing anything. Therefore, if the thermostat is set for 65 and the temperature is 65 plus or minus 3 degrees, nothing happens. If the temperature drops below 62 degrees, the heat goes on; if it rises above 68 degrees, the furnace shuts off. In this way, the heating system remains stable. However, if conditions change in the house (for example, the family insulates the attic), it is possible that the thermostat would need to be recalibrated or set at a slightly lower temperature to accommodate the change. After insulating and eliminating drafts, the house may be comfortable when the temperature is set at 63 degrees.

Changing the standard (moving the thermostat from 65 to 63 degrees) is accomplished through feedback. Feedback, in systems thinking, is positive when it produces change (the thermostat is set differently) and negative when it maintains the status quo (the thermostat remains at 65). When systems change they are called **morphogenic,** and when they stay the same they are called **homeostatic.**

To think about this within a family context, it is helpful to think about the rules that a family establishes for itself, a topic we revisit in Chapter 3. For example, the LeMoynes may have had a rule when Joel was young that he was not allowed to use swear words. Mark and Jean may have enforced this rule through punishment if they ever heard Joel swearing. In response to his parents' feedback, Joel would stop swearing, keeping the rule in place and maintaining the system. As Joel matured and came to work in the construction business with Mark, the system may not have needed the rule against swearing any longer. If Joel swore, his parents probably said nothing. Saying nothing in this case operates as positive feedback, changing the rule about swearing in the LeMoyne family system.

Equifinality   Open systems are characterized by the ability to achieve the same goals through different means, or **equifinality** (Littlejohn & Foss, 2011; von Bertalanffy, 1968). This principle applies to families in two ways. First, a single family can achieve a goal through many different routes. For example, if the Johnsons wish to send Jason to a preschool that is a little too expensive for their budget, Sonia could take a job, LaTasha could get a second job, they could economize on some of the things they spend money on, they could borrow the money from another family member, or they could take out a loan. There are several ways they could reach the goal of sending Jason to the preschool. Additionally, equifinality implies that different families can achieve the same goal through multiple pathways. For instance, families can report happiness given many different styles of family life. Some families may be happy with a lot of closeness and contact, whereas other families are content with more distance and less communication among the members. Systems thinking allows us to picture family interaction holistically, highlighting the important properties.

Limits of the Systems Approach Although systems theory offers a helpful framework for understanding family interaction, several researchers have critiqued it in a variety of ways. One overarching criticism is that it is too abstract to really guide research, and more narrowly focused theories would be more helpful to scholars (Galvin, Dickson, & Marrow, 2006). Other specific critiques of systems theory include: too much focus on (1) homeostasis at the expense of change, (2) pattern at the expense of unpredictability, (3) the system at the expense of the individual, (4) insensitivity to culture, and (5) its positivist intellectual tradition that puts the researcher outside the system in a search for objective truth about the system. We will briefly explain each of these five criticisms.

First, systems theory has been criticized for a focus on homeostasis that does not ring true to the experience of family life. Although systems theory views families as open systems that can be recalibrated, it pictures change as a disruption that must be controlled. As we discussed previously, systems thinking posits that the family tries to control and stabilize itself through calibration, changes only through positive feedback, and restabilizes afterward, creating a new homeostatic or steady state. In an interesting analysis of the metaphors used in systems thinking, Paul Rosenblatt (1994) considers what the metaphor of control obscures. He observes that the metaphor of control hides the fact that families are not governed by "static control structure[s] like a thermostat or a published legal code [and that the system] is constantly reengineered by family members" (p. 144). Thus, the metaphor draws our attention to one element of family life (stability) and away from another (change). When looking at the Murphy-Rodriguez family through the lens of systems theory, for example, we are tempted to look for the rules they have developed to keep the family on an even keel despite Amelia and Ray's divorce. An equal emphasis on family change would direct us to also look at the processes they develop to change their rules.

The second objection relates to the first. Here critics are concerned that the emphasis in systems thinking on pattern keeps us from seeing unpredictable behavior in families. As Rosenblatt (1994) argues, families have only so much energy, time, and desire to monitor their system. Therefore, "if control makes any sense in a family system, it may be a matter of haphazard sampling and occasional intense interest rather than constant monitoring" (p. 140). This haphazard sense of monitoring may easily lead to unpredictable and irregular results. When we look through a lens that directs us to observe regularities, we may find these even when they do not exist. Thus, we may see Mark and Joel LeMoyne's teasing and joking as part of a pattern, when in fact it is a random and seldom practiced behavior.

A third objection concerns the dichotomy between the system and the individual. Systems thinking underscores the importance of the whole, and some scholars think the emphasis has swung too far away from the individual. Although understanding the whole is vitally important, individuals within the whole also exert influence and have separate meanings for behaviors and events. Gerald Weeks (1986) argues that we should study neither the system nor the individual but rather find a way to integrate both perspectives. There is an interplay between Ray Rodriguez as an individual and Ray Rodriguez in relationship to Nolan Rodriguez as well as between Ray and the entire Murphy-Rodriguez family. We need to examine these dynamics. Also, some researchers, especially feminists, object to the removal of the individual from consideration in favor of a study of the relationship and patterns that exist in the relationship. They believe that this focus minimizes women's experiences of abuse and incest by avoiding placing responsibility on the perpetrators of this abuse and violence. In short, feminist researchers believe that systems theory does not account for power differences within the system and ignores the impact of the social context in which the system is embedded that disadvantages women and privileges men (Galvin, Dickson, & Marrow, 2006).

Somewhat related to the complaint of feminists, a fourth problem charges that systems theory is not sensitive to issues of cultural, socioeconomic, racial, and ethnic diversity. As Yerby (1995) observes,

> *While the systems model has focused on interaction in the nuclear family as an open system with relationships to the extended family and the environment, this definition of family is not widely agreed on by families themselves. . . . Boundaries between the generations are much more diffuse in Italian and African American families; in these subcultures the nuclear family often includes extended family members, friends, or both. (p. 345)*

The systems approach itself allows for examination of the cultural and historical context, because of the property of hierarchy. Yet systems practitioners have focused much more on microfunctioning within families, thus operating as though cultural differences did not affect family communication.

Finally, systems theory has been criticized for operating out of the positivist intellectual tradition, assuming there is a universal truth, and positioning the researcher outside the family, to observe and find the truth. You remember the analogy of the mobile advanced by Virginia Satir to describe the interdependence of the family system. Although that analogy is a useful one, it is clearly one that puts us, as researchers, outside the family. We see the mobile shimmer and move; we do not participate or feel its effects. Some researchers find this outsider position inaccurate. As we study the family we become a part of their system; we affect it and are affected by it.

Although not a perfect theoretical frame, the systems approach is still very useful to us as family communication students and researchers. From this approach, we can understand families as a set of interrelated people, forming a whole, organized in a complex fashion, radiating both inward and outward, creating boundaries and rules through a process of calibration, and taking many diverse paths toward outcomes. Further, the emphasis on interconnections, both among system elements and among different models from other fields of study, allows researchers to combine other approaches with systems theory to improve it as a lens for understanding family communication.

Social Construction Theory

Social construction theory focuses on the meaning-making function of communication that is lacking in the systems explanation, and this places it in the interpretative tradition. A central assumption of social construction is that people make sense of their experiences and their social world by talking about them—by offering descriptions, explanations, and accounts. In doing this, people actually construct their worlds by the shape they put on them through their talk (Gergen, 1985; Leeds-Hurwitz, 2006; Schwandt, 2000). An implication of this contention is the notion that people make these constructions in a social setting—they talk to others. Researchers who utilize social construction theory, then, are interested in how the family works together to create meaning, not just in how an individual member looks at family life.

This conceptual framework has its roots in the theory of symbolic interaction, which centered on the importance of meanings for human behavior. Meaning, at least for George Herbert Mead (1934/1956), a founder of symbolic interaction, came from symbols and their shared interpretation between people engaged in social interaction. Family researchers also showed interest in this focus. In 1926, Ernest W. Burgess argued that the family should be studied as a "living, changing, growing thing" because "the actual unity of family life has its existence . . . in the interaction of its members" (p. 5). With this call over 80 years ago, Burgess began the application of the symbolic interactionist approach to the family.

James White and David Klein (2002) suggest that a central division between symbolic interactionists focuses on whether interactions between people are the result of social expectations or are created and negotiated situationally by the actors. Researchers such as Peter Berger and Thomas Luckman (1966) adopt the latter view, developing the **social construction** approach. More recently, researchers such as Kenneth Gergen (1985) and Jane Jorgenson and Arthur Bochner (2004) have advanced social construction as a perspective for studying the "active, cooperative enterprise of persons in relationship" (Gergen, 1985, p. 267). This places importance not so much on shared meaning as on co-constructed meaning. As Victoria Chen and W. Barnett Pearce (1995) argue, meaning does not reside inside one person's head, waiting to be shared with another. Rather, meaning exists in the practice of communication between people. Shared meaning suggests that LaTasha Johnson has an individual meaning in her mind, and she is able to clearly convey it to Sonia so that the sisters share an understanding of LaTasha's original meaning. Co-constructed meaning rests on the notion of meaning being created between the sisters as they speak.

Thus, this approach suggests that the focus of concern for researchers should reside in the continuous flow of conversation between people (Ellingson, 2011). Emanating from this assumption are two notions. First, family communication researchers should study the routine, or the everyday talk that goes on in families (e.g., Burns & Pearson, 2011; Prentice, 2008). Second, we are making and remaking our social worlds through our interactions as well as being "ourselves made and remade by them in the process" (Shotter, 1993, p. 11). For example, in the Stamper family, the tradition is that each child takes a camping trip alone with their dad to celebrate their 10th birthday. When Melinda and her father return from their trip together, the family gathers to hear about it. As they tell about how Melinda fell into the lake when she was trying to untie the boat from the dock, other family members chime in and talk about how Melinda fell into the fountain at the Civic Center when she was three. The other children contribute tales of their camping trips with Dad, how he saved one from a bear who wandered into the campground and how bad his cooking was on each trip. As the family talks, they create a shared sense of themselves—that constitutes their identity as the Stamper family.

Student Perspective: Marnie

I certainly understand what we have been talking about in the social constructionist perspective. My family loves to tell stories, and I realize that much of how I came to understand what it means to be a member of this family, how to share love and affection, and just how to be a good person in this world came from listening to my mother and grandmother tell stories about my great-grandma Jennie. Jennie was a very determined woman, and she really loved her family. She wouldn't let anything stand in the way of her children getting what they needed. A favorite story was about how Jennie sold the furniture and all her jewelry so that her kids could all go to college. Some families might look at what she did differently, but it was clear that Jennie was a real hero in my family.

Given the importance of constructing meaning through family interaction, the social construction approach leads naturally to a study of the stories that families tell, which we will discuss in greater detail in Chapter 6. Further, storytelling encourages us to think in terms of multiple stories, stories from different cultures and different perspectives. It is possible to utilize social construction theory on its own, but combining social construction with systems thinking helps us to focus on families as meaning-making systems. Social construction draws the researcher into the system instead of viewing the family as an object to be studied by a detached observer, and it emphasizes the ongoing nature of family life. The addition of social construction to systems theory, then, helps address the criticisms that systems theory focuses too much on stability, ignores cultural context, and operates as though the researcher can find objective truth.

Although social construction is a very useful framework, it poses a few problems for researchers. These problems are mainly practical in nature, and they have resulted in fewer studies being conducted utilizing this framework fully. First, as with systems theory, some researchers believe that social construction is more abstract and descriptive than focused and explanatory. Second, social construction is a theory about words and behaviors in action, and this focus has methodological considerations for researchers. To use the theory aptly requires actually listening to people talk in the context of their family. This, however, is difficult for researchers to accomplish. As a researcher, it is a lot easier to interview people and ask them about how their family talks than it is to integrate oneself into a family and observe and participate in their talk. As a result, research in family communication often uses the language of social construction without following the methods that would be most appropriate within this framework (Leeds-Hurwitz, 2006).

Dialectics

In addition to systems thinking and social construction, dialectics is another frame for understanding questions about family communication. The **dialectic approach** maintains that family life is characterized by ongoing tensions between contradictory impulses. Dialectics theory (or relational dialectics) was a theory that Leslie Baxter and Barbara Montgomery brought to the field of communication in 1996. It is grounded in the interpretive-hermeneutic tradition because it focuses on meaning-making processes. To create the theory, Baxter and Montgomery adapted the ideas of the Russian philosopher Mikhail Bakhtin, who argued that the world is full of competing discourses, and that any one thing a person says is part of an utterance chain where

Student Perspective: Jolene

It's funny how I have fought so hard to be independent of my parents, and now they are saying to me that it is time for me to manage money on my own and not depend so much on them, and I actually miss having them tell me what to do. I kind of don't really want all this independence. I know it's time for me to be on my own, but I realize I sort of like having them to depend on too.

it is conditioned by what was said before it and acts as prologue for what is said subsequently. Further, these utterance chains cannot be understood apart from the cultural dialogue in which they are embedded. More recently, Leslie Baxter (2011) has refined and extended the theory while maintaining these basic tenets. Baxter is interested in what she calls the discursive struggle that occurs when people in unequal power positions voice contradictory utterances. For instance, if Melanie and Jodi wish to define family as two lesbian women and their adopted children, their utterance enters the struggle along with those of various politicians like Michele Bachmann and Mitt Romney who say that marriage (and family) only exist for heterosexual people. When some states legalize gay marriage, that forms another utterance in the discursive struggle. Baxter (2011) argues that meaning will eventually emerge from this struggle, although as Kristen Norwood and Leslie Baxter (2011) discuss, with any controversial topic, competing discourses may continue to occur.

Many different specific dialectics have been discussed as shaping relational life. The three most relevant to families are the **autonomy/connection dialectic** (our simultaneous desires to be independent of our families and to find intimacy with them); the **openness/protection dialectic** (our conflicting desires to be open and vulnerable, revealing personal information to our family, and to be strategic and protective in our communication); and the **novelty/predictability dialectic** (our conflict between the comfort of stability and the excitement of change) (Baxter, 1990). Other researchers have found additional dialectics in different contexts like friendship (Rawlins, 1992) and adoptive families (Harrigan & Braithwaite, 2010; Norwood & Baxter, 2011). The push and pull represented by the dialectics construct family life, and one of the family's main communication tasks is managing them. This approach considers homeostasis or stability to be an unnatural state—change and transformation are the hallmarks of family interaction in the dialectic perspective (Montgomery, 1992).

Although the tensions are ongoing, families do make efforts to manage them. Baxter (1988) identified four main strategies: (1) cyclic alternation, (2) segmentation, (3) selection, and (4) integration. **Cyclic alternation** occurs when families choose one of the opposites to feature at particular times, alternating with the other. For instance, when LaTasha and Sonia Johnson were adolescents they might have favored autonomy in their relationship; now that they live together and are both raising Jason, closeness might be their choice. As Jason gets older, the two sisters might move apart and emphasize their independence from each other.

Segmentation operates to isolate separate arenas for emphasizing each one of the opposites. For example, Mark and Joel LeMoyne might stress predictability in their working relationship and novelty for times they are in private. The third strategy, **selection**, implies a choice between the opposites. A family who chooses to be close at all times, ignoring their needs for autonomy, uses selection.

TABLE 2-2   Dialectic Tensions Shaping Family Life and Management Strategies

Tensions
Autonomy/connection
Openness/protection
Novelty/predictability

Strategies
Cyclic alternation: featuring one pole at one time in family development and the other at a different time.

Segmentation: featuring one pole in one domain of family life and the other in different domains.

Selection: choosing one pole at the expense of the other.

Integration
Neutralizing: compromising between the polarities and choosing a happy medium.

Reframing: transforming the dialectic so that it no longer seems to contain an opposition.

Disqualifying: choosing one pole for the general pattern, but exempting certain issues from this pattern (e.g., a generally spontaneous family that has strict rituals around birthday celebrations).

Finally, **integration** can take three forms: neutralizing, reframing, or disqualifying the polarities. **Neutralizing** involves compromising between the polarities. A family who chooses this strategy tries to find a happy medium between the opposites. The Murphy-Rodriguez family may decide they cannot really be close, yet because of their needs they cannot select autonomy either. Thus, they forge a moderately close relationship. **Reframing** refers to transforming the dialectic in some way so that the dialectic no longer seems to contain an opposition. One group of researchers (Wood, Dordek, Germany, & Varallo, 1994) discussed how couples in their study reframed by defining connection as including differences. Thus, the dialectic between autonomy and connection is redrawn as a unity rather than an opposition. **Disqualifying** operates by exempting certain issues from the general pattern. A family might be very open in their communication in general yet have a few taboo topics that are not discussed at all, such as sex and finances. Table 2-2 summarizes the dialectical tensions and strategies for dealing with them.

Leslie Baxter and Barbara Montgomery (1996) review these and other techniques for dealing with dialectical tensions. They argue that any techniques that family members use are (1) improvisational, (2) affected by time, and (3) possibly complicated by unintended consequences. By improvisational, Baxter and Montgomery mean that whatever people do to deal with a particular tension of family life, they do not alter the ongoing nature of the tension. For example, when the Murphy-Rodriguez family comes to a moderately close relationship to neutralize the tension, they have not changed the fact that closeness and distance continue to be an issue in their relationship. The aspect of time means that communication choices made by the family to deal with dialectics are affected by the past, enacted in the present, and filled with anticipation for the future. Finally, Baxter and Montgomery point out that a family may try to enact a strategy for coping with a tension, but it may not work out as the family intended. For example, Mark and Joel LeMoyne may feel they are coping with the novelty and predictability tension by opting for the segmentation plan we described earlier, but they may become dissatisfied because they spend so much time at work that they still do not get enough novelty in their relationship.

Dialectics are interactional (Rawlins, 1992) in that they are located within the context of the family—they are part of the family's interaction with one another. Some researchers have discussed other dialectics that affect the family. William Rawlins calls these contextual and says they derive from the place of the relationship (in our case, the family) in the culture. Rawlins lists two contextual dialectics—the public and the private and the ideal and the real. While perhaps a little less important to us than the interactional dialectics, these two do affect the family. The public and the private dialectic refers to the tension between the two domains, the family—a private relationship—and public life. Many other ways of thinking dichotomize the public and the private. Dialectical thinking shows us that family life is intertwined with public life. The dialectic between the real and the ideal concerns our idealized images of family life in conflict with our real experiences of family life. When we think of old television shows such as *Leave It to Beaver*, we receive an idealized message of what family life is like. We look at the families we live in; we have to contend with the troublesome realities that come along with our family. The tension between these forms this dialectic.

Dialectical process thinking allows us to think specifically about issues around which families will construct meaning. It also puts our emphasis on the interplay between change and stability. We do not have to choose between observing pattern or unpredictability because we recognize the presence of both within the family. Likewise, dialectical thinking reinforces the ecosystems approach, directing us to observe the interactions among the family, its individual members, and the larger social and cultural

Student Perspective: Ed

When we were talking about dialectics it made me understand my mom a little better. She wants me to be independent and she encouraged me to go to school a long distance from our home, but she also wants me to call home every Sunday and let her know what is going on with me here at school. I am thinking that is her way of reframing—showing me that independence can actually bring us closer together as we talk about the things I am learning about on my own.

systems in which it is embedded. This tack helps us focus on power issues and multicultural diversity. The main critique leveled against this theory is that it can support a potentially infinite list of dialectic tensions. Simply generating a list of tensions in family life is not especially explanatory, nor does it enable us to predict much about family communication behaviors, according to the critics of dialectic theory.

Developmental Theory

Developmental theory has a long historical tradition and it is rooted in the positivistic-empirical tradition because it seeks to find regular patterns related to developmental stages. This theory attempts to explain the way families change over time. It is embedded in four basic assumptions about family life—assumptions that some researchers believe in and other researchers find objectionable. First, the theory assumes that the process of family development is goal directed. In other words, as families change over time, they do so in order to reach some end or goal. Yet, many believe (from life experience) that family communication is messy and sometimes seemingly incoherent to us as participants. Many times family meaning is made after an experience by telling stories about it and constructing an acceptable framework for it. Ian Frazier (1994) wrote a book about his family after his parents' deaths. Frazier collected all of the family memorabilia he could find and did intensive research in order to make what he and his family had experienced meaningful. He speaks eloquently about the process:

> *I wanted my parents' lives to have meant something. I hunted all over for meanings of any kind—not, I think, simply out of grief or anger at their deaths, but also because the stuff they saved implied that there must have been a reason for saving it. The smell of an old hymnal, the weave of a black mesh hat veil, the tone of a thank-you note, each struck me with the silent force of a clue. Something was going on here. I believed bigger meanings hid behind little ones, that maybe I could follow them to a source back tens or hundreds of years ago. I didn't care if the meanings were far-flung or vague or even trivial. I wanted to pursue them. I hoped maybe I could find a meaning that would defeat death. (p. 39)*

Here Frazier articulates the desire for meaning but illustrates that it sometimes comes after the experience rather than as a goal that directs the family.

The second assumption that traditional family development theory makes is one of determinism. This means that necessary conditions and tasks must be met and accomplished during one stage for the family to successfully move to the next stage of development. For example, a parent who inadequately bonds with an infant is unlikely to bond with the child later. Many researchers are uncomfortable with this assumption because it suggests a predetermined course to family life that invalidates free choice.

A third assumption is that as the individual in the family develops, the whole family will develop or change. Again, many researchers find this assumption troubling. LaTasha Johnson may grow and develop in her confidence on the job, for example, without causing a movement in the process of the Johnson family's development. Although LaTasha's maturity may affect the Johnsons' communication, it does not necessarily propel them into a different phase of their development as a family.

The final assumption that grounds developmental theory is that the process of family development is a linear one. Thus families are seen to move in a forward, linear fashion through the life course. Like individuals, families are born, mature, and die. This assumption fosters the work in family development that attaches most stages in the model to the growth of children (for instance, the birth of the first child, the birth of the second child, the first child leaves home, the empty nest). The assumption carries with it an implicit definition of family excluding childless couples and gay and lesbian families, among others. The assumption of linearity also makes it difficult for researchers to talk about families like the Murphy-Rodriguez family. Divorce and new partners are somewhat difficult to accommodate in the traditional models of development based on stages.

These assumptions have left some researchers (e.g., Rodgers & White, 1993; White, 1991) troubled, and they have reworked this theory, remediating some of its problems. The result of their work is called **revised developmental theory.**

Basically, revised developmental theory concerns itself with the family's change over time. Further, change is continuous within this perspective. When we perceive stability, it is merely due to a very slow rate of change. Robert Rodgers and James White (1993) note, however, that not all change is developmental. Some change is random, some is maturational, and some allows the family to adapt to a changing environment. Developmental change is a probabilistic process (that is, it is not strictly determined) from stage to stage over the history of the family system. Rodgers and White offer a set of

Student Perspective: Peter

When we talked about development theory I really could not relate. I do not think too many researchers had a family like mine in mind when they worked on the stages of family development. First, my mom and dad get a divorce, and then my mom decides she is a lesbian. We lived for a long time with her first partner, Sylvia, but they have broken up now. I have moved out of the house, and my mom is now with Jeanine, and I think they have a good relationship. My girlfriend, Amy, comes from the type of family those developmental researchers were thinking about; she's had a hard time getting used to my family, but we seem natural to me.

FIGURE 2.1   Family Stages and Events in Family Development Theory

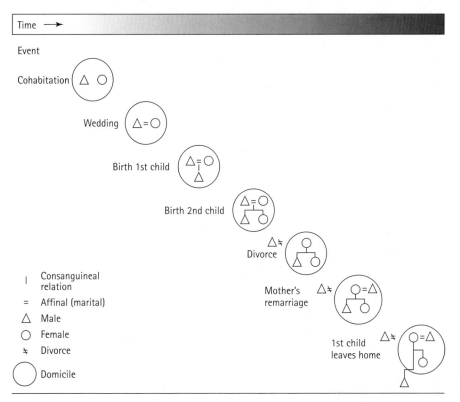

Source: From R. H. Rodgers & J. M. White, "Family Development Theory" in *Sourcebook of Family Theories and Methods,* eds. P. Boss et al. (New York: Plenum Press, 1993), 225–254.

family stages (including cohabitation, wedding, birth of first child, birth of second child, divorce, mother's remarriage, first child leaves home), noting that the family group structure must be considered in coming up with the stages (see Figure 2-1). Thus, the type of family and the cultural context of the family will suggest stages that are applicable to those families. Stages are linked by developmental events that form the transitions between stages. They state that "A developmental event carries with it the implication that there will be qualitatively different normative expectations in the role content of family relationships as a result of the event" (p. 238). Thus, when Joel LeMoyne moved out of his parents' house, it constituted a developmental event. But when Ray Rodriguez changed jobs, that was not a developmental event.

In this theory, developmental events are mapped across time and context (calendar or clock time, social process time, historical period, and cultural context) in order to understand how they affect communication behavior. The revised theory asserts that (1) previous stages influence present stages, (2) families develop in relatively consistent patterns over time, and (3) norms from other social institutions affect the timing and sequencing of stages in the family. These propositions rest on the following assumptions: (1) events are the transition points between stages, and (2) the order of stages in a family's life career is not invariant or irreversible. Thus, it is not a linear model.

The four theories we have reviewed are not the only ways to explain family communication, although they are widely used. In subsequent chapters we will refer to these and other more narrowly focused theories to help us understand family interaction.

METHODS OF INQUIRY

As we have seen, theories provide explanations about family communication and help researchers organize their studies. To study questions of family communication, researchers use a variety of methods. These may be divided into two main categories: **quantitative research** and **qualitative research**. Quantitative methods require researchers to gather observations that can be quantified (converted to numbers) and then analyze the numbers in order to make an argument about their meaning relative to a theoretical position. Qualitative methods help researchers understand how people make sense of their experiences. These methods do not depend on statistical analysis to support an interpretation, but rather require researchers to make a rhetorical appeal for their findings. Quantitative methods are seen as most appropriate for researchers who embrace a positivistic worldview, and qualitative methods as most appropriate for interpretive and critical researchers.

In practice it is a bit more complicated than this, and it's possible for researchers to blend methodologies from both the quantitative and the qualitative categories. This is often referred to as **triangulation,** or approaching the question with more than one method. Although triangulating is useful, it is sometimes difficult to achieve for two reasons. First, researchers are usually trained in only one approach, and it is difficult to learn a new set of methods on the job. But, perhaps more importantly, researchers believe that the two categories of methods represent two different intellectual traditions. Thus, it would be difficult for a researcher who believed in the utility of control and the possibility of discovering universal truth to adopt methods that ignored issues of researcher control and opted for multiple truths espoused by research participants. Conversely, researchers who focused on giving voice to their respondents may recoil at speaking for them by analyzing their words without concern for their interpretations.

Before we discuss the specific methods researchers use, we want to give you a broad overview of how theory is utilized by researchers. Sometimes a researcher (usually with a positivist-empirical intellectual tradition) will begin with a theory, deduce a hypothesis from it, design a study, collect data through some type of method, analyze the data, and come to conclusions that either support or cast doubt on the general propositions of the theory. This deductive model is what Paul Schrodt, Aimee Miller, and Dawn Braithwaite (2011) followed in their study about ex-spouses' satisfaction levels. Schrodt and his colleagues used theories from the social exchange perspective (which we discuss in Chapter 5). These theories provided guidance for them to predict (hypothesize) about how communication with former spouses about parenting decisions (called co-parenting) would relate to the ex-spouse's satisfaction. For instance, they hypothesized that when ex-spouses reported supportive co-parental communication, they would also report high levels of satisfaction. So, if Ted feels that his former wife, Carla, listens to him and expresses trust and cooperation when they talk about how to parent their 6-year-old daughter and 4-year-old son, Ted will say that he's satisfied with their relationship. Schrodt and his colleagues also hypothesized that the opposite would be true. Ted will be less satisfied if his co-parental communication with Carla is antagonistic.

The researchers collected survey data via a questionnaire, analyzed it statistically, and found that these two hypotheses were supported by the data. The fact that they found what the theory led them to predict allows them to say that the theoretical perspective of social exchange is useful for examining interactions about co-parenting, and that the propositions of the theory held true in their data.

Another way to use theory in researching families is usually employed by researchers within the interpretative or critical intellectual traditions. This approach does not begin with a theory and move to test hypotheses deduced from it, but rather operates inductively to generate a theory (usually called grounded theory) from a series of in-depth observations. An example of this approach comes from the work of Mark Young and David Kleist (2010). Young and Kleist interviewed six couples who said their relationship was healthy. The researchers conducted two rounds of in-depth interviews with the couples and then coded the interview transcripts so as to get at the underlying relationship processes that the couples described.

Young and Kleist followed qualitative methods and the interpretative tradition, stating, "Grounded theory methodology allows for the subjective nature of the research process. In using this methodology, it is necessary to use one's own experiences and emotions when coding and analyzing data. Rather than ignoring the researcher's personal reactions, they are documented and discussed either in peer triangulation, with the participants, or as a limitation" (p. 339).

The researchers examined their results and made several generalizations about healthy, functioning couples: they described their relationship with reference to the concept of security, and their processes were circular so that May, for example, would have positive perceptions about her relationship that would influence her expectations about it, and in turn those would influence how she communicated to her partner. Then these interactions would confirm and strengthen May's perceptions. These concepts and the circular process they describe formed the basis for their grounded theory of couple interaction.

As you can see, this process, the methods used, and the function of theory are all quite different from our earlier example of testing theory.

To give you a better picture of the methods researchers use in conjunction with theory, we will review two popular quantitative methods, **surveys** and **experiments**, and two well-regarded qualitative methods, **depth interviews** and **textual analysis**.

Surveys

Many researchers wishing to use quantitative methods opt for survey research. You probably have been a respondent in survey research, and perhaps you have even constructed a survey of your own to study a question for one of your classes. Typical survey research consists of a researcher administering a standardized questionnaire to a sample of respondents. The questionnaire may be a self-administered paper-and-pencil type, it may be administered face-to-face in a structured interview format, it may take place over the phone, or by using an electronic option such as Survey Monkey.

Surveys are often mailed if they are of the self-administered type, and then the researcher depends on the respondents to return the completed questionnaire. Researchers come up with a variety of clever ways to ensure a high return rate of questionnaires. They include providing stamped self-addressed envelopes, making the questionnaire a self-mailer so that envelopes are not needed, providing a monetary incentive, and administering follow-up mailings to nonrespondents as needed.

Surveys are best suited to research in which the individual is the unit of analysis. Although individuals can give information about groups to which they belong, like their families, researchers have to keep in mind that the data surveys generate are on an individual level. In such a case, researchers are learning what one member reports about the family, not necessarily about the whole family itself. Further, surveys are very useful for collecting data from a large population. Public opinion polls, such as Gallup and Yankelovich, are able to sample carefully to determine the opinions of all people in the United States, for instance.

Utilizing developmental theory, you might speculate (or hypothesize) that family life was a series of developmental stages that required different communication practices at each stage, and you might test that by asking people to fill out a survey. In the survey you might ask questions about assumed stages and about the type of communication that the family engaged in during each stage. You would then analyze participants' responses to see whether your hypothesis is supported by the data you have collected.

Experiments

Experimental research systematically manipulates the independent variable (for the study mentioned above that would be developmental stages) in order to see what its effects are on another variable, called the dependent variable (communication behaviors). Experiments involve researchers taking an action (the manipulation) and then carefully observing the results of that action. In an experiment, the researchers' goal is to keep everything constant except the variable being tested. In this way researchers hope to measure whether participants behave in the ways predicted by the theory the researchers are testing. For example, if researchers wished to conduct an experiment to test whether families communicated differently at different stages of family life, they might bring family members into the lab and ask them to role-play various situations depicting different developmental stages. Then they would analyze the communication the participants generated during the role-play to see whether it differed systematically based on the developmental stage. So you can see that a researcher could answer the same question (or test the same hypothesis) using either survey are experimental data.

Depth Interviews

Like surveys, depth interviews allow interviewers to question respondents in hopes of obtaining information about a phenomenon of interest. However, they differ from surveys in many significant ways. First, depth interviews are, at most, semistructured by the interviewer. They are seen by researchers as a collaboration between interviewer and participant, wherein what the participant wants to discuss is at least as important as the ground the interviewer had thought of covering. Researchers employing depth interviews are interested in the directions in which the respondents wish to take the interview. They are not as concerned with testing hypotheses as they are with finding out about the lived experiences of the respondent.

Second, depth interviews typically last between one and three hours. Researchers are more interested in obtaining rich, thick description from a smaller number of people than they are in collecting information from hundreds of respondents. Further, depth interviews are generally conducted in person. It may be possible to conduct depth interviews on the Internet (Garner, 1999), but this is a new concept and typically the personal contact is preferred.

Textual Analysis

Textual analysis requires a researcher to identify a specific text for scrutiny. Texts can be presidential speeches, television shows, advertisements, or any type of discourse that the researcher can focus on to illuminate. Researchers engaged in textual analysis must apply some type of analytic tool, usually rhetorical theory, in order to deconstruct the messages embodied within the text. Researchers interested in what advice is given to newlyweds about communication behaviors might use textual analysis to investigate popular advice books. In this type of study a researcher would probably examine the advice books to surface themes about what the texts considered positive and negative communication behaviors.

SUMMARY

This chapter introduced conceptual frameworks for examining family communication. Systems thinking, social construction theory, dialectics, and developmental theory all offer vantage points for understanding family communication. As we seek to understand the communication in our own families and in others, we need to realize that we are part of the ongoing conversation, and each family consists of multiple perspectives. As Yerby (1995) states, our ability to listen to the perspectives of others while voicing our own perspectives ultimately contributes to our ability to understand how we are connected to others. We also provided a glimpse at the ways in which theory is used by researchers.

We showed you how our assumptions shape our interest in the family and our reading of the research about family communication. We invite you to examine your own assumptions and the frameworks that shape your approach to family communication as you read the rest of the book.

KEY TERMS

autonomy/connection dialectic

boundaries

calendar or clock time

calibration

critical approach

cyclic alternation

depth interviews

developmental theory

dialectic approach

disqualifying

equifinality

experiments

feedback

hierarchy

homeostatic

implicit theories

integration

intellectual traditions

interdependence

interpretive approach

morphogenic

neutralizing

novelty/predictability dialectic

openness/protection dialectic

positivistic approach

qualitative research

quantitative research

reframing

revised developmental theory

segmentation

selection

social construction

social process time

subsystems

suprasystems

surveys

systems theory

textual analysis

theory

triangulation

wholeness

worldview

QUESTIONS FOR REFLECTION

1. Do you agree that a theory can help us understand family communication behavior? Why or why not?

2. Which intellectual tradition (positivist, interpretive, or critical) seems most compatible with the way you think? Why?

3. Does the analogy comparing a family to a system seem appropriate to you? Give some examples illustrating interdependence, calibration, openness, and other characteristics of systems in your family.

4. Does the notion of tension embodied in the dialectical approach make sense to you? Explain. Can you think of any other tensions besides the three given in the chapter that affect family communication? If you have experienced any of the tensions mentioned in the chapter, how did you manage them?

5. Do you believe families create reality (as the social construction approach advocates), or do you think families have to live in reality? Explain.

6. How has your family's communication changed over time? Can you link its changes to developmental stages? Can you come up with developmental stages for families other than those illustrated in Figure 2-1? What stages might cohabitating couples, lesbian families, or single-parent families experience?

7. Choose a theory of family communication and discuss a means of testing all or part of it.

8. What are the areas that families ask and theorize about that the four theories reviewed in the chapter don't address?

Chapter

3

EXAMINING STRUCTURE: ROLES AND RULES

Roles and Family Communication
Interpreting Family Roles • Examining the Assumptions of Roles
Gender Roles and Families • Reflecting on Roles

Rules and Family Communication
Interpreting Family Rules • Examining the Assumptions of Rules
Types of Communication Rules • Reflecting on Rules

Summary

Key Terms

Questions for Reflection

THE SONN FAMILY

Winnie Sonn has been married to Bradley Sonn for nearly 15 years. The Sonns have no children and live rather comfortably in an oceanfront condominium in the southeastern United States. Winnie's marriage to Bradley seems to mirror her own family-of-origin; her mom was a stay-at-home parent, and her father was rarely around because of his job responsibilities. Up to this point, it seems that Winnie is destined to follow in her mother's path. Aside from cleaning the condo, preparing the meals for Bradley, and taking care of the bills, Winnie doesn't do much with her time. She has reminded Bradley time and again about her pent-up frustration: She feels useless and trapped in the role of a 1950s wife. She has told Bradley that she really wants to get a job to keep her mind busy and to get her out of the house. Bradley, however, will not hear of it. His own family-of-origin was rather traditional, similar to that of his wife's, and he always thought that the husband should be the breadwinner. Bradley remains insistent that his wife not have a job outside of their home. He has always cherished coming home to dinner, having a glass of wine with Winnie, kicking back on the couch, and watching television with his wife. He couldn't imagine having it any other way. Despite Bradley's thinking, Winnie's plans are different from her husband's. She feels very restricted in her role as wife and wants to explore a more liberated life beyond the condo. Little does Bradley know that tomorrow morning, Winnie Sonn will go to her first job interview in 15 years.

THE LADZINSKI FAMILY

Two years after the death of his wife, Howard Ladzinski is still struggling with his new role as a single parent. With two children, ages 10 and 14, at home, he realizes that he must strive to balance work and home schedules. He is a little troubled about his relationship with his kids. His 10-year-old son seems withdrawn, and Howard and his daughter have had some angry exchanges. He recognizes his difficulty in communicating with his daughter in particular; in fact, he finds that she has developed her own rule for housekeeping, often doing much of the household chores when Howard is away. Although a babysitter is around the house after school, he realizes that his task as a single parent is an arduous one that requires careful attention. He hopes that he and his kids will begin getting along better soon.

DELTA PHI BROTHERS

Steve Knoller, Ben Wicker, and Antonio Gomez are members of the Delta Phi fraternity and they love to hang out with each other. Although they live in the residence halls and not in the fraternity house, they live on the same floor, take many of their classes together, and eat breakfast and dinner around the same time. They also find themselves playing out various roles during their personal time together. Because Steve is a psychology major, he is often sought after to help with relationship problems. Ben is rather quiet; therefore, the guys believe that he will be a great listener. And Antonio is excellent at smoothing out any personal conflicts, given the skills he learned in the university's mediation program, and his communication studies major. The guys know that they each have particular strengths, and are very willing to take on the roles others have given them.

In Chapter 2, we conceptualized families as systems, and in this chapter we explore the notion that family systems are rule-governed. Further, the family system is peopled by "players" who enact role behaviors that allow them to find their places in the family system. Thinking about individual family members as role players and rule followers allows us to remember the interplay between subsystems and the larger system as a whole.

Roles are critical components of family life and help the family function and develop, as they offer prescriptions for individual behaviors. Roles are not always easily accepted, however, and some conflict may result from roles that seem a poor fit with the player. For example, Winnie Sonn questions her role in her marriage and seems to be protesting the reasonableness of enacting the traditional female role. For Howard Ladzinski, his single-parent role is often clouded by his inability to understand what is expected of him. At times, his frustration gets the best of him since he has no experience with such a role. Finally, in the voluntary family of Steve, Ben, and Antonio, some conflict may occur if Ben wishes to speak out rather than continue his listening role, for instance.

Similarly, family rules offer guidance and prescriptions regarding the boundaries of appropriate behavior for family members. Family rules, therefore, are extremely important for family functioning, as they can establish stability, coordinate family behavior, and establish an overall framework for the family's interactions. Of course, families differ greatly in the flexibility of their rules and in the amount of negotiation taking place to establish the rules. For instance, in the Sonn home, the rules for dinner seem clear: Winnie will have dinner ready for her husband when he gets home from work. In contrast, Steve, Ben, and Antonio have to discuss and negotiate how to manage their mealtimes—they create their own rules.

Student Perspective: Alicia

We recently had complete chaos in our family. Last year, I went back to school after 13 years. Although my husband encouraged me to do so, it seems that he's having second thoughts. Now, he has to be the "mom" at times, and he has to do the cooking and cleaning. My favorite is how he complains about having to do the carpooling every other Monday. I have to laugh. Things are fine until he's required to take on Mom's role. I don't plan on stopping my schooling. I do plan on helping him out more.

This chapter will explore roles and rules and their relationship with family communication. Rules govern our communication, and our communication establishes our rules. Roles are created and sustained in interaction, but roles offer prescriptions and limits to an individual's communication behavior. For instance, if Howard Ladzinski believes a father's role should be one of all-knowing authority, it will be difficult for him to confess his confusion and uncertainty to his children. By defining roles and rules, examining assumptions behind each, and describing their importance to families, we will better understand the complex interactions that take place in families like those of Winnie Sonn, Howard Ladzinski, the Delta Phi fraternity brothers, and our own.

ROLES AND FAMILY COMMUNICATION

Interpreting Family Roles

For purposes of our discussion, we define **roles** as socially constructed patterns of behavior and sets of expectations that provide us a position in our families. As you will note, this definition reinforces one of our theoretical frameworks: social constructivism. Role behavior is socially constructed as we interact with family members. We learn various roles through our continuing interactions with family members.

Implicit in the social constructionist approach is the concept that it is through talking with others (or co-construction) that we make something (like a family or a role in a family) come into being (Leeds-Hurwitz, 2006). This is different from the approach of social learning theory (Kunkel, Hummert, & Dennis, 2006), which suggests we learn family roles through observing **role models,** or others who exemplify the behaviors of the role we expect to play, and by receiving instruction and rewards for playing a role correctly. For our purposes, both of these theoretical explanations are useful. Jane may learn how to be a wife, for instance, as she and her husband talk together. When he asks for her advice and she complies, they are co-creating their roles as a married couple. However, it is also true that while she was growing up Jane observed her mother and father interacting with one another, she has seen countless movies about married couples, and she lived with her older sister and her husband briefly before she married herself. In all these observations, she engaged in social learning about the role of a wife.

Both social constructivism and social learning explain how roles are inextricably linked to family communication. We learn our family roles as a result of our communication with others. Through both verbal and nonverbal communication, we receive instruction in how to behave in particular situations, and we create role behaviors in concert with our family members.

Three other processes related to roles are situated in communication: role taking, role evaluation, and role allocation. **Role taking,** or deciding to play a particular role, may occur mainly through intrapersonal communication, as a family member decides if he or she wants to be the peacemaker in a given situation, for example. **Role evaluation,** or deciding how well a role is being enacted, occurs both interpersonally and intrapersonally. For example, Tasha may think she is a very affectionate mother, but when her son tells her that she always frowns at him and makes him think she's angry, she may revise her evaluation of her mothering skills. **Role allocation, or a family's role assignment pattern, refers** to how the family distributes role behaviors. Communication, both verbal and nonverbal, accompanies this process. When Maria's mother died all of her siblings turned to her wordlessly, and she realized she was being anointed the mother-substitute for her brothers and sisters. When Theo needed his brother, Micah, to act as a teacher for him and socialize him into the ways of college life, he just told Micah that when he came to campus he'd be looking to him for help.

We are quick to note that not all family members are able to clearly talk about their family roles. For example, in many Salvadoran and Guatemalan refugee neighborhoods in the United States, roles are in flux because the lack of financial and material resources and the lack of English-language skills prohibit family members from communicating both within and outside the family boundaries (Baca-Zinn & Wells, 2005). Sometimes role behavior is out of the conscious grasp of family members. For instance, Antonio may not fully realize that he is seen as the conflict mediator for his chosen family of fraternity brothers.

In other cases, roles are difficult to articulate because they have not been clearly defined culturally. Amy Janan Johnson and her colleagues (2009) talk about this problem with reference to stepparents. They argue that stepfamilies may be seen as "incomplete institutions" and this makes it difficult for stepparents to talk about the role they play in relation to their stepchildren. Are they parent substitutes, friends, aunts/uncles, or something else? Johnson and her colleagues note that the lack of a clear cultural definition for a stepparent's role makes it difficult for stepparents to communicate with institutions outside the home. They comment that one striking example of this is the legal system, noting that for the most part, stepparents and their stepchildren are considered "legal strangers" (p. 307). Rebecca Speer and April Trees (2007) also examined role development in stepfamilies and concluded that stepchildren as well as stepparents feel a lack of clarity about how they are supposed to behave and feel in their roles within the family. This **role ambiguity** can cause problems for steprelations' sense of satisfaction with their new family.

Many family members, however, are very adept in communicating role messages. For example, as Howard Ladzinski thinks about his current situation, he is very aware of role considerations. He realizes that his wife's death has thrust new role behaviors on him, and he is concerned that he is not doing a very good job of fulfilling them. Further, he talks with his daughter about how she is stepping in to do many of the household tasks that were once part of her mother's role. Howard articulates the changes their family roles are undergoing as he tries to keep the family together after their loss.

Examining the Assumptions of Roles

In this section, we detail four assumptions of roles: (1) role position communicates value; (2) enacting a role is a process; (3) expectations, developed through communication, influence our roles; and (4) roles serve functions in the family. We realize that some of these assumptions overlap with others, but each helps us uncover the complexity of the relationship between family communication and role behavior.

Student Perspective: Min

I know that Asian families are not "known" to have single parents, but I'm a product of a single mother. As I think about what she was able to do—raising three kids with limited income—I am still in awe. My father was nowhere to be found, and we had no relatives in Northern California, the place where my siblings and I were born. So, we all joined in. At times, I felt like the disciplinarian when my mother worked, and I was only 14! At other times, I was the guidance counselor as I talked to my little brother about being teased at school because of our race. Then there was the time that I felt like the parent because I had to go to school to bail my other brother out of an after-school detention. I don't know how my mom juggled all those roles by herself all the time!

Role Position Communicates Value To understand this first assumption, think about those ideologies, people, and events in your current family or your family-of-origin that have high value. Roles are often created around important values in the family. We try to avoid the roles that are devalued in our family and choose to enact roles that are highly valued. Popular culture and a family's relational culture each help determine what roles will be valuable.

For example, Johnny Gillespie is the oldest son in a family of four children. As the oldest son, he is expected to go into business with his father. His parents believe that as the oldest child, Johnny should "carry the family torch" and sustain the legacy that his grandfather established. Consequently, Johnny's parents confide in him much more frequently and intimately than in his siblings. He has also been named the executor of the Gillespie estate. In sum, the role of the oldest child in the Gillespie home is highly valued, and comes with many responsibilities.

Cherishing a particular value at home may make you more willing to enact one role over another. Further, this assumption implies that roles and the behaviors attached to them carry with them value and prestige. In the Gillespie family, being the oldest child, the torch bearer, carries more status than being a middle child. However, it is also the case that high-prestige roles involve more pressure and responsibility for those who enact them. Further, some family members enact role behaviors that bring them low esteem within the family: the scapegoat, the irresponsible one, the scatterbrain, for example.

Enacting a Role Is a Process The second assumption guiding our understanding of roles pertains to the developmental approach we articulated earlier in this book. In Chapter 2, we noted that developmental change in the family system may occur at a family stage, such as marriage, a birth, or a death. This view also suggests that these stages are usually concerned with transitions. And it is these transitions—external and internal—that are viewed as bringing about changes in the internal family structure (Prentice, 2008), a structure that includes family roles.

To help you understand this assumption, reflect on the fact that through the course of your lifetime the roles you play will change. What may be appropriate for you at age 12, for instance, is likely to be inappropriate for you at the age of 40. As a 12-year-old, your role may simply be categorized as child. As a 40-year-old, however, you play more roles, which are normally much more complex, such as coworker, volunteer, parent, caregiver, and so forth. A tension may arise when a 40-year-old

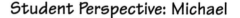

Student Perspective: Michael

My wife, Marcia, and I do not have what you would call a "perfect" marriage. I think we have some problems because we both work. It gets very tiring to figure out who's going to load the dishwasher, who's going to go grocery shopping, who's going to pick up the dry cleaning. We don't agree on a lot of the little things around the house. I wish we could figure out a way to share equally in the jobs around the house; the roles get pretty confusing. The bottom line is that we are both at important stages in our careers, and neither one of us wants to give up a promotion. I have to admit that I didn't expect this would be the way marriage would turn out. I know it isn't fair, but I kind of thought my wife would do a lot of these little things that take up so much time. I want to be a good husband and make things work, but it would be so much easier if Marcia didn't care about her career as much as I care about mine.

~/l\/l\~ **POPULAR PRESS PERSPECTIVES** ~/l\/l\~

Diane Mapes noted on msnbc.com (2009) that "the recession has dealt a lot of low blows in the past several months, but none so devastating, perhaps, as forcing adults to do the unthinkable: move back in with mom and dad." Mapes cites an August, 2008 Collegegrad.com survey that stated 77 percent of college grads were moving back home after school, up from 67 percent in 2006. She also notes that "from 2000 to 2008, multigenerational households increased by 24 percent, up to 6.2 million, according to AARP."

Mapes observes that this return to the childhood home can impact both parent and adult child behaviors. Usually the outcome is that both begin to act the same way they did when they lived together at an earlier time. One of the women whom Mapes quoted says she's happy for her mother's help, "but less thrilled about the 'growing pains.' But I'm still my mother's child. She's in mom mode, always."

Mapes also quotes Dr. Marion Lindblad-Goldberg, a clinical professor in the department of psychiatry at the University of Pennsylvania. Goldberg says, "Theoretically, by the time you reach adulthood, you're supposed to be at the same power level as your parents. But it's never like that. Parents can relate to their adult children when they're away from home. But in the home, particularly if it's the same home, the kid goes from being 28 down to 25 to 20 and ends up at 7."

Lindblad-Goldberg advises parents and adult children to sit with each other and talk about the situation. She comments that family is wonderful in that it provides adult children with support, but coming home requires a lot of talking, negotiating, and problem-solving to make it work. New roles and new rules have to be forged for parents and the adult children who return home to live during these tough economic times.

Diane Mapes, "Grown kids return to the nest–and regress: Moving back in with mom and dad sends relationship back in time." *msnbc.com.* June 22. 2009. Retrieved June 27, 2009.

returns home to his or her family-of-origin and is treated or feels like a 12-year-old—and in fact may begin enacting some of the same role behaviors that fit a 12-year-old!

The temporal nature of roles relates to the idea that people are not the roles they play. Roles are behaviors, and when people engage in these behaviors, we say they are playing a role. Yet they have the capacity to drop a given role and pick up another, or to modify the role, acting out some of the prescribed behaviors and not others. In their book about aunts, Laura Ellingson and Patricia Sotirin (2010) speak about encouraging readers not to think about the aunt as a person or even a role. Rather, they stress that the aunt is a practice or something people do. This is why they title their book *Aunting*. Aunting exists in the communicative practices that people engage in when they are in aunt/nephew/niece relationship with each other. In this way, as Ellingson and Sotirin argue, family becomes a dynamic experience. This perspective is aligned with our assumption that roles are processes that evolve over time and sets of behaviors that actors pick up and mold to their personalities or disregard when they become burdensome or outdated.

Expectations Influence Our Roles Family members are constantly influenced by expectations (Gardner, 2003). Whether a newborn or an elder family member, each family member will experience some sort of expectation of how to behave. **Role expectations** are internalized sets of beliefs about the way we will function in a particular role. Expectations may be very different from reality. Two people who are newly married may expect that they will know how to become effective parents, yet these expectations may be very different from the roles they will eventually enact.

One relevant example of how expectations influence roles pertains to the dual-earner couple. Patricia Roehling and Phyllis Moen (2003) report that because this couple is especially vulnerable to the problems of "mood and behavior" (p. 1) from workplace to home, role expectations are pronounced. And these role expectations both defy and support cultural stereotypes of husbands and wives. For instance, in the home, when a working wife is unavailable to care for the child, her husband is likely to serve as the caregiver. Yet, the presence of children may increase the amount of time that a wife will spend on housework, but not her husband's time. In other words, although a husband may be willing to care for his children while his wife is working, she still ends up doing most of the household chores. Nonetheless, Annis Golden (2001) granted that in dual-earner families, "adjustments to

Student Perspective: Beverly

Can I imagine any role conflict? Well, as a 57-year-old mother of three children, I can tell you that when my 46-year-old brother-in-law moved in with us because of cutbacks in mental health funding, our lifestyle changed forever. We had no idea that he would require so much attention. I can remember a night last summer when we got a call from the city police, and they informed my husband that his brother was urinating on a monument in the park. You can't imagine what kind of challenge we've found ourselves in! At this time in our lives, we thought we would be getting ready for retirement; now we find ourselves getting bogged down in caring for a man who needs help.

role redefinitions take place on an ongoing basis," and "individuals continually self-check their comfort with their roles and make adjustments" (p. 260). Further, Golden (2007) argues that men who assume caretaking responsibilities for their children may challenge expectations as well as live by them as they forge a masculine model of caregiving that differs from what feminine caregiving looks like.

Some expectations about role behaviors come from our own assessments, whereas others come from outside. Expectations may be clearly stated or inferred. As a 17-year-old, Caitlin is beginning to think seriously about what she will do once she graduates from high school. Because Caitlin's parents both hold graduate degrees—her mother is a college professor, her father is an attorney—and both sets of grandparents are college graduates, it's clear that Caitlin will most likely find herself in the college student role. The comments, stories, and suggestions made by her significant others will no doubt influence her own expectations about her roles and her future.

A cultural example may also help you understand the notion of expectations. Margarita Gangotena (2004) suggests that in many Mexican American households, when an outsider is welcomed into the family, he or she is integrated into the *compadrazgo* system, that is, a "co-parent" system. Biological parents expect that individual to function in a godfather or godmother role for the child, a relationship requiring obligations of upbringing should the parents die. Ultimately, the co-parent interacts with the child as a family member, assimilating into the family and assisting in its social constructions. Clearly, the expectations of others influence role taking here.

Tensions may be inherent in the expectations that shape our role behavior in families. **Role conflict** can occur, or a situation where someone experiences competing role-related expectations. Role conflict can take two forms. Sometimes two or more family members wish to enact the same role behaviors, thereby creating **interpersonal role conflict.** For example, a conflict could ensue if both Steve and Ben from the Delta Phi fraternity example at the beginning of the chapter decided that they wished to take on the behaviors of mediator. Instead of working to solve problems and deal with conflict, Ben and Steve could find themselves competing for who gets to be the one to come up with a solution. This type of role conflict is called interpersonal because it involves two or more people.

A second type of role conflict, **intrapersonal role conflict,** occurs internally within one family member. This happens when a person is called to perform a role that is incompatible with his or her personal perceptions, beliefs, or values. Karen Bullock (2004) suggests that many grandparents feel intrapersonal role conflict when asked to serve in the role of parent and caregiver of their grandchildren. In fact, given that grandparents are usually on a fixed income, have health-related problems, or do not have housing to accommodate the family, intrapersonal role conflict may be exacerbated. Bullock notes that for most of the women in her study, "the unexpected role of primary caregiver caught them unprepared, uninformed, and in need of social support" (p. 49).

An additional example of intrapersonal role conflict may come about when a child serves as the support for his or her parent. In some cases it may be productive for a child to learn skills by helping parents with caregiving of younger children, for example. But children who assume too many adult responsibilities can experience internal conflict as they cross into adult roles. This movement across the boundary between adult and child roles is called parentification (Byng-Hall, 2008) and can be detrimental. When children of immigrants have to act as translators for their parents, for instance, they may experience intrapersonal role conflict. Although they are children, they have more expertise than their parents, and they may become privy to information that their parents might have sought to keep from them had they stayed in their country of origin. For example, when Mila took her mother to the bank to act as a translator for her with the loan officer, she learned a lot more about her family's precarious finances than she would have normally known at age 13.

Katherine Miller and her colleagues (2008) noted that adult children of elderly parents also go through this role reversal if they become caretakers of their parents. They report that some of their respondents noted intrapersonal conflict in this role, but many appreciated the chance to parent their own parents.

Roles Serve Functions in the Family The systems approach we outlined in Chapter 2 suggests that the family grows and maintains itself through interdependency. Thus, each family member depends on the others to enact behaviors that keep the family going. Further, systems theory asserts that the family is a unique whole, not the sum of its parts. Therefore, each member's role enactments contribute to creating and maintaining the family. These principles give rise to the notion that family members will behave in ways that are needed by the system as a whole. Howard Ladzinski's continued employment allows him to provide for his family materially even though they are struggling emotionally. In some ways, even negative role behaviors may serve a function for a family. Howard's daughter's seeming lack of cooperation may be helping to divert the family's attention from their grief and focus the members instead on working through routine household tasks.

Not all roles function positively for the family, however. Some role behaviors have painful effects for the family as a whole and for individual family members. In some primary-parent systems, for instance, moms and dads must deal with the confluence of being financial provider, disciplinarian, teacher, confidant, and nurse. Teresa Chandler Sabourin (2003) concludes that "as a result of this role strain, single parents are more vulnerable to burnout, which means the parenting may be less consistent than in two-parent homes where role responsibilities are shared" (p. 53).

The McMaster model of family functioning (Epstein, Bishop, & Baldwin, 1982) provides five functions that families need to accomplish and posits that roles exist in the family to do this. The functions include adult sexual fulfillment and gender modeling for children, nurturance, individual development, kinship maintenance, and provision of basic resources. In the Phillips family when Jon Phillips goes to work to earn money and Edie Phillips spends time with her children, supporting their interests and nurturing them emotionally, they are providing most of the functions in the McMaster model by playing traditional gender roles.

Gender Roles and Families

Much discussion has taken place in popular culture regarding male and female roles. You've probably heard the old refrain that men and women are from two different planets. As students of family communication, we should be cautious about believing everything that is presented to us. First, there are significant methodological problems with much of the research related to male and female behavior (Barnett & Rivers, 2004). Second, Dan Canary and Kim Hause (1993) discovered that there are few important empirical differences in the communication of men and women. Further, other communication researchers remind us that claims of gender difference are often exaggerated; to be sure, most men and women are not that different from one another, although they are often treated very differently and have different socially constructed domains (Sterk & Turner, 1995). We might conclude that men and women are not from different planets, maybe just from neighboring states (Dindia, 2006; Golden, 2007).

Before embarking on a discussion of roles that men and women enact in the family, let's first define a few terms and explain some concepts further. **Gender roles** can be defined as the expectations assigned to masculinity and femininity. **Gender role socialization** pertains to the process by which men and women learn what roles are appropriate to their sex. For instance, in the United States, the gender role of a feminine person is nurturing, cooperative, and child-centered. A masculine individual would enact a role that includes independence, aggressiveness, and mechanical aptitude. Not all masculine individuals are males, and not all feminine individuals are females. Still, we believe that the U.S. culture and many other cultures have pretty clear expectations regarding men's and women's roles.

Deborah Kerfoot and Caroline Miller (2010) argue that gender can be seen as a cultural performance. Both men and women can perform masculinity or femininity, but, of course, when a male body performs femininity or a female body performs masculinity, they may be subjected to discipline by the greater culture given the expectations for men's and women's roles. Families often serve as the disciplinarians, providing early teaching about how to perform a gender that is appropriate to one's biological sex and congruent with cultural expectations.

Interestingly, co-cultural differences in gender roles have emerged. For instance, Ali Akbar Mahdi (1999) notes that there have been significant changes in gender roles within Iranian American families. Specifically, Mahdi contends that the roles of women and men have shifted tremendously over the past years in a few ways. First, male participation in household tasks has increased. Second, husbands find themselves in competition with their wives for social status and success. Mahdi concludes: "Role differentiation within the family is moving away from a traditional hierarchical division of male-dominated/female-subordinate roles toward a complementary one" (p. 184).

In one of the most comprehensive studies looking at culture and gender roles, Mihaela Robila and Ambika Krishnakumar (2004) looked at perceptions across a number of cultures—specifically, Bulgaria, Czech Republic, the former East Germany, Hungary, Poland, Russia, and Slovenia. The authors found that, overall, Bulgarians and Hungarians had the most traditional gender roles, believing that the family suffers if women have a full-time job, and a man's job is to earn money while a woman's job is to look after home and family. The East German respondents were the most egalitarian in their gender role expectations. Further, Robila and Krishnakumar discovered that the Czechs, Russians, Poles, and Slovenes held beliefs somewhat in between, from more traditional perceptions to more emancipated perceptions. Looking at these findings, the researchers state that the division of labor within these cultures is rather traditional as are the gender ideologies of both women and men.

In an interesting study of the Druze culture (a minority group in Israel who speak Arabic but maintain an esoteric religion that differentiates them from other Arab Muslims), Naomi Weiner-Levy (2011) illustrates how fathers enabled their daughters to transcend the traditional gender roles of their culture. Weiner-Levy points out that the Druze are a patriarchal society, but unlike most patriarchs, Druze fathers encouraged their daughters to seek higher education and break out of constraining gender stereotypes. The participants in Weiner-Levy's study "described their fathers as indulgent and supportive figures who encouraged their independence and permitted behavior that deviated from gender norms" (p. 142). The interesting finding in this study is that gender socialization was changed within the context of patriarchy.

Parents as Influences in the Home   Gender roles are socially constructed and are taught; they are not natural or inate. There is some disagreement among researchers about this statement. Some (e.g., Chodorow, 1978; Hartsock, 1987) believe that bearing and nursing children does shape a woman's world view in a way that is unique and not shared by men. Other scholars dispute this, noting that not all women bear children. These scholars (e.g., Alvesson & Billing, 2002; Kanter, 1977) argue that all people are shaped by what they do, and if they exchanged their activities, their orientations would change accordingly. The expectations for the roles of mother and father grow out

Student Perspective: Stuart

As a gay male in a three-year relationship, I am really bothered by all the hoopla over same-sex marriages. I don't ever want to take on a husband or wife role with my partner. It doesn't make sense. Why do gays and lesbians want to use matrimony to get their voice heard? It seems so contradictory to use a heterosexual way to intimacy when we're talking about homosexual people!

of social interaction and expectations; therefore, these roles often differ dramatically across cultures. In keeping with a social learning approach, a mother's or father's role will be based on stories that have been shared in the family about mothers and fathers as well as observation of parents, both real and fictional. If, for instance, you continually watched television shows or heard stories about moms who were at home all day, enacting the role of full-time housekeeper, you might be more likely to construct a traditional gender role for a mother. If you continually watched television programs or heard stories about dads who spent a great deal of time with their children perhaps even assuming their primary care, you may be more likely to construct a nontraditional gender role for a father. Clearly, then, our impressions of how men and women should behave in the family are a result of beliefs derived from interaction and observations.

Since gender roles are learned, it makes sense to discuss the sources of gender role socialization. Researchers studying the family have identified parents, schools, television, peers, religion, and toys as primary agents of socialization. Although gender communication scholars have identified a body of literature that concludes that biological sex does affect behavior (e.g., Ivy & Backlund, 2004), for our purposes, we will detail how gender roles are learned through interactions between parents and children (Table 3-1).

Whether intentionally or unintentionally, parents instruct their children about men's and women's roles and masculinity and femininity (Menvielle, 2004). These messages about masculinity and femininity are communicated to children very early in life. Even at birth, the gender role messages begin. James Doyle (1989) observes that once physicians and nurses check the genitals, a baby boy is described as "robust and strapping," and a female newborn is described as "petite and adorable." As the children get older—say by the time they're two—they appear to know their own sex and begin to acquire their gendered sense of self (Maccoby & Jacklin, 1987). Once at preschool age, girls and boys begin to be inundated with gender-based messages about their sex.

Parents are also central in communicating gender roles through differential treatment and perceptions of their daughters and sons. Boys and girls often experience two different worlds in the family. Those worlds are based on how parents treat them. Julia Wood (2013) reports that parents are likely to talk and interact more with their daughters and play more actively with

TABLE 3-1   Parents and Gender Roles

Parents respond differently to their children depending on whether they are male or female.
Example: When 15-year-old Jay went to his father, Marty, to ask him for help with his math homework, his dad told him to reread the chapter and figure out the word problems himself. When 12-year-old Jennifer asked Marty for help with her social studies assignment, her dad sat down with her for almost an hour, asking her questions along the way.

Parents have different expectations for their children depending on whether they are male or female.
Example: Upon the birth of their twins, Bob and Carol Boroski were elated that they now had two children, one boy and one girl. Smoking a cigar at work, Bob proudly told his coworkers: "I now have a beautiful model and a computer genius!"

Parents buy sex-typed toys for their children.
Example: When Myra Davis went shopping for her daughter's ninth birthday, she decided to buy her the child's deluxe kitchen set. A month earlier, she bought her son boxing gloves for his 11th birthday.

Parents assign household jobs differently to sons than to daughters.
Example: To get ready for their grandparents' 40th anniversary party, Wayne and Dana Hickman told their kids that they needed to help around the house. Wayne told his boys to rake the yard and not to forget to take out the folding chairs from the garage. Dana and her daughter, Samantha, were busy in the kitchen cleaning and finalizing the dinner preparations.

their sons. She indicates that fathers and mothers are selective in their expectations and treatment of their children by sex. Parents tend to emphasize strength and aggressiveness in their sons while expecting their daughters to be more delicate and weaker. Wood also observes that mothers typically have more face-to-face interaction with their children than do fathers.

In addition to differential perceptions and treatment, many mothers and fathers also buy sex-typed toys for their sons and daughters. Girls are usually given dolls, dress-up clothes, tea sets, kitchen utensils, even makeup. Boys receive trucks, plastic guns, boxing gloves, and footballs. At first glance these toys seem rather innocuous; what

Student Perspective: Ali

It's true. My parents always bought me "girl" things. And I know they treated my brother and me differently. One Christmas, I remember getting all of the Barbie stuff and the plastic kitchen, with all of the utensils. My brother got all of the G.I. Joe paraphernalia. Now that I get a chance to think about it, my parents were really treating us differently. They wanted me to play domestic, and they wanted him to stay active. I guess I'll try not to do that when I have children.

harm can toys bring to a child? Yet a closer look reveals that purchasing such toys for children reifies and exaggerates differences between the sexes (Messner, 2000).

A final way in which parents communicate messages about gender roles is in the way they assign household duties. Wood (2013) remarks that household jobs are assigned differently to daughters than to sons. Girls, as you may have guessed, are assigned domestic jobs such as washing clothes and dusting, and boys are assigned work such as taking out the garbage and shoveling snow. The implications of this task assignment are that girls are taught to be caregivers of people, such as the family, whereas boys are taught to be caregivers of things, such as the garage, yard, or car.

To better understand this task assignment, take the case of Howard Ladzinski in the vignette at the beginning of the chapter. Because Howard works full-time, he must try to ensure that whenever possible his children help around the house. To this end, his daughter frequently enacts traditional female role duties such as washing the laundry and vacuuming the living room. His son will periodically clean up the yard, raking in the fall and shoveling snow in the winter. This division of household chores is gender-specific, reifying the different domains of the sexes. The Ladzinskis are not unique, however, since research suggests that single fathers rely on their daughters to fulfill responsibilities inside the house (Davidson & Moore, 1996).

We might be tempted to think the gender socialization we have described is a modern phenomenon, but Thomas Socha and Julie Yingling (2010) remind us that during the Middle Ages mothers were preparing their daughters to manage a household, and fathers were preparing their sons for military life.

In examining family types and gender socialization, it is interesting to note that lesbian mothers do not assign such stereotypic domestic duties to their daughters or sons (Hill, 1988; Martin, 1993). Daughters, in particular, report that they have freedom of choice and satisfaction at home, dressing in less feminine ways and acting out in less stereotypic ways (West & Turner, 1995). Gay fathers are also very concerned about fostering equal responsibilities in the home (Benkov, 2003). April Martin (1993), in *The Lesbian and Gay Parenting Handbook,* notes that lesbian mothers and gay fathers accept a child's individuality, and many parents want to "make sure that they are also actively helping to combat the gender-role stereotypes that [their] children will pick up from the culture" (p. 213).

Finally, it is important to note that gender roles, and indeed the definitions of masculinity and femininity, are socially malleable, even if change is slow. Donald Unger (2010) in his book about fathering concludes that "a cultural space has begun to appear—small, irregular, spasming [sic] open and closed from time to time and place to place—in which it is at least sometimes recognized as acceptable, sometimes desirable, sometimes necessary, for men to openly demonstrate our softer side" (p. 194). In his study of fatherhood in Sweden, Thomas Johansson (2011) found similar changes taking place.

Johansson presents four case studies of four very different men who stayed at home to provide care to their children. Consistent across the case studies, according to Johansson, is the acknowledgement of "gender-neutral and equal parenthood" where mothering is not seen as significantly different from fathering.

Gender Schema Theory   To close this section, we wish to help you frame some of the findings we noted above. In *The Lenses of Gender,* Sandra Bem (1993) identified **gender schema theory** as a way for us to understand the organization of the world around masculinity and femininity. Specifically, she asserts that through a schema, we process and categorize interrelated beliefs, ideas, and events into what we consider to be useful and practical wholes. Thus, we may classify people by race, age, ethnicity, religion, and gender. Bem believes that although some of our beliefs, ideas, and events may not be relevant to gender, we, nonetheless, treat them all as if they were either masculine or feminine in orientation. That is to say, we may think and talk about such things as sports cars, stoves, dogs, cats, and so forth, filtered through our gender schemas. So we can decide as males, for example, whether we should be interested in the purchase of a sports car or a stove.

More contemporary understandings suggest a multidimensionality to gender schema (Tenenbaum & Leaper, 2002). Scholars now tend to agree that we have several gender schemas that are fluid and subject to change. Further, Harriet Tenenbaum and Campbell Leaper find that mothers may be more likely than fathers to hold nontraditional gender schemas. And, particularly in single-parent mother households, children hold less traditional gender schemas.

What does all of this mean with respect to family communication? Gender schema theory is one way to understand why some people categorize and classify behaviors into a gender-based system. Gender-typed behaviors in the family—from doing the dishes to changing the oil on the car to serving as the sole financial provider—are influenced by the gender schemas of family members. Family members who practice being flexible in their gender schemas are likely to have more expansive views of what it means to be masculine, feminine, male, female.

Student Perspective: Bruno

What can I say? I'm guilty. I raise my daughter in stereotypic ways. She gets Barbie dolls, kitchen stuff, and wears lots of pink. And you know what? It doesn't bother me. She is almost five years old and loves to play house. My wife and I don't discourage her from having fun. If it means that we are raising a girl in stereotypic ways, so be it. I really don't buy into all of this gender role parenting material. I know we are raising our daughter with a lot of love and care. It doesn't make a difference if she wears pink, now, does it?

Reflecting on Roles

Family roles are important for us to consider. They help us guide our behavior in the family, but they also "can restrict behaviors and limit spontaneity and creativity" (Socha & Yingling, 2010, p. 82). As you reflect on your current family and your family-of-origin, you will see that you and others have enacted various roles. Sometimes those roles were difficult; other times they were relatively simple to enact. Families in our larger culture must cope with a number of roles, given the uniqueness of the co-cultures around us. Families must be willing to communicate with each other about their role abilities—abilities often complicated by many variables. These variables may be external to the family boundaries or internal, such as the development of and adherence to family rules.

RULES AND FAMILY COMMUNICATION

Interpreting Family Rules

Just as roles serve important functions in our families, rules are also instrumental in structuring our family communication climate and behaviors. The interrelationship between rules and roles is clear: Rules flow from certain types of family roles, and certain types of family roles are shaped by family rules. In the Sonn home, for example, "car purchase decisions are Bradley's responsibility" may be interpreted as a rule, which in turn suggests that the husband is the vehicle caretaker and the decision-maker for this type of large purchase (role), and this role contributes to the existence of this particular rule. Also, just like the word *role, rule* is a complicated term that needs further clarification so we understand how rules relate to family communication. We believe that rules are discovered by examining repetitive patterns of behaviors in families. Through repetition, family members indicate that there are appropriate ways of interacting in their family. Since all families are unique, we will spend time discussing how families communicate that uniqueness and how families strategize their patterns of interaction. In Chapter 1 we argued that a family is a group of individuals who create and maintain themselves through interaction. In this section, we wish to expand this thinking, linking it to rules. Without doubt, rules govern the family system and are also linked with roles. In fact, Susan Shimanoff (1980) concluded that rules are used to fulfill roles.

Researchers have long been interested in the concept of rules. Donald Cushman (1977) is credited with providing early research on rules and personal relationships. Cushman believed that rules influence human action by governing and regulating it and by establishing its meaning. Shimanoff (1980) offers a definition of rules that we adopt for our discussion here. She argues that rules are prescribed guidelines for action and formally defines a **rule** as "a followable prescription that indicates what behavior is obligated, preferred, or prohibited in certain contexts" (p. 57). She theorized that rules help give meaning to our interactions.

Although not articulating the relevance of rules to families, Shimanoff's view has direct application to the study of family communication. In order to have a better grasp of the meaning and importance of rules in families, let's consider the important components of Shimanoff's interpretation of rules; that is, rules are followable, determining obligated, preferred, and prohibited behaviors in a particular context.

First, that *rules are followable* suggests that family members have a choice about whether or not to follow a rule. This notion suggests that a rule may also be broken or violated. For instance, the Becker family has a rule that when a school holiday season arrives, the entire family sits down and discusses possible places to go. The rule requires each family member to come to the kitchen table with some realistic suggestions for the family's vacation destination. If Lenny Becker decides that, as the father, he has every right to make a unilateral decision on the family holiday, then he has broken the family rule. Rules do not determine family behavior; they prescribe it. Family members have personal choice as to whether they will comply. Of course, sometimes members perceive that their choices are limited. Young children may believe that they have to follow family rules. Even adults may believe that, although they do not like a particular rule, they have to follow it. For example, the Osborn family has a rule that television is always turned off at dinnertime so the family can converse. Occasionally there is a show on at their dinner hour that Carol Osborn would like to watch. Yet she fears violating the rule because she doesn't want their dinner table talk to change. So, even though she's an adult, she complies even when she doesn't always want to.

Second, Shimanoff advanced that *rules prescribe behavior that is obligated, preferred, or prohibited.* Many families have rules that require family members to act or interact in certain ways. Obligated and preferred behavior should occur, whereas prohibited behavior should not occur. To understand the difference among the three, let's consider the Kesaris family. The Kesaris family lives day-to-day in homeless shelters in Baltimore. Still, the family members agreed early on that if one family member gets a job, at least 75 percent of the paycheck must go to a special "self-help" fund. This money would be put aside and kept in a safe place to help the family get some financial footing to eventually rent an apartment.

For the Kesaris family, then, a rule determined when and how future money would be used. The behavior may be obligated under the current family rule. In this scenario, obligated behavior means that a rule is enacted to protect the future of the family. Or, the Kesaris family may enact this rule as preferred behavior, clearly noting that the rule is not required, but highly recommended. After all, one family member might argue, they might need to spend more than 25 percent of their earnings now while they are still in the shelter. Finally, the family may prohibit any money spent on unnecessary

Student Perspective: May Julie

When I think about it, none of us really knew the rules that my stepdad had when he came into the family. How did he expect us to know that he wanted my brother and sister and me to stay quiet until the evening news was over? Or how were we to know that no one should eat the last ice cream bar unless we asked him first? If he had been more explicit in what he expected, we wouldn't have had so many surprises.

and frivolous items. This latter prescriptive behavior is much more direct than the previous two in that prohibited behavior means forbidden behavior. Thus, this type of rule requires negative sanctions if it is violated. Tom Socha (1991) commented that parents will often induce guilt as a negative sanction if rules are not followed.

In addition to the followability and prescriptive nature of rules in families, the third element of Shimanoff's rule definition pertains to context. Specifically, *rules are contextual.* In other words, rules vary according to situations, and not all rules cover all situations. Families differ in how they develop rules for different contexts. Rules may be either unique to a context or generalizable across many contexts. For example, the Ruhaak family members believe that the rules they have for dating are unique to their family. With a teenage daughter, Elizabeth and Terry Ruhaak must be concerned with how they will handle issues related to her dating. Their rules are clear: A young man may have a date with their daughter only after he first has dinner with the Ruhaaks and only after they speak to his parents first. This unique rule has sometimes complicated the dating process in the Ruhaak family, yet it remains in force. Although the dating protocol appears simple enough, a complex family conflict may emerge if any part of the rule is violated.

Think about stepfamilies for a specific example. When a stepfamily begins, the rules and roles are often confusing. What worked in one family may now seem unimportant or inappropriate in the reconstituted family. To be sure, the stepfamily configuration requires new rules and new roles. For example, when Alicia divorced her first husband and married another man with three children, Alicia's daughter, Paige, was having difficulty adjusting to her newly formed family. When a rule was developed that required family members to call for a meeting to express concerns, Paige felt prepared to openly express her uncertainty and anxiety with the family. In fact, only because there was a rule allowing free expression did Paige even have an opportunity to let her feelings be known to others.

In addition to a specific context, a family rule may be generalizable across additional contexts. In many Mexican American families, the grandparent is revered and sought after for advice and comfort. The family rule in many Mexican families, then, is to consult the oldest family member, since there is no substitute for wisdom and experience. This type of rule may also function in other contexts. In the classroom, older learners often provide important applications of theory. In the workplace, many coworkers with seniority have been important mentors to new workers. Even in our friendships, we seek out advice from those friends who are wise from experience.

Shimanoff has given us an important backdrop for discussing rules. Now that we have an understanding of what rules are, it's time to address the assumptions behind rules and their relationships to family communication. We should add that many rules that families currently employ have their roots in families-of-origin. Rules may be passed down many generations in families. We now turn our attention to some of the assumptions of rules and how they relate to family life.

Examining the Assumptions of Rules

In this section we need to reflect back to the definition of family that we articulated in Chapter 1. We stated, among other things, that a family helps to create and maintain itself by its interactions. We would like to expand that thinking by stating that rules help families create and maintain themselves.

By now, you should understand that rules are important to the family system. Consider the following examples of communication rules that may characterize your home:

- Don't interrupt when another family member is speaking.
- Tell the truth.
- Don't talk back to your parents or grandparents.
- Ask permission before borrowing something from a family member.
- Say "please" and "thank you."
- Speak to older family members respectfully.
- Defend your family to outsiders.
- Don't yell in the house.
- Call or text if you're going to come home after your curfew.

Rules such as these are general; you may find that more specific rules such as "Don't talk about Uncle Steve's divorce" are found in your families. It's clear that rules help families to create meaning, and families construct rules to clarify meaning.

We wish to uncover the complexities of rules in family life by examining four assumptions of rules relating to family communication: (1) rules may be explicit or implicit, (2) rules evolve over time, (3) rules work best when they consider needs of individual family members, and (4) rules are affected by cultural trends.

Rules May Be Explicit or Implicit   We began the chapter with Winnie Sonn. For Winnie, it appears that the rules about her duties are clear. Not everyone, however, lives in families with such clearly identified rules. For one family, the rules may be quite overtly stated; for another family, the rules are understood and unstated. These two types of rules are called explicit and implicit. **Explicit rules** are openly discussed by family members and agreed on by most family members. These types of rules are consciously referred to in family discussions. In some families, it is customary to have family meetings whereby family rules are formally (or informally) and explicitly stated. This type of meeting helps all family members to understand that there are prescriptions for appropriate family behaviors. Violations of these rules may have repercussions, depending on family decision making. Explicit rules are verbally stated, as in "no children are allowed to joke about sex in the presence of adults" or "everyone is expected to share the high point and low point of their week at Sunday supper."

Implicit rules are understood at more subtle levels and are unstated; they are communicated and understood nonverbally. Typically, these rules are not at issue in the family until one or more family members breaks them. Implicit rules can have as much importance as explicit rules. Consider an example from many Filipino households in the United States. Yen Le Espiritu and Diane Wolf (2001) report that a rule in many Filipino immigrant families is that family members look to each other to sustain themselves and maintain ongoing support. Although this is not an explicitly stated rule, it is understood to exist. What becomes important for family communication researchers is understanding the implicit rule governing this commitment toward family. Without this knowledge, researchers might erroneously assume that Filipino families are quite cohesive; in fact, living together may not reflect harmony as much as "Filipino ideologies of family cohesion, unity and loyalty, a Catholic aversion to divorce, and perhaps a greater need to cohere to the smaller family unit due to the absence of the wider family network" (p. 179).

Communicating explicit and implicit rules within and outside the family helps families to create and maintain themselves. Families are continually evolving, and rules help shape their evolution. Through rules, families communicate their uniqueness to themselves and to others. Explicit rules make it clear that there are expected and appropriate behaviors in a family. Implicit rules suggest that family members have a sufficient level of intimacy (a topic we will discuss in Chapter 5) that no verbal negotiation of rules is necessary. Through rules, family members help fashion how they interact with one another and how they manage problems in those interactions.

At times, rule setting can be a challenging and difficult process. What happens when individuals don't agree with the rules that have been set up in families? In an interesting study looking at stepfamilies, Tamara Afifi (2003) discovered that not everyone is happy with the rules pertaining to biological parents and stepparents. Children report "feeling caught" in the boundaries set up between custodial and noncustodial parents. Further, parents and/or stepparents report "feeling caught" between the children in the stepfamily. In order to extricate themselves from the dialectic tension of loyalty–disloyalty, stepfamily members established new boundary rules. Afifi notes that boundary turbulence happens when boundary rules and efforts to establish them are incompatible.

Because rules are conditional (McLaughlin, 1984), family members realize that they may need to be changed as the family's experiences change. Implicit rules may become explicit rules. For instance, when Carlos failed to follow an implicit rule that prescribed putting the toilet seat down after each use, his mother and sisters reminded him, thereby making the implicit rule an explicit rule. Further, tensions may exist between rules and the perceptions rule makers in the family wish to maintain. Although a family member may want to construct a particular rule, that same family member may also want to be perceived as flexible within the family. So, even if Julia would like to require that her partner's teenager not stay out later than 11 P.M., she also wants to be viewed as an accommodating and flexible stepparent who realizes that extenuating circumstances may occur, causing the rule to be modified. Julia has to struggle with competing desires.

Rules Evolve over Time   In Chapter 1, we noted that one of the premises operating in our discussion of families is that they evolve over time. We also believe this to be true with rules. Further, rules are often constructed with time changes in mind. That is, families provide for different curfews, privileges, and so forth for children as they age. Families-of-origin are significant influences in introducing us to some of the rules by which we currently operate in our families (Larson, Parks, Harper, & Heath, 2001). Many of these rules, however, are now considered antiquated because family members have changed. Many of the rules we abided by in our families-of-origin are simply not appropriate, relevant, or effective in our current family makeup. Therefore, in Renee's family of sorority sisters, she and her female friends have abandoned a common family-of-origin rule that stated that females marry and keep their birth names if they marry. Renee and most of her sorority sisters believe it's better to take your husband's name to create a sense of family unity. The old rule simply does not correspond with their current goals.

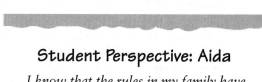

Student Perspective: Aida

I know that the rules in my family have changed since I was little. My younger sister today gets to stay out much later than I could. She also gets to take my dad's car on Saturdays to the mall with her friends. What's more, she dosen't have to do anything around the house. When I was her age, the rules were different.

It is true, however, that some of the rules that guided our families-of-origin remain in our current families. What was once effective may still be considered effective. For instance, a rule stating that every Sunday should begin with church services may be explicit in your present family. A rule requiring family members to schedule no meetings or appointments on Wednesday night in order to have dinner together may also be featured in some of today's families. One apparent reason why these rules remain intact is that the family-of-origin rule is ostensibly accepted by current family members, despite the rule's functionality. For example, Jeffry Larson, Michelle Taggart-Reedy, and Steven Wilson (2001) examined the effects of dysfunctional family-of-origin rules on the dating relationships of young adults within those families. They looked at **dysfunctional rules** as rules that hinder communication and increase opportunities for chaos and resistance (such as, "Don't feel or talk about feelings"). **Functional rules** are defined as fostering communication, strengthening relationships, and empowering family members to reach their goals (for example, "Look after others"). Larson and his colleagues discovered that dysfunctional rules were positively related to dating anxiety and negatively related to relationship satisfaction. That is, dysfunctional rules seemed to promote young people feeling nervous about the dating process. The authors question whether or not dysfunctional family rules that are rigidly adhered to will influence decisions to marry and, ultimately, the satisfaction within that marriage.

Rules derived from our families-of-origin may sometimes be in conflict with rules constituted in our present families. Although one or more family members may be comfortable employing a family-of-origin rule, not all family members may be as comfortable. Indeed, family members sometimes resist rules from the past, claiming that both individuals and rules should change. This interfacing of the past with the present can be frustrating to family members. **Rule negotiation,** or the ability to mediate potential conflicts pertaining to rule enactment, will be required if family members are to achieve a satisfactory level of communication. In addition, behavioral flexibility will also help work through potential family conflict.

To understand how rule tensions may occur and the importance of rule negotiation and behavioral flexibility, let's consider the Ironfield family. As a member of the Chickasaw community, the Ironfield family rules underscored the importance of kinship in decision making. Among other rules, all family members agreed that no family member would ever be romantically involved with someone outside the Chickasaw nation. Even the two teenage boys have openly agreed to this explicit rule. Although the boys knew that finding a date in a community of less than 5,000 nationally was going to be challenging, they agreed to honor this long-standing Ironfield rule.

One month before his 17th birthday, however, Duane Ironfield felt conflicted. He was very attracted to 16-year-old Suzan, only he knew she was Cherokee. Of course, he recalled the family rule and became troubled.

Yet instead of unilaterally developing his own rule, he went to his parents to see whether they would be able to rethink this rule. Much to his surprise, they were very proud that their son was mature enough to talk to them in this way, and they ultimately worked out a solution. Duane and Suzan could date, but his parents wanted to meet with her before the two went out on a date. Further, Duane's parents would have the right to stop the dating if there were troubling signals from Suzan's family. Duane agreed. Thus, through some effective rule negotiation and behavioral flexibility on the part of the parents, potential tension and anger were prevented. The Ironfield family system was maintained, even though a family-of-origin rule was revisited and ultimately changed to accommodate a new family development. As we discussed in Chapter 2, the Ironfield family system changed, or recalibrated, through positive feedback and rule modification.

Rules Work Best When They Consider Needs of Individual Family Members
A third assumption of rules is that they must take into consideration the needs of individual family members. Each family member is unique and has unique needs. As rules are developed and negotiated, it's important that all relevant voices in the family be heard and that the rules reflect the individuality of family members. Not everyone should or will take part in establishing rules. It is difficult to involve all family members in the process. You may have a grandparent with Alzheimer's disease or a four-year-old sister, and although these two may not take part in establishing rules, family rules should reflect their membership in the family.

How does one take into consideration the unique needs of family members when establishing rules? We first must note that the task can be difficult. After all, what is unique to one family member may not be understood by other family members. To make sure that rules acknowledge the uniqueness of others, family members must negotiate rules that correspond to differing needs. No family would expect the same level of table manners from a 1-year-old as from a 14-year-old. While moodiness might be excused in a young teenager, it probably would not be tolerated from a 24-year-old.

For example, Sandra Allen knows that as a single mother of four children, she is in a challenging situation. Her rule that none of the children should get an after-school job is one that disappoints her oldest son, Chip. Chip believes that as an honors student he has already proven he's a serious learner. He needs a job to start saving money for a car. Sandra, however, believes that school comes first, and refuses to budge on this rule. Chip will no doubt be further disappointed as he learns that his mother will not negotiate her rule. He judges her rule as inappropriate for him, and given his passion to drive, Chip may violate the rule. As you may surmise, this will probably cause great conflict in the Allen family. Considering individual needs suggests that Chip and his mother brainstorm ways that he could earn money for a car without putting himself

Student Perspective: Willy

Okay, I'll be the first to admit that I'm strict about rules in my home. But I know that while growing up, my mom let me get away with a lot. I won't let my teenage daughter get that much freedom; things are just too different today. I do think that I need to understand that she is a teenager who wants to go to the mall and I'm willing to let her do that. I also understand her need to talk on the cell or text her friends. But I won't let her go wild and go anywhere whenever she wants. We have rules at home that require her to "check in" every night before she goes to bed. I don't want our roles as parent and child to get mixed up anytime soon.

in danger. If they are successful, the rule may change in content, but Chip will respect it in spirit.

In addition, sometimes families find themselves in situations where they are unable to exert complete control over their rules. Christopher Jencks (1994) reported that communication in homeless families is particularly challenging. Since most homeless families travel from shelter to shelter, they are required to adapt to the rules of the shelter and sponsoring agency. The shelter's rules may contradict the family's rules, thereby creating some conflict. For example, if a shelter requires that all conversations cease by 10 P.M., this could be difficult for the Bianchi family. In earlier times, the Bianchi family decided to have nightly discussions while playing cards— games that lasted well into the late evening hours. The Bianchi family rule that "card playing can continue as long as we want" will inevitably cause some conflict in a shelter that does not allow interaction beyond 10 P.M.

Rules Are Affected by Culture Myron Lustig and Jolene Koester (1999) have commented that rules are determined by culture. Cultural events have inspired the development and enforcement of family rules. To be sure, all family rules are directly or indirectly responsive to the larger culture. Families do not exist in a vacuum. In Chapter 4, we note that family members interact both in and outside of the family and we will review how aspects of the external context affect the family's communication. Let's now discuss how culture influences family rules.

First, family rules reflect the generation and the times in which we live. For instance, rules concerning how to talk about sex in the family have changed over the years as the culture changed. In the 1960s, the so-called sexual revolution affected a great number of people in the United States. Many advocated open and frank conversations about sex, both within and outside of the family.

With a new, conservative Republican president in the 1980s, the cultural climate became more conservative, and the open talk about sexuality receded. The cultural messages focused more on a return to family values and a rejection of what was framed as destructive trends away from family life. Many families have retained such conservative views about issues such as sex and sexuality. However, YouTube and other public discussions concerning the sexual transgressions of public figures like Antony Weiner, John Edwards, and Arnold Schwarzenegger may have brought more frank conversations about sex into the family.

Sometimes rules associated with family sex communication need clarification. This situation is illustrated by the following dialogue between Ian and Jan Hart, a married couple with a 13-year-old daughter, Kendra:

IAN: I think we're at that time where you have to talk to your daughter about sex. It's clear that the boys want to date her.

JAN: Me?! What? Am I a *single* parent now? Why don't we both talk to her? I think we'd better do it together.

IAN: What about all of the female-related stuff? Don't you think you would be better off talking to her?

JAN: Ian, there is a lot more about sex than female stuff! I think we should make this an open discussion, telling her that we are here to answer any questions for her . . . if we can. Telling her that we are both here in case something happens is better. We both need to be present for this discussion, Ian.

IAN: Look, Jan, I'm still not comfortable talking about sex to my daughter. I really think that you're the better person to speak to her. I'll just make the whole thing uncomfortable.

JAN: Uncomfortable for whom? You? Kendra? Great! Now I have to take on something I'm not ready to deal with alone!

IAN: How about if you talk to her about sex and I'll talk to her about money? Deal?

JAN: No deal! No way!

The conversation between Jan and Ian is not uncommon in our country. Parents struggle with how to talk about sex with their children across many co-cultures in the United States. In fact, Clay Warren (1995) concluded that not only do few families have ongoing discussions about sex (about 12 percent), but also a large number of parents and children report dissatisfaction with the quantity and quality of family discussions about sex. Apparently, many parents struggle with what to say, who should say it, and what should guide the discussion. In other words, the rules need clarification.

For Ian, the rules were pretty clear. He felt that his wife should handle the discussion since they had a daughter who ostensibly warranted a private conversation about female "stuff." For him, the mother–daughter relationship implied conversations of this nature. Jan also saw the rules clearly, but her vision conflicted with Ian's. She believed that discussions about sex require that both parents be present.

Student Perspective: G. K.

I was completely overwhelmed when I moved into my stepmom's house. I had been an only child and had no idea that things would turn out as they did. The first night my dad and stepmom called me and my two step-sisters into the kitchen and pointed to the re-frigerator. There was a list of five "rules" that we were all to follow, including the parents. I was taken aback, because living with my dad had been pretty mellow. We knew that we had to stay out of each other's face and that was pretty much it. But this "five rules" thing sounded like things were going to be pretty uptight around the house. It turned out that I was right.

Inherent in this conversation is rule-governed behavior. For Ian, there are rules associated with sex communication in the family. One might be that "talk-ing about sex with Kendra is not my domain." It's pretty clear, too, that Ian believes that the role of mother fits nicely with this rule. At the end of the dia-logue, Ian appears to bargain with Jan by stating that he will talk to Kendra about money matters.

Jan believes that there are rules associated with talking about sensitive topics to their daughter. One guiding rule for Jan might be that "talking about sex with Kendra is both parents' responsibility." As you might have suspected, there is both role and rule conflict with the Harts. It's also interesting to note that traditional gender roles are fulfilled with this example. Ian maintained a traditional male orientation, wanting to discuss issues pertaining to money. Ian appeared to invoke a rule as the conversation materialized (Prusank, 1993). Jan, on the other hand, was seeking cooperation in the discussion (a traditional feminine behavior).

Popular culture also helps shape what rules a family will develop and follow. The media are powerful and influential forces in the United States. Media—particularly television—are also influential in the family as family members construct their rules. In fact, Ni Chang (2000) notes that rules *about* television are more important than ever, given the ever-increasing vio-lence in television programming. To this end, Chang argues that parents should only allow children to view educational television programming. Establishing such rules may seem odd to some of you. Yet, because television has been accused of "transforming family interaction" (Alexander, 1994, p. 281), the pervasiveness and influence of television needs to be managed with family rules.

Types of Communication Rules

All family rules have relevance for communication, because, as we mentioned in Chapter 1, all behavior has implicit communication properties. Yet, some rules govern family talk specifically, and in this section we will describe three general areas of communication rules: (1) rules governing what family members can talk about, (2) rules governing how family members can talk about these topics, and (3) rules governing to whom family members can talk about these topics.

Families also develop what R. D. Laing (1971) referred to as **meta-rules,** or "rules about knowing [and discussing] certain rules" (p. 111). Laing suggests that families not only make rules about communicating around certain topics and with certain people, but also create rules about whether or not to overtly acknowledge that they have these rules. Such a system requires three rules according to Laing: the rule itself (don't talk about sex); the first meta-rule (don't admit we don't talk about sex because there is a formal rule against it); and the second meta-rule (the first meta-rule does not exist).

> ### Student Perspective: Martin
>
> *I find it interesting to hear about taboo topics because I really don't think we have them in our family. I suppose there could be stuff I don't know about, but it is hard to believe that my mom holds back on much. She talks to me and my brother about everything— sex, drugs, money, stuff she did when she was young—everything. Maybe it's a black thing, I don't know, but there sure doesn't seem to be any topic that's off-limits in my house.*

Families have rules, either explicit or implicit, about what topics are taboo or off-limits for family discussion. The Ladzinski family, from the beginning of this chapter, may have decided to ban all sad talk about their mother's death. They are allowed to bring up happy memories of when she was alive, but talking about how much she suffered toward the end or how hard it is to cope without her is forbidden in the family. These **taboo topics,** or topics family members keep private to avoid negative reactions (Baxter & Wilmot, 1985), operate in the dialectical tension between openness and privacy. It is a cultural value in the United States that we value self-disclosure more than silence, but in fact, families need both to talk openly and to keep silent. This dialectic requires families to periodically revisit their rules about what can and cannot be spoken about in the family. In fact, Michael Roloff and Danette Ifert Johnson (2001) found that revisiting taboo topics may not be as problematic as one might imagine. They found that taboo topics that once were removed from conversations can be reintroduced. As long as the topic that led to its banishment was no longer relevant, when the relationship had become stronger, reintroducing taboo topics was received positively. So, it appears that although the Ladzinski family now views the death of the mother as a taboo topic, this topic may be reintroduced at a later time.

In addition to what can be discussed in the family, rules are also devised about how to talk about a variety of topics. For example, some families may allow only indirect or joking communication about topics such as sex or deep personal feelings. In our opening example of the Delta Phi fraternity, it is possible that Steve, Ben, and Antonio may develop a rule that allows them to talk about how they feel about their dates, but only in a relatively light manner. They are not allowed to cry or use extreme language to express to one another that they are upset about a partner. Rules dealing with how to talk about topics may specify how long conversations on certain topics can last and how the conversations can begin. If one member of a couple wants to lose weight, the rule may be that the topic can be brought up only by the person who wants to lose weight, not his or her partner, and the conversation can be terminated at any time by that person, and the partner has to stop talking about weight. Again, meta-rules may function to allow the family to believe their discussions are free to take any form, even though they are not.

Finally, communication rules may have to do with who gets to be included in certain conversations. "Don't tell your grandmother about this . . ." prescribes some family boundaries as well as constrains communication behaviors. Mark Karpel (1980) defines family secrets with these boundaries in mind. Karpel states that there are three types of secrets: individual, internal, and shared. Individual secrets require that only one family member know the information—so the constraint is total. If a partner had an affair and chose to keep it from everyone in the family, that would be an individual secret. The rule would exclude everyone from discussing that topic. Internal secrets are those shared by a subsystem of the family but kept from the larger system. Shared secrets are known by the whole family, but anyone outside the family is excluded. The rule mandates that family members not discuss the topic with those not in the family circle. Families that keep teenage pregnancies, child abuse, or alcoholism a secret from others have shared secrets. Often these shared secrets are taboo topics as well.

Reflecting on Rules

The rules in a family can be both difficult and easy to follow. For example, a rule that prescribes turning off the lights when leaving a room in the house is relatively easy to adhere to. A rule specifying that every Sunday the family gathers for a noon meal, however, might become difficult as children grow and have weekend activities that take them out of the house or as adults get new job responsibilities that necessitate travel over the weekends.

For some family members, explicit rules are necessary and help keep the family system maintained. For other members, explicit rules simply complicate an already overburdened system. Implicit rules can also be challenging in that not all family members may be aware of the rule. Rules allow family members to make sense out of the sometimes chaotic episodes that families experience. Rules also help family members understand another's behavior.

Family rules can be volatile at times, yet rules do help families further define themselves.

Almost all family types feel pressure to construct rules and roles that will facilitate communication rather than impede it. Ken Cissna, Dennis Cox, and Arthur Bochner (1990) noted that the parental and the spousal subsystems are "bound to come into conflict in every family" (p. 272). This conflict can be disturbing to the family, but it can be managed with rules about appropriate behaviors. With our earlier example of Ian and Jan, for instance, their potential conflict could be resolved with a family rule that specified what topics the parents would address with their daughter together, although once again, both will have to practice behavioral flexibility. Sometimes, however, flexibility may require a great deal of work. Rethinking family rules and roles may be satisfying for one family member but annoying to another. Change may come about slowly. Families may resist changing rules because of the tension between novelty and predictability. Rules provide stability and certainty, so they satisfy the family's desire for predictability. When rules are questioned or violated, family members may punish the violator verbally or nonverbally. These sanctions, or punishments, can keep the rule in place, keep the family stable, and follow the process we discussed in Chapter 2 about system calibration and recalibration. As we have discussed, however, sometimes even strong negative sanctions fail to keep the rule in place, and the family system changes.

SUMMARY

Roles and rules structure family interactions by giving family members directives and prescriptions for behavior. They both operate to limit behavioral options, providing families with a sense of predictability. In so doing, they allow a family to accomplish many important tasks, such as nurturance, individual development, and resource provision. Yet roles and rules are derived interactionally, so they have a reciprocal relationship with communication. They are both the product and the process of communication behavior in the family. In other words, the roles and rules that family members use to guide their communication behaviors are developed through communication in the family.

Additionally, roles and rules relate to one another in that many families develop rules about roles—when children reach college age they can sit at the adult table for Thanksgiving dinner, for example. Role behavior is rule governed to a large extent.

Families function through effective rule setting and role behavior, but not all rules or roles are productive for families. When either rules or roles are not working for families, they must be changed to avoid problems. Families that resist change may be caught in rigid applications of rules and roles that really do not help them at all. Changing rules and roles that no longer help the family is a difficult process for all families and, in some cultures, involves open discussion and negotiation. Sometimes implicit assumptions and expectations have to be made explicit in these discussions. Other cultures may be able to shift rules and recalibrate their system without much overt communication, because much is understood without words.

Roles and rules may also positively affect communication in the family. Families require some sort of framework by which to function, and roles and rules can provide this structure for the family system.

All families are unique in the role behaviors they enact and the rules they enforce. Yet, as we observed in this chapter, some regularities can be noticed in different co-cultures and cultural groups and across gender.

KEY TERMS

dysfunctional rules	role ambiguity
explicit rules	role conflict
functional rules	role evaluation
gender roles	role expectations
gender role socialization	role models
gender schema theory	roles
implicit rules	role taking
interpersonal role conflict	rule
intrapersonal role conflict	rule negotiation
meta-rules	taboo topics
role allocation	

QUESTIONS FOR REFLECTION

1. Consider the following claim: In order to be an effective family member, you should be able to take on multiple roles. Do you agree or disagree with this statement? What prompted your decision? What examples can you offer to justify your viewpoint?

2. What types of rules did you have in your family-of-origin? Were they developed by your parent(s) or guardian(s)? Did you follow them? If you have children or plan to have children, what types of rules will you integrate into your home?

3. Do you believe that all family members should agree on the rules in a family? Is it appropriate for the parent or guardian to establish the rules, or should children have input? Discuss your thoughts by incorporating examples.

4. What if you were asked to sit down with a family and identify the five most important rules for them to have in their family? Based on your reading of this chapter and your experiences, what advice would you give this family? What examples would you include in your discussion?

5. Because homeless families do not have as much autonomy as they would like and depend so much on shelters, do you believe that it is possible for homeless families to have particular roles and rules? What instances or examples can you offer for support?

6. Imagine that today you were asked to write something for a time capsule to be opened in the year 2020. Discuss the future of family roles in the United States. Reflecting on the cultural differences present in our country, what would you project will happen to roles in our larger culture in the future? Include examples in your response.

7. Discuss the changes in gender roles in the family since the 1950s. How do these changes affect family communication?

8. Suppose you were asked how roles in the office setting differ from roles in the home setting. What similarities could you point to? Differences? Provide examples.

9. Explore the challenges associated with the roles and rules when boomerang kids return home.

10. Discuss the different gender schemas that (may) occur over our life span. Include childhood, adolescence, adulthood, and late adulthood. Include examples at each stage and examine whether you believe people's gender schemas change or whether they are relatively stable. Comment on how you see gender schemas affecting a family's communication interactions.

Chapter
4

SOCIETAL CONTEXT FOR FAMILY COMMUNICATION

Televised Messages About Families
Families and Television Viewing
Televised Models of Family Communication
Early Images of Families on Television
Later Images of Families on Television
Recent Images of Families on Television
Future Images of Families on Television

Women's and Men's Movements and Their Influence on Families
Feminism and Women's Movements
The Male Voice and Men's Movements
Continuing Influence of Women's and Men's Movements

Government and the Family
Defining Family Policy • Marital and Family Rights
Child Concerns and Child Care

Summary
Key Terms
Questions for Reflection

THE VENEGAS FAMILY

Luís Venegas loves watching Thursday night television sitting next to his golden retriever. His work week is nearly over, and it is simply a matter of one more day before he can enjoy his weekend. For Luís, the Thursday night lineup is basically the beginning of his weekend. As a commercial comes on, Luís's 10-year-old son, Manny, comes into the room to ask him for help with his math homework. As the two sit on the couch together, the television program resumes, and Luís's once undivided attention to his son is now replaced with frequent quick glances to the screen. As Manny takes the homework sheet from his dad, he can't help but notice the comedy that occupies his father's attention. "Is this your favorite show, Papa?" his son asks. "Well, one of them. It's very funny," Luís replies, again diverting his attention back to the small screen. "But Mama says that these shows aren't good because they don't show people like us," his son quickly shoots back. Luís is growing impatient. "Mi hijo, we live in a country that gives us freedom to say what we want, to live in this home, and for you to go to school so that you can learn your math . . . which you should go do in your room right now." Luís gives his son a peck on the forehead as Manny goes upstairs. When another commercial interrupts the programming, Luís can't help but think about his son's comments. "Perhaps we are invisible," he thinks to himself.

THE PANIZZI FAMILY

Mary Kate and Gene Panizzi have never considered themselves culturally conservative, but they feel that the times have changed too quickly. For several years now, they have been on a quiet crusade with a few of their friends to try to get their voices heard. As parents of April, a 14-year-old, and Lucas, a preteen, they have become very concerned about the lack of responsibility within the media. At first they were disturbed about what they saw on television. With young people in the house, they found themselves both monitoring and turning off the set frequently. When the kids were on the computer, Mary Kate and Gene were astonished to find the relatively easy access they had to xxx-rated Web sites. The Panizzis are also troubled by the teen magazines that April has been buying; more than once they have seen ads that talk about the need for contraception before sex. Mary Kate and Gene did not want to be alarmists, but they were growing increasingly concerned about the lack of policing in the media. Mary Kate and Gene thought, "then we will do it for them."

THE DEERFIELD FAMILY

Nathan Deerfield never imagined himself a politically active person, but the recent drastic changes in family values required him to *take action. He and his 10-year-old son, Eddie, live together in a small apartment in St. Louis, and he is doing everything to give his son the sort of life that he never had. He works two jobs but makes sure he is home in time when Eddie comes home from school. Nathan is quite exhausted by dinner time, but he wants to make sure he spends every night with his son and would cancel anything work related just so he is home with Eddie each school night. It is his belief about the future of the family that motivates Nathan to board a bus one Tuesday evening and ride to Washington, DC, to march with Fathers USA, a national group of fathers dedicated to making sure men have opportunities for child custody and alimony payments from their ex-spouses. The way he sees society, Nathan Deerfield feels that family court judges don't understand fathers and instinctively award custody to mothers. He wants to help change public and legal perceptions, and this large march seems to be the perfect chance to do that. Nathan has other friends who are fathers and who he feels deserve to see their children. But they aren't able to because of court decisions. Further, he feels that many of these fathers are being exploited because they have little money but are required to pay exorbitant amounts of child support and alimony. So, using his vacation time and with a little help from his sister to watch Eddie, Nathan boards the bus in St. Louis and begins his journey toward helping other fathers achieve societal respect. In the meantime, he is privately hoping that he will be able to understand his own personal struggles on this trip as he tries to be the kind of dad his son deserves.*

We stated in Chapter 1 that families are partly defined by their internal interactions with each other and are influenced by internal behaviors. Throughout the book, we talk about a number of internal variables such as storytelling, conflict, intimacy, and stress. These are critical to examine if we are to have a comprehensive understanding of family life and communication within the family.

Yet, the family is influenced by external elements as well. Our interpretation of the family includes those events, issues, and elements that are outside of the family's boundaries. Families in the United States are continually affected by outside forces, and these outside forces are often affected by the family.

In addition, consider the impact of outside influences upon the co-cultural identity of the family. For instance, much research has been conducted on the intersection of African American life and the external context (e.g., Jackson, 2004; Miller, 2011). Thomas Socha, Janis Sanchez-Hucles, Jodi Bromley, and Brian Kelly (1995) discuss some family communication effects that result from being African American. They observe that in addition to all the other child-rearing challenges, African American parents also have to deal with the challenges of raising children with high self-esteem in a racist culture. Additionally, many African American families have to contend with the stress of living in unsafe neighborhoods and substandard housing (Patterson, 2012). The interrelationships among co-culture, society, and family communication cannot be ignored.

This chapter focuses on some important aspects of the family's external context. To give you a cross section of the many external influences on the family, we examine three areas: mediated messages, social movements, and family policy. These three areas encompass powerful forces on the family and represent the comprehensiveness of external contexts in family life.

To understand the mediated context, we discuss television, because "few contemporary forms of story-telling offer territory as fertile as television for unearthing public ideas about the family" (Taylor, 1989, p. 17). Or, as Nadine Gabbadon (2006) advances, "the images on television are essential to consider because together, they form a mirror (albeit a distorted one) of society" (p. 4). We specifically examine television situation comedies because they present pervasive messages about family life. The popularity of situation comedy has endured for many decades, and families have been depicted in a number of ways via the domestic comedy.

In addition to situation comedies, an important part of popular culture, **social movements,** or **rhetorical movements,** are also influential on the family. Charles Stewart, Craig Smith, and Robert Denton (2012) define these movements as consisting of collective processes aimed at arousing public opinion and changing society's norms and values. These movements are rhetorical because the communication involved mobilizes the public to change. Individuals involved in women's and men's movements, for instance, differ in how they interpret family life and how they share themselves in a family.

Finally, perhaps the most influential external context on the family is the government. Policies, regulations, and legislation may not seem particularly communicative. Yet, their effect on the communication within and outside of the family cannot be ignored. Interestingly, people in the United States elect the government and therefore, many believe that the government exists to serve its citizens. Yet, as we will learn, the government does not always make decisions that reflect family life as we know it today. For example, in our discussion of family types in Chapter 1, we identified the gay and lesbian family as a fast-growing family configuration in the United States. Yet, officially, it was not until the 2010 U.S. census that the federal government began to recognize the same-sex couple and same-sex–headed household. We will discuss this notion a bit later in the chapter.

The information in this chapter coalesces around systems thinking. We cannot, for instance, ignore the interdependent nature of our families with such social institutions as the media and government. Further, the issues we discuss in this chapter illustrate hierarchy, showing how the family system is nested within other, larger systems. It's also nearly impossible to ignore the wholeness properties of systems thinking. Examining each institution with an understanding of their joint effect on families helps clarify their importance and pervasiveness.

This chapter also has its roots in what Urie Bronfenbrenner (1979) calls "ecological systems" thinking. He believes that an individual's (e.g., child's) development is contingent on many social and cultural factors and events. Most relevant to the current discussion is what Bronfenbrenner terms "environmental systems:" (1) *microsystem*—the system in which the child lives (e.g., family, neighborhood, school); (2) *mesosystem*—the relationships between and among the different microsystems (e.g., mother's relationship to child may affect how child learns in school); (3) *exosystem*—the connection between an individual and a social setting in which that individual has no control (e.g., a parent who gets fired at work may affect the family communication at home); (4) *macrosystem*—the culture in which the family member lives (e.g., cultural values, customs, laws, socioeconomic status); and (5) *chronosystem*—the effect and patterns of time upon a family member (e.g., parental divorce may affect a child more profoundly in the first year than subsequent years).

Ecological systems theory has been applied to various societal events and relationships, including the Virginia Tech shootings (Hong, Cho, & Lee, 2011), bullying at school (Lee, 2010), and the family–school relationship in rural settings (Semke & Sheridan, 2011).

As you review the contents of this chapter, keep in mind these environmental systems since it is apparent that television, social movements, and governmental policies are embedded in Bronfenbrenner's theoretical framework.

TELEVISED MESSAGES ABOUT FAMILIES

Television has been instrumental in defining families and thus forms a significant part of the external context influencing family interaction. In fact, Janette Dates and Carolyn Stroman (2001) state that television "teaches us about us, as we talk about ourselves" (p. 207). In 1990, Jennings Bryant concluded that the family in the United States "is nearly 500 years old. Television is less than 50. Yet in the relatively brief time since the old timer [the family] has been invaded by the upstart [television], incredible changes in family life have taken place" (p. xiii). Clearly, the introduction of television has forever changed the way we view families and the way families are depicted to others.

As a population, our society seems to have a love affair with television. The numbers are difficult to ignore. The 2011 American Time Use Survey (*http://www.cro2.org/default.aspx?page=reviewdisplay&pid=3157450*) published by the U.S. government shows that people spend about 2.7 hours a day watching television. This accounts for about half of all adult leisure time. And, while television set usage has dropped a few percentage points over the past several years, nearly 98 percent of households still own a set (Szali, 2011). There are approximately 115 million television sets in U.S. homes (*http://blog.nielsen.com/nielsenwire/media_entertainment/number-of-u-s-tv-households-climbs-by-one-million-for-2010-11-tv-season*). Important to note is that despite the ever-present social media, television still captures the time and attention of children. In 2010, *Child Trends*, a national nonprofit and nonpartisan research organization, reported that children (ages 8–18) will spend approximately 4.5 hours a day in television viewing (*www.childtrends-databank.org/?q=node/261*). Further, David Murphey (2011) best creatively articulated the relationship of television to children: "Television is practically like wallpaper for many families with children" (*http://blog.childtrends.org/2011/06/06/the-problem-with-children-watching-television*).

It's clear that we all have the ability to be influenced by television and that television has been an integral part of family life since its inception. Although there are many television genres we could examine, we have chosen to limit our discussion to situation comedies. Television situational comedies that feature family life in general and family communication in particular are essential to consider. Foremost, the comedies provide us with models of what the family is like and models of how families talk about a variety of subjects. In a sense, sitcoms are a window into the issues of the day. Perhaps Robin Means Coleman (2000) sums up the value of examining family and situation comedy: "The situation comedy is significant because its humor relies upon, and is in response to, issues and problems found within the social structure" (p. 4).

Families and Television Viewing

How has television affected communication in the family? Television is a powerful medium and can influence the patterns of family communication. Although there are a number of issues we could explore, we will limit our discussion to one of the most taken-for-granted, but influential, television devices: the remote control.

Before beginning this discussion, we first acknowledge that television viewing has changed dramatically over the past decade. First, the advent of the smartphone (e.g., Android, iPhone, etc.) has prompted millions of people to adopt new viewing approaches, including watching television shows on their phones. Second, laptops, notebooks, and computer tablets (e.g., iPad, etc.) have become a primary choice for viewing (and streaming) television shows. Thus, it is clear that technology has influenced television habits and television viewing choices. Indeed, one can now be a "couch potato" without having a couch around!

Yet, despite the technology and technological advances, as we learned earlier, households in the United States are still addicted to watching television on a television set. Susan Whiting, for instance, observed in 2009: "Even as consumers increasingly turn to their PCs and cell phones for entertainment, they continue to spend more and more time with traditional TV—153 hours per month, as of the first quarter of this year" (*http://www.huffingtonpost.com/susan-whiting/tv-were-still-watching_b_208329.html*). Charlie Jane Anders (2010) agrees and succinctly states that "most people still want to watch television in their living rooms on their TV sets, not on their iPads or computer screens" (*http://io9.com/5636210/how-thenielsen-tv-ratings-work--and-what-could-replace-them*).

Young, middle-aged, and older family members are still turning on the TV, sitting on the couch, and watching the gamut of programming—from reality shows to crime dramas. And it is the remote control device (RCD) that has emerged as a source of influence on television watching.

Since the introduction of the remote control device, television viewing has been changed forever. This small television companion has become such a powerful unit of technology that James Walker and Robert Bellamy (2001) have referred to it as "subversive technology" (p. 77). William Urrichio (2005) believes that the RCD has provided a "viewer-dominant" ideology; the device allows television watchers to control both program and economic "flow" (p. 243). Johan Grimonprez (2010) believes that the remote control has forever changed the tenor, energy, quality, and length of television programming (*http://www.macba.cat/uploads/TWM/TV_grimonprez_eng.pdf*). These scholars all point to one conclusion: The RCD has permanently changed the television landscape.

What could this television device have to do with family communication patterns? Alison Alexander (1994) concludes that "families create communication patterns or practices in the televiewing context and the topic or function of these practices seem to occur across many families" (pp. 286–287). With respect to viewing, RCDs are considered the primary way to control viewing within the family (Walker & Bellamy, 2001), and researchers have been interested in knowing who controls the RCD and what impact it may have on family communication. In fact, there is what could be identified as "gendered technology" when discussing remote control usage. Donald Morley (1986) discovered that males usually control the RCD, and this control can be seen as a symbol of who has the most power in the family. In his study, Morley discovered that while males were very attentive to television, females were more likely to integrate domestic responsibilities and conversation into television viewing. Kathy Krendl and her colleagues (Krendl, Clark, Dawson, & Troiano, 1993; Krendl, Troiano, Dawson, & Clark, 1993) discovered that fathers were likely to control the RCD more often than mothers were. Gary Copeland (1989) concluded that in "socio-oriented" families, or families in which there is an attempt to control or reduce conflict, females were more likely to retain control of the RCD. In families with a greater perceived problem-solving ability and more open communication patterns, females were more likely to control the RCD (Copeland & Schweitzer, 1993). Finally, Christine Rosen (2004) reports research that has concluded that there is a modest difference between men and women in their remote control usage. Specifically, men were somewhat more inclined to change channels during prime-time viewing than women (approximately 37 percent of men changed the channel 10 times or more; 24 percent of women did). Yet, Jane Yenko (2011) cites research that shows men controlling the remote at a rate of two to one over women. She sums up the conundrum faced as the sexes deal with remote control use:

> *Some men go to such lengths as to hide the remote during bathroom breaks. Others take the batteries out when they leave the room. Some others even take the remote with them on business trips. As men and women come closer to equality in other areas of society, men seem determined to retain their dominance over the television set.*

How do these findings relate to family communication? First, with men dominating the remote control, there may be some signals that poor communication is evolving. Dominance is a male behavior and may serve to silence others (Ivy, 2012). If men are silencing family members by their remote control use, it's no wonder that many women are complaining about men "hogging" the RCD. Second, controlling what to watch on television and when to watch it may be indicative of relational control, a power strategy we address in Chapter 7. Elizabeth Perse and Doug Ferguson (1993) found that males received gratification when they used the remote control to annoy others in the room. This suggests that the RCD may serve as a metaphor in a family relationship; when the remote is clicked on, the relationship may be in need of help. To continue the metaphor, some "fine-tuning" of the family relationship may be needed. Of course, not all family relationships are in trouble when a father uses a remote control. Nonetheless, the remote control device can serve as an indicator of family issues needing attention.

Not all issues (or devices) pertaining to television result in negative family functioning. Television viewing can result in more satisfying family relationships, even though family members may not be aware of TV's impact. For instance, television can be an important vehicle for bringing families together (Alexander, 1994; Alexander & Kim, 2003). In fact, a 2010 survey of parents showed that television viewing was identified as a "WeTime" (family members coming together) activity by 86 percent of respondents—the highest response in the poll. Apparently, much of a family's time spent together is spent in front of a television set. This "co-viewing" experience (Alexander, 1994, p. 285) is essential as various family rules and communication patterns emerge from the viewing context. Imagine, for instance, watching two lead characters on a sitcom resolve a conflict related to their parenting skills. If one or more family members talk about that conflict, it becomes part of the family communication process. In other words, the television episode is now an "episode" in the family. Further, Alison Alexander concludes that issues pertaining to who controls viewing, the interpretation of content, and television's continual influence on the family system are important to consider when addressing television and families in the United States. In addition, television programming can influence a family's interaction, even when the television is not on and/or the family is not home. So, for example, when 16-year-old Paula Gunderson is not in front of the family television set, she might be talking to her friends about what was on her favorite television show or criticizing the fact that network television has gotten too liberal in its portrayals of sex. Therefore, although some researchers have commented on how frequently family members watch television, that viewing may serve as a springboard for additional family communication and communication outside the family context.

Televised Models of Family Communication

Television not only provides us with models of family types, it also serves a teaching function, modeling family communication behaviors that audience members may incorporate into their own family interactions (Levine, 2011). In this, television is a source of vicarious learning (Bandura, 1969), providing viewers with lessons about how to behave in situations they may not have actually experienced. However, as viewers observe TV models of family communication, they are not simply passive. They may compare what they see with their real-life families, engage in talk with their families about what is presented on TV, and select those TV models that best serve their purposes while ignoring other models (Austin, Roberts, & Nass, 1990). Along with one group of researchers (Perse, Pavitt, & Burggraf, 1990), we take a cognitive approach to media effects, emphasizing that viewers actively interpret and shape episodes of family interaction that they see on TV. These interpretations influence how significant the images are for viewers.

Our argument is that TV provides additional models, external to the family, that influence family interaction. That is not to say that family interaction is determined by televised examples. Yet despite this limited effects approach we take to the media, we believe television is still an important source of information for families about how to manage interaction. Therefore, we examine several themes that characterize communication in television families. These include (1) an emphasis on parental rationality and problem solving, (2) a value placed on harmony and low levels of familial conflict, (3) a large proportion of self-disclosive talk, and (4) talk that focuses on relational issues and excludes or minimizes talk about daily routines.

First, Richard Butsch (1992) points out that sitcoms mainly portray middle-class families. In these families, parents are depicted as calm and rational and capable of working as a team to help children solve their problems. Butsch notes that parents became more fallible in the 1970s and 1980s than they had been previously, but they "ultimately retain their roles as guides and models" (p. 112). They do this through communication patterns that show them answering children's questions, approaching problems calmly and rationally, joking but retaining their authority, and summarizing moral lessons for their children (Butsch, 1992). Marvin Moore (1992) concurs, pointing out that on successful family programming, family problems are easily solved, highlighting a problem–solution communication pattern. However, Butsch observes that these patterns do not always hold true when lower-class families are the characters in sitcoms. He points to the clownlike qualities of some lower-class fathers such as Al Bundy on *Married with Children,* a comedy from the 1990s. Nonetheless, because most television families are middle class, the image of parents as rational problem solvers remains strong.

Related to television's emphasis on problem solving is the value placed on harmony. Elizabeth Perse and her colleagues (Perse, Pavitt, & Burggraf, 1990) observe that family shows tend to depict low levels of conflict. Some estimates label 90 percent of TV conversations in families as affiliative rather than conflictual (Greenberg, 1982). Moore (1992) states that all types of television families surveyed during a three-week period in 1987 presented low levels of conflictual communication. When conflict did arise, it was portrayed in such a manner as to reinforce values of harmony, love, and trust.

Self-disclosures are frequently depicted in television families. Mary Anne Fitzpatrick (1988) notes that, on TV, relational partners are not reticent in expressing their intimate thoughts and feelings. In addressing mother–daughter conversations on soap operas, Tamar Liebes and Sonia Livingstone (1994) comment that daughters frequently self-disclose concerns about romantic relationships to their mothers. In keeping with our previously mentioned attribute of parental problem solving, Liebes and Livingstone observe that mothers are able to offer advice when their daughters disclose romantic problems because they understand their daughters perfectly.

Finally, television families most often talk relationally, omitting daily concerns from their conversations. Liebes and Livingstone (1994) find this point illustrated in their comparison of American and British soap operas. They observe that in British soaps "the characters face a wide range of serious but humdrum problems" (p. 733), such as unemployment, illness, and managing chores. Thus, on British soap operas, characters talk about going shopping, finding a babysitter, and doing the laundry. In shows in the United States, the authors point out, the upper-middle-class status of the characters relieves them from a focus on everyday routines and allows romance to dominate their talk. Liebes and Livingstone analyzed soap operas (daytime and prime time), but the surprise expressed over *Seinfeld*'s ability to base a show on "nothing," or the details of everyday life, indicates that these topics are novel on most of U.S. television.

Space limitations prevent us from discussing this topic in detail. We encourage you to consult additional resources (e.g., Dines & Humez, 2011) if you wish to have more information related to family life and television programming. Further, grab your DVD or subscribe to Hulu and if a show sounds interesting, rent it or download it.

Given the backdrop of television's teaching functions we have just provided, we now discuss a brief chronological review of family life as portrayed on television situation comedies. We highlight several representative shows to illustrate how the televised portrayal of family life has changed over time. We divide our discussion into early, later, recent, and future images of families on television.

Early Images of Families on Television

Keep in mind that television was still in its infancy in the 1950s. And many of the early television situation comedies actually came from radio, so much of the humor may be lost on you—as a student in the 21st century.

Some of the first images of television families may be a bit dated, but thanks to DVDs, videotapes, reruns, and cable, they remain current in the minds of many. In the 1950s, television sets were tuned into shows that placed fathers and fatherhood on the cultural agenda. Shows such as *Father Knows Best, Leave it to Beaver,* and *The Adventures of Ozzie and Harriett* occupied a prominent place in television history. First, these were among the first successful television shows that depicted families who were fast-becoming the norm in the United States: the suburban family. Second, these shows reflected the prominence of men's roles, following the post-World War II euphoria. In other words, now that men had returned home to their families after successfully defending freedom, they were becoming the focus of television programming (LaRossa, 2004), demonstrating their prominence in families and society.

These sorts of television shows were pivotal in communicating that it was possible to have a perfect family, complete with affluence, choice suburbs, clear lines of authority, and easy resolution to the (relatively simple) problems of life. In these 1950s situation comedies, women and men were relegated to traditional household duties. The father

Student Perspective: Gloria

In my family, sitting around watching other families talk on TV was a major activity. We spent a lot of our time together in front of the boob tube. In some ways, now that I think about it, it's kind of funny. Our whole family sitting in silence, watching how other families get along!

worked all day at the office, whereas the mother stayed at home, attending to domestic duties around the house. Although there were efforts to make family shows in the 1950s contemporary in thinking (there were minor marital disputes in some of the episodes), taken together

> these shows proposed family life as a charming excursion into modernity, but resting on the unshakable stability of tradition. Parents would love and respect each other and their children forever. The children would grow up, go to college, and take up lives identical in most respects to those of their parents. (Taylor, 1989, p. 27)

More important, Taylor notes that these families were almost always nuclear, white, and affluent. A few exceptions existed. First, *The Beulah Show,* which was the first network series to star an African American actress, premiered in 1951. However, the show presented only stereotypical images of African Americans. Another series featuring African Americans, *Amos 'n' Andy,* was also short-lived (two years). The show was not without its critics. In fact, the NAACP noted that the show portrayed the main characters only as clowns or crooks. A more scholarly criticism was advanced by bell hooks (1992a). She notes that *Amos 'n' Andy* presented contested images of the African American family, particularly in the character of Sapphire. According to hooks, young black women rejected Sapphire, seeing her as a bitch, a nag, a foil for black men. However, older black women saw the character differently. They identified with Sapphire's frustrations and woes, "and in opposition they claimed Sapphire as their own, as the symbol of that angry part of themselves white folks and black men could not even begin to understand" (p. 120). Yet, Alonzo Kittrells (2011, February 27) of the *Philadelphia Inquirer* states that "the only thing Black about the *Amos 'n' Andy* television show is the color of the actors and actresses. The dialect is Southern and not Black" (p. 3B). Further, Kittrells writes, "I find that most people who are critical of *Amos 'n' Andy* know about the show solely as a result of what someone told them or what they have heard" (p. 3B). This example illustrates television's complexity. As we argue throughout this chapter, the medium allows multiple interpretations of its images of the family, enabling many viewers to see the same show but to internalize it somewhat differently.

A small number of you may have favorite television shows from the 1960s. Understand that the 1960s was an era of civil and political unrest. Consider what occurred: the Stonewall riots (ushering in the gay rights movement); the assassinations of Martin Luther King, President John F. Kennedy, Robert Kennedy; and, of course, the Vietnam war. Because of this cultural turmoil, television executives were concentrating on making programming less "realistic" (that is, "good-feeling" TV shows). Escapism was paramount at the time. The 1960s featured sitcoms that, again, were made up of white, affluent families. Shows such as *The Donna Reed Show, Dennis the Menace,* and *The Patty Duke Show* really did not challenge the traditional nuclear family legacy begun in the 1950s. *My Three Sons* and *The Andy Griffith Show* showed some diversity with single fathers, and extended family members of Aunt Bea (*The Andy Griffith Show*) and Uncle Charlie (*My Three Sons*) provided household help. Each family was relatively affluent, however. *Petticoat Junction,* too, was a comedy that featured an extended family. While Kate raised her three daughters, Uncle Joe would help out whenever he could.

An interesting development in the late 1960s–early 1970s occurred in television programming. *Julia* (created by the writer of *The Beulah Show*) was not a typical sitcom in that it featured a young African American nurse who became a single parent after the death of her husband in Vietnam. For the first time in television history there was an effort to portray a cultural segment of the country outside of the white, affluent, nuclear family that had characterized the overwhelming number of television programs at the time. Further, according to Aniko Bodroghkozy of the Museum of Broadcast Communications (2011), the show also presented humorous situations dealing with race and helped to "diffuse anxieties about racial differences" (*http://www.museum.tv/eotvsection.php?entrycode=julia*).

The 1970s brought some significant changes in the way families were portrayed. Single parents were common (and their numbers were growing) and women were given featured roles. And one man became a household name: Norman Lear. Lear was responsible for a number of shows featuring African Americans: *The Jeffersons* (1975–1985), *Good Times* (1974–1979), and *Sanford and Son* (1972–1977). Respectively, the shows, sometimes called "ethnocoms," dealt with a wealthy couple and their grown son, a poor African American nuclear family in the Chicago housing projects, and a junk dealer and his son. Although some would applaud the development of such shows, others felt that, once again, stereotypes were plentiful. Ella Taylor (1989) remarked, for instance, that *The Jeffersons* often showed George, the lead character, spending his money in unwise ways. The *Good Times* family often used self-deprecating humor to trivialize poverty, street violence, and unemployment. And, although the show began with an emphasis on the parents, the popularity of the son's character caused a shift in focus, giving more emphasis to "shucking and jiving" and his trademark "DY-NO-MITE!" Once again, stereotypes emerged. In the case of *Sanford and Son,* Fred Sanford was somewhat of a buffoon, always faking a heart attack to gain attention from his son, Lamont. In addition, the show portrayed shrill women and conniving men.

The 1970s also featured the number one show of the decade: *All in the Family.* The premise of this satirical show was so controversial it was rejected several times before CBS decided to launch it. In fact, J. Fred MacDonald (1992) reported that the show ignited so much passion that CBS offered the following disclaimer: "The program . . . seeks to throw a humorous spotlight on our frailties, prejudices, and concerns. By making them a source of laughter, we hope to show—in a mature fashion—just how absurd they are" (p. 193).

Essentially, the show highlighted Archie Bunker, a "lovable bigot" who lived with his doting wife, Edith, their daughter, Gloria, and son-in-law, Michael. Michael Tueth (2004) believed that Archie Bunker made it a frequent undertaking to ridicule those who were fast becoming a vocal minority in U.S. culture, most notably feminists, Latinos, gun control advocates, and gay men and lesbians. These groups became Bunker's adversaries, and his rebuttals to them, many media critics argued, represented the beliefs of millions of viewers. The problems raised by the Bunkers had to be remedied easily so that a new family issue or crisis could emerge in the next episode. This was the case despite the fact that the Bunker family occasionally dealt with serious topics such as rape and aging. Of course, half-hour solutions are very common to sitcoms and very unlike life.

Clearly, the real families of the 1970s who encountered difficult issues (the arms race, drugs, and so on) could not find easy solutions, particularly during a decade in which passions were heated from the Vietnam War. While many enjoyed Norman Lear's efforts in satire, others may conclude that they did not advance a more compassionate understanding of minorities.

Television in the 1970s was also characterized by what Taylor (1989) calls prime-time feminism. Several comedies, in particular, prominently featured women. For example, *One Day at a Time* (1975–1984) showed how Ann Romano, a single parent of two teenage daughters, lands a job at an advertising agency, asks others to address her as "Ms.," and fights for child support from her deadbeat husband (O'Dell, 2011). Broadway actress Bea Arthur starred in one of the most pioneering of television sitcoms: *Maude* (another Norman Lear show, 1972–1978). Maude was not only portrayed as the "head of the family," but also as a feminist who eschewed the trappings of being a devoted and deferential wife. Married to her fourth husband, Walter, Maude was portrayed as an independent and sometimes aggressive woman. The show tackled a number of stressors that families experience, such as bankruptcy, abortion, menopause, and alcoholism. Today, these topics have found their way into television programming, but nearly 40 years ago, the mere discussion of some of these issues brought about efforts toward censorship. These two shows began public discussions about equality for women and triggered a reexamination of the roles of women in families during that time.

Like many of the shows we have discussed, people can also view one of the most popular shows of the 1970s, *The Mary Tyler Moore Show* (1970–1977), on cable. Mary Richards was a single professional woman who lived alone. Yet, as Bonnie Dow (1990) asserts, rather than breaking new ground, *The Mary Tyler Moore Show* actually was a familiar family sitcom. Dow argues that "a sitcom about a single, ambitious woman is daring until you surround her with a recognizable husband/father figure [Lou Grant] and a group of children to nurture. . . . In the end, Mary is threatening to no one" (pp. 269, 272). And Geoff Hammill (2011) of the Museum of Broadcast Communications called the show a working woman sitcom. He believes that Mary was "unattached and not reliant upon a man." But she never "rejected men as romantic objects nor abandoned her hopes one day of being married" (*http://www.museum.tv./eotvsection.php?entrycode=martylermo*). Dow (1995) later stated that Mary Richards was part of a traditional family portrait in that she symbolically served as a wife, a mother, and a daughter to those around her. Taylor (1989) argued that she was also a competitive sibling in her work-family.

Student Perspective: Bethany

I know we should have a more realistic reflection of families on TV, but I think one of the appeals of television is, it's escapist. It's so unreal it's fun to watch. Growing up, I saw so many shows about families who always got along and siblings who always treated each other with civility! My family's nothing like the Bradys, but it's relaxing to escape into mindlessness with them on the tube.

The 1970s also saw the premiere of *The Brady Bunch*—a show that lives on in reruns and in movies such as *A Very Brady Movie, A Very Brady Christmas,* and *A Very Brady Sequel.* The Brady family was a blended family with six children (three from Mom's first marriage and three from Dad's). Yet, the Bradys really had no more pressing problems in adjusting to their new family identity than having the two older children compete against each other in a school election. The new family formed seamlessly and effortlessly, and today seems far removed from the realities of family life.

Later Images of Families on Television

Television studios in the 1970s began portraying more diverse family forms, although some scholars have viewed their efforts as ultimately conservative and traditional. The 1980s, however, brought about a new way for families to be depicted on TV. Three shows examined by family communication researchers include *The Cosby Show, Roseanne, Murphy Brown,* and *The Golden Girls,* all popular shows of the time.

In *The Cosby Show* (1984–1992), Bill Cosby portrayed Cliff Huxtable, an obstetrician-gynecologist married to Claire Huxtable, an attorney. The pair had five children. This show was the top-rated television program in the 1980s and at its peak, about 25 percent of the U.S. population tuned in to watch it (Tueth, 2004). It focused on the life of an African American family. Interestingly, Bishetta Merrit (1991) notes that "the black experience on *The Cosby Show* emerges through subtle references" (p. 94). Merrit believes that the artwork on the walls, the antiapartheid symbols, the frequent references to historically black colleges, and the children listening to music produced by black artists (jazz and rap) created an implied image of African Americans in the United States. This helped to educate the viewing public as well as illustrate racial pride on the show. As we learned in Chapter 1, symbols can be powerful ways of communicating to others.

Michael Real (1991) believes that the Huxtable family was an innovation in television. The show was an opportunity to "invent new definitions of the black male and the black family" (p. 66). Timothy Havens (2000) was bolder in his analysis of the series: "*The Cosby Show* changed the face of American television and set a new standard for representing African American families in non-stereotyped roles" (p. 371). The show also dispelled several stereotypes that the larger culture has of African American families, namely, an absent father, an unstable family, uneducated family members, and poverty. The Huxtables were clearly father-oriented, stable, educated, and affluent. In almost every episode, the Huxtable children were taught such universal values as trust, honesty, and responsibility.

Some communication scholars believe that the show did have serious limitations, among them the fact that some of the somber realities experienced by African Americans were either obscured or ignored (Real, 1991; Tueth, 2004). Further, Muriel Cantor (1990) believed that Cliff, the father, was the center of most plotlines, thereby making him appear to be the most important family member. Additionally, the problems and situations in most of the shows were all easily solvable. These unrealistic solutions were probably due, at least in part, to the less than realistic portrayal of two professionals (a physician and an attorney) who were able to spend enormous amounts of quality time guiding and teaching their children. Nonetheless, the Huxtables remain forever etched in the minds of many viewers.

In addition to *The Cosby Show, Roseanne* (1988–1995) was one of the most watched television shows of the late 1980s and early 1990s. The show was produced by the same team that produced Cosby, although the Conner family in *Roseanne* were radically different from the Huxtables. Often called the blue-collar situation comedy, *Roseanne* dealt with a European American working-class family coping with paying bills, managing family problems, and raising children. This show was intriguing in that it used humor to help make lucid the challenges that the Conner family faced. In fact, Jeremy Butter (2011) observed that the parenting in the Conner family was often "sarcastic, bordering on scornful." The show presented compelling and provocative topics such as masturbation, birth control, domestic violence, PMS, and AIDS. These issues are faced by families every day and are not limited to a particular ethnic or racial group. The show, like *All in the Family* and *Maude,* served an important function, and that may partially explain why it sustained a top rating during most of its run on television.

Roseanne capitalized on the experiences of a large and diverse audience. The show was an effort to ridicule the glitz and opulence of early 1980s shows such as *Dynasty, Dallas,* and *Falcon Crest,* three shows featuring very rich families and their "struggles" with oil investments and wine vineyards! Roseanne and Dan Conner lampooned a society that was becoming fixated on mineral water, gourmet dinners, and jogging (Mayerle, 1991). Mortgage payments, physician's bills, and employment searches occupied the Conners. However, *Roseanne* had many detractors, primarily because of the characters' internal communication with each other. The heavy use of sarcasm, especially from the mother to her children, was offensive to many viewers, as it violated the idealized notion of loving family interactions presented in most other sitcoms.

Shows such as *The Cosby Show* and *Roseanne* have now disappeared into the realm of syndication and reruns. The Huxtables and the Conners, however, were pivotal in providing us with new and alternative visions of the family.

Efforts to diversify views of the family continued in the 1990s. This decade's sitcoms attempted to bridge the 1970s innovative formats and the 1980s diversity efforts. *Murphy Brown* is one such program. Set in Washington, D.C., the show depicted a news anchor caught between the perennial (and confusing) demands of family responsibilities and work responsibilities. The show asked the question, How can a professional woman single-handedly raise a child and have a successful news career?

Murphy Brown (1988–1995) became most prominent in 1992, when then Vice President Dan Quayle called the show's lead character a mockery to fathers because she had a child without being married. Quayle's comments were rooted in an indictment of an apparent "family values" void in Hollywood, saying that the show glamorized "something that is wrong with society" (Garment, 1992, p. B7). The specifics of the dialogue between Murphy (Candice Bergen) and Dan Quayle reached tens of millions of people in the first episode of the 1993 season, entitled "Murphy's Revenge." Using her television news show as a backdrop, Murphy lambasted Vice President Quayle by commenting on his rigid definition of the family and the challenges associated with being a single parent and a female in the United States. That particular episode caused politicians to reflect on the power of Hollywood and its potential for changing the status quo, and ultimately, the image of the contemporary family in our country.

Murphy Brown became a mother at the age of 42, an age when complications can occur from pregnancy and childbirth. Some applauded her decision to link feminist qualities of independence with feminine behaviors such as reproduction. However, Bonnie Dow (1995) contends that although Murphy was antichild for three years on the series, it was peculiar to see that having a baby suddenly gave her meaning. Dow continues by concluding, "She [Murphy] plays into stereotypes about the negative effects of feminism in a variety of ways" (p. 214). Having a baby on the show seemed to affirm that women were not complete if they did not have children. Further, it is interesting to note that once Murphy legitimated herself as a mother, the baby seemed to recede in importance on the show and was rarely involved in later episodes. The series did not focus on critical issues facing working single mothers.

Nonetheless, the show contributed significantly to redefining images of families on television. The producers and writers effectively used humor to respond to Vice President Dan Quayle's definition of family. William Benoit and K. Kerby Anderson (1996) conclude that Murphy's denial of Quayle's perception "was supported by the presentation of several single-parent families, all apparently loving and happy" (p. 80).

One additional comedy is also of note: *The Golden Girls* (1985–1992). NBC showcased four women in their senior years living together in Miami. *The Golden Girls,* featuring four widows, was an instant success. It was the first time that a major network had a successful comedy with senior citizens in all the lead roles. Like *Maude* and *Roseanne, The Golden Girls* tackled difficult subjects, including same-sex attraction, Alzheimer's, and grandparents' rights. The show was also an effort to understand the voluntary family, since only two of the characters were related (mother and daughter). In fact, the last line of one of the last episodes of the series demonstrated this voluntary close-knit family. When Dorothy, one of the lead characters, decides to leave the house after getting married for a second time, she states: "You'll always be my sisters. Always." For the first time in television, the country was able to watch a television show that portrayed the aging process in a thoughtful, articulate, and, of course, humorous way.

Recent Images of Families on Television

Since the beginning of the new century, television and situation comedy has evolved. The portrayal of families has been more reflective of the diversity of family types and individuals in society. In particular, two comedies show that to be a family, one doesn't have to be related by blood. A very successful hit for NBC was *Friends* (1994–2004), a show that focused on the friendships of six people who frequented each other's apartments and congregated at a local coffeehouse. The show represented the notion that individuals can consider themselves to be a family without clear biological or legal ties, similar to *The Golden Girls.*

Another comedy with a different view of the family was *Will and Grace* (1998–2006). This program centers around two people, one gay (Will) and the other heterosexual (Grace), who share an apartment as well as their romantic ups and downs. The show, following in the footsteps of *Ellen* (a show featuring a lesbian in the lead role), broke new ground in that it portrayed a gay man in a professional manner (Will is a Manhattan attorney). Despite this portrayal, some critics have blasted the show for not dealing with homophobia or AIDS, two leading issues in the gay community. Still, although Will's sexuality is part of each show's theme, it is not the overriding message being presented. Rob Owen (2000) of the *Pittsburgh Post-Gazette* quotes the creator of the series: "We're almost to the point where people identify with the [Will] character . . . that his sexual proclivity is secondary to the fact that they want him to have an emotional involvement."

One newer addition to the sitcom "family" is the Peabody award–winner *Modern Family*. The show, first aired in 2009, remains a groundbreaking comedy, featuring three different family types in the show's half-hour: gay-lesbian, traditional, and multigenerational. Further, culture is prominently addressed in the show as one of the central characters—a Colombian woman with a child from her first marriage—is married to a white male. What has made this show so popular—among both critics and viewers—is more than the comedy. As Glenn Whipp (2011) points out, the plot lines are realistic and compelling. Further, the show has an uncanny ability to discuss contemporary issues—including adoption by gay fathers, raising a stepson, and teenage sexuality—in sensitive, realistic, and (yes) humorous ways. Bruce Fieler (2011) of the *New York Times* also notes that "*Modern Family* may be most akin to family life . . . the goal [of the show] is to preserve the ideal of the family—conflicted, but functioning" (p. 1). As ParentFurther (2011), a family-centered think tank, concludes: "These families show what it means to be family and that's what matters most" (*http://www.parentfurther.com/blog/strong-modern-families*).

Future Images of Families on Television

What's in store for future television families is rather uncertain. We're confident that Hollywood will make efforts to reflect the diversity of families—if for no other reason than that it's a profitable undertaking. We've already learned in Chapter 1 that our country is getting more diverse and will continue to do so. While progress may come slowly, it will have to come. The competition from online resources will require TV to adapt—or die. Therefore, we can envision shows similar to *Modern Family* being developed and "repackaged" so they start to resonate with multicultural communities.

Television is a pervasive medium of popular culture—one that often focuses on the family. Our discussion here has only scratched the surface of televised images of the family. We have not spoken at all about family dramas nor children's daytime programming, both of which reflect many aspects of family life. Neither have we discussed the impact of such animated shows such as *King of the Hill, Family Guy*, nor television's longest running show, *The Simpsons*. Each of these, while sustaining a smaller audience than those on network television,

Student Perspective: Tabitha

I can't imagine a sitcom about my family. I guess you could call it The Zanies. We're a lot more chaotic than most families on TV. But we're a lot more boring too. We need some clever writers like they have on Friends *to make us sound funnier.*

has presented the nuclear family in a satirical, sometimes caustic manner. Again, we encourage you to review episodes of each show on your own to see if you draw any conclusions about family communication.

Yet, even from our brief review, several conclusions can be drawn. First, we believe that television sitcoms have not significantly demonstrated the challenges associated with being a single parent. Further, few television sitcoms have legitimately and realistically featured a multicultural family with parents or children. As Luís Venegas from our opening vignette realizes, Hollywood has also been negligent in producing few shows that address the racial and ethnic diversity of many families in our larger culture, namely, Native Americans, Latinos, and Asian Americans. The shows that do depict these co-cultures are frequently rooted in societal stereotypes and myths associated with that cultural group. As Dates and Stroman (2001) discovered, on television Native Americans are portrayed as alcoholics and poor, Latinos are shown as having little education, and Asian Americans are essentially invisible.

It would be refreshing to see efforts in developing situation comedies that tap into the reality of families who are Polish or Irish, and comedies that do not rely on stereotypes. To construct sitcoms that are also amenable to children's viewing (Buerkel-Rothfuss, Greenberg, Atkin, & Neuendorf, 1982) would be valuable. We agree with Sally Steenland (1995), who, over 25 years ago, concluded that the television industry "must expand its pool of storytellers and air more varied tales" (p. 188). Addressing diversity in family types and ethnicity would be a step in that direction, letting families see themselves reflected more accurately, albeit humorously, in televised sitcoms. Future sitcoms could stop solving all problems in less than 30 minutes, which trivializes family conflict. Especially when sitcoms deal with serious issues, it is problematic to find solutions so easily. Some viewers may be uncomfortable with their own communication skills because they are never as clever or adept as the families they watch weekly.

WOMEN'S AND MEN'S MOVEMENTS AND THEIR INFLUENCE ON FAMILIES

In this section, we discuss how women's and men's movements in the United States have affected family communication. Earlier we defined social movements as collective enterprises; people must come together for a common task or goal. Scores of social movements have existed in the United States since the country's beginning. Topics ranging from conservation to disability rights to global greed to nudism have been the focus of millions of people who have galvanized to form their collective identities. Further, it's important to point out that simply because there's a protest does not mean that it's a social movement. We agree with Rick Hampson (2011), citing Dan Schnur, differentiates between protest and movements: "The difference between an angry mob and a movement is a goal. . . . It's not enough to point out what's wrong. You need to affect the levers of power to change things (p. 3A)" We could explore dozens of movements in this section of the chapter, but we target two—women's movements and men's movements—whose goals are unique and usually implicitly related to family life. In our discussion, we point to two examples of social movements—the breast cancer movement and the Promise Keepers movement.

Social movements provide ways to enact changes in thinking about the status quo in our society. Social movements are not monolithic. Most social movements are concerned with reshaping collective identities and do not (and cannot) take place in a vacuum. Collective identities serve as a foundation for collective action (Reger, 2002, 2012). Social movements have multiple levels and are inextricably linked to the dominant culture, the state, and other social movements (Whittier, 2002).

Feminism and Women's Movements

For some, **feminism** connotes images of women who hate men and who do not want to share their lives with them. For others, however, the word encompasses a lot more. What is certainly true is that there is no one definition of feminism. There are lots of ways to be feminist, ranging from liberal to radical, eco-feminist, to separatist (Tong, 1989). Some would speak historically and classify the first wave of feminism in the 19th century as the beginning of women's basic political rights (Bem, 1993). The second wave began in the 1960s and "raised social consciousness still further by exposing—and naming—the 'sexism' in all policies and practices that explicitly discriminate on the basis of sex" (p. 1). Many feminists would say we are experiencing a third wave, begun in the 1980s, because much inequality has been addressed and feminists now need to focus on other issues like diversity and including men in the movement. Yet, Donna Sollie and Leigh Leslie (1994) note that, despite differences among the waves, feminists are deeply concerned with empowering women.

We believe feminism is a way of thinking that highlights the belief that men and women can assume equal power in society. Further, we see gender (as well as race, ethnicity, and class) as a site of struggle. This suggests that gender and the role prescriptions that accompany gender are socially constructed notions. Different interests struggle over who will be able to define gender, and in the past white, affluent, middle-aged men usually prevailed. Navita Cummings James (2011) talks about growing up as a black female "when Miss America was always white." Her point is that in the 1950s (and some would argue even today) standards of beauty and femininity were defined by European American features, making black women feel unfeminine or ugly.

Masculinity is also socially constructed, often through mediated images of models, including those that are fictional such as the Marlboro Man and those who have made money from their portrayals of masculinity, such as Bruce Willis or Vin Diesel. These emblems also highlight European American features, as well as other attributes such as silence and physical strength.

Feminism is integrally linked to **women's movements.** For our purposes here, we are using the two terms interchangeably, even though, as we have detailed above, there are different types of feminism and differing movements. Because of all this variety, we are following bell hooks's (1992b) convention of referring to "women's movements" rather than *the* women's movement.

Feminists vary in their willingness to redefine how we look at society and how we should view the family. That is, some wish to overhaul the family entirely, whereas others simply wish to make families more egalitarian. What feminism and women's movements mean to families in our country is that grandmothers', mothers', daughters', sisters', aunts', and nieces' voices should not be silenced in the family. For many feminists, listening to female voices will help us better understand some of the complexities of family life. More important, some feminists, such as Barrie Thorne (1992) and Judie Zeilinger (2012), believe that we can uncover ways of making families more stable and more satisfying to their members through feminist thinking.

Student Perspective: Rosie

They call my generation "selfish," but if it means that women have the right to be and do what they want, then go ahead and call us "selfish." I remember my mom always waiting on my father—hand and foot. If I ever get married, there is no way that I'll be doing that. Never. Period. My mom did it, my mom's mom did it, but my generation will stop it!

Feminists who are family researchers argue that we need to rid ourselves of the sentimentalized visions we have of families and highlight the inequities, dominance, power, and sometimes violence that can characterize family life as much as love can (Millman, 1994). In addition to noting the problems of family life, some authors advocate a grasp of family diversity because it is through understanding the mosaic of families that we begin to work through our problems in communication (Coontz, 2000a; Turner & West, 2011). Many individuals connected with women's movements also assert that the sentimental view of the family neglects families with gay men and lesbians, single parents, and racially diverse members (Millman, 1994; Peplau, 1994). In doing so, we eliminate a large and growing number of people who, each day, successfully communicate with their families.

Rethinking the Family Women's movements have been successful in getting our society to think about the value of women in families (see Table 4-1). Hester Eisenstein (1994) demonstrates how families are being reconstructed

TABLE 4-1 Goals of Some Women's Movements Relevant to the Family

---

1. Eliminate inequities in family (e.g., institute equal sharing of household tasks)
2. Break down power and dominance in family (e.g., share decision making in marriage)
3. Redefine prevailing family values (e.g., support lesbian mothers serving as co-parents)
4. Examine family relations and events from a female's perspective (e.g., impact on mother's job of having another child)
5. Promote women's knowledge about their bodies (e.g., sisters, mothers, and grandmothers undergoing a mammogram)

---

to address feminist issues. Two key assumptions guide her thinking on the family:

1. Feminists look at the family from a female perspective and, more specifically, from the perspective of women's experiences.
2. The family can be considered to be a set of relations and functions that have to be analyzed critically from the point of view of their effects on women and the options offered to women.

To understand each assumption and its relationship to communication in the family, we need to examine each a bit more in depth.

First, examining the family from a female perspective necessitates that researchers talk to women about what it means to be in a family. A feminist approach would advocate talking to single mothers to find out their feelings about the stresses and challenges pertaining to motherhood, rather than telling them to "snap out of it" in a caustic tone. Further, this assumption requires us to listen carefully as women describe the kinds of experiences they have had in families. This means seeing how women construct the experience of their family—a topic we have discussed throughout this book.

Was there ever a time when you spoke to your mother or your daughter or your sister about what it is/was like being a member of your family? Or, perhaps you have a grandmother to whom you have spoken about her reactions to being a matriarch in the family. Several questions may have come to your mind, questions that delve into beliefs, attitudes, and values of family life. General questions related to women's roles in the family, women's contributions to the family, and society's view of women may be particularly important with multiple generations of women in the home.

Additional questions might be more specific. How did you talk to your partner about your experience of pregnancy? Did you have trouble making yourself understood? Did you ever experience any uncertainty talking about decisions concerning birth control? If so, what communication tactics did you use to reduce this uncertainty? How did you and your family talk about the decision concerning whether you'd work or stay at home? What about episodes of rage or violence? How did you handle these, or how were they managed in the family? Did you ever disclose anything about these episodes to others? These are the sorts of communication-related questions that feminists are interested in when they talk about the family. These are also the types of questions that tap into specific feelings about being a female in a family and invite women to explain their experiences.

The second assumption of the family from a feminist viewpoint pertains to the way family life is analyzed. That is, what effects do events in the family have on women, and how are women's opportunities enhanced or squelched as a result of their family experiences? An example will help clarify this point.

Victoria and Hector, married 11 years, were each previously married. Together, they have four children living with them, three from their previous marriages. This Mexican American family is rooted in an important value: hierarchy. Because males in many Mexican American families are charged with preserving order and discipline and giving direction to the family (Cruz, King, Widaman, Leu, Cauce, & Conger, 2011), they are usually regarded as critical to preserving Mexican heritage.

Imagine Hector's surprise, therefore, when Victoria decided that she was going to enact a new discipline routine with their teenage sons. Victoria decided to disregard Hector's discipline plan (being grounded from social activities) and embark on an alternative disciplinary strategy: reexamination of the offensive behavior/remark and renegotiation of household duties. With this new way of addressing discipline, Victoria believes that the family will remain more communicative and more stable.

In this situation, Victoria is acting outside of her prescribed cultural role. We can only guess that Hector is frustrated by the newly enacted behavior and may even attempt to undermine it in order to restore his responsibility to the family. Feminists would be intrigued by how Victoria felt about her role, how she was able to go against her cultural value, and how she communicated her change to Hector. In essence, Victoria's thoughts on being both a spouse and a mother are of interest and value to feminists. Her ability to communicate these thoughts is relevant to family communication researchers.

Some feminists might argue that Victoria (and all women) are exploited in the family. As Barrie Thorne (1992) notes, this line of thinking focuses on how the ideology of the family is rooted in a sexual division of labor in which men are breadwinners and women are stay-at-home mothers. This ideology, Thorne observes, reinforces the economic and social exploitation of all women. Further, some feminists highlight how this traditional conceptualization of the family ignores diversity. African American, Latina, and Asian American feminists point out the white middle-class assumptions embedded in the dominant ideology of family. Against this backdrop, some feminists have called for the abolishment of the monolithic understanding of family that sustains gender oppression and renders class and ethnic differences invisible.

Women and the Breast Cancer Movement   We noted earlier that there is not "a" women's movement but several—each with particular goals and strategies. One recent social movement among women is the breast cancer movement (BCM). The movement does not really have a specific beginning, although the 1970s was the genesis of the women's health movement (Moffett, 2003). The movement was critical in providing a model for establishing organizations and coalitions pertaining to breast cancer research. The BCM really got traction with the inception of the Susan G. Komen Foundation. Named after a woman who "fought breast cancer with her heart, body, and soul" (*www.komen.org/AboutUs*), the organization has grown into a global leader in breast cancer research. Breast cancer awareness month occurs each October and at that time, millions of women (and men) focus on prevention, treatment, and general awareness of the disease.

The breast cancer movement has activism and volunteerism at its core (Brinkler, 2011). The movement is credited to be grassroots insofar as it

> *gave voice to women who had previously been silenced; educated women about their own bodies and the medical establishment; changed the way research for diseases is funded; demanded more humane treatment; and transformed a disease that was once shrouded in shameful secrecy into one with which companies like Kitchenaid and Yoplait are eager to be associated. (Blackstone, 2004, pp. 287–288)*

The movement has allowed women to feel more comfortable about their bodies, to communicate this level of comfort to other women (and men), and to encourage social change. As with most social movements, the breast cancer movement has intersected its efforts with governmental policy. Efforts have not been in vain. Nancy Evans (2002) reports that funding for breast cancer research increased from $90 million in 1991 to $800 million in 2001. This increase in money is due, in no small part, to the articulation of issues brought about by BCM participants.

Amy Blackstone (2004) notes that the movement is primarily comprised of two groups: patients/survivors and volunteers/activists whose primary identities focus on roles as wives and mothers. In her study of volunteers/ activists at the Susan Komen Breast Cancer Foundation, Blackstone suggests that workers frequently do not wish to be identified as political activists. She relates the words of one volunteer: "Obviously I care about this stuff but I'm just not that political" (p. 350). Regardless of their view, Blackstone notes that women's work at Komen is "about empowering women to believe in themselves, and their rights, so that they will take the initiative to advocate for their own health and ensure that their doctors assist them in this endeavor" (p. 359).

Contemporary applications of the BCM include writing and reading about the disease on the Internet. In a provocative study, Victoria Pitts (2004) explains how the Internet is being used by those who have breast cancer. Specifically, personal Web pages are being constructed that allow women to provide private narratives of breast cancer. Acknowledging that the Internet is being sought as a way for autobiographical stories to be written and shared, Pitts points out that women provide personal accounts, medical information, drug efficacy information, and ethical dilemmas as a way to gain empowerment. Pitts observes that the Web pages are challenging the "sick role" (p. 53) and indeed, "norms of female beauty and personal responsibility . . . are affirmed" (p. 36) within the BCM.

The future of the breast cancer movement is intimately linked with social and environmental justice (Barrie & Morrow, 2012). Organizations and coalitions are focusing their efforts on universal care of women across the world and on healthy working and living conditions. Further, getting to the environmental causes of breast cancer—from food to pesticides—is also a focus of attention. The relationship between this movement and the family cannot be ignored. Like many diseases, breast cancer can have long-term health effects. The stress associated with caring for a breast cancer survivor can be enormous. Aside from the obvious health issues, there are also economic and cultural implications to being diagnosed. For some, stress, conflict, and even bouts of verbal aggression may emerge as families reconcile the diagnosis and the treatment. For others, being diagnosed and living with the disease has enhanced the intimacy of the family. Breast cancer touches every member of the family. And the BCM has inspired millions of family members to aid in the understanding of breast cancer stories everywhere.

Criticisms of Feminism and Women's Movements   Feminists desire to give voice to women, enabling their experiences to be understood. In so doing, "women's ways of knowing" enhance family life. Not all have espoused this way of thinking, however. In fact, there are critics who believe that feminism actually undermines the family structure in the United States ("Some say Feminism has ruined men, what else has it ruined?") (Burroway & Sabato, 2011). Lenore Weitzman (1985) reports that the high divorce rate may be attributed to women and their desire to be in the workplace. Some believe that because women are the focus of women's movements, men's comments are belittled and neglected. Although we learned earlier that not all feminists advocate this women-only orientation, the perception by many is that the words and experiences of fathers and brothers are of little value.

A second criticism of feminism and women's movements relates to blame. Naomi Wolf (1993) talks about "victim feminism" and suggests that blaming does little to build bridges between women and men. Some critics of feminism and women's movements contend that women are inclined to blame men for problems they experience in and outside of families.

Despite the criticisms leveled against women's movements and the feminists associated with them, it is clear that women have gained significantly

TABLE 4-2   Goals of Some Men's Movements Relevant to the Family

1. Redefine the role of father and husband (e.g., support the stay-at-home dad)
2. Examine the roles of mother and wife and their relationship to the roles of father and husband (e.g., supporter of, or hindrance to, masculinity)
3. Reaffirm a man's importance to his family (e.g., primary financial provider)
4. Extend a man's rights within the family (e.g., fathers' rights in child custody cases)
5. Instigate psychological unity with other men (e.g., sharing stories with other fathers/husbands)

since the early days of suffrage. Women are not yet equal to men in terms of pay, job status, and employment opportunity, and their voices are still not fully heard. However, feminists have been instrumental in helping to redefine the family with women in mind.

The Male Voice and Men's Movements

To understand the influence that **men's movements** have had on families (see Table 4-2), we are reminded of the words of Michael Kimmel (1987): "Men are changing—not, perhaps, with the bang of transformation, but also not with a whispered hint of a slight nudge in a new direction" (p. 9). For Kimmel and others (e.g., Buchbinder, 2012), men are not Neanderthals locked in a 1950s model of relating. Rather, many men have been unlocking their past and, through men's movements, have been tapping into their future potential, working toward becoming better dads and learning to talk with their partners.

To begin, it's important to note that just as there are numerous types of women's movements, there are a variety of men's movements as well. It is not our intention to describe each and every movement; however, we wish to discuss three very different strains of men's movements: the pro-feminist orientation, the pro-masculinist orientation, and the Promise Keepers. To be sure, communication associated with and within these men's movements has been instrumental in helping to define families. Before discussing the three orientations, however, we need to briefly outline the development of men's movements in the United States.

Development of Men's Movements   Although women's movements have affected both public opinion and public policy, many people in our country are unfamiliar with the existence of men's movements. Perhaps one reason many people have not been aware of such efforts is the fact that the voices of men's movements have often been muffled. It is not uncommon for many in society to dismiss men who organize movements for themselves. Yet we cannot ignore the thousands of men who, beginning in the 1970s, formed groups to address the grievances and triumphs of men in the country. Further,

Gordon Schulz (2012) observes that men's movements are likely affecting the dynamics in many households.

If men's movements had their genesis 30 years ago, why haven't the media reported on this "male revolution"? Don Shewey (1991) suggests that the media have reported on men's movements, but only in a trivial way. Shewey writes that the media reports on men's movements possess "the piercing insight formerly found in articles about the women's movement that talked about 'bra-burning'" (p. 43). Helen Sterk (1993) comments that perhaps it is unwise to turn to the media for information and an analysis of a social movement: "Just as the mass media distort and ridicule feminism by associating it with torching underwear, so they distort and ridicule men's movement by associating it with white guys dancing around a fire in the night" (p. 1).

Student Perspective: Kenny

Great! Now women are mad that men have their own way of connecting with each other. In the past, women were mad that men didn't get "in touch" with their own feelings. Now, all over our country, men are getting together to privately talk about how they feel. I think women are mad because they can't be a part of these gatherings. I think it's great for men to go somewhere to explore their inner private side.

Pro-Feminist Approach   Men associated with the **pro-feminist approach** believe that sexism and patriarchy are particularly harmful to many males as well as females (Kaufman & Kimmel, 2011; Pease, 2009). James Doyle (1989) reported that the one-sided patriarchal system primarily benefits "a few privileged men while disadvantaging all women and most other men" (p. 309). It's important to note that the pro-feminist men's movement generally believes that nonwhites, gay men, the undereducated, and the poor are particularly vulnerable to the white male paradigm present in society. What's more troubling for the pro-feminists, Doyle notes, is the institutional support for such patriarchy, through many religions, political parties, and the U.S. economy.

Pro-Feminists and Family Communication   The relationship of pro-feminist men to the family can be seen through the example of Nick Collazo. Nick, a Long Island native, is the 44-year-old father of two children. Nick is married to Alex, the children's mother, a 40-year-old originally from Texas. On Tuesday evenings, after working all day as a bricklayer, Nick attends a gathering of men from all walks of life, including accountants, teachers, physicians, gardeners, and painters. During these meetings, Nick listens to his male associates who, like Nick, disclose their feelings about the power differential between men and women. He listens to his friend, Daniel, who tells of his female colleague at work and how she was passed up for a promotion.

He also listens to a story by another friend, Cyrus, who openly admits to once subscribing to the "male way of thinking," but who has found that such a mentality challenges his integrity and privileges the few. Nick also takes part in this week's discussion by addressing how competition at work has undermined his relations with both women and men. In the end, Nick returns home from this group with a better understanding of men, work, and family relations. He acts upon that appreciation by taking an active part in helping to get women's voices heard both at home and at work. In his male-dominated occupation, Nick knows that he will be challenged. Still, he is committed to an antisexist model of relating.

Pro-Masculinist Approach   In contrast to the pro-feminist approach is the **pro-masculinist** orientation. This orientation itself has several approaches. Some pro-masculinist males believe that men have been the victims of a social and legal structure (Rickabaugh, 1994). Warren Farrell (1987) and Herb Goldberg (1976) are credited with orienting individuals toward concern for men's rights within the family.

Other thinking associated with the pro-masculinist movement is more intrapersonal in nature. The poet Robert Bly was an early advocate of pro-masculinist thinking. Bly (1990) focused special concern on men losing their voice in a society that was fast becoming sympathetic to women's issues and concerns. Charles Stewart, Craig Allen Smith, and Robert Denton (2012) observe that Bly's writing was seen as a backlash to feminism and an effort to reclaim masculinity. In his popular book *Iron John,* Bly lamented the faceless men who were being influenced by dominant mothers, female lovers, and absent fathers. Using a Grimm Brothers fairy tale called Iron John, Bly contended that the only way for boys to progress into maturity is by bonding with the metaphoric father found in a male mentor. Men must descend into their spirits and connect with their deep masculine identity. Indeed, for Bly and others connected to pro-masculinity, the "inner wild man" must emerge. Employing rituals such as drum beating and sharing stories with each other will enable pro-masculinist men to construct "psychological unity" with other men (Rickabaugh, 1994, p. 461).

The pro-masculinist approach embraces the belief that men have been neglected in the larger culture. In fact, some researchers (e.g., Freedman, 1985) point out that the pro-feminist men could be considered perpetuators of such neglect, reinforcing stereotypes and negating men's beliefs. Pro-masculinists are preoccupied with making sure men continue to have their voices heard. Some focus on fathers' rights, others fondly recall the past when men were not considered the oppressors of women across the world.

Pro-Masculinists and Family Communication   For those men who desire to return to their masculine roots, eruptions in family communication may occur. For instance, a father who believes that he is oppressed by women (a belief articulated by Bly) would be less inclined to inaugurate or prescribe alternatives to sex-typed behavior in his children. Or it may be that because the pro-masculinist camp believes that males are subject to the power of women and come to depend on them, these same men are less inclined to bond with other men. Because men are turning to women for emotional fulfillment, men become uncomfortable with other men (Clatterbaugh, 1990). The implications of this in a father–son relationship become apparent. Although the masculine ideal is embraced, the father–son relationship is strained. Yet Bly is negative about the mother–son relationship as well. He describes the strain between fathers and sons as primarily the fault of mothers. Mothers turn their sons into "soft" men who see their fathers through their mothers' eyes. Bly argues that the boy must leave home to mature because home is "too close to the mother's pillow [a sexualized reference to the Oedipal complex] and the father's book of rules [making an association between fathers and discipline]" (p. 13).

Promise Keepers   From Israel to San Antonio, there is one men's movement—a Christian ministry—that has withstood criticism for over two decades: Promise Keepers (PK). Identified as a "biblical manhood [Christian] ministry" (Worthen, 2010), the group has, at its core, the fundamental belief that men in the family (fathers/husbands) should be held accountable for their actions. Christian togetherness is a hallmark of the movement. Men gather in large football stadiums and sports arenas and profess their allegiance to the Bible and the passages that invoke the role of men in the family. Founded by football coach Bill McCartney, the movement has evolved significantly over the years. Melanie Heath (2003) argues that the **Promise Keepers** "seek to transform and alter the norms of masculinity by challenging men to reestablish their leadership role in the family" (p. 423). Kurt Peterson (2010) advances the thought that a Promise Keeper "agrees to read the Bible regularly, bond with other males, practice sexual purity, build a strong marriage, serve his local church, break down racial barriers, and transform the world through moral and spiritual integrity" (p. 136). John Bartkowski (2000) notes that this movement's aim is to "rejuvenate 'godly manhood'" (p. 33). Indeed, among the many goals of this men's movement is the reestablishment of men to their family. And, as Rhys Williams (2000) reports, many in the media have dubbed this movement a bunch of "average Joes" who try to determine how to be better fathers, husbands, and Christians.

Promise Keepers rallies are characterized by one word: grand. They usually occur in football stadiums with tens of thousands of men present (women are not excluded from attending any of these gatherings; rather they have not been specifically invited to attend). PK men openly embrace other men in ways that appear to be culturally frowned upon. Melanie Heath (2003) writes that an expressive masculinity characterizes the movement. These discourses of masculinity are embedded in Biblical references. For instance, Bartkowski (2000) reports on the relationship between men and the women in their lives. He relates the words of Edwin Cole, a keynote speaker in the PK movement: "It is possible to get spirituality from women, but strength always comes from men. A church, a family, a nation is only as strong as its men. Men, you are accountable" (p. 35).

The Promise Keepers movement is a study of men's roles in the family and their relationship to God. In a study looking at members of the PK movement and their wives, Heath (2003) shares the words of one PK member:

[My wife] has more responsibility for the family as far as kid things. I shouldn't say—that doesn't take away responsibility from me. But, when it comes to answering to God, I am ultimately more responsible for the marriage in that way. (p. 438)

Spirituality guides virtually every aspect of PK. An emphasis on Christian unity is a hallmark of the movement. Efforts to include all denominations began in the early years of the movement in 1986 with one of the main stadium speeches called "The Highest Common Denominator: Uniting Together as Brothers in Christ" (Lockhart, 2000). This belief is underscored by the central promise of a Promise Keeper that pertains to "Biblical unity."

In addition to the Christian orientation of the PK movement, issues pertaining to race and ethnicity are also addressed by the leaders of the movement. William Lockhart (2000) claims that there are many speakers from various races and ethnicities at conferences. Further, Lockhart states that many stadium rallies include time for PK members to meet and pray with someone of another race. Improved racial relationships are a hallmark of the PK movement.

Promise Keepers is a men's movement that has been both praised and criticized. Stacia Creek (2009) concludes that although the group suffered some financial difficulties, it has undoubtedly "reemerged" and continues to influence millions of men committed to Christian principles. The decision to have a gathering of men furthering their commitment to their families (and Christian identity) appears to resonate well. Terry Todd (2009) argues that not only is Promise Keepers making a comeback from its heyday in the 1990s, but it has positioned itself as a Christian option in a post 9/11 world. He believes that PK is a "heady brew of muscular Christianity, personal transformation, and evangelical nationalism" (*http://www.alternet.org/belief/142000/warriors_for_christ%3A_is_promise_keepers_making_a_comeback/?page=1*). However, given that women are not invited to attend and given the patriarchal overtones of the rallies, the movement's value has been questioned. Although Rhys Williams (2002) notes that not all men who attend PK rallies are obsessed with patriarchy, "the dominant Promise Keepers messages promise a redemptive return to a God-ordained order" (p. 260). And, that order includes men as the unequivocal heads of the family. Despite these assessments, Promise Keepers is at the intersection of religion, men's movements, masculinity, and family life.

Criticisms of the Male Voice and Men's Movements   There has been extensive criticism of men's movements, much of which has been directed at the pro-masculinist orientation. Feminists have been especially critical of the motivations and meanings of Robert Bly. Margo Adair (1992), for instance, contends that "the concept of 'wild' emerges out of the assumption that nature needs to be controlled, otherwise 'she' will get out of hand" (p. 57). Elizabeth Dodson-Gray (1992) states that Bly and others assume that men can only find themselves by "leaving their mother's household. This is the old patriarchal script of masculinity being named only in opposition to anything female" (p. 162). Finally, Myriam Miedzian (1992) wonders whether Bly and others are more concerned with "proving their 'fierceness,' which, as they see it, differentiates them as 'real men,' than they are with encouraging good fathering, which they fear would render them 'effeminate'?" (p. 130).

Another criticism leveled at men's movements is that they not only leave out a positive role for women, but they also barely mention a place for gay men and men of color. Especially in the pro-masculinist branch, masculinity seems to be defined in a traditional manner—strength, wisdom, power, and heterosexuality compose the masculine profile (Wood, 2013).

Student Perspective: Bryan

It's very irritating to read about men's movements and read "homosexuality is okay—we accept gays," but then see a need on the part of the authors to be seen separately from them. As if to say, "It's okay in theory, but don't mistake us for homosexuals—we're straight." I'm not sure if people are just too wrapped up in sexuality or what.

Student Perspective: Tamara

I absolutely cannot believe how stupid I thought men's movements were until I started to think about them after class. I guess some of why I thought they were ridiculous may have had to do with how they were reported in the media. But I honestly thought that men have everything—what else do they want? But after thinking about it after our discussion, I guess it could be a good thing for men to think about masculinity and how it affects their family life. But I still don't know how I feel about all the blaming they do of women.

Continuing Influence of Women's and Men's Movements

Women's and men's movements will continue to play a role in our culture throughout this century. Women's movements have been instrumental in bringing about changes in the experiences of families. In fact, Barrie Thorne (1992) reports that feminism and women's movements have attempted to "dislodge beliefs that any specific family arrangement is natural, biological, or 'functional' in a timeless way" (p. 4). Men's movements, too, have recently gained media attention, and although much criticism has been offered, these movements have the potential to influence changes in the family (Staggenborg, 2010). Families living in the 21st century United States are contextualized by women's and men's movements. As we have mentioned, there are a number of additional types of women's and men's movements, including those associated with gay and lesbian groups and groups concerned about race, ethnicity, and class (Andrews, 2002; Bernstein, 2002). It is not possible for a family to communicate without acknowledging some issues dealing with women's and men's roles and responsibilities. Prior to these movements, these issues may have aroused little or no discussion in families.

GOVERNMENT AND THE FAMILY

Thus far, we have addressed how television and social movements have affected family communication. We now wish to delineate how government and its policies influence family life. Catherine Chilman (1988) concludes that "the chief goal of public policies concerning families is the promotion of family well-being" (p. 245). Although this sounds fine in theory, in practice there is much disagreement. For instance, what types of families are we talking about? As we have seen, there are a variety of family types in our larger culture, each striving to attain some sort of visibility. Another issue arising from family policies pertains to government's role in assisting families. In other words, to what extent do we want governmental assistance with families? How much money? For how long? The answers to these sorts of questions are difficult, because we first have to answer what a government is and how it should function in a country such as ours.

Various voices have been heard on the subject of family policy. One chorus (e.g., *www.childpolicy.org*) sings the praises of governmental intervention, believing that in a capitalist society, tax money should be used to help those in need. Of course, some of you might wonder who it is we need to be helping and for what length of time this assistance should continue. For example, are you in favor of extending welfare payments to single, young, poor women with babies, or do you believe that these women should be required to work and manage their family after work? The choices are not so clear, as there are many factors to consider.

A second choir of voices has also been heard (*www.citizenlink.com*). This group believes that because we are an individualistic country (that is, we are responsible for ourselves), governmental assistance runs counter to our core values. In fact, some scholars (Moen & Schorr, 1987) note that the Social Security Act of 1935 was developed to ensure economic independence of the elderly. It wasn't until much later that the Social Security program began to serve families.

Defining Family Policy

For purposes of our discussion here, we need to define **family policy.** Shirley Zimmerman (1992) is credited with the broadest interpretation, defining it as "everything that governments do that affect families, directly or indirectly" (p. 3). Chilman (1988) elaborates on others' interpretations of family policy, concluding that many writers view family policy as "activities funded and sponsored by government that affect families directly or indirectly, intentionally or unintentionally, whether or not these policies have specific family objectives. . . . family policy is both a perspective and a set of activities" (p. 249). The sorts of activities to which she refers are family planning services, food stamps, income maintenance, foster care, adoption, homemaker services, child care, child development programs, family counseling and therapy, and employment services. This interpretation of family policy uniquely intersects the interests of various communities, including the scientific, political, public advocacy, and corporate communities.

Of the dozens of issues and topics we could explore within family policy, we wish to focus on some of the more prominent family policy issues affecting communication within families. These subject areas have invited a great deal of cultural conversation—sometimes resulting in very heated discussions. Our focus is on heterosexual unions and covenant marriages, same-sex unions and gay marriage, and a topic that affects both: child care.

Marital and Family Rights

Covenant Marriages An intimate and romantic bond between a man and a woman in the United States usually results in marriage. With that, this bond typically results in a couple conceiving one or more children. This pattern has described life in the United States since colonial times. What has evolved, however, are the specific customs and rituals surrounding marriage that continue to be redefined and re-created. As Paula Kamen (2003) suggests,

> *Today, even for the most traditional couples, marriage, like the American family, has changed. Just as young women have more choices about their sexual behavior and principles, they also have more freedom to tailor their family according to their own personal preferences. (p. 153)*

This freedom, though, is not without its costs, and marriage appears to be taking a hit. According to Frank Furstenberg (2003), "public concern over changes in the practice of marriage is approaching hysteria" (p. 171). Furstenberg argues that there has been a prodigious amount of research and popular press articles looking at the "marriage crisis" resulting in different interpretations of the future of marriage. Sharon Jayson (2010) observes that "marriage is increasingly optional and could be on its way to obsolescence" (p. A1). In Chapter 1, we addressed the notion that cohabitation is increasing and therefore the marriage rates seem to be declining. In fact, Haya El Nasser and Paul Overberg (2011) place the marriage "crisis" in a difficult financial picture for many families: "Marriage is losing ground to a grinding economic slowdown" (p. A1). The vulnerability of marriage (and spouses) has been discussed by Frank Fincham (2004). He observes that in marriage, we share our goals, aspirations, and values with our spouse. Although this is a lofty marital goal, it does, nonetheless, render the couple rather vulnerable. Fincham contends that when spouses reveal their private selves to each other, it can serve to both unite and divide them. The challenge is to avoid the inevitable tensions that accompany marriage and the decision to stay with someone for the rest of one's life. One way that society believes it is meeting those challenges is with the codification of a marital form: covenant marriages.

In the 1990s, state legislators around the country began experimenting with an alternative to domestic relations law. Covenant marriages were born out of what some felt was a need to control the spiraling divorce rate, increases in cohabitation rates, nonmarital fertility, and "alternative" family arrangements (Cade, 2010). Spearheaded mostly by Christian organizations, covenant marriages were seen as a way to reestablish a pro-family environment in a society that was moving away from a conventional view of family configuration. As we argued in Chapter 1, the nuclear family form has decreased significantly over the years, but considerable effort has been made to restore its prominence once again. Covenant marriages began because a number of legislatures and community leaders felt that the institution of marriage was in jeopardy, and the state needed to wrest control of a tradition that is held so dear by so many.

What is a covenant marriage? **Covenant marriages** are guided by the belief that people should not be easily granted a divorce. Therefore, more stringent terms for entering and leaving a marriage exist. Laura Sanchez and colleagues (2002) report that among these terms are (1) premarital counseling, (2) a signed affidavit agreeing that marriage is a lifetime commitment, (3) a complete disclosure of personal history that may adversely affect the relationship, (4) an agreement to a monitored separation prior to divorce, and (5) marital counseling before a divorce could be approved. Divorce may be granted when infidelity, physical or sexual abuse, a felony conviction, or long-standing abandonment can be authenticated. Covenant marriage status can be granted to currently married couples who wish to engage in this piece of marital and family legislation.

The effects of covenant marriages on family life and family communication have been debated. Ashton Applewhite (2003) believes that this state-sanctioned family policy will hurt children. She asserts that covenant marriages keep couples who argue together, resulting in a tense home environment for children. With recurring parental conflict, Applewhite contends, children will be exposed to difficult family circumstances that may leave children in intact families but in homes filled with "turmoil or icy silence" (p. 192). Further, Applewhite believes that the whole notion of a covenant marriage tends to marginalize both the roles of women and men. For instance, although some women's advocacy groups believe covenant marriages allow women more opportunity to negotiate financial settlements if divorce occurs, Applewhite notes that husbands may not enjoy the same legal recourse. Also, Applewhite suggests that because divorce is disproportionately initiated by women, covenant marriages may undercut a woman's need to extract herself from a difficult marital union.

John Crouch (2003) disagrees that covenant marriages would negatively affect family life and family communication. He advocates for this family legislation as one way to make sure that couples understand that marriage is a lifelong commitment and that this family arrangement will allow couples to "prudently invest themselves in the marriage" (p. 187). Agreeing and abiding by covenant principles, spouses will be more likely to restore self-control; feeling "victimized" will be difficult to claim in covenant marriages. Further, Crouch specifically identifies the premarital education as an opportunity for improved family communication. In addition to teaching couples how to "fight fair," these premarital sessions will include "interrogations and psychological profiling that will give the couple a lot more information on how they will get along, whether their priorities are compatible, and whether their plans are realistic" (p. 188).

In sum, states such as Louisiana, Arizona, and Arkansas have enacted covenant marriages to give married couples an alternative to the conventional marital arrangement. Although this legislative action has not spurred an outcry for additional marital arrangements, what covenant marriages did do was provide states the opportunity to offer their citizens marital and divorce reforms in an era of high divorce rates. Writers like David Jeremiah (2011) believe that "God designed marriage to be a permanent union" (p. 113). To this end, some contend that taking part in a covenant marriage makes spiritual sense. Although not everyone agrees with the principles guiding this family policy, the questions raised are important to consider in these changing times.

Same-Sex Unions and Gay Marriage   In Chapter 1, we noted the increasing rise of gay- and lesbian-headed households in the United States. Interestingly, despite this rise, the federal government does not recognize this family configuration in its policies. If anything, the government—under both Democratic and Republican presidents—has upheld the notion that gay and lesbian couples (and their families) should not be recognized with respect to legal rights. In other words, although gay marriage is legal in several states and the District of Columbia, the federal government does not recognize the legality of the union. Evan Wolfson (2011) decries what could be described as a double standard when discussing gay marriage and "straight" marriage: "In the United States, we don't have second-class

TABLE 4-3 Some Benefits of Marriage in the United States

Income tax deduction

Obligations of financial support for each other

Automatic inheritance rights when a spouse dies without a will

The right to sue for injuries to the other spouse

The right to private sexual activity together

The right to share joint parenting, custody, and visitation rights

The right to adopt

Employment-related benefits

Sick and bereavement leave

Survivor rights to insurance and retirement plans

Private company benefits (e.g., frequent flyer miles, family discounts)

The ability to have children without legal advice

The ability to live with a partner without suspicion

The ability to make medical decisions

The ability to have spouse visit in hospital intensive care unit

citizens and we shouldn't have second-class marriages" (*http://www.usnews. com/debate-club/should-gay-marriage-be-legal-nationwide/without-nation- wide-gay-marriage-us-government-discriminates*). Although she wrote this many years ago, April Martin's (1993) words seem to have merit to many: "Heterosexuals who are planning to become parents do not usually consult their lawyers first. They don't have to. The laws which protect the families they create are already in place" (p. 156).

A number of gay and lesbian individuals, couples, and organizations have recently urged states to allow gay men and lesbians to get married. Why? Four reasons stand out. First, there are the legal benefits of marriage (see Table 4-3). Second, publicly demonstrating an exclusive and committed bond that is only permitted to one group of individuals (heterosexuals) is unequal and unethical (Shelton, 2013). Third, marriage "normalizes" gay and lesbian couples (Savin-Williams & Esterberg, 2000). Finally, marriage for gay men and lesbians is the next step in the decades-long gay rights movement. As Victoria Clarke and Sara-Jane Finlay (2004) advance, in the 1970s, gay/ lesbian politics centered around respect and being left alone; today, the goal is inclusion and recognition.

The evolution of the quest for gay marriage appears to have begun in Hawaii when, in 1996, the Hawaii Supreme Court stated that the state's refusal to grant marriage licenses to three same-sex couples violated the sex discrimi- nation clause in the state's constitution. The court stated that Hawaiian offi- cials did not prove a "compelling government interest" in barring same-sex marriage. Hawaiians later voted to amend the state's constitution and effectively made the court's decision null and void. Hawaii's dialogue and debate on this issue prompted state and national legislators to pass the Defense of Marriage Act (DOMA). In 1996, President Clinton signed the act into law. DOMA prevents same-sex marriages from becoming legal under federal law. Over 35 states currently have statutory defense of marriage acts.

Hawaii, however, was just the beginning. Two landmark decisions by the courts put gay and lesbian unions back on the agenda. First, in 2000, the Vermont Supreme Court ordered the state to extend all the rights and privileges it extends to married men and women to gay and lesbian couples. Although the state was not required to use the word *marriage* and offered "domestic partnership" as an alternative, the effects of the ruling could not be ignored. Eventually the state settled on *civil unions* for same-sex recognition. Although Vermont's decision to allow civil unions was deemed difficult and divisive, it was the 2004 decision by the Massachusetts Supreme Judicial Court that has attracted the most attention and seems to have caused the biggest cultural reverberation. The court decided that there was no compelling reason to deny gay men and lesbians the right to marry. But, unlike Vermont, the court did not allow the state to use any alternative language such as "civil unions" or "domestic partnerships" to describe the relationships. Soon after its decision, over 1,500 same-sex couples applied for marriage licenses (Bayles, 2004). Further, considering that the court's action initially prompted great public outcry (and even a proposal to remove four of the justices who supported the decision), Fred Bayles notes that the furor calmed a bit: "What generated front-page headlines has slipped to wedding announcements in the back of newspapers" (p. 2D).

Since the 2004 decision in Massachusetts, as we noted earlier, several states and Washington, D.C. have enacted laws allowing gay men and lesbians to marry. There are some, like David Frum, former special assistant to President George W. Bush, who believes that "the case against same-sex marriage has been tested against reality. The case has not passed its test" (*http://www.cnn.com/2011/OPINION/06/27/frum.gay.marriage/index.html*). And, with large (e.g., New York) and small (e.g., Iowa) states legalizing gay marriage, with the majority of Americans supporting laws allowing gay men

Student Perspective: Robbie

My cousin is gay, and we all pretty much don't care about that. What really bothered my family, though, was that he and his partner wanted to get married and wanted all of us to come to the ceremony. It was like he didn't know that we don't think they should get married. I'm not prejudiced, but I think there should be a limit to how much gays and lesbians get. I'm married and it doesn't make sense to me.

and lesbians to marry (*http://www.gallup.com/poll/147622/first-time-majority-americans-favor-legal-gay-marriage.aspx*), and with television programming featuring more gay and lesbian characters (Gilbert, 2011), we could assume inevitable universal acceptance of the right for gay marriage. Yet, there continue to be congressional efforts (called the Marriage Protection Amendment) to write into the U.S. Constitution a definition of marriage as a union between a woman and a man. While the House of Representatives and the Senate have, upon several opportunities, failed to secure sufficient votes for passage, this issue is far from over. The words of Margaret Somerville (2011) resonate with millions of people: "Society should not be complicit in intentionally depriving children of a mother and a father. We must consider the ethics of deliberately creating any situation that is otherwise" (*http://www.mercatornet.com/articles/view/the_case_against_same-sex_marriage*).

Child Concerns and Child Care

On Saturday, June 1, 1996, over 200,000 people gathered for the rally called Stand for Children. Robert Pear (1996) reported that the event was supported by very diverse groups, including the Girl Scouts, Catholic Charities, and the U.S. Conference of Mayors, as well as numerous churches and schools. The overarching purpose of such a gathering was to refocus the nation's attention on its children. Organizers were concerned that with the proposed congressional cuts to children's services and programs, the United States was exacerbating the social and economic worries associated with being or raising a child. Further, many of those in the most difficult situations are members of racial and ethnic minority groups whose children will account for 50 percent of the child population by 2030 (*www.childrensdefense.org*).

Although the rally for children occurred a number of years ago, many organizations such as the Children's Defense Fund continue to believe that children across the United States warrant special attention. For instance, in 2011, the Fund reported the following about the state of children today (*www.childrensdefense.org/data/keyfacts.asp*):

- There are over 16 million children living in poverty, accounting for 22 percent of the total number of children in the United States.
- Every 32 seconds a baby is born into poverty, 2,692 each day.
- There are more poor Hispanic children than any other minority group. Black and Hispanic children are more than twice as likely to be poor as White, non-Hispanic children.
- One in 7 children never graduates from high school.
- Children in female-headed families are four times as likely to be poor as children in married-couple families.
- Nearly 70 percent of poor children live in families where at least one family member works.

These numbers point to the fact that millions of children are being cared for by relatives, nannies or babysitters, before/after school personnel, and child care center employees. These individuals can both implicitly and explicitly influence the child and his or her communication.

One reason child care is so important in family communication is that governmental involvement in family policy addressing child care has come under scrutiny. Lillian Rubin (1994), in *Families on the Fault Line,* notes that "decent affordable child care is scandalously scarce, with no government intervention in sight for this crucial need. In poor and working-class families, therefore, child care often is uncertain and inadequate" (p. 244). Mona Harrington (2003) candidly concludes: "Our family care system is collapsing . . . we need new support systems to enable families to provide good care for their members" (p. 156). Yet, to some extent, the government does intervene. Three ways seem evident: (1) subsidies through block grants to states for child care, (2) a tax credit to parents who spend money on child care, and (3) support for employers of parents who provide on-site child care. Perhaps the latter—corporate support—explains why companies such as Pfizer, AOL, Bank of America, Kraft Foods, Ford Motor Company, Procter & Gamble, and American Express have been named among the 100-best family-friendly companies in the United States by *Working Mother* magazine (*www.workingmothers.com/node/116542/list*). Among other family-friendly policies, the magazine notes that these companies provide significant support for child care in the form of "flex time" (work schedule responsive to family needs) and on-site child care facilities.

As we addressed earlier, the cost of child care can be exorbitant for millions of families. The U.S. Census Bureau (*www.census.gov/newsroom/pdf/cspan_childcare_slides.pdf*) indicates that on average, for some families between 6 and 9 percent of monthly income is spent on child care. In some low-income families, that number can grow to more than 25 percent (Harrington, 2003). The number of dollars that families dedicate to child care often competes with a mortgage payment as the single biggest monthly family expenditure. Additional problems compound child care issues. These include a high turnover in child care personnel, low wages provided to child care workers, the lack of quality child care centers, dramatic variations across states in regulating child care, and expenses associated with finding a licensed child care facility (Bloch, 2012).

Child Care and Family Communication   The future of child care is in the hands of the culture it serves. That is, because child care is a pressing legal, political, and family issue, our society will have to continue to unravel its complexity. And, as we learn to better understand child care, we will consequently better understand family communication patterns and practices. Communication functions significantly in child care and in child care practices (Socha & Yingling, 2010). To illustrate the intersection of child care and family communication, we address how child care affects the communication in single-parent families and dual-income families.

Many families struggle with child care demands and must adjust to difficult challenges. Perhaps the stress of child care is most evident in single-parent families, with mothers in charge. Specifically, working mothers are generally responsible for decisions regarding when a child needs child care, the availability of quality child care, and cost considerations (Johnson, 2000). Indeed, the cost of child care is a significant factor for single mothers as they determine their child care needs. We are reminded of the comments of Beverly, a 30-year-old mother of three children: "We barely make it now; if I stop working, we'd be in real trouble" (cited in Rubin, 1994, p. 93). Families such as Beverly's must juggle the communication stresses of multiple roles—financial provider, disciplinarian, medical attendant, and trusted guardian—often without a large network of support. As we note in Chapter 7, parents need some social support, such as a network of relatives, to help manage the challenges in family life. For single parents, relatives may serve as child care providers. Although we have tens of thousands of child care facilities, relatives frequently become primary child care providers for family members. In fact, the Urban Institute (*www.urban.org*) notes that between 7 and 14 percent of child care providers are relatives. Such support, no doubt, helps to reduce the negative effect in families, which, in turn, assists parents such as Beverly in handling her child care challenges.

In addition to single-parent families, those families with dual incomes also are influenced by decisions related to child care. Ted Huston and Erin Kramer Holmes (2004) specifically address the division of labor associated between working fathers and mothers. In their research, they found that wives preferred their husbands to become more involved in child care but the husbands were hesitant to do so since women "often gain considerable satisfaction from doing the job themselves" (p. 122). Huston and Holmes posit that many fathers are reluctant to help in child care tasks, and when they do get involved, they are likely to complain, criticize, and become less in love with their wives. In fact, Huston and Holmes argue that the more reluctantly husbands are drawn into child care duties, the more negatively they evaluate their marriages. This may be partially explained by looking at the results of a study by Francine Deutsch (1999). In an ethnographic study of shared parenting, she discovered that when a husband did get involved with such tasks as diapering a child, his wife would redo what he had just completed. Interestingly, although many wives prefer that their husbands be part of child care responsibilities, this involvement may result in more marital tension. As we learn in Chapter 7, power is often part of decision making in families. Therefore, in order to work through any conflict pertaining to differing perceptions of child care responsibilities, husbands and wives will have to negotiate their decisions.

Future Needs in Child Care Governmental policy associated with children and child care will continue to elicit conversation. Once again, as with

```
┌──────────────────────────────────────────────────────────────────┐
│              ⁓ⱮⱮ⁓ POPULAR PRESS PERSPECTIVES ⁓ⱮⱮ⁓                  │
│                                                                    │
│  The importance of the intersection between families, communication,│
│  and the school is underscored in an essay appearing on the website of│
│  the Public Broadcasting System. Written from the perspective of a │
│  teacher, the essayist articulates the critical nature of keeping the lines│
│  of communication open between schools and families. Communication │
│  skills, including informal chats during drop-off and pick-up of children,│
│  active listening skills (e.g., not being distracted by the telephone or text│
│  messages), and group parent meetings are identified as important to│
│  facilitate the communication process. The author continues and notes│
│  that dealing with anger and crises, in particular, needs special attention.│
│  Taking a deep breath, paraphrasing, and owning one's anger are crucial│
│  to making sure that anger is kept to a minimum in the family-school│
│  relationship. With respect to difficult and challenging family crises, the│
│  author posits that many conflict-resolution skills can be adapted.│
│  ─────────────────────────────────────────────────────────────    │
│  Establishing strong family-school communication. Retrieved from *http://www*│
│  *.pbs.org/wholechild/providers/f-s.html*                          │
└──────────────────────────────────────────────────────────────────┘
```

marital and family rights for gay men and lesbians, this topic elicits potent response from all sides of the policy spectrum. Some child care advocates believe our country has done little to promote quality child care while others believe that such expansion will result in a federal budget out of control. Throughout these discussions are the tens of millions of families who struggle with the availability, costs, and accessibility of care. As we learned earlier, their dialogues within the family system are frequently fraught with tension, conflict, and the need to navigate tough discussions.

Student Perspective: Meg

I think it would be harmful to family communication if the family lived on welfare for a long period of time. How could the family have any self-respect if they weren't able to get off welfare at some time and go to work? If they all felt bad about themselves, they would probably get in fights with each other and take it out on one another.

It's clear the United States does not have a coherent policy regarding child care. And despite the conflicting views on its need, all signs point to the difficulty of establishing one. Stephan Klasen and Hermann Waibel (2013) believe that child care problems become more poignant when we look at the numbers of homeless families and children. Society is replete with examples of the frustrating loop of homelessness and child care. A homeless mother, for example, wishes to find a job. Yet, because she has young children, she must also simultaneously find child care. Because most homeless facilities do not care for children, she searches for help. Yet, this search prevents her from looking for a job, and if/when she gets a job, she has to spend most of her money on paying for child care. To address this cycle of despair, Christopher Jencks (1994) states that we must remain focused on the children and their well-being. He cautions that "our dilemma, both as individuals and as a society, is to reconcile the claims of compassion and prudence" (p. 122).

SUMMARY

This chapter has introduced you to three significant aspects of a family's external context: television, women's and men's movements, and government policy. Through an examination of situation comedies since the 1950s, we have provided a glimpse of how families have been portrayed by the television industry and how these portrayals relate to interaction in the family.

Next, although they can differ greatly in their goals and intended responses, we have illustrated how women's and men's movements have been and continue to be influential in family life. Women's movements have traditionally focused on the role of women in the family, their needs, experiences, and aspirations. Men's movements can vary greatly, with one movement arguing for a redistribution of power in the family to redress the inequities women have suffered, while other movements want to reestablish men's centrality in families.

Finally, we presented governmental and legal issues related to families, namely, marital and family rights, indicating the difference in rights guaranteed to heterosexual and homosexual couples. We also examined the challenges associated with child care and how the government currently addresses this problem and what we can expect in the future.

The communication in families can be influenced by several aspects of our larger culture. These external influences continue to shape the way families are heard and treated and how they interact.

KEY TERMS

covenant marriages

family policy

feminism

men's movements

pro-feminist approach

pro-masculinist approach

Promise Keepers

rhetorical movements

social movements

women's movements

QUESTIONS FOR REFLECTION

1. Identify two current television sitcoms that highlight two different types of family communication patterns. Explain by referring to specific episodes.

2. Do you believe that television will become more or less influential in the future? Explain your answer.

3. Two social movements are discussed in this chapter. Can you imagine a future social movement that could relate to family interaction? For example, how might gay and lesbian rights or environmental activism affect family communication?

4. Some people believe that our government should stay out of families. Do you agree? In all cases? In none? In some? Which areas warrant government involvement?

5. Should the courts decide whether children can live apart from their biological parents? Should we have laws relating to how families conduct their private lives (how many children to have, how a pregnant woman should behave vis-à-vis drinking and smoking, and so on)? Explain your point of view.

6. What impact do you think feminism has had on interaction within the family? What impact have men's movements had? Why do you think this?

7. Do movements such as those represented by Promise Keepers do more to unite or to divide families? Explain your response and provide examples to justify your thoughts.

8. Explain what the following statement means: "Caught in the crossfire of child care issues is the child." Based on information in this chapter, what does it mean to you? Do you agree or disagree with the claim? What examples can you provide to support your views?

9. Suppose you have been asked to chair an advisory group in your community that looks at ways to talk about family life on television. How would you go about coordinating these discussions and what guidelines would you follow?

10. The breast cancer movement is identified as an example of a rhetorical movement aimed at women's health. What benefits exist when people talk about social movements pertaining to health? What risks exist? Use examples in your response.

Chapter

5

COMMUNICATING INTIMACY

THE MIRANDE FAMILY

José Mirande, 43, and his wife, Judy Perlman Mirande, 40, are co-owners of a popular restaurant outside of Washington, DC. They have one son, Adam, who is attending college in the Midwest. Judy is upset that José won't confide in her about his financial concerns. The restaurant business is demanding, and often the couple work 12-hour days, 6 days a week. They are usually quite busy on their one day off as well, because that is when they visit other restaurants in the area, to see their friends and check out the competition. Judy knows that José is worried about continuing to work so hard as they get older and about continuing to bring in enough money to support their current, rather lavish lifestyle, yet he won't say much when she asks him to talk to her about it.

THE MARKS FAMILY

Elizabeth Marks loves her children more than anything else in her life. She is so proud of all four of them, and she enjoys spending time with them all together as well as individually. Now that Rebecca, Melanie, Paul, and Jordy are all in their 20s, Elizabeth is enjoying them on a whole different level. She finds their adult interests and pursuits fascinating, so she is looking forward to lunch with her youngest son, Jordy. When Jordy arrives at the restaurant, he looks harried, and Elizabeth wonders if there is a problem that has prompted his asking her to lunch. She feels vaguely uneasy as she waves him over to her table. Jordy hurries over and sits down. After eating, Jordy clears his throat and says, "Mom, I have something to tell you. I am not sure how you'll take this, but I love you and I want you to really know me and be a part of my whole life." Elizabeth tries to smile in a supportive fashion, but she feels so unsure. What is coming? Jordy leans forward and puts his hand over his mother's on the table. "Mom, I am gay," he says in a low voice.

THE WALTER FAMILY

Max Walter playfully pushes his younger sister, Sabrina, as they work together to finish their Saturday chores. "Hey, Bree, get going with that dust rag," Max jokes. Max, 15, and Sabrina, 13, have to vacuum and dust the living room and pick up their own bedrooms every Saturday before they can go out and follow their own pursuits. Sabrina laughs at Max and throws the dust rag at him. The two hurry to get the living room in good enough shape to pass their mother's weekly inspection. Just as they are about to finish, their younger brother, Joe, comes in with a can of Coke. Sabrina runs to slide a coaster under the can so Joe won't mess up their clean surfaces. Joe looks at Sabrina and laughs, "You are really becoming crazy clean, Sis." Sabrina replies that Joe would be a cleaning freak too if he couldn't go out until their mom thought everything in the living room and bedrooms was perfect. Max and Sabrina exchange smiles and knowing glances, aware that next year when Joe turns 10, he will be on cleaning detail, too. As they smile at each other, they each feel grateful to have the other to share the work. Even though they occasionally get on each other's nerves, they also know it is nice to be able to depend on each other. As if they had read each other's minds, they high-five each other and yell for their mother to come in and perform the inspection.

When we think abstractly about the subject of this chapter—intimacy— we may think in terms of big events. Serious declarations of love and commitment probably characterize our impression of intimacy. Yet, as the Mirande, Marks, and Walter family vignettes illustrate, families are routinely engaged in activities that intensify their sense of closeness and intimacy with one another, co-creating their sense of each other and their family as a whole. For example, the simple conversation between Max and Sabrina Walter brings them closer together in their mutual appreciation and their recognition of their shared circumstances.

Scholars (e.g., Burns & Pearson, 2011) have become interested in **everyday talk** in families and define it as habitual, mundane communication of various types, including joking around, gossiping, and recapping the events of the day. Some researchers (e.g., Duck, Rutt, Hurst, & Strejc, 1991; Schrodt, Soliz, & Braithwaite, 2008) argue that this type of communication affects the health of relationships in families and other interpersonal contexts. These researchers note that it is important to have simple, everyday encounters like the ones we have profiled in our opening vignettes in order to have family intimacy and satisfaction. Michael Burns and Judy Pearson (2011) found, for instance, that participating in everyday talk increases family satisfaction and intimacy for many families.

This focus on routine, mundane communication and intimacy correlates well with Oliphant and Kuczynski's (2011) observation that it isn't strictly the content of people's communication that makes it intimate, "but rather that individuals perceive that they are participating in the process of creating shared meaning about the interaction. Conversely, an interaction may be considered nonintimate when individuals perceive that they or the other person are refusing to participate in shared meaning or are imposing, misunderstanding, or rejecting shared meaning" (p. 1106). As you can see, Oliphant and Kuczynski's comments are congruent with our theoretical framework of social construction.

It is also the case that there's a difference between intimate communication and intimate relationships. For instance, Joe and Theresa are married, so by definition they have an intimate relationship. Yet, during an average day, the way they talk to one another probably includes a lot of nonintimate conversation. They no doubt spend some time planning who will take their daughter,

Linda, to nursery school and what to buy at the grocery store. They might also gossip about how they heard yelling coming from their next-door neighbor's house last night. They may spend some time telling each other what happened at their respective workplaces, perhaps complaining about coworkers who aren't keeping up their share of the workload. Yet, in addition to everyday talk, people in families also engage in a variety of behaviors that both develop and reflect that their relationship is different from a less intimate one. Family members do declare their love, engage in fierce conflict, and offer self-disclosures, which distinguish their communication from less intimate relationships.

Further, as Sean Horan and Melanie Booth-Butterfield (2011) point out, we can (and should) distinguish between feeling affection and communicating affection. They state that "affectionate communication should represent the outward expression of one's internal feelings of affection, yet these two experiences may not always be congruent" (p. 79). For instance, Wes may have warm, fond feelings toward his brother, Joel, but not express them (and perhaps Wes even tells Joel he hates him or teases him mercilessly). Or, conversely, Beth may be feeling frustrated with her husband but choose not to express it because she doesn't want to get into an involved discussion. Beth might simply tell her husband, "Good night, I love you," and not share her frustration.

You are probably getting the idea from this brief introduction that intimacy is a more complicated topic than it first appears. But one thing most people agree upon is that intimacy is revealed, developed, and maintained in a relationship through verbal and nonverbal communication behaviors (Horan & Booth-Butterfield, 2010). To clarify how intimacy and family communication relate, we will do the following in this chapter: (1) offer an interpretation of the terms *closeness* and *intimacy*, (2) discuss how culture affects intimacy and intimate communication within families, (3) review theoretical perspectives on intimacy and closeness, and (4) examine communication behaviors used to reflect and create intimacy and closeness within a family.

INTERPRETING INTIMACY AND CLOSENESS

Although there are some conceptual differences, for our purposes we refer to *closeness* and *intimacy* as synonymous. A close relationship, then, is characterized by intimate behaviors (affectionate talk, for instance) and intimate experience (or the positive feelings families derive from engaging in intimate behaviors) (Prager, 1995). Researchers expect that some closeness characterizes the family, yet the concept itself is difficult to define, and conceptualizations of intimacy vary (Harvey & Weber, 2002; Patrick, Sells, Gordano, & Tollerud, 2007; Reis & Patrick, 1996).

Most scholars would agree, however, that closeness is manifested in a high level of mutual knowledge and influence, a sense of the dependability of the relationship (Floyd, 1996), mutual devotion, sharing, commitment

(Spooner, 1982), a long-term timeline, providing both history and expectations of a future (Oliphant & Kuczynski, 2011), and strong desires to interact with each other (Sternberg, 1986). These qualities are exemplified in the following definition:

> *Intimacy is an interpersonal process within which two [or more in the case of a family] interaction partners experience and express feelings, communicate verbally and nonverbally, satisfy social motives, augment or reduce social fears, talk and learn about themselves and their unique characteristics, and become "close" (psychologically and often physically: touching, using intimate names and tones of voice . . .). (Reis & Shaver, 1988, p. 387)*

This definition highlights concepts that are compatible with our approach in this text: the notion of process and the centrality of communication. Closeness represents the family members' acceptance of their interdependence—their sense of their history together and their confidence in their shared future. Distance is not simply the opposite of each of the characteristics of closeness. Rather, distance involves a reluctance to acknowledge mutual needs and interdependence.

Family intimacy involves a sense of commitment and devotion (Weigel, 2003; Weigel & Ballard-Reisch, 2008). Commitment implies a focused energy directed toward maintaining and enriching the family: "Commitment represents extended time orientation, and highly committed individuals should accordingly behave in ways that are consistent with this perspective, acting to ensure that their relationships endure and are healthy" (Rusbult, Drigotas, & Verette, 1994, p. 123). Devotion rests on the development of attachment and dedication to the family. However, as we have indicated previously, simply because the family comprises intimate *relationships* does not mean that all the members feel devotion and intimacy, nor do they always express these things to one another. And sometimes, the family is the setting for violence and strong negative emotions (Montalbano-Phelps, 2003). As Sally Planalp (1999) points out, close relationships by definition require the participants to coordinate many important issues over a long period of time: "Relationships that facilitate or interfere with so many important, long-lasting concerns are capable of evoking powerful emotions and are sources of our greatest delights and distresses" (Planalp, 1999, p. 25).

Andrea Joseph and Tamara D. Afifi (2010) explore how the family functions to provide both stress and relief from stress in their study focused on military families. Joseph and Afifi note that "during a service member's deployment, couples must maintain their relationship while coping with distinct stressful circumstances" (p. 413). However, they also found that one way for wives to reduce the stress they experienced while their husbands were deployed was to engage in intimate communication such as self-disclosure, and allow their husbands to help them cope.

CULTURE AND INTIMACY

In addition to the overall complexity of defining intimacy and intimate communication, our task is further complicated by a variety of factors that affect the definition of intimacy. In this section, we will discuss how culture (both national culture and co-culture) impacts expectations for and expressions of intimacy and closeness.

You may remember in Chapter 1, when we defined family, we did not specify that affection or love was a defining characteristic. Yet, when most people in the United States think about the family, they think of love and similar emotions. When family communication students are asked to devise their own definition of the family, they generally come up with a definition that includes a sense of affection among the members. The notion that love is a critical part of the definition of family was articulated as early as 1913, when Bronislaw Malinowski wrote an influential book called *The Family Among the Australian Aborigines*. Malinowski, an anthropologist, argued that the family was a universal human institution, functioning across time and culture to nurture children. In making this argument, Malinowski described three features of family life that he believed stemmed from the family's nurturing function. One of these features, germane to our discussion here, was a particular set of emotions—family love and closeness.

Malinowski argued that, through the process of child rearing, both parents and children develop a sense of closeness and love for one another. This emotional bond serves as a kind of reward for the parents for all the time and energy invested in nurturing children. Further, Malinowski believed that the long, intimate nature of child rearing fostered close emotional ties between the spouses as well. More recently, many researchers have concurred with this notion (see for example, Foley & Duck, 2006; Kuczynski, 2003).

The expectation for loving closeness to be a hallmark of families is pervasive, but, as we know, it is not always found in practice. Some families are very estranged, at least some of the time. Further, the expectation of love and affection is not necessarily universal, in the way Malinowski asserted. Nicholas Kristof (1996) reported in the *New York Times* on Japanese marriages, noting their stability.

Student Perspective: Chloe

I understand what we said in class about how different cultures see family closeness differently. And I know there are a lot of families right here that beat their kids and do terrible things. The newspaper has horror stories in it every day about kids killing their parents and parents abusing their kids in awful ways. I know all that, but I cannot get it out of my mind that in order for a family to really be a family, they should all love each other. My own family is very loving and affectionate. We really like to be with each other. I guess that's how I think every family should be.

‿ⅉⅉⅉ⟋ **POPULAR PRESS PERSPECTIVES** ‿ⅉⅉⅉ⟋

The *New York Times* online examined intimacy between siblings in an article by Alexis Clark called "Separated in Foster Care, Siblings Reunite in Camp." Clark tells about siblings who do not live together because they have been placed in different foster homes, and who are able to spend some quality time together at Camp to Belong. Camp to Belong was founded by Lynn Price in 1995 in Las Vegas. Ms. Price was herself a former foster child, and she was separated from her sister while they were growing up. Ms. Price is quoted about how much that separation affected her, and how she felt she missed out on experiences and interactions with her sister that would have built intimacy.

She says, "I realized that my sister and I had no memories of when we were kids. There were no memories of birthday parties, sharing clothes, or helping each other with homework, or talking about boys. I thought about the kids who will miss out on something that is so critical to their growth and feelings of unconditional love."

One of the New York campers, Robin, age 11, said that a highlight of camp was swimming with his brother, Alex. They have been separated for a year, but see each other every other weekend. Then Alex observes that these visits are not for sure, mentioning that sometimes they are cancelled.

The New York camp is sponsored by the Parsons Child and Family Center in Albany where Joanne Trinkle is the director of special projects. Trinkle was motivated to start a Camp to Belong in New York after meeting Lynn Price at a conference. Ms. Trinkle commented that after their meeting, "Her camp just stayed in the back of my mind. For me, my relationship with my brothers is the cornerstone of my life. So, to have the opportunity to bring siblings together to do things that are normal and that are fun was really important to me."

Alexis Clark, "Separated in foster care, siblings reunite in camp." *New York Times* (online). September 16, 2011. Retrieved October 1, 2011.

Kristof comments, "It does not seem that Japanese families survive because husbands and wives love each other more than American couples, but rather because they perhaps love each other less" (p. 12). He concludes that the secret to staying married in Japan has little to do with love. Instead, the secret of long marriages is rooted in low expectations for the relationship (so there is no disappointment), patience, and the shame of getting divorced, which affects your family, your community, and your work life. Stephanie Coontz (2003) concurs, stating that the expectation for love in North American marriages is not shared in many Asian cultures. Further, in some cultures and co-cultures,

"I love you" is not spoken. It is either implied or thought to be unnecessary (Coontz, 2003). These cultures, primarily Asian, place value on the unstated, or what members of the culture are expected to just understand through contextual clues (Matsunaga & Imahori, 2009).

Most of the research conducted on family communication that is published in the United States examines U.S. families (Turner & West, 2011). This is unfortunate because culture pervades all aspects of family life, especially with regard to what family members believe is the ideal or "right" way to communicate with one another (Matsunaga & Imahori, 2009). Of course, there is a great deal of variability within cultures, especially those that are diverse like the United States, and it is important to remember that research findings focusing on one culture, like the Asian culture for instance, may ignore differences among the variety of Asian cultures like Chinese, Japanese, or Filipino families. However, it is useful to acknowledge the impact that cultural teaching makes on family communication practices.

For example, Masaki Matsunaga and Tadasu Todd Imahori (2009) found that Japanese and U.S. family members differed in their perceptions of ideal ways of communicating based on differences in individualism and collectivism in the cultures. Sachiyo Shearman and Rebecca Dumlao (2008) assert that Japanese culture puts a high premium on harmony, and young adults in Japan are expected to develop harmonious relations with parents. On the contrary, U.S. culture prizes autonomy, and young adults are expected to become independent and separate from parents as they mature. Shearman and Dumlao note that these differing cultural values have an impact on the way family relationships are communicated and the way conflict is conducted in the family.

Robin Clair (2011) cites Stella Ting-Toomey who described how marriages should be maintained in Chinese culture. Clair notes that Ting-Toomey said, "The primary defining theme of a good relationship is being able to anticipate your partner's need and fulfill it. And so [Ting-Toomey's] mother often set a bowl of steaming noodles in front of her father before he ever mentioned being hungry and he in turn often brought a sweater to his wife in the cool evening hours before she ever shivered" (p. 58). In the United States, most middle-class European Americans would advocate open communication in marriage and suggest that married couples cannot read each others' minds as Ting-Toomey's example advocates.

Some research focuses on how co-cultures within the United States might differ with respect to family communication issues. Lawrence Kurdek (2008) asserts that Black and white individuals experience marriage differently, with Blacks having a more negative impression of marriage, a higher divorce rate, and a lower overall marriage rate. Kurdek suggests that this may be due to the fact that "they are socialized in different social, cultural, and historical contexts that influence how marriage and family life are viewed" (p. 52). In the context of mothers and daughters, Barbara Penington (2004) found that African American and European American mother–daughter pairs thought about closeness and distance differently. African American mothers conceive of closeness more in terms of being "best friends" with their daughters while European American mothers expressed that less so. At the same time, African American moms are more authoritarian and insistent on their daughters developing survival skills and self-esteem, which would move them toward autonomy.

Culture also affects emotional expressiveness. As John Gottman, Lynn Katz, and Carole Hooven (1997) observe, cultures vary a great deal in the value they place on emotional expression compared with emotional inhibition or control. Masako Ishii-Kuntz (1997) asserts that Chinese American families express intimacy less frequently than do European American families. Affection is not displayed openly in Chinese American families because this behavior is considered childish and in bad taste. Thus, Chinese American parents tend to teach their children to inhibit and control such expressions. Further, Coontz (2003) notes that social class also makes a difference in expressing intimacy, as working-class families are generally found to be less emotionally expressive than middle- and upper-class families.

EXPLAINING INTIMACY IN FAMILY COMMUNICATION

Many theories attempt to explain the relationship between family communication and closeness. In the following pages we will review how one theory we discussed in Chapter 2, dialectics, explains intimacy in the family. We'll also present two new frameworks, attachment theory and social exchange, to help us understand this topic. Finally, we introduce a model, the Circumplex Model, which illustrates intimacy in the family.

The Dialectic Approach

As we discussed in Chapter 2, we take a dialectic approach to the study of family communication. Further, as our opening vignettes illustrate, the same communication encounter simultaneously represents messages of *both* interdependence *and* differentiation. For example, José Mirande's silence about his business worries may express both his desire for closeness with his wife, Judy (as in protecting her from problems), and a desire for independence from her (as in keeping to himself some aspects of their life as business and family partners).

Leslie Baxter (2011) says that people in relationships are always making meanings that "are wrought from the struggle of competing, often contradictory, discourses" (p. 2). She has identified one of the most salient struggles in relationships as being between autonomy (an individual's need to be independent) and connection (the need to feel connected in a relationship). The critical tasks for family members concern dealing with both their need for closeness and their desire for independence. As Jordy Marks from our opening vignette looks at his mother and waits for her response, he thinks that he told her about himself for two reasons. First, he loves her and wants to be connected to her. Second, he wants to be free to recognize his individuality and have his mother acknowledge it as well. In a dialectic sense, Jordy's disclosure accomplishes both a bonding function ("I'm telling you something important about myself") and a differentiating function ("Telling you this shows how different we are").

According to a dialectic perspective, closeness and distance are opposing tensions that construct all family relationships. Yet, although they are in opposition to each other, they work together in creating a relational culture (Wood, 1982). By this we mean that developing a close relationship is not like moving along a continuum, whereby each act of closeness banishes distance. The two are ever present in family relationships (Segrin & Flora, 2005). Closeness focuses on what the family members share; distance differentiates among family members.

For example, when José and Judy Mirande, from our scenario at the beginning of this chapter, respond to their money worries and busy lifestyles differently, they are emphasizing some of their independence—that is, they handle problems differently. When Max and Sabrina Walter, from one of the other vignettes that began this chapter, exchange knowing looks and smiles as they watch their younger brother, they highlight their similarities and interdependence. When Elizabeth hears her son's disclosure, she experiences a mix of many feelings, but chief among them is her sense of closeness to and distance from Jordy at that moment.

Negotiating the tensions between closeness and distance varies across families. This negotiation is affected by several factors within the family. For instance, certain relational events may cause a family to reflect differently on their constructions of closeness and distance. Glen Stamp (1994) suggests that the birth of the first child is such an event. The addition of a child to the family system usually means that the couple draws closer in some ways. First, the couple may feel closer because a new life has entered the world. Second, the couple needs to work closely together to coordinate schedules and caretaking. In this second aspect, the couple is interdependent, yet it may not be a rewarding closeness. Couples may feel trapped and begin to remember fondly what it felt like to be partners before the birth of the child. They may contrast these two senses of interdependence in such a way that distance is actually created between them. It is common for families with infants and families with many children to feel that the quality of their lives suffers from all the day-to-day coordination they must arrange. Thus, closeness is featured, but it is also redefined into something less positive than the closeness of a couple without children.

Further, differing circumstances may cause differences in conceptualizing closeness and distance. For example, couples in which both members have careers may frame the dialectic between closeness and distance differently than couples in which one partner stays at home while the other works outside the home (Medved & Kirby, 2005). Couples who commute long distances for work and families who maintain two residences for professional reasons may also construe the dialectic differently (Govaerts & Dixon, 1988).

The dialectic approach is fairly easy to talk about, but it is also somewhat difficult to conceptualize because we are used to thinking about family closeness in either monologic or dualistic terms (Baxter & Montgomery, 1996).

Monologic Thinking **Monologic thinking** about closeness suggests that families will develop closeness as they have mutual influence over one another, share values and beliefs, and like and love one another. Baxter and Montgomery (1996) point out that this perspective views closeness as occurring along a linear continuum. Thus, the more influence, sharing, and positive emotions that exist, the more closeness in the family; whereas independence, difference, and negative emotions act as threats to closeness, making the family more distant. This approach privileges harmony and positive affect in family life.

Student Perspective: Tavo

That monologic thinking is kind of hard to shake. I am used to evaluating how close families are, somehow. My mother is always saying how loving our family is compared to my cousin's family. Puerto Ricans put a big value on close families, and it's kind of a bad thing that my cousin's family doesn't hang out together. Also my cousin talks back to my aunt and uncle sometimes, and that is a big negative. My mom always says how nice it is how we kids are so loving, polite, and respectful, not like my cousin Jorgé.

Monologic thinking is prevalent in our language when we speak metaphorically about relationships that "get close" or "grow apart." When we think monologically about closeness in families, we have a tendency to evaluate families on the closeness scale—the Walters may seem like a closer family than the Mirandes, for instance.

Dualistic Thinking **Dualistic thinking** about closeness, unlike the monologic approach, recognizes the importance of negative emotions and differentiation in close relationships. Dualism does not espouse the linear thinking that posits a move toward closeness or a move away from it. From this perspective, differentiation and separateness are seen as healthy aspects of close relationships, aspects that keep them from becoming too enmeshed. This type of thinking is related to the Circumplex Model (Olson, Sprenkle, & Russell, 1979) that we will discuss later in the chapter.

Further, some research suggests that negative interactions in the family can serve positive functions for relationships. The willingness to voice negative feelings is seen as a vote of confidence that the relationship is strong enough to withstand difference (Metts & Bowers, 1994). John Gottman (1994a) points out another benefit of anger and negative emotions between spouses. On the basis of some longitudinal research on marriage, Gottman argues that anger may cause short-term "misery" for a couple, but in the long run it may actually improve the relationship.

Other research that supports the dualistic approach acknowledges that people vary in their desire and need for closeness. Much research examining gender in relationships is rooted in the dualistic perspective (Gilligan & Machoian, 2002). This research advances the notion that men are

Student Perspective: Loreli

When I think about my parents, I do see that women and men are opposites or, at least, different. My mom is so concerned about all us kids and the family sticking together. She puts a high value on togetherness. When she talks to us, she's always asking how our relationships with our friends are, and she's checking up to see if we've called our grandparents lately—all those relationship concerns. When Dad talks to me, he wants to know things like how I am managing my money, how I am doing in school, and what I am planning for a summer job. He focuses on me as a separate individual, whereas my mom sees me connected to all sorts of relationships.

socialized to value autonomy over connection, whereas women receive just the opposite socialization. From this perspective, the degree of distance and closeness in a heterosexual couple's relationship depends on gender, not on inherent features of the relationship itself. For example, some theorists would analyze the situation we described in the Mirande family at the beginning of this chapter in gendered terms. Judy Mirande wishes to communicate about their financial situation and other worries because in communication she will develop closeness with José. José, on the other hand, wishes to maintain autonomy concerning financial issues and so does not wish to talk about these worries. Additionally, for some men, talking about something may not be a favored means of developing intimacy (Unger, 2010). You can see how this analysis illustrates dualistic thinking about closeness and distance. They are conceived separately as the property of Judy and José, rather than in a dynamic interplay permeating Judy and José's relationship and communication with one another.

As we suggested earlier, this dualistic approach may privilege a woman's way of expressing closeness and intimacy. Some researchers (e.g., Bem, 1993) argue that since the Industrial Revolution in the United States, we have conceived of life as divided into public and private spheres. Women have received power and authority in the private sphere and men in the public. Thus, women's ways of expressing love and intimacy (properties of the private sphere) have been seen as the right ways. This may unfairly degrade the way men express intimacy (Punyanunt-Carter, 2007). These researchers point to a bias in favor of direct verbal expression for communicating intimacy at the expense of indirection, nonverbal expression, shared activities, and idiosyncratic communication. All of the latter behaviors are ways fathers express intimacy to their sons (Buerkel, 1996). Aside from disadvantaging men, this bias illustrates dualistic thinking, focusing on what individuals bring to the conversation, not on what they create through interaction.

Other researchers suggest that life cycle or developmental stages affect needs for connection and autonomy. Fran Dickson (1995) and Judy Pearson (1992) both found that long-term marriages reflected themes of connectedness over separateness. Yet, events may intervene in long-term marriages that will affect these findings. Dawn Braithwaite (2002) observes that when one spouse is in a nursing home and the remaining partner experiences "married widowhood," some women feature distance rather than closeness in their relationships. Braithwaite refers to these couples as the "no couplehood" type, and they are characterized by comments like: "I feel very little closeness to him," "There's nothing there," "Obviously, I love him, but there's no closeness, no intimacy."

Dialectic Thinking   Although we can derive insights about intimacy in the family from both the monologic and dualistic approaches, **dialectic thinking** focuses more closely on the complex nature of separateness and connectedness in the family. Intimacy is seen not as the absence of distance, but rather, intimacy and distance are seen as simultaneously operating in family relationships. Margarita Gangotena (2004) asserts that formal greeting rituals in Mexican American families are intended to preserve both familiarity and distance. Because the rituals are affectionate and include touch, they create connection. Because they are ritualized, they also create some distance. Families who end phone conversations by saying "I love you" enact a similar ritual.

Lynda Ashbourne (2009), a family therapist, illustrates the dialectic of closeness and distance when she describes a mother and her 17-year-old daughter who came to consult with her about their relationship. Ashbourne stated, "The profound emotion in the room spoke to the history they shared, the misunderstandings and differences that challenged them, and the underlying connection that remained in spite of those challenges. While they expressed, sometimes loudly, a desire to be apart, they also described, more quietly, the significance of this relationship and their belief that it would last forever" (p. 211). In this case study, Ashbourne observed how both mother and daughter expressed strong emotions and the tension of competing desires.

Student Perspective: Rhetta

When my parents got divorced, it was a really sad time. But I have to say they worked hard to make the best of it. They did redefine their relationship, so it readjusted the balance between closeness and distance that we have been talking about. When they were married, I guess they were overly close. Now they seem to be very friendly while still being quite separate. Living in different houses helped them be nicer to each other, I think. It's funny. I remember my grandmother saying, "If they can get along so well, why don't they stay married?" I felt that way at the time myself, but now I see that it was their autonomy that allowed them to regain a bit of closeness.

You might think that the mother–daughter relationship is a natural for this dialectic and that perhaps other family relationships do not illustrate it so completely. But, Leslie Baxter and Dawn Braithwaite (2002) argue that marriage partners also illustrate dialectical tensions through specific rituals. For instance, Baxter and Braithwaite discuss the ritual of marriage renewal ceremonies as a way to show that a couple's marriage is at once stable and evolving.

Elizabeth Graham (1996, 2003) argues that this same tension characterizes the relationship of divorced couples. Graham found that many tensions were reported by divorced couples, but the one between connection and autonomy was the most frequently stated. She concludes that "the act of divorce often is an expression of the need for autonomy, but yet, many still feel the pull toward connection because some former spouses continue to have relational expectations as their lives are still enmeshed" (1996, p. 12). Graham's respondents clearly illustrated the interplay between separateness and connection in their desires for creating a state of "separate togetherness" (Masheter & Harris, 1986).

Managing Tensions Although dialectical tensions are ongoing features of relational life—that is, they are never settled—families do make efforts to deal with them (Ashbourne, 2009). We can arrange some of the research on the language of family intimacy around the strategies we outlined in Chapter 2: cyclic alternation, segmentation, selection, disqualifying, reframing, and neutralizing (Baxter, 1988). In so doing, we must keep in mind that much of this research was not actually conducted from a dialectical perspective. Despite that, it is still possible to see how the findings relate to the notion of the interplay between closeness and distance.

Cyclic Alternation In Chapter 2 we said that cyclic alternation occurred when families feature one of the opposites at particular times, alternating with the other. For instance, while Elizabeth Marks is adjusting to her son's disclosure, she may draw closer to him to show him that she still loves him. After some time passes, they may distance themselves a bit, to signal a return to their "normal" ways of relating to each other.

When families try spiraling back and forth between the two poles of the autonomy–independence dialectic, they enact many different communication behaviors to accomplish this cyclic alternation. For example, when attempting to be close to an adult daughter diagnosed with breast cancer, a mother may simply spend time listening to her daughter talk, or joke around, or offer concrete help, or show affection through hugs or saying "I love you" (Fisher, 2010). Carla Fisher also found that both mothers and adult daughters who were diagnosed with breast cancer saw "being there" as a way to be close, but also thought "giving space" helped their sense of intimacy. These two alternating approaches could be considered as forming a dialectic tension.

In attempts to cycle back to a closer phase of a relationship, families may well employ many communication behaviors that represent intimacy to them. For example, if Judy Mirande, from the beginning of the chapter, becomes concerned that she and José are becoming too distant, she may refer to him as "Chief," a nickname they established when they were dating and in their early marriage. Judy would hope that José would remember the closeness they shared then and they would begin moving closer again. She might also begin saying "I love you" before they go to sleep each night—a practice they engaged in early in their relationship but have not kept up. By invoking communication behaviors that are indicative of closeness, Judy tries to cycle back to a period of relative closeness.

Segmentation The segmentation technique isolates separate spheres for closeness and autonomy. In the earlier example, Judy Mirande may have a problem accomplishing her goals if José is operating with a strategy of segmentation. José may have decided to emphasize separation in their work life and closeness in their home life. Thus, he is content to keep financial problems private from Judy. He may respond in loving fashion to nicknames and declarations of affection in their home, but if he is following segmentation, he still may not confide in Judy about financial issues relating to their restaurant.

Kim Hause and Judy Pearson (1994) found that older couples seemed to handle the dialectic between autonomy and connection through segmentation. They designated some activities as together time and others as separate time. They often maintained three sets of friends—yours, mine, and ours—for their separate spheres of activities.

In Chapter 3 we discussed how families make rules governing what to talk about. These rules may specify taboo topics that are not supposed to be discussed in the family. Taboo topics may also function to segment areas of closeness and distance. Lynda Ashbourne (2009) discusses how older adolescents keep some areas of their lives private from their parents by segmenting and creating taboo topics. Ashbourne notes that this is appropriate because the adolescent period, developmentally, is one of constant negotiation of individuality and connectedness.

Student Perspective: Damien

I have noticed whenever my girlfriend, Lara, and I haven't been getting along too well, she will start to call me by a special name she has for me. It became my nickname after we had been dating for six months and we were really getting serious. She stopped using it all the time after a while, but she does use it sometimes in the way we talked about in class. I know she is trying to move closer together whenever she calls me that private name. It always works, too!

Selection Some families choose to manage the tensions between closeness and separation through selection—they select one of the two and ignore their need for the other. In their study of the communication patterns of abusive and nonabusive couples, Teresa Sabourin and Glen Stamp (1995) found that abusive couples seemed to favor selection as a strategy for managing the dialectic. They state, "The oppositional nature of the abusive couples' responses may be related to an imbalance of either too much or not enough closeness" (p. 225). Sabourin and Stamp noted that the abusive partners disagreed with each other about their daily routines and about perceptions of their relationship. By maintaining separate versions of these things, as opposed to collaborating on shared perceptions, these couples seem to be privileging autonomy.

Baxter and Montgomery (1996) suggest that this pattern is not too useful for families because the interplay between autonomy and connection is inherent in relationships. Thus, it is shortsighted to ignore one of the polarities in the dialectic. Nonetheless, some families attempt to do so.

Because many people in the United States place a high cultural priority on closeness of family relations, at least when children are young, some families respond by emphasizing connection at the expense of autonomy. They do not totally forget about autonomy, but connection is considered much more important. For example, the Belton family insists on eating their dinner together every weekend. The seven of them limit their outside friendships so as not to disturb the closeness among the family members. The fireplace in their family room is decorated with the family motto: All for one and one for all. In the kitchen, there are tiles painted with the slogan PABANOW, a word made by combining the first letters of their seven first names. The Beltons engage in a great deal of private talk, and people outside the family circle always feel a little excluded when they are around the Beltons. By dwelling exclusively on ways to maintain and nurture their closeness, the Beltons select it over their need for autonomy.

When families become estranged, they ignore their need for closeness. If Elizabeth Marks does not respond well to Jordy's disclosure and asks him to give

---

Student Perspective: Mandy

It's interesting to reflect on how my husband and I have changed in our 30 years of marriage. When we first married, we were intense in our closeness—we really had no boundaries between us. Then I started working, and we kind of informally decided to keep our work lives a bit separate from one another, but weekends were our time. We banned all talk about work and just renewed our closeness to each other. But then our jobs got really demanding, and sometimes one of us had to go into the office on weekends, and then Jim began traveling a lot for work. We kind of drifted for a while, and it got to feeling lonely. Now we have recommitted to each other and to keeping our weekends for us. But it's easier to do that now because we are pretty secure in our careers. Earlier it would have been hard to do that.

her time and space to adjust, Jordy might respond to her distancing moves by distancing himself as well. The two might retreat into their own thoughts and pursuits, selecting distance over closeness. Some families lose touch with one another as their choice of distance becomes a way of life.

Disqualifying   A fourth pattern for managing the closeness–distance dialectic is disqualifying, or exempting certain issues from the general pattern. For example, a family with a general pattern of closeness may disqualify this pattern when it comes to certain situations. In one of our chapter-opening vignettes, Sabrina and Max Walter are close and enjoy a warm relationship. But Max may not want to have Sabrina know all about his relationships with girls. If the two follow a pattern of disqualification, they may tell each other everything except about the topic of romantic relationships.

Reframing   In reframing, the family combines the two poles into a unity (Hughes, 2010). This integrating approach redefines the dialectic so that it no longer seems to contain an opposition. Some of the elements of a family's private communication may act to reframe and unify the tensions of closeness and distance. For example, when Judy Mirande calls her husband by the affectionate nickname "Chief," she combines elements of individuation and connection. Connection is symbolized by reference to their closeness—only intimates call each other by pet names. Connection is also evoked because the nickname recalls an earlier time in their relationship when they were developing intimacy. Yet, the name also symbolizes features of José's individual personality and thus heightens a sense of individuality and differentiation in their relationship. The simple use of a nickname accomplishes a unifying function as it celebrates both polarities at once.

> ### Student Perspective: Nola
>
> *My sister is really good at complimenting me on things she thinks I do differently than she does. She will often say, "I could never have the guts to do what you do," or "I really like how you rearranged the furniture in your room. I never would have thought of doing it that way." I like getting these compliments, but sometimes I think she pays too much attention to how we are different. There are lots of things we do the same, too.*

Some communication rituals in families also operate as reframing devices. Families that gather at dinner to update each other on what they each did in their day reframe the oppositions. By discussing in turn the events of their individual days, they highlight autonomy. Yet, by bringing their different experiences into the family circle, they privilege connection as they integrate each other's differences into the fabric of their shared life as a family.

Dialectic tensions also permeate adoptive family relationships, when the families are formed through visible adoptions. **Visible adoptions**, according to Kathleen Galvin (2003), are those where the members' ethnic features make it visually obvious that the members are not biologically related. Meredith Harrigan and Dawn Braithwaite (2010) found that parents tried to reframe the tensions in ways that helped these adoptive families forge closeness and a sense of family identity. These tensions included oppositions such as pride and imperfection about the child's birthplace. Parents said that they talked about the child's birthplace as somewhere that was "important, worthy, and valuable, yet imperfect" (p. 133). In doing this, parents tried to integrate a sense of pride in where their children came from with a sense of realism about it.

Reframing involves the coordination of the tension—interdependence fostered from individual differences and individuation nurtured from a strong base of connection. When family members compliment one another, they show that they see each other as separate but connected. When Nancy tells her daughter, Tamara, that she is very impressed with how disciplined she is with her schoolwork, Tamara feels affirmed by her mother (connection) but also recognized as a separate individual with different work habits, perhaps, from other members of the family. Of course, not all compliments function to set members apart from one another. Sometimes compliments only emphasize connection—"I am so proud of how you are carrying on the Gomez family tradition," for example.

Neutralizing Finding a compromise between the two polarities rather than reframing them is neutralizing. In our earlier discussion of divorced partners, the notion of a separate togetherness relates to neutralizing. The couple is not completely connected, yet not completely separate either—it is somewhere in between. The Mirandes, from the beginning of the chapter, may come to some compromise on how much to talk and connect with one another about issues of money that are causing them problems. Sabourin and Stamp (1995) note that nonabusive couples seemed more likely than abusive couples to find a "happy medium" approach. When nonabusive couples described the routines of their day, they tended to listen to one another, agree with some of what the other said, and then offer their own

---

Student Perspective: Kamehla

In my family we use all the strategies at one time or another. When my brother, Nolan, got in trouble with gangs, we kind of shut him out for a while. But then we moved to a mode of working really hard to get him back with the family, and for a time we all stuck to him like glue. He couldn't move without one of us on his tail. Then we settled into a compromise position, and that's where we are now. Nolan is staying out of trouble, but he is really different from the rest of us kids, and sometimes we talk about that. It's funny how people can come up in the same family and yet be so different.

TABLE 5-1 Managing the Dialectic Tension Between Closeness and Distance

STRATEGY	EXAMPLE
Cyclic alternation	Elly is close to her sister, Sue, as an adult. She was very distant from her when they were children.
Segmentation	Rob is close to his cousin when they're on their grandpa's farm together, but when he sees him in town, he's distant.
Selection	The Meyers family is very distant—no matter what. They've chosen one extreme.
Disqualifying	The Randolph family is very close; they tell one another everything except they never talk about money.
Reframing	Michael and Andrea Soliz believe they become closer when they do different things all day at work and then have experiences to share with each other when they do get together.
Neutralizing	Paula wants to spend all her time with her twin brother, Paul. Paul wants a lot more distance. They compromise and spend less time than Paula wants but more than Paul wants.

interpretations. Sabourin and Stamp state that this give-and-take process, rather than complete agreement or open conflict, represents a neutralizing approach.

In the Wright family, for example, neutralizing is used to mediate between the differing perspectives between Charlie Wright and his son, Noel. Charlie expects his son to be present for all dinners and to share anecdotes about his day and his feelings. Noel has difficulty doing that, in large part because he believes his father would not want to hear that he is thinking about quitting school and going to work in his girlfriend's father's construction business. Because Noel feels his individuality will cause problems, he tends to stay away from the family. The Wrights neutralized this tension by having Noel come to dinners but keeping the dinner table conversation somewhat impersonal. This compromise seems to be working for the time being but may have to be revisited as the time draws nearer for Noel to make a decision. See Table 5-1 for examples of all six strategies.

Attachment Theory

Although the dialectic approach works well to explain aspects of intimacy in family relationships, it is not the only way researchers have sought to understand family closeness. **Attachment theory** forms another approach for this purpose. A theory in the positivistic-empirical tradition, attachment theory explains and predicts the relationship among affect or bonding and behaviors and thoughts. In the earliest conception of attachment theory, John Bowlby (1969/1982, 1973) sought to explain why children develop strong attachments to their mothers, or other caregivers, and cry upon separation from these attachment figures. Further, Bowlby argued that children develop attachment styles based on how available and responsive their caregivers have been, and thus the quality of the first love relationship between infant and caregiver is critical in establishing a pattern for the infant's future attachments. Bowlby's approach is consistent with the general systems perspective that we presented in Chapter 2.

Attachment theory suggests that there are several behavioral systems that are universal across species, although there may be subtle differences exhibited by individuals or within certain groups, like primates, for example. Some of these behavioral systems include those related to feeding, reproduction, caregiving, attachment, fear, exploration, sociability, and so forth. Bowlby (1973) asserts that behavioral patterns associated with each of these systems fulfill the biological function of ensuring the survival of the species. For example, attachment behavior protects infants and children from a wide variety of dangers.

Attachment theory proposes that the systems of attachment, fear, exploration, and sociability exhibit a complicated balance that helps a child develop needed coping skills under the protection of the attachment figure (Ainsworth, 1967). For example, when a child's attachment and fear systems are minimally invoked, the exploratory and sociability systems can be activated easily and vice versa. The fear system acts to terminate exploratory and sociability behaviors and at the same time activates the attachment behavior system. The effect, in Mary Ainsworth's (1967) terms, is that the child is "using the mother as a secure base for exploration" (p. 27). Further, strongly activating the exploration system may reduce activation of the attachment system. When parents watch their children exploring a playground and meeting new children, they notice that the sense of attachment to them is rapidly reduced. These observations provided the foundation for a typology of infant–caregiver relationships consisting of *secure* relationships (confident infant, responsive caregiver), *anxious-ambivalent* relationships (temperamental infant, inconsistent caregiver), and *avoidant* relationships (undemonstrative infant, undemonstrative caregiver) (Ainsworth, Blehar, Waters, & Wall, 1978).

The theory asserts both that adult attachment is a result of these patterns set in childhood and that the patterns remain relatively stable over time (Hazan & Shaver, 1994; Shaver, Hazan, & Bradshaw, 1988). Following from these assumptions, researchers have posited attachment types for adults (Bartholomew & Horowitz, 1991) including *secure* (comfortable with both autonomy and intimacy), *preoccupied* (preoccupied with intimacy), *dismissing* (dismissing of intimacy), and *fearful* (fearful of intimacy). However, some research demonstrates that these patterns are changeable (Le Poire, Haynes, Driscoll, Driver, Wheelis, Hyde, Prochaska, & Ramos, 1997).

Communication may play an important role in revising and developing attachment styles (Bretherton, 1990; Edwards, 2011; Ragsdale, Brandau-Brown, & Bello, 2010; Trees, 2000). Additionally, Anthony Roberto and his colleagues (Roberto, Carlyle, Goodall, & Castle, 2009), found that parents of children with secure attachment styles were lower in verbal aggression than parents of children with preoccupied, dismissing, or fearful styles.

Attachment theorists would explain José Mirande's (from our opening vignette) style of intimacy with his wife, Judy, by examining his relationship as an infant with his caregivers and then by noting what modifications Judy's interactional style may have made as they forged their relationship together. As you can see, this is not opposed to the analysis that would be offered by a dialectic scholar, but it simply focuses on a different aspect of intimacy.

Social Exchange Theory

Another theory that aims to explain intimate relationships and the communication within them is **social exchange theory.** Actually, the social exchange approach encompasses several theories, one of which we will review here—interdependence theory (Thibaut & Kelley, 1959). This theory, also rooted in the positivistic-empirical tradition, is based on the notion that people think about their relationships in economic terms. In this way, they keep count of the costs of the relationship and compare these to the rewards that the relationship provides. The worth of a relationship is its rewards minus its costs. As you can imagine, some relationships cost more than the rewards they provide, and some are more rewarding than costly. Social exchange theory calls the former negative relationships and the latter, positive. Further, the theory predicts that, in general, people will stay in positive relationships and try to get out of negative ones.

To exemplify costs and rewards, the central concepts of this theory, let's examine the O'Neill family based on social exchange. Patricia and Conner have been married for 12 years, and they have three children ranging in age from 3 to 8 years old. Patricia is a stay-at-home mom, and Conner has been working as an electrician. Recently, however, he has been laid off from the job he's held for the past 6 years. If we examined Patricia's cost/benefit ratio for her relationship with her husband, Conner, we'd see that there are several costs involved. Currently, since Conner is out of work, there is a cost in trying to keep up appearances, paying the bills, keeping the children from becoming worried, and getting along with Conner when he is depressed about his lack of job prospects. Yet, the relationship also offers rewards. Patricia and Conner have been together for a long time, and they share many happy memories. They have fun together when they can forget the job situation. Conner is a loyal husband and a great father—the kids adore him. Before she met Conner, Patricia felt she would never find anyone who really understood her.

The situation is further complicated by the notions of comparison level and comparison level for alternatives (Thibaut & Kelley, 1959). These two ideas make the calculation of the worth of the relationship more complex than simple subtraction and addition. The **comparison level** is a standard representing what a person feels she or he should expect regarding costs and rewards from a relationship. Thus, if Patricia grew up expecting that marriage is a relationship in which a wife should sacrifice for her husband and children, then her standard for costs may be fairly high. She may also believe that in return for these sacrifices wives should be put on a pedestal by their husbands. In this case, Patricia's comparison level for rewards is also rather high. If her actual marriage rewards her as much as or more than she expected and costs her what she expected or less, Patricia will likely be very satisfied with her marriage, even if it has significant costs.

Comparison levels are different for different people, because they are derived from individuals' past experiences. Yet, part of an individual's past experience is rooted in cultural values and teachings and popular cultural representations of relationships. To the degree that people share cultural beliefs and watch the same television shows and films, comparison levels will converge. If Patricia watches many romantic comedies, for example, she might come to believe that her marriage is not romantic enough and that Conner is not available enough for her. If she has a group of women friends who all watch the same shows, they may all feel that they are not being rewarded enough in their marriages compared with the cinematic representations. This is similar to the dialectic between the real and the ideal that we have discussed previously.

Comparison level for alternatives measures how people evaluate a relationship compared with realistic alternatives to that relationship. The comparison level for alternatives predicts how likely it would be that Patricia would leave Conner based on her evaluation of other possible relationships. This calculation explains why people stay in relationships that appear very negative to outsiders. If the partners do not see a chance for a better alternative, they will stay in the relationship that they have. Children have little opportunity to achieve alternatives to their families. Thus, although some children run away from home, most children believe their family life is normative and therefore stay within their families.

Through all these calculations, social exchange theory purports to explain why people stay in intimate relationships, why they leave, and why they feel satisfied or dissatisfied with them. Like attachment theory, social exchange thinking does not completely contradict the other theoretical frameworks that we have presented as much as it offers another way of viewing intimate relationships.

The Circumplex Model

The Circumplex Model of family functioning was developed in 1979 (Olson, Sprenkle, & Russell, 1979) and has been refined many times in the intervening years (Olson & Gorall, 2003). It has been an extremely important model in the family systems tradition. David Olson and his colleagues contend that family life is conducted along two critical dimensions: adaptability and cohesion. The model is especially appealing to communication researchers because of Olson's claim that communication is the vehicle allowing families to change their position on the adaptability and cohesion dimensions. When combined, the two dimensions create a typology of family functioning based on how adaptable and cohesive they are.

Adaptability is the ability of a family to recalibrate (in systems terms) in response to stress. Families are more adaptable when they are able to change rules, roles, and so forth in response to crises. For our purposes in this chapter, the more important dimension in Olson's model is cohesion. **Cohesion** refers to the degree of emotional connection the family experiences. As Olson and his colleagues (1979) put it, cohesion represents "the emotional bonding members have with one another and the degree of individual autonomy a person experiences in the family system" (p. 5). Further, "cohesion focuses on how systems balance separateness versus togetherness" (Olson & Gorall, 2003, p. 516).

By examining how families exhibit cohesion, Olson and his associates observe that there are five levels of cohesion ranging from extremely low cohesion (disconnected or disengaged families) to extremely high cohesion (enmeshed or overly connected families). In between these two extremes are low to moderate cohesion (somewhat connected families), moderate cohesion (connected families), and moderate to high cohesion (very connected families). This creates five family types based on closeness (see Figure 5-1). Families in the middle three types are considered balanced, and those on the two extremes are unbalanced. Olson and his colleagues argue that the middle types are more likely to have optimal family functioning while the unbalanced types are seen as problematic if they continue over time. This situation is complicated by the fact that in the Circumplex Model, the researchers weren't simply interested in cohesion, so in Figure 5-1 you can see that there are 5 types of families based on adaptability as well. This makes for 25 types of families, 9 of which are considered balanced along both dimensions.

The way this model presents cohesion is not totally different from the perspective of dialectics theory, but its emphasis on balance does provide an important distinction. Balance is viewed as the preferred state in the Circumplex Model. This is unlike the dialectical perspective, which views the interplay of contradiction as a key element to relational life.

FIGURE 5-1 Couple and Family Map

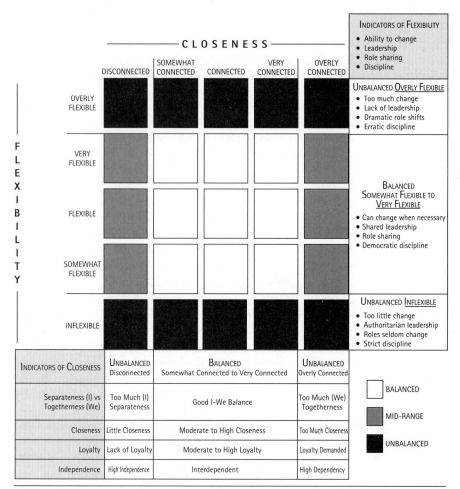

Source: From D. H. Olson & D. M. Gorall, "Circumplex Model of Marital and Family Systems" in *Normal Family Processes,* 3rd edition, ed. F. Walsh (New York: Guilford, 2003), 517.

EXPRESSING INTIMACY IN THE FAMILY

We have discussed the nature of intimacy within the family and explored some theoretical frameworks seeking to explain issues of intimacy and closeness, but our major focus in this text is on how communication behaviors structure intimacy for family members. For example, we are interested in interpreting the dialectics in family members' nonverbal communication. These behaviors may create both closeness and separation between members of the family. For instance, when Miguel frowns, turns away, and shrugs, his sister, Ana, knows exactly what he is feeling. Thus, Miguel's nonverbals signal closeness between the siblings: They can understand each other without words. But Ana also knows that when Miguel expresses those nonverbals, they mean that he doesn't want to talk and needs to be alone. Thus, the nonverbal signals communicate separation at the same time that they indicate how close the two are because of how well they know each other. On this topic, and throughout all our discussions, it is the interaction between people in families that forms our emphasis.

Mark Knapp and Anita Vangelisti (2009) provide a long list of communication behaviors that manifest intimacy and closeness. Some of these include (1) declarations of commitment and affection ("I love you"), (2) use of positive absolute statements ("you're the best sister anyone could have"), (3) use of personal idioms or private language, (4) giving comfort and support, (5) playfulness, (6) nonverbal intimacy and sexuality, and (7) self-disclosures. We agree with Knapp and Vangelisti, as well as other researchers, that intimate relationships are constructed and reflected through the exchange of communication. Yet, it is important to realize that this list, or others we could generate, is affected by many variables. Previously we discussed how important culture can be to understanding intimate communication within the family. Here we briefly mention how issues of gender may impact family intimacy.

Many researchers' notion of the feminine sex role includes a focus on emotional expressiveness (Wood, 2013). Some scholars have argued that the social division of labor that promotes women as nurturers in the family and men as providers actually devalues some of the more indirect methods that men employ for expressing affection (Pasley & Minton, 2001). In a study of men's responses to the loss of their fathers, Neil Chethik (2001) discovered that sons reported a variety of their fathers' behaviors as expressions of affection, including taking them to activities such as auto races and baseball games, as well as simply conversing together. Arlene Istar Lev (2010) comments that this feminine bias especially impacts gay men who wish to become fathers. She notes that "gay fathers are caught between gender-based sexism that presumes men are unable to nurture children and homophobia that assumes gay men are child molesters" (p. 272). Thus, as we review these expressions of intimacy, we must be mindful that gender interacts with communication, often resulting in different styles for men and women.

In addition, Gottman and his colleagues (1997) argue that meta-emotions are critical in understanding how families communicate emotion. **Meta-emotions** are emotions that people have about emotions. As Gottman, Katz, and Hooven state, "Some people are ashamed or upset about becoming angry [for example], others feel good about their capacity to express anger, and still others think of anger as natural, neither good nor bad" (p. 7). As these researchers explain, how family members express an emotion will be best understood in the context of their meta-emotions. For example, José Mirande, from our opening vignette, may feel he needs Judy's love and support yet he also may have a meta-emotion of shame at his feelings of dependence. The meta-emotion, according to Gottman and colleagues, guides his choice to avoid talking about their financial situation when Judy asks him about it.

We will briefly review seven behaviors that Knapp and Vangelisti (2009) mention as indicative of intimate relationships: declarations of commitment, positive absolute statements, private language, messages of comfort and support, playfulness, nonverbal intimacy and sexuality, and self-disclosure.

Declarations of Commitment

The first behavior, declarations of commitment, seems an obvious choice. When relationships are close, partners are expected to declare this by saying "I love you," "I feel so close to you," "I love our life together," and so forth. Some evidence (e.g., Wood, 2013), however, suggests that women are more adept at these direct emotional expressions than are men and that this may cause some difficulties in their romantic relationships. In a qualitative study geared toward exploring how a newlywed couple defines commitment, Daniel Weigel (2003) reports that the wife in the couple (more so than the husband) favors these types of declarations as a way of communicating commitment. She mentions that she always signs notes to him, "I love you." Further, she states that saying "I love you" directly is a very strong statement to her that she doesn't take lightly.

Positive Absolute Statements

The use of positive absolute statements refers to phrases such as "you are the best daughter in the world!!" and "I love you the most!" In these types of phrases, intimates announce the strength of their bond. Mark Knapp and Anita Vangelisti (2009) note that using unqualified absolute statements is another method for communicating commitment in a relationship. They suggest that it is part of a series of communication behaviors that can help a person more effectively communicate a sense of commitment. When people speak in absolute terms about their relationship or their relational partner, they convey their certainty about the strength of their bond. Judy Pearson (1996) observes that long-term happily married couples tend to distort their perceptions and comments in a positive manner. She reports that the couples she interviewed who considered themselves happily married after 50 years appeared to skew the experiences and behaviors they shared in a positive direction. They said about their partners that they were "wonderful, wonderful," "the most beautiful person in the world," and that they "looked terrific," among other things. As Julia Wood (1995) observes, idealizing communication operates to intensify a sense of intimacy within relationships. "It isn't just a good relationship—it is the best ever; she isn't just intelligent— she's the brightest woman I've ever known; he isn't simply fun to be with— he's the most engaging person around" (p. 215). These idealizing comments structure and express intimacy and closeness within relationships.

Private Language

One of the most interesting connections between language and relational developments lies in the taken-for-granted aspects of communication (Sillars, Shellen, McIntosh, & Momegranate, 1997). In these "understood" components, relational partners exhibit their interdependence with one another. As Sillars and his colleagues illustrate, these elements often result in idiosyncratic talk reflecting the private culture of the family with many shared associations. Private language may take many forms: nicknames, investing ordinary words with personal meaning, and invented language, among others. In some families, private or inside jokes act as a private language (Boyd, 1996). Nicknames are perhaps the most common type of idiosyncratic language within families. Nicknames may be more or less personalized. For example, "sweetie" connotes that a personal relationship exists, but many intimate relationships may use that code. When Elizabeth Marks, from our opening vignette, calls her son "Googie," she is referring to a childhood mispronunciation, and thus that name both connotes the closeness of their relationship and marks the uniqueness of their bond. She may invoke this childhood nickname to reassure Jordy that she loves him without reservation.

Ordinary words may have transformed, private meanings within families (Hopper, Knapp, & Scott, 1981). In this situation, partners may be able to converse about outsiders in their presence. Julia Wood (1995) recounts how her father used the term "duffer rebuffer" to refer to getting rid of dull people. When they were listening to people he found dull, he would ask Wood if she had seen the duffer rebuffer. Wood claims that she and her father enjoyed the joke without offending anyone. In one of your authors' families, the phrase "look on sky balloon is hanging" was used to express that someone had just uttered an incomprehensible statement.

Finally, intimates may actually create words and derive a true personal language. Twins are especially noted for a type of "twinspeak" that constitutes a complete language that is known only to the twins themselves (Bishop & Bishop, 1998).

Messages of Comfort and Support

Intimates are expected to extend help to one another when it is needed. Your family is the group of people who are supposed to support you no matter what. This illustrates the enduring aspect of the intimate bond. Kathleen Galvin and Charles Wilkinson (1996) observe that nurturing communication sends messages that the partners care about one another. They further conclude through their work with families that if 10 percent of a family's communication is nurturing, the family is a healthy one, because the members will feel valued and cared for. When family members experience stress, they turn to their family for comforting messages (Burleson, 1994). Knapp and Vangelisti (2009) state that "we can reasonably expect that a couple's skill with comforting messages is a crucial barometer of intimacy, and each partner's ability to manage this style of communication will have a lot to do with how the relationship is maintained" (pp. 307–308). Sally Planalp (1999) notes that one reason we talk to our family members about our problems and our feelings is because we know we can rely on them for comfort and support.

Some researchers (e.g., Nicolas, Desilva, Prater, & Bronkoski, 2009; Planalp, 1999) also observe, however, that there may be a downside to seeking support from family members. Family members may become too close to the problem, and a certain "emotional contagion" or "empathic family stress" may occur. For example, if José, from the beginning of our chapter, confides in his wife, Judy, about his money worries, this may tap into fears that Judy herself shares. Then, together, they may define the problem as more critical than it actually is, as their fears feed upon each other. Additionally, family members may be part of the problem. José may not want to seek support from his wife because part of his worry centers on continuing to support her and their son. The primary danger in seeking support from your family is that the burden may become too great for them. This is often the case when divorced parents seek support from their children and tell them more than they want or need to know about the problems in the marriage and in the subsequent situation.

Playfulness

A sense of play characterizes emotionally healthy intimate relationships (Baxter, 1992). William Doherty (2001) notes that developing skills in play is one way for fathers to become more involved and connected with their children. Sabrina and Max Walter, from our opening vignette, interact in a playful fashion. Their sense of shared experience adds to their ability to tease and play with each other, building a foundation of intimacy. Carol Bruess and Judy Pearson (1997) report that intimate couples exhibit many types of rituals. Among these rituals are play rituals, which represent fun for the couple. These play rituals may take the form of kidding, teasing, silliness, and banter. Clyde Hendrick and Susan Hendrick's (1996) research on styles of heterosexual love may point to some gender differences in playfulness. Hendrick and Hendrick found six different love styles characterizing the participants in their research, who were predominately white, middle-class college students in the United States. One of these six styles they called ludus, which they defined as love as a game, played as a pleasant pastime. They found that men engaged in the ludus style of love far more than did women.

Nonverbal Intimacy and Sexuality

A sense of access to the physical space of intimate partners characterizes intimate relationships. And certainly intimacy within the family does not depend exclusively on verbal communication. Nonverbal behaviors communicate intimacy in many ways, some overlapping those we have discussed previously. For example, interactional definitions of social support involve verbal and nonverbal expressions of affirmation, caring, and assistance to someone dealing with a stressful event or life problem. April Trees (2000) found that adult children were affected by their mothers' nonverbal supportiveness, specifically their mothers' vocal warmth and proxemic attentiveness.

One of the critical aspects in nonverbal intimacy concerns participants' ability to read or decode the signals accurately (Knapp & Vangelisti, 2009). Some evidence (Pearson, West, & Turner, 1995) suggests that wives are better at decoding their husbands' nonverbal signals than vice versa. Touch is often considered the "language of physical intimacy" (Galvin & Brommel, 2000). A discussion of touch includes touch that may be sexual in nature. Here we note that **sexual communication,** by which we mean both talk about sex and sexual relations, characterizes intimate relationships, although not all relationships that involve sexual contact are truly intimate in all the ways that we have discussed in this section. Further, some inappropriate sexual contact within families constitutes abuse and is not appropriate as an expression of intimacy. For adult partners, however, sexual communication can be a powerful bridge to intimacy. We talk further about sexuality as a communication issue within families in Chapter 9.

Self-Disclosure

Self-disclosure is a communication behavior often related to the development and maintenance of intimacy. The word *intimacy* derives from the Latin words that mean "to make known," and **self-disclosure** is defined as voluntarily telling another person private information that the other could not easily obtain any other way (Derlega, 1984; Nakanishi & Johnson, 1993). Thus, the relationship between the two terms is clear, and self-disclosure has traditionally been considered a skill needed to nurture healthy intimate relationships (Jourard, 1971). Yet, we do know that sometimes people tell perfect strangers private information, and it may also be the case that we know a great deal of private information about someone whom we do not really like all that well. Therefore, the relationship between self-disclosure and intimacy is not a perfect equation. Also, as we have discussed throughout this text, self-disclosure is a communication behavior that is affected by cultural norms. Sally Hastings (2000), for example, asserts that Asian Indians' sense of appropriate self-disclosure differs greatly from that of North Americans. Gender may also affect people's attitudes toward self-disclosure, as well as their practice of this communication behavior. Women and men may self-disclose about different personal information, and women seem to be the recipients of more self-disclosures than are men (Pearson et al., 1995). Although, as Katherine Dindia (2000) observes, the differences between the genders in relation to self-disclosure are relatively small, and they are moderated by the sex of the recipient of the disclosure.

Further, some cautions need to be sounded about indiscriminate self-disclosure (Henwood, Giles, Coupland, & Coupland, 1993). Yet, the positive effect of self-disclosure on intimate relationships also has been well documented (Fitzpatrick, 1987; Galvin & Brommel, 2000). This leads to what Lawrence Rosenfeld (2000) refers to as the approach-avoidance relationship most people have toward self-disclosure. The rewards of self-disclosing can be great in terms of increased intimacy within an important relationship, but the risks of rejection and derision are equally great. Sandra Petronio (2000) theorizes that as a result of this tension, people balance privacy and openness through boundary structures, such as decisions about with whom the private information is co-owned and boundary rules that are created to "regulate the flow of information to and from others" (p. 39).

People practice self-disclosures, according to Petronio (2000) and others (e.g., Dindia, 1998), through managing the boundaries between privacy and openness. Through this process some information is shared, and other information becomes off-limits or taboo. In family relationships, research suggests that self-disclosures are related to the type of family relationship involved, as well as various outcomes like relational satisfaction. People tend to self-disclose more to spouses than to parents, siblings reported greater satisfaction in their relationships with each other when there is greater self-disclosure, and parents reported that they are more open with their children than vice versa (cited in Martin, Anderson, & Mottet, 1999). Further, siblings are less likely to avoid disclosures with each other than with their parents (Guerrero & Afifi, 1995).

Given that the type of family relationship seems important, Matthew Martin and colleagues (1999) investigated self-disclosures in stepfamilies. Earlier research (Galvin & Cooper, 1990) suggested that, given the nonvoluntary nature of stepfamilies, openness would be reduced for the first five years of the family's existence. In Martin and colleagues' (1999) work, self-disclosure was positively related to a sense of perceived understanding in the stepchild–stepparent relationship, and this was especially true for stepdaughters. John Caughlin and colleagues (2000) found that the degree of openness (or the number of secrets, the topics of secrets, and the function of secrets) was consistent across stepfamilies, nuclear families, and single-parent families. They did discover that people in stepfamilies are more likely to disclose secrets to members of their original families than to family members who are new to them.

In sum, self-disclosure is a complex communication practice that tends to increase with increased intimacy and also serves to motivate increased intimacy. However, it may also occur without the context of an intimate relationship, or it may actually decrease intimacy. Self-disclosure seems to operate dialectically with self-protection or suppression. How this dialectic is activated may depend on a complicated system of rules, relationships, and boundary structures moderated by individual differences such as culture and gender.

SUMMARY

In this chapter we have examined how family members construct a sense of closeness and intimacy with each other through communication. We discussed the important role that culture plays in shaping expectations of family closeness as well as providing models for expressing closeness and intimacy. We have observed that intimacy and distance can occur (and most likely always do occur) simultaneously within families. We take the position that negotiating closeness is a primary task of all families, and it is never ending. Family systems, throughout their developmental life, continually cope with distance regulation. Further, we have argued that regulating distance and closeness forms an important dialectical tension for families—a tension that can be managed in many ways but one that is inherent to the family relationship. As the family system calibrates and recalibrates (makes rules) around the issue of connection and autonomy, it enacts communication behaviors that often encode elements of both simultaneously.

Thus, families engage in the interplay of closeness and intimacy rather than become intimate and stay that way (or become distant and maintain that). As families interact they create a relational climate that contains both intimacy and distance. Some members may not be satisfied with the climate as it exists, and then they may engage in interaction, trying to modify the climate. Families need flexibility and a willingness to negotiate closeness and distance to their own satisfaction.

We noted that attachment theory, social exchange theory, and the Circumplex Model address the issue of intimacy in slightly different ways than the dialectic approach, although they are not always mutually exclusive. Finally, we recounted seven communication behaviors that family members use to create and reflect a sense of family intimacy.

KEY TERMS

adaptability	everyday talk
attachment theory	meta-emotions
cohesion	monologic thinking
comparison level	self-disclosure
comparison level for alternatives	sexual communication
dialectic thinking	social exchange theory
dualistic thinking	visible adoptions

QUESTIONS FOR REFLECTION

1. Why is it difficult to define intimacy? Based on your family experiences, do you believe that you can identify the level of intimacy you have with each family member? If appropriate, does this level differ from what you experienced in your family-of-origin? What examples can you point to?

2. Do you agree that closeness and distance form an ongoing dialectic in the family? Why or why not? Give some examples of communication behaviors that encode messages of both distance and intimacy in the family.

3. Develop your own definition of intimacy. What sorts of family experiences can you provide to support your perspective?

4. List the five levels of cohesion described in the Circumplex Model. How do they differ from one another? How does this view of intimacy in the family differ from the dialectic approach?

5. Refute or defend the following statement: Maintaining distance in a family relationship can sometimes result in a more satisfying relationship. Provide examples to support your thoughts.

6. Do you subscribe to the dialectic approach, attachment theory, social exchange theory, the Circumplex Model, or some other model? Why or why not? What elements of your chosen theory work best to explain family intimacy?

7. In this chapter, we mentioned seven behaviors that researchers say communicate intimacy. Can you think of times when these would not help develop intimacy in a family? Can you think of other communication behaviors that were not mentioned that should be added to the list?

8. How might you revise the Circumplex Model to incorporate different cultural preferences for intimacy? Create a new model to illustrate this.

Chapter
6

TELLING STORIES AND MAKING MEANING

Understanding Family Stories
The Family as Subject • Sequence of Events
Significance • Performance • Dramatic Element • Fluidity
Negotiated Meaning

Functions of Family Stories
Building Identity • Creating Links Among the Past, Present,
and Future • Teaching Lessons and Morals
Negotiating Dialectical Tensions and Managing Difficulties

Types of Family Stories
Courtship Stories • Birth Stories • Survival Stories
Stories on the Margins

Other Meaning-Making Practices
Family Theme • Family Ritual • Family Myth • Family Metaphor

Summary

Key Terms

Questions for Reflection

THE MCINTOSH FAMILY

Rita McIntosh, age 64, sits by the phone in her condo waiting for her son, Alex, to call for his regular weekly check-in with her. Since her husband, Paul, died last year, her five grown children have really been good about calling, visiting, and making sure that she is doing well. Of course, Rita misses Paul a great deal, but she finds it very comforting that her children are so solicitous and caring. Rita thinks back to the time when she lived in their large house, and all the kids were running around, driving her crazy. She smiles and realizes that it was all worthwhile—her kids are fine adults, and all have a strong family feeling. Then Alex calls, and the two of them have a long talk, including many laughs over a favorite story about the kids and Paul getting the Christmas tree late one year. As the story goes, when they found their choices were limited, they came home with a lot of branches and built their own tree in the living room. Rita loves that story.

THE NICHOLS-RESNICK FAMILY

Mindy Nichols and Jerry Resnick have lived together for six years. They are thinking about getting married and have been talking about it for several weeks now. Today they are going to a birthday party at Mindy's sister's house. Almost all of Mindy's large extended family members will be there, and they have decided to talk to some of Mindy's sisters about their marriage plans. When they get to the party, it's in full swing, and there's so much noise and chaos that they can't talk to anyone about anything too serious.

But after they have dinner and the birthday cake's been served and the presents opened, they find an opportunity to corner Mindy's sister, Rachel. When they tell her what they're thinking about, she's overjoyed. Immediately, she calls her husband, Cal, over and tells Mindy to tell him. Cal smiles at the news and turns to Rachel. "Remember the day we decided to get married, and we came over to your folks' house and tried to tell them about it?" he asks. Rachel, Mindy, and Jerry all laugh, and they each start telling a favorite part of the story. Mindy and Jerry catch each other's eye: They thought about this story before they came to the party tonight, and they were determined they wouldn't repeat it exactly. They wanted their engagement story to be more dignified.

Rachel's parents were having a party the night Rachel and Cal got engaged, and people were practically falling out the windows when Rachel and Cal got home. Music was blaring, and the party was pretty chaotic. After trying to tell her parents unsuccessfully for an hour, Cal pulled the plug out of the stereo and yelled the announcement to everyone who was standing nearby. While Rachel, Cal, Mindy, and Jerry were retelling the story, some of Mindy's other relatives came over and chimed in, reminiscing about that funny event.

Then Mindy told the others that she and Jerry were thinking about getting married themselves. The relatives were all excited to hear that. Her Uncle Charles started telling about the day he first met Jerry, and the whole group starting laughing again.

THE WASHINGTON FAMILY

Mark and Su-Lin Washington, married for 20 years, have two children, Lee, 15, and Brenda, 12. Today they are attending Su-Lin's father's funeral. In the car on the way home at the end of a long day, the couple retells the familiar story of their courtship. They reminisce about how hard it was to convince Su-Lin's parents that she and Mark, an African American, could make a good life together. There were times they thought they would never get Su-Lin's family to agree to their relationship. Su-Lin's father, especially, found it difficult to accept Mark. He wanted Su-Lin to marry a Chinese man. He had already spoken to one of his friends about arranging a marriage between Su-Lin and his friend's son, Wei-Jong. Mark and Su-Lin smile as they recount how Su-Lin's mother interceded with her father to allow them to date. Mark laughs, remembering how impatient he used to be with the slowness of getting an answer from Su-Lin's father. "Yes," Su-Lin agreed. "You could never tell what my father thought, and he took a very indirect route to tell us. We never really heard his 'inside' feelings. Luckily my mother helped behind the scenes to bring my father and me together." Lee and Brenda repeat the last words of the story in a chorus with their parents: "Thank goodness Grandma Tong wasn't as Chinese as Grandpa Tong or we wouldn't be a family today!"

In 1968, Muriel Rukeyser observed that "the universe is made of stories, not atoms." In this chapter, we examine the importance of stories (and other meaning-making communications) for families. Previously (see Chapter 2) we discussed an assumption highlighting the family as a meaning-making system, one that changes as people's interactions change. In Chapter 1 we reviewed some axioms of communication, including the notion that families derive meaning from verbal and nonverbal codes. This chapter builds on these assertions and turns our attention to how families use stories and other meaning-making processes to accomplish a variety of functions.

As we approach the family as a meaning-making system, we are taking a social constructivist position on family communication. As we discussed in Chapter 2, the theoretical position advanced by Peter Berger and Hansfried Kellner (1964) conceptualizes marriage as a conversation between the partners, in which they set the norms and standards for their own relationship. By approaching the family in this way, we see that the interpretations people attach to codes are the most important element in the communication process. Further, this interpreting is done on the basis of the social context in which the communication behavior takes place. For example, in the Washington family described at the beginning of the chapter, Grandpa Tong's objections to Mark are seen, somewhat affectionately, as part of his cultural background. Other families might interpret Grandpa Tong's behavior differently, which would change the tone and meaning of the story.

Further, we are also taking a narrative approach in this chapter because social construction's focus on meaning making leads us naturally to an examination of people's stories (Boss, 2002). Karla Mason Bergen (2010) observes that when people form and tell family stories, they are influenced by their own personal experiences as well as stories told by the culture, which are known variously as "canonical stories," "cultural scripts," or "master narratives." **Master narratives** are "stories drawn from the cultural store that circulate widely within a society and embody its shared understandings" (Nelson, 2001, p. 152). In this way, master narratives reflect the values of the dominant culture. Additionally these narratives create norms for what are acceptable and unacceptable behaviors in the family. Bergen notes that wives who are absent from home because they commute to work create personal stories to help explain why their lived experiences diverge from the master narrative of marriage.

Finally, we approach this subject from a cultural perspective. First, we note that the family's relational culture affects (and is affected by) communication behaviors. One of the attributes of an intimate relationship is a private or idiosyncratic language. For instance, when Cal reminds Rachel about the day he proposed, he may only have to say "Remember the chaos" for Rachel to know exactly what he is talking about. She and Cal have told this story many times before, and Cal's point is quite clear to her. Another English speaking couple would understand the words, "Remember the chaos," but would not interpret them in the same way.

Moreover, relational culture is only one part of the cultural context that affects a family's communication and meaning-making. Race and ethnicity are also factors. Thus, the Washingtons, in our earlier example, may interpret their story as they do in part because Su-Lin is Chinese American. Confucian morality, governing most traditional Chinese American families, places a great emphasis on family obligations and honoring ancestors (Hardway & Fuligni, 2006).

There is some evidence that family stories are universal and are represented in all cultures. Although individual cultures may enact storytelling differently or may interpret stories differently based on unique cultural mores, family stories persist across cultures. For example, Bernie Sloan (1999) notes that in Irish families storytelling is a way of life, harking back to the tradition of Irish ballad makers. Carma Bylund (2003) found that although ethnicity may affect some functions of family stories (for example, the Latino family she studied did not say that passing down family history was an important function of their family stories, whereas the African American and European American families did), family stories were equally integral to all the families' lives and cultures. Stephanie Wright (2008) states that one important function of storytelling in immigrant families is the transmission of cultural values, both to adjust to an adopted culture and to retain key values of the original culture. Cheshire's (2001) study of narrative in American Indian families, for instance, pointed to a strong desire to ensure the maintenance and survival of their culture through storytelling, among other practices.

Walter Fisher (1987) has suggested that human beings are, by nature, storytellers and that we live our lives in narrative. Fisher argues that we know the world as a set of stories, and we pick and choose among these stories, selecting those that seem most true and probable to us. Other researchers (e.g., Bergen, 2010; Thorson, 2012; Wright, 2008) agree with Fisher. Meredith Marko Harrigan (2010) asserts that narrative is "integral to the human experience" (p. 24), used across cultures to understand family, individual, and cultural meanings. Kristin Langellier and Eric Peterson (2004) observed that "people make sense of their experiences, claim identities,

Student Perspective: Eliana

I always tell my husband that I really knew I was a member of his family when I started to hear the family stories for a second and third time. I was just an outsider at first, hearing the stories. I became an insider when I could recognize the stories and even join in. It was funny, but the third time I heard his great-uncle tell the story about how he handled the cow rebellion when he was the governor of Nebraska, I really did feel I belonged in this family. Then, later, my husband and I would retell this story (and others) to our kids—now it's "our" story. I can see how communities are built this way.

Student Perspective: Mariah

Stories are so important in my family. Every time there are two or more of my family members together in a room, someone is telling a story. We love to relive funny things that have happened, and a lot of our stories are about that—sometimes poking fun at my brother, Abe, who always seems to get in trouble in a kind of humorous way. But we also tell stories to remember important people that the younger generation doesn't really know, like my great-great-aunt Zilla. She was a former slave, but she was feisty and never let anyone get the best of her. There are a lot of stories about how Zilla outsmarted folks.

Student Perspective: Rafe

In my family I know our deep religious beliefs affect our stories, and maybe that is also because we are Latinos. Almost every story my family tells shows how God looks out for us and helps us, even when we do stupid things. We are always saying that God puts us in certain situations, and God helps us out of them as well. One story we always tell is about when my sister, Lala, almost set our kitchen on fire because she forgot and left a pan on the stove with just a little grease in it. The grease soon burned away and the pan started smoking. Just before everything burst into flames, our friend Tobias came to the kitchen door and Lala had to go back in there to let him in, so she saw the pan and saved the house from burning. God had to have brought Tobias to our door.

interact with each other, and participate in cultural conversations through storytelling" (p. 1).

Elizabeth Stone (2008) has defined **family stories** as those "bit[s] of lore about a family member, living or dead . . . [that have] worked [their] way into the family canon to be told and retold" (p. 5). When you think about your own family, you probably can remember stories that are told and retold at family gatherings. Stone asserts that these stories communicate more than a plotline—they also communicate who we are, what we value, and how we should live our lives. As Robert Bellah and his colleagues note in *Habits of the Heart* (Bellah, Madsen, Sullivan, Swidler, & Tipton, 1986), family stories bind families to one another in "communities of memory," acknowledging the past and creating hope for the future.

In this chapter we (1) discuss the characteristics of family stories; (2) review the functions of family stories; (3) examine types of family stories; and (4) contrast family stories with similar symbolic behaviors that develop a family's sense of themselves.

UNDERSTANDING FAMILY STORIES

As we begin our discussion exploring the concept of family stories, it is important to first note how valuable family stories are for identity development, relational satisfaction, and overall personal growth according to many researchers (e.g., Adams, 2008; Ellingson & Sotirin, 2010; McNay, 2009). Patrice Buzzanell and Lynn Turner (2012) observe that families seek meaning and identity through narrative. This is no doubt the case because of the characteristics that distinguish family stories from other, less formative, family interactions. We turn now to an examination of each of the following characteristics of family stories: They feature a family member or several members; involve a plotline of some type; develop around something significant for the family; exist in performance; contain an element of drama; and are somewhat fluid over time.

The Family as Subject

Rita Buchoff (1995) observes that the "featured characters," or subjects, in family stories are family members, living or dead. While cultural stories—stories we read in books, hear in songs, see on television or in the movies—are also important to us, they are not the same as family stories because the characters in them are not related to us as part of our family. Yet, this generalization may not hold true across all cultures. This may be especially the case with Native Americans. Lois Einhorn (2000) states that some Native American stories may sound like the cultural stories we mentioned above because they refer to unrelated people or to animals in a parable form. Yet, Einhorn argues these can be considered family stories because of the inclusive meaning Native Americans have for families. Native Americans consider human relatives as family, but they go beyond that to include the physical, natural, and spiritual worlds:

> *To Native Americans, then, family relationships stretch across time and distance and include flora and fauna as well as people. Carter Camp, Ponca, offered this example: "Just as our grandfathers are us, we are our grandchildren. In this way the grasshopper, the sweetgrass, the rabbit, the clover and the sage are part of us." He illustrated his point, continuing, "As when my brother Crowdog came home from prison. He stepped from the car and went to the trees around his homeplace. He put his arms around each and told them he was home. He spoke to his grandfathers, his separation from them had hurt." (p. 38)*

Thus, stories about trees and animals can represent family stories in the Native American tradition.

Elizabeth Stone (2008) describes the appeal a story about her great-grandmother had for her as a child by saying first that the story seemed to be about the "genesis" of her family and, second, that her great-grandmother was a wonderful, admirable character in the story. And, as Stone says, the story showed a person who was someone she aspired to be like, "and most important, [someone she] felt [she] *could* be like. She [Stone's great-grandmother] wasn't distant like a film star or imaginary like a fairy-tale heroine. She was real. And she was my relative" (p. 4).

Richard Price (2003) observes that because family stories are peopled by characters related to the tellers and the listeners, they provide a gift to both parties. A little bit of their humanity is exchanged in telling stories about relatives past and present and that makes the telling and listening a pleasure.

Student Perspective: Sam

One story my family always likes to tell is about me, when I was maybe five years old. Our family had gone on a vacation to Florida, and my parents had left me at the pool with my 10-year-old sister, Megan. Megan was supposed to be watching me, but she couldn't come in the pool because she had poison ivy all over her arms. I was supposed to stay in the shallow end of the pool. But after I had been there for a while, I noticed a bunch of kids jumping off the low diving board at the other end of the pool. There was an adult waiting for the kids in the water, and he caught them as they jumped in and guided them over to the side, where they climbed out and went back to the board and did it again. It looked like a lot of fun to me, and I figured that the man was hired by the pool to catch little kids. So I climbed out and made my way over to the low board. Megan was reading a magazine, and she didn't notice me. I jumped joyfully off the board, but the man had left with his kids, and I didn't know how to swim! I guess Megan looked up at that moment because she ran over to the side of the pool and leaned over me as I bobbed up and down and made it over to the side and out of the pool. Boy, she was really yelling at me. Everybody likes to tease me about how I learned to swim by putting my faith in a "catcher" who wasn't there for me after all.

We can assume that the pleasure Alex and Rita McIntosh take in the story about the Christmas tree that we mentioned at the beginning of this chapter has to do with the fact that they are the characters in the narrative. As Buchoff (1995) notes, family stories appeal to us because we, or those related to us, play the starring roles. In hearing stories about ourselves and our family members, we learn about our own behavior as well as connect ourselves to our family culture.

Sequence of Events

The story that Sam tells in the accompanying box is about himself and his family, and it also follows a sequential pattern. One thing leads to another as Sam reveals the **sequence** of events that were involved in this episode at the pool. The story has a beginning—when Sam's parents leave him playing at the pool under his sister's supervision. The story has a middle—when Sam gets the idea to jump off the diving board and have the man catch him. And the story has an ending—when Sam bobs safely to the side of the pool while Megan shouts at him. The sequence that Sam's story follows is linear, in that the events are organized in chronological time, but that is not the only pattern that family stories take. Some stories involve flashbacks and flash-forwards, as storytellers weave their tales. Even in Sam's story, he comments on the episode in the present by noting how his family still teases him about his naive belief in the kindness of strangers. This movement to the present in Sam's story comes at the end, so he still maintains a chronology from the past to the present. But sometimes storytellers might make the present comment on the story before telling it, thus altering the sequence a bit.

All stories have a sequence. Whether the story moves in a linear fashion, or adopts a more circular form, listeners are able to discern a beginning, a middle, and an end to family stories. If listeners do not "get" the sequence, they will usually ask questions of the storyteller. For example, in the Van Deer family, Grandmother Van Deer likes to tell stories about when she was a young girl growing up in Holland. Once, after telling a brief story about walking home from school each day with her friend Ella, her granddaughter asked, "So, what's the point, Grandma?" To the granddaughter, this particular story did not have a satisfactory ending—it seemed to be missing something. The storyteller was asked to provide the missing elements, making the story whole. Jane Jorgenson and Arthur Bochner (2004) assert that family life is a struggle to impose a narrative structure on the messiness of unexpected events and lived experience. They argue that families work to accomplish this by constructing stories that have some coherent plotline or sequence. As they note, "Each family must imagine, create and/or sustain symbolic images that draw past and future into the present" (p. 517). Allison Thorson (2012) agrees, suggesting that **accounts** are a special class of narrative that are created to explain and control events that need to be turned and shaped by tellers.

Some researchers assert that sequencing family stories is a function of gender. Some evidence from folklorists and sociolinguists suggests that women organize stories more around details and less around temporal order of events, compared with men (Hall & Langellier, 1988). Women often organize stories in an episodic fashion (Sullivan & Goldzwig, 1996), relying on their listeners to fill in textual gaps. When women and men tell family stories together, they often divide storytelling roles. Men provide the plotline, giving the story a linear sequence, while women provide the contextual material, circling around the linear plot (Baldwin, 1985).

Significance

Elizabeth Stone (2008) notes that stories vary in terms of how elaborately plotted they are and observes that some of her own family stories relied on a well-developed scene, whereas others were merely character sketches of family members. Stone argues that these short, loosely plotted tales qualify "as stories in the way haiku qualify as poems" (p. 5). What must be present for lore to be characterized as a family story, however, is not so much plot as **significance.** Family stories endure in family groups because, in Stone's words, "they matter."

Jennifer Bohanek and her colleagues (2008) comment that family stories form a window into families' lives because they account for something that is important to the family. Families, of course, vary in what is important to them and thus in what's a likely issue for storytelling, but here we

---

~~~~ POPULAR PRESS PERSPECTIVES ~~~~

Jonathan Shorman reports in *USA Today* about a study showing how telling stories may be of help to terminally ill patients. Shorman cites a study done by Canadian researchers focusing on what they call "dignity therapy." This therapy guides patients through a conversation with a trained interviewer aimed at eliciting their life story. The conversation is recorded and then edited into a transcript that patients can share with their families. The study involved 441 patients and ages ranged from 18 into the 90s, with an average age of 65.

The lead researcher, Harvey Chochinov of the University of Manitoba, is quoted as saying that dignity therapy contributed to self-reported well-being significantly more than standard end-of-life care. Shorman says that "Chochinov called the patients' experiences extraordinary. One man, who had battled alcoholism much of his life and was estranged from most of his family, wanted his grandchildren to know who he was so they could choose a different path." Chochinov notes that patients all tell unique stories that are meaningful in their distinctiveness. Shorman concludes that "behind dignity therapy is the idea of 'generativity,' which the study defined as the ability to guide the next generation, and how patients may be comforted knowing they are creating something that will last beyond their death."

Jonathan Shorman, "'Dignity Therapy Gives Comfort to Dying Patients," *USA Today* (online). July 11, 2011. Retrieved July 21, 2011.

---

will discuss one aspect of significance: power, or the practice of control and authority.

Family Stories Name Practices of Control and Authority   Glen Stamp and Teresa Sabourin (1995) discuss a painful aspect of the significance of family stories. In analyzing the narratives of husbands who abuse their wives, Stamp and Sabourin conclude that abuse may be legitimized through family stories. When abusive men have witnessed abuse in their families-of-origin, this abuse is most likely reinforced through stories, according to Stamp and Sabourin. Further, as Kristin Langellier and Elizabeth Peterson (1993) assert, "Family storytelling names practices of social control. Stories and storytelling both generate and reproduce 'the family' by legitimizing meanings and power relations" (p. 50). This issue relates to the significance of family stories and also points to a potential dark side of family stories.

Yet, as Elinor Ochs and Lisa Capps (1996) illustrate, storytelling does not have to dwell on the dark side of power. Power relations "on a seemingly benign but nonetheless consequential level, [are revealed when] parental accounts of family incidents . . . carry more legitimacy than those told by children" (p. 33). Ochs and Capps suggest that power is reproduced through family stories by what they call **narrative asymmetry.** Narrative asymmetry exists in the unequal distribution of three elements: (1) *narrative rights,* or who gets to tell a story; (2) *narrative timing,* or who determines when a story is told; and (3) *narrative reception,* or who is the primary recipient or listener for stories. Analyzing a family in terms of its narrative asymmetry provides a sense of its power structure. Ochs and Capps observe that there is cultural variability in family power relations.

In many cultures, children may be denied narrative rights. Ochs and Capps state that in the Xavante culture in Brazil, adolescent males must go through a formal rite of passage before they can recount narratives. In other cases, in the United States for example, the ritual is not formalized, but adults may simply preempt children's stories by taking over the story once a child begins it or by being the ones to initiate the narrative (such as, "Molly, tell your father what happened in school today"). By initiating stories in this way, adults exert power over narrative timing as well.

Additionally, Ochs and Capps focus on narrative reception, arguing that the primary listener has the right to "provide feedback on a narrative contribution, for example, to align and embellish; to question, tease, and refute; or to ignore" (p. 35). This places the listener in a powerful position. In European American families, narratives are often told by mothers and children to fathers. In contrast, Japanese families tend to involve fathers much less in storytelling, and mothers and children select each other as primary listeners. Thus, power structures reproduce differently in these two cultures.

In a study examining how families crafted stories about the job loss of their major wage earner, Patrice Buzzanell and Lynn Turner (2012) found that the person who lost the job (in all cases, it was the father/husband) was the major storyteller. This privilege accorded to the father "sometimes diminished others' discursive and material contributions to the family" (p. 294). Buzzanell and Turner observed patterns showing that the man of the family was the primary author of the families' stories, and the other family members provided support for him and his version of the story. They listened to him and focused on his reactions and emotions, rather than weaving their own impressions into the story. Family members reported that they felt the need to empathize with the husband/father and to "get in synch" with him. In this way, in these U.S. families, fathers were given narrative rights and determined narrative timing.

Family stories provide significance to families through a variety of means, inculding naming practices of control and authority. As Stone (2008) notes, when stories no longer speak to something significant to the family, they tend to disappear and are no longer told.

Performance

Because we are concerned with communication in this book, we like the distinction that Mary-Jeanette Smythe (1995) makes when she compares Walter Fisher's (1984, 1987) and Robert Rowland's (1987) concepts of narrative. Smythe observes that Fisher's approach is broad and inclusive, whereas Rowland's focuses, more specifically, on "the talk that forms a story" (p. 246). This attention to the performance of storytelling allows us to examine the connections among storytelling in the family and the social functions that are served by storytelling, according to Smythe and other researchers (e.g., Langellier & Peterson, 2004). Joseph Veroff and his colleagues (1993) also comment on the performance aspect of stories when they state that narratives differ from accounts found in sources such as diaries because narratives imply an audience, whereas diaries involve more private, unspoken cognitions. For families, the telling and retelling of stories—the **performance**—is just as important (or more important) as knowing them.

This distinction between performance and cognition implies that individual family members may reflect on family stories somewhat differently, a subject we will discuss at greater length a little bit later in the chapter. Despite differences in cognition, however, the performance of family stories is agreed upon collectively. That is to say, the family members are in accord concerning the telling of the story. For example, as Cal and Rachel, from our story at the beginning of the chapter, talk about telling her parents about their engagement, they focus on the same elements of the plot, characters, and sequence.

Sometimes family stories are performed jointly, as with Cal and Rachel, or by groups of family members, each chiming in to tell a favorite part; but often these stories have a single storyteller. However, as Veroff and his colleagues (1993) argue, even when only one person tells a story, its inception and construction may have been collaborative. Many family members may have contributed their ideas and embellishments to a story that one designated storyteller retells.

Student Perspective: Akiko

In my family my grandmother and grandfather were the main storytellers. Although, now that I think about it, I guess it was more my grandmother. My grandfather just came in once in a while and provided a detail here and there. My grandmother came to the United States in 1910 from Japan as a picture bride. She and my grandfather had never met—they had just exchanged pictures. At first their marriage did not go well. My grandfather had expected a gentle, docile woman, and my grandmother was too strong-minded for him. For her part, my grandmother really struggled with English; she found the language difficult and often wondered why she had come to the United States. Despite all this, their marriage endured for over 50 years. Mostly the stories my grandmother told us had happy endings.

Elizabeth Stone (2008) argues that most often the role of family storyteller is assumed by women in the family. She observes that stories are told about both men and women, but the tellers are most frequently female. In her study of long-lasting marriages, Fran Dickson (1995) observed that even when men and women told their stories together, women often dominated the storytelling.

Stone's (2008) book on family stories, *Black Sheep and Kissing Cousins: How Our Family Stories Shape Us,* is the result of many interviews she conducted throughout the United States, asking people to tell her their family stories. She states that she did not begin her project believing that more women than men were family storytellers, but that is the message she got from her respondents. A quote from one of the men she spoke with provides an example of the insight she heard repeatedly about the sexes:

> *"From everything I've studied or seen, I would expect the men to be the storytellers. In tribes, the* griots *who tell the family genealogy are always men, but that's not my experience. If I want family history, I go to the women. If I want to hear about the men, I still go to the women. It's my aunts who tell stories about my father. Never my father himself." (p. 20)*

Stone concludes that as long as families are perceived as women's sphere, women will be the major storytellers.

Bohanek, Marin, & Fivush (2008) investigated how emotions were incorporated into family stories that parents told to their children. They were interested to see if gender made a difference in how and how much emotion was expressed. They found, contrary to their expectations, that in the same family, mothers and fathers tended to express emotion similarly. There seemed to be a "family style" relative to emotion talk in narratives. However, they also found that overall, mothers talked more about emotions than fathers did. This is not surprising, they concluded, because mothers tend to do the majority of "emotion work" and storytelling in families.

Dramatic Element

Family stories usually have some quality of **drama**—a sense of suspense or conflict, for example. Of course, family stories vary in their dramatic aspects. Sometimes the dramatic quality of the story is enhanced by the way the story is told. Some family storytellers have a flair for the dramatic and assume different voices as they almost act out the stories they tell. When more than one family member participates in the telling, stories can deepen in dramatic quality. For example, Elinor Ochs (1989) has been studying family storytelling at the dinner table and has identified what she calls the family detective story. The reason Ochs calls this type of narrative a detective story is because of the storytelling process, not the content of the story. She says that typically in this interaction someone begins to tell a story, leaving out some important pieces of information, and the other family members do not just listen quietly but "co-narrate" by asking the storyteller questions aimed at bringing out all the parts of the story. As Ochs (1997) later observes, "Collaborative storytelling helps to create solidarity" (p. 201). Ochs observes that this structure of storytelling, **slow disclosure,** resembles many literary and cinematic plots. Slow disclosure and listener participation can heighten the suspense and dramatic quality of family stories.

Pamela Benoit and Kimberly Kennedy (1998) illustrate the dramatic quality of family stories in their analysis of a story they call "the broken leg." This story is about a traumatic event in which a son is severely injured in a sledding accident. The drama of the story is further heightened by the fact that the boy's brother at first does not realize how serious the injuries are, nor do his parents. Additionally, the drama intensifies because the story is conjointly told by the mother and the brother. As they interweave their versions of what happened on the sledding hill (the brother's perspective) and what happened at the hospital (the mother's perspective), their competition for a "telling space" provides suspense. Some researchers (e.g., Bohanek, Fivush, Zaman, & Lepore, 2009) argue that collaborative storytelling involving children as collaborators is critical for the children's sense of well-being and emotional adjustment.

Some evidence suggests that there may be cultural variations in the performative characteristic of famliy stories. Karla Scott (1995) and Thomas Kochman (1981) both argue that African Americans may be more animated and confrontational than European Americans. Scott's and Kochman's work indicates that African Americans may be more inclined to drama than European Americans. Michael Hecht and his colleagues (Hecht, Larkey, & Johnson, 1992; Hecht, Ribeau, & Alberts, 1989) investigated African Americans' preferred communication behaviors for achieving satisfaction in interethnic conversations. They found a need for expressiveness, which might indicate that African Americans are comfortable with dramatic communication. Joseph Veroff and his colleagues (1993) report on an unpublished study they conducted contrasting the marriage narratives of black and white newlywed couples. They did not find striking differences in dramatic style between the two races, but the section of the narrative dealing with the wedding itself was judged to be more dramatic in the black couples' stories.

Fluidity

Elizabeth Stone (2008) explains **fluidity** of family stories best when she comments that even after we leave our original families we carry their stories with us, and they continue to matter to us but sometimes in new ways. Thus, stories change over time and are shaped and reshaped as the need arises. When Opal's daughter, Vanessa, was born, Opal's mother told a lot of stories about Opal's birth. By the time Vanessa was 10, birth stories were replaced by stories about Opal's childhood. Opal's mother recycled stories about her daughter's childhood to parallel her granddaughter's growth and development. Stone says we may "claim" some of our family stories at times of life transitions and "put our own stamp on them, make them part of us instead of making ourselves part of them. We are always in conversation with them one way or another" (p. 8). It is interesting to think of ourselves in conversation with our stories, and this notion focuses on the importance of process in the practice of storytelling, as well as in other areas of family communication.

Several researchers have noted that often members of the older generation are the main family storytellers (e.g., Benoit, Kennedy, Waters, Hinton, Drew, & Daniels, 1996; Nydegger & Mitteness, 1988). The fluidity of stories is illustrated when the grandparents die and the next generation begins telling the stories. In passing the storytelling torch generationally, the stories are adapted to the new tellers—embellished and tailored to the new generation's experiences.

Sometimes stories change because the listeners grow and change. Sharon Fiffer (1996) comments on this when she reflects on a story her father told her when she was 14. The story was a family secret about how Fiffer's paternal grandmother had given her youngest son to her brother and his wife to adopt. Fiffer's grandmother had been very ill and recently widowed when she was persuaded to become her son's aunt and keep a family secret. After Fiffer learns this story, she has difficulty understanding its meaning, and she observes, "I couldn't reconcile my stern but loving sewing teacher with a mother who could give up her baby boy. I was old enough to know the family secret, but I still had a teenager's heart, all soft sentiment, little hard compassion. I didn't get it. It didn't add up" (p. xiii). Years later as she tells this story to her children, she understands it and shapes it differently than when she first heard it.

Family therapists often focus on this characteristic of family stories and encourage family members to "re-author" dominant narratives so they become more productive and helpful to the participants in therapy (Chrzastowski, 2011). These therapists, known as narrative therapists, define families as a collection of specific stories, rather than simply a group of related people. As Szymon Chrzastowski notes, "a portion of these stories still need to be uttered, while a part are well-known: old stories retold countless times, each time in a new way. This new way of retelling stories allows them to be reinterpreted in a way that will better serve the person [in therapy]" (p. 637). Because family stories are fluid and subject to multiple interpretations, they are amenable to therapeutic uses such as Chrzastowski describes.

Negotiated Meaning

We mentioned earlier that stories are characterized by their performable nature—they are told aloud to listeners. This makes them different from the private thoughts and accounts that individual family members possess. Stone (2008) argues that families share a sense of what their stories mean, and this is what enables stories to be such powerful shapers of a family's sense of identity. Stone asserts that in her research she checked meanings with family members and discovered that while people did not always relate identical versions, the different versions were usually congruent and compatible with one another. It is possible for some family members to place more importance on slightly different elements of a story than other members do, but in general families share an understanding of what their lore is telling them.

This does not mean that all family members accept the lessons and values put forth in family stories. Many families have rebellious members. Yet, even when individual members reject the family values or meanings advocated in stories, they understand what they are. Thus, family meanings are known, even if rebuffed. Further, it is possible for individual family members to understand the **collective meaning** and then to shape it in their own individualistic way. As Elinor Ochs and Lisa Capps (1996) state, the meanings people take from stories are mapped onto their personal experience, perhaps resulting in only "partially overlapping" meanings.

In the Tucker family, a favorite story concerns Great-Grandfather Enos Tucker, who was the president of a bank that failed during the Depression. The story recounts how, when the bank failed, Great-Grandfather paid all his customers 100 cents on the dollar, bankrupting the family but maintaining the family's honor. The shared meaning here focuses on dignity and honor, no matter what the personal cost. Todd and Jeffery Tucker, the great-grandsons of Enos, both understand and accept this family value. However, Todd has adapted it to mean that money is irrelevant to honor, whereas Jeffery has focused on making money in an honorable way.

In describing how couples and families work together to create stories about family experiences, Barbara H. Fiese and Arnold J. Sameroff (1999) introduce the concept of narrative interaction. In this process, families work together to co-construct a story they can agree on and that represents their values. However, Fiese and Sameroff note that this interaction process may not always be accomplished smoothly. Families may conflict over story versions and meanings. Sometimes family members may actively disconfirm another's story. Further, race may affect how couples perform narrative interaction. Marianne Dainton (1999)

Student Perspective: Marta

I was thinking about the idea we discussed that family members all "get" the same basic meaning out of stories told in the family. I was trying to decide if all of us kids would agree about our family's meaning, based on the stories we've heard. I called my sister, Camille, and we talked about it for a while. It was pretty amazing how much we did agree on what our stories meant. I think the reason why we do is because these stories are repeated so often, and sometimes the "moral" is even stated by the storyteller. You'd have to really not be paying attention not to figure it out after kind of having it drilled into your skull!

TABLE 6-1   Characteristics of Family Stories

Subject: The story is about a person (or persons) who are part of the listener's family. Aunt Ida, Great-Grandpa Charlie, or the fraternity brother who graduated in 1963 are all appropriate subjects for family stories.

Sequence: Family stories have some type of coherent plotline that moves through time. Family stories may be chronological, or they may contain flashbacks and/or flash-forwards.

Significance: The story is important for the family in various ways including naming practices of control and authority.

Performance: Family stories must be told and retold in front of an audience (who may participate in the telling).

Dramatic element: Family stories contain some dramatic quality such as conflict, suspense, or humorous plot twists.

Fluidity: Family stories change over time if necessary—some elaborations, renovations, and omissions characterize the stories as time passes.

Negotiated meanings: Family stories are characterized by some sense of meaning shared (if not accepted) by family members.

observed that European American couples conflicted with each other less than did African Americans in telling courtship and marriage stories. Although European American couples did interrupt each other in telling their narratives, they did so less than African Americans did. Biracial couples were very interactive in telling their stories, but their interruptions tended to be in the form of elaborations rather than conflict.

An understanding of family stories is grounded in a clarification of several characteristics that elaborate our definition of family stories—subject, sequence, significance, performance, drama, fluidity, and negotiated meanings. Table 6-1 summarizes these important characteristics of family stories.

FUNCTIONS OF FAMILY STORIES

Family stories shape the private world of the family by developing the "family worldview" (Sluzki, 1983). In so doing, family stories serve several important functions. They provide a sense of identity, link families from the past through the present and into the future, teach lessons, as well as negotiate tensions and manage family difficulties. We will briefly review each of these functions.

Building Identity

Family stories help families define, articulate, and refine their sense of collective identity, and in doing so, they contribute significantly to the system's meaning. For example, the parents in the Liss family survived the Holocaust. Some research (Turner, 1997) suggests that Holocaust survivors either tell incessant stories about their experiences or make the Holocaust a taboo topic. In either case, children of Holocaust survivors display great interest in stories about their parents' experiences. In the Liss family, stories about the parents' lives during the war were shared, but the stories focused mainly on the luck the Lisses had in escaping rather than on the horrors they lived through. In telling their children about how lucky they were to survive and how they persevered through danger and death in order to make it to the United States and begin a life together, Ellis and Ruth Liss establish a sense of their family as special—both severely tested and uniquely blessed. This theme of luck in the face of great trauma shapes the Liss family's identity in a much different way than would stories of survival at enormous cost.

Stories also help individual family members to shape their personal identities. In a family like the Lisses, the children may see themselves as responsible for their parents' continued luck and happiness. Indeed, some children of Holocaust survivors report that their parents' stories made them see themselves as caretakers and made teenage rebellion difficult (Turner, 1997). In a different example, the story Sam told about jumping in the pool in Florida offers messages about how Sam's family sees him and how he might shape his own identity. He is described as adventurous, too trusting of others, yet resourceful. In the story, Sam puts himself in a dangerous situation by being somewhat naive, but he is able to get to safety without anyone's help after all. Sam's story implies a criticism of his behavior while also providing a sense of his strength.

Although some family stories ridicule family members, most present the family in a positive light or flatter individual members by highlighting their strengths. Even in those stories that point out flaws in the family or in individual members, often the overall message is positive. In Sam's story, as we pointed out previously, his actions are the source of humor for the family, but the outcome of the story shows him prevailing. In showing the family as attractive and admirable, family stories provide families with esteem as well as identity. That is, not only do family members understand their identity through stories, but they are made proud of this identity as well.

Navita Cummings James (2004) describes how family stories can develop a sense of esteem within the family consciously by refuting the dominant culture's negative messages. James talks about how her parents spoke frequently about race in an effort to challenge the cultural messages of the 1950s and 1960s of "what it meant to be 'colored' or 'Negro'" (p. 62). James observes that her father's stories focused on the evils of whites. Despite her father's skills as a pilot and a carpenter, racial discrimination caused him to struggle, usually failing to be paid what he was really worth. James's mother's stories emphasized different things than her father's. "For example, she stressed how my grandmother helped poor Whites. My mother did not believe in any way that Blacks were inferior to Whites. She was very proud of her family, and there was no false humility here" (p. 63). James concludes that from the stories of her youth she developed beliefs about being black—that blacks are just as good and often morally superior to whites, that they have to fight for their rights and be prepared to be twice as good as whites to be considered half as good. Although her family stories prepared her for racial discrimination, they also countered notions that blacks were inferior and thus developed esteem within the family.

Creating Links Among the Past, Present, and Future

Researchers (e.g., Ballard & Ballard, 2011; Goodall, 2005, 2006; McNay, 2009) speak of **narrative inheritance** or the lore that elders pass on to family members. This narrative inheritance is the storehouse of stories that help us make sense of the present and the future by contextualizing them through the past. Further, this linking function relates to the previous identity-building function. As Robert Ballard and Sarah Ballard observe, the act of storytelling provides "the site where [their family] jointly, interactionally, collaboratively, and in a shared way make[s] sense of the narrative we have inherited while simultaneously constituting who we are—our identity—as a family" (pp. 73–74).

Richard Price (2003) comments eloquently on the connecting function of family stories when he describes the enjoyment he has in telling his young daughters stories about himself, his father, and his grandfather. Price states,

> *Everyone knows the pleasure of being on the receiving end of narrative hand-me-downs. But as I took in my daughters' attentive faces, the terse nods of absorption, the slightly parted lips, the pre-setting of the laugh muscles around the mouth and eyes, all the ways that I could see the stories ingested, the kick for the teller became ineffably obvious. "I love you" is just a phrase, the quacking of a duck, of a thousand ducks; so here, take this small chip of my life, it's yours now, too. And there's plenty more where that came from. (p. B3)*

Lucas Bietti (2010) notes the referential function of family stories as helping families remember events and experiences and creating shared memories among family members. The connecting or linking function we're discussing here also serves that referential function in that family stories keep memories alive long after those who have actually experienced them are gone. Further, family stories serve a socializing function by telling new family members about the family lore. This socializing function is also similar to the linking function as the links may be horizontal in time as well as vertical. That is, a new member marrying into a family, for instance, is connected to the family through hearing its stories.

In their study of the communication of aunts and their nieces and nephews, Laura Ellingson and Patricia Sotirin (2010) argue that aunts often serve the function of kin keepers. They act as agents of "continuity and connection in extended family networks" (p. 150). In this role, they contribute to the processes of linking families across generations and weaving an intergenerational family narrative.

Teaching Lessons and Morals

Elders in families often instruct directly by telling their children how to behave in various situations. But perhaps even more frequently they instruct indirectly, by telling stories that incorporate moral lessons or family codes. Walter Kawamoto and Tamara Cheshire (1997) interviewed Frank Merrill, a respected elder in their Native American community. One of the things they asked him was to tell them about his family. In his reply, Merrill observed:

> *When I was brought up, my grandparents did most of the disciplining. The grandparents are usually the ones who end up being the teachers. I think that is where the respect for the elders came in a long time ago. They used to set me down if I did something wrong, and a lot of times they'd tell me stories of how to gather my food if I was alone, and if I was playing around when I was supposed to be working, they'd tell me coyote stories, about how this coyote didn't do his work and the outcome would be where we learned the lesson. (p. 30)*

As Merrill suggests, adults often use parables to develop a sense of morality in their children.

In the McIntosh family, who appear at the beginning of this chapter, the family story focuses on the importance of the past. Further, the fact that the story Rita and Alex share highlights the values of familial love, togetherness, and humor indicates that these are the lessons the McIntosh family take from the past. As Genie Zeiger (2000) notes, family stories convey "ancestral lore and wisdom," providing lessons for living a moral life.

Negotiating Dialectical Tensions and Managing Difficulties

In Chapter 2 we explored the theory of dialectics, which holds that family life is characterized by seeming oppositions that coexist in a both/and fashion rather than an either/or relationship. We reviewed some of the major dialectics permeating family interaction: autonomy and connection, openness and protection, and novelty and predictability. Earlier in this chapter, when we pointed out that stories are fluid and changeable, we were implying that stories can provide help for negotiating dialectical tensions. Elizabeth Stone (2008) states this point eloquently as she illustrates how the fluidity of family stories helps people manage to be both a part of and separate from their families:

> *Eventually we come of age and tell the story of our own lives in which the past has become our prologue; we have our own family and*

invent an ethos for it. This is the stage of transformations, willed or unwilled, the point at which we make our own meanings. Our meanings are almost always inseparable from stories, in all realms of life. And once again family stories, invisible as air, weightless as dreams, are there for us. To make our own meanings out of our myriad stories is to achieve balance—at once a way to be part of and apart from our families, a way of holding on and letting go. (pp. 243–244)

In a simple way, when Jerry and Mindy, from the beginning of our chapter, talk about her brother-in-law's proposal, they may also be managing the tension between autonomy and connection. They experienced togetherness with Mindy's family, but they manage their lives a bit differently. Their laughter at the story is part enjoyment and part distancing themselves from that behavior.

When storytellers vary a favorite story, they are playing with the tension between novelty and predictability. Well-known family stories are often co-narrated, as we pointed out earlier. The interplay between and among the tellers may highlight both predictability and spontaneity. For example, when Rita and Alex McIntosh, from the beginning of the chapter, tell the familiar story of the Christmas branches, they may take turns adding details. They enjoy both the repetition and the predictability of the story. But occasionally, one of them might vary the sequence or add a slightly new twist to the story. In this way, the story evolves both predictably and creatively.

Student Perspective: Paula

It struck me when we talked about how sometimes stories get told so much they get boring, and then the family changes the story a little to make it more interesting again. That is just what happened in my family. My uncle Ronnie always tells the same story about the time he was in the Navy and had to cook for a whole ship. The story goes on and on about what he cooked and all the problems he had. Well, one day my mother started telling the story with Ronnie. She had it down word for word, and she wouldn't stop even though it was plain Ronnie wasn't too happy. Finally he got the hint and added some new material just so she couldn't be talking in time with him. The next time he told the story it was a little different; he added some new parts and left out some details. But it was odd, because I kind of missed the old way the story was told, so I added in some of the old stuff that he left out.

In addition to negotiating the expected tensions that characterize family life, stories are also used to manage a range of difficulties that families encounter. April Trees and Jody Koenig Kellas (2009) comment that "narratives help people make sense of difficult experiences" (p. 91), and they cite other researchers who state that disclosing difficulties is beneficial for people's physical and psychological health. Thus, Trees and Koenig Kellas investigate whether jointly told family stories have beneficial effects on the family's relational culture. They found that when families tell stories of shared difficult experiences, they do reap benefits if the stories are told with perceived supportiveness and coherence.

Several researchers (e.g., Alemán & Helfrich, 2010; Lindenmeyer, Griffiths, Green, Thompson, & Tsouroufli, 2009; Sirota, 2010) have examined how family stories are used to manage the uncertainties and concerns related to illness. In an autoethnography, Melissa Wood Alleman and Katherine Helfrich (who are mother and daughter) write about their own family's narrative inheritance related to dementia. Both Melissa's grandmothers (and Katherine's mother and mother-in-law) suffered from dementia before their deaths. As Alleman and Helfrich quilt their stories together they discover "the therapeutic value of telling difficult stories together" (p. 20).

Gino Giannini (2011) explores how narrative helps bereaved parents cope with the loss of a child. Giannini interviewed 10 people (five married couples) who had lost a child between the ages of 3 and 22. He found that the parents found comfort in telling their stories and in so doing were able to engage in the process of recovery.

TYPES OF FAMILY STORIES

There are infinite types of family stories, but some stock genres recur across many families (Stone, 2008). These include stories of courtship, birth, and survival. In addition, we will discuss another type: stories on the margins.

Courtship Stories

We are calling stories about first meeting, love, dating, and wedding ceremonies **courtship stories**. These stories instruct family members in the meaning of love, marriage, and the interplay between cultural expectations and more idiosyncratic family mores and customs. Courtship stories are, like all family stories, about matters of significance to the family. When these stories are not told or given cultural support, as in the case of a divorced couple or a gay or lesbian couple, the family loses a narrative resource.

As Elizabeth Stone (2008) suggests, courtship stories "offer at least one possible way to enter into this intricate dance; they suggest what to feel about love, how to recognize it, what to do with it" (p. 74). Stone offers the example of Jane Gilbert, who learned from stories of her grandparents' courtship and marriage that love should be approached slowly and reasonably. "Flyaway passion was a danger to family stability: it led to divorce, abandonment, and agricultural ruin" (p. 55). Therefore, the story of how Gilbert's grandparents had grown up together, always known each other, became sweethearts, and then married, illustrated to Gilbert the approved family script for courtship and love.

The story about the Gilbert grandparents was reinforced by the story of Jane Gilbert's maternal grandparents, the Picketts. They also had always known each other; and the story is told that one day Gilbert's grandfather, Henry, was visiting her grandmother, Opal, before their marriage, and Opal's mother asked Henry if he didn't think it was time he and Opal got married. Henry replied that he guessed it was; so they did. Gilbert related to Stone that these stories warned against romantic, passionate love and opted for the comfort and security of rational decision making in matters of marriage. The moral of these stories seemed especially clear to Gilbert because her grandparents had both had long, and seemingly happy, marriages.

Hassan's comments refer to how stories mediate between cultural expectations and family expectations. In Hassan's family, the move from Lebanon to the United States involved a welter of expectations grounded in the family's culture of origin, new culture, and the family itself. Hassan observes that the family had to forge new expectations that allowed them to be comfortable in the United States without doing a disservice to their Lebanese heritage.

Student Perspective: Hassan

The stories that warned against romantic love were very interesting to me because my grandmother always told about how her marriage to my grandfather was arranged by the Imam. I think she and my grandfather were happy together, but her stories really didn't focus on happiness. What was the important thing was keeping the culture and Islam and the community. My grandmother often said that parents know better than 19-year-old children what is best. Yet her own children did not have arranged marriages, and my uncle didn't even marry an Arab. Grandma has changed her views a little, but she still likes to tell stories that show that the older generation knows best and romantic love is not a big deal.

Birth Stories

Stories focusing on the birth of children are a second common family story genre. These **birth stories** often create a sense of how each child fits into the family, the roles they are expected to play, and some of their parents' hopes and dreams for them. Stone (2008) tells of Dan Vernale, whose birth story convinced him that he was a special son. He was born after two other brothers had died at birth, and the stories feature the great anticipation that attended his birth and the great joy that the family felt when he survived. Vernale comments to Stone that "the message was: 'You're special, you're unique . . .' I knew I was going to make it big. The family almost invested its own success in what I would do" (p. 178). Vernale's story illustrates the power of the birth story to shape its listeners and its protagonist.

Some children do not hear stories of their own birth because they are adopted, and their parents do not know much about the birth. Or their birth may have been traumatic in some way—they were premature, conceived when their parents were not married, or their parents are now divorced and don't wish to remember events that happened while they were married. There are many reasons why birth stories may not be shared, but again, an important resource may be lost to the family. Certainly, since birth stories help the protagonist gain a sense of identity, it is unfortunate when they are not told.

Families do tell stories about adopting children. These stories do not focus on the physical birth but, rather, on the process of adoption itself. Many times these stories center on how much the parents wanted a child, how hard they looked for a child, and how happy they were when they found the child they adopted. These stories are often called **entrance narratives** (Kranstuber & Koenig Kellas, 2011) because they focus on the child's entrance into the adoptive family.

Haley Kranstuber and Jody Koenig Kellas tested the assumption, shared by many previous researchers, that these narratives have long-lasting effects on the adopted child's later life, influencing his or her adjustment and well-being as an adult. They investigated the entrance narrative from the adopted child's perspective (rather than the parents') and asked 105 adults who had been adopted as children to tell their entrance narrative. They discovered that these narratives focused on seven different themes (from chosen child to rescued child). Three of these themes significantly impacted self-concept in adulthood. When entrance narratives reflected the theme of *chosen child* (i.e., the adoptive parents specifically chose the adopted child to be part of their family) or *difference* (i.e., the adoptive child was unique or special because of being adopted), the adults in this study reported positive self-concept development, as measured on self-esteem and generalized trust instruments. However, when the theme was *negative reconnection* (i.e., the adoptive child expressed concerns about finding and reconnecting with birth parents), self-concept was negatively impacted in the participants' scores. The researchers conclude that the entrance narrative is a powerful family story for adopted families, and communication research can help adoptive families construct healthy messages to shape these stories in beneficial ways.

Survival Stories

Survival stories teach family members how to cope in a world that is not always welcoming and charitable. Survival in these stories may be literal, as in stories Holocaust survivors tell, or it may mean surviving in the sense of achieving or maintaining dignity or comfort. These stories offer illustrations of coping strategies from the family's own history. Chang-Rae Lee (1996) describes how his mother's stories of her girlhood during the Japanese military occupation of Korea operated as survival stories in his family. His mother's passion as she told these stories influenced Chang-Rae and convinced him to have pride in his Korean heritage and language:

> *My mother often showed open enmity for the Japanese, her face seeming to ash over when she spoke of her memories, that picture of the platoon of lean-faced soldiers burning books and scrolls in the center of her village still aglow in my head . . . , and how they tried to erase what was Korean by criminalizing the home language and history, by shipping slave labor, draftees, and young Korean women back to Japan and its other Pacific colonies. How they taught her to speak in Japanese. And as she would speak of her childhood, of the pretty, stern-lipped girl (that I only now see in tattered rust-edged photos) who could only whisper to her sisters in the midnight safety of their house the Korean words folding inside her all day like mortal secrets, I felt the same burning, troubling lode of utter pride and utter shame still jabbing at the sweet belly of her life, that awful gem, about who she was and where her mother tongue and her land had gone. (p. 31)*

Lee's recounting of his mother's story focuses both on literal survival, because it was a military occupation in which some Koreans lost their lives, and on the ability to maintain a sense of self and dignity in the face of a world that was demeaning and out of control. Survival stories help families to see their strengths and learn coping skills.

Stories on the Margins

Jane Jorgenson and Arthur Bochner (2004) coined the term **stories on the margins,** and they observe that stories about love, courtship, marriage, birth, and parenting establish an overarching story about the perceived "natural" course of family life. Jorgenson and Bochner argue that this "natural" story "promotes ways of thinking and talking about families [that] may discourage or ignore alternative depictions and narrative forms" (p. 528). Stories on the margins give voice to these ignored or silenced experiences.

Jorgenson and Bochner refer to several stories of this type that scholars have studied: a woman's decision to get a divorce after being raped by her husband (Riessman, 1992); couples who have been unable to conceive a child (Walkover, 1992); terminating an unexpected pregnancy (Ellis & Bochner, 1992); and child abuse (Kiesinger, 2002). Additional stories might include adoptions that fail, miscarriages, family violence, family illness, and so forth.

Stories on the margins are not advanced solely to focus on negative family experiences. Rather, Jorgenson and Bochner are interested in illuminating that

> *families routinely breach conventions and expectations, cope with exceptional and transformative crises, invent new ways of acting and speaking when old or traditional ways fail them, and are stunningly adept at making the absurd sensible and the disastrous manageable. (p. 530)*

Thus, stories about transnational adoptions, gay and lesbian courtships, and transgendered family members represent topics that are outside the more traditional arc of family life represented by the master narratives we discussed at the beginning of the chapter. As a result, they are less often told and are, thus, marginalized. Yet, Jorgenson and Bochner note that it is too simplistic to evaluate family events as "traditional" or "normal" or even "positive" or "negative." All of family life is complicated and contains struggle. Families may strip some of that complexity away when they tell a story to make it seem neater, and they may shy away from stories that shine a light on marginal experiences, but that doesn't mean they don't experience some of them or that even positive stories may contain some trauma and vice versa.

Further, Karen Gainer Sirota (2010) asserts that telling stories on the margin (she is particularly interested in stories of families who have a member diagnosed with autism) can be transformative, providing families with hope. Sirota notes that when children with autistic spectrum disorders are included as co-narrators in family stories, it is productive and encouraging for the family as a whole, as well as individual members within the family. Lori L. Montalbano-Phelps (2003) agrees and argues that telling stories on the margin (she is interested in stories about family violence) may represent a method for moving toward healthier families. Researchers suggest that telling family stories about experiences that have previously been marginalized will go a long way toward widening our acceptance of what constitutes "normal" family events as well as helping families feel positive and hopeful about themselves and their circumstances.

OTHER MEANING-MAKING PRACTICES

In this section, we review the relationship between stories and other communication practices that also function to create a family's collective identity: family theme, family ritual, family myth, and family metaphor. All of these concepts, like family stories, contribute symbolically to the family's sense of collective identity. All of them relate to family stories, and there is some overlap among them. Yet, each is also unique as well. By comparing and

TABLE 6-2 Other Meaning-Making Practices in the Family

Family themes: Statements about reality and its relationship to the family, such as "The world is a tough place, and the Mathews have to stick together" or "The Samuels have been blessed, and we have to give back to the community." Themes are less elaborate than stories.

Family rituals: Repeated, patterned communication events, paying homage to a person, idea, or thing (like the family itself). Rituals can take three forms: everyday interactions, such as prayers before sleep; traditions, such as yearly family reunions; and celebrations, such as Thanksgiving or Kwanzaa. Rituals may include stories and may also be the topic for other stories.

Family myths: Beliefs that the family members hold about themselves that are selective or constructed to represent the family in a way that may not be true but serves a function for the family. If the Meyer family believes it is charitable, but really has not given to charities for three generations, it has a family myth. Myths may be perpetuated by family stories, but not all family stories are in the service of a myth.

Family metaphors: A linguistic comparison between the family and some other event, image, object, or behavior. For example, families might compare themselves to a leaky boat, a bag of popcorn, a circus, a blue sky with cottony clouds, a picnic, an orchestra, and so on. Metaphors are less elaborate than stories.

---

contrasting family stories to these other concepts, we will get a clearer sense of what family stories are all about. Table 6-2 summarizes the four other meaning-making practices in the family.

Family Theme

The concept of **family theme** was first articulated by Robert Hess and Gerald Handel in 1959. They discussed themes as performing a centering function for a family, suggesting that families develop themes that provide "some fundamental view of reality and some way or ways of dealing with it" (p. 11). Thus, the Washington family, from the beginning of the chapter, may possess a theme revolving around the importance of fighting for love and not giving up on the one you love despite outside interference or objections. This theme reflects the family's values and suggests prescriptions for behaviors that conform to those values. When family members do not behave in accordance with a family theme, it is likely that some disturbance occurs.

Like stories, themes are both created through conversation among the family members and used as guides for family communication, although the theme itself need not be specifically stated by the family. If a couple has a theme that the only way they will succeed in the world is if they stick together, their talk will reflect this theme. They may say things like "We have to let your parents know we are united on this" or "I think the best thing about us is how we share the same goals" or "We have always agreed on the basics even when we had little disagreements about nonessentials."

These types of communication behaviors reflect and are congruent with their theme. Additionally, other communication between them has served to shape the theme. For instance, Lorna tells Amelia about the couples she knows who have been more concerned with their own careers than their relationships and how she disapproves of that. In talking this way, Lorna is advancing ideas that create the theme "we need to stick together." If Amelia agrees, she is supporting the development of that theme. If she disagrees, the couple would have to engage in more negotiation about the appropriate theme for their relationship. Negotiation about a family theme may be both implicit and explicit.

Family themes, then, are like family stories in that they function to establish what is significant for the family group. They also, like stories, offer some behavioral prescription or guidance about how family members should live and conduct themselves in given situations. And, like family stories, family themes are both developed in conversation and used as guides for conversation. Stories, however, are more elaborate than themes because they involve characters and plotlines. Further, as we discussed previously, stories are performed orally, whereas themes may be implicit and not stated specifically. That is, a family may know that its theme is to question authority, but no one in the family may ever say that theme aloud. It operates in the family, guides interaction, and focuses the family's attention on their values, but they simply never explicitly discuss it. Stories, on the other hand, do not exist for the family until they are told. Finally, stories may serve as sources for theme development. When Rita McIntosh, from the beginning of this chapter, tells her children about how hard her parents worked to scrape by and provide for their kids, she is establishing the idea that hard work is valued in their family. Perhaps a family theme will arise from this value.

Family Ritual

Leslie Baxter and Catherine Clark (1996) observe that family rituals are important to the family system in many ways, including how they can "produce and reproduce a family's culture or sense of its identity, and socialize family members in how to conduct social relations" (p. 254). In these functions, family ritual also resembles themes and stories. In the definition offered by Baxter and Clark for **family ritual**, "a recurring, patterned communication event whose successful enactment pays homage to some highly valued person, concept, or thing . . . typically the family unit . . ." (p. 255), we also see similarities to family stories.

Steven Wolin and Linda Bennett (1984) offer a category system of family rituals, which includes everyday patterned interactions such as bedtime or dinner time, family traditions such as reunions, yearly vacations or anniversaries, and family celebrations such as Thanksgiving and the Fourth of July. Celebrations differ from traditions in that the former are culturally sanctioned whereas the latter are more idiosyncratic to the family. From this category system, we can see that stories can be one part of the "patterned communication" that forms the ritual. For example, bedtimes may include stories, the Thanksgiving dinner table may provide a popular stage for storytelling (Benoit et al., 1996), and family reunions promote reminiscing and the retelling of favorite family stories (Leach & Braithwaite, 1996). Rituals may also provide subject matter for family stories. Thus, the McIntosh family, from the beginning of the chapter, tells a story about what occurred one Christmas (the family ritual of celebration).

In a qualitative review of 32 articles about family rituals published since 1950, Barbara Fiese and her colleagues (2002) observed that, like family stories, rituals are an important resource for families. Their study pointed to several similarities between stories and rituals. First, they noted that rituals were symbolic communications that formed around something of importance to the family. Additionally, rituals were seen as linking generations together when they were passed down from generation to generation. So, in the Mahler family, the Christmas tree is always decorated on the same day in December, and the youngest child always places the angel on top of the tree while being held up by the oldest family member. Finally, Fiese and her colleagues assert that family rituals provide a sense of family identity. In addition, family rituals are also created through family communication and guide family communication (Baxter, et al., 2009).

Student Perspective: Pooja

In my family, we had a complex set of themes, I think, and they mainly came from stories my mother told us. I guess the two main themes were never forget who you are—you are Indian, and you can speak out—you will be heard. Almost everything my parents said and did, from food, clothing, language, and friends, ensured that we were not to forget that we came from India. Plus, we always went back to my parents' home in India once a year to visit relatives. But in addition, my mom told a lot of stories about growing up in India and how my grandparents lived in a mud hut and how she played in the dirt all the time. The second theme came a lot from my parents' encouragement of me and my sisters. They always wanted to hear what we had to say. But it was also a big part of a story she told about my grandmother's death and how, as she and her sisters tended their mother on her deathbed, she promised Grandma she'd keep telling her stories. She always ended this by saying, "See, you can die, but your voice can continue."

Family Myth

Beliefs about the family that are selective or constructed to represent the family in a way that may not be objectively true but serves some function for the family (Ferreira, 1963) are **family myths**. Myths are perpetuated

Student Perspective: Kip

My family always likes to tell a simple story about how our dinner time ritual included a lot of joking and laughing. In this story we usually recall how my dad would always make some joke about the food—like making a choking noise and practically falling off the chair whenever we had artichokes. The story also highlights how I would often do little comedy routines at the table, mimicking Mel Brooks. Usually I could make my sister laugh so hard she would spit out the milk she was drinking.

Student Perspective: Deena

It was funny to learn about family metaphors because my family actually talks about that at home. It is just my mother and my sister and me, and we are always saying how we are just like a sorority. Since it is all women at our house and my mom is really young (she's only 15 years older than I am), we are always joking about how we are this sorority house. We talk about our secret handshake and our initiation rites (even though we really don't have any of that). We even have a name for our sorority: Alpha Alpha Alpha, because we all three want to be number one!

through family stories. For example, it is important for the Gerard family to see themselves as civic minded, although they really do relatively little in their community. Thus, the Gerards spend much time telling and retelling the story of how Great-Grandpa Gerard came to the town over a hundred years ago and helped start one of the first businesses, which helped get the town going economically. In this story, the Gerard family is able to perpetuate the myth that civic responsibility is a family trait.

Sometimes family stories maintain family myths by what they exclude as well as by what they include. For example, in the Saunders family, Gramps Saunders is seen as a family hero, and many stories are told about him and his activities. Gramps was an inventor, an early advocate of healthy lifestyles, an athlete, and an amateur chef. The Saunders family delights in telling stories about all of these attributes of Gramps's life. However, Gramps Saunders was also a poor money manager who lost most of the family's fortune and a bad husband who cheated on his wife. The negative aspects of Gramps's life and character are taboo topics in the Saunders family, and these stories are never told. Thus, the myth of Gramps as a hero is maintained for the family.

Family Metaphor

Metaphors, defined as "understanding and experiencing one kind of thing in terms of another" (Lakoff & Johnson, 1980, p. 5), also function to create a sense of reality for those employing them. As users hear themselves speaking metaphorically, they participate in a transformational process whereby the experience and its comparison interact with one another, creating a sense of reality. In a sense, metaphors operate to persuade us of the validity of the comparison being made (Sopory, 2008). A **family metaphor**, then, is a linguistic comparison the family makes between themselves and some other event, image, object, or behavior. Families make this comparison because the metaphor sheds some light on their collective identity and provides richness to their understanding of who they are (Jones, 1982). For example, the McIntosh family may see themselves as a tree with strong roots, because closeness and family love are so important to them. The Nichols-Resnicks may compare themselves to a circus because of all the chaos in their extended family. The Washington family might choose a different comparison, seeing themselves as a flower bouquet, because they are made up of different elements that look beautiful together.

Metaphors may or may not be invoked in family stories, but they do affect a family's communication behaviors, including family narratives. In his work on relational metaphors, William Owen (1985) argues that couples often develop metaphors for their relationships and reflect these metaphors in their language choices. Families who see themselves as a well-oiled machine will probably extend that metaphor by saying things like, "We're really swinging into high gear," "We need periodic maintenance," or "We have our timing perfectly synchronized."

Helen Black and her colleagues (Black, Moss, Robinstein, & Moss, 2011) suggested that the metaphor of her father as the "cement" of the family infused one of their respondents' story of his recent death. Further, these researchers noted that the metaphor of the father/husband as the "cement" holding the family together was shared by the other surviving family members and played itself out in their narratives as well. Several members included their fears of the family "coming apart" in their stories.

Family metaphors, along with themes, rituals, and myths, are part of the symbolic culture that surrounds and defines the family. Each of these concepts relates to family stories: Themes are reinforced by stories, rituals contain stories and provide the subject matter for other stories, myths are maintained through particular stories and the exclusion of other stories or story elements, and metaphors provide linguistic comparisons that may stimulate stories.

SUMMARY

Human beings are storytellers, and we understand ourselves and our situations through stories that make sense of our experiences. Our grasp of life's meaning is usually inseparable from our stories about life. Stories offer us a sequence that shapes reality for us and then becomes our reality. Through stories, families participate in a communication practice that both circles backward to illuminate family history and reaches forward to influence future communication interactions. Through stories, families come to understand one another and themselves—they create a collective identity or a relational culture. Family stories offer family members a sense of identity, a connection to other family members through time, a set of prescriptions for behaviors, and methods for coping with the tensions and difficulties that are part and parcel of family life. Stories offer families guidelines for how to behave in the world.

Family stories are unique narrations containing a cast of characters from the family's past and present. These narrations offer a plot focusing on issues of central importance to the family. Through this plotline, lessons are taught, and family members understand how they are supposed to conduct themselves to be in accord with the family identity. Further, family stories are performances—they exist to be told and shared. Gertrude Stein (cited in Cahill, 1975) once observed, "Everybody's life is full of stories. Your life is full of stories; my life is full of stories. They are very occupying, but they are not really interesting. What is interesting is the way everyone tells their stories" (p. 43). Family stories can be performed in ritualistic ways or more spontaneously, but they must be performed.

Family stories have a dramatic quality, evolve over time, and depend on the meanings negotiated by listeners and tellers. Stories may be about an infinite number of topics, but some recurring genres include courtship, birth, and survival stories. Some stories are outside these genres. Stories on the margins include stories about issues and events that are not included in the "normal" progression of family life. Yet, we have advanced that this "normal" progression is problematic. This is the case because it strips away the complexities that mark our real lived experiences of family. Family stories are rich resources of entertainment, pleasure, and sometimes pain for family members. But, even when stories pain us or make us sad, they function to provide us with significant lessons and connections.

KEY TERMS

accounts	fluidity
birth stories	master narratives
collective meaning	narrative asymmetry
courtship stories	narrative inheritance
drama	performance
entrance narratives	sequence
family metaphor	significance
family myths	slow disclosure
family ritual	stories on the margins
family stories	survival stories
family theme	

QUESTIONS FOR REFLECTION

1. Think about the story of your birth or adoption. What does it tell you about your own identity and that of your family?

2. Choose any favorite family story. How does it fit the characteristics we discussed in the chapter of subject, sequence, significance, performance, drama, fluidity, and meaning?

3. We argue in this chapter that stories tend to establish congruent meanings for individual family members. Do you agree that all the people in your family would interpret the meaning of your stories similarly? If not, what do you think that means? Are family stories less important if we disagree about their meaning?

4. In this chapter we make the assumption that all families tell stories. Do you agree with that? Do you know any families that do not engage in this communication practice? What does that mean for the family's communication behavior in general, if they don't tell stories?

5. We suggest that courtship, birth, and survival stories are typical genres. Can you think of other story types? What are they?

6. Think of a persistent family story in your own family. How has it accomplished the functions of family stories—establishing identity, developing connections through time, teaching lessons, and managing dialectics and difficulties?

7. How does culture make a difference in family storytelling practices? Explain with examples.

Chapter

7

EXPRESSING CONFLICT, POWER, AND VIOLENCE

THE SCOTT FAMILY

Emily Scott, 45, wakes up at 7 a.m. and calls to her husband, Charles. Because Emily has multiple sclerosis, she waits for Charles to come and help her up. Once Emily is in her wheelchair, Charles wheels her to the bathroom in their specially outfitted home. Charles adjusts the shower for Emily and then goes to the kitchen to make the coffee and prepare breakfast while she takes her shower. While Charles finishes making breakfast, Emily wheels herself into the kitchen.

She sees that Charles has poured her coffee and put some cream into it. She feels her irritation growing and says, "Charles, I can't believe you haven't remembered that I hate cream in my morning coffee." Immediately she feels angry, and Charles looks on in disbelief as she bursts into tears. He remains silent as she rails against him for a host of things he's forgotten to do for her. Finally, he snaps back at her that maybe she should hire a professional caregiver. Then he stomps out the door. He's back in five minutes and they both apologize.

THE JORDAN FAMILY

Jeffery Jordan and his wife, LuAnn, are arguing again. They have been having the same argument for the last two years. Ever since they adopted Elijah, they have disagreed about how to handle the racial difference between their new son and themselves. They had put their name in for a baby and had expected to wait for a long time, but Elijah was available only three weeks after they first contacted the agency. It was such a whirlwind that they hadn't had time to discuss how to deal with the fact that they are white and he is black. Jeff wants to operate from a color-blind stance and just ignore their differences. He thinks that this will be the best thing for their family. But LuAnn feels that Elijah needs to know about his heritage. She wants to have a black family mentor them, but Jeffery thinks that would be a big intrusion into their personal lives, and he is afraid that Elijah would bond more with the black family than with LuAnn and him. It is very frustrating, and now that Elijah is almost three, they have to decide how they are going to handle this. It is an unusual situation for Jeff and LuAnn because before this they had hardly ever argued—they seemed to agree on most things before. But this is the biggest issue they've had to face, and it is disappointing to both of them that they cannot figure out a way to deal with their differences. The constant bickering about the topic is wearing them down.

THE THOMAS FAMILY

James and Judy Thomas live in a stepfamily with five children (two children from each previous marriage and one of their own). Married for five years, James and Judy are acutely aware of the challenges they face. Recently, James's 13-year-old daughter, Cynthia, said she wanted to get a nose ring. Cynthia's request has erupted into a major family argument. James is fairly agreeable to her request, yet her stepmother, Judy, is not. Some of the other children have entered into the discussion, expressing their opinions about what Cynthia should do. This discussion is beginning to dominate the family's time together. Judy has found herself resentful of James's position on this subject. She is concerned that he is taking his daughter's side over hers. She wonders whether this is a sign of the future of their relationship. This was an issue she had worried about before they married—it is really tough to merge two families with two different styles and views on almost everything. She shrugs and sighs to herself, thinking what a joke the term "blended family" is turning out to be in this situation.

Many people like to say that they have happy families and refuse to engage in conflict, power struggles, or violence. However, this is simply not the case with most families. While physical violence does not characterize all families, all families experience some conflict and power issues. Power is inherent in family systems. Researchers have focused a great deal of attention on conflict in families, making it one of the most studied variables in the area of family communication (Shearman, Dumlao, & Kagawa, 2011). Further, as Holly Recchia, Hildy Ross, and Marcia Vickar (2010) assert, power is the variable that allows us to understand differences among conflict interactions between family members. Although husbands and wives might have similar amounts of power in some relationships, our opening vignette about Charles and Emily Scott shows that illness, for example, can affect the power balance, and thus the conflict interaction.

Although violence is not as pervasive as conflict and power issues are, it too invades many families in the United States. A conservative estimate is that 1.5 million women a year and over 800,000 men in the United States experience family violence (Feingold, 2000), and this violence can be an important indicator of other forms of family violence, including child abuse and elder abuse. According to Angela Swanson and Dudley Cahn (2009), every ten seconds in the United States, a child is abused by a family member. Approximately 15.5 million children in the United States experience home lives where their parents engage in violence (Minze, McDonald, Rosentraub, & Jouriles, 2010). Nancy Eckstein (2009) reports on a little discussed phenomenon, adolescent-to-parent abuse. She notes that the National Family Violence Survey reported that 2.5 million parents were hit by their adolescent children, and 900,000 of them suffered severe physical abuse at their children's hands.

Olga Barnett and her colleagues (2005) observe that family violence has probably always existed, but in earlier times it was seen simply as a social condition rather than the social problem it is known as today. The history of childhood is replete with horror stories about abuse that was tolerated around the world and in the United States. Until the mid-to-late 1800s, wife abuse was not noticed at all in the United States because the subjugation of women was considered appropriate behavior. Only recently have we begun to classify abusive acts against family members as problematic. The World Heath Organization did not make an official recognition of family violence as a global health issue until 2002 (Barnett, Miller-Perrin, & Perrin, 2005).

In some ways, conflict and power (and to a lesser extent, violence) are part of family interaction by definition. Earlier in this text, our definition of family placed a high premium on the interaction among family members. And, the more interaction that takes place among people, the more opportunities there are for disagreements. Further, systems theorists point out that family members are interdependent. Conflict occurs in interdependent relationships—you rarely express disagreement with someone you don't depend upon in some way. Additionally, our definition posits that families create boundaries, that is, ways of determining who's in and who's out of the family. This process of setting boundaries provides fertile ground for additional disagreements. Finally, as families evolve through time (a third component of our definition), families will change. The very presence of change provides additional conflict arenas. Some family members may be very receptive to changing and developing, whereas others may be very unwilling to change. Even welcomed changes (a desired move to a better job, leaving the old neighborhood for a lovely new home, or welcoming a much-wanted child into the family) bring with them situations that may lead to conflict.

Conflict and power are intertwined in families, although not all power issues involve conflict. For example, a young child may accept a parent's power and go to bed at the time the parent decides. Yet when conflict develops, power and perceptions of power are central. In other words, conflict in a family may result in a power struggle. For example, Jeffery and LuAnn in our chapter-opening scenario have a **content-based conflict:** a disagreement over the subject of whether or not to draw attention to their son's race. As they argue, however, it is possible that their positions will become rigid if they perceive that a compromise will erode their individual power. Their argument may be prolonged and transformed from one about what's best for Elijah to one about who has the power to make this decision. In many cases, issues of power may lie at the source of family conflicts. For some family members, the goal of conflict is to assert their power. Cynthia Thomas, for instance, may want to be a powerful individual even more than she wants to have a nose ring.

If power and conflict get out of hand, it is possible that violence will occur. Linda Ade-Ridder and Allen Jones (1996) state that "embedded within acts of violence are inferences of power and control" (p. 72). Some researchers argue that violence is an interactional event, arising out of communication episodes such as conflict or discipline (Cupach & Olson, 2006; Socha & Yingling, 2010). A child's misbehavior, for instance, may be viewed very unfavorably by a parent if the parent feels that the child is causing unnecessary conflict in the family. For some parents, violence is an outlet for coping with children who disrupt family interaction patterns. And there is some research showing that abusive parents lack the communication skills to appropriately discipline their children when they misbehave or to soothe and calm them when necessary (Anderson, Umberson, & Elliott, 2004).

Understanding the processes of conflict, power, and violence and their relationship to communication practices helps us understand the family. Conflict can be constructive or destructive and each family member must be prepared for the repercussions of disagreeing with others in the family (Socha & Stamp, 2009). Each person in a conflict has some sort of power, although as Wilmot and Hocker (2011) noted, the power potential may shift during a conflict. The way family members communicate violence may be verbal, physical, and/or sexual. Yet, however inexcusable each act remains, the violence serves to demonstrate a family member's way of resolving conflict and asserting power.

Clearly, conflict, power, and violence can be inextricably, although not inevitably, linked within some families' communication, and it is equally clear that conflictual communication, power struggles, and violence are disconcerting, troubling, and unsettling to most family members. Yet, it is useful to keep in mind as we review the material in this chapter that "we may have overdramatized the prominence of conflict in family life" (Sillars, Canary, & Tafoya, 2004, p. 413). In a study surveying married people, the self-reported incidence of conflict was relatively low. Even though very few respondents said they never had conflict with their partners, 80 percent reported that they had unpleasant disagreements no more than once per month (McGonagle, Kessler, & Schilling, 1992, cited in Bradbury, Rogge, & Lawrence, 2001).

To begin to understand the nuances associated with these three behaviors, we first discuss the impact of culture on conflict, power, and violence. Then we examine conflict, interpreting what it means, and explore two models of conflict and responses to family conflict. Next, we discuss power, explaining its presence in the family system and its relationship to decision making. Finally, we identify several assumptions underlying violence,

Student Perspective: Robin

My mother and I never used to talk about our problems. Now, after a lot of counseling, we openly talk about all of our problems. This has started a great deal of conflict in our relationship. Before, she kept everything inside, and I could only guess what she was thinking. Now, she blurts out everything she thinks, which is just as bad as when she was silent. I'm not sure how to work this out, except I am pretty happy that we are at least talking. But I really don't know where this mother–daughter relationship is going if she keeps telling me everything she likes and doesn't like. Sometimes it's better just to be quiet.

explaining how this social problem and extreme form of communication is manifested in families across the United States.

CONFLICT, POWER, VIOLENCE, AND CULTURE

Before delving further into this chapter, it's important to note that several of the conclusions emanating from research on family conflict, power, and violence are rooted in a Western model of thinking. Throughout this book we embrace the notion that the United States is comprised of myriad co-cultures, containing families who are influenced by their unique cultural heritage. We realize the dominant ideology in the United States is one that is most influenced by Western, European American, middle-class values and thinking.

And, although there is value in understanding the way a majority of people manage conflict, power, and violence, if we focus on that exclusively, we run the risk of becoming culturally self-centered. This **ethnocentrism** impairs our understanding of communication in the family. We believe that defining and interpreting conflict, power, and violence must be tempered with an understanding of how we (and others) have been influenced by our culture. As difficult as that may be, we need to interpret the theory and research with our biases in mind.

As we have mentioned in previous chapters, the United States is considered an **individualistic culture** in which direct communication and individual goals earn favor; **collectivist cultures**, such as Japan, place more emphasis on group goals and a "we-ness" or a sense of the community (Shearman, Dumlao, & Kagawa, 2011). These values may result in fewer overt conflicts in these cultures. Japanese and Iranians usually avoid self-assertion and are not usually direct in their communication (Shearman & Dumlao, 2008; Zandpour & Sadri, 1996). Yet some conflicts may be generated by changing values within a culture. Gary DeCoker (2001) points out that gender roles are changing in Japan, and more women are working outside the home. Conflicts may arise because this change is more strongly endorsed by Japanese women than Japanese men.

As we have noted previously, national culture is only one type of cultural difference affecting families' interactions. Within the United States, co-cultures, or ethnic backgrounds, exert strong influences on families' attitudes and behaviors regarding conflict. One study examining co-cultures' effects on family conflict (Dixon, Graber, & Brooks-Gunn, 2008) concluded that, congruent with their cultural values, African American girls and Latinas showed more respect toward their mothers' authority than did European American girls. Further, this respect affected how mothers interpreted conflict with their daughters. African American and Latina mothers reported less frequent conflicts with their adolescent daughters than European American mothers did. In addition, when African American and Latina mothers thought their daughters were not respecting their authority properly, they said their conflicts were most intense. This study also showed that African American and Latina mothers engage in stricter disciplinary behaviors than do European American mothers while none of the co-cultures demonstrated differences in maternal nurturance (according to the mothers' reports) or in overall mother–daughter relationship quality (according to the researchers' observations). As the authors point out, "respect, obedience, and cultural traditions are seen as important social conventions that parents and children within particular ethnic groups abide by" (p. 8).

As you read and apply the following information to your lives, keep in mind that the way we look at conflict is culturally conditioned. Further, the way power is manifested can be dramatically different from one family to another; often a family's cultural background affects a power decision. Finally, violence must be considered in a cultural context (Vissing & Baily, 1996). Barbara Aswad (1997) observes, for example, that Arab Americans may seem aggressive and boisterous to those outside their group. Further, she notes that the generalizations about Arab culture, with its value on the extended family, may sometimes obscure "the fact that there can be conflicts and problems with dominance, control, and abuse among Arab American family members" (p. 231). Culture, therefore, is integral to our review of the research findings that pertain to conflict, power, and violence.

Additionally, even in the United States there are researchers who would argue with Hocker and Wilmot's assertion that directness, clarity, and assertiveness are essential skills for managing family conflict. Some have advanced that family conflict is too emotional and ambiguous for participants to remember to use assertiveness skills such as using "I" statements (that is, acknowledging your own attributions: "I am troubled by this" rather than "You make me so mad") (Sillars & Weisberg, 1987). Laura Stafford and Marianne Dainton (1994) observe that being aware of culturally sanctioned skills for conflict communication does not mean that family members will actually use them during their conflicts.

CONFLICT IN THE FAMILY

Interpreting Conflict

To suggest that most families engage in conflict is to state the obvious. As Rebecca Dumlao and Renee Botta (2000) conclude, "People first learn about how conflicts work and how to resolve interpersonal problems with their families" (p. 175), and "family communication environments would seem to provide important training grounds for future management of conflicts" (p. 184). Tom Socha and Julie Yingling (2010) observe, children's conflict behaviors are greatly affected by the role models provided by their parents, particularly their fathers. Further, Tamara Afifi and her colleagues

(2011) found empirical support for the assertion that how parents manage conflict affects children's physical and mental health. Other researchers (Xing, Wang, Zhang, He, & Zhang, 2011) argue that this generalization has to be interpreted in the context of culture and gender. They found that in China for instance, girls were more influenced by their parents' aggressive conflict behaviors than boys. Yet many family members would like others to believe that they function without any conflict. Many believe that conflict is a bad thing, and when conflict is present there is no hope of maintaining a happy, productive family unit. Self-help books even proclaim that it's possible to be conflict-free in intimate relationships. We do not agree. In fact, we believe—like other communication researchers—that conflict is inevitable in intimate relationships. Conflict simply occurs and may have many results within the family.

Conflict can be productive. Conflict may serve to clarify family boundaries and foster interdependence of family members (Cupach & Canary, 1997; Wilmot & Hocker, 2011; Noller, Feeney, Peterson, & Sheehan, 1995). The way a family member interprets the conflict and the way conflict is handled will determine how effective it is in a family. We believe that managing conflict competently "can lead to stronger relationships, alternative ways of seeing a tough problem, and durable solutions" (Cupach & Canary, 1997, p. 6). Indeed, family members can function more effectively when they understand what conflict is and how it influences the family system.

Although we believe that conflict can be a productive family occurrence, we must reiterate that conflict also often undermines family satisfaction and unravels relationships that family members wished to maintain. Further, family members cannot always predict whether conflict will escalate destructively. For example, as Jeffery and LuAnn Jordan, from our opening vignette, argue about how to best raise their adopted son, neither one can confidently predict at the outset of their conflict whether their disagreement will escalate into significant misunderstanding. Further, research by Christin Bates and Jennifer Samp (2011) suggests that even when a member of a couple rehearses and plans for a conflict interaction, that does not necessarily lead to the desired outcome.

One of the factors that affects whether a conflict will be destructive or constructive for the family relates to the type of conflict it is. There are many ways to put family conflicts into categories. Here we introduce you to a simple family typology that has two categories: solvable and perpetual (Gottman, 1999). *Solvable conflicts* are those that a family can solve with the right communication tactics and responses, and these are the types of conflicts that can be productive for a family. For instance, if Jeffery and LuAnn Jordan demonstrate good listening behaviors and fight fair with each other, they may well come out of this argument about their son with a new appreciation for each other's viewpoints and a creative plan for coping with their interracial family.

Perpetual conflicts are more difficult as they are rooted in conflicting values, roles, and personality issues. And, as the name implies, they recur

~^w\~ POPULAR PRESS PERSPECTIVES ~^w\~

Recently (April, 2012) in the *New York Times Online* Laura Holson noted that social media provide another source of couples' conflict. Holson comments that "relationships are hard enough. But the rise of social media—where sharing private moments is encouraged, and provocative and confessional postings can help build a following–has created a new source of friction for couples: what is fair game for sharing with the world?" Holson mentions several famous couples who have fought with one another concerning what one of them has posted online about the other. For example, Rosanne Cash, the daughter of the late Johnny Cash, frequently talks about her marriage and her husband, a musician, on her Twitter account. Her husband, John Leventhal, does not appreciate all that she shares online. As Holson recounts it:

> *Ms. Cash said in an interview that another time she wrote about her husband taking a nap. When he showed up at the studio, the sound engineer was puzzled, since he had just read Ms. Cash's post online. "I thought you were taking a nap," the engineer said to him. "John called me and he was really annoyed," she recalled. "He said, 'Don't tell people I'm taking a nap!'"*

Holson notes that this "oversharing" online can be the sources of many conflicts between couples. She concludes that "if one half of a couple is not interested in broadcasting the details of a botched dinner or romantic weekend, Facebook postings or tweets can create irritation, embarrassment, miscommunication, and bruised egos." Holson also notes that this type of conflict is not confined to famous couples, and she interviewed more than a dozen other couples who admitted that disagreements about how much to post online are common. Some of the couples mentioned that the best way to avoid these types of conflicts is to establish rules about online posts right away before one person is annoyed.

For example, Holson observes that "some couples seek to preserve intimacy by establishing rules early on. Jen Dunlap, who lives in Brooklyn, took a trip to Turks and Caicos in May 2009 with her new boyfriend, Chris Sullivan, an actor and musician. Before they left, she said, Mr. Sullivan asked her not to post photos on Flickr of the couple kissing. 'I feel like people don't want to see it,' Mr. Sullivan said."

Laura Holson, "'What were you thinking?': For couples, new source of online friction." *New York Times* (online). April 25, 2012. Retreived May 17, 2012.

in the family's communication because they aren't clearly solvable. So they will not be resolved easily, if at all. John Gottman (1999) estimates that over half of marital conflicts are perpetual, and couples should just figure out ways to live with them (like making them the focus of humor) because they won't go away. If LuAnn and Jeff's conflict about raising Elijah is deeply rooted in value differences, then they may have a perpetual conflict, which will be much more challenging to their relationship. Many researchers (e.g., Bevan, 2010; Johnson & Roloff, 1998) have examined what they call **"serial arguments"** (or ongoing, unresolved conflict that recurs within the relationship), which are similiar to Gottman's notion of perpetual conflicts.

Conflict has been defined in a number of ways. Communication researchers cannot agree on a single definition that encompasses all interpretations of the term. In fact, some definitions are so complex that some interpersonal conflict researchers believe there is a sense of mystery surrounding the concept (Canary, Cupach, & Messman, 1995). We believe we need to employ a clear and concise definition of conflict. To this end, we define **conflict** as an interaction process whereby family members perceive a disagreement about goals, rules, roles, culture, and/or patterns of communication.

In defining conflict in this way, we realize that we have taken an expansive view. To help you understand our perspective, we will delineate two key elements of our definition, process and perception. We view conflict as a process because we believe that conflict develops over time. In Chapter 2 we described the developmental view of families; that is, families change over time. As families change, so do their conflict episodes. To suggest that the family remains static undermines systems principles pertaining to the family, which we have previously articulated in this book. For example, Amy Dickinson (2000) observes that conflict among siblings is an inevitable part of family life for families that include more than one child. She notes, however, that over time these conflicts ebb and flow.

It's important to point out that family change is both random and maturational. The same could be said about conflict. Conflict is often random in families, spontaneously occurring at both opportune and inopportune times. Annetta Miller (2000) notes that parents are concerned with their children's messy bedrooms, and they actually rank this as the single biggest family battlefield, ahead of curfews, dating, and drug use. Miller observes that this battle can break out at any time and seems to permeate parents' relationships with their children. Yet this conflict also has a maturational aspect, in that over time the conflict changes focus. Early in children's lives, parents emphasize clean rooms as a way to teach their children good habits. Miller argues that when children become adolescents, many parents enforce room cleanup in an effort to assert power. Yet many teens think of their rooms as their own space and may consider them "metaphors for their blossoming independence" (p. 76). Thus, as children grow, the conflict changes somewhat at its core, although the topic remains the same.

The second aspect of our definition of conflict is perception. The first important element here is that conflict may exist both because family members actually disagree about something and because they (mistakenly) believe they disagree. Thus, if Judy Thomas, from the beginning of the chapter, thinks her husband supports Cynthia's request for a nose ring, Judy and James may engage in conflict even if James really does not want Cynthia to pierce her nose. A second implication of this element concerns the intensity of the disagreement. All conflicts need not be vehement. At times, we may simply not agree with a family member, but neither one of us is interested in escalating the conflict. If Emily Scott (in our earlier scenario) disagrees with her husband, Charles, about how to spend an unexpected inheritance, the two may simply state their own conflicting positions and then come to a mutual agreement. Other conflicts are more serious, and

Student Perspective: Judine

My sister, Jolene, and I could fight about what day it is. Once we had a fight about whether our dog's hair was too matted. Our brother, Jeff, heard us and couldn't stop laughing. Even Jolene and I had to stop and laugh. Who cares about 90 percent of the stuff we argue about? But we are always squabbling about something. I know it drives my mother nuts. She keeps saying that sisters should support each other and take care of each other and not fight all the time like we do. But I think Jolene and I are okay. We love each other, and we don't get all bent out of shape about our fights. It's not that big of a deal to us, and it's kind of how we relate to each other.

family members may become rather intense and rigid in their positions, making resolution seem much more unlikely. Individual perceptions of intensity play a role here as well.

A third implication focuses on the potential for variability in people's perceptions about a conflict. As Miller (2000) notes when discussing parent–child conflicts about messy rooms, what is considered messy to one person may not be to another. Miller quotes one daughter whose mother finds her bedroom a disaster area: "I think of myself as an artist. My whole room is a reflection of my tastes in art and music" (p. 76). Linda Sampson Lay (2000) writes about money as a source of power and conflict within families. She observes that perceptions of control and ownership of money may vary within marriage.

Models of Family Conflict

Now that we have presented you with an idea of how we interpret conflict, it's appropriate to discuss two models of conflict. The first model refers to the marital context because that is how John Gottman (1994b) derived this model. Yet, as Craig Fowler and Megan Dillow (2011) observe, it is likely that these conflict behaviors are established during a couple's premarital years, at "various stages of a romantic involvement" (p. 17). As we have discussed previously, we recognize that cultural differences affect the validity of these models. Both of these models are most appropriate for mapping conflict in European American middle-class families.

The Four Horsemen of the Apocalypse Model   Gottman (1994b) presents a lucid way of examining the conflict in millions of marriages in the United States. Gottman called it the **Four Horsemen of the Apocalypse model**, because he believes that there are four disastrous stages in which a spouse will sabotage any attempts at productive communication during a conflict. In explaining each stage of the model, he contends that these behaviors will become entrenched, resulting in an escalation of tension in a marriage. Gottman explains, "As each horseman arrives, he paves the way for the next" (p. 72). In order, the four stages of the Four Horsemen of the Apocalypse model are criticism, contempt, defensiveness, and stonewalling.

Criticism includes attacking a spouse's personality or character, "usually with blame" (Gottman, 1994b, p. 73). Gottman believes that criticizing is an inevitable part of all marriages, even those assessed to be healthy. He reasons that criticizing is so close to complaining that many spouses simply cannot and often do not differentiate between the two. There are differences, however, between criticism and complaining. Criticism involves making an accusation, whereas complaining is "a negative comment about something you wish were otherwise" (p. 74). For simplification, Gottman notes that complaints usually contain the word *I*, and criticisms are often accompanied by the word *you*. When Patricia and Albert argue about whether they should file for bankruptcy, it would not be uncommon for Albert to state to Patricia, "I am so sick of our money problems. You never had a knack for managing money. It's no wonder we are in this situation!" So, following one premise of this model, the complaint (I) is embedded within a criticism (you) of Patricia's financial skills.

Sometimes partners "hear" a criticism implied by the other's complaint. So, for example, if Albert said, "I wish we had more money!" Patricia might interpret that as a criticism of her money-management skills.

The second stage of Gottman's (1994b) model is called **contempt**. In this stage, partners insult and "psychologically abuse" each other (p. 79). Employing both verbal and nonverbal communication, spouses show contempt by identifying their partner as incompetent, lazy, and even stupid. Gottman likens this process to pushing a partner's "anger button." Contempt occurs because criticism went unchecked and the conflict escalated unresolved. Among the most common signs of contempt are insults and name-calling, hostile humor, mockery, sneers, or eye rolling.

The third stage, **defensiveness**, is essentially going from bad to worse in the conflict. Defensive behavior in a marriage occurs when neither spouse is willing to take responsibility for his or her behavior. Denying responsibility, making excuses, disagreeing, cross-complaining, repeating yourself, and whining are all included in the defensive stage. Defensiveness can be understood by examining the following brief dialogue between Patricia and Albert:

PATRICIA: We are filing for bankruptcy—not because I don't know how to take care of finances, but because you are too lazy to get a real job! A waiter! Give me a break!

ALBERT: Right! And your job in retail really rakes in the dollars! I'm a waiter because I love people. Besides, how am I supposed to finish college working 40 hours a week making minimum wage? I can't go to school full-time and work full-time!

PATRICIA: All I know is that I can't believe that you have any self-respect or concern for our marriage. Being a waiter does not show a serious financial commitment to making this marriage work! And I'm sick and tired of coming home to a mess. At least while you read your little textbooks, you can throw a load of laundry in!

ALBERT: Knowing that all you do is ring up people at a cash register all day makes me happy that I am doing something with my life!

Clearly, Patricia and Albert are demonstrating a great deal of defensiveness, contempt, and criticism in their conflict behavior. Their defensive posturing obstructs their ability to deal effectively with their problems.

The final stage, or fourth horseman, of this model is called **stonewalling**. Gottman (1994b) notes that this stage usually occurs while the couple is talking. Imagine speaking to a stone wall rather than another person. This is precisely what occurs in this stage. The listener responds to the speaker with trite and meaningless expressions such as "Uh-huh" or "Hmmm." This results in restricting the communication needed in intimate relationships.

Gottman notes that in marriages men are more likely to become stonewallers than women and that husbands react physiologically to marital tension, more so than their wives do. This reaction includes higher blood pressure and higher pulse rates. Gottman reasons that men may feel a greater and more instinctive need to flee intense conflict situations. Running away from the conflict by becoming a stone wall may be perceived as relatively benign; yet not providing feedback may seriously jeopardize a long-term intimate relationship.

The Four Horsemen of the Apocalypse model is one way to help explain destructive conflict in marital interactions. Gottman (1994b) is clear in noting that what makes these stages particularly deadly is that they "create a continuing cycle of discord and negativity that's hard to break through" (p. 97). This model also points to possible links among conflict, power, and violence, as destructive conflict involves power struggles and may escalate into verbal aggression or violence.

The Explanatory Model of Interpersonal Conflict   A more global model for conflict is one proposed by William Cupach and Dan Canary (1997). Although not specifically designed for the family context, its components are applicable to countless families across the United States. In the **explanatory model of interpersonal conflict,** the authors claim that to best understand the conflict going on in relationships, one has to examine the conflict episodes. They identify five conflict processes and outcomes: distal context, proximal context, conflict interaction, proximal outcomes, and distal outcomes. Let's briefly address the components of this explanatory model.

First, Cupach and Canary (1997) note that the model begins with a **distal context** for conflict. They argue that distal refers to the background or personalities of individuals. This context includes prior successes or failures in handling conflict, as well as the "relational environment" in which conflict occurs. In families, each member has a unique disposition that relates to his or her propensity for engaging in conflict. For instance, Kathryn is an extremely nonconfrontational person. Her sorority sisters recognize this and further realize that she will avoid conflict at all costs, even to the degree that it may jeopardize her own integrity. Her close friends, Trina and Renee, do not instigate disagreements with Kathryn because they know that such disagreements may result in her becoming very distressed. In this instance, Trina and Renee acknowledge the distal context of their relationship with Kathryn. The two also realize that if conflict were to ensue among the three of them, it would not be productive or constructive.

The second component of Cupach and Canary's model is termed **proximal context** and refers to the goals, rules, emotions, and attributions of individuals. In each conflict, family members bring with them various goals and rules. These goals and rules may be formulated or prioritized differently from one person in the family to another. Emotions include anger and guilt, and attributions are explanations of another's behavior. Ryan and his brother Jarrad rarely speak to each other. The 27-year-old twins live about 11 miles apart and speak to each other only if they see each other on the street or in a store. It was surprising for Ryan, then, when he received a phone call from Jarrad. Ryan immediately became suspicious and his suspicions were

---

Student Perspective: John

When I heard about the stonewall in class, things about my first marriage really clicked in my mind. I always ran away from arguments with Elise, and I could literally feel my blood pressure elevating whenever I thought we might get into a serious fight. She sometimes would be following me out the door of a room trying to get me to talk about something, and I would be speeding away as fast as I could. Fortunately, things are a lot better in my second marriage. Connie and I try to talk things out as soon as possible so I don't get too anxious about us fighting. It seems to be working.

confirmed when Jarrad asked to borrow $1,000 from him. Apparently, Jarrad's car was about to be repossessed by the bank. An argument arose, and Ryan accused Jarrad of speaking to him only when he needed money. Jarrad said that the two of them needed to forget the past and work on the future. Ryan felt that Jarrad was a jerk for calling him and quickly hung up the phone. In this instance, Ryan thought Jarrad's behavior was due to desperation (attribution), prompting an angry reply from Ryan (emotion). Ryan also thought Jarrad's goal was to get money. Further, Ryan saw Jarrad as violating their rules, which specified distance and minimal communication between them.

Conflict interaction, proximal outcomes, and distal outcomes round out the remainder of the model. **Conflict interaction** refers to the strategies, message tactics, and communication patterns used in a conflict. We will address some of those tactics in the next section. **Proximal outcomes** are the immediate results or consequences of a conflict episode. These outcomes also evolve during a conflict episode. **Distal outcomes** are the results of the conflict that are removed and delayed. At times, the effects of conflict are not readily apparent. These effects may include personal growth and the development or renegotiation of family rules.

An example will help clarify these last three pieces of the explanatory model. Jake and Suzanne have been married for eight years. Suzanne is about 40 pounds over her ideal weight, and Jake has been nagging her to lose weight for the last four years. He believes that she will feel much better if she loses weight. Suzanne, however, consistently tells Jake to stop harassing her because of her weight and that she will lose weight only if her physician tells her to do so. Besides, she says she feels great and does not need someone telling her how to feel. Integrating the model into this example, Jake has employed a variety of conflict tactics, including guilt and aggression. Proximal outcomes are clear, since Suzanne has not, and apparently will not, lose weight. Finally, the distal outcomes—those that are delayed—will not be fully understood for some time. If Suzanne continues to reject Jake's suggestion, the distal outcome from the conflict could be quite problematic. It is possible that Jake will become annoyed at Suzanne for failing to heed his advice. Or maybe Jake will come to understand Suzanne's point of view and stop nagging her to change her weight. Perhaps Suzanne will feel even more positive about herself and her sense of what is right for her by rejecting Jake's suggestion. Or she may later decide to lose weight, taking Jake's comments to heart. The distal outcome is not immediately clear because conflict has latent effects (Cupach & Canary, 1997).

Responses to Family Conflict

Although the Four Horsemen of the Apocalypse model and the explanatory model do not fully capture all the nuances of interpersonal conflict in families, they do illustrate that conflict is a complex and diverse process. However, as we've mentioned, we should not be confident in applying all of this information to every culture and co-culture. They simply give us a starting point for understanding conflict in the family. Next, we'll examine how people respond to conflict.

A great deal of research focuses on this topic. Much of this research reveals interpersonal styles and tactics for managing conflicts (such as avoiding, confronting, or collaborating). We use *styles* and *tactics* together here, but they do have slightly different meanings. Styles are habitual or patterned responses to conflict, whereas tactics are the smaller, individual moves that people enact to carry out their style. Linda Putnam and Charmaine Wilson (1982) found three basic dimensions underlying conflict styles and tactics: nonconfrontation, solution orientation, and control. We highlight these styles in Table 7-1. Nonconfrontation includes avoidance, withdrawal, and indirectness, among other tactics. Michael Roloff and Denise Cloven (1990) discuss "the chilling effect" that occurs when family members avoid conflict for fear of the strong negative reactions it will provoke. Avoidance is often associated with negative outcomes, especially if the topic of the conflict is serious, or if the expectations in the family involve talking about problems and disagreements (Samp & Abbott, 2012). This association of avoidance with negative outcomes may even hold true across cultures (Song & Zhang, 2012).

The solution-orientation dimension underlies tactics such as reasoning, compromise, and expression of mutual agreement. Researchers suggest that this approach has many advantages, as it is useful for showing respect and gaining commitment to the solution. But approaching conflict from a solution orientation requires a great commitment of time and energy. Further, Hocker and Wilmot (2010) point out that some people

TABLE 7-1   Conflict Styles

STYLE	TACTICS	EXAMPLE
Non-confrontation	Indirectness, withdrawal, detachment, retreat, flight, avoidance	Maria changes the subject when her sister begins to criticize her.
Solution orientation	Reasoning, logic, compromise, negotiation	Ted and Mark agree to take turns choosing their vacation spot for the next several years.
Control	Blame, accusation, condemnation, criticism, attack	Howard belittles Rhonda's job when she wants him to consider moving so she can accept a promotion.

Source: Adapted from L. L. Putnam & C. E. Wilson, "Communication Strategies in Organizational Conflicts," in *Communication Yearbook 6,* ed. M. Burgeon (Beverly Hills, CA: Sage, 1982), 629–652.

use "pseudocollaboration" as a way of maintaining a power imbalance. For instance, Emily Scott, in our example at the beginning of this chapter, had a frustrating morning because of her disability. She might have begun the argument with her husband because she's is sick and tired of being so dependent on him. If Charles responded in a rational manner, trying to show her some areas where she is independent, Emily may feel worse than ever. Charles's obvious superiority in physical ability is compounded by his reasonable, collaborative approach to the conflict, and Emily is left in a less powerful position, at least temporarily.

The control dimension encompasses tactics such as personal criticism, rejection, hostile jokes, and blame. These approaches are often thought of as negative, or "dirty fighting," although researchers suggest that they may have some advantages. These tactics may be useful for letting people know how important the issue is, because competitiveness or control can be a sign of commitment. When LuAnn and Jeff, from our example at the beginning of this chapter, hold strongly to their own positions on raising Elijah and reject the other's opinion, it is clear to both of them that this is an important issue in their relationship.

Conceptualizing responses to conflict as falling along one of the above three dimensions helps illustrate behaviors but also poses several problems. We see four issues that complicate the styles approach. First, conflict is a process and it changes over time. The relatively static notion of styles/tactics does not seem to capture the changing nature of conflict. For instance, Emily Scott's sense of her abilities fluctuates over time, and although she may feel powerless and dependent one day, a few days later she may feel stronger and more capable. These changes in Emily's perceptions will undoubtedly affect her approach to conflict. Further, in a single conflict, Emily may change her approach as her sense of the conflict changes. She may start out avoiding or confronting, and then she may later decide to collaborate with her husband to manage her mobility problems. You will recall that the developmental approach espoused in this text suggests that families evolve over time. When a couple has been together 3 years, their approach to conflict will be different from when they have been together 30 years. Further, the dialectic approach argues that families ebb

Student Perspective: J. J.

My father is definitely a dirty fighter. He always uses sarcasm and rejection whenever we disagree about anything. It is kind of a pain to fight with him, but I do know what to expect. I don't have any expectations that he will listen and be reasonable, but I guess that's just Dad. I remember one Saturday morning when he met my new girlfriend, Gwen. I told him we were going away for the weekend to ski, and he just went off on me! Gwen heard words she didn't know existed. I ended up staying home that weekend.

and flow between forces of togetherness and forces of division. As families manage the tension between this dialectic, they may need differing approaches to conflict at different times.

A second problem with the styles and tactics approach is that it is not sensitive to differing situations—even those occurring in relatively proximate time. For example, LuAnn and Jeffery probably handle conflicts at work much differently than they are managing their conflict over raising Elijah. Undoubtedly, Cynthia Thomas discusses differences with her friends in a much different way than she does with her stepmother.

Third, our emphasis on social construction leads us to conclude that much of what happens in family conflict is the result of relational dynamics enacted in communication behaviors. That is, how Cynthia and Judy conduct their conflict over the nose ring is more a function of what happens between them as the disagreement unfolds than a result of their preferred conflict styles. Perhaps Cynthia wishes to avoid a fight, but when she hears her step-mother say that nose rings are "disgusting" she is unable to stop herself from yelling back that they are not. And, as some researchers argue, there are other contextual issues that affect family conflicts. For example, Donna Pawlowski, Scott Myers, and Kelly Rocca (2000), found that siblings' conflict behaviors were influenced by their overall sense of their relationship with another. Some researchers have found it's more useful to think about conflict patterns (like demand-withdraw) than individual styles to account for the relational nature of conflict (Shimkowsk & Schrodt, 2012).

This third problem with the skills and tactics approach is illustrated by Ascan Koerner and Mary Anne Fitzpatrick's (2002) comment that "the impact that specific behaviors have also depends on when they are performed in an ongoing conflict episode" (p. 234). For instance, suppose Judy says to Cynthia that maybe she could get a clip-on nose ring as a trial because she is trying to be conciliatory and meet Cynthia halfway, and Cynthia scornfully says "that's a ridiculous idea." Now suppose that Judy yelled at Cynthia in a sarcastic manner that maybe she should get both eyes pierced and put a hoop around her neck while she was at it, and Cynthia provided the same response ("that's a ridiculous idea"). Although Cynthia's responses are the same, they would take on different interpretations. In the first instance, Judy might be angered that Cynthia has rebuffed her honest effort to work things out. In the second example, Judy could think that Cynthia was justified in her response.

Finally, the research on styles and tactics is grounded in a European American tradition that values directness and speaking one's mind even at the expense of harmony. Other cultural traditions cultivate different values and have different approaches to conflict as a result. For example, Chien Lin and William Liu (1993) discuss the value of *hsiao* or respecting and honor-ing one's family elders, which characterizes intergenerational relationships among Chinese families. Lin and Liu report that *hsiao* requires that children show parents "selfless devotion and an attitude of loving warmth and rever-ence" (p. 272). This places a premium on harmony that would be displaced if there were open conflict between parents and children. Further, even within European American families, the value of open discussion about conflict may be grounded more in ideology than in reality.

We need to keep these four issues in mind when we think about conflict response styles. We believe that with behavioral flexibility, family members become more mature in the way they respond to the conflictual process. Changing and adapting to conflictual environments are critical to a productive outcome. As Anita Vangelisti (1993) reported, family members may **reframe** or change the way they view problematic situations in their families, thereby changing their behaviors in conflict situations. When the Norris family framed their move from Chicago to Boston as "a crisis," they behaved differently than when they changed the frame to "a challenge." Of course, a critical issue is getting the whole family to frame the event in a similar way. Nadine Norris will still have conflict with her teenage son, Jerimiah, if he maintains the crisis frame about their move. However, the notion of reframing helps us avoid some of the problems with conflict response styles we outlined above.

POWER IN THE FAMILY

Interpreting Power

Intertwined with our discussion of conflict is the notion of power. Although we do not assert that power underlies every communication episode, it is particularly salient in conflict. The way power is manifested in the family, however, varies considerably from one family to another. Possessing and displaying power differs according to the goals, rules, roles, culture, and patterns of communication in each family. Further, power may be distributed differently at various times in the evolution of a family. That is, a father may be viewed as a powerful family member in the early stages of a family's development; yet as he ages, his power base may dissipate dramatically. This power may then shift to another family member, perhaps an older sibling or the mother.

Student Perspective: Katie

I never thought in my 58 years that I would lose power to a 9-year-old child. When I was babysitting my son's boy, I asked him whether he had a girlfriend. Well, if looks could kill, I would be dead now. Max gave me a deadly dirty look and told me that whether he had a girlfriend was none of my business— it was his personal life. I told him that was very fresh to talk to his grandmother like that. He repeated that it was his personal business. So I never did find out if he had a girlfriend, and he didn't apologize. He certainly had more power in that conversation.

Before we go any further with a discussion of power, let's first provide an interpretation of what it is. Like many terms in the communication literature, power is a difficult and slippery concept to define. As Timothy Loving and his colleagues note (2004), power is difficult to define and measure because it is multidimensional. Further, conceptualizations of power are often presented from either a sociological or a psychological viewpoint. Definitions from these orientations do not focus on the communication process, thereby overlooking the interactional focus in power relationships (Noller & Fitzpatrick, 1993). Taking a communication perspective that frames power as an ability, **power** can be defined as the capacity to influence another's goals, rules, roles, and/or patterns of communication. Family members with power gain compliance and/or change the behaviors, beliefs, opinions, and values of others (Kimoto, 1997). This definition has some important implications: (1) power may or may not be exercised (Levine & Boster, 2001) and (2) power is perceptual. First, by calling power a capacity, we acknowledge that a family member may be able to influence others but, for some reason, may choose not to do so. For example, parents may keep their opinions silent in order to let their children learn on their own rather than being influenced by them. Second, power depends on the perceived power relationships among the participants. For instance, if Courtney believes that her father will punish her if she comes home after 11 p.m. and she comes home from her date by 11, then her father has **implicit power**; that is because Courtney perceives him to have power over her, she conforms to his wishes even when he doesn't state them. Basic to this understanding of power is the notion of control; Courtney's father controls her behavior. This is the case both because he exercised power by setting a curfew and because Courtney believes her father has the power to constrain her behavior with curfews.

Implied in the example we just discussed about Courtney and her father is another important consideration about power. This consideration, *relational power,* underlies a slightly different framework for family power. In our previous definition, we framed power as an ability that one person has to influence others. Yet, the example of Courtney and her father illustrates that power can productively be seen as a process between people as well. In other words, when family members attempt to influence each other, they are always constrained by the other's responses. No one in the family can have influence unless another agrees to be influenced.

However, a family member's agreement to be influenced isn't a simple matter of free will. Many issues complicate this decision. For instance, parents have legitimate power (French & Raven, 1959), and many children don't have the resources or the desire to contest that. Denise Solomon, Leanne Knobloch, and Mary Anne Fitzpatrick (2004) mention that another source of power that is difficult to ignore is *dependence power.* A person gains dependence power if he or she is more willing to end the relationship than is the person's partner.

Power and Decision Making

A great deal of the research on family power focuses on how power is exercised in decision-making situations. This body of research measures power by who prevails in a decision. Using this line of thinking, decision making is seen as a power outcome. For example, the Thomas family, from the beginning of the chapter, is poised to make a decision about Cynthia's request to pierce her nose. If Judy Thomas has her way, Cynthia will not get her nose pierced. Power researchers would then conclude that Judy has the power in the family. Although this helps us understand some things about power and decision making, it obscures questions pertaining to process. That is, a family in which family members readily accept a parent's will differs communicatively from a family in which a parent's decision prevails after a great deal of tension and conflict. In turn, these two families differ from another family in which the parent makes the decision after a great deal of family negotiation and discussion. The decision makers in all of these families are the parents (outcome), but the process within each family varies greatly. Focusing on process allows us to take a communication perspective on decision making and power.

Although we all have a commonsense notion of the meaning of decision making, for clarity, we will adopt John Scanzoni and Karen Polonko's (1980) definition. **Decision making** is the process of getting things done in a family when the cooperation of two or more members is needed. This definition implies the enormous range of issues about which families decide. Decision-making topics range from the seemingly simple to the very complex. Families decide where to go on vacation, what to have for dinner, who should walk the dog, how children should be disciplined, how budgets should work, and how sexuality should be discussed, among other things. Every day brings a variety of decisions for families.

Student Perspective: Abdul

I am interested in how decision making is different here from in my country. At home, my father has all the power. He owns his own business, and all my uncles and cousins work for him. My mother would never think of telling him how to do anything, let alone forcing her will on him. As in most Middle Eastern cultures, my father, because he's male, can speak with confidence and authority, knowing my mother will not argue. For instance, my father decided I would come to the United States for school. I really don't know if my mother thought that was a good idea—she never said a word, and it would have been totally out of character if she did.

We could conclude that families reel under the "tyranny of the trivial" in having to deal frequently with so many small decisions. Family systems generally work out a pattern for managing decisions to keep from having to enter into negotiation on every issue. For example, Susan and Charlie may have agreed early in their marriage that Susan will decide on every household expenditure under $500. This pattern saves the couple from talking about each small decision, reserving their energy for larger issues.

Decision-Making Processes

Families use a variety of processes for actually coming to a decision. Many families have a habitual process that they use whenever they need to make a decision. Other families vary in the way they approach decision making depending on the type of decision, their mood, their stage of development, and so forth. In this section we will review five possible processes that families use in reaching decisions, including appeals to authority and status, rules, values, use of discussion and consensus, and de facto decisions.

However, we note that some of these processes may not generalize to a wide variety of family types. For instance, Jennifer Chabot and Barbara Ames (2004) analyzed the decision-making processes concerning having children in lesbian couples. They induced a circular process model that really doesn't resemble any of the five approaches detailed below. So, as we enlarge our concept of what and who constitute family, we will have to enlarge our understanding of the decision-making processes families actually use. We discuss this further a bit later in the chapter.

Student Perspective: Duncan

My family certainly followed the authority process in making decisions. And my mom was the absolute authority. And she could let you know it in a nanosecond if you got out of line. Once my brother thought he would test her by telling her that he had decided he wasn't going to go to college. Man, you could have heard her for a mile! She let him have it and told him in no uncertain terms that she was the boss here and he had no business making a decision like that. All his pitiful comments about it being his life and all just didn't work and really sounded lame. She reasserted her authority for sure, and no one really questioned her on that again in our house. I don't know exactly how she managed to keep on top of all of us kids— I have five brothers and sisters—but she did, and she was always the boss.

Authority and Status Appeals to authority and status allow family decisions to occur as a result of the will of the person in the family with the most status and/or authority. For example, in the Thomas family, from the beginning of our chapter, decision making may be vested in James Thomas. His daughter may be guided by what he says is right. In this case, since James says the nose ring is okay, Cynthia will go ahead and get it.

If James had said no, Cynthia would have obeyed because of his authority. This mode of decision making works for a family as long as all the members agree about who has the most status and authority. In the example of the Thomas family, we see that Judy Thomas is not pleased with granting James authority to sanction this decision about Cynthia's nose ring. When family members disagree about who has the authority to make a decision, they may engage in serious conflict.

Further, the authority approach may be more complex than simply investing a particular member with the most status and/or authority. Some families may have designated certain areas of decision making that are the province of one member and some that belong to other members. For example, many households divide the labor and delegate authority to the person who is in charge of a particular area. If a husband is in charge of maintaining the family automobiles, he may have authority over car-buying decisions. However, he may have no authority over issues concerning the children; for instance, a decision about curfews might be out of his jurisdiction. In this process, everyone in the family might have authority over some decision-making concerns. Some families grant authority and status to members based on expertise. Thus, if Molly Brent, Sam Brent's 17-year-old daughter, knows a great deal about computers and the Internet, she may be the one who decides what type of computer the family will buy and what Internet provider to use.

Rules   Many families use rules to make decision making easier. As you noticed in Chapter 3, rules create structures that help families function. Some specific rules may provide methods for dividing family resources. When the Michaels family's grandmother died without specifying how her possessions should be divided among her children, Tara Jordan and her husband, Jamie, and Jerry Michaels and his wife, Bethany, used a system of rules to divide the estate. They all four went to Grandma Michaels's apartment. The rule was that each person would alternate in choosing something they wished to keep. If someone else wanted what had been chosen, they could offer to trade, but the first person had the right of refusal. In this fashion they divided their inheritance without much conflict. Sometimes parents tell children that one child may divide the cookies or cut the cake, and the second child gets to choose which portion to take.

Rules may also structure decision-making discussions. For example, Matthew McCann and David Blair maintain rules about equal participation in a decision-making conversation. They will not come to a decision until they have both had an approximately equal say about the topic. The Spitz family has a rule specifying that each member of the family has to say something before a decision can be reached. Other families have time limits for the process and a decision has to be reached when the time has lapsed.

Values   Decisions based on values are exercised in families that have strongly articulated principles. These principles may be explicitly stated or indirectly communicated, perhaps through family stories or other meaning-making practices. Some of these principles may derive from organized religion, some from a commitment to social justice, racial equality, or some other cherished value. For example, when parents are deciding about schooling for their children, some may choose religious education or homeschooling based on a dedication to their values. Families may also choose to volunteer, donate money, take in foster children, and so forth as a result of their value system. In the Scott family, from the beginning of this chapter, Charles's decision to stay with his wife despite her disability is a decision based on valuing commitment, enduring love, and loyalty.

Discussion and Consensus   Decisions founded in discussion and consensus are related to decisions based on values. Families that use discussion and consensus as their mode of reaching a decision are committed to the principle of democratic process. It is important to these families that all members have a voice and that members feel that they contribute to the eventual decision. Families utilizing discussion and consensus may convene family meetings to discuss a decision that needs to be made. If the Thomas family, from the beginning of this chapter, wanted to adopt this process, they would call a family meeting and let everyone have a voice in discussing whether Cynthia should get a nose ring. The process of coming to a consensus would necessitate that the family continue discussing the decision until all members are satisfied with the outcome. This type of decision-making process works best when the family is comfortable with sharing power.

De Facto Decisions   De facto decision making occurs when the family does not actively engage in a specific decision-making process and the decision gets made by default. For example, when May and Theo wanted to buy a new stove, they discussed their options. They found a stove on sale that they could afford, but they could not absolutely agree to buy it. While they waited around, trying to decide about the purchase, the sale ended and they did not get the stove. In another example, Roberto is trying to decide about taking a new job and moving his family from Ohio to Florida. He doesn't know what to do and receives conflicting input from his family about the decision. If he lets the deadline pass for acting on the job offer, the decision is, in effect, made without the family actually stating that they have decided not to move. De facto decisions allow family members to escape responsibility for the repercussions of a decision, because no one actively supported the course of action taken.

Some families discuss their processes and have an overt, preferred mode of decision making. Other families simply fall into one or another process without thinking about it much. Additionally, many families may say they prefer to reach a decision through a discussion with all family members, yet the family power relations are such that discussion only confirms what the father, for example, wants as the outcome. In this manner, the family may preserve an illusion of openness while actually using an authoritarian process for coming to a decision. Barbara Risman and Danette Johnson-Summerford (2001) talk about **manifest power** and **latent power**. Manifest power is present in decision making by authority because it involves imposing one's will on others. Latent power, sometimes called unobtrusive power, exists when the "needs and wishes of the more powerful are anticipated and met" (p. 230). When families profess a democratic style of decision making, but really acquiesce to the will of an authority figure, latent power is being exercised. Families make countless decisions using power relations and the processes we have described here. Often the process engaged in by family members reveals more about them and affects them more profoundly than the outcome.

Factors Associated with Power and Decision Making

We conclude our discussion of family power and decision making with an examination of two critical factors that affect the process. These factors include family types and culture.

Family Types   As we discussed in Chapter 1, there are many family types. For the purposes of this discussion, we will review the literature on gay and lesbian couples and stepfamilies, two types that are often overlooked in communication research and in the media. To begin, we are quick to point out that we agree with the research that says, "there is no 'typical' gay or lesbian couple" (Steen & Schwartz, 1995); therefore, the following information generalizes and should not be considered as universally true. In their pioneering research, Philip Blumstein and Pepper Schwartz (1983) analyzed 12,000 questionnaires sent to couples in the United States. In addition to receiving and analyzing questionnaires for heterosexual couples, the authors also analyzed over 1,700 responses from gay and lesbian couples. At that time, this population was virtually ignored by researchers, and to this day, Blumstein and Schwartz's research remains groundbreaking.

Numerous findings from this research are particularly relevant to issues of power in gay and lesbian couples. For instance, like some heterosexual couples, gay and lesbian couples are interested in maintaining equality in their relationships. Yet as much as they wish for such equality, inevitably some power differential occurs in their families. For example, among gay couples, a man is more likely to leave the relationship if he is less powerful than his partner. Less powerful is defined as being "less educated, less forceful and aggressive, or with a lower income" (Blumstein & Schwartz, 1983, p. 317). Further, some gay males reported that they have gained the right to exercise power and control in decision making if they earn more than the other. In fact, the partner with the higher income is often a significant influence on financial decision making, and he expects to have "complete authority" in decision making (p. 59). At times, however, the partners work to change this pattern, and somehow "gay men find some way to establish the balance of power" (p. 59), although they reject traditional family setups such as a provider role and a nonworking partner.

For lesbian couples, money is not a central issue nor does it play into a power struggle in their families. Interestingly, lesbian couples were the poorest of all the types of couples studied by the research team, and gay couples were the wealthiest. Blumstein and Schwartz (1983) noted that lesbians are particularly conscious about issues pertaining to money and power equality, thereby deemphasizing the traditional model of women's financial dependence on another. Yet power issues are not absent in lesbian relationships, although they may not focus on money. When relationships break up, the partner who leaves is characterized as the more powerful, the more forceful, and the one who did less housework. Mignon Moore (2008) found that, within black lesbian couples, power related to parenting decisions usually resided with the biological parent. This greater power was also associated with doing more household chores, even though the provider role was equally shared between the partners.

Other findings support much of Blumstein and Schwartz's conclusions. For instance, Michelle Huston and Pepper Schwartz (1995) noted that for most gay male couples, power and decision-making ability resides with the partner who makes more money. Specifically, they state that the man who makes more money has more power. Huston and Schwartz believe that lesbians do not place as much emphasis on money and power since they actively minimize power differences. As the authors conclude, "The notion of using money as an instrument of control is ideologically repulsive" (p. 109) to lesbians.

Student Perspective: Chris

I just don't get it with my gay guy friends. I mean, some of them have been together for years, and all they do is fight. My friends Chuck and Carlton have fought about curtain colors, box seats at baseball games, and even what to serve at Sunday brunch! My partner, Karissa, and I have been together for almost three years, and we have only fought once. Of course, we fought over what to get Chuck and Carlton for their anniversary gift! Seriously, those guys seem to have a power struggle every time they're together. I'm glad my relationship is a lot less stressful.

Research articulated by Letitia Peplau and Kristin Beals (2004) discovered that gay men and lesbians reject traditional heterosexual values pertaining to division of power. Specifically, the researchers note that "many lesbians and gay men seek power equality in their relationships" (p. 239). They also concluded that generally, both gay men and lesbians rate equality as very important, yet lesbians rate it a bit higher than gay men. Finally, in line with the conclusions of Blumstein and Schwartz (1983), Peplau and Beals discovered that income may affect the power in gay relationships and have a less significant effect in lesbian relationships.

One final area to explore with gay and lesbian couples pertains to conversational dominance. Sarah Steen and Pepper Schwartz (1995) noted that "one good indicator of the allocation of power within a relationship is the use of interruptions" (p. 322). To this end, they concluded that with gay couples, the individual who was perceived to have more power did the interrupting. Lesbian couples, however, did not subscribe to conversational dominance, perhaps because dominance is often associated with males (Pearson et al., 1995). In addition, Huston and Schwartz (1995) acknowledge that many gay men see conversations as competition, wishing to "win" points, whereas lesbians demonstrate conversational support throughout their interactions with other women and, at times, with other men. As you can tell, gay and lesbian couples respond to power and decision making in ways that are both unique and similar to other family types.

We now turn to a discussion of stepfamilies to gain some sense of how power and decision making function in this family type. Like gay and lesbian families, stepfamilies are a unique family type in the United States. At the beginning of a new marriage, spouses in a stepfamily are inclined to use powerful strategies to identify the differences between them (Papernow, 1993). That is, a spouse is likely to be direct in his or her communication, but this directness can prompt family conflicts. Decisions made with this direct form of communication may elicit a sense of **powerlessness**, or a lack of freedom to make and act on one's own choices.

In addition, power plays a role in the way some children discover that they are about to become part of a stepfamily. For many children no prior discussion takes place about how the transition to a new family will occur, when it will occur, or how the new family type will be handled. Clearly, these children have been placed in a situation that denies them any opportunity to be part of the decision-making process. For instance, because stepparents often balance a desire to build a warm relationship with a desire to establish authority (Noller & Fitzpatrick, 1993), parents may be required to exercise some power without considering the child's input.

Finally, recall that boundaries are a part of the way we define families. The way boundaries are set in stepfamilies may require some assertions of power by both spouses (Ahrons, 1994). Nancy Burrell (1995) claims that in stepfamilies boundary issues may include membership, time, space, and authority. Struggles arise, therefore, when children are not prepared for a new parent to revamp family boundaries. For instance, when a child is accustomed to easy access to her single parent, how should that child behave when new boundaries are set for her in the new family? If 15-year-old Jacqui were used to walking into her mother's bedroom any time she wished to talk to her mother, how will she respond to closed doors and more limited access to her mother as her mother establishes a subsystem with her new husband? Imagine Jacqui's response to the newly created boundary set for her. These and other issues provide challenges to stepfamilies related to power and decision making.

Culture   Communicating power through decision making varies a great deal in different cultures. Although no culture is monolithic and there is variability within and between cultures, cultural values affect how families approach the task of decision making. The exercise and distribution of power is also influenced by culture. For example, Steven Gold (1993) quotes a Vietnamese refugee who describes how the Vietnamese family solves problems and makes decisions. Gold reports the refugee as saying, "To Vietnamese culture, family is everything . . ." (p. 304). The priority that the Vietnamese place on the family acts as a standard for evaluating decisions and solutions to problems— are they good for the family as a whole? Also, the Vietnamese use a form of delegated authority to deal with decisions. Female family members are in charge of money matters and are referred to as "Noi Tuong, or 'Chief of Domestic Affairs'" (Finnan & Cooperstein, 1983, p. 31). Although Vietnamese wives are not expected to be breadwinners, they are in charge of making decisions about and managing the money their husbands earn.

M. J. Hardman (1995) reports that the Tupe women of South America make most of the decisions in their families. She describes an experience she had when she was studying the Tupe people in the 1950s. When she told a Jaqaru woman that she (Hardman) and her husband were in a commuter marriage, requiring them to have limited time with their children, the Jaqaru woman found Hardman's problem difficult to understand. Hardman relates that the woman told her, "Well, you just tell him where he should live" (p. 153). Jaqaru women are used to possessing power and making family decisions. This may be due in part to the fact that they are major business entrepreneurs in the Andes and other parts of the world.

From studying African American families, John McAdoo (1993) argues that black families must cooperate in decision making because, for most families, both spouses have had to work to help overcome the husband's lower wages. McAdoo suggests that African American families depend on spousal cooperation because of the threats to the family from outside in the form of institutional racism and economic constraints. When families have to devote so much energy to survival, they are not in a position to compete among themselves for power. Further, African American values, according to McAdoo, place a premium on cooperation for the good of the family. Stanley Gaines (1995) concurs with McAdoo's assessment, stating that the collectivistic values of African Americans "promote egalitarian decision-making processes" (p. 71) between spouses.

Hilary Lips (1994) reports studies of some rural Mexican American families that illustrate both an ideology of male dominance in power and decision making and the divergence from that ideology that occurs within the family. Although both men and women in these families perceive that it is unfeminine and undesirable for women to assert independence and assume power, in practice, couples report that most family decisions are handled jointly by husbands and wives. Thus, the ideology of male power is not actually adhered to in family decision making in these rural Mexican American families. Yet, the ideology is maintained because the families assert that husbands always have the last word in family decisions. Lips notes a similar pattern in Greek village women who have a great deal of power in family decisions because of the land they bring to the family as a dowry. Despite their actual power, however, they report that their husbands have the formal authority within the family.

While the above examples illustrate differing distributions of power and decision-making authority, Mahboub Hashem (1997) explains that in some Lebanese American families much of the necessity for family decision making is subsumed by the church. Hashem notes that religion influences every aspect of Lebanese families' lives, instructing the members in issues such as "birth, death, baptism, confirmation, circumcision, education, courtship, marriage, divorce, the use of contraception, and inheritance" (p. 100). Given this strong church influence, fewer aspects of family life are left to individual family decision making.

Power and Relational Control

One aspect of power that communication researchers pursue relates to patterns of control in couple relationships. Communication scholars argue that control is established through repeated patterns of talk that regulate authority in the relationship (Millar & Rogers, 1976; Rogers & Farace, 1975). **Relational control** refers to power distributions that place the individuals as either equal, subordinate, or superior to one another in their interactions. In their 1975 and 1976 studies, Edna Rogers and her colleagues asserted that these power distributions emerge from the interaction between the partners and are not properties of the individuals. Relational control results from a reciprocal process enacted in the couple's conversations with each other.

Rogers and her colleagues analyzed couples' conversations to determine patterns of relational control. To illustrate this, imagine the following conversation between Matthew and David concerning the hiring of a housekeeper:

MATTHEW: David, I can't understand why you are so resistant to this idea. We have the money to do this, and it would make things so much easier around here. You and I both work hard—what's wrong with hiring a little help?

DAVID: I just think it's too intrusive to have someone coming into our home, for one thing. I feel like we should be able to keep things up on our own. And I also would like to use that money for something else. What about a nice trip or saving it for when one of us needs a new car?

MATTHEW: Okay. I guess I can't say I don't understand your position anymore. But I still think we need to do something about making life a little easier for us and keeping the place from looking like a pigsty. We could always use more money, but we are saving a bit each month, and at this point, I would rather come home to a clean house each night than go on a trip. Isn't there some way we could work this out? How about just trying a housekeeper for a short time to see how we like it?

DAVID: Maybe that would work. I really have trouble with this idea, but I know you want it a lot. I guess I could live with it on a trial basis for the next month. But I get to veto this if it doesn't seem to be working after a month.

MATTHEW: Great. I have someone who was highly recommended. We'll talk about it again after we've tried it out for the next month and see what we think.

DAVID: Okay.

This dialogue illustrates a fairly equal power distribution. By analyzing what each partner says in response to the other, we can see that both David and Matthew respect each other and are not actively trying to constrain the power of the other. This is different from a dialogue in which one partner threatens the other if she or he doesn't comply or when one partner responds to the other's request for a dialogue with passive agreement. Rogers and her colleagues (Millar & Rogers, 1976; Rogers & Farace, 1975) call the responses of Matthew and David **one-across** because the power is evenly distributed across the couple. If one of them threatened the other, that would be labeled **one-up** because the threatener would be trying to gain power over the other. If the threat were responded to with agreement (Matthew: "If we don't hire a housekeeper, I'm moving out." David: "Okay, Matthew, if you feel that strongly we'll hire somebody"), the agreement would be labeled a **one-down** statement because David accepted Matthew's right to be more powerful in this situation.

By examining the pattern across a conversation, relational control is determined. By **pattern**, we mean the interlocking series of responses in a dialogue. We can determine pattern only by seeing how someone responds to someone else. For example, Matthew and David would have very different patterns if Matthew said, "I want to hire a housekeeper" and David replied (1) "Okay, you're the boss"; (2) "That is the most ridiculous extravagance I can imagine—absolutely not"; or (3) "I'm not sure we can afford it, let's look at our budget."

The work by Rogers and her colleagues in this area of relational control provides empirical evidence for Paul Watzlawick and his colleagues' (1967) assertion that all relationships are either complementary or symmetrical. **Complementary relationships** are those in which the partners are opposite to each other; that is, one person is assertive and the other is passive. In **symmetrical relationships**, the partners mirror each other; that is, one person demands power and the other demands it too. Patterns of relational control are dependent on the conversational moves of the partners. The ways couples define the power distributions within their relationships may be fraught with struggle and negotiation or may seem almost effortless. Certainly, relational control is an issue that recurs for couples. As they evolve, grow, and continue communicating, new power distributions may be needed.

VIOLENCE IN THE FAMILY

Interpreting Violence

We are keenly aware that not all episodes of conflict and power involve violence. Yet we also recognize that some conflict and power issues may be manifested by interpersonal violence. We would be remiss in neglecting this extreme form of conflict and power sometimes referred to as "the dark side of family communication" (Olson, Wilson-Kratzer, & Symonds, 2012). Further, some researchers (e.g., Babcock, Waltz, Jacobson, & Gottman, 1993; West, 1996) argue that the link between power and violence may explain why some husbands abuse their wives and others do not. Julie Babcock and her colleagues found evidence supporting their hypothesis that "violence may be compensatory behavior to make up for husbands' lack of power in other arenas of marriage" (p. 40). These researchers see powerless husbands as more likely to abuse than husbands who are more powerful, relative to their wives. Interestingly, violence is a relatively new area of investigation in family communication research yet one that is crucial to examine. Sally Planalp (1993) and other scholars have contended that since researchers have already dedicated themselves to looking at healthy relationships, it is incumbent on them to examine the unhealthy (violent) relationships.

We wish to clarify how violence relates to family communication. We believe that there is no excuse for violent behavior in any family. Yet, we recognize that family members enact violent behaviors every day in millions of households. There is no shortage of explanations for family violence, but none is fully satisfactory. Some evidence suggests, however, that a good explanation for family violence should be rooted in interpersonal communication processes. These

Student Perspective: Jenni-Marie

The first time he hit me, I thought it was because he had been out with his buddies drinking. I can take some of that crap when he's drunk. But the second time came less than a week later, and after that, I said, "no way." I have too much self-respect to stay with someone who is screwed up enough to think hitting is a way to show love. Once I left, though, he got mad. I really didn't know if he was going to follow me everywhere or if he'd go ahead and try to hit me again. I still stay with my best friend, and it's been about six months since we split up. To be honest, I'm afraid.

have been shown to be powerful predictors of family violence (Anderson, Umberson, & Elliott, 2004; Wilson, Norris, Shi, & Rack, 2010).

Mark de Turck (1987) reported on the **frustration-aggression hypothesis**, which advances the premise that when personal goals are blocked, frustration sets in, resulting in people becoming more aggressive, more threatening, and ultimately violent. Michael Roloff (1996) explored the **catalyst hypothesis** and argued that under certain conditions coercive communication serves as a catalyst to violence in the family. Other researchers have spoken of violence from an individual perspective, depicting it as a **skills deficiency** (Infante, Chandler, & Rudd, 1989). This explanation asserts that people resort to violence because their communication skills are too limited to sustain an argument in other ways. This explanation prompted communication researchers to prescribe effective communication strategies for conflict. However, teaching someone to become more effective in communication may not always result in a positive family experience. Becoming verbally proficient, for instance, may also allow someone to become verbally manipulative and exercise undue relational control (Millar & Rogers, 1987), which evokes defensiveness in family relationships (Stamp, Vangelisti, & Daly, 1992).

Other explanations for family violence include a relational approach, similar to a systems approach and like the relational control model we discussed earlier, which suggests that violence is inherent in the dynamics between people. Often the idea of social learning and intergenerational transmission is invoked, suggesting that those who receive violent treatment in turn treat others violently. All these explanations have their strengths and weaknesses. For our purposes here, we need not choose among them. Instead, we wish to examine the communication surrounding family violence, whatever its cause.

The working definition of violence that we will follow is one offered by Dudley Cahn (2009). He asserts that **family violence** is "imposing one's will (i.e., wants, needs, or desires) on another family member through the use of verbal or nonverbal acts, or both, done in a way that violates socially acceptable standards that are either (1) carried

Student Perspective: Sabastian

My family came from Puerto Rico about 11 years ago. To be honest, I still have a hard time understanding women in this country. They don't try to understand the fact that I come from the island and that even though I am over 30 years old, I try to respect my ancestors. I know women here don't like hearing my stories about how men relish the hardworking image of being a male. To Puerto Rican men, having a machismo image is very important. I know that threats and angry talk may catch some women off guard here, but it's really a man's way of keeping his dignity and showing that he has virility. What's wrong with respecting the traditional Puerto Rican way?

out with the intention or the perceived intention of inflicting physical or psychological pain, injury, and/or suffering, or (2) in the case of incest, of sexually exploiting a relative of one's own or of one's significant other under 18 years of age" (p. 16). This interpretation of violence gives us some idea of the complexity of the act. Family violence, by this definition, is a communicative event that can be verbal and/or nonverbal, is embedded in multiple contexts (the family and the larger society), and may be intentional on the part of the abuser or perceived as an intentional act by the abused.

Assumptions Behind Family Violence

Our approach to family violence is rooted in four premises, which we describe below. We have also highlighted these assumptions in Table 7-2.

We Live in a Violent Society   Each day, millions of people in this country open their newspapers and click the remote control to find stories and images of violence. From September 11, 2001, to school and workplace shootings, to bombings at abortion clinics, violence pervades our country. We also learn about suicide bombers in the Middle East, political unrest in many countries in Africa, and the war in Afganistan.

TABLE 7-2   Assumptions Regarding Violence and Why They Exist

---

Assumption 1: We live in a violent society.
Possible reasons: Violence is everywhere in our country. Top-rated television shows and films are often violent in nature. We open newspapers and turn on news reports with violence vividly portrayed in their stories. We play violent video games. Some states allow handguns to be carried. Few messages involving negotiation are represented in the media. We have become a society that is emotionally exhausted from receiving so many violent messages.

Assumption 2: Violence is gendered.
Possible reasons: Women are the targets of violent behaviors by men. Judges seldom impose serious sentences on violent offenders. Current laws assisting women in violent domestic episodes are often weak across the country. An insufficient number of women are in decision-making roles whereby laws pertaining to violence may be redefined and rewritten.

Assumption 3: Violent episodes may be perceived differently.
Possible reasons: People's cultures, family backgrounds, and past experiences provide them with differing viewpoints for assessing the degree of violence that exists in an encounter.

Assumption 4: Family violence is not an isolated event.
Possible reasons: Violence is embedded in family life. It affects and is affected by the process of interpersonal communication used by the family. It is also influenced by the cultural traditions and issues of power and control within the family. Additionally, violence takes place at the complex intersection of the family and all the other suprasystems in which the family is nested.

Television is a powerful communicator of images. These images may include explicit aggression and violence. In fact, a national study conducted at four large universities demonstrated that television violence may pose a substantial risk to television viewers (Wartella, 1997). In particular, Ellen Wartella argues that the context in which violence appears on television poses negative consequences for viewers because the perpetrators of violence often go unpunished, and negative repercussions of violent events are rarely portrayed. In addition to television, violence and violent actions can be viewed on YouTube and other Internet sites. Video games also provide violent images, as well as the opportunity for game players to (vicariously) participate in violence.

Movies are violent as well, and they reach millions of people on a daily basis. Young and old alike pay money each week to see their "action heroes" assault and murder others. Clearly, the media are a significant source of violent episodes. What these images suggest is that violence is commonplace in the United States. This pervasiveness of violence in the society is complicated by laws and moral sanctions against violence. We experience a tension between teachings against violence and the evidence of violence surrounding us.

Violence Is Gendered Julia Wood (2013) argues that **gendered violence** pertains to "physical, verbal, emotional, sexual, and visual brutality that is inflicted disproportionately or exclusively on members of one sex" (p. 291). Although family violence touches everyone, male and female, research verifies that females are disproportionately the targets of such violence (Cahn, 2009; Margolin, 1992). Further, women are more likely than men to be seriously harmed by family violence (e.g., Cascardi, Langhinrichsen, & Vivian, 1992; Stets & Straus, 1990). Some evidence (Finkelhor, 1983) argues for the view that violence is committed in relationships with large power differentials and by the partner who has the greater power. Male–female relationships in U.S. culture (as well as others) are framed by an unequal distribution of power favoring males (Bograd, 1984).

Perhaps because of these power discrepancies, there are people who feel women are to blame when they are treated violently. As astonishing as this may sound, some researchers tell us that men often view women as "bait, servers, and sexual prey" (Yancey-Martin & Hummer, 1995, pp. 421–423). With such a perception, it's little wonder that some people view violence against women as justified. With regard to allocating blame for violent episodes, however, it is important to remember that there is a difference between having the power to choose to take an action and having the power to determine the consequences of that action. In other words, there's a difference between Sara taunting her husband, Jeff, about his low-paying job and Jeff beating Sara for her cruel remarks. Sara may have made a mistake in speaking so callously to Jeff, but this misjudgment does not justify Jeff's violent actions. Some researchers have called for an end to viewing women as co-creators of a violent environment (Spitzack & Carter, 1987). In addition, Nina Reich (2002) has investigated the impacts of labels on women who have suffered abuse. She notes that gendered violence is exacerbated by the use of the term *victim,* and many women prefer the label *survivor.*

Violent Episodes May Be Perceived Differently   Interpretations of what constitutes violence vary across individuals and households. For instance, a mother may think that slapping her child's face when she begins crying in the grocery store is necessary to keep the child quiet. The cohabiting partners who frequently argue over finances may not feel that their regular verbal assaults on each other are violent but simply part of what couples go through when there's not enough money. Or couples who have recently taken in an elderly grandparent may not see anything violent about tying her hands to her wheelchair to make sure that she doesn't harm herself. Examples such as these occur daily in our country, and people differ in their assessment of the violence in them.

   Of course, the era or time in which we live makes a significant difference in judging violent episodes. Acceptance of family violence in the 1950s was certainly greater than it is today. Family shelters were rare in the 1950s. Domestic violence laws were either weak or nonexistent (Chafe, 1974; Coontz, 1992; Mintz & Kellogg, 1988; Seward, 1978). And the prevailing cultural script prescribed privacy, not disclosure (Mintz & Kellogg, 1988), undoubtedly obscuring much of the violence that occurred within families.

   Cultural variation may further affect perceptions of violent behavior. As newspaper columnist Ellen Goodman (1997) queried in an essay about female genital mutilation, what do you do "in a world where one culture's tradition may be another's cruelty?" (p. 14A). Goodman quotes a Somali father living in Houston who said that seeing that his daughters are circumcised (or mutilated, depending on your perspective) is his "responsibility." He told a reporter, "'If I don't do it, I will have failed my children'" (quoted in Goodman, p. 14A). Goodman points out that cultures can change what they value and that many traditions, such as Chinese footbinding and Indian widows throwing themselves on their husbands' funeral pyres, are no longer practiced. Yet, cultural change is not an easy process, and concerns about family violence have to be negotiated against a backdrop of cultural sensitivity.

Family Violence Is Not an Isolated Event   The notion that family violence is not an isolated event relates first to our definition of violence from a communication perspective. When we direct our attention to violence in this way, we concur with Dominic Infante and his colleagues (1989), who claim that "when violence occurs it is not an isolated event in [a family's life], but is embedded firmly in the process of interpersonal communication which people use to regulate their daily lives" (p. 174). Thus, violence does not manifest itself out of nowhere. It is, rather, interwoven into all aspects of a family's interaction, especially with regard to messages about power and control.

Linda Ade-Ridder and Allen Jones (1996) observe that, seen in this way, violence is a maintenance behavior. That is, violence reasserts or reestablishes an abuser's power over a victim, keeping a power hierarchy in place.

Second, this assumption follows the systems perspective by noting that the violence affects all in the system and resounds through all the sub- and suprasystems making up the family's ecology. The family itself is affected, of course, as are all of its members. Family communication spirals out in relationship to the violence. For example, victims of abuse become hypervigilant, scanning abusers' nonverbal communication for signs of what might be coming next (Ade-Ridder & Jones, 1996). Additionally, the community is involved, both as the context for the abuse and as potential support for the family (Vondra, 1990). The suprasystems and subsystems that surround a family all affect and are affected by family violence.

Verbal Aggression

The notion that some family members become physically violent is well documented, albeit the numbers may underrepresent the scope of the problem because of unreported instances. However, a family with a verbally aggressive member is not as well documented. This may be due to the fact that verbal aggression is accepted as a natural part of family life. For instance, Yvonne Vissing and Walter Baily (1996) commented that "parents may believe that they are better parents if they punish a child verbally instead of hitting the child" (p. 85).

Further, Dominic Infante, Scott Myers, and Rick Buerkel (1994) conclude that the family may be the most likely context in which verbal aggression is found because family members have a lower need for social desirability, or the need to respond to others in a way that will elicit favorable impressions. In Chapter 1 we stated that family is defined, in part, by having a rich history and the expectation of a long future. Because family members believe in their future together, they are somewhat released from the need to be pleasing to one another in order to stay together. Several studies show that married couples communicate more negatively to one another than they do to strangers (e.g., Birchler, Weiss, & Vincent, 1975). Dudley Cahn (2009) observed that the sense of connectedness that defines a family may make it a crucible for verbal aggression and violence because members can feel trapped by the connection and thus become frustrated and then aggressive.

Verbal aggression is defined as those messages directed to others that are sent to intentionally hurt another person (Infante & Rancer, 1996). Such messages are aimed at attacking a person's self-concept and are often called put-downs (Infante, 1995; Infante & Wigley, 1986). Infante (1995) notes that the psychological pain experienced by targets of the verbal aggressor include feelings of inadequacy, humiliation, depression, despair, hopelessness, embarrassment, and anger. Verbally aggressive messages include blame, character attacks, competence attacks, physical appearance attacks, teasing, threats, and sexual harassment. As we're able to see, verbal aggression is an important area to consider in family communication because it leads to negative relational outcomes, consistently jeopardizes the family system, and may be a precursor to more severe abuse (Brule, 2009).

Researchers have already embarked on a program investigating the influence of verbal aggression in family relationships. Conclusions reveal that verbal aggression is an unwelcome behavior in homes. We briefly describe four lines of research here to give you a sense of the breadth and depth of the research programs. First, Michael Beatty and Jean Dobos (1992a, 1992b, 1993) have studied father–son relationships, looking at sarcasm, criticism, and disconfirmation from a verbal aggression framework. The research team concluded that sons report lower relational satisfaction with their fathers when fathers are perceived to employ criticism and sarcasm.

In addition to Beatty and Dobos, Teresa Chandler Sabourin and her colleagues (Sabourin, 1996; Sabourin, Infante, & Rudd, 1993; Sabourin & Stamp, 1995; Stamp & Sabourin, 1995) have also investigated verbal aggression based on the catalyst hypothesis we discussed earlier. They conclude that verbal aggression is a catalyst to physical aggression in many marriages (for example, the wife initiates a verbally aggressive comment only to be followed by the husband's physically violent reaction). Sabourin and others also discovered that verbal aggression can lead to perceptions of relationship termination and that verbal aggression can be treated with interventions that focus on communication.

Additional research by Matthew Martin and others (Martin & Anderson, 1995; Martin, Anderson, Burant, & Weber, 1996; Martin, Anderson, Weber, & Burant, 1996), grounded in the notion of intergenerational transmission, reveals that mothers who manifest verbal aggressiveness had daughters and sons who also report being verbally aggressive. Siblings report a similar use of verbal aggression, and when stepparents are verbally aggressive, their stepchildren also admit to being verbally aggressive. In a related study, Martin (with Carolyn Anderson and Kelly Rocha, 2005) also found verbal aggression in sibling relationships to be negatively related to satisfaction, trust, and credibility. That is, in their study of over 280 siblings, the researchers concluded that perceptions of frequently used verbal aggression techniques—manifested by one sibling to another—influenced the negative perceptions that one sibling had on the satisfaction, trust, and credibility of the other sibling.

Finally, research by Loreen Olson (2002, 2009) and others (Olson, 2004; Olson & Braithwaite, 2004) examines tactics and communication competence in verbally aggressive conflicts. These studies are marked by an acknowledgment of the importance of emotion in conflict and the finding that respondents often reported that the use of verbal aggression was appropriate and functional in their conflict interactions. Respondents noted that aggression was especially effective when it was a change from the aggressor's normal conflict behavior. This made the partner pay attention.

SUMMARY

This chapter has focused on the relationships among conflict, power, and violence. With respect to conflict, we presented two primary models of conflict and several responses to family conflicts. Power in the family was also examined, identifying the interrelationship between power and decision making and explaining how family types and culture influence the power and decision making within families. We also explained research on power and relational control. Finally, to illustrate the pervasiveness of family violence, we identified assumptions our culture holds about family violence. As we noted, perpetrators of violence are never justified, nor should victims of violence be blamed for another's violent act.

Although conflict, power, and violence are not always interconnected, we have shown how associations frequently exist among them. A conflictual family event may be the result of a power differential between family members and can erupt into a violent or verbally aggressive episode. Conflict, power, and violence are embedded in the interpersonal communication between and among family members. Without an understanding of how they contribute to family life, we cannot be confident that we have an accurate picture of what takes place in families. Comprehending the reasons why conflict, power, and violence occur in a home may be challenging and uncomfortable. Yet, this understanding is necessary to uncover the complexity of families and their communication patterns.

KEY TERMS

catalyst hypothesis

collectivist cultures

complementary relationship

conflict

conflict interaction

contempt

content-based conflict

criticism

decision making

defensiveness

distal context

distal outcomes

ethnocentrism

explanatory model of interpersonal
    conflict

family violence

Four Horsemen of the Apocalypse
    model

frustration-aggression hypothesis

gendered violence

implicit power

individualistic culture

latent power

manifest power

one-across

one-down

one-up

pattern

power

powerlessness

proximal context
proximal outcomes
reframe
relational control
serial arguments

skills deficiency
social desirability
stonewalling
symmetrical relationship
verbal aggression

QUESTIONS FOR REFLECTION

1. It should be clear that conflict can be negative in many families. Comment on how conflict can be beneficial to family life. Discuss specific instances to support your views.

2. Explain how children can acquire power in their families. What specific examples can you draw on to justify your thinking? Do you believe that children can ever have too much power in their families? Too little?

3. There appears to be an increase in family violence in our country. Do you believe that personal issues or societal issues are more responsible for this apparent increase? If you had a best friend who was in a violent home, what suggestions would you make to him or her?

4. Based on your own family experiences—either in the past or currently—do you believe that your family members respond to conflict effectively? Ineffectively? What specific examples can you give to support your answer? Be sure to limit your example(s) to an appropriate area for discussion.

5. We have argued that verbal aggression is a negative behavior in families. Yet many family members feel that yelling and swearing are acceptable ways to communicate in their families. What do you believe about yelling and swearing? Criticism and sarcasm? Are there instances when these verbally aggressive behaviors are appropriate to use in a family? Explain by using examples.

6. Is there a difference between violence and abuse? Can a family member be violent but not abusive? Abusive but not violent? Are they too similar to differentiate? Use examples as necessary.

7. Defend, criticize, or modify the following statement: Conflict, power, and violence are necessarily interrelated. Discuss your view by using examples.

8. Articulate why culture needs to be considered when discussing conflict, power, and violence.

Chapter
8
COMMUNICATING UNDER STRESS

THE MICHAELS FAMILY

Laura and David Michaels are at their kitchen table with their calendar laid out. Laura asks David whether he knows what his travel schedule will be for the next three months. David says he will check with the band's manager and be able to tell her next week. Laura sighs and starts to put the calendar away. David comes around the table and gives her a hug: "I know this is hard, honey, but probably next year we can stop touring and just put out one new CD." Laura smiles but pushes David away: "I know this band is what you want, David, and don't get me wrong, I am really happy you guys are doing so well. But it's just hard for me to get anything done when you're gone all the time, and I have to take care of Tiffany and Alice all by myself." As if on cue, the two-year-old and five-month-old make noises indicating they are waking up from their nap. David laughs: "You sit, Laura. I'll get the girls." As Laura sits at the table listening to her daughters, she thinks about the combination of great things—the band's growing fame and earning power, her two daughters' births, their new house outside of Seattle—that somehow have a downside to them too. When David comes back with the girls, she says, "Maybe we should move back to Oregon so we could be closer to my parents."

THE GILMARTIN FAMILY

Colleen Gilmartin owns a convenience store next to the city's largest high school. She bought the store after her husband left the family many years ago. The store does a brisk business, especially during the noon hour when the students come in droves to get their sodas, candy bars, hot dogs, and hot pretzels. During the day, Colleen's daughter, Lindy, 16, attends Pond Cove High School, and her other daughter, Danielle, 4, stays at home with Colleen's mother and dad. Colleen didn't always envision letting Danielle stay with her grandparents, but these days, she couldn't simply walk away from the store. The store is located in a strip mall, and the building's owner is raising the rent. She opens the store at 6 for the morning coffee rush and closes around 11 at night. It is a long day, but Colleen knows she will be able to sell the business one day and spend a lot of time with her daughters. Colleen has to make sure she works in the store during the noon rush because many of the high school students frequently lift a candy bar or two without paying. In addition to working at the store, Colleen also volunteers as a teacher's helper at Pond Cove. She also has agreed to serve as this year's holiday chairperson for the upcoming dance sponsored by the chamber of commerce. Colleen wonders whether or not she is overextended. She feels her commitments are important, but she also knows that as a single mother, she needs to be there for her two daughters. She muses about the problems of single motherhood and wishes she had someone to talk to about the girls, her worries about stretching herself too thin, her financial obligations, and just life in general.

THE VICTOR-PARRISH FAMILY

Josie Victor and Andrea Parrish have been living together for five years. They have begun to plan a commitment ceremony to celebrate their love for each other and their faith in the stability of their relationship. This is an important step for both of them, and they are very excited about the ceremony—they have a Unitarian minister who is willing to conduct it. After the ceremony, they plan to have a large party for their friends. Josie's two children—Beth, 12, and Scott, 9—live with Josie and Andrea, except on the weekends they visit their dad, Josie's former husband, Ed. Ed thinks the commitment ceremony is disgusting. He disapproves of Josie and Andrea's relationship, and he has been making negative comments about it to the kids. After they returned from their last visit at Ed's house, Beth told Josie she didn't think she wanted to be a part of the ceremony.

T he Michaels, Gilmartin, and Victor-Parrish families all experience some stress related to their daily interactions and tasks. All families do. Family stress is inevitable because stress often comes from change, and the family system changes over time. As we have discussed throughout this text, everything at issue in family life, and most especially, family communication, is an evolving process. This process approach puts a premium on evolution and change. Change, however, represents a disturbance in the status quo. This disturbance is often accompanied by feelings of uncertainty (Babrow, Hines, & Kasch, 2000; Ford, Babrow, & Stohl, 1996), and because uncertainty is uncomfortable for people (Berger, 2009; Soloman, 2008), we are motivated to reduce it. In fact, **certainty**, or a belief in your ability to predict and control your experiences, is associated with mental health and social adjustment (Brandes, Franck, & Pieper, 2010).

Yet the dialectic approach that we describe in this text argues that there is a tension between certainty and uncertainty—between novelty and predictability—both of which inform family life and a family's approach to change and the stress accompanying it. Families need both change and stability, and therefore, it is not useful for us to think about eliminating change and stress from family life. Some degree of stress is a normal part of life, a part of an important family dialectic. What's important is that stress not take over a family but, rather, that a family take over the stress.

When families include children, the children's growth marks off developmental stages, each of which brings change. Thus, Laura Michaels's perception of stress in her family has something to do with being a parent of preschoolers. Colleen Gilmartin's stress level is explained, in part, because her children are young and growing, a time of life marked by limit testing as well as physical and psychological changes. As her daughters get older, their needs and demands change, generating some stress within the family system. Changes in life stages are, of course, not confined to children. As adults age, retire from the workforce, and face the death of elderly parents, they are catapulted into change and stress.

Further, the developmental model is complicated by layering individual development over family stages. For example, as we discuss a bit later in this chapter, teenage parents may experience more stress than parents in their 30s (Whitson, Martinez, Ayala, & Kaufman, 2011). As Alan Sillars and William Wilmot (1989) observe, "Older parents are more likely to have completed their education, to be well established in their careers, and to be less stressed and more stable in a variety of respects" (p. 229). Additionally, remarriage may place older individuals in the position of parenting young children, or it may create families with both preschool and young adult children. These variations of the developmental model may recycle stages that some family members have already experienced. Although this does not eliminate stress, prior experience—with the "terrible twos," for example—may provide some resources for dealing with stress.

Changes occur when growth occurs and also, unexpectedly, in both positive and negative ways. We often think of unexpected change in terms of crises, such as a sudden death or illness, or a disaster, such as a flood or tornado. Yet families can also receive pleasant surprises. For example, a promotion at work may come when a worker is not expecting it. A family could receive a phone call informing them that a distant relative they didn't even know they had has left them a large inheritance. A mother may go to the doctor and discover that her multiple sclerosis has gone into remission, and she gets a clean bill of health. A couple who believed that they could not get pregnant gets the good news that they are, in fact, expecting a child. These events are not part of normative growth; they are happy surprises, but they still involve change and interrupt the course of events, and thus involve stress.

Families are buffeted by changes, although sometimes change occurs so slowly that family members do not notice it at first. Children's growth is like that. Parents often exclaim that they thought childhood would last forever, and then one day they turned around and all the children were grown. Change is a normal characteristic of family life, but it produces stress that the family must respond to in some way. This is the essence of our next discussion.

In this chapter we will (1) provide an interpretation of family stress, (2) examine several underlying assumptions about family stress, (3) discuss the relationship between communication and managing developmental stress, and (4) discuss the relationship between communication and managing unpredictable stress.

INTERPRETING STRESS

In this section, we explain our approach to the concept of family stress by illustrating two important distinctions in the research on stress. The first centers on disentangling the concepts of stressor and stress. The second focuses on the differences between normative, or developmental, stressors and nonnormative, or unpredictable, stressors.

Distinguishing Between Stressor and Stress

Many family scholars involved in research on stress adopt a philosophy whereby specific areas of interest are grouped under the general label *stress* (McCubbin, Cauble, & Patterson, 1982). *Stress* is thus used as a generic term to mean the "stimuli producing stress reactions, the reactions themselves, and the various intervening processes" (Lazarus, 1966, p. 27). Other scholars, and we include ourselves among them, have made an effort to distinguish the stressor from the reaction, or stress, that is produced in the family. Although the research is more than 50 years old, Rueben Hill's (1958) early model of family stress provides a conceptual framework for distinguishing between the stressor and the stress reaction.

Hill's **ABC-X model,** shown in Figure 8-1, focuses on three concepts: A represents the *event,* or **stressor,** that causes a change in the family system; B represents the family's *resources,* or strengths, for coping with the change; and C represents the *perception* that the family has of the change. These three concepts relate to produce X, which is the degree of **stress,** or discomfort, experienced in the family system. These concepts and the distinction made between the stressor and the stress are important to us because they

FIGURE 8.1 The ABC-X Family Stress Model

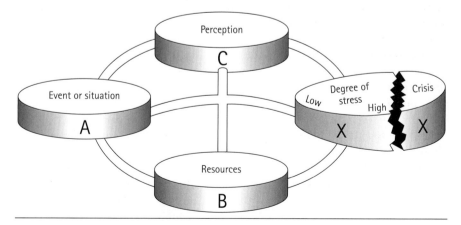

Source: From P. Boss, *Family Stress Management* (Newbury Park, CA: Sage, 1988).

are congruent with our social constructivist approach to the family. A family's relational culture will make a great deal of difference in how much stress a family feels in response to changes. As Pauline Boss (2002) puts it,

> *A stressor event is an event that has the potential to cause change in the family because it disturbs the status quo. The event also has the potential to raise the family's level of stress, although it does not necessarily do so every time. The degree of stress caused by the event depends not only on the actual magnitude of the event, but, also, on the family's perception of that event. (p. 48)*

You can see how this approach fits in with our emphasis on the family as a relational culture. The material we discuss in Chapter 6 on storytelling suggests that families develop collective, symbolic realities through communication practices. It stands to reason that these realities would affect how the families process change and respond to stressors.

Boss (1988) points out that not all families respond in the same ways to similar stressors, further justifying the distinction between the two concepts. For example, one family may treat moving to another city as an adventure, while another family responds unhappily and with anger to a proposed move.

Not all families treat the death of a family member in the same way either. Clearly, the death and dying process is one that is overwhelmingly stressful for members of various cultures. But it is important to note that not all cultures share the same value system in this process. Robert Blank (2011), for instance, posited that "in many Asian cultures, it is perceived as unnecessarily cruel to directly inform the patient of a cancer diagnosis" (p. 205). This is in contrast, argues Blank, to the forthrightness in medical diagnoses expected by most co-cultures in the United States. Although losing a family member to death is a stressor—a turning point in family process—different families manage death

Student Perspective: Yolanda

My friends could never understand how my family dealt with problems. We just have a very fatalistic attitude—what will be will be. We hardly ever get stressed out over things that probably would bother other families a lot. Maybe it has to do with the stories we have had passed down from the older generations who lived through slavery and times when we basically had no civil rights. The lesson my family took from these stories was that life is hard, but we will persevere. In a way, we also learned not to "sweat the small stuff." In knowing some of the horrible things our ancestors lived through, we would have to come up with something pretty big to have it worth getting stressed about. My mom always says when something bad happens, "It's inconvenient." Somehow that doesn't seem worth a lot of stress.

quite differently. Some differences may be a function of culture or ethnicity. Elliott Rosen and Susan Weltman (1996) point out that rituals may help Jewish families reduce the stress or discomfort of death. Rosen and Weltman observe that the complexity of the rituals and their clear prescriptions can reduce some of the uncertainty attending a death in a Jewish family. At least the family has a clear mourning ritual to follow in the aftermath of death.

Monica McGoldrick (2004) and Ken Hardy (2008) state that some of the stress surrounding death may be reduced in Irish American families because of Irish attitudes about life and death as well as clearly articulated rituals for dealing with funerals. McGoldrick's observations about the Irish support this thinking:

> *The Irish believed that it was important to have the window open at the moment of death so that the spirit could escape. They placed salt or tobacco on the body. They also made a point of sending two people out to tell all the neighbors, and also the livestock and the bees, of the death. At the funeral itself, the hearse and mourners typically drove around the neighborhood, passing all the places where the deceased had lived or spent time, including schools and the pubs he or she frequented. (p. 143)*

While a death in the family represents change and uncertainty, cultures that provide families with ritual also provide some certainty and predictability. This perhaps mediates the amount of stress felt in the system. Further, cultures with values that celebrate death as a release from the suffering of life may help to reduce the stress that families experience.

To further bolster the argument that a family's relational culture affects its response to stressors and the stress level they experience, consider how the same stressor may affect a family differently at different times. That is, as the family changes and modifies its culture, the family members perceive and respond to stressors differently. For example, the Michaels family, from the beginning of the chapter, has recently moved away from Laura's family, narrowing the boundaries of the family, at least temporarily. Laura's perception of stress is probably colored by her sense that her family includes only two adults now, one of whom is usually unavailable because he is traveling. If Laura were near her mother and father and could count on them for social support, she might feel less stress in the same situation.

Developmental stages also affect both the family's culture and the family's response to stress. For instance, in the Victor-Parrish family, from the beginning of the chapter, a great deal of the perception of stress regarding the commitment ceremony centers on the fact that Beth is 12 years old. If she were younger (or possibly older, as in her 20s), the sense of stress might be lessened. Since Beth is on the threshold of adolescence, she is experiencing myriad physical, emotional, mental, and social changes herself, all of which have some effect on the family system (Willis, 2011). Given all the changes that go along with the adolescent stage, the commitment ceremony may simply be one change too many.

Finally, stressors produce change in the family system. Mary Guindon and Barrett Smith (2002), for example, indicate that loss of employment tends to exacerbate a person's stress. They point out that "when job loss occurs, particularly when it is involuntary, perceived stress may exceed the person's ability to cope with the demands of the environment" (p. 75). Guindon and Smith note that a lack of resources, including family support, can result in headaches, sleep disorders, depression, and mental illness. In research on how job loss affects family communication, Patrice Buzzanell and Lynn Turner (2003) discovered that some people felt that job losses like seasonal layoffs were normal and did not really change the way their family communicated. They knew the employer would be rehiring them, and they built the layoff into their family routine. However, for other workers in this study, a job loss represented a major upheaval that changed virtually everything about the way the family communicated, at least for a period of time.

During the "great recession" of 2010, the stress in the family was palpable as more employers began to downsize and job losses began to affect family members everywhere. During that time, families had to retool past practices (such as purchasing, credit use, etc.) (and continue to do so), which influenced their communication patterns. Such an area has been ripe for both research and editorial commentary. As Shu-wen Wang, Rena Repetti, and Belinda Campos (2011) conclude: "The work-family interface and the transmission of stress between these two contexts is a rich area for investigations of family health and functioning" (p. 442). Writers have chimed in on this relationship in prescriptive and theoretical ways. For instance, Lindsay Olson (2011) states, "Losing a job is a loss, similar to losing a person to death. You have to allow for the grieving process and find your new normal" (*http://money.usnews.com/money/blogs/outside-voices-careers/2011/10/20/how-to-cope-with-the-stress-of-unemployment*). Further, she believes that at times, a spouse (or partner) may communicate his or her anxiety related to the unemployment. Olson cautions that finding routine, focusing less on staying unemployed (and more on getting a job), and volunteering with family events (at school or home) will help relieve some of the stress.

Amanda Gunn (2007) quotes the words of several employees who lost their jobs. Their emotions and obvious stress communicate a great deal about the experience and upheaval that scholars claim take place: "They needed to consider our feelings, our families, our families are gonna suffer." "There's a sad day coming. We know how to put our arms around each other and pray for the strength to keep the family together. We keep the family together." And, finally, "It's not my American Dream. How do I feel about it? It can be overwhelming, it could be history taking place" (p. 11).

Distinguishing Between Developmental and Unpredictable Stressors

Some researchers have made efforts to classify stressors (and the stress that may accompany them) into categories (e.g., Henry, Plunkett, Robinson, & Sanchez, 2011). The two categories of **developmental or normative stressors** and **unpredictable or nonnormative stressors** are common classifications. Stressors are seen as normative if they are part of the human developmental process. Thus, birth, death, a young adult leaving home or getting married, and older adults retiring from the workforce are all seen as predictable life events. They cause change and disturb the status quo, but they are expected in the course of family life. Unpredictable stressors are those that are unexpected and are the result of some unique set of circumstances for which the family is relatively unprepared. The family home burning down, a family member's disabling accident, or winning the lottery are all unpredictable stressors.

The distinction between the two types of stressors is not always completely clear. For instance, the commitment ceremony that Josie and Andrea are planning, in the chapter opening vignette, seems to be a developmental occurrence. When two adults wish to spend their lives together, they get married. In Josie and Andrea's case, however, marriage is not a legal option. As lesbians, Josie and Andrea's developmental change is unsupported by the larger culture and, thus, is unexpected. In our example of the Michaels family, we see developmental change (the birth of children) exacerbated by unpredictable change (the sudden fame of David's band). As these two types of stressors intertwine, it is frequently difficult to maintain the distinction between them.

Although it may sometimes be unclear as to whether a stressor is normative or not, we need to keep in mind that we are the final judge of what is normative in the family. We can usually make the distinction in our own families.

Student Perspective: Gordon

One really wild thing about my coming up here to school was how it was completely planned. My family was in on all the decision making, and my mom and my grandma said how proud they were of me all the time. They talked a lot about how this signified a big change in my life and in our family's life. I am the first person in my family to go to college, and it's a major turning point. But as the time for my leaving got closer, my mom and grandma and even some of my brothers and sisters acted like my going away was a total shock. They acted all surprised that I was really going to go, and they even acted a little mad that I would leave. Sometimes they made small digs at me—that I would be this big, stuck-up old college man the next time they saw me. Go figure.

ASSUMPTIONS ABOUT STRESS AND STRESSORS

So far, we have noted that stress is inevitable in families, that it can emerge from both positive and negative family events, from expected or predictable events as well as unexpected ones, and that stress and stressors differ in that stress is based on the family's perception of events, whereas stressors are the events themselves. We turn next to three assumptions guiding our thinking about stress. As we explain each, keep in mind the various family types that we examined in Chapter 1. Although we explore stress in a general sense, much of the information can be applied to specific families. We examine three assumptions: (1) stressors are in the eyes of the family member, (2) family stressors are shaped by the internal and external context of a family, and (3) communication is at the heart of family stress management.

Stressors Are in the Eyes of the Family Member

As we noted in Chapter 2, the family can be viewed as a system. One of the important principles of a system is wholeness. Through this principle, we understand that the family system has a character of its own. Further, family members tend to see stressors similarly, although not completely alike. This line of thinking is consistent with the reasoning we advanced in Chapter 6 about the family's relative unity in interpreting the meaning of a family story. The notion of a family perception or a family reality does not mean that every individual in the family behaves in the same way relative to a stressor. It does mean that the family members all understand the meaning a stressor has for their family. Thus, for example, both David and Laura Michaels, from our chapter opening scenario, could explain the stressor that is currently affecting their family. They also could describe the family perceptions about how serious the stressor is. That does not mean they agree on how to deal with it or will act similarly to reduce the stress accumulating from it.

Family Stressors Are Shaped by Internal and External Contexts

As with many other issues that we have discussed, the family's perception is developed in an interplay between the internal system and the external systems in which it is embedded. As we will discuss in Chapter 8, the family does not act in isolation. Some of the ideas family members bring to the family are shaped by external elements such as messages heard on television or through social movements. Here, we assume that the family's response to stressors is conditioned by its own relational culture in dialogue with the wider culture outside of the family.

Boss suggests that the family's **external context** consists of the following frameworks: historical frame, economic frame, developmental frame, hereditary frame, and cultural frame. These frameworks form a superstructure that houses the individual family. Families have no real control over these frameworks. They are givens as the family deals with and formulates its responses to stressors. We will discuss each framework in turn to give you an idea of how they operate to shape a family's perceptions.

Historical Frame   The historical frame refers to the time in history in which a family lives and experiences a stressor (or stressors). For instance, over the past several decades, the United States was involved in several wars, including wars in Afghanistan and Iraq. While military deployment is understood to be a part of being an active-duty military person, the stress, nonetheless, remains palpable. Steve Wilson and his colleagues (2011) discovered that children in military families experienced stress at both the point of deployment and point of return. Worrying about the parent at home, arguing more with brothers and sisters, and feeling more responsible for daily chores were among the many deployment stressors children reported. Brandi Frisby and her research team (2011) also report stress within military personnel. Specifically, the researchers discovered that given the higher divorce rates of military romantic couples, it is likely that the couples are not managing their stress effectively and that they are experiencing high levels of stress when they are not engaged in everyday talk/ordinary conversations. It should be clear that the historical period of living during a time of war deployment affects the stress and the perceptions of stress for those family members involved in a war.

Economic Frame   The economic framework is closely related to the historical frame. It encompasses the economic conditions in the family's community. For example, in communities across California and the Northwestern United States, economic conditions were very good in the late 1990s. The tech industry was doing quite well, and Wall Street seemed to respond positively to what was happening in Silicon Valley. When the technological industry went bust in the early 2000s, people were scrambling to find jobs. What jobs were available to individuals with graduate degrees paid far less than the jobs that were lost. The impact of job loss and underemployment within some communities has been especially stressful, a topic we return to a bit later in the chapter.

Fran Dickson (1995) comments on the economic frame in her observations about couples who have been married for more than 50 years. She notes that the Depression and World War II affected these couples and influenced how they view the quality of their relationships. By extension, we might argue that these events could shape their perception of stress as well. Dickson observes that couples who lived through the Depression learned how to be thrifty and to make do with less than couples today do. Perhaps a financial setback would not seem as stressful to those couples. Boss (1988) also suggests that losing a job during the Depression might have had a different meaning for families than losing a job in a time period such as the early 21st century, when the unemployment rates are relatively low.

Developmental Frame   The developmental frame refers to the stage of life a family is in when the stressor occurs. Colleen Gilmartin is worrying about the intersection between her job and her family. At this developmental juncture, with two children at critical developmental times, and as a single parent, the loss of her business would inevitably cause more stress than at another time—for instance, when the girls were younger and Colleen's husband was still living with her and bringing home additional income.

The developmental stage of a family suggests the importance of resources a family can bring to bear on the stressor. Consider, for example, the effects of immigration on various families. Those individuals who enter the United States because of political persecution or war may initially have difficulty assimilating. But, after some time of being in the country, these immigrants may have acquired jobs, money, education, and social support, all of which will affect the stress level of various family members.

Hereditary Frame   The hereditary framework acknowledges that long life and good health are, in part, a function of heredity. Good health removes one stressor (illness) and provides strength to families for coping with other stressors. In the Nickels family, it is a source of pride that they come from "good stock." Both sets of grandparents lived healthy lives and died in their 90s. Obviously, families that experience multiple generations of hereditary illness have more stressors than healthier families. For example, Kay Bruno's mother, grandmother, and two of her aunts died at relatively young ages from breast cancer. Now that Kay is 30, the age her mother first discovered her cancer, she is anxious about her own health and is thinking about having a mammogram. While she worries about this, she has withdrawn a little from her husband, Carl, and their three sons. Adopted individuals who do not know the medical histories of their birth families report stressful feelings related to this uncertainty.

Student Perspective: Sam

I feel so useless to my mother. I mean here she was—after leaving Saigon with my grandparents many years ago—working three jobs just so that I could go to college. She kept telling me just to study hard and do my best. I don't have a job, I take four classes a week, and I try to make it home to my mom's house at least twice a year. I can't wait to get a job, make money, and pay for my mom to stay at home. I don't want her working on people's fingernails her entire life.

Cultural Frame   Culture plays a large role in transmitting values to families and aids in the management of family stress. Many of these values contribute to the family's perception of, and reaction to, a stressor. For example, Vietnamese families have many strengths that they derive from their cultural heritage that could be useful in dealing with stressors (*http://www.globalsecurity.org/ military/world/vietnam/rvn-family.htm*). First, the value of family cohesion and familism means that the extended family can be counted on to come together, offering support in times of crisis. Second, the Vietnamese American family has the capacity to adapt, particularly given that most refugees to the United States "lacked education, job skills, and measurable economic resources [and] also suffered from the trauma of war and flight and from the severe emotional stress that they experienced at refugee camps" (Zhou, 2001, pp. 187–188). Vietnamese Americans' strong commitment toward maintaining cultural identity helps ease stressful situations. Finally, Kristi Hagans, Michael Hass, Phuong Lee, and Kristin Powers (2011) comment that fluent bilingualism (or speaking both Vietnamese and English) significantly bolsters self-esteem, decreases depression, and enhances the educational opportunities of young people. Maintaining "the mother tongue," then, may help in reducing the stress associated with assimilation and communication with others.

Internal Context The family receives messages from each of these external frameworks, but family perceptions are not shaped by the external context alone. The family's **internal context**, or relational culture, developed through stories, themes, metaphors, rituals, myths, and conversations, also sends powerful messages. Catherine Chilman, Elam Nunnally, and Fred Cox (1988) present several factors in the internal context that are important to acknowledge: (1) family size and structure, (2) the personality and cognitive functions of family members, (3) previous life experiences of family members, (4) family member's perceptions of the magnitude of the stress, and (5) the boundaries, rules, patterns of interaction, and available resources present in the family.

The two contexts, internal and external, relate to and impact each other. Certainly, the family's relational culture is affected by the external context. In some instances, this interplay itself is a

Student Perspective: Mirela

Coming to the United States from Bosnia was not a real choice. We had to leave, and of course, it's safer here. But there are so many differences that sometimes it is terribly confusing and upsetting. Everything happens so fast when you arrive here. No one stops to let you catch your breath the way they would in my country. When you are in your own country you have your house, you have a cow, you have a car. But here, we have nothing of value. Here when you work, you are not sure how long you will be working. It depends on whether the company has jobs. Someone could come tomorrow and say, "Tomorrow we are closing the company." It was different at home—you had rights. In Bosnia everyone had health care, here no. It is hard. I am counting on my children. They will take care of me.

stressor. In immigrant families, for example, when the values of the adopted culture do not reinforce those derived from the native culture, the conditions exist for stress (Bush, Bohon, & Kim, 2010).

Communication Is at the Heart of Family Stress Management

Our final assumption about stress is that family perceptions are developed through communication, and this communication can exacerbate family stress or be used as a coping resource to manage stress. As the ABC-X model shows, family stress is a function of family perceptions and family resources in response to a stressor. Thus, we place communication centrally in the process of family stress management. Through interaction, families may develop a sense of the stressor. For example, if Josie Victor, from the beginning of our chapter, talks to her daughter, Beth, about Beth's feelings, and Beth expresses them forcefully and strongly, Josie may perceive the stressor as more serious than she did before the conversation. If Josie and Beth get into a major conflict over this topic, communication may actually contribute to increasing the stress level felt in the family. If Josie and Andrea sit down and strategize some ways to make Beth feel more comfortable, this conversation may serve as a coping resource that reduces the stress that the family experiences. If Andrea takes Beth out for ice cream and the two of them have a pleasant conversation, again, communication can reduce the level of stress in the family. Thus, communication is central to the process of experiencing and managing family stress.

COMMUNICATION AND DEVELOPMENTAL STRESSORS

As we observed earlier in this chapter, it's not always easy to distinguish between developmental and unpredictable stress. It is useful to examine the life trajectory if we want to understand some of the regularity in changes that families experience. As James White (1991) argues, "The theory of family development cannot answer all of the questions about family change. Some changes are random, other changes are the result of cross-institutional adaption. But some changes are developmental in nature" (p. 240). We will examine three broad stages that capture some of the most important of these developmental changes: young families, growing families, and older families. In each stage we will list some of the main developmental stressors and the communication resources that can be brought to bear in managing these stressors.

Developmental Stressors in Young Families

When a family is just starting out, or young, decisions about marriage, cohabitation, and whether to have children often provide a confounding opportunity for the family (Jayson, 2010). The family members must begin the reality construction that they will continue throughout their lives. Of course, most young families are predicated upon older families who have gone before them, so when adults come together to form a family, they bring with them the stories, myths, and rituals of their families-of-origin. Some of this **symbolic baggage** is helpful to the new family, but it also provides them with the challenge of merging and reformulating the symbolic content so that it will represent the new family. Some cultures, notably Latino and African American cultures, focus more on the extended family than do others. When extended families share living space, and new members are brought into the family, the task is not to reform the story of the family but to socialize the newcomer to the existing family story. Communication behaviors that help young families in these tasks include storytelling, invoking family themes and family metaphors, and using negotiating skills similar to those we covered in our discussion of conflict management in Chapter 7.

A number of young families choose to remain child-free (in the 1990s, these couples were called DINKS, or "double income, no kids," families). Although these couples have chosen to avoid parenting (and the subsequent parental stress), they nonetheless experience developmental stress, including coping with the aging/illness of their parents. Few childfree couples are prepared to deal with the stresses of dealing with an ailing parent because they often lack the resources, services, and finances to do so. In fact, Gail Sheehy (2010) in *USA Today* points out that women, in particular, feel the effects of this stressful caregiver role. She notes that not only is there a financial toll, but also a psychological consequence in the form of depression and low self-esteem. We return to the topic of caring for aging family members a bit later in this chapter.

If children are brought into the family, the family must manage the transition to parenthood. As Elizabeth Menaghan (1982) notes, "Life is never quite the same again after one becomes a parent" (p. 105). Some past research (e.g., Ruble, Fleming,

Student Perspective: Hector

It was really interesting when my wife and I had our first child. I was not really expecting a lot of change in our life, and I felt that the baby would be more of my wife's responsibility on a day-to-day basis. I sort of remembered back to my father's treatment of me and the idea in the Puerto Rican culture that the man is more in charge of material things for the family, while the woman keeps the home fires burning. I wasn't prepared for how I'd feel when Amalia was born and I saw her and held her. I did some fast changing about what I thought was the role of the father. And Tessa, my wife, and I had to talk about that, because she didn't really expect me to be so involved. It helped that we had several friends who had kids at the same time Amalia was born. Luckily, those new fathers felt a lot like I did, and we were able to talk it out with them, too.

Hackel, & Stangor, 1988) reports a decline in marital well-being after the birth of a child, particularly since new parents often lack the education, skills, and social support needed to sustain the presence of the child. Tim Dun (2010) states that "the first child stresses the parental relationship (e.g., marriage) and each parent individually" (p. 195). Yet, as Ted Huston and Anita Vangelisti (1995) note, this decline may be attributable to measurement and methodological issues rather than to a real drop in marital satisfaction. Huston and Vangelisti conclude that parenthood undoubtedly affects marriage but does not necessarily undermine it.

Parenthood may not be a negative stressor for all couples, bringing with it a decrease in marital satisfaction, but it causes change. At the least, it changes the couple's allocation of time, and parents report that they spend less time in conversation with each other than do nonparents (Huston & Vangelisti, 1995). As couples make this transition, they must also deal with other communication-related issues, including renegotiating their roles, as they now add parenting to their repertoire.

Hector's observations (in the student quote) indicate two important communication considerations during the transition to parenthood. First, gender role attitudes may affect how couples handle the transition and how they perceive the stress it generates. Couples who share traditional gender role attitudes find the transition less stressful than those with less traditional attitudes (Huston & Vangelisti, 1995). When partners share traditional role prescriptions, the patterns they establish about the division of labor, before children, serve them well as they make the transition (Mattingly, 2010). These patterns and role prescriptions involve little need for renegotiation. Thus, partners do not have to spend their time discussing this issue after they have or adopt children.

Hector's comments also underscore an important communication resource that families can avail themselves of if they do not perceive the parenthood transition as stressful—social support. Generally speaking, **social support** is the process of using communication to help another person manage stress. Social support involves activating a social network of friends (and family) to help manage the ebbs and flows of uncertainty that accompany changes. Social support also involves messages of relational loyalty, reassurance, generosity, encouragement, and knowledge (Goldsmith, McDermott, & Alexander, 2000). Thus, as Hector and his wife struggle with their new roles and with Hector's unexpected definition of his role, they talk to friends and family members who help them understand and clarify their feelings. For these challenges and others, friends serve as an informal, yet critical, support group who can mediate difficult decisions (Manne, Ostroff, Sherman, Glassman, Ross, Goldstein, & Fox, 2003).

Developmental Stressors in Growing Families

As families with children grow, they have to provide for the children's needs at their various stages of development. For our purposes, we will discuss two stages and the main developmental tasks involving communication—preschool children and adolescence. When children are young, parents need to help them learn language skills as well as set boundaries for them, generally socializing them into the approved social and cognitive competencies of their culture (Burleson, Delia, & Applegate, 1995). Brant Burleson and his colleagues (1995) note that the socializing process, making children functional communicators in their culture, is accomplished in the family through communication behaviors—disciplining, persuading, comforting, and informing, among others. Stress may accompany these developmental demands when children do not seem to be learning the lessons parents are offering. In this situation, parents need a large repertoire of teaching behaviors at their disposal so they can shift from one to another to find the one that's most effective. Also, parents with young children generally find the social support offered by other parents of young children, friends, and members of the extended kin network to be helpful in managing stress (Cobb, 1982).

During the adolescent period, families need to help children renegotiate rules and roles, help with identity exploration, and teach problem-solving skills (Noller, 1995). Also, self-esteem enhancement is critical. Particularly given cultural differences, self-esteem becomes crucial. As Rhunette Diggs (1999) comments, "Black and White adolescents . . . see their race, in general, as a significant frame of reference, and this consciously impacts their self-feelings" (p. 118). Diggs notes that parents, in particular, are instrumental. For African Americans, mothers hold special importance, and for European Americans, fathers are central in influencing self-esteem.

Further, during the adolescent period, families must pay special attention to the dialectic of autonomy and connection, as adolescence highlights this tension in the family system (Cooper, Grotevant, & Condon, 1983). In accomplishing all these developmental tasks, the potential for family stress is high. Indeed, some researchers note that the adolescent period entails significant stress, with one writer conceptualizing this time as similar to "being pecked to death by ducks" (Penington, 1997). Nonetheless open communication generally leads to beliefs of more equity between parent and child (Vogl-Bauer, Kalbfleisch, & Beatty, 1999).

Student Perspective: TJ

It was a sunny day, I remember. But the day was anything but bright. At precisely 4:30 p.m., my boss called me into his office to tell me that the company wasn't doing that great and that they had to let some guys go. Because I was the lowest in seniority, I was part of the "chosen few." Yep. That was not a good day. I went home and didn't tell anyone in my family nor my girlfriend. About a week later, I met with a counselor at my community college, and a month after that, I enrolled to get a degree. I've tried to move on here. Sure, I'm in college now, but that day still haunts me. I got fired.

Adolescence is a period when stress is often managed, at least by the adolescents, through topic avoidance (Afifi & Afifi, 2009; Afifi & Guerrero, 2000; Mazur & Ebesu Hubbard, 2004). Topic avoidance, however, is not the same as secrets because secrets imply that one family member hides information from other family members. Topic avoidance may include secrets, but it is more general. It also includes topics that members are all aware of but are avoiding because they are likely to cause conflict or embarrassment, for example, or because they simply want to avoid talking about them. In fact, Michelle Mazur and Amy Ebesu Hubbard (2004) found that adolescents will lie, reject the topic discussion either directly or indirectly, and even end the conversation. At times, adolescents reported using verbally aggressive communication such as yelling or being sarcastic to a parent. There are times when adolescents do communicate with their parents on potentially sensitive topics (Caughlin & Malis, 2004), but teens tend to use topic avoidance quite selectively.

Developmental Stressors in Older Families

The developmental needs of older families revolve around the dialectics and renegotiation of roles. Multigenerational relationships between couples, siblings, and parents and children are all affected by the aging process (Price & Humble, 2010).

Changes in Couples' Relationships   As partners in a relationship age, retire, and spend more time together, they must learn new ways of communicating that are effective in this new stage of life. Fran Dickson, Allison Christian, and Clyde Remmo (2004) present a number of challenges that later-life couples face. They conclude that "aging creates multiple stressors that later-life couples need to incorporate into their adult lives" (p. 156). The research team noted that many couples struggle with a number of stressors. We briefly explore two: relational roles and partner/romantic sustainability.

First, Dickson and her colleagues (2004) observe that new relational definitions need to occur as a result of the changing household roles. Redefining this relationship usually occurs once the husband retires. Dickson and her colleagues suggest that to avoid conflict and additional stress, couples need to negotiate their roles. For instance, after Dwayne retired from his job at the car dealership, he didn't know what to do with his time. He sat at home, expecting his wife, Claire, to come home from her job for lunch each day and eat with him. Claire, though, had plans of her own. Instead of retiring and sitting at home, Claire continued working as a receptionist at her job and as a volunteer at the Agency on Aging. She had no plans of coming home each day for lunch. The stressor of having Dwayne at home expecting his wife to undertake specific domestic roles was more than Claire could take. If Claire and Dwayne negotiate their responsibilities in the home and accommodate both spouses' concerns, the stress is likely to be reduced.

Another issue facing couples in later years is achieving focus on the partner and sustaining a romantic relationship with him or her. Dickson and her colleagues (2004) believe that people generally think that "once children are launched from the nest, the marriage changes from a child-focused marriage to a partner-focused marriage" (p. 156). That does not occur, however, because many couples are, for instance, still preoccupied with college tuition bills, wedding events, and grandchild-related activities. In other words, the child still lives on in the relationship, prompting couples to ignore their own needs.

Student Perspective: Jean

I know I've got to be the only grandmother in this course. That makes me especially able to comment on this topic. At 14, I was in charge of taking care of my mother, who was an alcoholic and who always fell down. I can vividly recall walking her three blocks to the hospital one January and telling Admitting that my dad left us years ago and I was her "guardian." At age 14, I was my mother's mother! At 56, I now take care of my son's two kids, since he picked up a second job and his wife works all day as a college secretary. I don't know what I'll be doing if and when I'm 70. I sure hope I'll be in Florida taking care of myself instead of taking care of my family!

In addition, Dickson and her colleagues (2004) claim that "later-life couples struggle with renewing romance and sustaining a pleasurable sexual relationship" (p. 157). Why? First, health-related issues may influence whether romance is present in the relationship. If couples are not physically well, it's likely they are not willing to be romantic. Second, there may be an uncomfortable feeling about reigniting romantic feelings that have been dormant for years. Despite being together for quite some time, couples may still cling to the belief that romance is not integral to a long-term relationship.

We cannot ignore the stress that later-life couples experience. Stress seeps into couples' lives both in a predictable and unpredictable manner. Scholars tell us that, generally, women are culturally charged with caretaking responsibilities in the United States (Ivy, 2012). Interestingly, if women are not valued for their caregiving contributions, an already stressful situation may generate additional stress. Yet, some writers, like Leonard Hansen (*www.agingcare.com*), have noted that men are now becoming caretakers in ways that society has not seen. Although women tend to continue to provide more intimate care than men (such as dressing and feeding), men organize medications, provide transportation, and do the grocery shopping almost as much as women. Nonetheless, women continue to serve as the primary caretakers of aging parents (Sheehy, 2010). As Mona Harrington (1998) asserts: "We need new support systems to enable families to provide good care for their members—on terms of equality for women. We have to decide as a society about shifts in responsibility for caretaking, shifts in resources, and shifts in costs" (p. 1).

Changes in Siblings' Relationships   Seventy to 80 percent of elderly adults have at least one living sibling (Schwartz & Scott, 2013), making this a common relationship of older families, but one in which the rules and roles are unclear, sometimes causing stress. As siblings age, their contact with one another changes (Goetting, 1986). In early and middle adulthood, contact may be less frequent, mediated by distance, jobs, and other relationships. In later adulthood, especially as they may need to deal with the deaths of elderly parents, contact tends to increase, and the ties between siblings become closer. H. Michael Zal (1992) indicates that elderly siblings can provide communicative and social support to one another during times of developmental stress.

This support may come from the symbolic realm more than the physical. Marie-Louise Mares (1995) observes that siblings may not share in actual caregiving behaviors as much as they support each other through "the socio-emotional role of reminiscence" (p. 353). Siblings are able to engage in storytelling that invokes pleasant memories, helping them to manage current stressors. Victor Cicirelli and Jon Nussbaum (1989) assert that, because of siblings' long and unique history, they engage in reminiscence at many points during their lives, but this communication practice seems to be even more important in old age.

However, siblings do not always support one another, and their failure to do so can be a major source of stress in the family. The reason may be that as siblings reach adulthood, the maintenance of their relationship becomes more voluntary (Goodboy, Myers, & Patterson, 2009; Mikkelson, Mysers, & Hannawa, 2011). In addition, perceptions and priorities differ. In the Hoffman family, for instance, stress accumulated during Carolyn Hoffman's prolonged bout with Parkinson's disease. The siblings, Lee and Fredrick, had always been close, but they constructed the meaning of their mother's illness differently and participated unequally in her care. Lee found it difficult to understand how Fredrick could take a vacation when their mother took a turn for the worse and had to be hospitalized for dehydration. Lee took a short leave from her job in California and joined her mother in Chicago to provide care during this crisis. Fredrick did not feel the need to do so and continued with his plans for a vacation in Maui. Lee resented her brother's attitude and behavior, and this caused some conflict and stress between them, which affected Carolyn as well.

Ethnicity influences the intersection of stress and sibling relationships. For instance, one reason why African American elderly siblings experience less stress than other cultural communities relates to "the drive to maintain strong family relationships and to utilize those relationships before consider-ing outside sources" (Stewart, 2010, p. 321). Latino immigrant families, because of the presence of other family members residing in the United States, do not experience stressors to the same extent that, say, Asian immigrants face (Bush, Bohon, & Kim, 2010). Within Asian immigrant families, Bush et al. (p. 303) argue the following:

> [U]nlike Chinese, Japanese, and Korean immigrants, most of whom left their home countries voluntarily to seek better economic and educational opportunities, a majority of Southeast Asians [e.g., Vietnamese, Cambodian, Laotian, and Hmong] arrived in the United States after being "forced" to leave their countries.

Therefore, the introduction of new people, values, customs, and patterns of interaction prompts much more stress since these cultural groups have had little exposure to or preparation for Western practices. Familial values no doubt influence which cultures promote closer and less stressful sibling relationships. Some research suggests that sibling relationships are affected by community values as well as ethnic values. Patricia Suggs (1989) found no differences in African American and European American elderly siblings all living in rural communities. Both groups were closer when they offered each other mutual helping behaviors.

Changes in Parents' and Children's Relationships Corinne Nydegger and Linda Mitteness (1988) observe that the dialectic tension between closeness and distance is not resolved as families age. These researchers conceptualize the dilemma by noting that frequent contact is desired by elderly parents and their children, but it can cause friction. Nydegger and Mitteness note that, despite the myth of the happy family, interactions between elderly parents and their adult children are by no means uniformly positive.

Because this stage of life presents many opportunities for stressors, it is natural that adult children and elderly parents experience some stress in their relationship. Nydegger and Mitteness (1988) suggest that families at this stage develop strategies to manage stress, especially around the ongoing dialectics of openness and privacy and autonomy and connection. The researchers argue that family conversation offers complex mechanisms for moderating these tensions and other stressors in this relationship. One technique that Nydegger and Mitteness explain is avoidance etiquette, somewhat similar to topic avoidance. These researchers found that adult children and elderly parents collude to avoid topics that may prove stressful.

Perhaps nowhere is this more evident than in the caring for an aging relative. Caring for an aging parent has taken on new meaning in the 21st century. Longer life expectancy, medical advances, and a healthier older population are causing new stressors. In her book *Necessary Losses,* Judith Viorst (1987) sums up the meaning of this stress when she remarks that "watching our once-so-powerful parents marked by the passage of time, we may mourn the mother and father who 'used-to-be'" (p. 4). Those in this era of life have been caught in what Dorothy Miller (in 1981) referred to as the **sandwich generation**, that is, middle-aged parents are sandwiched between concerns for their growing children and concerns for their aging parents. Throughout this book, we have exemplified this complex lifespan experience for families. Caretaker and caregiving stress cannot be overemphasized; such family assistance has seen a sharp increase over the years because people are living longer. In 2012, the National Alliance for Caregiving (*www.caregiving. org/research*) noted that there were over 65 million caregivers in the United States, or almost 30 percent of the U.S. population. In 2005, that number was 34 million. The rising numbers suggest inevitable challenges as family members navigate the economic, familial, role, and health stressors related to aging.

Caregiver stress has been the topic of numerous studies. Perhaps one of the most provocative conclusions in the literature is that caregivers who view themselves with stress are more likely to be unhealthy, more depressed, and indeed have higher mortality rates (Herzog, 2010). Researchers have acknowledged that caregivers rarely have time to take care of their own health needs, resulting in less concern about their well-being. The implications of increased mental and physical problems can be best understood by considering the following observation: "It is useful to think of caregiver stress not as an event or as a unitary phenomenon [but rather as] a mix of circumstances, experiences, responses, and resources that vary considerably among caregivers and that, consequently, vary in their impact on caregivers' health and behavior" (Pearlin, Mullan, Semple, & Skaff, 1990, p. 591).

Nydegger and Mitteness (1988) observed in their interviews that families may manage the stress of this developmental stage through the strategic use of "empty" discourse. **Empty speech** includes meaningless phrases, cliches, deferential politeness, small talk, and other forms of trivial interaction. Nydegger and Mitteness note that this empty talk is not actually meaningless; it enables family members to engage in conversation (promoting a sense of connection) while avoiding stressful topics and without actually divulging private information (maintaining a sense of privacy and autonomy). The researchers comment that, particularly for elderly parents, "the fact of contact is likely to matter more than its substance" (p. 710). Thus, for elderly parents and their children, empty speech, or small talk, is functional, as it is in other relationships. In all cases, empty speech provides contact and develops the relationship dimension of communication that we discussed in Chapter 1.

Some Conclusions About Developmental Stressors

Families are faced with stressors that are often caused by a changing society. As families evolve, they face predictable developmental stressors, such as getting married or having a baby. Stressors can be disquieting, even if the event is joyous. For family members who enjoy flux, stressors can be a welcome alleviation from boredom. Not all family members, however, are able to cope with these developmental changes in their family system. Unique communication patterns and role flexibility are required to offset potentially devastating developmental stressors in a family.

COMMUNICATION AND UNPREDICTABLE STRESSORS

Just as predictable family events can cause stress for families, unpredictable events can also greatly affect the family system. In this section, we address how the family makes sense and constructs meaning out of nonnormative stressors. Unpredictable stressors are the unexpected events in a family's life that force a family to respond with appropriate emotions and/or resources. Thus, for Marla Wilbanks the unpredictable stressor of her daughter's death at age 12 from a car accident requires Marla to set clear boundaries and employ all her resources. She may activate her social networks and talk to friends she hasn't seen for years. Her whole family will need to recalibrate in order to respond to the stressor. A child's death is unpredictable and seems "out of order."

Families in the United States are especially vulnerable to unpredictable stress because of the pressure placed on them by society. As Judy Root Aulette (1994) asserts, "In our society, families are the social institutions that are frequently called on to provide a lifeboat in an economic crisis" (p. 323). Aulette believes that when we combine the pressure on families to provide economic survival with the inability of large numbers of families to provide that support, we have the recipe for great family stress.

Student Perspective: Diane

The way we handled my parents' divorce was strange at best. We had no idea that they were going to separate, and when I was about 14, my sister and I were called outside on the patio. Both my parents told us that they weren't getting along and that it was time for them to separate. After we got over the shock of it, my sister and I were told that they had decided to divorce instead! That was less than three weeks after they told us that they were going to separate. At that age, we had no idea what the difference was. The only thing we knew was that we were not going to be the same family again.

It is important to understand unpredictable stress, because many family events that are unexpected or uncontrollable usually elicit negative responses (Turner & Finkelhor, 1996). As we mentioned in Chapter 7, verbal aggressiveness and violence affects the fabric of family life. If unpredictable stress is not handled competently, such negative communication behaviors may be more likely to be a part of the lives of many families.

Unpredictable family stress comes in many forms. For the purposes of our discussion, we focus on two prevailing and often troubling forms of unpredictable stress: divorce and homelessness. These types of stress may be called crisis periods in a family's life. Although many spouses and children find themselves in a divorce situation, not all families are equipped to handle the potential stress associated with divorce. In addition, no family wants to be on the street, in need of food, clothing, and shelter. Divorce and homelessness are also interrelated in that without an appropriate economic opportunity following divorce, poverty and homelessness may set in, particularly for single mothers and their families. Let's examine these two unpredictable stressors and their impact on families and family communication.

Divorce

In the United States, marriage is usually seen as a lifelong commitment between intimate partners. Not all married relationships, however, remain close. Unresolvable conflicts, a topic we discussed in Chapter 7, often result in couples being incapable of maintaining their family system. It seems inevitable, then, that with conflicts enduring for extended periods of time, married partners often turn to divorce.

Divorce is considered to be an unpredictable stressor for a few reasons. First, despite its relatively high numbers, divorce can take families by surprise. As Julia Lewis, Judith Wallerstein, and Linda Johnson-Reitz (2004) observed, "the actuality of divorce is an unwelcome shock with no preparation" (p. 200). In other words, many couples may not have considered divorce, regardless of the extent and pervasiveness of their conflict.

A second reason why we consider divorce an unpredictable stressor relates to the notion that married couples enter their marriages with a relatively optimistic view of their future together (Fine, Ganong, & Demo, 2010). We don't usually hear marriage vows qualified with "if we don't get along, we can divorce after a year or so." Therefore, when unmanageable conflict occurs, some reconciliation is necessary. This scenario is similar to what social exchange theorists believe happens with divorced couples. Often, one or both married partners will assess the quality of the relationship by assessing whether the relationship is profitable; that is, they will consider the ratio of costs to rewards. At times, partners realize that there are alternatives to the current relationship and opt for divorce. Estimates of the number of divorces in the United States are rather complex. Newspapers, Internet sites, television, and magazines are replete with divorce statistics. Many accounts are exaggerated so that a story can be told. Some writers have even called divorce "an American tradition" because they believe it is so common in our society (Riley, 1992).

Calculating the numbers of divorces in our country is not a pure science; in fact, it's rather messy. Some writers include divorce rates, and other estimates include divorce projections. For our purposes, it's fruitful to point out that there are over 1.18 million divorces annually and that there is an average of 3.4 divorces for every 1,000 U.S. citizens (National Center for Health Statistics, 2012). Further, it's important to recognize that "marital unhappiness" as a reason for divorcing is a nebulous phrase. It could refer to a number of issues, including socioeconomic status and income, abuse, childlessness, and a host of other factors. Clearly, then, when reflecting on the information associated with divorce statistics, and as we learned in earlier chapters, it's important to consider much more than what is presented to us in the media. For a comparison of marriage and divorce rates, examine Table 8-1.

Divorce should not be seen as an isolated event in the family system. Rather, in keeping with the spirit of our theoretical orientation, we believe that divorce should be thought of as part of a family's transition and part of the changes that occur in family relationships (Ahrons & Rodgers, 1987; Hetherington, 2002). It's understandable that our society has equated divorce with catastrophe. In Chapter 4, we identified the importance of the media in communicating images about the family. We're sure you can point out numerous examples from television talk shows and self-help books showing that couples who divorce are in for a gloomy experience. Sometimes, that's true. Families may not be in a position to accept the blurring of boundaries and role strains that accompany most divorces. Other times, however, divorce is an appropriate, albeit difficult, outlet for couples who cannot endure or control the stress taking place within their families. Divorce does not shut down the family system permanently. Rather, ex-spouses may initially deal with lingering resentments and anger. But, many couples begin their recovery by the end of the second year, and "by six years after divorce, 80% of both men and women have moved on to build reasonably or exceptionally fulfilling lives" (Hetherington, 2002, p. 153).

Student Perspective: Graham

The day my wife told me that she wanted a divorce I thought that I was going to lose it. I thought our marriage was going fine. I know hindsight is 20/20, but I guess the warning signs were there. We had sex about once a week (or less), and she took on longer hours at the clinic. She said she wanted to save money for a vacation. She did go on a vacation eventually, only she went without me. She said she needed time to "get in touch with herself." Today, we have been divorced for about four years, and I still feel like a sucker. I still believe in true love, and I still think that I'll meet "Ms. Right." To be honest, though, I think of her a lot, and it makes it kind of difficult when I meet a woman and subconsciously compare her to my ex-wife.

When discussing divorce and stress, we necessarily have to focus on two subsystems in the family: the spousal subsystem and the parent–child

TABLE 8-1 Marriages and Divorces—Number and Rate by State: 1990 to 2009

State	MARRIAGES						DIVORCES					
	Number (1,000)			Rate per 1,000 population			Number (1,000)			Rate per 1,000 population		
	1990	2000	2009	1990	2000	2009	1990	2000	2009	1990	2000	2009
United States	2,443	2,239	2,077	9.8	8.3	6.8	1,182	(NA)	(NA)	4.7	4.1	3.4
Alabama	43.1	45.0	37.3	10.6	10.1	8.3	25.3	23.5	20.2	6.1	5.5	4.4
Alaska	5.7	5.6	5.5	10.2	8.9	7.8	2.9	2.7	3.3	5.5	3.9	4.4
Arizona	36.8	38.7	35.3	10.0	7.5	5.4	25.1	21.6	23.1	6.9	4.6	3.5
Arkansas	36.0	41.1	31.6	15.3	15.4	10.7	16.8	17.9	16.3	6.9	6.4	5.7
California	237.1	196.9	213.9	7.9	5.8	5.8	128.0	(NA)	(NA)	4.3	(NA)	(NA)
Colorado	32.4	35.6	37.4	9.8	8.3	6.8	18.4	(NA)	21.2	5.5	4.7	4.2
Connecticut	26.0	19.4	19.8	7.9	5.7	5.9	10.3	6.5	10.8	3.2	3.3	3.1
Delaware	5.6	5.1	5.1	8.4	6.5	5.4	3.0	3.2	3.4	4.4	3.9	3.6
District of Columbia	5.0	2.8	1.9	8.2	4.9	4.7	2.7	1.5	1.3	4.5	3.2	2.6
Florida	141.8	141.9	141.2	10.9	8.9	7.5	81.7	81.9	79.9	6.3	5.1	4.2
Georgia	66.8	56.0	63.6	10.3	6.8	6.5	35.7	30.7	(NA)	5.5	3.3	(NA)
Hawaii	18.3	25.0	22.2	16.4	20.6	17.9	5.2	4.6	(NA)	4.6	3.9	(NA)
Idaho	14.1	14.0	13.9	13.9	10.8	8.9	6.6	6.9	7.7	6.5	5.5	5.0
Illinois	100.6	85.5	72.7	8.8	6.9	5.6	44.3	39.1	32.7	3.8	3.2	2.5
Indiana	53.2	34.5	52.9	9.6	7.9	7.9	(NA)	(NA)	(NA)	(NA)	(NA)	2.4
Iowa	24.9	20.3	21.2	9.0	6.9	7.0	11.1	9.4	7.3	3.9	3.3	2.4
Kansas	22.7	22.2	18.5	9.2	8.3	6.5	12.6	10.6	10.3	5.0	3.6	3.7
Kentucky	49.8	39.7	33.4	13.5	9.8	7.6	21.8	21.6	19.9	5.8	5.1	4.6
Louisiana	40.4	40.5	28.7	9.6	9.1	7.1	(NA)	(NA)	(NA)	(NA)	(NA)	(NA)
Maine	11.9	10.5	9.4	9.7	8.8	7.2	5.3	5.8	5.3	4.3	5.0	4.1
Maryland	46.3	40.0	32.4	9.7	7.5	5.8	16.1	17.0	15.2	3.4	3.3	2.8
Massachusetts	47.7	37.0	36.7	7.9	5.8	5.5	16.8	18.6	12.7	2.8	2.5	2.2
Michigan	76.1	66.4	53.1	8.2	6.7	5.4	40.2	39.4	32.5	4.3	3.9	3.3
Minnesota	33.7	33.4	28.4	7.7	6.8	5.3	15.4	14.8	(NA)	3.5	3.2	(NA)
Mississippi	24.3	19.7	14.5	9.4	6.9	4.8	14.4	14.4	12.2	5.5	5.0	4.1
Missouri	49.1	43.7	39.8	9.6	7.8	6.5	26.4	26.5	23.3	5.1	4.5	3.7
Montana	6.9	6.6	7.1	8.6	7.3	7.4	4.1	2.1	3.9	5.1	4.2	4.1

State	MARRIAGES						DIVORCES					
	Number (1,000)			Rate per 1,000 population			Number (1,000)			Rate per 1,000 population		
	1990	2000	2009	1990	2000	2009	1990	2000	2009	1990	2000	2009
Nebraska..............	12.6	13.0	12.5	8.0	7.6	6.7	6.5	6.4	5.4	4.0	3.7	3.4
Nevada...............	120.6	144.3	108.2	99.0	72.2	40.9	13.3	18.1	17.7	11.4	9.9	6.7
New Hampshire........	10.5	11.6	8.5	9.5	9.4	6.4	5.3	7.1	4.9	4.7	4.8	3.7
New Jersey...........	58.7	50.4	46.3	7.6	6.0	5.0	23.6	25.6	24.0	3.0	3.0	2.8
New Mexico...........	13.3	14.5	10.2	8.8	8.0	5.1	7.7	9.2	8.0	4.9	5.1	4.0
New York.............	154.8	162.0	120.1	8.6	7.1	6.4	57.9	62.8	46.1	3.2	3.0	2.6
North Carolina.......	51.9	65.6	65.8	7.8	8.2	6.7	34.0	36.9	36.7	5.1	4.5	3.8
North Dakota.........	4.8	4.6	4.3	7.5	7.2	6.6	2.3	2.0	1.6	3.6	3.4	2.9
Ohio.................	98.1	88.5	64.8	9.0	7.8	5.8	51.0	49.3	36.9	4.7	4.2	3.3
Oklahoma.............	33.2	15.6	23.5	10.6	(NA)	6.9	24.9	12.4	16.9	7.7	(NA)	4.9
Oregon	25.3	26.0	23.5	8.9	7.6	6.6	15.9	16.7	13.3	5.5	4.8	3.9
Pennsylvania.........	84.9	73.2	64.2	7.1	6.0	5.3	40.1	37.9	28.8	3.3	3.1	2.7
Rhode Island.........	8.1	8.0	6.5	8.1	7.6	5.9	3.8	3.1	3.3	3.7	2.9	3.0
South Carolina.......	55.8	42.7	29.2	15.9	10.6	7.4	16.1	14.4	12.2	4.5	3.8	3.0
South Dakota	7.7	7.1	5.9	11.1	9.4	7.2	2.6	2.7	2.6	3.7	3.5	3.3
Tennessee	68.0	88.2	55.2	13.9	15.5	8.4	32.3	33.8	25.8	6.5	5.9	3.9
Texas................	178.6	196.4	179.8	10.5	9.4	7.1	94.0	85.2	76.9	5.5	4.0	3.3
Utah	19.4	24.1	23.9	11.2	10.8	8.2	8.8	9.7	10.7	5.1	4.3	3.6
Vermont	6.1	6.1	4.7	10.9	10.0	8.7	2.6	5.1	2.1	4.5	4.1	3.5
Virginia.............	71.0	62.4	54.1	11.4	8.8	7.0	27.3	30.2	28.5	4.4	4.3	3.7
Washington...........	46.6	40.9	40.4	9.5	6.9	6.0	28.8	27.2	26.3	5.9	4.6	3.9
West Virginia........	13.0	15.7	12.4	7.2	8.7	6.9	9.7	9.3	9.2	5.3	5.1	5.2
Wisconsin............	38.9	36.1	30.3	7.9	6.7	5.3	17.8	17.6	17.3	3.6	3.2	3.0
Wyoming..............	4.9	4.9	4.7	10.7	10.0	8.2	3.1	2.8	2.8	6.6	5.8	5.2

NA not available.

Source: U.S. National Center for Health Statistics, National Vital Statistics Reports (NVSR), *Births, Marriages, Divorces, and Deaths: Provisional Data for 2009,* Vol. 58, No. 25, August 2010, and prior reports.

subsystem. As family systems thinking suggests, the marital relationship and the parent–child relationship are interrelated and interdependent; stress, therefore, within one subsystem will affect the other subsystem. Each relationship undergoes unique changes when coping with the stress brought on by divorce. Further, the consequences of divorce for each subsystem merit attention.

Spouses and Divorce   Partners who divorce differ in their ability to handle the breakup. Researchers have concluded that men are in a better position to handle the stress of a divorce than are women (Amato, 2000; Peterson, 1989; Rubin, 1994). The primary reason for this conclusion is that men are more able to sustain their financial level following divorce than women are. Since a large number of children remain with their mother after a divorce, women must take on that added economic responsibility. The financial responsibility of single mothers is especially relevant to our discussion because, following a divorce, 29 percent of women live below poverty level compared with 12 percent of men (Krieder & Fields, 2002). This financial strain increases stress because more time is needed to address costs pertaining to transportation, housing, and general living expenses.

There are additional stressful consequences of terminating a marriage. Foremost, spouses with children must deal with custody issues. Catherine Saillant (2000) in the *Los Angeles Times* notes that ex-spouses fight fiercely over custody agreements and that "children are being shuttled more frequently between parents' homes as moms and dads fight for the greatest share of time" (p. 1). Courts, overwhelmingly favor mothers over dads in granting custody. In 68 percent to 88 percent of cases, moms are given primary custody, while men gain primary custody 8–14 percent of the time (Kenny, 2011).

Things may be beginning to change, however. For instance, in response to the number of fathers who fail to get child custody, groups such as the National Fatherhood Initiative and the Fatherhood Coalition have been established, in part to assist fathers in their custody pursuits. Organizations dedicated to advancing fathers' rights are gaining attention and success both in child custody cases and in the perceptions of fathers as capable parents. Fathers may need some help, according to Matthew Purdy (2000) of the *New York Times*. He states that "if mothers teeter on the high wire stretched between home and work, fathers are like Mr. Potato Heads, endlessly trying out combinations of parts" (p. 21).

Although it may appear that single fathers are usually more capable of financially handling divorce than are single mothers, some family scholars believe that this is a cultural misconception. Linda Nielsen (1999), for example, believes that 80 percent of women remarry within a few years of divorce and eventually regain their financial standard of living; for men who remarry, they "cannot provide their new family with as high a standard of living as they gave their former wife and children" (p. 142). Further, Matthew

Weinshenker (2011) contends that single dads are more likely to be below the poverty line. As Nielsen states, misconceptions related to divorced fathers are "demeaning, demoralizing, and disenfranchising" (p. 139).

Although some researchers contend that fathers are shortchanged in a divorce, much of the research on postdivorce relationships has discussed the effects of divorce on mothers and their children (e.g., Afifi, Afifi, Morse, & Hamrick, 2008; Walker, Logan, Jordan, & Campbell, 2004). To better understand this intersection among gender, divorce, and stress, consider the experiences of Patti and Hank Jackson. When Hank and Patti decided to divorce after their three-year marriage, Patti immediately filed for custody of their two-year-old child, Leda. When the judge granted both the divorce and full custody to Patti, the mom's challenges had just begun. She was given about $350 a month for child support, and she knew she would have to get another job to keep the bills paid. Working at her job as a receptionist during the day, she privately wondered whether her job, her lack of time with Leda, her rent, and other bills were finally taking their toll. So, what was supposed to be an opportunity for growth and change in her new family configuration resulted in more stressful times for Patti Jackson.

In Chapter 1, we noted that single parents often struggle with the challenges brought on by emotional, psychological, and financial responsibilities. Single mothers like Patti Jackson must be able to adapt to task overload, financial challenges, and an unclear future. As we previously mentioned in this chapter, social support can help offset this family stress. Supportive communication in the form of concern, solidarity, sympathy, and understanding can be monumentally helpful to a distressed individual. Of course, better-paying jobs and jobs with opportunities for advancement also help. Further, awarding appropriate child support and ensuring compliance with child support payments are also critical. And, although there is some variation in the level of social support that single moms and single dads receive, the reality is that, on average, both family types warrant both research and community attention as these single parents are prone to stress.

Children and Divorce   Fine et al. (2010) conclude that although some variation exists in family custody arrangements, approximately two-thirds of children reside with their mother, 10 percent reside with their father, and the remaining either have a joint custody arrangement or some other configuration. And, although "parent-child communication plays an integral role with divorce-related stress" (McManus & Nussbaum, 2011, p. 501), when spouses with children divorce, children become affected. But too often we are inclined to think that children are incapable of handling the divorce and that their communication competency will be forever damaged. Some children do have a difficult time adjusting to their parents' divorce as we will learn later. Yet, some researchers acknowledge that it is not the divorce per se that causes adjustment problems for children, but rather the emotional tones and relational turbulence that parents manifest (Timmer & Veroff, 2000). In addition, if adjustment problems do occur, they are usually a result of the child's development. That is, a 3-year-old will respond to a divorce very differently than will a 13-year-old. Examining our opening story of Colleen Gilmartin, we see that her daughters, Lindy and Danielle, are at different developmental points. As a teenager, perhaps Lindy will be able to find support from peers who have already experienced divorce. Danielle, however, as a preschooler, may be more challenged in that her peers may ask her where her father is at family events. Someone at this developmental stage will need a great deal of attention—something that Colleen seems to be considering.

With this in mind, what does research report with respect to how children process and manage their parents' divorce? There are some mixed signals in the scholarship. First, one set of writers believes that divorce negatively affects children, reducing relational quality between parent and child (Lewis, Wallerstein, & Johnson-Reitz, 2004). Succinctly underscoring this position, Julia Lewis and her colleagues (2004) report that "divorce results in a lowering of the quality of the child's relationship with the mother as well as with the father" (p. 206). In other words, divorce has lasting negative consequences for children. Some writers (Arditti, 1990; Wallerstein, Lewis, & Blakeslee, 2000) note that children of divorced parents can suffer lasting stress that affects the way they view their own social skills and their prospects for having a satisfying marriage themselves. Further, if there are high levels of conflict between parents before and after the divorce, adverse conditions arise for children. Ironically, interspousal conflict is often cited as a reason for divorce, yet even after divorce some couples continue to be conflict-ridden. The impact of this tension on children can be great. The effect of the age of the child at the time of the divorce has also been investigated. Judith Wallerstein (1985) discovered that children of about nine years old and up were experiencing emotional residue about a decade after a divorce. These children were even assessing the future of their own personal relationships. Overall, this line of thinking suggests that all children—regardless of age—have a more difficult time adjusting to divorce than do adults.

The research on divorce by Judith Wallerstein, Julia Lewis, and Sandra Blakeslee (2001) has received an inordinate amount of media attention. Theirs was hailed as a landmark study because it followed the children of

Student Perspective: Monica

The day that my mom left was the hardest, no doubt. My dad sat in the bathroom and cried. I wanted to cry with him, but he wouldn't let me in. I think that my mom would never have left if she had seen what it did to my sister and my dad. We've really done remarkably well, though. But there isn't a day that I don't think about my mom. I'm an adult right now, but I still feel like that 11-year-old New Hampshire girl who watched her mom leave on a summer day many years ago.

~ POPULAR PRESS PERSPECTIVES ~

Divorce in the military is apparently on the upswing. In a report in *USA Today*, Greg Zoroya notes that in 2011, the military divorce rate reached its highest level in over a decade. Zoroya observes that the divorce rate of those enlisted edges out the civilian divorce rate (3.7 percent and 3.4 percent, respectively). The Army's rate is 3.7 percent, the Navy's divorce rate is 3.6 percent, the Air Force's rate is 3.9 percent, and the Marines average around 3.8 percent.

Zoroya quotes Army chaplain Carlton Birch. Birch posits that as wars in Iraq and Afghanistan draw down and end(ed), "we're going to put more families together who haven't been used to being together." Zoroya's report, based on "interviews and Pentagon data," suggests that as troops withdraw from war, the United States will see increased divorces from those who served. He also concludes by stating that "one in 10 split marriages among enlisted women will terminate."

Greg Zoroya, "Military Divorce Rate at Highest Level since 1999," *USA Today*, December 14, 2011.

---

divorced parents 25 years after the divorce. Yet, before we readily accept the conclusions of Wallerstein and colleagues (2000), it's important to note that the research has been challenged (Amato, 2003; Cherlin, 2000). Andrew Cherlin (2000), for example, believes that the method undertaken by Wallerstein and colleagues is seriously flawed. Most important, Cherlin indicts Wallerstein and her colleagues for their claim that their research was undertaken with "typical American middle-class families" (p. 64). Cherlin notes that large percentages of mothers and fathers were found to have had "histories of mental illness," thereby rendering her sample (the children) not generalizable. Eschewing the scholarly arguments and focusing more on a cultural response, writer Katha Pollitt (2009) suggests several ways to ameliorate the negative effects of divorce on children:

> *If the concern is really with children, especially poor children, we could improve their lives tremendously by concentrating on the things we actually can achieve. Healthcare. Excellent schools with music and drama and art and gym and after-school programs. Neighborhoods safe enough for kids to play outdoors and air clean enough so they don't get asthma. Libraries. Summer camp. Counseling for kids in trouble—and their parents. Economic support for families, married or not. Housing for all. Free college. A public works job for anyone who wants one. All those necessities that, in America, are seen as the responsibility of individual families. (http://www.thenation.com/article/can-marriage-be-saved-1)*

A second theme in the literature pertains to what we alluded to earlier: The ramifications of divorce are associated with what occurs simultaneously with the dissolution. The types of physical and emotional conditions created by parents are instrumental in how divorce affects the children. Paul Amato (1993) outlines several of these issues:

1. *Interparental conflict:* If parents are prone to arguing, children are prone to its negative effects.

2. *Additional life stress:* Divorce can create additional stressors such as problems with school and peers and adjustments to new surroundings.

3. *Economic loss:* The effects of divorce usually result in a child living in a single-parent home, which often means that this family has fewer economic resources than children living in intact homes.

4. *Poor parental adjustment:* Parents who are having a difficult time with the divorce will most likely influence their children's adjustments.

5. *Parental competence:* Parents who have the skills to deal with divorce effectively will have considerable influence on how well the children manage the divorce.

Amato's suggestions fall directly in line with what communication scholars have been arguing for quite some time: The effects of divorce on children have most to do with the communication abilities of both parents, before, during, and after the divorce (Ahrons, 2011; McManus & Nussbaum, 2010). That is, the negative effects of divorce on children can be mitigated by talking sensitively, openly, and sensibly within the family system and engaging in predivorce communication strategies (Fine et al., 2011).

Honesty is also integral to how children respond to the divorce. For instance, Candice Thomas, Melanie Booth-Butterfield, and Steve Booth-Butterfield (1995) argue that parents who are deceptive in revealing their plans for divorce will be negatively perceived by children. The researchers caution that parents should be open with children who are old enough to manage this family transition. Tamara Afifi and Paul Schrodt (2003) discovered that children often feel "caught" between their parents. That is, "parents' conflict and negative disclosures toward one another can spill over onto children" (pp. 142–143). Despite parents' best intentions of not dragging their children into the middle of a divorce, Afifi and Schrodt found that children who are torn between parents tend to avoid those topics that might be seen as provoking conflict. Further, when children are involved in a divorce, they serve as a mutual conversational topic, thereby maintaining an open line of communication between ex-spouses (Metts & Cupach, 1995). David Demo (1992) discovered that with both parents creating a nurturing atmosphere for their children—an atmosphere with low levels of interparental conflict—children will be better able to adjust to a divorce. Finally, E. Mavis Hetherington and colleagues (1993) propose that if parents consider the child's developmental ability when discussing divorce, the adverse effects will be greatly reduced. In sum, as a divorce gets under way, parents who create a trusting, comfortable, and welcoming relationship with their children will promote a less traumatic experience for the children.

Final Thoughts on Divorce   The family system certainly is altered with the introduction of a divorce and eventual recalibration. But not all systems break down, and not all family members are incapable of maintaining a balance. Certainly, members of the family will be challenged by divorce. Still, researchers have found that open, sensitive communication during the dissolution process can counter negative repercussions. Further, some researchers have discovered that individual or family counseling, family life education, and mediation can help ease the burden (Bueler, Betz, Ryan, Legg, & Trotter, 1992; Emery, 1988).

The dissolution of a relationship can be devastating, or it can be managed effectively. Families who have gone through a divorce are families who have been reconfigured. This reconfiguration involves listening to parents, children, new partners and their children, friends, and social support systems as the marital dissolution is contemplated and carried through (Coleman & Ganong, 1995).

Homelessness

Little is known about homeless families from a communication perspective. There are several reasons why these families are virtually unknown and untapped by family communication researchers. First, accessibility to homeless families is limited since most are constantly on the go, moving from one shelter to another. Second, to get a sense of the kinds of stress that homeless families experience requires frequent visits to the same family over and over again. Because homeless families are always moving (Connolly, 2000), it's very difficult to follow up on initial interviews. Finally, investigating homeless families involves some ethical considerations. For example, what do researchers do with the information they collect? Include it in a communication journal with a limited readership? Or should researchers present information to government agencies? What about nonprofit shelters that work with homeless families on a daily basis? These are some of the concerns family researchers struggle with when studying homelessness.

In Chapter 1, we noted that we are genuinely interested in listening to homeless families because their voices often go unnoticed. For the purposes of this discussion, we will not delve into the root causes of homelessness nor address statistics associated with this stressful event. That information is available elsewhere (Hombs, 2011). As we observed earlier, we discuss homeless families in this section on unpredictable stressors because we believe few families expect to be homeless. Elizabeth Lindsey and Christine Sanchez (2010) indicate that among the precipitants to homelessness are eviction, job loss, abusive relationships, inability to pay rent, and unsafe living conditions. Although we realize that some family members are born into these categories, still these are unforeseen events in most families in the United States.

Homelessness and Stress   No other families in the United States experience as much stress as families who are homeless. The National Alliance to End Homelessness (*http://www.endhomelessness.org/section/about_homelessness/ snapshot_of_homelessness*) reports several sobering statistics related to the number of homeless people in the United States:

- Approximately 540,000 people experience homelessness on any given night.
- Of that number, over 230,000 are people in families.
- 17 percent of the homeless population are considered chronically (or permanently) homeless.
- 12 percent of the homeless population are military veterans.
- 25 percent of the homeless population have serious mental illness.

It should be apparent that homeless families are an at-risk cultural group that experiences daily challenges of finding food, shelter, and education, in addition to responding to health-related concerns and psychological problems. These stressors make homeless families stress-ridden. Mary Ellen Hombs (1990) comments that "not only do people continue to be pushed into the streets, but for some, escape from the streets seems nearly impossible" (p. 2). It doesn't help, of course, that as Linda K. Fuller (1999) remarks, the image of homeless people has been less than desirable. She contends that words such as *hobo, vagrant, panhandler, bum, vagabond, drifter, street urchin, beggar, runaway,* and others have placed homeless people in a highly charged category. With such a dire forecast for survival, it's important that we talk about the homeless. Further, as we mentioned in Chapter 1, families with children represent the fastest-growing segment of homeless people (Shields & Warke, 2010), and therefore we must begin to understand how homeless families function.

As you read and reflect about the following information, keep in mind that, like nearly everything else in family communication, homelessness is affected by culture. These cultural differences are especially important to acknowledge as we consider child rearing (Pérez, 2001). Of the many areas pertaining to the homeless that can be addressed, we wish to focus our attention on how homelessness affects single mothers and their families. Given that women head the overwhelming majority of homeless families, we focus the following on this critical demographic.

Single Mothers, Children, and Homelessness   The U.S. Department of Housing and Urban Development reports that the average monthly income for homeless families (headed by women) is $475 (*http://www.huduser.org/ publications/homeless/homelessness/ch_2e.html*). Couple this meager sum with the inability of most of these women to secure a job, to find childcare, to go to school, among other things, and it is plain to see that an inordinate amount of stress permeates this family type. It is already challenging enough to be a single parent, as we argued in Chapter 1, let alone a single *homeless* parent. It is important, therefore, to consider the words of Elizabeth Lindsey and Christina Sanchez (2010): "While mothers who are homeless with their children may have difficulty fulfilling some aspects of their roles as parents, many are able to keep their families intact and find ways to cope with the stress of homelessness and conditions that precipitate homelessness" (p. 340).

Student Perspective: Gwen

I'm not stupid. I know that our country is the richest country on earth. Why, then, do we let people walk the streets, give them nowhere to live, and then tell them that we aren't going to help them? Sometimes I hate living in a country where we don't take care of our own. I remember when I went to Minneapolis one weekend, I guess I was around 9 or 10 years old. I saw a young couple—maybe in their early 20s—with four very young kids. I remember one girl because she was about the same age as I was then. That image of them standing in front of a nice hotel asking for money has never left me. We need to do more for the homeless in our society.

Because single-mother families are the most common homeless family type, let's explore this population in some detail. First, researchers are clear in recognizing the importance of community shelters in the homeless mother's life. One popular misconception associated with homeless moms is that a shelter is the first choice for housing. In fact, shelter life is not conducive to healthy parent–child relationships (Lindsey & Sanchez, 2010). Further, Mikki Meadows-Oliver (2003), points out that moving to the shelter was the "last resort" (p. 132) for homeless mothers; indeed, most sought out friends and family members before arriving at the shelter. Second, because many homeless mothers are on the streets, problems exist that have to be managed. Lisa Cosgrove and Cheryl Flynn (2005) report that once a homeless mother and her family find a shelter, she inevitably loses all sense of family stability. Lisandro Pérez (2001) notes that the homeless mother must surrender to the shelter's rules. For instance, some shelters do not allow mothers to babysit for each other's children. Further, there are rules associated with when a mother is required to wake up each morning. Rules associated with hygiene, cooking responsibilities, child discipline, overnight privileges, phone use, and alcohol/drug use are also part of many shelters. Despite the breadth and depth of rules, Friedman observes (through her interviews with homeless moms) that "no mother interviewed thought the shelters should do away with all rules. They believed that some rules were essential. Although shelter rules were difficult to deal with, mothers understood the need for rules that increased the predictability and safety for themselves and their children" (p. 125).

Although rules may not be entirely frowned upon by homeless mothers, rules do, nonetheless, restrict and control a mother and her family. This loss of freedom often leads to feeling stressed, and this stress is on top of the stress that mothers already experience after losing their homes and becoming homeless (Meadows-Oliver, 2012). One poignant reminder of the stress a homeless mother feels is exemplified by Elizabeth:

> *You pray to God because He don't say no. You are hungry. You can't pay the rent. You cannot buy the shoes your child needs. You cannot understand the rules. You cannot keep the cat or TV. You need to pray! Help me, God! Help me see the day! Help me see the light! Help me to go over. Don't forget me. Please do not do that! (quoted in Kozol, 1988, p. 141)*

For an indication of the most frequently reported stressors of homeless parents, review Table 8-2. For Elizabeth and thousands more single

TABLE 8-2 Stressors Most Frequently Reported by Homeless Parents

STRESSOR	PERCENTAGE OF RESPONDENTS REPORTING
Insufficient money	70.3
Moved to new residence	70.3
Arguments with partner	49
A lot of problems unsolved	43.2
Not enough food for family	43.2
Going on welfare	37.8
Arguments between children	32.4
Arguments with children	32.4
Being in debt	32.4
Fights with in-laws or relatives	32.4
Family member seriously ill or hurt	29.7
Separation or divorce	29.7
Out of work for extended period	27
Change in job	21.6
No safe place for children to play	21.6
Problems with friends or neighbors	21.6
Eviction	18.9
Safety hazards in the home	18.9
Death of family member	13.5
Unable to heat or cool home	10.8

Source: J. C. Torquati, "Personal and Social Resources as Predictors of Parenting in Homeless Families" in *Journal of Family Issues 23* (2002): 463–485.

mothers, a constant struggle for daily support is tempered by a sense of hope through prayer. We will revisit the importance of religion in a family's life in Chapter 9.

Parenting effectiveness sharply decreases when families are homeless. It's clear from Elizabeth's thoughts and from her daily search for a better world that her role as a parent becomes secondary to her role as a provider. That is, finding the basic needs—food, shelter, clothing—takes priority over trying to socialize children when they are part of this chaotic and uncertain environment.

Much of the preceding information on the challenges experienced by homeless moms can be further understood by examining one of the few pieces of communication scholarship in the area of homelessness. In an important study by Fran Dickson and her associates (2011), five themes emerged that related to the communication challenges associated with being homeless: (1) maintaining privacy (e.g., attempting to parent in private, not public), (2) seeking out surrogate parents (e.g., including others to watch the children when the parent was busy), (3) managing health issues (e.g., maintaining cleanliness, coping with physical/mental health challenges, dealing with drug and/or alcohol abuse), (4) managing legal issues (e.g., trying to use law enforcement to secure child support), and (5) maintaining stability (e.g., avoiding shuttling from one shelter to another). In a classic study of mother–child interactions in a homeless shelter (Boxill & Beaty, 1990), two different mothering role themes were discovered. First, **public mothering**, or the absence of any privacy for family communication, may occur. As the researchers comment, "Every aspect and nuance of the mother/child relationship occurs and is affected by its public and often scrutinized nature" (p. 58). With social services staff, shelter staff, and other shelter members and families visible and available, a mother cannot privately act out expressions of compassion without witnesses. In some cases, shelter rules required mothers and children to remain together at all times. Consequently, children are exposed to an assortment of emotional displays, including watching mothers cry, feel nervous, or show signs of irritation (Meadows-Oliver, 2003). Further, mothers may feel awkward disciplining their children in front of others. This public accessibility to private parenting may inhibit child development and fragment family boundaries and eliminate family rules (Lindsey & Sanchez, 2010). In other words, public mothering interferes with a parent's need to restrain or reward her children as necessary.

In addition to public mothering, a second mothering role theme discovered by Nancy Boxill and Anita Beaty (1990) is called **unraveling**. In unraveling, a mother confers her maternal role on her older children, primarily older teenage girls. The mother allows her oldest child not only to dress and bathe her siblings, but also to discipline them if necessary. The authors note that in reality, the mothers were simply grateful for some extra help in parenting responsibilities. One mother of four children, however, relates the stress and pressure on her 10-year-old child:

Older kids are under stress, especially when it comes to them trying to control the smaller ones. And a lot of times, if we, as parents, take our stress out on our older kids because we think that they supposed to help, you know, try to keep under control the smaller ones, you know, like a lot of times I forget that my older child is not a mama. You know, she's not the child's parent, that's my duty. She's 10, you know, and I can't do that to her. (quoted in Averitt, 2003)

Further, mothers are trying to not only juggle the roles associated with being a single parent, but also the responsibilities of competing demands, such as looking for housing, working with public assistance, getting along with other parents in community shelters, and attending shelter meetings where necessary (Pérez, 2001). The dialectical tension of maintaining authority with their children and simultaneously answering to other adults (such as case workers and shelter personnel) is one that mothers must manage. Interestingly, unraveling may provoke a closer relationship between mother and child (Boxill & Beaty, 1990).

One additional communication behavior characterizes many shelter-based homeless mothers: guarding (Meadows-Oliver, 2012). **Guarding** entails a protection of sorts whereby moms make efforts to provide safety and security to their children in the unfamiliar and often violent homeless shelter. Meadows-Oliver discovered that not only were moms protecting their children from the inherent dangers related to shelter living but also insulating their kids from witnessing their own emotional displays. Because shelter rules require children to be with their parent at all times, the children are exposed to the raw emotions that any homeless mom would inevitably experience: fear, sadness, regret, frustration, and anger. Yet, mothers try to guard their children from seeing such emotions. Perhaps the comment by a homeless mom interviewed by Shirley Thrasher and Carol Mowbray (1995) sums up the importance of guarding in a homeless shelter: "A lot of times, I am just crying. And when I begin to cry they start to cry. I hate for them to see me this way" (p. 97).

Final Thoughts on Homelessness   We, like many of our family communication colleagues, believe that homeless families will continue to be a challenging group to study. First, there is the ethical dilemma of potential exploitation of these families through our studies. Second, homeless citizens are justifiably suspicious of researchers, given the perceptions of some writers that homeless people are homeless because they choose to be (Horowitz, 1990).

As communication scholars wrestle with the implications of homelessness in society, the everyday struggles of being a member of a homeless family will continue. We agree with Mitch Snyder and Mary Ellen Hombs (1990), who state, "we must begin to act as though it is our sister or brother, our mother or father, our son or daughter, or we ourselves who huddle silently" (p. 20).

SUMMARY

This chapter has examined developmental and unpredictable stress. We have presented information about stress and stressors and differentiated between stress that accompanies change and growth and stress that is unforeseen or unexpected. We have noted that eventually all family systems have some sort of stress and that stress does not always function negatively in a system. The birth of a child or a job promotion are examples of stressors that are frequently viewed very favorably. We described the ABC-X model of family stress to give you a sense of how family stress is perceived and received. Further, divorce and homelessness were discussed as unpredictable stressors on family life.

Stress in the family affects the family's ability to maintain itself as an effective system. In most cases, responsive and sensitive communication will ease the possible burden a stressor may have on the family unit. Of course, traumatic stressful events such as homelessness may never be eased in a family. Stress and stressors also pressure a family to change and grow. As Steve Duck (1992) commented, "Many life events are *undesirable* . . . but they also have a second element, which is *change*" (p. 199). Stressors require the family to respond to, adapt to, and respect life processes.

KEY TERMS

ABC-X model

certainty

developmental or normative stressors

empty speech

external context

guarding

internal context

public mothering

sandwich generation

social support

stress

stressor

symbolic baggage

unpredictable or nonnormative stressors

unraveling

QUESTIONS FOR REFLECTION

1. How does the dialectical tension between certainty and uncertainty relate to developmental stress? Be sure to include examples in your response.

2. Discuss whether or not you believe divorce is a developmental or an unpredictable stressor in a family. Is it possible to predict that about half of all marriages will dissolve? Or is divorce still an unexpected event? Incorporate examples as necessary.

3. Why is a happy family event thought to elicit stress? What specific family communication patterns can you identify to demonstrate this stress-inducing event? Give examples.

4. How does the divorce rate in our country redefine who the contemporary family is? Do you believe that divorce is a problem, or just another family event? Explain by including examples.

5. Defend or criticize the following statement: "The homeless are homeless, you might say, by choice." Do you agree or disagree with this statement? How does your response fit in with the economic opportunities for all U.S. citizens?

6. Differentiate among the young family, the growing family, and the older family and their relationship to developmental stress. Is one family more prone to stress? How severe is the stress for each family? Be sure to include examples as you respond.

7. Discuss predictable and unpredictable stressors that a newly arrived immigrant to the United States might feel.

8. Review our different family types from Chapter 1. Compare and contrast among the types and unique stressors that accompany each family type.

9. How does gender influence how family members handle stress?

10. In addition to divorce and homelessness, discuss additional unpredictable stressors that families may experience.

Chapter
9

MANAGING CHALLENGING DIALOGUES

Religion and Spirituality in the United States
Family, Religion, and Culture • One Nation Under God
Families and Religious Convictions • Marriage and Religion
Messages About Women and Religion
Religion and the Internet
Conclusions About Faith and Families

Family Communication and Sexuality
Sexual Scripts and Sexual Communication
Sexual Communication and Marriage
Sexual Communication and Culture

Summary

Key Terms

Questions for Reflection

THE STEINBERG FAMILY

When Carol and Ben Steinberg were dating in their 20s, they never gave much thought to the situation they find themselves in now. Carol has been a practicing Catholic her entire life, a woman who has been committed to her church's teachings and practices. Although she has maintained her church membership, in recent years, she has had considerable trouble with the church's statements on the role of women. Nonetheless, after marriage, Carol assumed that because of her lifelong devotion to Catholicism, she and Ben would raise their son, Ethan, to be Catholic. After all, she thought, although they are an interfaith family, Ben is not an observant Jew and rarely follows the traditions associated with Judaism. Ben, however, feels that given that Ethan is male and given Ben's upbringing in a Jewish household, he and Carol will naturally want Ethan to be raised Jewish. Of course, Ben's Orthodox parents often addressed this subject in subtle ways to Ethan's parents. Because both Carol and Ben are concerned that Ethan may be confused about being raised to identify with both faiths, the Steinbergs now must determine a particular religious identity that supports the values of everyone involved.

THE JASPER FAMILY

Beverly sits at the Thanksgiving table looking at her large extended family. She can't help but smile as she hears Grandma Helen tell one of her "Little Lena" stories. She also feels a warm sense of connection as she watches her daughter, Jessica, help her own son, Ricky, with his bib. And then there is Beverly's son Jake, who is growing ever more frustrated as he tries to get someone to pass him the sweet potato casserole. Although Beverly's husband died four months earlier from a heart attack, she tries to stay focused on the true meaning of being a family: togetherness. Her sentimental feelings, however, are soon shattered as Jake yells across the table, "There's no way I'll ever step foot in a church. The people who go to church each Sunday are bigots the rest of the week." Ruth, his sister-in-law, butts in: "Excuse me, Jake, but I think that you got it wrong. The people who don't go to church are going to have to face their Maker." The two begin their traditional shouting match over values. "And what about sex?" Jake asks loudly, "Your church says not to have sex before you're married, and you and my dear brother lived together for four years before you got married! Talk about hypocrisy." Ruth would never let her "in-law" have the last word: "Look, first that conversation is better left with the kids gone, and second, we lived together because we wanted to save money." "Right," Jake says. "And you really saved a lot of money buying that king-size bed for your apartment, huh?" Beverly finally interrupts them: "If you two want to argue again this year, take it outside.

Right now, we're not going to discuss religion or sex." Under his breath, everyone can hear Jake say, "We never did discuss religion or sex in our family."

THE EMMERLING FAMILY

Buck and Debbie Emmerling are worried about their daughter, Joy. In retrospect, they fear they may have sheltered her too much. As a 15-year-old, Joy is beginning to be interested in sex. They feel confused as they read the papers and watch the news with stories about unwanted pregnancies, abortion, and young teenage girls. Joy is a straight-A student, and although Buck and Debbie feel that she is a smart girl, they are also anxious about whether or not they protected her too much. They can't help but think that she will eventually want to experiment, and yet they also think it's ridiculous that a girl so young would even want to have sex. In their day, it would be quite unusual for a 15-year-old to be sexually active. Today, though, things are different. They know that Joy understands a lot about sexual issues since she is taking a health class, and she hangs out with girls who are older. The two are nervous about broaching the topic with their daughter since they don't want to come across as awkward and uncomfortable. Buck and Debbie also fear that Joy may already have experimented with her boyfriend. Getting their feelings and concerns across to their only child appears to be a serious problem for the couple.

Many times, family members find themselves challenged, frustrated, and confused. Throughout this book, we have presented you with a large number of issues facing families. We have noted that changing demographics, social norms, and family forms provide families with communication challenges. Families continue to redefine themselves as they adjust to these myriad challenges.

Indeed, there are a number of challenges facing all families in the United States today. Although some families face these problems head on, other families virtually ignore them or choose to focus on other issues. Yet, whether discussing religion or sex, as Jake and Ruth Jasper do in our opening story, the way families manage challenging situations can have lasting consequences. As Steve Duck and Julia Wood (1995a) comment, "Responses to challenges reflect and reshape individual relationship histories and carry repercussions not only for particular relationships but more generally for partners' relationships with other people" (p. 20).

Among the toughest communication topics facing families are religion and sex. Both resonate deeply in the fabric of family life, and both seem to serve as probable polarizing agents within the family (as seen with the

Jasper family). For instance, when parents try to talk to their children about one of these topics, the result is often a stilted and awkward conversation. The difficulty of discussing these issues rests largely with the lack of norms associated with religion and sex in the family. That is, coordinating any interaction pertaining to these two important topics usually depends on family rules, roles, and patterns of communication. Culture is also important to acknowledge, as we will discuss later. The problem for many families, however, is that such topics command some pretty thoughtful talk: Parents, children, and other family members need to think through their own biases and past experiences with sensitivity. Also, in many families, such topics may demand an immediate response. For the Steinbergs, affiliating with a religion at a young age is critical, since early socialization patterns are a foundation for adult patterns of behavior. And the Emmerlings' inexperience and delay in talking about sex to Joy may have dire consequences for her.

Challenging dialogues characterize family life, yet the way such conversations are facilitated differ from one family to another. For some, the boundaries may be quite penetrable among family members, resulting in open and direct communication between parent and child. For others, a great deal of innuendo and implicit talk may have to take place. Still others may resolve the situation by simply avoiding it. We believe that family members must reconcile the challenging conversations in their families. Managing these challenges can be beneficial in a few ways. First, some families may reawaken a connection that they may have forged earlier in their lives. Second, simply ignoring these challenges now carries far-reaching effects. Children, for instance, can learn about sex and sexuality via the Internet. With little or no accountability, having the Internet serve as a cyber-parent only exacerbates the challenges facing families today.

Student Perspective: Anthony

I go home to my mother's house during Christmas, and each year, I can't believe how different my brother and I are. We are only two years apart in age, and yet we have such a different view of things. We both used to think that religion was bogus and anyone who followed a religion had to be nuts. So now I sit with the family, and he starts this stuff about how he found God and that God is the almighty. I sit across from him at the table and can't believe we're related. He seems so self-righteous about it. I try to respect other people's views on religion, but I hate it when people wear it on their sleeves.

Religion and sex are only two of the numerous topics that may be difficult to integrate into the family system. There is no magic reason why these two areas are so complex and challenging to many families in our country. What may be universal across families, however, is that both areas offer family members an option. That is, once old enough, family members are able to choose which, if any, religion with which to identify. Also, having sex necessarily involves a choice, even though sexuality is primarily biological (Strong, DeVault, Sayad, & Yarber, 2005). Further, because some family members will not agree on the choices made by others, the topics of religion and sex enhance opportunities for family dialogue.

In our definition of family, presented in the first chapter, we noted that families create and maintain themselves through their own interactions. We believe that most families have difficulty discussing religion and sex; yet most families have poignant experiences with these topics.

Interestingly, at times, the areas of spirituality and sexuality intersect, prompting some difficulties. For instance, if you are a supporter of same-sex marriage, you may have a hard time listening to your minister or priest discuss the societal decay related to gay and lesbian couples getting married. In many families, values related to sex, sexuality, and sexual identity have their genesis in church teachings. This chapter provides a beginning as you prepare yourselves to delve thoughtfully into these vexing topics and their relationship to family communication.

We begin our discussion with an examination of the role of religion and spirituality in the family, a complex and deep theme. Keep in mind that the topic of family communication and religion is "uncharted territory on the landscape of diversity" (Diggs & Socha, 2004, p. 259). Alan Mikkelson and Colin Hesse (2009) observe, "Although religion and religious communication are an important part of people's everyday lives, they often feel uncomfortable when religious issues surface in conversations" (pp. 40–41). Kathleen Galvin (2004) is even more direct on the paucity of research in this area: "The extent to which religious beliefs impact family interaction remains remarkably understudied" (p. 680). Given these comments and the notion that there is a unique and complicated interrelationship among religiosity, families, and communication, we offer the following to help you unpack this complex connection.

RELIGION AND SPIRITUALITY IN THE UNITED STATES

Since the birth of the United States over 225 years ago, the freedom to worship as each one pleases has been protected, ensured, and even embraced. The U.S. Constitution guarantees freedom of religious assembly, and most families in our country embrace some notion of religious affiliation. Indeed, the United States is a religious nation.

The Gallup polling organization, in 2011, found that among adults, 90 percent believe in God, with women constituting 94 percent and men 90 percent of that total. Belief in God is highest in the Midwest, the East, and South (respectively) and lowest in the West (approximately 60 percent believe). Moreover, 71 percent contend that religion is losing its influence on American life (up nearly 50 percent in 2005).

In addition, a Gallup/USA Today poll in 2010 also found significant variation among generations in terms of daily prayer: (1) The Greatest generation (born before 1928) had a 74 percent daily rate, (2) The Silent generation's (1929–1945) rate was 71 percent, (3) the Baby Boomers' (1946–1964) rate was 62 percent, (4) Generation X (1965–1980) had a 54 percent daily prayer rate, with (5) Millennials (those born in 1981 or later) having the lowest prayer rate (41 percent) (*http://www.pewforum.org/Age/Religion-Among-the-Millennials.aspx*).

Clearly, the United States is a religious country with a variety of religious identities to consider (see Table 9-1 for a breakdown on church membership in the United States). Yet, despite the apparent pervasiveness of religion, not everyone agrees with the notion that religiosity and/or spirituality results in a harmonious culture. Indeed, Robert Putnam (2010), in his influential book,

TABLE 9-1 Membership in Church Denominations

Church Denomination	Members (thousands)
Roman Catholic	68,202
Southern Baptist	16,136
United Methodist	7,679
Church of Jesus Christ of Latter-Day Saints (Mormon)	6,157
Church of God in Christ	5,499
National Baptist Convention, USA	5,197
Evangelical Lutheran Church in America	4,274
National Baptist Convention of America	3,500
Presbyterian (USA)	2,675
African Methodist Episcopal	2,500
National Missionary Baptist Convention of America	2,500
Lutheran Church—Missouri Synod (LCMS)	2,278
Episcopal	1,951
Pentecostal Assemblies of the World	1,800
Churches of Christ	1,639
Greek Orthodox Archdiocese of America	1,500
African Methodist Episcopal Zion Church	1,400
American Baptist Churches (USA)	1,308
Jehovah's Witnesses	1,184
Church of God (Cleveland, Tennessee)	1,074
Christian Churches and Churches of Christ	1,071
Seventh-Day Adventist	1,060
United Church of Christ	1,058
Progressive National Baptist Convention	1,010

Source: Adapted from E. Lindner, *The Yearbook of American and Canadian Churches* (Nashville, TN: Abingdon, 2012).

American Grace, articulates the notion that religion can be a dividing force in the country. He argues that it's customary to find religious polarization, resulting in individuals taking sides on socially important issues such as gay marriage, abortion, prayer in public schools, the role of women, and so forth. Religion and spirituality continue to play a critical part in the human experience. As Robert Pollock (2002) concludes, "It is probably true to say that religion has produced a greater mass of literature, opinion, hate, strife, wars, persecution, absolute drama, and love than almost any other subject" (p. xii).

The U.S. Information Agency (*http://www.usinfo.state.gov/journals*) reports that there are around 2,000 religious denominations in this country, affecting tens of millions of people. Religion remains prominent in family relationships and exerts considerable influence on family members. Religion affects how families consider cultural and demographic events. For example, the largest of the religions—Catholicism—has been especially influential. Bradford Wilcox (2012) and colleagues conclude that Pope John Paul II was especially vocal about family-related issues such as divorce, sexuality, and marriage. Interestingly, however, Catholics in the United States are generally more liberal than the Vatican. Consequently, the U.S. Conference of Catholic Bishops generally encourages its congregations to work toward personal holiness but also to support those who don't live up to the Church's values and beliefs (p. 493). We will return to Catholicism and the family a bit later in the chapter.

Finally, from a developmental perspective, religion and spirituality commitments differ across the life span. Sueli Petry (2011) offers the following important conclusions (as always, keep in mind the significant cultural influences as you consider these points):

- From infancy to pubescence, children are reliant upon their parents' spiritual beliefs.

- As adolescence begins, children can become more autonomous and seek religious experiences on their own.

- As young adults move away from their families-of-origin (vis-à-vis college or entering the workplace), they may simultaneously move away from their religious beliefs.

- Middle-aged people (45–65 years old) rarely undergo major spiritual changes because they have already made life decisions (e.g., launching children, getting married) based upon religious foundations.

- As old age sets in, while people may not become more "religious," they attempt to make sense out of their lives using a spiritual lens. As Petry notes, "we all want to believe that our life has meaning and love."

Despite these variations across our lives, Petry points out that "children [and people] of all ages have the capacity for spiritual thoughts and beliefs, and very often their spirituality can help them" (p. 136). For a composite view of how religious practices and rituals change across various points in a life span, see Table 9-2.

TABLE 9-2   Religious Practices for Families Throughout a Life Span

---

What do they do? (What religious practices were most often mentioned, respectively?)
"Practicing what you preach"
Prayer (personal, couple, and family)
Sacred ritual (i.e., Shabbat meal, Family Home Evening, Ramadan)
Service and involvement throughout the week
Study of sacred texts (the Holy Koran, the Torah, the New Testament, and so on)
Church/synagogue/mosque attendance
Singing of sacred music

Why do they do it? (What purposes, motives, and meanings were connected to these practices?)
To transmit religious beliefs to the rising generation
To teach the rising generation a moral way of living
To promote family closeness, cohesion, and solidarity
For a sense of personal and/or family meaning
For a sense of multigenerational connection
To promote and build a sense of common history
As a coping resource for stress or in challenging times
To provide an example for children
To promote separation from contemporary culture without segregation
Because children "push" or "pull" you into it
To facilitate conflict resolution
To promote empathy, patience, gratitude, and discipline (i.e., through fasting)
To influence change in situations outside the realm of personal influence
To foster a sense of personal relationship with and connection to God

What are some costs associated with religious practices and involvement?
Bigotry and prejudice from outsiders
Money (participants donated an average of 10 percent of their incomes)
Time (required for personal, family, and faith community practices)
Effort, preparation, and organization
Recurring scheduling conflicts between outside entities (e.g., school, work, social
    activities, athletic or extracurricular participation) and sacred days
Constant conflict between sociocultural norms and religious ideals

What benefits did parents attribute to religious rituals and practices?
Relaxation, the ability "to breathe"
A structure and "rhythm to life"
Better physical, mental, and/or spiritual health and quality of life
Recovery from drug and/or alcohol addiction
Improved (direct and indirect) parent–child communication
Stronger marriage relationship
A sense of comfort
A personal relationship with and connection to God

Source: L. Marks, "Sacred Practices in Highly Religious Families: Christian, Jewish, Mormon, and Muslim Perspectives," *Family Process,* 43 (2004): 217–232.

Family, Religion, and Culture

As we noted earlier, culture is ever-present in discussions related to religion and spirituality. Families from various co-cultures, in particular, manifest their beliefs and practices in, and commitment to, a "supreme being"/God in different ways. For instance, the Barna Group (a nonpartisan research organization) (*http://www.barna.org/barna-update/article/13-culture/286-how-the-faith-of-african-americans-has-changed*) has found that African American beliefs and practices differ significantly from those of whites in a number of ways. Consider the following statements and the percentage of agreement between two cultural groups (and the U.S. respondents overall):

> **"The Bible is totally accurate in all the principles it teaches."**
> African Americans (66%), Whites (46%), U.S. (49%)
>
> **"You have a personal responsibility to tell others your religious beliefs."**
> African Americans (46%), Whites (32%), U.S. (34%)
>
> **"Your religious faith is very important in your life."**
> African Americans (86%), Whites (70%), U.S. (72%)
>
> **"The single most important purpose in life is to love God."**
> African Americans (85%), Whites (63%), U.S. (66%)

These responses suggest that African Americans place a premium on their commitment to their faith and their belief in God.

A number of Native American families have adopted nontraditional religious associations. Jessica Tinklenberg Devega and Christine Ortega Guarkee (2012) posit that among the 250,000 Native Americans in the U.S., most tribes have no written scriptures or dogma. Rather, oral transmission of history of practices, values, and customs was the primary means of educating family members. Many Native American families are **pantheistic**, meaning that there is a divine understanding of the world by looking at and embracing the planet and all that it offers (e.g., mountains, plants, animals, trees, etc.). Walter Kawamoto and Tamara Cheshire (1997) report that some Native American families have Christian orientations, but others have abandoned Christianity because of its role in oppressing Indian communities. B. A. Robinson (2001) reports that religion in the Native American communities evolved to match the tribe's needs and ways of living. Robinson eloquently notes that the "sacred texts" for many Native Americans have been preserved through storytelling and that various tribal nations have different views of the Creation. One provocative view notes that in the beginning, the world was populated with humans who were subsequently transformed into animals. This transformation is one reason Native Americans feel a close ancestry bond with animals. Perhaps Noah Augustine (2000) in the *Toronto Star* best addressed the relationship of religion to his Native community:

> *Despite being born into a strong Catholic family, I choose to honor our Great Spirit—God—through the practices of ceremonies originally given to the First Peoples of this land. Rather than going to church, I attend a sweat lodge; rather than accepting bread and toast from the Holy Priest, I smoke a ceremonial pipe to come into Communion with the Great Spirit; and rather than kneeling with my hands placed together in prayer, I let sweetgrass be feathered over my entire being for spiritual cleansing and allow the smoke to carry my prayers into the heavens. I am a Mi'kmaq, and this is how we pray. (p. A17)*

In addition to African Americans and Native Americans, Masako Ishii-Kuntz (1997b) has examined Japanese Americans and religious life. Ishii-Kuntz contends that scores of Japanese American families are not strongly influenced by religion; nonetheless, the Japanese cultural values of loyalty, harmony, and ethics are rooted in Confucianism and Buddhism. Shinto, too, has influenced Japanese Americans. Shinto means the way of the gods and is a belief that life and spirit simultaneously exist in inanimate objects such as rivers, rocks, and trees (Aston, 2012). Rock gardens and bonsai trees might be considered manifestations of the dedication to Shinto. Although Europeans tried to spread Christianity to the Japanese islands, they were largely unsuccessful, as evidenced by the fact that less than 1 percent of Japanese call themselves Christian. Finally, H. Neill McFarland (1991) argues that Japanese American families who advocate a Buddhist orientation may have in their homes a *butsudan,* an altar made up of Buddhist images. He continues: "One of the most important family-centered rites is the annual summer Bon festival, when spirits of the deceased are welcomed home for a visit with special food offerings and other signs of respectful attentiveness" (p. 18). Clearly, then, many Japanese American families today continue spiritual traditions originating back in 6th century B.C.

One additional co-cultural family-religion connection we wish to address is the Mexican American family. For many Mexican American families, Catholicism is revered through participation in a number of celebrations. Among them is the *quinceañera,* a mass in honor of a young woman's rite of passage from youth to adulthood. This event is part of a "sacramental constellation" embraced by many Mexican Americans (Rodriguez, 2012). The event occurs on the young woman's 15th birthday, and the family gives thanks to God for the young woman's advancement into adulthood. It should be pointed out that although Mexican Americans overwhelmingly subscribe to Catholic practices, Yolanda Sanchez (1997) comments that the number of social justice programs sponsored by Protestant religions and their relationship to this co-culture has resulted in a number of Mexican Americans converting to Protestantism from Catholicism. Sanchez also reports that women in the family are pivotal in religious upbringing. Believing that medicinal herbs can cure such things as fear, women frequently engage in faith healing, which is an extension of the family's belief that Catholicism is rooted in folk remedies and herbal cures. Sanchez observes that for women to serve as *curanderas,* or folk healers, they must be born into a family of folk healers so that the mentoring process can get under way quickly.

In unique ways, several co-cultures in the United States have invoked a personal response to religion and have embraced some sort of spiritual connection to a deity. Clearly there are a number of other groups that we could address, and we encourage you to further consider the influence that religion has on members of diverse families.

One Nation Under God

Although we realize that not all people subscribe to a religion or a supreme deity, the United States continues to be a culture dedicated to the existence of God. God pervades our relational, political, and popular culture. For instance, after a sneeze or when individuals leave an interaction, people often say "God bless you." In the political environment, each session of the U.S. Congress begins with some sort of prayer, and many political candidates customarily conclude their speeches with "God Bless America." On paper money, "In God We Trust" appears, and despite efforts to eliminate the phrase, the Pledge of Allegiance contains clear references to God ("one nation under God").

Other God-related references exist, even with those cultural groups who are unaccustomed to invoking God. In times of despair, **agnostics** (those who neither affirm nor deny the existence of God) and **atheists** (individuals who deny or disbelieve the existence of God) may reference God to make a point and may pray at times (Shook, 2011). Finally, over the years, Hollywood and New York City—not usually viewed as cradles of religiosity—have found value (that is, money) in producing television shows (such as *Joan of Arcadia, Touched by an Angel, Highway to Heaven*), films (*The Passion of the Christ, The Last Temptation of Christ,*

Student Perspective: Leo

I was raised thinking that I had no other choice but Judaism. It was incredible when I went to college to hear about and see so many other religions. I remember my freshman year when I went home for Thanksgiving. I told my mother that I had been going to a Buddhist temple the past four weeks. She about cried. I told her that I was 18 and needed to explore all religions. I tried to tell her that Buddhists believe in self-empowerment and respect diversity. She didn't buy it. She made me feel like I committed some crime. I really don't know how we're going to get through this one; religion is one of those issues where people go crazy. I don't think I'll do this to my kids.

Oh God!), and Broadway musicals (*Jesus Christ Superstar, Godspell*). The perception remains that God exists and is part of the cultural fabric of the United States.

Families and Religious Convictions

Many family celebrations in our country are religious. Marriage, baptism, and death ceremonies often involve religious clergy of some kind and may assume religious associations. In fact, many family rules, roles, norms, and patterns of communication are based upon something related to religion. For example, in the Kanowitz family, an explicit family rule is that each family member reserve Sundays to attend church together. This church celebration is followed by a breakfast each Sunday at a local restaurant. In the Bernabei family, each of the six children was baptized into the Catholic Church, although as adults, two of the six are now Buddhists. For five Jewish fraternity brothers, every Friday night is a chance to get together to reflect on the challenges of being Jewish on their college campus. Finally, although their financial and emotional situation is disquieting, Rita Lowry and her family attend church services at a religious center each Saturday night. She believes that her family's homelessness is only a temporary condition and that with faith their circumstances will soon change. For these families, David Knox and Caroline Schacht (2012) suggest that the relationship between a family system and its religion is reciprocal, each influencing the other. We further conclude that through religion, many families are able to survive their losses, manage their difficulties, and celebrate their fortunes.

Religion can unite and divide. As we have observed, not all members of our complex society believe similarly in God, nor do they worship in the same way. For some families, their religion determines how they view such issues as marriage, childbearing, women's and men's roles, power, and procreation. For the Steinbergs, from the chapter's opening, raising their son as Catholic or as Jewish is seen to have lasting repercussions. Either affiliation will affect how Ethan perceives a variety of issues.

Religious communities often dictate or strongly suggest how their members should believe and behave. Still, we should add that some religions are rather tolerant of conflicting attitudes. The Quaker religion, for instance, serves God's "will," and to this end, divergent viewpoints or dissenting opinions are honored. Listening and understanding are key to respecting individuality (Clarkson, 2012). Such religious traditions as Judaism, Christianity, Hinduism, and Buddhism differ in their interpretations and prescriptions for their followers. Also, within each tradition, variations exist. That is, local religious traditions and practices often differ from each other.

Families often find themselves at the crossroads of religion and their own unique values, morals, and behavior. Different family types in particular vary in their experiences with, exposure to, and interpretation of religious opportunities. Perhaps no family type has experienced more challenge with religious institutions than gay and lesbian families. For instance, many gay and lesbian households frown on religions that preach from Leviticus 20:13: "If a man also lie with mankind, as he lieth with a woman, both of them have committed an abomination: they shall surely be put to death." Despite the societal dialogue on the contemporary applications of Biblical teachings, many gay fathers and lesbian mothers have found themselves turned away at a church door because of their sexual identity. As Laura Benkov (1994) asserts, "Biblical references are often the sole justification for antihomosexual sentiments" (p. 46).

Gay and lesbian family members find that a number of religiously conservative groups and churches oppose the development and existence of their families. That is, these institutions feel that gay men and lesbians should not be legally permitted to parent children. Some people, for example, conclude that children were meant to be nurtured by a man and woman together, and any variation of this is a distortion of sexuality. Even former U.S. presidential candidate Rick Santorum, a devoted Catholic, commented in 2012 upon the need for children to have both a father and mother and not same-sex parents (Memoli & Barabak, 2012). Santorum cited a research study that prompted him to conclude that children with imprisoned fathers who abandoned them were still better off than if they had no father at all. Further, in some religious circles, there is outright discrimination against the participation of gay men and lesbians in church ministries. Deepa Bharath (2011) reports that the Crystal Cathedral leadership "strongly encouraged" the church's choir members to sign a "convenant" that notes, among other things, that sexual intimacy is (per God's word) only between one man and one woman, celebrated in the bonds of marriage. Finally, consider these words, published by the pastor of a church in Santa Ana, California:

Homosexuals ought not be admitted to the fellowship of the church or ordained to ministerial office, for they are placed outside the bounds of God's kingdom altogether.

Although many religions and houses of worship sincerely consider homosexuality an abomination, many gay and lesbian families continue to seek out hospitable spiritual surroundings. These families have found comfort and support among many United Methodists, reformed Jews, Unitarian Universalists, and in the United Church of Christ. In addition, Catholic gay men and lesbians and their heterosexual allies have formed Dignity/USA, a progressive national lay movement that advocates for change in the Catholic Church's teaching on homosexuality. In addition to Dignity/USA, gay and lesbian families have also viewed Metropolitan Community Churches to be affirming and inclusive. It's important to point out that many mainstream religions may vary tremendously at the local level. The extent to which religious groups welcome gay and lesbian families, then, may be more a product of the pastor's or rabbi's beliefs than those at a national or international level.

In addition to gay and lesbian families, couples who cohabit may find themselves at odds with a number of mainstream religions in the United States.

In particular, contemporary Catholicism poses some great problems for cohabitors. Although many cohabitors believe that living together is a different path toward marriage (although not all cohabitors get married), the Catholic Church still considers it "living in sin." Having previously been married, then, Carol Travis would have to receive an **annulment**, or a symbolic nullification of her first marriage, before she could receive any sacraments of the church—including matrimony. In fact, a father or mother in a stepfamily who is a practicing Catholic should have had his or her previous marriage annulled.

Unlike gay and lesbian families and cohabiting couples, single moms and dads may find more inviting religious communities. Michelle Anthony and Ken Canfield (2011), for instance, report that churches across the United States are now opening their doors to offer what are called "single-parent ministries." Many churches—from Presbyterian to evangelical Southern Baptists—are welcoming single parents and their children. With babysitters on hand, moms in particular are being taught how to budget. Patrik Jonsson (2000) argues that while Catholics have tried to reconcile the difficulty of illegitimacy and divorce, many Protestant churches have openly addressed teenagers, single adults, and their children. Still, not all religions are welcoming. Consider the pastor of a church in Waterville, Maine, who claimed that there are people who need help "all around us. . . . There's [*sic*] prostitutes, drug addicts, single moms, alcoholics, you name it" (Aligning single mothers with individuals who have an addiction or who are engaging in illegal activities gives a clear sense of how single mothers are viewed by this church). Despite these words, single parents now experience more religious acceptance, but the process has been quite slow. Although the social and religious stigmas associated with being a single parent are slowly being substituted with more embracing views, this and other family types will continue to question and sometimes fully reject church teachings.

Marriage and Religion

As we mentioned in Chapter 1, most people in our country get married and, usually, marriage is sanctioned through some religious official. Through marriage, a couple announces to others that they have coalesced into a partnership, complete with financial and social benefits. As we noted in earlier chapters, however, not everyone is afforded this opportunity. In fact, as mentioned earlier, the Defense of Marriage Act passed by the U.S. Congress specifically points out that marriage is limited to a man and woman, regardless of more liberal interpretations of the marriage vow. In this instance, as has been historically the case, the government intervened in a religious event.

Despite efforts to separate church and state—a constitutional requirement—the United States has been interested in preserving the institution of marriage, even protecting it. In fact, if there was any doubt whether marriage was a state-controlled institution, consider the fact that in 2012, the National Conference of State Legislatures (NCSL) devoted an entire section of its Web site to defining marriage. The NCSL is clear in identifying marriage as a governmental institution by stating that "state legislatures have been deeply involved in the public debates about how to define marriage" (*http://www.ncsl.org/issues-research/human-services/same-sex-marriage-overview.aspx*). Interestingly, many politicos argue against "government intrusion" in a person's personal life, but seem comfortable with such "intrusion" as it relates to the intimacy between two adults. For some, states should not be in the business of being "marriage police" (*http://www.ontheissues.org/2012/Ron_Paul_Civil_Rights.htm*). Lora Liss (1987) reports that since the 1800s, the United States Supreme Court has maintained control over individuals and their individual decisions to marry. From polygamy to divorce, the court has ensured that marriage is protected in our society.

Liss (1987) contends that the U.S. legislation as it affects the family is rooted in several myths: (1) a return to more traditional family values and gender roles would save many marriages and protect children; (2) the sexual revolution of the 1960s caused the rise in unwed mothers; (3) most women have a man to support them; (4) women benefit from receiving alimony and child support; (5) women can find jobs—dollar for dollar of what a man earns—if a divorce occurs; and (6) in the typical family, children are raised by their biological parents. Although Liss acknowledges changes in societal attitudes and legal opinions, a tension still exists between the old and new morality within the judiciary.

With this high level of societal support for the institution of marriage, we would expect most people to be successful in securing a lifetime partner. However, for many reasons, including infidelity and violence, couples divorce, despite the fact that most religions do not encourage or permit divorce. The fact that the Catholic Church does not "allow"

Student Perspective: Winnie

When I decided to march in front of the capitol, I knew this would be the first time I would show my face supporting homosexual marriages. As a straight woman, I thought I would have some credibility. I have so many gay and lesbian friends who have been in their relationships for decades and who want to have the same benefits as we straight people have. It's pretty sad that everyone complains about how gays and lesbians don't stay in relationships, and when they want a chance to prove that they have long-term commitments, society says it can't allow that. I guess I wonder what I would do if I were involved with a woman and we wanted to get married— probably move out of the country to a more tolerant land.

divorce forces many Catholic families either to leave the church (and its sacraments) or to petition for an annulment after the divorce is final. This may explain why Catholics are less likely to divorce than are Protestants. For those affiliated with the new Christian right, in a consolidation of "parachurch organizations" such as Focus on the Family, divorce is perceived as an "erosion" of the family (Hadden, 1983). Intriguing data, however, suggest that some faiths may not be able to influence divorce rates. Conservative Christians, for example, while overtly opposed to divorce, have higher divorce rates than other faith groups, and even higher rates than atheists and agnostics (*http://divorcerate2011.com/divorce-statistics/divorce-rate-by-age-or-religion*). In addition, although the Church of Jesus Christ of Latter-Day Saints (Mormons) explicitly tells its members that divorce is abhorrent and that few divorces are justifiable, the divorce rates of Mormons mirrors closely that of the general population (*http://mormonexpression.com/blogs/2011/07/09/more-than-6-of-temple-married-mormons-get-divorced/*). Finally, although the divorce rate in many Arab American communities remains low compared to that of other co-cultures, it is on the rise (Bayor, 2011).

With a large number of U.S. families associated with some religious denomination and the prevalence of religious marriage ceremonies, we would expect divorce to be an aberration. However, marriage still remains challenging to many couples. As a result, families need to reconcile their need to divorce and their need to follow their religion. This tension is highlighted in the following dialogue between Estelle and Enrique, a Mexican American couple who have been married for 11 years. The two have a 7-year-old daughter, Maria.

ESTELLE: Believe me, we have no choice. The way we act now will affect Maria forever. Let's be mature about it, okay?

ENRIQUE: Let's just agree to keep her from feeling any of this pain. Can we do that?

ESTELLE: We can try. It's going to be another story, though, with the priest. We should go together to tell him that we've thought this through, and it's for the best that we divorce. What do you think his response will be?

ENRIQUE: Who cares? It's our relationship. He hasn't lived with us. If he turns his back on us, he turns his back on Maria.

ESTELLE: Enrique, it's the church! We shouldn't be so arrogant! We must make amends with our God.

ENRIQUE: I will with my God, Estelle, but I probably won't ever make amends with my church.

Estelle and Enrique are clearly challenged by both their interpersonal relationship and their relationship with their church. Across the country, countless couples experience this confusion. Mexican Americans particularly may be troubled by the canons of Catholicism. As Julian Samora and Patricia Vandel-Simon (1993) admit,

> There exists a chaotic void between the demands of the formal institution and the everyday life experiences of the people. . . . If there is any hope of true acceptance for and by Mexican American Catholics, the institutional church and its structure will have to change. (p. 233)

The relationship between marriage and religion is further complicated by **interfaith marriages,** or unions that include at least two different religious identities. Interfaith marriages have been studied thoughtfully by Patrick Hughes and Fran Dickson (2005). This research is pioneering insofar as it is one of the few series of scholarly works examining the role that religion plays in marital relationships. Hughes and Dickson (2005) report that interfaith couples exhibit extrinsic (outward) and intrinsic (inward) religious orientations, and these orientations influence the conflict in their marriage. Hughes and Dickson (in press) observe that when a partner desires a change in the marriage, extrinsic interfaith partners—who are likely to practice their faith in public settings—expect collaboration over religious issues (for example, worshiping) in their marriage. Intrinsic interfaith partners—practicing their faith independently—may be less likely to desire a change. This research is an important beginning to unravel the complex intersection of religion and marriage.

As we noted, most people in the United States get married. Many marriages, however, end in divorce, and consequently families often scramble to ease the emotional, financial, and religious pain inflicted on their members. With couples reneging on the ever-popular "till death do us part" matrimonial vow, religious leaders must continually assess the spiritual reasons surrounding their teachings on divorce and the practicality of such religious standards.

Messages About Women and Religion

In Chapter 4, we identified the Susan G. Komen Foundation as an example of a social movement dedicated to empowering and assisting women with

---

Student Perspective: Miriam

I sit in class and I can't believe it sometimes when the others talk about how their parents influenced their religious beliefs. When I was younger, my dad never took me to any church. I was never told that God existed. I did have some friends who were Catholic, but I wasn't allowed to go to church with them. In fact, my dad kept telling me something like "there is no God" or "If God was here, why did he let your mom die so young." I think he was really mad at God, and as his only kid, I had to deal with the fallout of how he felt. Today, I do go to church but raise my two daughters to respect all religions and even those people who do not belong to or follow a religion.

Student Perspective: Christine

I'm 31 years of age and demand that I be treated the same as men. Yet, when I look around, I don't see many religions doing this. I did go to a synagogue one time, and there was a female rabbi. To be honest, I was a bit taken aback. I didn't even know that women were allowed to be rabbis; I was very excited to see that the Jewish religion is getting more progressive. Even though I know that not all temples have female rabbis, it's nice to see some ancient religions become more contemporary. I also know that there's a lot more that needs to be done to get women involved in their religions. Why aren't there female priests, for example?

breast cancer. While the organization has had unequivocal success in the breast cancer movement, it has also found itself in the midst of much controversy. In 2012, the organization decided to cut funding to Planned Parenthood, an organization headed and staffed by women, with a predominately female clientele. Planned Parenthood received over $500,000 in grants annually from Komen, primarily to fund cancer screenings and fund education for low-income women (Morgan, 2012). Yet, the decision to defund the women's organization drew much scrutiny after it was reported that the Catholic Church exerted pressure upon Komen over the years to stop supporting Planned Parenthood because some Catholic bishops believed that money to the organization might end up funding research on stem cells collected from fetuses (Komen also felt that the grant-making policies were also questionable). In the end, Komen reversed its decision after much public and media outcry, given the type of services that Planned Parenthood provided to marginalized communities. Many citizens, including scores of Catholics, were insulted by the move and perceived it as yet one more misogynistic behavior prompted by the Catholic Church (*http://ohiodailyblog.com/content/wouldnt-you-know-it%3F-catholic-bishops-involved-komen-debacle*).

Many women across the United States have found religions to be personally challenging and inhospitable. The Komen–Planned Parenthood mess is one reason for this frustration. In a real sense, **patriarchy,** or the rule of men that subordinates women, permeates many religious communities. Most religions in the United States rely on the Bible (and its many translations) for their source of inspiration. Because Biblical scripture proclaims that woman (Eve) was made from Adam's rib, women's subordinate condition is argued to be the word of God. According to Ephesians 5:21–32, "Wives should be submissive to their husbands . . . because the husband is head of his wife." Additional masculinist references can be found when examining the phrasing used in churches and temples across our country. For example, God is often referred to as "He," the "Lord," and "Our Father." Many women, then, find themselves a part of a patriarchal, yet very personal, religious experience when they enter a church or temple or mosque.

The hierarchy of many religions is dominated by men. The Pope, the head of the Catholic Church, arguably the most recognized person in the world, has always been male. His subordinates—cardinals, archbishops, bishops, and priests—are also all male. In fact, with the largest number of U.S. citizens belonging to the Catholic religion, millions of people who attend church each Sunday never see a woman in a position of power in their church. We should add that women play a more prominent role in the Unitarian Universalist Church, the Episcopal Church, and even some Jewish temples, where women serve as clergy for millions of worshipers.

The legitimation of women in religious roles affects the family and can create tension. For instance, although families align themselves with some sort of religious worship, family members may be troubled by the patriarchal overtones of their particular religions. Men and women are often challenged by the opposing needs of fostering their faith and adhering to sexism, which goes against their beliefs. For those Catholic couples who practice birth control (such as the pill), the dissonance is palpable. Because Catholic doctrine considers contraception to be an egregious sin, Catholic women who wish to use the pill will have to reconcile the religious, biological, and political discrepancy. It's intriguing to note that some surveys point out, "Even among married Catholic women, only 3 percent practice natural family planning, while a majority uses contraceptives that the Church hierarchy routinely denounces" (Jones & Dreweke, 2011, p. 7). As a result, religious messages emanating from many families are dissonant: Go to church, but be cautious in believing in everything you see and hear.

Yet, women's participation in religious services outpaces men's participation. Gerald Zelizer (2002) notes that the national trend is that a "substantially higher percentage of women attend church regularly on Sunday, read the Bible, pray in any given week, or set spiritual goals for themselves" (p. 23A). In fact, Maureen Fielder (2010) concludes that women around the world are more committed to religion than are men. Although our discussion of the Promise Keepers provides some evidence that things may be changing with respect to men and religious participation, we still live in a society where "religion tilts to the female side" (Zelizer, 2002, p. 23A).

Although women find themselves more involved in religious activities, many women continue to feel shut out. Consequently, an irony exists. Joan Aldous (1983) believes that although women are the primary teachers of religion in their homes, their voices often remain silent because they are teaching lessons of patriarchy. As Aldous asserts, "Women, because they have always had less power and status than men, have been the ones most affected by events over which they lack control" (p. 74). In the eyes of many religions, women's opinions are important, yet, ironically, they are not articulated nor solicited by many mainstream religions.

Although we have pointed out that many religions are masculinist, we should add that change is occurring. Two changes have taken place within the Catholic Church, the largest religious denomination in our country.

The U.S. Catholic bishops have endorsed a gender-neutral language policy urging that sexist language be eliminated in all services. Therefore, church lectors are encouraged to eliminate references to "mankind" and to "brethren" and employ more gender-neutral language. Women now constitute a large number of church advisory board members. Further, efforts are under way to place women in more prominent roles in the Catholic religious service. Women are ministering altar wine and reading the Scripture lesson. They have also gained access serving Holy Communion, the most sacred of all Catholic events. Of course, not all parishes embrace these changes. However, perhaps because of public reaction or perhaps because of the perception that Pope John Paul II was a "staunch defender of the dignity of women" (Campbell, 2011), women today are discovering changes in the spiritual environment of the Catholic Church.

The changes going on within centuries-old religions such as Catholicism have a great deal to do with **religious feminists.** Teresa Marciano (1987) writes that feminists have urged "reinterpretations of theology that will lead to equal shared access to opportunities for action, leadership, sacramental participation, and church policy formation" (p. 304). Marciano and others report that feminists question current Biblical translations that do not respect earlier Biblical writings showing women serving in leadership roles. Marciano notes that both Christian and Jewish feminists have promoted changes in male-biased liturgies. Clearly, women are finding warmer surroundings in religion today. Much more needs to be done, however, to retain women's current involvement and secure their future participation.

Religion and the Internet

The interface of religiosity, family, and the Internet is a topic worthy of an entire book! The advent of cyberfaith communities around the country and the globe has resulted in people of all ages, cultural backgrounds, and identities using the Web for spiritual and religious purposes. First, it's important to distinguish between online religion and religion online. Bernard Jansen, Andrea Tapia, and Amanda Spink (2010) posit this difference: "Religion online is defined as meaning that which provides a Web seeker information about a religion or congregations, and online religion is defined as referring to that which invites the Web seeker to participate in religious activities online" (p. 41). We include both in this discussion.

Justin Farrell (2011) stated that the number of religious congregations with Web sites has tripled (1998–2006) with more than 10,000 congregations adding a Web presence each year. In Farrell's groundbreaking study, he discovered that podcasts, video sermons, blogs, and downloadable choir music with QR codes were readily available among the 600 Web sites he analyzed. Farrell found that among many denominations, the Web sites were not considered to be an electronic brochure but rather a "portal of action" (p. 85), meaning opportunities to donate, watch a sermon, hear announcements, participate in Bible study, keep up with fellow church members, and so forth. Farrell clarifies that the Web sites are not used as "virtual churches" but rather as supplements to the real experiences of the congregation.

A host of additional religious technological opportunities have also been undertaken, including the Vatican's Web TV channel and Twitter campaign during Lent, an iPhone "prep" application for confessions (although all sacraments must be bestowed in person), search-engine algorithms to steer people toward salvation, online streaming of sermons, and even #TOF, which is a campaign/competition that asks people to write a statement of faith and pass it along in 140 characters or less (Cheong, 2011; Grossman, 2012). Christopher Helland (2004) tells us that major and minor Christian denominations—in addition to Jewish, Muslim, Hindu, and Buddhist religious traditions—utilize the Internet in both public and private ways. Many religions have provided their followers with the opportunity for public comment. For example, the Catholic faith first provided an electronic gathering place in 1995 with the development of the Vatican's (home of the Pope) official Web site (*www.vatican.va*). Other traditions have also established their own Internet connections, from the Alpha Church (*www .alphachurch.org*), an online Christian global church, to a Pagan-centered Web site (*http://thepwa.net*), which bills itself as a nontheological site dedicated to those who advocate the goddess who is immanent in all things (Griffin, 2004). These diverse electronic gatherings have given family members the chance to worship as they please. Helland argues that those "religious seekers and spiritual entrepreneurs" will continue to utilize the Internet because they wish to maintain religious customs "on their own terms" (p. 34).

Virtual religious communities affect the contemporary family in a few ways. First, having religious information immediately accessible to families can create a community of religious discourse (Griffin, 2004). Many of you grew up in families in which your parents would take you to a mosque, church, or synagogue. Some of you may have been enrolled in a religious school; others may have participated in religious education before, during, or after religious services. These faith episodes may have been your sole exposure to understanding your faith.

Today, Internet engines have driven religion into the home. Different generations can access a number of different Web sites to gain more understanding of their own religion or the religions of the world. Family members with Internet access are now able to read about such religions as Taoism, Confucianism, or the Peyote religion, for instance, which were once far-reaching and misunderstood. Rituals, customs, and discourses of various religions are now better understood because the Internet has brought these practices into millions of family homes. As Marc MacWilliams (2004) notes, a "virtual pilgrimage" (p. 223) occurs for many families as they "satisfy spiritual curiosity" (p. 225).

A second way in which the Internet influences a family's religious life relates to younger family members' assertion of religious independence. That is, young people are provided with an opportunity to cultivate their identities online. Identity management (Coupland & Nussbaum, 1993; Goffman, 1959) provides us with the ability to function within various communities. In identity management, we decide how our behavior will influence the perceptions of others. Further, we begin to clarify our own individuality. Mia Lovheim (2004) articulates the view that because the Internet offers young people the chance to see "cool" ways of expressing one's spiritual beliefs vis à vis graphics, chat rooms, and downloads, religious identity may be prone to change. Young women and men are attracted to and even seduced by this visual-auditory medium that entices them into unexplored spiritual journeys.

Consider, for instance, what happens to Adam during his first week at college. Being raised a Methodist, Adam was accustomed to attending church services every Sunday with his family. Yet, once he began college, Adam was introduced to a Web site that was dedicated to the "busy religious college student." He began to "attend" the Web site every weekend and found himself questioning some of the religious principles and values he learned while growing up. Adam eventually began chatting with several other like-minded college students in virtual discussion forums and began to question his belief systems pertaining to such topics as gay marriage, cohabitation, and even the existence of Hell. He felt that what his parents taught him seemed rather outdated and ill-informed.

Clearly, Adam is beginning to foster an identity different from his parents. This sort of metamorphosis, Lovheim (2004) notes, frequently provides younger people with a chance to explore their personal values and assert individual responsibility over their spiritual journeys. Today, then, young people who were raised in families who attended weekly religious services and adhered to a religion's beliefs and practices are now creating their own religious rituals, symbols, and practices, thanks in some part to the availability of the Internet.

We have only touched on the impact that religion and faith have on families in the United States. And we have addressed primarily prominent Western religions, while recognizing that millions of families subscribe to Eastern religious teachings as well. Still, we have provided an important snapshot of how some families are influenced by their religious convictions and how religion plays a role in family communication.

Challenges to religious teachings abound across co-cultures. For instance, although many Eastern religions such as Hinduism and Buddhism are prominent among Japanese and Chinese Americans, times are changing. As Shobha Pais (1997) acknowledges, "Although children participate in the family's religious activities, the dominance of Western culture may render them unable to internalize these religious beliefs" (p. 175). Most likely, religion will continue to confound families in our society while it continues to be a vital part of family discussions.

Conclusions About Faith and Families

Families across the United States continue to face and prepare for spiritual and religious challenges. The dialectical dilemma facing them becomes clear: How do citizens in an individualistic country such as the United States reconcile a collectivist orientation to faith and religion?

First, religion and faith are idiosyncratic. The personal decision to subscribe to a mainstream religion, for instance, requires us to respect individual decisions associated with the religion. At all times, we must acknowledge that spirituality and faith are very private arenas for a number of families. We should be careful to avoid judgment, then, when Luke and Michael, a gay couple and practicing Catholics, decide to serve on the church's advisory board. Obviously, for them, being gay and being Catholic are not incompatible. Although their actions contradict prevailing cultural scripts, they believe that their religious convictions are deeply personal.

A second conclusion relevant to families and religion pertains to the number of religions practiced in the United States. It should be apparent that, just as families do, religion takes many forms. There is "something for everyone." For some, being religious is not as important as being spiritual, and we have seen that in some co-cultural groups, spirituality may not have any connection with mainstream religion. This is perplexing to some, and yet, with thousands of religions, churches, denominations, faith groups, religious bodies, tribes, and cultures, it should come as no surprise that our society is filled with faith options. Some of you may believe that our society has gone too far in allowing all voices to be legitimized and protected under the U.S. Constitution. Others of you, however, may feel that the diversity in religion and spirituality is simply a response to the diversity found in the U.S. population. Whether family members adopt the former way of thinking or the latter, or some sort of middle ground, they should be acutely aware of the multitudes of religious opportunities available today.

A third conclusion regarding religion and family life is based on the conversations taking place in families today. As we mentioned earlier, religion can both divide and unite us. This is seen nowhere more clearly than in the decisions family members make when it comes to subscribing to a religion. Children generally affiliate with the same religion as their parents. Yet there are times when children choose to abandon the religion of their family-of-origin and instead forge a different path toward spiritual fulfillment. Family members may openly disentangle themselves from mainstream religions, such as the child who once at college decides to forego attending religious services. Other family members may choose to learn about other spiritual ways, including less popular religions. Still other family members may openly reject any religious association and deny the existence of a supreme being.

The dialogues that take place around these decisions can be quite perplexing and demanding. We have already noted that children develop spiritual values and practices along their lifespans. And we presented research that showed that parental influence upon children's religiosity typically wanes as children grow up. So it should be no surprise that a parent may feel frustrated, angry, confused, or betrayed if a child embarks upon a religious path that is not aligned with the path of his or her parent.

Further, overall conversations related to the value of religion seem to be inevitable when dealing with children of different ages. For instance, what difficulties lie ahead for atheist or agnostic parents when making decisions about their children's spiritual journey? Think about the challenges related to interfaith families (as exemplified with the Steinbergs from our opening) as they determine the religious direction of their children. The restructuring of the family, various spiritual options, and shifts in family roles have prompted children to embark on autonomous spiritual paths. It is important, first, for both parent and child to recognize the intimate nature of spirituality and religion and, second, for parents to remain supportive as children stake out an approach to faith.

The interface of religion and family life reflects the changes going on in a number of religions across the country. Some religions are beginning to disengage from their past. It is clear that many religions are beginning to reshape their dogma and practices in response to public opinion and cultural patterns. As we have mentioned, Catholicism and other religions are reassessing their inclusion of women in church protocol. One significant change in Catholicism is of particular note. In 2011, the U.S. Conference of Catholic Bishops approved translating the mass into Spanish to address the increased presence of Latinos in American churches. Such a move would likely have been provocative years ago, particularly in Anglo-centric communities.

Student Perspective: Diane

It really amazed me when I introduced my boyfriend to my parents, and they got all bent out of shape because he isn't Jewish. I was totally surprised by their reaction. We have never really been a religious family, and I didn't know this was a big deal to my mom and dad. I guess in high school the issue never came up, because we lived in an area with a lot of Jewish people and most of my friends were Jewish and the guys I dated were all Jewish too. But that wasn't because I thought it was important—it just worked out that way. So their reaction to Tim was a big shock to me. We never talked about religion much when I lived at home, and this isn't really the way I wanted to start the conversation. I am not sure where we will go with this. I am not about to let their prejudices stop me from dating Tim, though. My folks will have to get over their bias and treat Tim better. It's not like he is an anti-Semite or anything!

FAMILY COMMUNICATION AND SEXUALITY

The challenge associated with sexuality is depicted by Ellen Berman and David Wohlsifer (2011): "The interaction between body's changes, and the individual and family's knowledge, experience, relationship, and culture make sexuality a highly complex and variable phenomenon" (p. 103).

Perhaps no issues elicit more provocative discussion—internal and external to the family—than those pertaining to sex and sexuality. Over the years, we have heard countless messages from family members about how sex codes are integrated into their family system. The Sexuality Information and Education Council of the United States (SIECUS) Web site (*www.siecus.org*) (2012) effectively demonstrates the role that families and other cultural institutions play in developing an individual's sexuality: "Sexuality education is a lifelong process that begins at birth. Parents, family, peers, partners, schools, religion, and the media influence the messages people receive about sexuality at all stages of life. These messages can be conflicting, incomplete, and inaccurate." Melanie Booth-Butterfield and Robert Sidelinger (1998) underscore the importance of family communication about sex when they state, "interactional patterns in the family shape both the relationships with the family, and serve as mediators influencing children's attitudes and subsequent behaviors" (p. 296). And, as we discussed in Chapter 5, sexuality and conversations about sex can be important behaviors in developing and maintaining intimacy.

Yet talking about sex is often a complex dialogue. Buck and Debbie Emmerling, in our opening vignette, provide an example of the difficulty parents face when discussing sex and sexuality with their children. For them and other family members across our country, communicating about sex is a necessary but difficult process. Effective communication about sex and sexuality is based on a parent's family-of-origin and background, the receptivity of the child, and the emotional atmosphere of the home. Too often, however, these are (and have been) troubled areas, resulting in family members receiving sexual messages that are convoluted, confusing, frustrating, and sometimes inaccurate.

Families communicate messages about sex and sexuality in many ways. How effective family members are in communicating about such issues as conception, pregnancy, contraception, sexual dysfunctions, abortion, sexual coercion, and masturbation depends on their willingness and ability to tread on difficult ground. When family members refuse to engage in conversations pertaining to sex and sexuality, the ramifications can be overwhelming.

Sexual Scripts and Sexual Communication

The way sexual subjects are introduced and treated in a family's discussion is a result of **sexual scripts,** or a person's past or present sexual motivations, behaviors, and experiences. F. Scott Christopher and Susan Sprecher (2005) note that sexual scripts are learned from society and are influenced by the five

---

⌇⌇⌇ POPULAR PRESS PERSPECTIVES ⌇⌇⌇

In an essay in the *Wall Street Journal Online,* Mary Eberstadt discusses whether or not the "sexual revolution" has been good for women. She is emphatic in noting that because of a variety of factors, the answer is a resounding "not sure." Eberstadt notes that "the sexual revolution has transformed economics, culture, and law." She further contends that many social issues—including same-sex marriage and abortion—have divided the country. Such division has resulted in women being less happy about a number of issues. In addition, she presents research that shows that women's happiness (a "personal, imponderable thing") is slowly declining over time, despite "advances in the work force and education." In sum, Eberstadt attempts to show that the "sexual revolution" has not been an "event" that has resulted in happiness for women (and men). She frames most of her comments within a larger context called "the war on women" and advances that such a "war" needs more community conversation rather than "shortsighted political theatrics."

http://online.wsj.com/article/SB10001424052702304724404577297422171909202.html

---

questions Who? What? When? Where? and Why? Maria Alvareaz and Leonel Garcia-Marques (2011) state that sexual scripts "influence the actions of the individual and provide a structure for understanding and anticipating the behavior of others" (p. 358). Clearly, sexual scripts "arise from, explain, and accomplish sexual activity" (Metts & Cupach, 1989).

Families differ in their reactions to and interpretations of sexual scripts. Some family members may reject society's sexual script, choosing to develop an idiosyncratic and relationship-specific script. Other family members may be more comfortable adhering to a public sexual script. Chances are that we are each products of some combination of the two. Some parents may be extremely open in conversing about sexuality issues, whereas other parents may choose to be

Student Perspective: Derrick

We really have a terrible time talking about sex in my family. First, my parents never even mentioned the word sex, and when I would bring it up, they would change the subject right away. I think one reason why they didn't talk about it is because their parents never talked about sex to them. It's strange that what our parents do with us, we do with our children. But when it comes to sex, it's too dangerous these days to ignore the topic. I know if and when I have kids, I will definitely bring it up. There's no way that I'm going to have children who feel embarrassed about talking to their father about sex. I may not have all the answers, but at least I can tell them that I'll try to find them out.

more restrictive and closed in their **sexual communication,** or talk about issues pertaining to sex, sexuality, and intimacy. Each approach has consequences. Openness about sex results in more satisfying and quality relationships in the family, whereas a family system that shuts out discussions of sex is vulnerable to family conflicts (Strong, DeVault, & Cohen, 2010). We are reminded, however, of the comments by William Cupach and Brian Spitzberg (1994): "Privacy and the bolstering of one's separate identity are integral to personal and often relational, well-being" (p. 317). That is, at times, an open and expressive orientation may serve to undermine family functioning.

The way sex is discussed is usually a result of the rules governing such conversations in a family. Indeed, sexual communication in a family is rule bound. The St. Lawrence family, for instance, believes that sex is a topic better left unspoken or a topic to be learned in physical education class in high school. This rule is implicitly understood by the family and has never been challenged. The Fitzgerald family is more explicit in their rules about sexual communication. Family members overtly discuss dating, cohabitation, sexual activity, homosexuality, and heterosexuality. The parents have even gone so far as to swim nude with their children in their pool, feeling that the human body should be celebrated and not hidden. Although you may not identify or agree with either family's rule system, the decision to remain silent or open about sex differs from one family to another.

As we have discussed, sexual communication in a family can take many forms—there may be open discussions, or there may be little, if any, discussion. Family communication researchers have discovered that sexual communication is important in families. Jennifer Heisler (2009) concludes that while some parents may wish to communicate about sex and sexuality to their children, they often lack the knowledge, have a limited repertoire to draw upon, or are "paralyzed by embarrassment" (p. 297). In her research, Heisler found that the average age for beginning sexual activity was about 17 years old, mothers talked about sexuality more often than fathers, and that three primary topics emerged as most frequently discussed in parent-child sexual communication (morals, relationships, and pregnancy).

Other family communication research is important to address as it relates to sex and sexuality. For example, Heather Powell and Chris Segrin (2004) discovered that communication practices with peers influenced the sort of communication that college students undertook related to sexuality, HIV, and AIDS. Orratai Rhucharoenpornpanich and colleagues (2012), studying the Thai culture, found that while parents discussed body changes and dating with their children, the parents were less inclined to talk about sex, birth control, and/or HIV. In one of the first studies of its kind in family communication literature, Kristen Norwood (2012) examined transgender identity and its "presence" in families. She discovered that transgender identity could be considered a family stressor (see Chapter 8) because family members were trying to make sense of this identity in their families and this prompted them to renegotiate identity and family relationships. Norwood observes,

"Family members struggled to honor their familial relationships, roles, and obligations in the face of social stigma, religious commitments, and other personal beliefs that seemed to work against support of their [transgender] family members' transitions" (p. 90). Finally, examining the mother-daughter relationship, Tina Coffelt (2010) says that in very close relationships, mothers and daughters have no great difficulty discussing sex. Coffelt found that this dyadic type first acknowledged that sex is a "natural" topic in relationships. They then openly discussed the challenges related to talking about sex. Finally, using a dialectical model (see Chapter 2), Coffelt noted that mothers and daughters framed the conversations about sex as challenging *and* not challenging rather than as challenging *or* not challenging.

Clay Warren (1995) explains that a large percentage of both children and parents report dissatisfaction with the quantity and quality of family sex communication. He notes that parents are crucial barometers of how messages pertaining to sex will be processed; if parents intend to control sexual attitudes and behaviors of their children, children will view that effort as repressive. Warren concludes that "mutual dialogue is the key factor essential to satisfaction with family discussion; children are most satisfied with their family sex communication pattern when parents help them feel free to initiate discussions" (p. 182).

How do families attain the healthy and mutually satisfying dialogues to which scholars refer? Warren (1995) argues that parents are instrumental in sex education. He presents a number of suggestions: (1) Start talking; (2) once parents start talking, they should make an effort to continue; (3) start early; (4) both parents should talk, if the family has two parents; (5) sons as well as daughters should be part of the discussion; (6) establish mutual dialogue; (7) create a supportive environment; (8) remember, if parents don't successfully influence their children, someone else will; (9) keep in mind that discussing sex does not promote promiscuity; and (10) remember that discussing sex early will likely make discussion less anxiety filled. Although some people may see these suggestions as little more than common sense, as we have seen (and as some of you have experienced), talking about sex can be a very difficult undertaking for parents and other family members. Openness to a child's thoughts and experiences and respect for a parent's background and comfort level are critical to a satisfying sexual communication episode. In other words, considering a family member's sexual script may enhance the opportunity to socially construct a family environment of sensitivity and frankness with a topic too many families fail to discuss. This social construction may facilitate meaning within the family.

Thoughtful communication about sexuality in the family may influence not only children's sexual behavior, but also the way they view their own sexuality. In their best-selling book *How to Talk with Your Kids about Sex,* John Chirban & Dr. Phil McGraw (2012) contend that learning and talking about sex are not tantamount to giving permission to engage in sexual activities. Nonmarital sex occurs with young people not only because of sex education at home, but also because there is more acceptance of this sexual behavior in the courtship process (Cate & Lloyd, 1992). Further, individual factors (previous sexual experiences, sexual attitudes, personality characteristics, and gender), relationship factors (level of intimacy and length of relationship), and environmental factors (physical surroundings, presence of others, cultural affiliation) all contribute to decisions about nonmarital intercourse (Sprecher, 1989; Sprecher & McKinney, 1993). So, many factors, including family communication, affect individual decisions about sexual behavior.

Sexual Communication and Marriage

Patricia Chisholm (2003) writes that one expectation of marriage is that intimacy and social support will be expressed through sex. To be sure, marriage carries with it some challenging dialogues, most notably, how to integrate sexual issues. Susan Sprecher and Kathleen McKinney (1993) conclude that what a couple does in their sex life together and their feelings about their sexual activity are likely to affect the overall quality of their relationship. Sexual communication in marriage has changed over the years, in that wives and husbands are discovering a need to understand the other's sexual script. These days, understanding a partner's sexual past is critical to "healthy passions" (Adelman, 1992).

Researchers are inconsistent in pointing out how the frequency of sex leads to marital satisfaction. Some researchers observe that married couples wish to have sex frequently. In fact, Phillip Blumstein and Pepper Schwartz (1983) discovered that "married couples feel so strongly about having sex often that those who say they have it with their partner infrequently tend to be dissatisfied with their entire relationship" (p. 201). The authors interpret this statement further and conclude that other factors affect marital satisfaction: "From our vantage point, it looks like other problems come into the bedroom" (p. 201). Other writers conclude that frequency of sex and a willingness to talk openly about sexual scripts result in more sexual satisfaction (Theiss, 2012).

Contradictory evidence about frequency of sex and marital satisfaction also exists. For some couples, child rearing, fatigue, and work-related duties interfere with their sex life. Yet a lack of sex does not translate into a lack of marital happiness. In other words, satisfaction in marriage and with sex has little to do with frequency of sex but rather compatibility of sexual desires. In fact, incompatibility of sexual desires can be the beginning of the end of a marriage (Sprecher & McKinney, 1994). Finally, Ted Huston and Anita Vangelisti (1991) found that affectional expression was positively related to marital satisfaction, not simply sexual interest or frequency of sex. Thus, we see that sex in marriage is complicated because a sexual relationship may not necessarily mean a satisfying relationship. That is, because a married couple engages in sex does not mean that they are satisfied.

As we learned in Chapter 1, there are numerous types of families in our society. Similarly, there are different types of marriages, each of which must consider issues pertaining to sex and sexuality. Let's briefly address what communication-related problems can occur with couples in a few types of marriages. Pepper Schwartz (1994) discusses two types: traditional and peer. **Traditional marriages** are marriages in which male and female roles are divided in expected and stereotypic ways. Schwartz reveals several problems with these marriages, which number in the millions in our country. She identifies five communication dilemmas in sexual communication among traditional married couples: (1) failure of timing, (2) failure of intimacy, (3) failure of sexual empathy, (4) failure of reciprocity, and (5) overromanticism. For **peer marriages,** or marriages in which both partners have equal control and equal influence in family decision making, Schwartz believes that mutual respect and pride in one another characterize the sexual relationship. Further, relational hierarchy and dominance are broken down in favor of sexual equality.

Although we may be inclined to believe that all marriages should be peer marriages, reflect back to what we have stated all along in this book: Each family is unique. No two family members think and behave alike, and the rules, roles, and norms of interaction can differ tremendously. Therefore, it's reasonable to conclude that some marriages work quite well as traditional marriages and that others do not effectively function as peer marriages. Research by Mary Anne Fitzpatrick (1988), discussed in Chapter 1, clearly supports this belief. Further, Schwartz (1994) contends that among the challenges to peer marriages are career and identity costs associated with living in this marriage type.

One final area related to marriage and sexuality is important to note but not normally discussed in families: extramarital infidelity. Extramarital affairs took center stage many years ago in the United States during the impeachment hearings of President Clinton. Since that time, the topic has resurfaced, notably during the 2012 presidential election campaign with the media focusing on the infidelity of two Republican candidates, the former Speaker of the U.S. House of Representatives, Newt Gingrich, and the former CEO of Godfather's Pizza, Herman Cain. Of course, infidelity is not relegated to politicians only. Millions of families have acknowledged and dealt with extramarital (or extra *relational*) relationships. (Recall that cultural values and customs influence the perceptions and experiences of what we are calling "infidelity"). Although some partners are in an open relationship (Knox & Schacht, 2011), most couples—married or cohabiting—do not develop such sexual scripts. Let's talk about this topic a bit further.

You could easily surmise that sexual norms in the United States were quite different in the early 1900s than they are today. Aside from the dramatic shift in terms of openness, individuals born into the same family over different generations may differ significantly in their sexual beliefs and values systems (Berman & Wohlsifer, 2011). Yet, considering the polling related to how the United States views extramarital affairs, not much has changed in terms of the population's perception. For instance, in 2001, the National Opinion Research Center (2001) reported that between 1972 and 1982, 56 percent of those surveyed felt that extramarital affairs were either "always wrong" or "almost always wrong." In 2009, the Gallup Organization reported that 92 percent of those surveyed found extramarital affairs to be morally wrong (*http://www.gallup.com/poll/121253/extramarital-affairs-sanford-morally-taboo.aspx*). What's important to note is not necessarily the percentage who view infidelity as wrong. Rather, consider the impact of such behavior on the communication in the family. This impact can manifest in a variety of ways: divorce, renegotiation of relational rules, examination of family configuration, intervention of professional counseling, among others. Our focus here is on how a behavior—one that many family types deal with—affects the family members and the family dynamics. It appears that this topic will always be with families in the United States since "the tension between security and adventurousness in sexuality is a consistent theme in couples, in individuals, and in cultural/religious strictures on sexual behavior" (Berman & Wohlsifer, 2011).

Finally, we note that a recent twist on the infidelity experience is with cybersex. The Internet—as we argued earlier in the chapter—has forever changed the cultural mores of society. The Harris Poll Online (Sex and the Internet, 2000) found that 60 percent of women and 41 percent of men believe that having cybersex is synonymous with infidelity. Online betrayal is viewed harmless by some and an act of violation by others. As cyber-infidelity becomes more prevalent and researchers study it further, it will be important to assess what constitutes online infidelity, the extent of its pervasiveness, and whether men and women continue to look at this topic differently.

The implications of extramarital sex for the marriage subsystem have been studied. Researchers have discovered that the tendency to engage in infidelity is linked to how satisfied a spouse is in his or her marriage (Reiss, 1990), although not all unsatisfying marriages result in an extramarital affair (Buss,

Student Perspective: Mlefe

Leaving South Africa, I heard that the United States was such a liberal place to live— that people are always talking about sex and that there are even prostitutes who come up to your car when it is stopped at a light. When I got here, my eyes were opened wide. This country is so conservative when it comes to sex. It's strange: There is so much sex on TV, yet I've been in families where sex is not even mentioned. I have a friend from the South whose family has a rule that they shouldn't talk about sex unless it's with their minister! My closest friend here told me that his father talked to him but never once mentioned any words like orgasm *or* masturbation. *I never imagined that America was like this when I lived in South Africa.*

1994). Further, an extramarital encounter does not necessarily mean the end of a relationship, although we're sure that some relational partners rethink the future of their marriage if infidelity is discovered or revealed.

Married partners are an especially challenging subsystem in the family system. They must continually negotiate their sexual scripts in order to achieve respect and understanding. Further, the rules that the couple introduce into the relationship affect the satisfaction of their sexual communication. Indeed, a married couple must coordinate meaning (Cronen, Pearce, & Harris, 1982) in their sexual relationship.

Sexual Communication and Culture

Before closing this section on sex and sexuality, we'd like to discuss the different racial and ethnic interpretations and experiences related to sexual communication. This is a consequential discussion since there are cultural differences in understanding sexual communication in the United States. The media are clearly influential in perceptions both within and outside of the United States (Jurkowitz, 2001). However, various co-cultural groups think and behave differently. As always in discussions about family communication, we have to be careful about assuming a monolithic view in a diverse world. Yet the ever-shrinking global village does bring some threats to our diversity. As Yahya Kamalipour (1999) concludes, the values and customs of indigenous cultures have been "Americanized" to the extent that their unique traditions and narratives are now in danger of being homogenized.

We are cautious in dealing with this topic because we agree with Anthony Cortese (1989), who asserts that there is no adequate theoretical model that accurately depicts racial and ethnic differences and similarities in sexuality. Cortese notes that most of the pioneering studies on sexuality (for instance, Kinsey studies, Hunt studies) neglected to include African Americans, among other racial populations, in their surveys. Further, he contends that most sexuality studies have used middle-class Caucasians and have failed to include first-person thoughts and feelings from other groups and classes. In the following discussion, and as we have maintained throughout this book, many findings pertaining to race and ethnicity are necessarily globalized and may not apply to every member of the racial or ethnic group.

With respect to this topic, however, a few relevant findings merit attention. Mexican American families operate under the assumption that sexual issues will not be discussed (Zambrana, 2011). Robert Francoeur (1987) writes that "Mexican American men also place a high value on many children and thus often refuse to use contraception" (p. 525). This patriarchal tradition, Francoeur believes, is beginning to erode with younger and more educated urban Puerto Ricans and Cuban Americans refusing to adopt this family script. Griselda Chapa (2011) believes that this is a stereotype ("womanizing Don Juan") of men based on an outdated view of Latino families. She argues that the Catholic Church, a religious tradition identified by many Latinos, is more influential in contraception use in the family. Since the Catholic Church forbids use of contraceptives, men may simply be subscribing to religious dogma. In the end, Larry Rohter (2012) contends that Latino men are granted more sexual freedom than women, making decision making related to sex a masculinist experience.

We find more agreement by scholars on how Japanese American families handle sexual communication issues. For instance, because Asian Americans tend to be less individualistic than other co-cultures (Jandt, 2012), Japanese American families are inclined to view their family in relationship to other families. Because fathers tend to protect their family's reputation (Newman, 2012), family members will privately discuss sexual concerns, problems, or experiences within the confines of the family. Masako Ishii-Kuntz (1997) feels that sexual expression within the Japanese family is a very private matter. Again, however, like many Mexican American families, Ishii-Kuntz believes younger generation Japanese families are adopting more liberal views on issues pertaining to sex and sexuality.

In addition to Mexican Americans and Japanese Americans, other ethnic and racial groups handle issues pertaining to sexual communication in different ways. To understand how Arab American families, for instance, manage their sex codes, consider the Haddad family. Samuel and Judy Haddad have a 15-year-old daughter, Mary. The parents are very concerned about Mary as she begins to mature into a young woman. Samuel and Judy know that young men will soon call at their house frequently and will want to ask their daughter out on dates. This troubles the parents greatly. In fact, both parents have vowed to scrutinize phone calls to Mary and monitor her dating practices closely. Having Mary go out with a group of friends is the parents' preference. How feelings, patterns of communication, and family rules will be carried out in their family, however, remains to be seen.

Sam Kubba (2011) contends that a large percentage of Arab parents arrange the marriages of their children. Therefore, it is not uncharacteristic that the Haddads are cautious with their daughter. Because many Arab American parents watch their daughter's intimate behavior more closely than they do their son's (Nanji, 1993), it's likely that both Samuel and Judy will continue to ensure that Mary maintains self-respect and does not dishonor the Haddad family name with careless sexual behavior. Dalel Khalil (2008) reports, however, that many young Arab American women conceal their dating from their parents, especially if they are dating outside of their ethnic group. We can see that Mary Haddad and her parents may soon experience family conflict owing to cultural expectations.

For many Asian Indian immigrants living in the United States, because discussions of sex and sexuality are not usual in this cultural group, it is difficult to accurately assess their sexual attitudes and values (Kaduvettoor-Davidson & Inman, 2011). Research indicates that a large percentage of Asian Indian males have engaged in sexual relations before marriage, and, ironically, most of these males expect their future wife to be a virgin (Sujay, 2011). Despite living in a country where women are afforded sexual options, this sexual double standard is rooted in a culture with a traditional male role of dominance in spousal relationships.

Although a number of other cultures could be addressed, we close by noting that when discussing sexuality and culture, we necessarily draw on generalities. We are reminded that even within cultures, variations can and usually do exist. Nonetheless, we hope we have given you a sense of how some co-cultures send and receive messages about sex and sexuality.

SUMMARY

In this chapter, we introduced some complex and challenging dialogues that are an important part of family life. We recognized that religion and sexuality frequently influence family communication; many family members differ greatly on how to approach these topics within their family system. Religion and faith are highly personal, and the extent to which family members worship and believe in a deity can have an impact on how effectively family members function. We also discussed how sexual communication within a family varies. Some families openly discuss issues pertaining to sex and sexuality, whereas others are apprehensive, nervous, or philosophically opposed to such discussions. Certainly cultural values influence dialogues about sex and sexuality.

Earlier in the chapter, we noted that religion and sexuality often intertwine. This meshing requires careful attention to family rules, the roles carried out in the family, available norms, and any predictable patterns of interaction that may be a part of these challenging conversations. In addition, without considering the cultural influence on families, we won't have a fair or accurate understanding of how these areas influence families in all corners of our society. The United States, with over 300 million people, will always have families trying to reconcile their challenging dialogues. The process is ongoing and requires sensitivity, acceptance, and nurturance from all family members.

KEY TERMS

agnostics

annulment

atheists

interfaith marriages

pantheistic

patriarchy

peer marriages

religious feminists

sexual communication

sexual scripts

traditional marriages

QUESTIONS FOR REFLECTION

1. What do you believe is the most difficult dialogue in your family? How have you managed it? Discuss your response by incorporating examples.

2. Defend or criticize the following statement: Families are getting frustrated with organized religions. Provide examples to support your views.

3. Discuss how sex and sexuality were introduced in your family-of-origin. Do you believe that today's families are open in discussing sex and sexuality? Describe your answer by including examples.

4. Do you believe that the United States should abandon all officially sanctioned references to God? Why or why not?

5. How will families in the future deal with religion and sexuality?

6. Were you surprised by the various perceptions of extramarital sex? Why or why not? What would you project in terms of future extramarital affairs? How will family communication be affected by this behavior?

7. Discuss whether you consider cybersex between and among relationally committed people to be dishonest.

8. Examine the intersection between religious identity and sexual behavior. How do they relate? What overlap exists between the two?

9. What would you say to someone who believes that religion is slowly declining in the United States? Explain your response with examples.

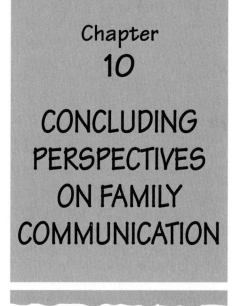

Chapter

10

CONCLUDING PERSPECTIVES ON FAMILY COMMUNICATION

The Future of Family Communication Research
Explanations for Family Communication
Family Communication in Neglected and Understudied Populations
Work–Life Issues

Cultural Discourse About the Family
The Impact of Technology on Family Life • Co-Parenting

Thinking About Family Communication: Four Conclusions
Recognition of Diversity in Family Communication
Recognition of the Challenges of Family Communication
Recognition of the Value of Family Communication in Our Society
Recognition of Changing Times

Summary
Questions for Reflection

THE BLANCHARD FAMILY

After school, Bobbie Blanchard stuffed her books and papers into her backpack and headed home. When she arrived, her grandmother was in the kitchen making a stew for dinner. It smelled great, and Bobbie put her backpack down and washed up. Then she began to set the table as she did every night. "Grandma, how many of us will there be for dinner tonight?" Bobbie asked. That was one thing Bobbie really loved about her family— there were always people coming over, and you were never alone. "Well, Bobbie," her grandmother said. "It'll be you, me, Uncle Terry, Aunt Belle, and your brother Curtis." When the family all sat down to eat the savory stew, Bobbie told them about her homework assignment. Mr. Spector had asked the class to write an essay predicting the future of families. Bobbie was supposed to write about what family life will be like in 100 years. She was to discuss what the demographics might be, what activities families might engage in, and how families will communicate 100 years in the future. Uncle Terry laughed, "That is sure different from the kind of homework I had when I was in the sixth grade, Bobbie!" But Aunt Belle and Bobbie's grandma took the assignment seriously and began speculating about how people would be able to design their children to order. Curtis wondered whether brothers would be able to add to the design. He poked Bobbie in the ribs and told her she would have turned out a little different if he could have had a say in the matter. They all laughed, and Bobbie figured she would have to think about the essay on her own.

KATE HOBSON AND GUY HERNANDEZ

Kate Hobson and Guy Hernandez had begun living together at the beginning of the fall semester, and they were still finding out a lot about each other and figuring out how to handle their new living arrangement. For the most part it was working well, and Kate and Guy thought that living together had made them a great deal closer. But now Kate was concerned. She was telling Guy about her family communication class. In the lecture today, the professor had quoted research findings indicating that people who live together for a while and then decide to get married are more likely to divorce than married couples who don't live together first. But if those who already plan to get married then live together first, living together doesn't have any negative impact on their marriage. Kate and Guy hadn't really talked about marriage, but Kate hadn't ruled it out either. Now she was hearing that their living arrangement might be dooming their chances for a successful marriage. Guy smiled at Kate. "First of all," he said, "they didn't do that research on us. I am sure we could beat the odds if we decided to get married. But second of all, are we ready to think about marriage? I thought things were going great just the way they are."

Kate laughed. "Yes, things are going well. But I can't help thinking about the future. I think I will do a little more research and find out how they did this study." Guy agreed that might be a good idea. "Maybe I should sign up for that family comm course next semester," Guy said.

PROFESSOR JON SASSI

Professor Jon Sassi organized his data and put together a flowchart. He planned to meet with a new research assistant tomorrow to outline her duties for this semester. Professor Sassi is working on a research project examining the issues that arise in gay and lesbian families with kids after parental separation. He observed that gay men and lesbians do not have a good model for keeping both adults involved in the lives of any children they may have raised together, although he knows that some couples manage the breakup well. Sassi is specifically interested in the communication strategies that gay and lesbian couples use to restructure their families after they break up. He wondered whether these strategies differ from how heterosexual couples manage divorce and child custody issues. Sassi sees the problem as one of shifting boundaries in the family system. He has done a great deal of library research on the topic, and he is eager to get his research assistant up to speed so he can begin interviewing people and get this project under way.

Like Bobbie Blanchard, Kate Hobson, Guy Hernandez, and Jon Stassi, we are all students and practitioners of family communication. All of us live in some type of family where we communicate with the other members for various reasons. Further, like the characters in our opening stories, we all puzzle over family communication questions. Sometimes, our research in this area is confined to our own experiences, but often, like Professor Stassi, we become more systematic in our inquiry and examine family communication more broadly and inclusively.

In this text we have focused on the importance of family communication. It enables family members to accomplish the critical tasks invested in the family as an institution, including socializing members, providing emotional support, and aiding in the development of the younger members. Additionally, there is a "constitutive link between communication and families" (Vangelisti, 2004, p. xiii). This means that communication creates and maintains family identity. Families develop characteristic communication patterns to cope with the big issues of family life, such as conflict and affection. Further, families deal with more mundane practices like greetings and dinner conversation through communication. These communication patterns, in turn, establish and continue a sense of the family's personality or identity. In a way, these communication patterns constitute what a family is—they define the family.

THE FUTURE OF FAMILY COMMUNICATION RESEARCH

Our aim in this book has been to blend theory, research, and practical examples to give you a clear understanding of the role of family communication in a diverse society. Because this book is based on research, we would like to provide some thoughts on the future of scholarship in family communication. In a sense, we are posing challenges for those individuals—like yourself—who are interested in family life in the United States. Our hope is that some of these suggestions, recommendations, and conclusions will be useful as you begin your own thinking about family communication research. The following three general research areas are informed by the many findings and examples contained in the previous chapters of this book. Family communication research has just begun to tap the exciting promise of the field. As you read and think about these suggestions, keep in mind our overarching belief that all future research about family communication should continue to discuss the complexities associated with culture, race, ethnicity, and family forms. Dr. Sassi's research from our chapter opening is an example of this type of research.

As we have learned throughout this book, open, direct communication can have various meanings in different cultures. If we are to remain sensitive to the different co-cultures and their families in the United States, research must begin to address the variation in how communication functions within those families. For instance, self-disclosure may be a valuable behavior in many families, but Pauline Agbayani-Siewart and Linda Revilla (1995) report that verbal communication is deemphasized in many Filipino American families. To this end, "spouses are hesitant to confront one another with problems" (p. 163). Sally Hastings (2000) found that Asian Indians value self-suppression and strategically avoid self-disclosures. Family communication scholars should recognize that the same behavior will be evaluated differently in different families. Thus we must always take culture into consideration when interpreting findings.

It is also important to keep Diggs and Socha's (2004) advice in mind when examining the effects of culture on family communication. They advise that researchers need to question their "own ethnic thinking and its impact on who they study, what they study, and how they study various phenomena" (p. 255). Rhunette Diggs and Thomas Socha note that openly examining our own cultural ways of knowing will help us include more diversity in our research and will provide opportunities for us to interrogate cultural assumptions we might bring to our conclusions. For instance, it is important that we don't judge the results of our studies of diverse populations by one measure that fits with only one group's values. Eddie Diez Martinez Day and Marie José Remigy (1999) observe that the Mexican and French children they studied defined family based on their own family experience. When children lived with two parents, they thought family meant two parents living with children. When they lived with a single parent, they were less likely to think that a family had to be defined by two parents. Day and Remigy remained open to their respondents' different definitions rather than pre-defining family in a manner that would have excluded one segment of their sample.

Through our research for this book, we have found the following areas to be promising for more research: explanations for family communication or the development of family theory, explorations of family communication in neglected populations, and work–life issues.

Explanations for Family Communication

In Chapter 2, we discussed the role of theory in understanding family communication. The need to understand why families communicate the way they do is very strong. Good explanations guide our observations and help us sort out and make sense of what we have seen. Earlier we noted that the complexity of family communication and all of the variables impinging on it make it difficult to know when to generalize. Theories of family communication help us in this regard. We are not necessarily encouraging new theoretical development in family communication research. Rather, we believe that much will be accomplished by combining theories (as we have done in this text) and by testing and retesting existing theory. Although we believe that further testing of theory will help us better understand family life, such an undertaking is often avoided by researchers. As James White and David Klein (2002) conclude, "It is much more glamorous to work on something that nobody else has worked on before" (p. 238).

The work of refining current theory can begin by assessing its importance and relevance. For instance, although the dialectic theory of Leslie Baxter and Barbara Montgomery has effectively framed a number of studies in family communication, and we have used it in this book, the theory could undergo even further refinement. As Baxter and Montgomery (1996) admit, "We do not view our articulation of a dialogic alternative as finalized or definitive, indeed, to do so would violate the indeterminacy that characterizes all dialogues" (p. xv). Therefore, even some of the more established theoretical approaches to family communication should continue to evolve. And this call has been addressed by some (see Baxter, 2011).

We also believe that theory can have additional importance when it is introduced into studies involving various cultures. In fact, some writers have argued that since racism and sexism often pervade a number of cultural arenas, we are especially in need of theory to explain their meaning in different cultural frameworks (West, 1996; West & McCall, 1997). Culture, as a variable, is important for theoretical thinking and should be incorporated into theories we use to explain family communication. In this way, as we have suggested, we will be aided in the generalization process. For example, Kathleen Galvin (1999) observes that we may understand dialectics in a new way if we apply it to the study of African American families in order to illuminate race as a critical family variable. The dialectics of integration and segregation may help us understand tensions inherent in our culture and tensions that permeate family communication within a multicultural society.

In addition, we need to think about theories that incorporate a diversity of perspectives. As we discussed in Chapter 2, theories grow out of intellectual traditions that carry with them certain assumptions about human beings. Glen Stamp (2004) studied what intellectual traditions grounded studies in the family literature. He found, overwhelmingly, that researchers adopted a positivist/empirical approach when studying the family. Over 90 percent of the 1,254 articles he surveyed were identified as growing out of this intellectual tradition. Only 6.46 percent of the sample were identified as interpretive/hermeneutic, and fewer than 2 percent were from the critical tradition. There is some indication (Baxter & Braithwaite, 2006) that when only family communication research is studied, the number of empirically grounded studies decreases (to approximately 76 percent of the total studied), but this perspective still informs the majority of research undertaken in the family area.

We need to think about how embracing other perspectives might enable us to understand and explain family communication more comprehensively. A balanced representation of all these intellectual traditions would allow for a dialogue among scholars, which would be productive for our research findings (Baxter & Braithwaite, 2006). As White and Klein (2002) observe, the trend is now for a new respect for diverse philosophies and approaches to theory and theory-building. They acknowledge that this means there will be no one grand theory explaining everything about families but rather more mid-range and mini-theories to accommodate the complexity of family interaction. Further, these theories are more often than not, according to White and Klein, going to be grounded in critical and interpretive philosophies.

Finally, we may want to think about applying some theories that have a long history in other areas to our studies of family communication. As Leslie Baxter and Dawn Braithwaite (2006) suggest, theories like symbolic convergence theory and goals-plans-action theory can be applied to communication in families with good results.

Family Communication in Neglected and Understudied Populations

Many areas of family life and many family types have been virtually ignored by family communication scholars. For example, researching communication behaviors in at-risk families will result in a more comprehensive understanding of family life, and in this book we have introduced you to marginalized families in our society. Yet, very little communication research has investigated families who are homeless or families at or below the poverty line. The communication of at-risk families may or may not be similar to that of other families. Possible research questions include the following: Are there marked differences between communication rules in homeless families and families with homes? Are the discipline practices of homeless parents similar to those of parents who are not homeless? Does homelessness affect the ways family members express affection to one another? How does homelessness affect role behavior in families? The answers to such questions will not only be thought-provoking but may assist us in responding to a serious social dilemma in our larger culture.

Similarly, research examining the impact of aging on family communication is a relatively overlooked area with great research potential. More than 25 percent of the U.S. population is 65 years old or older (Dickson, Christian, & Remmo, 2004). Longer life expectancies have led to more children knowing and being cared for by grandparents and great grandparents (Turner, 2012). Additionally as life expectancies creep up each year as a result of new medical technologies, families must be prepared to deal with aging family members. Throughout this book, we have noted that older family members are changing the profile of the contemporary family in the United States. Extended family configurations are increasing, and families are developing new ways to handle this cultural shift. At the same time that life expectancies are increasing, family size is decreasing, with more and more couples having fewer and fewer children (Fishman, 2012). These demographic trends are prompting what Ted Fishman calls "the challenge of our age." We must learn how to live in extended families again, and how to develop close-knit community ties to replace the shrinking number of blood ties that may exist for social support.

With 90 percent of care for elderly persons coming from families, caring for aging and elderly family members is fast becoming a cultural trend. Robert Del Campo, Diana Del Campo, and Marcilla DeLeon (2000) observe that nearly 25 percent of households are caring for older family members. Further, Del Campo and his colleagues state that U.S. citizens who are 85 years old and older "constitute the fastest-growing segment of the older population" (p. 1). To place this in context, let's briefly discuss what the implications are for caretakers of elderly family members.

In years past, caring for elderly family members was an easier process than it is today in many middle-class families. Years ago gender roles in many families in the United States were less abstract and fluid than they are today. Men were the primary financial providers for families, and women were the primary homemakers. This translated into women usually staying home, caring for the children. Although an aging family member certainly would have changed the family dynamics, traditional family arrangements seemed to be more equipped to handle this family event. Today, however, things are entirely

Student Perspective: Patsy

The first thing I thought about when you mentioned aging family members is when my grandma came to live with my family when I was around 11 years old. My grandpa had died, and I remember that a few years after that Gram would have trouble getting downstairs to do her washing and ironing. She loved her basement because it sort of represented a quiet place for her to escape to. One day I remember her coming over to our house for Sunday lunch (she lived across the street and came over quite a bit), and she told my mom that she didn't think she could live by herself anymore. Gram was heartbroken because my grandpa was no longer with her, but she also felt that she couldn't climb up and down the stairs by herself any longer. I recall my dad and mom crying with her at the kitchen table. Maybe it was a realization that we all need family in difficult times.

different. Del Campo and his colleagues (2000) articulate the difficulties many adult caregivers face: working full-time, caring for the finances of the aging family member, keeping up with the family member's home and its general repairs, and providing transportation (for example, to the pharmacy, grocery store, dentist, physician). These responsibilities are compounded by the need to shuttle children to and from school and after-school activities, check children's homework, and attend to regular household tasks. Finally, there are the potential difficulties of arranging one's work schedule to accommodate and accomplish each of these duties. Del Campo and his colleagues (2000) conclude by noting that "after these tasks are accomplished, whatever time (if any) is left is spent with a spouse or on personal pursuits" (p. 2). Thus, there is a delicate balance between being responsible for an aging family member and maintaining one's own family unit.

In order to ameliorate some of the challenges facing caregivers of aging family members, a number of Web sites have been constructed that address this family circumstance (e.g., *www.usa.gov/Topics/Seniors.shtml, www. seniors.org,* and *www.careguide.org*). In addition, the American Association of Retired Persons (AARP) provides a number of suggestions for effectively caring for an aging family member, which are given in Table 10-1.

Our discussion thus far focuses on caring for an aging family member within one's household. However, as the AARP notes, in today's mobile society, it is common for family members to live at a distance from a member who is in need of assistance. Because long-distance caregivers are not able to personally visit and provide care on a regular basis, they can feel guilty for not spending more time with the family member. The AARP suggests that long-distance caregivers consider the suggestions listed in Table 10-2. Caring for an aging family member has to be handled with thoughtful consideration for not only the individual needing care but also the immediate family members whose lives will most likely be affected for a long period

TABLE 10-1   Suggestions for Handling the Care of an Aging Family Member
(In the Family Household)

Determine Whom to Involve

Consult more than immediate family and close friends. Community and religious organizations are frequently available allies. Suggest small ways to help, including watering lawns and flowers, running small errands, and taking care of pets.

Ask For Help When Needed

Don't feel that you have to have all the answers and all the resources. Seek out people who have extra free time, such as retirees.

Involve the Aging Family Member When Possible

Unless the family member has some cognitive dysfunction, include him or her in your decision making regarding things such as assisted care, meal preferences, and so forth. The aging family member should always be properly aware of any legal decisions you make and should have a central voice in those decisions.

Be Careful of Starting Disputes

Strategize what you want to say to an aging family member. Use a relaxed approach and anticipate reactions. Be prepared to avoid long-standing family disputes in decision making.

Take Care of Your Own Needs

Recognize the strain of caretaking and be especially aware of your limits. Give yourself credit when you do something worthwhile, and reward yourself with free time as necessary. Learn coping skills and seek out community support for your efforts. Take care of your health, including diet, sleep, and exercise.

---

of time. Most of the suggestions in Tables 10-1 and 10-2 focus on communication practices (see *www.aarp.org* for more information).

Jon Nussbaum (1991) and his colleagues Mary Lee Hummert and John Wiemann have been instrumental in helping us understand the roles that loneliness and aging play in families (Hummert, Nussbaum, & Wiemann, 1994). Although we all realize that our parents, we ourselves, and our extended family networks will age, many of us are ill prepared to deal with the stress associated with the aging process. Not all of the effects of aging are stressful. At times, laughing with aging relatives as they share personal narratives can be beneficial to family members. Further, since the elders of the family are often the tellers of family stories and the keepers of family history, it is important to investigate how narratives are passed from generation to generation, as well as how elders are treated in different families when they share family stories. In an era when baby boomers are themselves aging, life spans are increasing, and Alzheimer's disease affects many elderly persons, we are in great need of securing additional research in this area. As Hummert, Nussbaum, and Wiemann (1994) comment, "The richness of the aging process is perhaps best demonstrated by the adaptive interpersonal behaviors of older adults as they cope with various pleasures and difficulties in life" (p. 4).

TABLE 10-2 Suggestions for Handling the Care of an Aging Family Member (Outside the Family Household)

Make the Most of Your Visits

Talk with the family member when you do visit him or her. Observe important issues, such as eating and exercise habits, home safety, and task management. Try to allow yourself sufficient time to make important decisions about future arrangements. Include time to socialize and to enjoy each other's company.

Gather Information on the Community

Use phone and Internet resources to determine which places can provide services to the family member. Research agencies and compare costs and availability. Consider waiting lists. Work with local aging agencies in locating credible and responsible geriatric care managers.

Work with the Family Member to Help Her or Him Accept the Services You Find

Be sure to secure important medical information, such as doctor names and phone numbers. Be sure to compile a list of all medications and allergies. Develop a legal document that identifies financial issues important to both of you. Be sure to have copies of wills, birth certificates, and insurance cards.

Be Careful of Starting Disputes

Regardless of distance, it's possible to make the family member angry. Avoid those heated discussions, be sensitive to the life experience of the family member, and tread carefully in legal and financial matters.

Identify People Your Family Member Can Call On

Be prepared to introduce yourself to a family member's friends or other relatives. Keep a list of their phone numbers handy. If you can't reach the family member and are concerned, calling his or her friends or other family members can help calm you while you're not there. These individuals may also be able to help out in an emergency.

Know When Your Help Is Needed

Over the miles, a family member may communicate various impressions. Don't be alarmed by issues that the family member is able to resolve, and stay involved in the issues that may ultimately require your assistance. Keep informed, but maintain respect for the family member's life.

Related to issues of aging, communication researchers need to explore family relationships of later-life adults. In particular, this necessitates an emphasis on marriage, divorce, and remarriage in later life (Dickson, Christian, & Remmo, 2004) as well as grandparent–grandchild relationships (Soliz, Lin, Anderson, & Harwood, 2006; Turner, 2012). When examining marriage in later life, Fran Dickson and her colleagues note that many stressors attend these marriages. For instance, older adults must contend with end-of-life issues, may have to struggle to re-create a partner-focused rather than a child-focused relationship, and may have to let go of past marital disappointment brought to light by the reflection that comes with aging. All of these stressors are mediated by communication and provide a rich research agenda. As Fran Dickson, Allison Christian, and Clyde Remmo (2004) conclude, "Future research needs to examine the impact of the challenges that face later-life individuals and couples" (p. 166).

Grandparenting is an important and meaningful process, representing a growing relationship. Peter Uhlenberg and James Kirby (1998) estimated that almost 70 percent of children are born into families with all their grandparents living. By age 10, 40 percent of all children still have all their grandparents alive. Tavia Simmons and Grace O'Neill (2001) note that many of these grandparents and grandchildren live together. They estimated that 3.9 million households in the United States contained both grandparents and grandchildren in 2000. Nearly half of all grandparents living with their grandchildren are custodial grandparents (Simmons & Dye, 2003).

Despite the prevalence of this intergenerational relationship, communication researchers haven't investigated it much. Jordan Soliz, Mei-Chen Lin, Karen Anderson, and Jake Harwood (2006) comment that there are many reasons for this lack of attention: It's been conceptualized too simplistically as an idealized relationship punctuated with treats and cozy, loving interactions; it's overshadowed by the parent–child relationship; and the Western emphasis on the nuclear family has diminished researchers' interest in grandparents. However, Soliz and his colleagues suggest that this is an unfortunate situation. Researchers should begin putting grandparents and grandchildren on their agenda. There is much to be learned about what makes this a special, satisfying relationship and the communication variables that relate to more or less satisfaction in this relationship.

Changing demographics in the United States do not only pertain to age. Communication in biracial families forms a rich area for future research for many reasons, not the least of which is the fact that the number of biracial families is increasing fourfold on the average in the United States (U.S. Census Bureau, 1990). According to Michael Lind (1998), 1 out of every 25 married couples in the United States is interracial. Communication researchers need to discuss the communication variations within bi- and multiracial families. Families consisting of more than one race must deal with issues related to language and communication. Moreover, because various races have various interpretations of relational development (Williams, Clinton, & Wyatt, 1995), it would be worthwhile to assess the rule construction and rule adherence within multiracial families.

Although stepfamilies have not been totally ignored in the family communication research, much more attention could be paid to this family form. Chapter 8 focused on stress—expected and unexpected—in families. One stressor we discussed was divorce. We believe that an important line of inquiry for future research focuses on the reconfiguring of family life and family communication after divorce or multiple divorces. As we mentioned previously, the number of those getting divorced is not as important as what goes on during and after a divorce. Research by Elizabeth Graham (1996, 2003) and Sandra Metts and William Cupach (1995) are welcome additions to the literature on postdivorce relations. We suggest examining the role of divorce from the eyes of the children involved as well. All too often younger people are not surveyed for their impressions and experiences. If conducted ethically and thoughtfully, research studies discussing findings emanating from the voices of children will be extremely useful to many community resource agencies as well as to communication theory.

Divorce and remarriage bring with them a host of new and evolving relationships. Communicating across these reconfigured families is a challenge and an area ripe for research. As Tamara Afifi and Kellie Hamrick (2006) note, studying communication processes and practices in postdivorce families can give us insight into why some families are successful at reconfiguring their families and others are not. Even though the circumstances may be similar, families respond quite differently to postdivorce challenges. Questions ranging from the names for the new "kin" created through remarriages to the disclosure of divorce decisions provide fertile ground for communication research. Further, as Professor Sassi's research project, discussed in the chapter opening, illustrates, reconfigured gay and lesbian families provide another unique context for examining family communication.

We have spoken about homeless families, aging families, biracial families, and stepfamilies as fertile ground for communication researchers. These are certainly not all the understudied populations to which researchers can turn their attention. In addition, there are many family relationships that are extremely important to people's lives but that remain relatively unexplored. Aunts and their nieces and nephews (Ellingson & Sotirin, 2010) form one such relationship, and siblings are another (Fingerman & Hay, 2002; Mikkelson, Myers, & Hannawa, 2011). Most people live in families with aunts and siblings, but we have not fully examined the very important communication practices that constitute these relationships. We're sure you can think of memorable communication with aunts, siblings, grandparents, or some other relative. These are the interactions family communication researchers need to explore in the future.

Work–Life Issues

Family communication researchers need to complement the work that organizational communication scholars have begun. These scholars are exploring conflicts that arise when family life encroaches into the job arena (Ashcraft, 1999; Farley-Lucas, 2000; Jorgenson, 2001; Kirby, 2000; Kirby & Krone, 2002; Medved, 2004; Medved & Heisler, 2002). This body of research examines how managers deal with problems of home life that intrude into workers' job responsibilities. Further, organizational communication researchers have been interested in how policies have been constructed to moderate challenges between home and work life. Family leave policies, for instance, are of interest to these scholars. Yet, little empirical work has investigated the impact of the organization making inroads into our family lives. Here is a good opportunity for family communication researchers to make a contribution. Future research should question the ways in which families use communication to separate and manage their home lives and their work lives.

Throughout history in the United States, tensions between public and private as well as issues of race and class have cast the family in a variety of positions with regard to the workplace. For white, middle-class families within the last 100 years, family has been conceived of as radically different from the workplace. Home has been seen as the safe haven from the storm of the work world. Recently, however, the meanings and boundaries distinguishing these domains have been complicated in discussions about work–life issues, dual earner or dual career couples, telework, and various flexible work arrangements (e.g., Edley, 2004; Kirby, Golden, Medved, Jorgensen, & Buzzanell, 2003). If workers do their jobs in their homes, how is the separation maintained?

Further complicating the situation is the fact that in some popular and scholarly discussions, work relations are looked to for remedies to the stress and tensions of family relations. These discussions posit that connections at work are more stable and reassuring than those outside of work (Hochschild, 1997). At the same time, "balancing" work and home life has come to be considered a critical "problem" with families becoming isolated from community networks (Fondas, 1995) and "family time" structured in opposition to work time (Ciulla, 2000).

Perhaps the most popular metaphor in both scholarly and popular discourse is that of "balancing work and family." Communication researchers can investigate this metaphor to see if it is helpful or if it simply encourages us to add another obligation—the obligation to "balance" disparate demands (Sotirin, Turner, & Buzzanell, 2005). Some researchers have questioned whether balance as an end is attainable within isolated nuclear family units (Duckworth & Buzzanell, 2009). The irony of balance may be that this state is never achieved; balancing life–work demands is an exercise in futility. Communication researchers need to investigate whether balancing is the best metaphor to use and also how families achieve a sense of satisfaction with work and home issues. Communication practices surely must be used in this process, and how that is accomplished suggests an important research agenda.

CULTURAL DISCOURSE ABOUT THE FAMILY

The previous section on research areas leads us to a consideration of what people are currently discussing about family life. Future areas of research are often grounded in current areas of public debate. Out of the many topics that occupy public concern, we turn now to consider two: technology and co-parenting.

The Impact of Technology on Family Life

Technology affects family communication in many ways, some of which include: the impact of computers, social media, smartphones, e-mail, remote control devices, iPods, and so forth. But technological advances also strike at the very definition of family and human life. These potential effects of technology are being mulled over in the popular press. Margaret Talbot (2001) discusses cloning and its relationship to the family in an article in the *New York Times Magazine.* Talbot recounts how, after a 10-month-old baby boy died, his grieving parents strongly believed that his genes "were crying out, as a ghost might, to express themselves again in this world. The idea preoccupied them that their little son's genotype deserved another chance, that it had disappeared by mistake and could be brought back by intention" (p. 40). Talbot notes that, had the couple's son died sometime in the more distant past, the couple's conviction that he deserved another chance to live would have had to fade away. But with our current technological power to clone, the parents were able to turn to a group, the Raelians, to try to marry their conviction to our technological advances.

Bioethicists, according to Talbot (2001), have for the most part endorsed cloning as a "reproductive right," framing it as an extension of other technologies intended to help infertile adults. Ronald Green, a professor of ethics at Darmouth and an adviser to a company called Advanced Cell Technologies, states that there are three groups of people who might benefit from cloning: (1) couples in which the woman lacks viable eggs or the man lacks viable sperm, (2) lesbian parents (and to a lesser extent gay men, since they would still need a female surrogate), and (3) people with serious genetic disorders who still wish to have a biological child (cited in Talbot, 2001).

Student Perspective: David Alan

I couldn't believe the discussion we had about cloning. I do not think that will ever happen—at least I hope it doesn't. I don't even like the fact that couples can know what sex their child will be in advance. When my brother and his wife had their baby last year, all their friends made fun of them because they didn't want to know whether it was a boy or a girl before the baby was born. They took a lot of heat for being "old-fashioned." I don't get it. It seems antireligious to me because of that creepy feeling of "ordering" a child's personality and looks. It's really strange.

Talbot interviewed Rael, the founder of the Raelians, who told her that cloning is simply the wave of the future. He compared the qualms that Talbot raised with the resistance people felt when the first test-tube baby was born. Now, as he notes, test-tube babies are commonplace. The same will be true of cloning, he asserts. Talbot (2001) suggests that Rael is "merely the surreal version of other more respectable biotech utopians" (p. 68), and she notes that UCLA's Gregory Stock told her that new reproductive technologies will replace sex as the means of reproduction. Sex will be solely recreational, as we will be too concerned with our children to leave their fate to "a random meeting of sperm and egg" (p. 68). Bobbie Blanchard's grandmother and aunt, from our opening vignette, agree about future parents having the ability to choose their children's attributes. Talbot cites Lee Silver, a molecular biologist at Princeton University, who says that parents will be able to choose genes that increase musical, athletic, and cognitive abilities in their children.

The Raelians plan to use surrogate mothers to carry the cloned embryo, and in the case of the family who lost their 10-month-old son, they have surrogates lined up to serve after they create a clone from one of the dead boy's cells. Further, they have a list of 100 people, including some homosexual couples, who have expressed an interest in expanding their families through cloning. They claim to prefer this technique to using a sperm bank because it gives them the ability to have a child with their own genes.

Talbot (2001) concludes with the thorny psychological and sociological problems a family with cloned members will have to face. She questions how the cloned child will feel, "being forced to play out some complicated re-enactment of a parent's or dead relative's life" (p. 68). Further, she raises the issue of creating "genetic haves and have-nots." Finally, she notes the feeling shared by many, that science "is accelerating beyond our capacity to comprehend it—let alone control it" (p. 68). In the midst of this accelerating pace, we have to question whether family relations will be inexorably altered if some members are specifically created according to others' desires. How, for example, will parents discipline children that they have cloned from the tissue of their deceased siblings? How will children react to

Student Perspective: Louie

I know a lot of the students in class disagreed with me, but I have to think that the Raelians make some sense. Before when I had heard about cloning it didn't mean much to me. It seemed to just be about a bunch of scientists and sheep. And I guess I thought it was really in the realm of science fiction. But when I read about the Raelians it really made me think. Now it seems like it is a realistic possibility to clone someone. I know lots of others in class thought cloning sounded gross and maybe even against religion. But maybe no one else in class has lost a sibling like I have. I know I would do anything to get Angie back, even something as far-out sounding as cloning. And I know my parents would, too. It did seem like Angie was taken away from us before she should have been—she was only eight years old. If there really were a way to take her genes and make someone just like her, I would jump at the chance to do it. She was the best little sister in the world.

the knowledge that they are duplicates of a child that died? How will parents encourage athletic ability, for instance, if they are responsible for selecting the exact genes that produce it? How will families communicate religious principles about the origin of life and the will of God when humans utilize technology in this fashion? Clearly, this is an area in which discourse about the family, communication within the family, technology, and religious beliefs and spirituality all intersect (Tierny, 2007).

Co-Parenting

Co-parenting, which occurs when biological parents ask close friends or relatives for assistance in the lifelong care and nurture of their children, is a topic that has also entered public discourse. Further, it is closer to actualization than some of the technological advances we have just discussed, because there are many families living with co-parenting systems currently. In fact, as Andy Steiner (2001) observes, co-parenting is actually an old concept. The tradition of asking close friends of family to play a key role in a child's upbringing goes back to the fourth century. There are even words for people who play such a role, *comater* and *copater,* that can be traced to the end of the sixth century. And, as Georgiana Arnold and Princess Jackson-Smith (2001) state, there has always been a tradition in the African American community of single women without children interacting with the children of their friends and family members.

The cultural tradition of co-parenting within the African American community is also discussed by Bryant Alexander and H. Paul LeBlanc (1999), who state that in the African American community a system of shared values allowed other adults to discipline children in place of their biological parents (*in loco parentis*). Alexander and LeBlanc's respondents spoke to them about the family traditions that promoted family values within their household and noted that these were reinforced within the larger community. They point out that "family was practiced throughout the community and not just within the close confines of the home" (p. 200). Thus, a sense of shared parenting was encouraged along the lines of the African proverb that it takes a village to raise a child.

Student Perspective: Emma

When I read about the co-parenting idea, I thought that everything old is new again. I am a returning student in my 50s, and when I was raising my children in the 1960s, we lived on a commune. Everyone called us hippies, but now I see it's called co-parenting. But whatever you call it, it does make a lot of sense. No one person can do everything that children really need, and it is certainly nice to help out. Plus, taking care of kids and the home can be a lonely and isolating thing; it's great to have other adults around to talk and share the load with.

Andy Steiner (2001) observes that co-parents can be a huge help to single parents, dual-career families, and families living far from their extended biological families. In many ways, the co-parenting arrangements that Steiner reviews suggest a change in the definition of family along the lines we have stressed in this text. For example, Steiner writes of Holly Coughlin, who co-parents Chantz, the nine-year-old son of her ex-partner. Coughlin no longer keeps in touch with her ex, but she has remained close with Chantz's mother, Coughlin's ex-partner's former wife. Coughlin and this woman share time with Chantz, attending school conferences and dinners together. Steiner reports that one difficulty of their relationship is the lack of relational names for each other. They reject *co-parent* because it sounds too formal, so for Coughlin they use *ate,* a Filipino word for an older woman who cares for a child although she is not related by blood. Coughlin refers to Chantz as *ading,* which is Filipino for a younger person who is a close friend.

In other examples, co-parenting is more an extension of family definitions we have always held. Steiner (2001) also writes about a lesbian couple, Cynthia Scott and Cathy Hoffman, who are godmothers to Hannah and Natalie Owens-Pike. They suggest that they are not godmothers who teach the girls religion or take them to Sunday school, but rather they are like a "second set of parents" (p. 72). Steiner notes that for Scott and Hoffman, who have chosen to have no children of their own, being godmothers allows them to have children in their lives without all of the responsibility of being full-time parents.

As Princess Jackson-Smith says in her article with Georgiana Arnold, "not having had children has allowed me to arrange my life in a certain way, but if I care about my world then I still am responsible to society. I have the time, energy, and financial leeway that lots of parents don't have, and I can share these with children in my community" (Arnold & Jackson-Smith, 2001, p. 79). Jackson-Smith notes that she and her husband have a five-year-old "friend" whose single mother must travel for business at times. Jackson-Smith and her husband often have their friend stay with them while his mother is out of town. In this co-parenting arrangement, the biological mother gets support, the child receives care, and the Jackson-Smiths enjoy the companionship of this child without the full responsibility for his care. Co-parenting is another aspect of family life that has entered the public discourse and that provokes thought about our definitions of family life and our expectations for the future of family configuration and interaction.

THINKING ABOUT FAMILY COMMUNICATION: FOUR CONCLUSIONS

We have introduced a number of significant issues related to families in this text, and now we wish to discuss four conclusions that guide our thinking about communication in the family. As we discuss these conclusions, keep in mind that we do not pretend to have all of the answers regarding so complex a subject as the family. Your own thoughts and experiences are enormously important. As we have noted, knowledge exists in the space between our own lived experience and the experiences of families that are very different from our own. Throughout this book we have tried to engage you in thinking beyond your own direct experiences with families. By introducing you to a variety of different kinds of families, we hope we have broadened your understanding of family communication.

Recognition of Diversity in Family Communication

As we mentioned in Chapter 1, there are many ways to classify families, based on race, ethnicity, demographics, and interaction type (such as closed, open, random, or separate, independent, and traditional). Each classification refers to families with different identities and goals, most of which affect their communication behavior. Although this multiplicity of family life and its effects on communication may seem confusing, we argue that such diversity is cause for celebration, not trepidation. When Mr. Spector gave Bobbie's class the homework assignment in our opening vignette, he was interested in examining the diversity inherent in families now and in the future. By understanding more about the variety of influences on family communication, we can be more precise in our conclusions about how families communicate.

However, we also understand the difficulty in generalizing across families based on any of these classifying variables. For instance, not all African American parents discipline their children similarly (Socha, Sanchez-Hucles, Bromley, & Kelly, 1995), nor do all Jewish families practice their religion in the same way. As Fred Jandt (2004) concludes, "The diversity within cultures probably exceeds the differences between cultures" (p. 8). Nonetheless, we have tried to identify findings that have empirical support from a variety of research studies. Although we acknowledge the diversity *within* various cultures and co-cultures, we also acknowledge the need to provide some generalizations about these groups for discussion purposes. Thus Professor Sassi's research, in our chapter opening, will help us understand gay and lesbian families, although his findings will not hold true in *all* such families. In this endeavor, your role as a critical thinker becomes very important.

Understanding family diversity and how it affects family communication is challenging. Sometimes our efforts are hampered by false assumptions we bring to the task. These false assumptions may be grounded in outdated stereotypes of various racial and ethnic groups; intolerance toward some family types, such as cohabitors or gay and lesbian families; or ethnocentrism. We hope we have given you some tools throughout this text that will help you understand how families align with, and diverge from, their cultural values. At least, we hope you are now less likely to assume that all families behave just like your family, or that they should. Family communication is shaped by a family's makeup, which includes culture, race, ethnicity, religion, and many other elements. Thus, there are similarities in the ways that Irish Catholic families communicate, for example, that result from their similar backgrounds. However, we always include the caveat that no two families have an identical makeup. Therefore, not all Irish Catholic families will be completely alike in their communication behaviors, because of differences such as how many generations they have been in the United States, what region of the United States they settled in, or how strongly they adhere to their religion. As Guy Hernandez from our opening vignette suggests, not all cohabiting couples will behave in the same way either. Despite research to the contrary, Guy asserts that he and Kate have the ability to have a successful marriage if they want one.

Recognition of the Challenges of Family Communication

The ability to articulate views, defend positions, and clarify misconceptions through communication is seen by many as the cornerstone of effective family functioning. Expressive and well-timed self-disclosure has also been shown to help couples in troublesome times. Further, the ability to communicate positive comments to others contributes to another's positive self-concept. Sven Wahlroos (1995) remarks that "the key to improvement of family relationships—and thereby to emotional health in general—lies in communication" (p. 3). Such a claim finds grounds in an optimistic view privileging direct and open communication.

Yet, as we have mentioned before, different families view communication differently. Open communication is not always practiced or embraced similarly across diverse cultures. Further, even in cultures that value direct communication, family communication is not always positive or life enhancing. Communication knits the fabric of family identity and satisfaction, but communication may unravel that fabric as well. We note Steve Duck's (1994b) thoughts about the negative side of relationship development: "For some people, intimacy and closeness are terrifying . . . ; for others, love is maniacally disruptive and jealousy provoking . . . ; for others, the thought of acceptance is deeply revolting" (pp. 5–6). We are reminded of those family members who teach other family members distrust. We can also point to individuals who use their communication skills for manipulation. Further, we can each probably identify at least a few people who have coerced others through their communication. Saying "I need you" or "I want a divorce unless you do what I say," for instance, can exert force on listeners, changing their behaviors. We need to recall, then, that communication is in the eyes (and ears) of the beholder. As we have argued in this book, communication has a negative side for families, and not all family problems are resolved by more communication (Olson, Wilson-Kratzer, & Symonds, 2012).

The role that violence plays in the family is fast becoming a well-researched area, shining a light on a very challenging aspect of some families' lives. In Chapter 7, we noted a number of research teams in family communication who have committed a great deal of time, energy, and emotion to studying family violence. From verbal aggression to overt brutality, the violent acts that take place on a daily basis in families across our country have been revealed. As personally challenging as this research is, we hope to see further research on family violence.

By taking a communication perspective on violence in the family, we conceptualize it as an act with an intention or a perceived intention. Further, we see violence as verbal, nonverbal, or both. Additionally, family violence can be viewed from three dimensions of communication: instrumental, relational, and identity (Cahn, 2009). The instrumental dimension of communication focuses on solving problems, attaining goals, and accomplishing tasks. Dudley Cahn (2009) notes that violence may occur in the family along this dimension when abusers believe they cannot reach their goals because of a potential victim's actions. The relationship dimension of communication concerns creating and maintaining a sense of commitment between people. Cahn observes that abusive families may use relationship issues as the stimulus for abuse (jealousy, for example), and he contends that abuse in the family has relationship implications (it may result in separation, for instance). Finally, the identity dimension of communication centers on communicators maintaining their desired images within interactions. This dimension may emerge in abusive families in two ways, according to Cahn. First, abuse may erupt when abusers feel their identity or self-esteem is attacked in some way. Second, abuse in the family affects the members' sense of identity. Victims may ask themselves what is wrong with them and what did they do to deserve the abuse, for instance. Thus, Cahn relates these three dimensions of communication directly to family violence.

When we conclude that family communication can be negative, we mean to state that family interaction is more complex than simply speaking our minds. Speaking our minds often makes us vulnerable. The more we talk, the more vulnerable we can become. Further, the same behaviors may function differently at different times, making it impossible to impose simple prescriptions on family communication. In some families, perhaps in all families, some of the time, a lack of communication and a lack of clarity can prevent conflict. Sometimes communicating clearly and directly can cause conflict and dissent. Thus, we must recognize the complexity of family communication to understand how families function. Laura Stafford and Marianne Dainton (1994) observe that the dark and bright sides of family interaction operate in dialectical tension with one another, allowing most family members to experience negativity without necessarily suffering extreme adverse effects.

Recognition of the Value of Family Communication in Our Society

Many of us realize the importance that family interaction has in our lives. This is probably the case for two reasons. First, family, as an institution, holds an important place within U.S. culture. Maintaining family relations seems to be a cultural expectation in our society. Over 90 percent of all Americans marry during their lifetimes. Although, as we have discussed throughout this text, "contemporary family arrangements in the United States are diverse, fluid, and unresolved" (Stacey, 1994, pp. 645–646), the notion of some type of family grouping still persists for people. Mr. Spector's assignment to Bobbie Blanchard's class, from our opening vignette, reflects a presumption that the family, albeit in altered forms, will continue to be an important social institution in the future.

Second, the interaction patterns learned in one's family-of-origin endure for most people. This statement has two implications. First, according to a social learning model, people tend to learn interaction from the interaction they experience and observe in their early lives. Thus, for example, families who talk about current events at their nightly dinner table establish the importance of family talk for their members, as well as put a value on connecting family interaction to the wider world. The second implication centers on the effect of communication on individual development. The social constructivist approach we have described in this text grows out of a symbolic interactionist perspective, which argues that an individual's sense of self develops in interaction with significant others. Family members fit this category. Thus, family interaction contributes to a sense of individual identity and self-worth for family members.

Recognition of Changing Times

Throughout this book, we have noted that family systems continually evolve. Through this evolution, family members attempt to make sense of their experiences. Families must adapt and evolve as they grow. Growth brings change, and change necessitates adaptation. As the systems model proposes, families recalibrate their communication behaviors as the system evolves. In addition to internal changes, however, families also must respond to external events, many of which challenge a family's communication patterns. As Lillian Rubin (1994) asserts, "What happens in the social, economic, and political world outside the family affects life inside" (p. xiv). Two issues we focused on in this text illustrate Rubin's observation.

First, families must balance their own approaches to family life and communication with idealized versions. We have argued that society has an idealized image of what a family "should" be. As Stephanie Coontz (1992) asserts, there are a number of "myths and half-truths that surround our understanding of American families" (p. 6). Outdated views and antiquated orientations may explain the existence of these illusions. We believe that many

Student Perspective: Dante

I'm an art major, and I never thought this family communication course would make a difference in my life. Was I wrong! During Thanksgiving, I noticed a lot of the stuff we learned going on in my family. There was my sister talking about her miscarriage (self-disclosure), my niece and nephew fighting over the remote control (conflict), my brother telling us the trouble he's having being both a father and a husband (dialectics), and my aunt Karina telling us about her honeymoon with Uncle Bap (storytelling). I can't believe this stuff is all around us and we all take it for granted.

~\|\|\~ POPULAR PRESS PERSPECTIVES ~\|\|\~

In 2009, Brad Stone noted in the *New York Times* that "breakfast can wait. The day's first stop is online." Stone was writing about the trend in families to stay connected to some electronic device during all their waking hours. For instance, Stone profiles the Gude family of East Lansing, Michigan, who remember a time not so long ago when they and their two sons ate breakfast together while engaging in conversation. But, as Stone notes,

> *That was so last century. Today, Mr. Gude wakes at around 6 a.m. to check his work e-mail and his Facebook and Twitter accounts. The two boys, Cole and Erik, start each morning with text messages, video games, and Facebook. The new routine quickly became a source of conflict in the family, with Ms. Gude complaining that technology was eating into family time. But ultimately even she partially succumbed, cracking open her laptop after breakfast. (n.p.)*

Stone continues to discuss how technology has "shaken up" many families' routines and rituals. In the Gude family, for example, texts are now a common way for the family to interact with one another. The two sons sleep with their phones at their bedside, and Mr. Gude sends them texts to wake them up in the morning. "We use texting as an in-house intercom," he said. "I could just walk upstairs, but they always answer their texts." The Gudes recently began shutting their devices down on weekends to allow for a return to family time.

Brad Stone. "Breakfast can wait. The day's first stop is online." *New York Times* (online). August 9, 2009. Retrieved April 3, 2011.

---

people in the United States operate under a limited vision of what a family looks like. The media perpetuate a narrow vision of the family and do not present the rich diversity of family life for us to view. This challenges families to find ways to talk about the roles and relationships they experience but do not see in the idealized family.

Second, as the external context changes around the family, demands are placed on the family requiring flexible and creative communication. Technology often complicates family life. The interface of technology with reproduction illustrates why families are often faced with difficult choices. For instance, medical technology has radically altered the conception process. Alternative insemination, in vitro fertilization, and surrogate motherhood are a few of the ways in which childbirth has been redesigned. In addition, genetic counseling has found its way into the conversations of couples seeking children. As recently as 30 years ago, these processes were not an option; today, millions of couples are engaging in these alternatives for human reproduction. Discussing these options across generations and incorporating these nontraditional conception methods into our definition of the family are challenges for many. In addition, communication technologies have altered the ways that families connect with one another (see Popular Press Perspectives box).

In sum, family communication needs to be envisioned in its complexity, embracing much diversity, providing many challenges, holding a strong significance for family members, and responding to many ongoing changes related to the family's external context.

SUMMARY

Currently in the United States we are experiencing unprecedented redefinitions and reinterpretations of what constitutes a family. Simultaneously, we experience confusion over how to examine and understand the communication that takes place within the family. Here, we have discussed a number of directions for future research in family communication. Further, we discussed three trends that are part of our cultural discourse about the family. These three trends point the way toward the future and shape the present. Finally, we drew four conclusions about family communication. We recognize that our suggestions, recommendations, and considerations are not exhaustive—they are a beginning. We hope, as you have read through the book, you have also thought about areas that would be fruitful for further investigation and that provoked your thinking about the future.

As we close this book, we encourage you to keep an open mind as you and others discuss the future of our families and communication within the family. You can help shape how conversations about the family evolve, your voice can be a powerful contributor to daily public and family discourse. And with the great diversity of families in our society, much more research, thinking, and discussion must take place. As we suggest, family communication is complex, significant, and challenging. We hope taking this course and reading this book have inspired you to think critically and carefully about family communication in your own life and across the diverse tapestry of families in the United States and other cultures.

QUESTIONS FOR REFLECTION

1. Give one to three concrete examples of the ways a recognition of diversity would enhance our understanding of family communication behaviors.

2. Explain how acknowledging the negative side of family communication helps us to understand communication patterns in families.

3. What questions would you generate for future research on family communication? What areas do you think are most important to study? Why?

4. Do you agree with Guy Hernandez that he and Kate could beat the odds and have a successful marriage? What would influence you to accept or reject research findings such as those Kate learned about in class?

5. What questions might you research to take a communication perspective on aging families?

6. How might you research a specific family communication challenge, such as telling children about sexuality and sexually transmitted diseases?

7. What difference does it make if we have commonly accepted relationship terms for relations like co-parents? Generate some labels for relationships that do not currently have labels—for example, what relationship does Holly Coughlin have to Chantz's biological mother?

8. What do you think about the prospect of "replacing" deceased family members with clones? Does it matter if the deceased died at 10 months or 38 years? How would cloning affect family communication patterns in your opinion?

9. What theoretical insights have helped you understand family communication practices?

Glossary

ABC-X model A model that explains stress (X) as the result of a stressor (A) combined with a family's perceptions of the stressor (C) and their resources for dealing with it (B).

accounts A special class of narrative, created to explain and control events by the teller.

adaptability A family's ability to recalibrate to respond to stress.

agnostics Individuals who believe there is no proof of God's existence but that God might exist.

annulment A symbolic termination of marriage, indicating that the marriage never existed in the eyes of the church.

atheists Individuals who deny or disbelieve the existence of God.

at-risk families Families whose members, for a variety of reasons, face a high probability of not attaining the basic diet, skills, and credentials society considers necessary for survival.

attachment theory A theoretical perspective explaining adult behaviors by analyzing attachments formed to caregivers in childhood.

autonomy/connection dialectic One of the major tensions characterizing family life. This dialectic represents our simultaneous desires to be independent of our families and to find intimacy with them.

binuclear family Two divorced parents in two different households, with each household sharing responsibility for the children.

biological extended families Families that can include parent(s) and children living together as well as other blood/legal relatives such as aunts, uncles, and grandparents.

birth stories Family stories that retell the circumstances of a child's birth. Often these stories form an important source of identity, creating a sense of how children fit into the family, the roles they should play, and their parents' hopes and dreams for them.

boomerang kids A variation of the extended family. Boomerang kids are adult children who return to their family-of-origin to live with their parents. They may bring children of their own with them. *See also* nesting.

boundaries A property of systems theory holding that families develop boundaries, but because families are open systems, the boundaries are relatively permeable.

boundary ambiguity Lack of clarity concerning who is and is not a part of the family. This may occur in situations of divorce, remarriage, death, and so forth. The ambiguity can be a source of stress for family members.

calendar or clock time   Time measured in equal units. All days have 24 hours, all hours have 60 minutes, and so forth.

calibration   A system principle that involves setting the range of accepted behavior in the family. Calibration involves checking the scale and monitoring feedback to allow for control of this range.

catalyst hypothesis   An explanation for violence positing that coercive and aggressive communication acts as a precursor or catalyst to physically violent episodes in the family.

certainty   The belief in your ability to predict and control your own experiences.

closed family   One of Kantor and Lehr's (1975/1985) family types. The closed family is characterized by fixed space, regular time, and steady energy.

co-culture   Groups of individuals who are part of the larger culture but who—through unity and individual identification around attributes such as race, ethnicity, sexual orientation, religion, and so forth—create unique experiences of their own. These experiences form norms, values, and social structures different from those characterizing the national culture.

cohabiting couples   Two adults with a romantic interest in each other living together without being legally married sometimes referred to as paperless marriage.

cohesion   The degree of emotional connection a family experiences.

collective meaning   A congruent and compatible interpretation of repeated family stories developed by family members.

collectivist cultures   Cultures that place more value on the group than on the individual. Group goals are privileged over individual goals.

common-law marriage   A variation of cohabitation. This type of marriage exists without the formality of a ceremony, and some states, such as Texas, recognize common-law marriage as legal when both partners publicly identify themselves as married.

communication   The process of meaning-making.

comparison level   A standard representing what a person feels she or he should expect regarding costs and rewards from a relationship.

comparison level for alternatives   Measures how people evaluate a relationship compared with realistic alternatives to that relationship.

complementary relationship   A relationship characterized by partners' opposing behaviors. For example, if one partner exhibits passive behaviors while the other is aggressive, their relationship is complementary.

contemporary nuclear family   A family composed of a married couple living with their biological children, but the financial provider may be the mother and the father may stay at home as the caregiver for the children, or both parents may work. *See* dual-career family.

conflict   A process whereby family members perceive a disagreement about goals, rules, roles, culture, and/or patterns of communication.

conflict interaction An element in Cupach and Canary's (1997) model of interpersonal conflict. It refers to the strategies, message tactics, and communication patterns used in a conflict.

contempt The second stage in Gottman's (1994b) model of conflict, in which partners insult and "psychologically abuse" each other. Contempt represents an escalation in the conflict.

content-based conflict A disagreement over a specific subject.

courtship stories Family stories that focus on first meeting, love, dating, and wedding ceremonies. These stories instruct family members in the meaning of love, marriage, and the interplay between cultural expectations and more idiosyncratic family mores and customs.

covenant marriages A relationship that both partners voluntarily enter into. In most cases it requires that couples receive premarital counseling and agree that they may be divorced only after being separated for two years, or if adultery, abandonment, imprisonment, commission of a felony, or domestic abuse can be proved.

critical approach An intellectual tradition positing that knowledge cannot exist apart from ideology; critical theorists are concerned with the ways that the powerful shape knowledge to keep themselves in power. The critical approach implies activism or change to the status quo. Also known as critical theory.

criticism The first stage in Gottman's (1994b) model of conflict. Criticism involves attacking a partner's personality or character, "usually with blame."

culture A way of life that groups hold in common; an organizing concept that creates communities around common languages, symbols, foods, religions, belief systems, and so forth.

cyclic alternation A strategy for managing the dialectic tensions of family life. Cyclic alternation occurs when families choose to feature one of the opposing terms in the tension at particular times, alternating with the other. When families feature closeness with young children and independence when the children are older, they employ cyclic alternation.

decision making The process of getting things done in the family when cooperation of two or more members is needed.

defensiveness The third stage of Gottman's (1994b) model of conflict. In this stage, the partners are unwilling to take responsibility for their behaviors. Defensiveness is characterized by denying responsibility, making excuses, disagreeing, cross-complaining, repeating, and whining.

depth interviews A method that allows interviewers to question respondents in the hopes of obtaining information about a phenomenon of interest.

developmental or normative stressors Life events that may cause change and disruption in the family but are predictable as part of the human growth process.

developmental theory A theory explaining family communication by assessing the developmental stage of the family.

dialectic approach   An approach to understanding family interaction that says that family life is characterized by ongoing tensions between contradictory impulses. Common dialectics exist between closeness and distance, novelty and predictability, and openness and self-protection. Contradictory impulses are seen as normative in family interactions from this perspective.

dialectic thinking   An approach to family functioning that posits the both/and quality of oppositions, locating the dynamic interplay between the opposites in social interaction.

disqualifying   Part of the integration strategy for managing dialectics. Disqualifying neutralizes the dialectic by exempting certain issues from the general pattern. For example, a family might be open in general but have one or two taboo topics that are disqualified from the general pattern of openness.

distal context   An element in Cupach and Canary's (1997) model of conflict. Distal context refers to the backgrounds or personalities of the people in conflict, as well as prior successes or failures in handling conflict. It is the overall "relational environment" in which the conflict occurs.

distal outcomes   An element in Cupach and Canary's (1997) model of conflict. Distal outcomes are the results of the conflict that are not readily apparent at the time of the conflict. They may be removed or delayed, such as personal growth or the development or renegotiation of family rules.

drama   A feature of family stories indicating a sense of conflict or suspense embedded in the narrative. Drama may also be enhanced by the performance of the story; for example, the storyteller may "act out" the story while retelling it.

dual-career family   A family where the husband/father and wife/mother both work outside the home and both act as primary caregivers of children at home. *Also called* two-income family.

dualistic thinking   A perspective on oppositions in family life, such as closeness and distance. Dualism sees closeness and distance (or any opposition) as separate aspects, both of which are needed by families to some degree.

dysfunctional rules   Rules in the family that hinder communication and increase opportunities for chaos, fear, and resistance.

empiricism   An intellectual tradition that assumes there are objective truths that can be uncovered about an object of study. Researchers operating from this tradition strive to be objective and work for control over the important concepts in the study. *See also* positivistic approach.

empty speech   Meaningless phrases, clichés, deferential politeness, small talk, and other forms of trivial interaction. Empty speech allows family members to make connections through communicating while avoiding stressful topics and disclosures.

entrance narratives   Stories explaining how a child came to be adopted into a new family.

equifinality   A principle of the systems approach to families. Equifinality means that families can reach the same or similar ends in a variety of ways. Thus families can be happy yet enact very different communication behaviors that bring them happiness.

ethnocentrism   An exclusive focus on one ethnicity, ignoring others.

everyday talk   Habitual, mundane communication within families. Includes such things as joking, gossiping, and recapping the events of the day.

experiments   Experimental research systematically manipulates the independent variable in order to see what its effects are on another variable, called the dependent variable. Experiments involve the researcher taking some type of action (the manipulation) and then observing the results of that action.

explanatory model of interpersonal conflict   Cupach and Canary's (1997) model of interpersonal conflict, which focuses on conflict episodes and consists of five processes and outcomes: distal context, proximal context, conflict interaction, proximal outcomes, and distal outcomes.

explicit rules   Family rules that are openly discussed by family members. These rules are consciously referred to in family discussions; they are verbally stated.

external boundaries   Limit markers separating family members from those considered outside the family. Boundaries may be literal, such as fences that keep neighbors out of the family's space, or symbolic, such as silence that discourages interaction between people. There also may be rules telling members not to talk about a divorced relative, keeping him or her out of family membership.

external context   The suprasystems in which a given family system is embedded. The external context consists of the following: historical frame, economic frame, developmental frame, hereditary frame, and cultural frame. They form the givens that a family has to deal with as it copes with stress.

families of procreation   *See* traditional nuclear family.

family metaphor   A linguistic comparison between the family and some other event, image, object, or behavior. Less elaborate than family stories, family metaphors are one way that families create meaning.

family myths   Beliefs that families hold about themselves that are selective or constructed to represent the family in a manner that may not be true but is functional for the family.

family-of-origin   The family in which one has been raised.

family policy   All the things that governments do that affect the family either directly or indirectly.

family ritual   A repeated, patterned communication event, paying homage to a person, idea, or thing. Rituals can form around everyday interactions, family traditions, or celebrations.

family secrets   Information with clear prescriptions about how and with whom it can be shared. A secret can be individual (only one family member knows it), internal (only a few members know it), or shared (the whole family knows it, but no one outside the family can know it).

family stories   Lore about family members, living or dead, and/or family events that become part of the family canon and are told and retold.

family theme   A statement about reality and its relationship to the family. A theme serves a meaning-making function for the family and resembles a motto for the family.

family violence   When a family member imposes his or her wants, needs, or desires on others with the intention (or perceived intention) of doing physical or psychological harm or exploiting them sexually.

feedback   One of the principles of systems thinking. Feedback is the mechanism that allows the system to recalibrate or to stay the same. Positive feedback produces change in the system, whereas negative feedback maintains the system.

feminism   A social movement focused on the position of women in the culture. There are multiple types of feminism, for example, liberal, radical, eco-feminist, and separatist. Although these types differ greatly, they are all deeply concerned with empowering women.

fluidity   A feature of family stories indicating that they adapt and change over time.

Four Horsemen of the Apocalypse model   A model of marital conflict proposed by Gottman (1994b) consisting of four stages of escalating intensity: criticism, contempt, defensiveness, and stonewalling.

frustration-aggression hypothesis   An explanation for family violence positing that violence is the result of blocked personal goals, which cause frustration. Frustration causes aggression and, ultimately, violence.

functional rules   Rules in the family that foster communication, strengthen relationships, and empower family members to reach their goals.

gay and lesbian families   Families that include two people of the same sex who maintain an intimate relationship and who may or may not serve as parents to at least one child.

gendered violence   Violence that is inflicted disproportionately on the members of one sex, usually women.

gender roles   The expectations assigned to masculinity and femininity by a culture or co-culture.

gender role socialization   The process by which we learn our gender roles.

gender schema theory   Bem's (1993) explanation for why we classify so much of the world and our behaviors into masculine and feminine categories. Gender schema theory posits that we develop mental schemata for masculinity and femininity. We then filter our decisions through these schemata, deciding, for example, if certain activities are appropriate for us based on whether we see them as masculine or feminine.

genogram   A family diagram that visually depicts family communication patterns and relationships across at least three generations.

guarding   Provision of safety and security to a mother's children in a homeless shelter.

heterosexism   The assumption that heterosexuality is universal. Our culture and its behaviors are rooted in ways that promote heterosexual ways of thinking and relating.

hierarchy A principle of systems thinking holding that all systems have sub-systems and are embedded in suprasystems.

homeostatic A description of the steady state. When no recalibration is instituted and systems are maintained, they are homeostatic.

homophobia The irrational fear of homosexuals and homosexuality. Many people who are homophobic are unconscious of their fears.

implicit power When a family member conforms to another member's wishes without the second member having to state them explicitly.

implicit rules Family rules that are understood without overt statement. They are communicated and understood nonverbally.

implicit theories Explanations we carry in our head helping us to make sense of the world around us. They are informal and not rigorously tested.

independent couples One of Fitzpatrick's (1977, 1988) couple types. The independent couple is characterized by the belief that individual freedom should not be constrained by marriage. Independents value psychological closeness with some physical distance, and they are not conflict avoidant.

individualistic culture A culture, such as the one in the United States, in which individual goals are valued more than group goals, and overt, direct communication is prized.

integration A strategy for managing dialectic tensions. Integration involves a move to pull the opposing elements of the tension together in some way. Integration can take three forms: neutralizing, reframing, or disqualifying.

intellectual traditions A general way of thinking that has been held in common by a community of scholars.

interdependence A principle of systems thinking holding that the behaviors of system members co-construct the system, and all members are affected by shifts and changes in the system.

interfaith marriages Unions that include at least two different religious identities.

intergenerationality Establishing a legacy that affects the development of individual family members and the patterns of adjustment found in subsequent family generations.

internal boundaries Limit markers within a family. Boundaries may be literal, such as closed doors inside the home, keeping family members apart; or symbolic, such as silence that discourages interaction between family members.

internal context The relational culture of a family. The internal context is developed through stories, themes, metaphors, rituals, myths, and conversations.

interpersonal role conflict A type of role conflict in which two or more family members wish to enact the same role behaviors.

interpretive approach An intellectual tradition holding that truth is subjective and co-created by the participants. Researchers in this tradition view themselves as participants and believe that theory is best induced from observations and experiences they share with the family or families being studied. Sometimes referred to as hermeneutics.

intrapersonal role conflict   A type of role conflict in which one family member is called on to perform a role that does not feel right for some reason.

involuntary family   A group of people defined as a family by birth and/or law.

latent power   Sometimes called unobtrusive power; exists when the needs and wishes of the more powerful are anticipated and met.

manifest power   Manifest power is present in decision making by authority because it involves enforcing one's will against others.

married couples   Two adults living together, having declared their love by a legally sanctioned matrimonial bond.

master narratives   Stories coming from the social cultural backgrounds of a family. These are shared by the majority of the members of a given culture.

men's movements   Social movements that focus in some way or another on the grievances and triumphs of men in the United States. These movements also concentrate on the relationship between men and women, both as it is currently constructed and as members of the movements believe it should be constructed.

meta-emotions   Emotions that people have about emotions.

meta-rules   Rules about rules. Meta-rules tell the family if, when, and to whom they are able to acknowledge the existence of a rule.

monologic thinking   An approach contrasted to dialectics. Monologics suggests that as families develop closeness they will necessarily become less distant. As families move toward one pole in an opposition, they move away from the other.

morphogenic   A component of systems theory that means change. At times, systems must change, or become morphogenic, in order to adapt to the environment.

narrative asymmetry   The power differential that may exist when family stories are shared. Asymmetry is achieved when there is an unequal distribution of narrative rights, narrative timing, and narrative reception.

narrative inheritance   The lore that elders pass on to younger family members.

nesting   An unexpected return to the family of adolescents or young adults who family members previously thought had left permanently. *See also* boomerang kids.

neutralizing   A form of integration that involves compromising between the polarities of a dialectic tension.

nonverbal codes   Facial expressions, body positions, vocal inflections, and gestures as forms of communication behavior.

novelty/predictability dialectic   One of the major tensions characterizing family life. This dialectic represents our simultaneous desires for stability with our families and for change within our families.

one-across   A message or response that suggests that power in a relationship is evenly distributed between the partners.

one-down   A message or response that suggests that power in a relationship is not equally shared; one partner is trying to be in a less powerful position relative to the other.

one-up   A message or response that suggests that a partner in a relationship is trying to gain power (and control) over the other partner.

open family   One of Kantor and Lehr's (1975/1985) family types. The open family works toward goals using movable space, variable time, and flexible energy.

openness/protection dialectic   One of the major tensions characterizing family life. This dialectic represents our simultaneous desires to be open and vulnerable and to be strategic and protective within our families.

pantheistic   A divine understanding of the world by embracing nature and all that it offers.

paperless marriage   *See* cohabiting couples.

patriarchy   The governance of men to the extent that women are subordinated. Patriarchy has been identified with many churches and religions.

pattern   The interlocking series of responses in a dialogue.

peer marriages   Identified by Schwartz (1994), this form of marriage is one in which both partners have equal control and equal influence in family decision making.

performance   The oral telling and retelling of family stories.

popular culture   Messages sent about the family through television, radio, newsprint, and other forms of mass media.

positivistic approach   A philosophical position that assumes there are objective truths that can be uncovered about family interaction and that the process of inquiry that discovers these truths can be value neutral. It is also known as empiricism.

power   The capacity to influence another's goals, rules, roles, and/or patterns of communication in a family. *See also* relational control.

powerlessness   The lack of freedom to make and act on one's own choices.

pro-feminist approach   An approach associated with the men's movement that identifies sexism and patriarchy as harmful to both males and females.

pro-masculinist approach   An approach associated with the men's movement that adheres to placing men and males' issues as central to social and legal systems. Poet Robert Bly has been a leader in the pro-masculinist approach.

Promise Keepers   A men's movement that challenges men to reestablish their leadership role in the family as well as their responsibility to their families based on their relationship to God.

proximal context   An element in Cupach and Canary's (1997) model of conflict referring to the goals, rules, emotions, and attributions of individuals in conflict. These goals or rules may reformulate or be prioritized differently from one person to another.

proximal outcomes   An element in Cupach and Canary's (1997) model of conflict. Proximal outcomes are the immediate results or consequences of a conflict episode. These outcomes can evolve during a conflictual episode.

public mothering   A term developed by Boxill and Beatty (1990) that describes a type of mothering undertaken by mothers in homeless shelters. Public mothering is the absence of any privacy for family communication, requiring the mother to engage in parenting skills in public.

qualitative research   Undertaken by researchers wishing to understand how people make sense of their experiences. This research does not depend on statistical analysis to support an interpretation, but rather requires researchers to make a rhetorical appeal for their findings. This research is seen as most appropriate for interpretive and critical researchers.

quantitative research   Requires researchers to gather observations that can be quantified (converted to numbers). Researchers then analyze the numbers in order to make an argument about their meaning relative to a theoretical position. Quantitative research is most often done by researchers who embrace a positivistic worldview.

random family   One of Kantor and Lehr's (1975/1985) family types. The random family exhibits dispersed space, irregular time, and fluctuating energy. These families can be highly unpredictable.

reframe (reframing)   To change the way problematic situations are viewed, creating a more positive frame. The term is also used to mean a specific form of the integration strategy for managing dialectic tensions. In this sense, reframing refers to transforming the dialectic in some way so that it no longer seems to contain an opposition.

relational control   Power distributions that place the individuals in a relationship as equal, subordinate, or superior to one another in their interactions.

relational culture   Discussed by Wood (1982), this is the family's shared understandings of what family relationships mean and how they function.

religious feminists   Discussed by Marciano (1987), these are individuals who have urged reinterpretation of Biblical passages in order to allow for women's greater participation in church activities and church policy.

revised developmental theory   An updated version of developmental theory asserting that (1) family life stages can influence each other, (2) families develop relatively consistent interaction patterns over time, and (3) norms from other social institutions affect the timing of stages in the family.

rhetorical movements   *See* social movements.

role allocation   The family's role assignment pattern; how the family distributes role behaviors.

role ambiguity   A lack of clarity regarding how one is supposed to behave and feel in one's family role.

role conflict   A condition in which there is potential for contradiction or incompatibility in role-related expectations.

role evaluation   Deciding how well a family member plays a role.

role expectations   Internalized sets of beliefs about the way we will function in a particular role.

role models   Individuals who we believe exemplify the behaviors of the role we expect to play.

roles Socially constructed patterns of behavior and sets of expectations that provide us a position in our family.

role taking The decision to play a particular role.

rule Described by Shimanoff (1980), a rule is a prescribed guideline for action. Rules are (1) followable; (2) prescriptive of obligated, preferred, or prohibited behaviors; and (3) contextual.

rule negotiation The ability to mediate potential conflicts pertaining to rule enactment.

sandwich generation Middle-aged people concerned about their aging parents and their growing children.

segmentation A strategy for managing the dialectic tensions of family life. This strategy operates to isolate separate arenas for emphasizing each side of an opposite. For example, two individuals might stress predictability in their work relationships and novelty in their social relationships.

selection A strategy for managing the dialectic tensions of family life. This strategy implies a choice between two opposites. If a family chooses to be close at all times, ignoring autonomy needs, they are engaging in selection.

self-disclosure Voluntarily telling another private information that the hearer could not easily obtain any other way.

separate couples One of Fitzpatrick's (1977, 1988) couple types. The separate couple is conventional in some aspects of marriage (such as, wife taking the husband's name) but also opts for both psychological and physical distance at times.

sequence An element of family stories, sequence is the way a story unfolds—some stories are linear, others are circular. Sequence refers to the arrangement of the elements of a story.

serial arguments Ongoing unresolved arguments that intrude repeatedly in a relationship.

sexual communication Interactions about sex, sexuality, and intimacy.

sexual scripts Discussed by Sprecher and McKinney (1993), these are a person's past or present sexual motivations, behaviors, and experiences.

significance An element of family stories, significance refers to the extent to which family stories matter to family members. Significance may be achieved when stories (1) provide a sense of identity for the family, (2) teach lessons for behavior and promote a family code, (3) develop family esteem, and (4) name practices of control or authority in the family.

single-parent households Families that consist of one adult and at least one child.

skills deficiency An explanation for family violence that asserts that people resort to violence because their communication skills are too limited to sustain an argument in other ways.

slow disclosure Part of the drama in performing a family story, discussed by Ochs (1989), this is the methodical unfolding of a story. Slow disclosure includes individuals leaving out some parts of a story and other individuals "filling in" to complete the story.

social construction A theoretical perspective that centers on the importance of meanings for human behavior.

social desirability Responding to others in order to elicit favorable impressions.

social exchange theory A theoretical perspective asserting that relationships develop when the rewards outweigh the costs.

social movements Collective processes aimed at arousing public opinion and changing societal norms and values. *Also known as* rhetorical movements.

social process time A dimension of time that refers to how family members use their family experiences as a way to divide time.

social support Associated with reducing stress, this is the process of using communication to help another person. Often, a social network of friends is activated to help manage uncertainty.

stepfamily Family with at least two adults who provide continued care for at least one child who is not the biological offspring of both the adults. Also called a blended family, reconstituted family, or remarried family.

stonewalling The final stage in Gottman's (1994b) model of conflict in which a speaker figuratively speaks to a "stone wall." The listener responds with trite and meaningless expressions, restricting the communication between the two.

stories on the margins Stories revealing family experiences outside the boundaries of cultural conventions and expectations.

stress A family's perception of and/or response to disruption, disturbance, or pressure in the family, which may positively or negatively influence family life.

stressor An event that causes a change in the family system.

subsystems Smaller units that are part of the hierarchy of a system.

suprasystems Larger units that contain a system; suprasystems are composed of subsystems.

surveys Typical survey research consists of a researcher administering a standardized questionnaire to a sample of respondents. The questionnaire may be of a self-administered paper-and-pencil type, or may be administered face-to-face in a structured interview format, or may take place over the phone or online.

survival stories Stories that teach family members how to cope in a world that is not always welcoming and charitable. Stories about experiencing the Holocaust and slavery are examples of survival stories.

symbolic baggage Stories, myths, rituals, and so forth that emanate from experiences within a family-of-origin. Symbolic baggage may be both helpful and challenging to a newly formed family.

symmetrical relationship A relationship in which partners mirror one another. For example, a symmetrical relationship exists if one person defers decision making and the other defers it as well.

systems theory A theoretical framework asserting that families are best understood as whole, interdependent entities that constantly adapt to a changing environment.

taboo topics   Topics that family members keep private to avoid negative reactions.

terrain of struggle   Developed by Coontz (1988), the terrain of struggle refers to the process of cultural comparison to define a complex term such as *family*.

textual analysis   Textual analysis requires that a researcher identify a specific text for scrutiny. Texts can be presidential speeches, television shows, advertisements, or any type of discourse that the researcher can focus on to illuminate. Researchers engaged in textual analysis must apply some type of analytic tool, usually rhetorical or critical theory, in order to illuminate the messages embodied within the text.

theory   An abstract system of concepts with indications of the relationships among these concepts; theories help us to understand a phenomenon.

traditional couples   One of Fitzpatrick's (1977, 1988) couple types. The traditional couple emphasizes stability more than spontaneity in their marriage, exhibits interdependence and sharing, and endorses community customs related to marriage.

traditional marriages   Identified by Schwartz (1994), traditional marriages are those in which male and female roles are divided in expected and stereotypic ways.

traditional nuclear family   A family composed of a married couple living with their biological children, where the husband/father works outside the home, and the wife/mother works in the home as mother and homemaker.

triangulation   Approaching a question with more than one method, usually by blending methodologies from both the quantitative and the qualitative categories. Although useful, it is sometimes difficult to achieve for two reasons. First, researchers are usually trained in only one type of method, and it is difficult to learn a new set of methods "on the job." Perhaps more importantly, researchers believe that the two categories of methods represent two different epistemologies and ontologies.

unpredictable or nonnormative stressors   Unexpected life events that may cause change and are the result of some unique set of circumstances for which the family is relatively unprepared.

unraveling   A term developed by Boxill and Beaty (1990) that describes the process a homeless mother goes through when she confers her maternal role on her older children. Unraveling usually includes dressing, bathing, and even disciplining children if necessary.

verbal aggression   Messages directed to others that are sent with the intention of hurting them.

verbal codes   The words we use and their grammatical arrangements.

visual adoptions   Adoptions in which the family members' ethnic features make it obvious by sight that the family is not a biological one.

voluntary family   A group of people whom you consider to be family, arising from a personal decision to include these individuals as family members.

wholeness   A system principle that suggests we learn more about the family by seeing all the members interacting together than we would by simply observing one or two alone. The "whole is greater than the sum of its parts."

women's movements   Social movements consisting of many different strains but all placing women as central. A women's movement seeks to listen to women's voices and attend to women's issues. *See also* feminism.

worldview   A way of observing and making sense of the world in which an individual lives; a lens for sense-making.

References

Adair, M. (1992). Will the real men's movement please stand up? In K. L. Hagan (Ed.), *Women respond to the men's movement* (pp. 55–68). San Francisco: Harper.

Adams, B. N. (1988). Fifty years of family research: What does it mean? *Journal of Marriage and the Family, 50,* 5–17.

Adams, T. (2008). A review of narrative ethics. *Qualitative Inquiry, 14,* 175–194.

Adelman, M. B. (1992). Healthy passions: Safer sex as play. In T. Edgar, M. A. Fitzpatrick, & V. S. Freimuth (Eds.), *AIDS: A communication perspective* (pp. 69–90). Hillsdale, NJ: Erlbaum.

Ade-Ridder, L., & Jones, A. R. (1996). Home is where the hell is: An introduction to violence against children from a communication perspective. In D. D. Cahn & S. A. Lloyd (Eds.), *Family violence from a communication perspective* (pp. 59–84). Thousand Oaks, CA: Sage.

Affifi, T., & Steuber, K. (2009). Keeping and revealing secrets, *Communication Currents, 4,* p. 1.

Afifi, T. D. (2003). "Feeling caught" in step-families: Managing boundary turbulence through appropriate communication privacy rules. *Journal of Social and Personal Relationships, 20,* 729–755.

Afifi, T. D., & Hamrick, K. (2006). Communication processes that promote risk and resilience in post-divorce families. In M. Fine & J. H. Harvey (Eds.), *The handbook of divorce and relationship dissolution* (pp. 435–456). Mahwah, NJ: Erlbaum.

Afifi, T. D., & Olson, L. N. (2005). The chilling effect in families and the pressure to conceal secrets. *Communication Monographs, 72,* 192–216.

Afifi, T. D., & Schrodt, P. (2003). "Feeling caught" as a mediator of adolescents' and young adults' avoidance and satisfaction with their parents in divorced and nondivorced households. *Communication Monographs, 70,* 142–173.

Afifi, T. D., Afifi, W. A., Morse, C. R., & Hamrick, K. (2008). Adolescents' avoidance tendencies and physiological reactions to discussions about their parents' relationship: Implications for postdivorce and nondivorced families. *Communication Monographs, 75,* 290–317.

Afifi, T. D., Granger, D. A., Denes, A., Joseph, A., & Aldeis, D. (2011). Parents' communication skills and adolescents' salivary-amylase and cortisol response patterns. *Communication Monographs, 78,* 273–295.

Afifi, W. A., & Afifi, T. D. (2009). Avoidance among adolescents in conversations about their parents' relationship: Applying the Theory of Motivated Information Management. *Journal of Social and Personal Relationships, 26,* 488–511.

Afifi, W. A., & Guerrero, L. K. (2000). Motivations underlying topic avoidance in close relationships. In S. Petronio (Ed.), *Balancing the secrets of private disclosures* (pp. 165–180). Mahwah, NJ: Erlbaum.

Afifi, W. A., & Steuber, K. R. (2010). The cycle of concealment model: An examination of how secrets, and the strategies used to reveal them, affect family relationships over time. *Journal of Social and Personal Relationships, 27,* 1019–1034.

Agbayani-Siewert, P., & Revilla, L. (1995). Filipino Americans. In P. G. Min (Ed.), *Asian Americans: Contemporary trends and issues* (pp. 134–168). Thousand Oaks, CA: Sage.

Ahrons, C. (2011). Commentary on "Reconsidering the 'good divorce.'" *Family Relations, 60,* 528–532.

Ahrons, C. R. (1994). *The good divorce.* New York: HarperCollins.

Ahrons, C. R. (2004). *We're still family: What grown children have to say about their parents' divorce.* New York: HarperCollins.

Ahrons, C. R. (2011). Divorce: An unscheduled family transition. In M. McGoldrick, B. Carter, & Nydia Garcia Preto (Eds.), *The expanded family life cycle: Individual, family, and social perspectives* (pp. 292–306). Boston, MA: Allyn & Bacon.

Ahrons, C. R., & Rodgers, R. H. (1987). *Divorced families: A multidisciplinary developmental view.* New York: Norton.

Ainsworth, M. D. S. (1967). *Infancy in Uganda: Infant care and the growth of love.* Baltimore, MD: Johns Hopkins University Press.

Ainsworth, M. D. S., Blehar, M. C., Waters, E., & Wall, S. (1978). *Patterns of attachment: A psychological study of the strange situation.* Hillsdale, NJ: Erlbaum.

Albelda, R., Himmelweit, S., & Humphries, J. (2004). The dilemmas of lone motherhood: Key issues for feminist economics. *Feminist Economics, 10,* 1–7.

Alberts, J. K., Tracy, S. J., & Tretheway, A. (2011). An integrative theory of the division of domestic labor: Threshold level, social organizing, and sensemaking. *Journal of Family Communication, 11,* 21–38.

Aldous, J. (1983). Problematic elements in the relationships between churches and families. In W. V. D'Antonio & J. Aldous (Eds.), *Families and religion: Conflict and change in modern society* (pp. 67–80). Beverly Hills, CA: Sage.

Alemán, M. W., & Helfrich, K. W. (2010). Inheriting the narratives of dementia: A collaborative tale of a daughter and mother. *Journal of Family Communication, 10,* 7–23.

Alexander, A. (1994). Television and family interaction. In G. Handel & G. G. Whitchurch (Eds.), *The psychosocial interior of the family* (pp. 281–296). New York: Aldine De Gruyter.

Alexander, A., & Kim, Y. (2003). Television and family. In J. J. Ponzetti (Ed.), *International encyclopedia of marriage and family* (pp. 202–223). New York: Macmillan.

Alexander, B. K., & LeBlanc, H. P. (1999). Cooking Gumbo–Examining cultural dialogue about family: A black-white narrativization of lived experience in southern Louisiana. In T. J. Socha & R. C. Diggs (Eds.), *Communication, race, and family* (pp. 181–208). Mahwah, NJ: Erlbaum.

Alvarez, M., & Garcia-Marques, L. (2011). Cognitive and contextual variables in sexual partner and relationship perception. *Archives of Sexual Behavior, 40,* 407–417.

Alvesson, M., & Billing, Y. D. (2002). Beyond body-counting: A discussion of the social construction of gender at work. In I. Aaltio & A. J. Mills (Eds.), *Gender, identity and the culture of organizations* (pp. 72–91). London: Routledge.

Amato, P. (1993). Children's adjustment to divorce: Theories, hypotheses, and empirical support. *Journal of Marriage and the Family, 53,* 22–38.

Amato, P. (2000). Diversity within single-parent families. In D. H. Demo, K. R. Allen, & M. A. Fine (Eds.), *Handbook of family diversity* (pp. 149–172). Oxford: Oxford University Press.

Amato, P. R. (2003). Reconciling divergent perspectives: Judith Wallerstein, quantitative family research, and children of divorce. *Family Relations, 52,* 332–339.

Anders, C. J. (2010). How the Nielsen TV ratings work and what could replace them. Retrieved from *http://io9.com/5636210/how-the-nielsen-tv-ratings-work-and-what-could-replace-them.*

Anderson, K. L., Umberson, D., & Elliott, S. (2004). Violence and abuse in families. In A. L. Vangelisti (Ed.), *Handbook of family communication* (pp. 629–645). Mahwah, NJ: Erlbaum.

Andrews, K. (2002). Social movements and policy implementation: The Mississippi civil rights movement and the war on poverty. *American Sociological Review, 66,* 2–22.

Anthony, M., & Canfield, K. (2011). *A theology for family ministry.* Nashville, TN: B & H Publishing Group.

Applewhite, A. (2003). Covenant marriage would not benefit the family. In A. Ojeda (Ed.), *The family: Opposing viewpoints* (pp. 189–195). San Diego, CA: Greenhaven Press.

Arditti, J. (1990). Noncustodial fathers: An overview of policy and resources. *Family Relations, 41,* 154–162.

Armendariz, A. (2010). Tracking unmarried, same-sex couples using social maps. Retrieved from *http://californiawatch.org/dailyreport/tracking-unmarried-same-sex-couples-using-social-maps-4233.*

Arnold, G., & Jackson-Smith, P. (2001, February). A kid on the side. *Utne Reader, 103,* 78–79.

Ashbourne, L. M. (2009). Reconceptualizing parent-adolescent relationships: A dialogic model. *Journal of Family Theory & Review, 1,* 211–222.

Ashcraft, K. L. (1999). Managing maternity leave: A qualitative analysis of temporary executive succession. *Administrative Science Quarterly, 44,* 240–280.

Aston, W. G. (2012). *Shinto: The way of the gods.* London: Longmans, Green.

Aswad, B. C. (1997). Arab American families. In M. K. DeGenova (Ed.), *Families in cultural context: Strengths and challenges in diversity* (pp. 213–237). Mountain View, CA: Mayfield.

Augustine, N. (2000, August 9). Grandfather was a knowing Christian. *Toronto Star,* p. 2.

Aulette, J. R. (1994). *Changing families.* Belmont, CA: Wadsworth.

Austin, E. W., Roberts, D. F., & Nass, C. I. (1990). Influences of family communication on children's television interpretation processes. *Communication Research, 17,* 545–564.

Averitt, S. S. (2003). "Homelessness is not a choice!" The plight of homeless women with preschool children living in temporary shelters. *Journal of Family Nursing, 9,* 79–100.

Babcock, J. C., Waltz, J., Jacobson, N. S., & Gottman, J. M. (1993). Power and violence: The relation between communication patterns, power discrepancies, and domestic violence. *Journal of Consulting and Clinical Psychology, 61,* 40–50.

Babrow, A. S., Hines, S. C., & Kasch, C. R. (2000). Managing uncertainty in illness explanation: An application of problematic integration theory. In B. B. Whaley (Ed.), *Explaining illness: Research, theory and strategies* (pp. 41–68). Mahwah, NJ: Erlbaum.

Baca-Zinn, M., & Wells, B. (2005). Diversity within Latino families. In A. S. Skolnick & J. H. Skolnick (Eds.), *Family in transition* (pp. 389–415). Boston, MA: Allyn & Bacon.

Baker, S. (2011). Married couples now number minority in U.S. households. Retrieved from *http://www.theblaze.com/stories/married-couples-now-number-minority-in-us-households.*

Baldock, C. (1999). *How to succeed as a single parent.* London: Sheldon Press.

Baldwin, K. (1985). "Woof!": A word on woman's roles in family storytelling. In R. A. Jordan & S. J. Kalcik (Eds.), *Woman's folklore, woman's culture* (pp. 149–162). Philadelphia, PA: University of Pennsylvania Press.

Ballard, R. L., & Ballard, S. J. (2011). From narrative inheritance to narrative momentum: Past, present, and future stories in an international adoptive family. *Journal of Family Communication, 11,* 69–84.

Bandura, A. (1969). Social learning theory of identificatory process. In D. A. Goslin (Ed.), *Handbook of socialization theory and research* (pp. 213–262). Chicago, IL: Rand McNally.

Barbarin, O. (2002). *Mandela's children.* New York: Routledge.

Barna Group. (2009). How the faith of African-Americans has changed. Retrieved from *http://www.barna.org/barna-update/article/13-culture/286-how-the-faith-of-african-americans-has-changed.*

Barna Group. (2011). Regional shifts in religious beliefs and behavior since 1991 revealed in new Barna report. Retrieved from *http://www.barna.org/faith-spirituality/512-regional-shifts-in-religious-beliefs-and-behavior-since-1991-re-vealed-in-new-barna-report.*

Barnett, O., Miller-Perrin, C. L., & Perrin, R. D. (2005). *Family violence across the lifespan: An introduction* (2nd ed.). Thousand Oaks, CA: Sage.

Barnett, R. C., & Rivers, C. (2004, September 3). Men are from earth, and so are women. It's faulty research that sets them apart. *The Chronicle Review,* p. B11.

Barrie, A., & Morrow, M. (2012). *The breast cancer field manual.* Lanham, MD: Rowman & Littlefield.

Bartholomew, K., & Horowitz, L. M. (1991). Attachment styles among young adults: A test of a four-category model. *Journal of Personality and Social Psychology, 61,* 226–244.

Bartkowski, J. P. (2000). Breaking walls, raising fences: Masculinity, intimacy, and accountability among the Promise Keepers. *Sociology of Religion, 61,* 33–53.

Bates, C. E., & Samp, J. A. (2011). Examining the effects of planning and empathic accuracy on communication in relational and nonrelational conflict interactions. *Communication Studies, 62,* 207–222.

Baumann, A. A., Kuhlberg, J., & Zayas, L. H. (2010). Familism, mother-daughter mutuality, and suicide attempts of adolescent Latinas. *Journal of Family Psychology, 24,* 616–624.

Baxter, L. A. (1988). A dialectical perspective on communication strategies in relationship development. In S. Duck (Ed.), *A handbook of personal relationships* (pp. 257–273). New York: Wiley.

Baxter, L. A. (1990). Dialectical contradictions in relationship development. *Journal of Social and Personal Relationships, 7,* 69–88.

Baxter, L. A. (1992). Forms and functions of intimate play in personal relationships. *Human Communication Research, 18,* 336–363.

Baxter, L. A. (2011). *Voicing relationships.* Thousand Oaks, CA: Sage.

Baxter, L. A., & Braithwaite, D. O. (2002). Performing marriage: Marriage renewal rituals as cultural performance. *Southern Journal of Communication, 67,* 94–109.

Baxter, L. A., & Braithwaite, D. O. (2006). Introduction: Meta-theory and theory in family communication research. In D. O. Braithwaite & L. A. Baxter (Eds.), *Engaging theories in family communication: Multiple perspectives* (pp. 1–15). Thousand Oaks, CA: Sage.

Baxter, L. A., & Clark, C. (1996). Perceptions of family communication patterns and the enactment of family rituals. *Western Journal of Communication, 60,* 254–268.

Baxter, L. A., & Montgomery, B. M. (1996). *Relating: Dialogues and dialectics.* New York: Guilford.

Baxter, L. A., & Wilmot, W. (1985). Taboo topics in close relationships. *Journal of Social and Personal Relationships, 2,* 253–269.

Baxter, L. A., Braithwaite, D. O., Kellas, J. K., LeClair-Underberg, C., Normand, E. L., Routsong, T., & Thatcher, M. (2009). Empty ritual: Young-adult stepchildren's perceptions of the remarriage ceremony. *Journal of Social and Personal Relationships, 26,* 467–487.

Baxter, L. A., Bylund, C. L., Imes, R. S., & Scheive, D. M. (2005). Family communication environments and rule-based social control of adolescents' healthy lifestyle choices. *Journal of Family Communication, 5*, 209–227.

Bayles, F. (2004). Gay marriage debate quiet for now. Retrieved from *http://www.usatoday.com/news/nation/2004-06-16-gay-marriage-usat.x.htm.*

Bayor, R.H. (2011). *Multicultural America: An encyclopedia of the newest Americans.* Santa Barbara, CA: ABC-CLIO/Greenwood.

Beaton, J., Norris, J. E., & Pratt, M. W. (2003). Relationships between adult children and their parents: Unresolved issues in adult children's marital relationships involving intergenerational problems. *Family Relations, 52*, 143–153.

Beatty, M. J., & Dobos, J. A. (1992a). Adult sons' satisfaction with their relationships with fathers and person-group (father) communication apprehension. *Communication Quarterly, 40*, 162–176.

Beatty, M. J., & Dobos, J. A. (1992b). Relationship between sons' perceptions of fathers' messages and satisfaction in adult son-father relationships. *Southern Communication Journal, 57*, 277–284.

Beatty, M. J., & Dobos, J. A. (1993). Direct and mediated effects of perceived father criticism and sarcasm on females' perceptions of relational partners' disconfirming behavior. *Communication Quarterly, 42*, 187–197.

Bellah, R. N., Madsen, R., Sullivan, W. M., Swidler, A., & Tipton, S. M. (1986). *Habits of the heart: Individualism and commitment in American life.* New York: Harper & Row.

Bellamy, R. V., & Walker, J. R. (1996). *Television and the remote control.* New York: Guilford.

Bem, S. L. (1993). *The lenses of gender: Transforming the debate on sexual inequality.* New Haven, CT: Yale University Press.

Bengtson, V. L. (2001). Beyond the nuclear family: The increasing importance of multigenerational bonds. *Journal of Marriage and the Family, 63*, 1–15.

Benkov, L. (2003). Reinventing the family. In A. S. Skolnick and J. H. Skolnick (Eds.), *Families in transition* (12th ed., pp. 415–435). Boston, MA: Allyn & Bacon.

Benkov, L. (1994). *Reinventing the family.* New York: Crown.

Benoit, P. J., & Kennedy, K. (1998). *"The broken leg": Family values in stories.* Paper presented at the annual meeting of the National Communication Association, New York, NY.

Benoit, P. J., Kennedy, K. A., Waters, R., Hinton, S., Drew, S., & Daniels, F. (1996). *Food, football and family talk: Thanksgiving rituals in families.* Paper presented at the annual meeting of the Speech Communication Association, San Diego, CA.

Benoit, W. L., & Anderson, K. K. (1996). Blending politics and entertainment: Dan Quayle versus Murphy Brown. *Southern Communication Journal, 62*, 73–85.

Bergen, K. M. (2010). Accounting for difference: Commuter wives and the master narrative of marriage. *Journal of Applied Communication Research, 38*, 47–64.

Berger, C. R. (2009). Message production processes. In C. Berger, M. Roloff, & D. Roskos-Ewoldson (Eds.), *Handbook of communication science* (pp. 111–127). Thousand Oaks, CA: Sage.

Berger, C. R., & Calabrese, R. (1975). Some explorations in initial interaction and beyond: Toward a developmental theory of interpersonal communication. *Human Communication Research, 1*, 99–112.

Berger, P. L., & Kellner, H. (1964). Marriage and the construction of social reality. *Diogenes, 46*, 1–23.

Berger, P. L., & Luckman, T. (1966). *The social construction of reality.* Garden City, NY: Doubleday.

Berman, E., & Wohlsifer, D. (2011). Sexuality and the family life cycle. In M. McGoldrick, B. Carter, & Nydia Garcia Preto (Eds.), *The expanded family life cycle: Individual, family, and social perspectives* (pp. 103–115). Boston, MA: Allyn & Bacon.

Bevan, J. L. (2010). Serial argument goals and conflict strategies: A comparison between romantic partners and family members. *Communication Reports, 23,* 52–64.

Bharath, D. (2011). Crystal Cathedral board picks diocese over Chapman. Retrieved from *http://www.ocregister.com/articles/chapman-327576-cathedral-board.html.*

Bharath, D. (2011). Schuller Sr. speaks out against church's anti-gay covenant. Retrieved from *http://www.ocregister.com/news/schuller-292476-church-covenant. html#.*

Bietti, L. M. (2010). Sharing memories, family conversation and interaction. *Discourse and Society, 21,* 499–523.

Birchler, G. R., Weiss, R. L., & Vincent, J. P. (1975). Multidimensional analyses of social reinforcement exchange between maritally distressed and nondistressed spouse and stranger dyads. *Journal of Personality and Social Psychology, 31,* 348–360.

Bishop, D. V. M., & Bishop, S. J. (1998). "Twin language": A risk factor for language impairment? *Journal of Speech, Language, and Hearing Research, 41,* 150–160.

Black, H. K., Moss, M. S., Rubinstein, R. L., & Moss, S. Z. (2011). End of life: A family narrative. *Journal of Aging Research,* 1–7.

Black, J., Bryant, J., & Thompson, S. (1998). *Introduction to media communication.* Boston, MA: McGraw-Hill.

Blackstone, A. (2004). "It's just about being fair": Activism and the politics of volunteering in the breast cancer movement. *Gender and Society, 18,* 350–368.

Blank, R. (2011). End of life decision making across cultures. *The Journal of Law, Medicine & Ethics, 39,* 201–213.

Blau, D. (2001). *The child care problem: An economic analysis.* New York: Russell Sage Foundation.

Bloch, M. N. (2012). *Governing young children, families, and their care.* New York: Palgrave Macmillan.

Blumstein, P., & Schwartz, P. (1983). *American couples.* New York: Morrow.

Bly, R. (1990). *Iron John: A book about men.* Reading, MA: Addison-Wesley.

Bochner, A. (1976). Conceptual frontiers in the study of communication in families: An introduction to the literature. *Human Communication Research, 2,* 381–397.

Bochner, A. (1985). Perspectives on inquiry: Representation, conversation, and reflection. In M. L. Knapp & G. R. Miller (Eds.), *Handbook of interpersonal communication* (pp. 27–58). Beverly Hills, CA: Sage.

Bodroghkozy, A. (2011). Julia. Retrieved from *http://www.museum.tv/eotvsection. php?entrycode=julia.*

Bograd, M. (1984). Family systems approaches to wife battering: A feminist critique. *American Journal of Orthopsychiatry, 54,* 558–568.

Bohanek, J. G., Fivush, R., Zaman, W., & Lepore, C. E. (2009). Narrative interaction in family dinnertime conversations. *Merrill-Palmer Quarterly, 55,* 488–515.

Bohanek, J. G., Marin, K. A., & Fivush, R. (2008). Family narratives, self, and gender in early adolescence. *Journal of Early Adolescence, 28,* 153–176.

Bond, J. T. (2002). *Highlights of the national study of the changing workplace.* New York: Families and Work Institute.

Booth-Butterfield, M., & Sidelinger, R. (1998). The influence of family communication on the college-aged child: Openness, attitudes, and actions about sex and alcohol. *Communication Quarterly, 46,* 295–308.

Boss, P. (2002). *Family stress management,* Thousand Oaks, CA: Sage.

Boss, P. G. (2002). *Family stress: Classic and contemporary readings.* Thousand Oaks, CA: Sage.

Boss, P. G. (1988). *Family stress management.* Newbury Park, CA: Sage.

Boss, P. G. (2000). *Ambiguous loss: Learning to live with unresolved grief.* Cambridge, MA: Harvard University Press.

Boss, P. G. (2001). *Losing a way of life?: Ambiguous loss in farm families.* Minneapolis: University of Minnesota Extension Service.

Bowlby, J. (1969/1982). *Attachment and loss: Vol. 1. Attachment.* New York: Basic Books.

Bowlby, J. (1973). *Attachment and loss: Vol. 2. Separation: Anxiety and anger.* New York: Basic Books.

Bowlby, J. (1980). *Attachment and loss: Vol. 3. Loss.* New York: Basic Books.

Boxill, N. A., & Beaty, A. L. (1990). Mother/child interaction among homeless women and their children in a public night shelter in Atlanta, Georgia. *Child and Youth Services, 14,* 49–64.

Boyd, J. (1996). *"Somebody has to be the hamster": Inside jokes in families.* Paper presented at the annual meeting of the Speech Communication Association, San Diego, CA.

Boykin, W. A., & Toms, F. D. (1985). Black child socialization: A conceptual framework. In H. P. McAdoo & J. L. McAdoo (Eds.), *Black children: Social educational and parental environment* (pp. 33–51). Beverly Hills, CA: Sage.

Bradbury, T., Rogge, R., & Lawrence, E. (2001). Reconsidering the role of conflict in marriage. In A. Booth, A. C. Crouter, & M. Clements (Eds.), *Couples in conflict* (pp. 59–81). Mahwah, NJ: Erlbaum.

Braithwaite, D. O. (2002). "Married widowhood": Maintaining couplehood when one spouse is living in a nursing home. *Southern Communication Journal, 67,* 160–179.

Braithwaite, D. O., & Baxter, L. A. (Eds.). (2006). *Engaging theories in family communication: Multiple perspectives.* Thousand Oaks, CA: Sage.

Braithwaite, D. O., McBride, M. C., & Schrodt, P. (2003). Parent teams and the everyday interactions of co-parenting children in stepfamilies. *Communication Reports, 16,* 93–111.

Braithwaite, D. O., Olson, L. N., Golish, T. D., Soukup, C., & Turman, P. (2001). "Becoming a family": Developmental processes represented in blended family discourse. *Journal of Applied Communication Research, 29,* 221–247.

Brendes, L., Franck, E., & Peiper, J. (2010). *Why self-esteem needs self-certainty: Social identity processes in organizations. Working paper 135.* Zurich: Institute for Strategy and Business Economics.

Bretherton, I. (1990). Open communication and internal working models: Their role in the development of attachment relationships. In R. A. Thompson (Ed.), *Nebraska Symposium on Motivation: Socioemotional development.* Lincoln: University of Nebraska Press.

Brinker, N. (2011). *Promise me: How a sister's love launched the global movement to end breast cancer.* New York: Three Rivers Press.

Bruess, C. J., & Pearson, J. C. (1997). Interpersonal rituals in marriage and adult friendship. *Communication Monographs, 64,* 25–46.

Brule, N. J. (2009). Adolescent-to-parent abuse: Abused parents' perceptions of the meaning and goals of adolescents' verbal, physical, and emotional abuse. In D. D. Cahn (Ed.), *Family violence: Communication processes* (pp. 179–204). Albany, NY: SUNY Press.

Bryant, J. (1990). Preface. In J. Bryant (Ed.), *Television and the American family* (pp. xiii–xvii). Hillsdale, NJ: Erlbaum.

Buchbinder, D. (2012). *Studying men and masculinities.* New York: Routledge.

Buchoff, R. (1995). Family stories. *The Reading Teacher, 49,* 230–233.

Bueler, C., Betz, P., Ryan, C. R., Legg, B. H., & Trotter, B. B. (1992). Description and evaluation of the orientation for divorcing parents. *Family Relations, 39,* 460–465.

Buerkel, R. A. (1996). *Intimacy in the father-son dyad: The role of verbal and nonverbal idiosyncratic communication in father-son relational intimacy.* Paper presented at the annual meeting of the Speech Communication Association, San Diego, CA.

Buerkel-Rothfuss, N. L., Greenberg, B. S., Atkin, C. K., & Neuendorf, K. (1982). Learning about the family from television. *Journal of Communication, 32,* 191–201.

Bullock, K. (2004). The changing role of grandparents in rural families: The results of an exploratory study in southeastern North Carolina. *Families in Society: The Journal of Contemporary Social Services, 85,* 45–54.

Bulmer, S. (2011, May 4). Same-sex parents manage stigma, "normal" lives. *The Daily Iowan,* 1.

Burgess, E. W. (1926). The family as a unity of interacting personalities. *The Family, 7,* 3–9.

Burleson, B. R. (1994). Comforting messages: Significance, approaches, and effects. In B. Burleson, T. L. Albrecht, & I. G. Sarason (Eds.), *Communication of social support: Messages, interactions, relationships, and community* (pp. 3–28). Thousand Oaks, CA: Sage.

Burleson, B. R., Delia, J. G., & Applegate, J. L. (1995). The socialization of person-centered communication. In M. A. Fitzpatrick & A. L. Vangelisti (Eds.), *Explaining family interactions* (pp. 34–76). Thousand Oaks, CA: Sage.

Burns, M. E., & Pearson, J. C. (2011). An exploration of family communication environment, everyday talk, and family satisfaction. *Communication Studies, 62,* 171–185.

Burrell, N. A. (1995). Communication patterns in stepfamilies: Redefining family roles, themes, and conflict styles. In M. A. Fitzpatrick & A. L. Vangelisti (Eds.), *Explaining family interactions* (pp. 290–309). Thousand Oaks, CA: Sage.

Bush, K. R., Bohon, S. A., & Kim, H. K. (2010). Adaptation among immigrant families: Resources and barriers. In S. Price, C. A. Price, & P. McHenry (Eds.), *Families and change: Coping with stressful events and transitions* (pp. 285–310). Thousand Oaks, CA: Sage.

Buss, D. M. (1994). *The evolution of desire: Strategies of human mating.* New York: Basic Books.

Butsch, R. (1992). Class and gender in four decades of television situation comedy: *Plus ça* change. . . . *Critical Studies in Mass Communication, 21,* 387–408.

Buzzanell, P. M., & Turner, L. H. (2003). Emotion work revealed by job loss discourse: Backgrounding-foregrounding of feelings, construction of normalcy, and (re)instituting of traditional masculinities. *Journal of Applied Communication Research, 31,* 27–57.

Buzzanell, P. M., & Turner, L. H. (2012). Effective family communication and job loss: Crafting the narrative for family crisis. In F. C. Dickson & L. M. Webb (Eds.), *Communication for families in crisis: Theories, research, strategies* (pp. 281–306). New York: Peter Lang.

Bylund, C. L. (2003). Ethnic diversity and family stories. *Journal of Family Communication, 3,* 215–236.

Byng-Hall, J. (2008). The significance of children fulfilling parental roles: Implications for family therapy. *Journal of Family Therapy, 30,* 147–162.

Cade, R. (2010). Covenant marriage. *The Family Journal, 18,* 230–233.

Cahill, S. (Ed.). (1975). *Women and fiction: Short stories by and about women.* New York: Mentor.

Cahn, D. D. (2009). An evolving communication perspective on family violence. In D. D. Cahn (Ed.), *Family violence: Communication processes* (pp. 1–24). Albany, NY: SUNY Press.

Campbell, C. C. (2011). Pope John Paul II: Staunch defender of the dignity of women. Retrieved from *http://www.washingtonpost.com/blogs/on-faith/post/pope-john-paul-ii-staunch-defender-of-the-dignity-of-women/2011/04/29/AFZvlDFF_blog.html*.

Canary, D. J., Cupach, W. R., & Messman, S. J. (1995). *Relationship conflict*. Thousand Oaks, CA: Sage.

Canary, D. J., & Hause, K. (1993). Is there any reason to research sex differences in communication? *Communication Quarterly, 41*, 129–144.

Cantor, M. G. (1990). Prime-time fathers: A study in continuity and change. *Critical Studies in Mass Communication, 7*, 275–285.

Cascardi, M., Langhinrichsen, J., & Vivian, D. (1992). Marital aggression: Impact, injury and health correlates for husbands and wives. *Archives of Internal Medicine, 152*, 1178–1184.

Cascone, G. (2003). *Life al dente: Laughter and love in the Italian-American family*. New York: Atria.

Cate, R. M., & Lloyd, S. A. (1992). *Courtship*. Newbury Park, CA: Sage.

Caughlin, J. P., Golish, T. D., Olson, L. N., Sargent, J. E., Cook, J. S., & Petronio, S. (2000). Intrafamily secrets in various family configurations: A communication boundary management perspective. *Communication Studies, 51*, 116–134.

Caughlin, J. P., & Malis, R. S. (2004). Demand/withdraw communication between parents and adolescents: Connections with self-esteem and substance use. *Journal of Social and Personal Relationships, 21*, 125–148.

Caughlin, J. P., & Petronio, S. (2004). Privacy in families. In A. L. Vangelisti (Ed.), *Handbook of family communication* (pp. 379–412). Mahwah, NJ: Erlbaum.

Chabot, J. M., & Ames, B. D. (2004). "It wasn't 'let's get pregnant and go do it':" Decision making in lesbian couples planning motherhood via donor insemination. *Family Relations, 53*, 348–356.

Chafe, W. (1974). *The American woman: Her changing social, economic, and political roles, 1920–1970*. New York: Oxford University Press.

Chang, N. (2000). Reasoning with children about violent television shows and related toys. *Early Childhood Education Journal, 28*, 85–89.

Chapa, G. (2011). Family planning. In S. Loue & M. Sajatovic (Eds.), *Encyclopedia of immigrant health* (pp. 677–681). New York: Springer.

Chen, V., & Pearce, W. B. (1995). Even if a thing of beauty, can a case study be a joy forever? A social constructionist approach to theory and research. In W. Leeds-Hurwitz (Ed.), *Social approaches to communication* (pp. 135–154). New York: Guilford.

Cheong, P. H. (2011). Religion and social media: Got Web? *Media Development, 58*, 23–36.

Chesire, T. C. (2001). Cultural transmission in urban American Indian families. *American Behavioral Scientist, 44*, 1528–1535.

Chethik, N. (2001, January/February). Fathers, sons, and loss. *UUWorld, 15*, 16–23.

Children's Defense Fund. (2004). Key facts about American children. Retrieved from *www.childrensdefense.org/data/keyfacts.asp*.

Chilman, C. S. (1988). Public policies and families. In C. S. Chilman, E. W. Nunnally, & F. M. Cox (Eds.), *Variant family forms: Families in trouble* (pp. 245–253). Newbury Park, CA: Sage.

Chilman, C. S., Nunnally, E. W., & Cox, F. M. (1988). Introduction to the series. In C. S. Chilman, E. W. Nunnally, & F. M. Cox (Eds.), *Variant family forms: Families in trouble* (pp. 7–14). Newbury Park, CA: Sage.

Chirban, J., & McGraw, P. (2012). *How to talk with your kids about sex*. Nashville, TN: Thomas Nelson.

Chisholm, P. (2003). Sex & marriage. In K. Gilbert (Ed.), *The family* (pp. 136–139). Guilford, CT: McGraw-Hill/Dushkin.

Chodorow, N. (1978). *The reproduction of mothering: Psychoanalysis and the sociology of gender.* Berkeley, CA: University of California Press.

Choi, K. H., & Seltzer, J. A. (2011). *Race, ethnic, and nativity differences in the demographic significance of cohabitation in women's lives.* Los Angeles, CA: California Center for Population Research.

Christopher, F. S., & Sprecher, S. (2005). Sexuality in marriage, dating and other relationships: A decade review. In J. K. Davidson & N. B. Moore (Eds.), *Speaking of sexuality: Interdisciplinary readings* (pp. 117–131). Los Angeles, CA: Roxbury.

Chrzastowski, S. K. (2011). A narrative perspective on genograms: Revisiting classical family therapy methods. *Clinical Child Psychology and Psychiatry, 16,* 635–644.

Cicirelli, V. G., & Nussbaum, J. F. (1989). Relationships with siblings in later life. In J. F. Nussbaum (Ed.), *Life-span communication: Normative processes* (pp. 283–299). Hillsdale, NJ: Erlbaum.

Cissna, K. N., Cox, D. E., & Bochner, A. P. (1990). The dialectic of marital and parental relationships within the stepfamily. *Communication Monographs, 56,* 44–61.

Ciulla, J. B. (2000). *The working life: The promise and betrayal of modern work.* New York: Three Rivers Press.

Clair, R. P. (2011). The rhetoric of dust: Toward a rhetorical theory of the division of domestic labor. *Journal of Family Communication, 11,* 50–59.

Clarke, V., & Finlay, S. J. (2004). "For better or worse?" Lesbian and gay marriage. *Feminism & Psychology, 14,* 17–23.

Clarkson, T. (2012). *A portraiture of Quakerism.* New York: Tredition Books.

Clatterbaugh, K. (1990). *Contemporary perspectives on masculinity.* Boulder, CO: Westview.

Cobb, S. (1982). Social support and health through the life course. In H. I. McCubbin, A. E. Cauble, & J. M. Patterson (Eds.), *Family stress, coping, and social support* (pp. 189–199). Springfield, IL: Thomas.

Coffelt, T. (2010). Is sexual communication challenging between mothers and daughters? *Journal of Family Communication, 10,* 116–130.

Cohen, J., (2004, December 23). E-mail doesn't take a holiday. *New York Times,* pp. E1, E4.

Coleman, M., & Ganong, L. H. (1995). Family reconfiguring following divorce. In S. Duck & J. T. Wood (Eds.), *Confronting relationship challenges* (pp. 73–108). Thousand Oaks, CA: Sage.

Coleman, M., Ganong, L., & Fine, M. (2004). Communication in stepfamilies. In A. Vangelisti (Ed.), *Handbook of family communication* (pp. 215–232). Mahwah, NJ: Lawrence Erlbaum.

Coleman, R. M. (2000). *African American viewers and the situation comedy.* New York: Garland.

Collins, P. H. (1990). *Black feminist thought: Knowledge, consciousness, and the politics of empowerment.* New York: Routledge.

Conlin, M. (2003, October 20). Unmarried America. *Business Week,* pp. 106–111.

Coontz, S. (1988). *The social origins of private life: A history of American families, 1600–1900.* London: Verso.

Coontz, S. (1992). *The way we never were: American families and the nostalgia trap.* New York: Basic Books.

Coontz, S. (2000a). Historical perspectives on family diversity. In D. H. Demo, K. R. Allen, & M. A. Fine (Eds.), *Handbook of family diversity* (pp. 15–31). Oxford: Oxford University Press.

Coontz, S. (2000b). *The way we never were: American families and the nostalgia trap.* New York: Basic Books.

Coontz, S. (2003). Diversity and communication values in the family. *Journal of Family Communication, 3,* 187–192.

Coontz, S. (2003). The American family. In K. R. Gilbert (Ed.), *Annual editions: The family* (pp. 2–7). Guilford, CT: McGraw-Hill.

Cooper, C. R., Grotevant, H. D., & Condon, S. M. (1983). Individuality and connectedness in the family as a context for adolescent identity formation and role-taking skills. In H. D. Grotevant & C. R. Cooper (Eds.), *Adolescent development in the family: New directions for child development* (pp. 43–59). San Francisco, CA: Jossey-Bass.

Corbin, K. (2011). More boomerang kids returning home after college. Retrieved from *http://www.schools.com/articles/more-boomerang-kids-returning-home-after-college.html.*

Cortese, A. (1989). Subcultural differences in human sexuality: Race, ethnicity, and social class. In K. McKinney & S. Sprecher (Eds.), *Human sexuality: The societal and interpersonal context* (pp. 63–90). Norwood, NJ: Ablex.

Cosgrove, L., & Flynn, C. (2005). Marginalized mothers: Parenting without a home. *Analyses of Social Issues and Public Policy, 5,* 127–143.

Coulter, A. (2009). *Guilty: Liberal victims and their assault on America.* New York: Three Rivers Press.

Coupland, N., & Nussbaum, J. F. (Eds.) (1993). *Discourse and lifespan identity.* Newbury Park, CA: Sage.

Creek, S. (2009). Promise Keepers. In J. O'Brien (Ed.), *Encyclopedia of gender and society* (pp. 34–44). Thousand Oaks, CA: Sage.

Cronen, V. E., Pearce, W. B., & Harris, L. M. (1982). The coordinated management of meaning: A theory of communication. In F. E. X. Dance (Ed.), *Human communication theory* (pp. 61–89). New York: Harper & Row.

Crouch, J. (2003). Covenant marriage would benefit the family. In A. Ojeda (Ed.), *The Family: Opposing viewpoints* (pp. 185–188). San Diego, CA: Greenhaven Press.

Cruz, R. A., King, K. M., Widaman, K. F., Leu, J., Cauce, A. M., & Conger, R. D. (2011). Cultural predictors of positive father involvement in two-parent Mexican-origin families. *Journal of Family Psychology, 25,* 731–740.

Cupach, W. R., & Canary D. J. (1997). *Competence in interpersonal conflict.* New York: McGraw-Hill.

Cupach, W.R., & Olson, L.N. (2006). Emotion regulation theory: A lens for viewing family conflict and violence. In D. Braithwaite & L. Baxter (Eds.), *Engaging theories in family communication: Multiple perspectives* (pp. 213–228). Thousand Oaks, CA: Sage.

Cupach, W. R., & Spitzberg, B. H. (1994). Dark side denouement. In W. R. Cupach & B. H. Spitzberg (Eds.), *The dark side of interpersonal communication* (pp. 315–320). Hillsdale, NJ: Erlbaum.

Cushman, D. (1977). The rules perspective as a theoretical basis for the study of human communication. *Communication Quarterly, 25,* 30–45.

Dainton, M. (1999). African-American, European-American, and biracial couples' meanings for and experiences in marriage. In T. J. Socha & R. C. Diggs (Eds.), *Communication, race, and family: Exploring communication in black, white, and biracial families* (pp. 147–165). Mahwah, NJ: Erlbaum.

Daly, K. (2003). Family theory versus the theories families live by. *Journal of Marriage and the Family, 65,* 771–784.

Davidson, J. K., & Moore, N. B. (1996). *Marriage and family.* Dubuque, IA: Brown.

Davis, R. L. (2010). *More perfect unions: The American search for marital bliss.* Cambridge, MA: Harvard University Press.

Day, E. D., & Remigy, M. J. (1999). Mexican and French children's conceptions about family: A developmental approach. *Journal of Comparative Family Studies, 30,* 95–112.

DeCoker, G. (2001). Japanese families: The father's place in a changing world. In T. F. Cohen (Ed.), *Men and masculinity* (pp. 207–218). Belmont, CA: Wadsworth.

Del Campo, R., Del Campo, D., & DeLeon, M. (2000). Caring for aging family members: Implications and resources for family practitioners. Retrieved from *www.ces.ncsu.edu/depts/fcs/pub/2000/caregiving/html.*

Demo, D. H. (1992). Parent-child relations: Assessing recent changes. *Journal of Marriage and the Family, 54,* 104–117.

Derlega, V. J. (1984). Self-disclosure and intimate relationships. In V. J. Derlega (Ed.), *Communication, intimacy, and close relationships* (pp. 1–9). Orlando, FL: Academic Press.

de Turck, M. (1987). When communication fails: Physical aggression as a compliance-gaining strategy. *Communication Monographs, 54,* 106–112.

Deutsch, F. (1999). *Having it all: How equally shared parenting works.* Cambridge, MA: Harvard.

DeVega, J. T., & Guarkee, C. O. (2010). *All you want to know but didn't think you could ask: Religions, cults, and popular beliefs.* Nashville, TN: Thomas Nelson.

Dickinson, A. (2000, May 22). Family fighting. *Time, 150.*

Dickson, F. C. (1995). The best is yet to be: Research on long-lasting marriages. In J. T. Wood & S. Duck (Eds.), *Under-studied relationships: Off the beaten track* (pp. 22–50). Thousand Oaks, CA: Sage.

Dickson, F. C., Borowsky, J. P., Baldwin, K. T., Corti, J. K., Johnson, D., Lawrence, L., & Velasco, J. (2011). Communication challenges of parenting in homeless families. In F. C. Dickson & L. M. Webb (Eds.), *Communication for families in crises: Theories, research, strategies* (pp. 337–360). New York: Peter Lang.

Dickson, F. C., Christian, A., & Remmo, C. J. (2004). An exploration of the marital and family issues of the later-life adult. In A. L. Vangelisti (Ed.), *Handbook of family communication* (pp. 153–174). Mahwah, NJ: Erlbaum.

Diggs, R. (1999). African American and European American adolescents' perceptions of self-esteem as influenced by parent and peer communication and support environments. In T. S. Socha & R. C. Diggs (Eds.), *Communication, race, and family* (pp. 105–146). Mahwah, NJ: Erlbaum.

Diggs, R. C., & Socha, T. (2004). Communication, families, and exploring the boundaries of cultural diversity. In A. L. Vangelisti (Ed.), *Handbook of family communication* (pp. 249–266). Mahwah, NJ: Erlbaum.

Dilworth-Anderson, P., Burton, L. M., & Johnson, L. B. (1993). Reframing theories for understanding race, ethnicity, and families. In P. G. Boss, W. J. Doherty, R. LaRossa, W. R. Schumm, & S. K. Steinmetz (Eds.), *Sourcebook of family theories and methods: A contextual approach* (pp. 627–646). New York: Plenum Press.

Dindia, K. (1998). "Going into and coming out of the closet": The dialectics of stigma disclosure. In B. M. Montgomery & L. A. Baxter (Eds.), *Dialectical approaches to studying personal relationships* (pp. 83–108). Mahwah, NJ: Erlbaum.

Dindia, K. (2000). Sex differences in self-disclosure, reciprocity of self-disclosure, and self-disclosure and liking: Three meta-analyses reviewed. In S. Petronio (Ed.), *Balancing the secrets of private disclosures* (pp. 21–35). Mahwah, NJ: Erlbaum.

Dindia, K. (2006). Men are from North Dakota, women are from South Dakota. In K. Dindia and D. J. Canary (Eds.), *Sex differences and similarities in communication* (pp. 3–20). Mahwah, NJ: Erlbaum.

Dines, G., & Humez, J. M. (2011). *Gender, race, and class in media.* Thousand Oaks, CA: Sage.

Dixon, L. D. (2004). A house as a symbol, a house as a family: Mamaw and her Oklahoma Cherokee family. In A. Gonzalez, M. Houston, & V. Chen (Eds.), *Our voices: Essays in culture, ethnicity, and communication* (pp. 144–148). Los Angeles: Roxbury.

Dixon, S. V., Graber, J. A., & Brooks-Gunn, J. (2008). The roles of respect for parental authority and parenting practices in parent-child conflict among African American, Latino, and European American families. *Journal of Family Psychology, 22*(1), 1–10.

Dodson-Gray, E. (1992). Beauty and the beast: A parable for our time. In K. L. Hagan (Ed.), *Women respond to the men's movement* (pp. 159–168). San Francisco, CA: Harper.

Doherty, W. J. (2001, January/February). Towards confident fathering. *UUWorld, 15,* 31.

Doherty, W. J., Boss, P. G., LaRossa, R., Schumm, W. R., & Steinmetz, S. K. (1993). Family theories and methods. In P. G. Boss, W. J. Doherty, R. LaRossa, W. R. Schumm, & S. K. Steinmetz (Eds.), *Sourcebook of family theories and methods: A contextual approach* (pp. 3–30). New York: Plenum Press.

Dow, B. J. (1990). Hegemony, feminist criticism, and *The Mary Tyler Moore Show. Critical Studies in Mass Communication, 7,* 261–274.

Doyle, J. A. (1989). *The male experience.* Dubuque, IA: Brown.

Duck, S. (1992). *Human relationships.* London: Sage.

Duck, S. (1994b). Stratagems, spoils, and a serpent's tooth: On the delights and dilemmas of personal relationships. In W. R. Cupach & B. H. Spitzberg (Eds.), *The dark side of interpersonal communication* (pp. 3–24). Hillsdale, NJ: Erlbaum.

Duck, S., & Wood, J. T. (1995a). For better, for worse, for richer, for poorer: The rough and smooth of relationships. In S. Duck & J. T. Wood (Eds.), *Confronting relationship challenges* (pp. 1–21). Thousand Oaks, CA: Sage.

Duck, S., Rutt, D. J., Hurst, M. H., & Strejc, H. (1991). Some evident truths about conversations in everyday relationships: All communications are not created equal. *Human Communication Research, 29,* 5–40.

Duckworth, J. D., & Buzzanell, P. M. (2009). Constructing work-life balance and fatherhood: Men's framing of the meanings of both work and family. *Communication Studies, 60,* 558–573.

Dumlao, R., & Botta, R. A. (2000). Family communication patterns and the conflict styles young adults use with their fathers. *Communication Quarterly, 48,* 174–189.

Dun, T. (2010). Turning points in parent-grandparent relationships during the start of a new generation. *Journal of Family Communication, 10,* 194–210.

Eberstat, M. (2012). Has the sexual revolution been good for women? No. Retrieved from *http://online.wsj.com/article/SB10001424052702304724404577297422171909202.html.*

Eckstein, J. J. (2009). Exploring the communication of men revealing abuse from female romantic partners. In D. D. Cahn (Ed.), *Family violence: Communication processes* (pp. 89–111). Albany, NY: SUNY Press.

Edley, P. P. (2004). Entrepreneurial mothers' balance of work and family: Discursive constructions of time, mothering, and identity. In P. M. Buzzanell, H. Sterk, & L. H. Turner (Eds.), *Gender in applied communication contexts* (pp. 255–273). Thousand Oaks, CA: Sage.

Edwards, A. P., & Graham, E. E. (2009). The relationship between individuals' definitions of family and implicit personal theories of communication. *Journal of Family Communication, 9,* 191–208.

Edwards, J. (2011). The use of music therapy to promote attachment between parents and infants. *The Arts in Psychotherapy, 38,* 190– 195.

Einhorn, L. J. (2000). *The Native American oral tradition: Voices of the spirit and soul.* Westport, CT: Praeger.

Eisenstein, H. (1994). Reconstructing the family. In G. Handel & G. G. Whitchurch (Eds.), *The psychosocial interior of the family* (pp. 363–374). New York: Aldine De Gruyter.

Eklund, M. A. (1996). *Understanding Southwest urban Hispanic women's sources of health information.* Paper presented at the annual meeting of the Organization for the Study of Communication, Language, and Gender, Monterey, CA.

Ellingson, L. L. (2011). Interviews as embodied communication. In J. F. Gubrium, J. A. Holsten, A. Marvasti, & K. M. Marvasti (Eds.), *Handbook of interview research,* 2nd ed. Thousand Oaks, CA: Sage.

Ellingson, L. L., & Sotirin, P. J. (2010). *Aunting: Cultural practices that sustain family and community life.* Waco, TX: Baylor University Press.

Ellis, C., & Bochner, A. P. (1992). Telling and performing personal stories: The constraints of choice in abortion. In C. Ellis & M. Flaherty (Eds.), *Investigating subjectivity* (pp. 79–101). Thousand Oaks, CA: Sage.

El Nasser, H., & Overberg, P. (2011, May 26). Fewer couples embrace marriage; more live together. *USA Today,* A1–A2.

El Nasser, H. (2010, March 2). Multiracial no longer boxed in by the U.S. Census. *USA Today,* 1A–2A.

El Nasser, H., & Overberg, P. (2011, August 9). How America changed. *USA Today,* 1D.

Emery, R. E. (1988). *Marriage, divorce, and children's adjustment.* Newbury Park, CA: Sage.

Epstein, N. B., Bishop, D. S., & Baldwin, L. M. (1982). McMaster model of family functioning. In F. Walsh (Ed.), *Normal family processes* (pp. 115–141). New York: Guilford.

Espiritu, Y. L., & Wolf, D. L. (2001). The paradox of assimilation: Children of Filipino immigrants in San Diego. In R. G. Rumbaut & A. Portes (Eds.), *Ethnicities: Children of immigrants in America* (pp. 157–186). Berkeley, CA: University of California Press.

Evans, N. (2002, March 31). The whispering is over. *YES!, Spring 2003,* p. 1.

Fagan, P.T. (2010). The real root cause of violent crime: The breakdown of the family. Retrieved from *http://goodnewstucson.wordpress.com/2010/05/05/the-real-root-cause-of-violent-crime-the-breakdown-of-the-family.*

Farley-Lucas, B. (2000). Communicating the (in)visibility of motherhood: Family talk and the ties to motherhood with/in the workplace. *Electronic Journal of Communication/Revue Electronique de Communication, 10.*

Farrell, J. (2011). The young and the restless? The liberalization of young evangelicals. *Journal for the Scientific Study of Religion, 50,* 517–532.

Farrell, W. (1987). *Why men are the way they are.* New York: McGraw-Hill.

Feingold, M. H. (2000). Everything's not O.K. at home. *Clinical Pediatrics, 39,* 41–42.

Ferreira, A. (1963). Family myths and homeostasis. *Archives of General Psychiatry, 9,* 257–463.

Feuer, J. (1991). Melodrama, serial form, and television today. In L. Vande Berg & L. A. Wenner (Eds.), *Television criticism* (pp. 163–177). White Plains, NY: Longman.

Fieldler, M. (2010). *Breaking through the stained glass ceiling: Women religious leaders in their own words.* New York: Seabury Books.

Fieler, B. (2011). What "Modern Family" says about modern families. Retrieved from *http://www.nytimes.com/2011/01/23/fashion/23THISLIFE.html?pagewanted-all.*

Fiese, B. H., & Sameroff, A. J. (1999). The family narrative consortium: A multidimensional approach to narratives. *Monographs of the Society for Research in Child Development, 64*, 1–36.

Fiese, B. H., Tomcho, T. J., Douglas, M., Josephs, K., Poltrock, S., & Baker, T. (2002). A review of 50 years of research on naturally occurring family routines and rituals: Cause for celebration? *Journal of Family Psychology, 16*, 381–390.

Fiffer, S. S. (1996). Introduction: Skeletons. In S. S. Fiffer & S. Fiffer (Eds.), *Family: American writers remember their own* (pp. vii–xv). New York: Pantheon Books.

Fincham, F. D. (2004). Communication in marriage. In A. L. Vangelisti (Ed.), *Handbook of family communication* (pp. 83–103). Mahwah, NJ: Erlbaum.

Fine, M. A., Ganong, L., & Demo, D. H. (2010). Divorce: A risk and resilience perspective. In S. J. Price, C. A. Price, & P. C. McKenry (Eds.), *Families and change: Coping with stressful events and transitions* (pp. 211–233). Thousand Oaks, CA: Sage.

Fingerman, K. L., & Hay, E. L. (2002). "Searching under the streetlight?": Age biases in the personal and family relationships literature. *Personal Relationships, 9*, 415–433.

Finkelhor, D. (1983). Common features of family abuse. In D. Finkelhor, R. J. Gelles, G. T. Hotaling, & M. A. Straus (Eds.), *The dark side of families: Current family violence research* (pp. 17–28). Beverly Hills, CA: Sage.

Finnan, C. R., & Cooperstein, R. (1983). *Southeast Asian refugee resettlement at the local level* (Office of Refugee Resettlement Report). Menlo Park, CA: SRI International.

Fisher, C. L. (2010). Coping with breast cancer across adulthood: Emotional support communication in the mother-daughter bond. *Journal of Applied Communication Research, 38*, 386–411.

Fisher, W. R. (1984). Narration as human communication paradigm: The case for public moral argument. *Communication Monographs, 51*, 1–22.

Fisher, W. R. (1987). *Human communication as narration: Toward a philosophy of reason, value, and action.* Columbia: University of South Carolina Press.

Fishman, T. C. (2012, March 14). Challenge for our (ripe old) age. Retrieved from *http://www.usatoday.com/news/opinion/forum/story/2012-03-14/old-age-retirement-baby-boomer/53535784/1.*

Fitzpatrick, M. A. (1977). A typological approach to communication in relationships. In B. Rubin (Ed.), *Communication yearbook 1* (pp. 263–275). New Brunswick, NJ: Transaction Books.

Fitzpatrick, M. A. (1987). Marital interaction. In C. Berger & S. Chaffee (Eds.), *Handbook of communication science* (pp. 564–618). Newbury Park, CA: Sage.

Fitzpatrick, M. A., & Badzinski, D. (1994). All in the family: Interpersonal communication in kin relationships. In M. L. Knapp & G. R. Miller (Eds.), *Handbook of interpersonal communication* (pp. 726–771). Thousand Oaks, CA: Sage.

Flora, J., & Segrin, C. (2000). Affect and behavioral involvement in spousal complaints and compliments. *Journal of Family Psychology, 14*, 641–657.

Floyd, K., & Morman, M. T. (2003). Human affection exchange: II. Affectionate communication in father–son relationships. *Journal of Social Psychology, 143*, 599–613.

Floyd, K. (1996). Communicating closeness among siblings: An application of the gender closeness perspective. *Communication Research Reports, 13*, 27–34.

Floyd, K., & Parks, M. R. (1995). Manifesting closeness in the interactions of peers: A look at siblings and friends. *Communication Reports, 8*, 1–8.

Foley, M. K., & Duck, S. (2006). That dear octopus: A family-based model of intimacy. In L. H. Turner & R. West (Eds.), *The family communication sourcebook* (pp. 183–199). Thousand Oaks, CA: Sage.

Fondas, N. (1995). The biological clock confronts complex organizations: Women's ambivalence about work and implications for feminist management research. *Journal of Management Inquiry, 4,* 57–65.

Ford, L. A., Babrow, A. S., & Stohl, C. (1996). Social support messages and the management of uncertainty in the experience of breast cancer: An application of problematic integration theory. *Communication Monographs, 63,* 189–207.

Forest Institute of Professional Psychology. (2011). Articles. Retrieved from *http://www.forest.edu/lib_find_articles.aspx.*

Fowler, C., & Dillow, M. R. (2011). Attachment dimensions and the Four Horsemen of the Apocalypse. *Communication Research Reports, 28,* 16–26.

Francese, P. (2004). Marriage drain's big cost. *American Demographics, 26,* 40–41.

Frazier, I. (1994). *Family.* New York: Farrar Straus & Giroux.

Freedman, C. H. (1985). *Manhood redux.* Brooklyn, NY: Samson.

French, J. P. P., & Raven, B. (1959). The bases of social power. In D. Cartwright (Ed.), *Studies in social power* (pp. 150–167). Ann Arbor, MI: University of Michigan Press.

Frisby, B. N., & Sidelinger, R. J. (2009). Parents' post-divorce relationships: Maintenance with former in-laws. *Ohio Communication Journal, 47,* 77–95.

Frisby, B. N., Byrnes, K., Mansson, D. H., Booth-Butterfield, M., & Birmingham, M. (2011). Topic avoidance, everyday talk, and stress in romantic military and nonmilitary couples. *Communication Studies, 62,* 241–257.

Frum, D. (2003). Legalizing same-sex marriage would harm marriage. In A. Ojeda (Ed.), *The Family: Opposing viewpoints* (pp. 201–206). San Diego, CA: Greenhaven Press.

Fuller, L. K. (1999). From tramps to truth-seekers: Images of homelessness in the motion pictures. In E. Min (Ed.), *Reading the homeless: The media's image of homeless culture* (pp. 159–174). Westport, CT: Praeger.

Furstenberg, F. F. (2003). The future of marriage. In A. S. Skolnick & J. H. Skolnick (Eds.), *Family in transition* (pp. 170–176). Boston, MA: Pearson.

Gabbadon, N. (2006). *From "Good Times" to bad: Changing portrayals of the African American sitcom family.* Paper presented at the annual meeting of the International Communication Association, Dresden, Germany.

Gaines, S. O., Jr. (1995). Relationships between members of cultural minorities. In J. T. Wood & S. Duck (Eds.), *Under-studied relationships: Off the beaten track* (pp. 51–88). Thousand Oaks, CA: Sage.

Galvin, K. (2003). International and transracial adoption: A communication research agenda. *Journal of Family Communication, 3,* 237–253.

Galvin, K. M. (1999). Epilogue: Illuminating and evoking issues of race and family communication. In T. J. Socha & R. C. Diggs (Eds.), *Communication, race, and family: Exploring communication in black, white, and biracial families* (pp. 229–232). Mahwah, NJ: Erlbaum.

Galvin, K. M. (2004). The family of the future: What do we face? In A. L. Vangelisti (Ed.), *Handbook of family communication* (pp. 675–697). Mahwah, NJ: Erlbaum.

Galvin, K. M., & Brommel, B. J. (2000). *Family communication: Cohesion and change* (5th ed.). New York: Longman.

Galvin, K. M., & Cooper, P. (1990). *Development of involuntary relationships: The stepparent/stepchild relationship.* Paper presented at the annual meeting of the International Communication Association, Dublin, Ireland.

Galvin, K. M., & Wilkinson, C. A. (1996). The communication process: Impersonal and interpersonal. In K. M. Galvin & P. Cooper (Eds.), *Making connections: Readings in relational communication* (pp. 4–10). Los Angeles: Roxbury.

Galvin, K. M., Dickson, F. C., & Marrow, S. R. (2006). Systems theory: Patterns and (w)holes in family communication. In D. O. Braithwaite & L. A. Baxter (Eds.),

Engaging theories in family communication: Multiple perspectives (pp. 309–324). Thousand Oaks, CA: Sage.

Gangotena, M. (2012). The rhetoric of *la familia* among Mexican Americans. In A. Gonzalez, M. Houston, & V. Chen (Eds.), Our voices: *Essays in culture, ethnicity, and communication* (pp. 113–119). New York: Oxford University Press.

Gardner, M. (2003). Weighing the price of "perfect" in family life. In K. R. Gilbert (Ed.), *Annual editions: The family* (pp. 10–15). Guilford, CT: McGraw-Hill.

Garment, S. (1992, May 22). After the snickers, a serious issue. *Los Angeles Times,* B7.

Garner, A. C. (1999). Negotiating our positions in culture: Popular adolescent fiction and the self-constructions of women. *Women's Studies in Communication, 22,* 1–27.

Gergen, K. (1985). The social constructionist movement in modern psychology. *American Psychologist, 40,* 266–275.

Gheaus, A. (2011). Arguments for non-parental care for children. *Social Theory and Practice, 37,* 483–509.

Giannini, G. A. (2011). Finding support in a field of devastation: Bereaved parents' narratives of communication and recovery. *Western Journal of Communication, 75,* 41–564.

Gilbert, M. (2011). Openly gay on TV. Retrieved from *http://articles.boston.com/2011-10-16/ae/30286928_1_openly-gay-actor-graham-norton-jesse-tyler-ferguson.*

Gilgoff, D. (2004). The rise of the gay family. *U.S. News and World Report, 136,* pp. 40–45.

Gilligan, C., & Machoian, L. (2002). Learning to speak the language: A relational interpretation of adolescent girls' suicidality. *Studies of Gender and Sexuality, 3,* 313–333.

Goetting, A. (1986). The developmental tasks of siblingship over the life cycle. *Journal of Marriage and the Family, 43,* 409–421.

Goffman, E. (1959). *The presentation of self in daily life.* Garden City, NY: Doubleday.

Gold, S. J. (1993). Migration and family adjustment: Continuity and change among Vietnamese in the United States. In H. P. McAdoo (Ed.), *Family ethnicity: Strength in diversity* (pp. 300–314). Newbury Park, CA: Sage.

Goldberg, H. (1976). *The hazards of being male.* New York: Signet.

Golden, A. G. (2001). Modernity and the communicative management of multiple roles: The case of the worker-parent. *The Journal of Family Communication, 1,* 233–264.

Golden, A. G. (2007). Fathers' frames for childrearing: Evidence toward a "masculine concept of caregiving." *Journal of Family Communication, 7,* 265–285.

Goldner, V. (1985). Feminism and family therapy. *Family Process, 24,* 31–47.

Goldsmith, D. J., McDermott, V. M., & Alexander, S. C. (2000). Helpful, supportive and sensitive: Measuring the evaluation of enacted social support in personal relationships. *Journal of Social and Personal Relationships, 17,* 369–391.

González, A., Houston, M., & Chen, V. (2011). Introduction. In A. González, M. Houston, & V. Chen (Eds.), *Our voices: Essays in culture, ethnicity and communication* (pp. 1–13). Los Angeles: Roxbury.

Goodall, H. L., Jr. (2005). Narrative inheritance: A nuclear family with toxic secrets. *Qualitative Inquiry, 11,* 492–513.

Goodall, H. L., Jr. (2006). *A need to know: The clandestine history of a CIA family.* Walnut Creek, CA: Left Coast Press.

Goodboy, A. K., Myers, S. A., & Patterson, B. P. (2009). Investigating elderly sibling types, relational maintenance, and lifespan affect, cognition, and behavior. *Atlantic Journal of Communication, 17,* 140–148.

Goodman, E. (1997, March 28). Finally, a law to curb female genital mutilation. *Milwaukee Journal Sentinel,* p. 14A.

Goodwin, P. Y., Mosher, W. D., & Chandra, A. (2010). Marriage and cohabitation in the United States: A statistical portrait based on Cycle 6 (2002) of the National Survey of Family Growth. Retrieved from *http://www.cdc.gov/nchs/data/series/sr_23/sr23_028.pdf.*

Gordon, A. (2004, June 11). What are we doing to our kids? *Toronto Star,* p. 1D.

Gorrell, C. (2000, November/December). Live-in and learn. *Psychology Today,* p. 33.

Gottman, J. M. (1994a). *What predicts divorce?* Hillsdale, NJ: Erlbaum.

Gottman, J. M. (1994b). *Why marriages succeed or fail.* New York: Simon and Schuster.

Gottman, J. M. (1999). *The marriage clinic: A scientific based marital therapy.* New York: Norton.

Gottman, J. M., Katz, L. F., & Hooven, C. (1997). *Meta-emotion: How families communicate emotionally.* Mahwah, NJ: Erlbaum.

Govaerts, K., & Dixon, D. (1988). ". . . Until careers do us part": Vocational and marital satisfaction in the dual-career commuter marriage. *International Journal for the Advancement of Counseling, 11,* 265–281.

Graham, E. E. (1996). *A state of exquisite imbalance: Dialectic contradictions in post divorce relationships.* Paper presented at the annual meeting of the Speech Communication Association, San Diego, CA.

Graham, E. E. (1997). Turning points and commitments in post-divorce relations. *Communication Monographs, 64,* 350–368.

Graham, E. E. (2003). Dialectic contradictions in postmarital relationships. *Journal of Family Communication, 3,* 193–214.

Greenberg, B. S. (1982). Television and role socialization: An overview. In D. Pearl, L. Bouthilet, & J. Lazar (Eds.), *Television and behavior: Ten years of scientific progress and implications for the eighties* (pp. 179–190). Washington D.C.: Government Printing Office.

Griffin, W. (2004). The goddess net. In L. L. Dawson & D. E. Cowan (Eds.), *Religion online: Finding faith on the Internet* (pp. 189–203). New York: Routledge.

Grimonprez, J. (2010). Remote control: On zapping, close encounters, and the commercial break. Retrieved from *http://www.macba.cat/uploads/TWM/TV_grimonprez_eng.pdf.*

Grossman, C. L. (2012). More churches turning to high-tech outreach. Retrieved from *http://www.religionnews.com/faith/clergy-and-congregations/more-congregations-turn-to-facebook-web-high-tech-outreach.*

Guerrero, L. K., & Afifi, W. A. (1995). What parents don't know: Topic avoidance in parent–child relationships. In T. J. Socha & G. H. Stamp (Eds.), *Parents, children, and communication: Frontiers of theory and research* (pp. 219–245). Mahwah, NJ: Erlbaum.

Guindon, M. H., & Smith, B. (2002). Emotional barriers to successful reemployment: Implications for counselors. *Journal of Employment Counseling, 39,* 73–82.

Gunn, A. (2007). *"It's not my American dream": Working class people share their experience of job loss.* Paper presented at the annual meeting of the National Communication Association, Chicago, IL.

Hadden, J. K. (1983). Televangelism and the mobilization of a new Christian right family policy. In W. D'Antonio & J. Aldous (Eds.), *Families and religions: Conflict and change in modern society* (pp. 247–266). Beverly Hills, CA: Sage.

Hagans, K., Hass, M., Lee, P., & Powers, K. (2011). Developing school psychology in Vietnam. *Communique, 39,* 8–10.

Hall, B. (2005). *Among cultures: The challenge of communication.* Ft. Worth, TX: Harcourt.

Hall, D. L., & Langellier, K. M. (1988). Storytelling strategies in mother-daughter communication. In B. Bate & A. Taylor (Eds.), *Women communicating: Studies of women's talk* (pp. 107–126). Norwood, NJ: Ablex.

Hammill, G. (2011). Mary Tyler Moore. Retrieved from *http://www.museum.tv/eotv-section.php?entrycode=marytylermo.*

Hampp, A. (2011, April 18). Why viewers and marketers are loving "Modern Family."*Advertising Age, 82,* 4.

Hampson, R. (2011, October 10). Anti–Wall Street protests face question: Now what? *USA Today,* 1A–2A.

Handel, G., & Whitchurch, G. G. (1994). Introduction to the fourth edition. In G. Handel & G. G. Whitchurch (Eds.), *The psychosocial interior of the family* (pp. xiii–xix). New York: Aldine De Gruyter.

Hardman, M. J. (1995). "And if we lose our name, then what about our land?" Or what price development? In L. H. Turner & H. M. Sterk (Eds.), *Differences that make a difference: Examining the assumptions in gender research* (pp. 151–162). Westport, CT: Bergin & Garvey.

Hardway, C., & Fuligni, A. J. (2006). Dimensions of family connectedness among adolescents with Mexican, Chinese, and European backgrounds. *Developmental Psychology, 42,* 1246–1258.

Hardy, K. (2008). Race, reality, and relationships: Implications for the re-visioning of family therapy. In M. McGoldrick & K. Hardy (Eds.), *Re-visioning family therapy* (pp. 76–84). Thousand Oaks, CA: Sage.

Harper, J. (2001, September 3). Some things are secret, and that's no white lie: Communication in marriage. Retrieved from *http://www.questia.com/library/1G1-76729720/some-things-secret-and-no-white-lie.*

Harrigan, M. M. (2010). Exploring the narrative process: An analysis of the adoption stories mothers tell their internationally adopted children. *Journal of Family Communication, 10,* 24–39.

Harrigan, M. M., & Braithwaite, D. O. (2010). Discursive struggles in families formed through visible adoption: An exploration of dialectical unity. *Journal of Applied Communication Research, 38,* 127–144.

Harrington, M. (1998). The care equation. Retrieved from *www.prospect.org/print/v9/39/harrington-m.html.*

Harrington, M. (2003). Improved day care would benefit the family. In A. Ojeda (Ed.), *The family: Opposing viewpoints* (pp. 155–159). San Diego, CA: Greenhaven Press.

Hartsock, N. M. (1987). The feminist standpoint: Developing the ground for a specifically feminist historical materialism. In S. Harding (Ed.), *Feminism and methodology* (pp. 157–180). Bloomington, IN: University Press.

Harvey, J. H., & Weber, A. L. (2002). *Odyssey of the heart: Close relationships in the 21st century.* Mahwah, NJ: Erlbaum.

Harwood, J. (2004). Relational, role, and social identity as expressed in grandparents' personal web sites. *Communication Studies, 55,* 300–318.

Hashem, M. (1997). The power of Wastah in Lebanese speech. In A. González, M. Houston, & V. Chen (Eds.), *Our voices: Essays in culture, ethnicity, and communication* (pp. 99–104). Los Angeles: Roxbury.

Hashem, M. (2011). The power of wastah in Lebanese speech. In A. Gonzalez, M. Houston, & V. Chen (Eds.), Our voices: *Essays in culture, ethnicity, and communication* (pp. 113–119). New York: Oxford University Press.

Hastings, S. O. (2000). Asian Indian self-suppression and self-disclosure. *Journal of Language and Social Psychology, 19,* 85–109.

Hause, K., & Pearson, J. C. (1994). *The warmth without the sting: Relational dialectics over the family life cycle.* Paper presented at the annual meeting of the Speech Communication Association, New Orleans, LA.

Havens, T. (2000). "The biggest show in the world": Race and the global popularity of *The Cosby Show. Media, Culture & Society, 22,* 371–391.

Hazan, C., & Shaver, P. R. (1994). Deeper into attachment theory: Authors' response. *Psychological Inquiry, 5,* 68–79.

Hecht, M. L., Larkey, L. K., & Johnson, J. N. (1992). African American and European American perceptions of problematic issues in interethnic communication effectiveness. *Human Communication Research, 19,* 209–236.

Hecht, M. L., Ribeau, S., & Alberts, J. K. (1989). An Afro-American perspective on interethnic communication. *Communication Monographs, 56,* 385–410.

Heisler, J. (2009). Family communication about sex: Parents and college-aged offspring recall discussion topics, satisfaction, and parental involvement. *Journal of Family Communication, 5,* 295–312.

Helland, C. (2004). Popular religion and the World Wide Web: A match made in (cyber) heaven. In L. L. Dawson & D. E. Cowan (Eds.), *Religion online: Finding faith on the Internet* (pp. 23–35). New York: Routledge.

Hendrick, C., & Hendrick, S. S. (1996). Gender and the experience of heterosexual love. In J. T. Wood (Ed.), *Gendered relationships* (pp. 131–148). Mountain View, CA: Mayfield.

Hendrix, K. G. (2012). Home as respite for the working-class academic. In A. Gonzalez, M. Houston, & V. Chen (Eds.), *Our voices: Essays in culture, ethnicity, and communication* (pp. 240–246). New York: Oxford University Press.

Henwood, K., Giles, H., Coupland, J., & Coupland, N. (1993). Stereotyping and affect in discourse: Interpreting the meaning of elderly, painful self-disclosure. In D. M. Mackie & D. L. Hamilton (Eds.), *Affect, cognition, and stereotyping: Interactive processes in group perception* (pp. 269–296). San Diego, CA: Academic Press.

Hertz, R. (1986). *More equal than others: Women and men in dual-career marriages.* Berkeley, CA: University of California Press.

Herzog, M. J. (2010). Family, stress, and intervention. In S. Price, C. A. Price, and P. McHenry (Eds.), *Families and change: Coping with stressful events and transitions* (pp. 399–418). Thousand Oaks, CA: Sage.

Hess, R., & Handel, G. (1959). *Family worlds.* Chicago, IL: University of Chicago Press.

Hetherington, E. M. (2002). Marriage and divorce American style. Retrieved from *www.prospect.org/print/V13/7/hetherington-e.html.*

Hetherington, E. M., Law, T. C., & O'Connor, T. G. (1993). Divorce: Challenges, changes, and new chances. In F. Walsh (Ed.), *Normal family processes* (pp. 208–234). New York: Guilford.

Hicks, T. (2011). Discipline: Making time out effective for children. Retrieved from *http://www.helium.com/items/2081927-discipline-children-make-timeout-effective.*

Hill, M. (1988). Child-rearing attitudes of black lesbian mothers. In Boston Lesbian Psychologies Collective (Eds.), *Lesbian psychologies: Explorations and challenges* (pp. 109–129). Urbana, IL: University of Illinois Press.

Hill, R. (1958). Generic features of families under stress. *Social Casework, 49,* 139–150.

Hochschild, A. R. (1989). *The second shift: Working parents and the revolution at home.* New York: Viking.

Hochschild, A. R. (1997). *The time bind: When work becomes home and home becomes work.* New York: Henry Holt.

Hocking, J. E., & Lawrence, S. (2000). Changing attitudes toward the homeless: The effects of prosocial communication. *Journal of Social Distress and the Homeless, 9,* 91–110.

Holson, L. (2011). Who's on the family tree? Now it's complicated. Retrieved from *http://www.nytimes.com/2011/07/05/us/05tree.html?pagewanted=all&_moc.semityn.www*

Hombs, M. E. (1990). *American homelessness: A reference handbook.* Santa Barbara, CA: ABC-CLIO.

Honeycutt, J. M., & Brown, R. (1998). Did you hear the one about?: Typological and spousal differences in the planning of jokes and sense of humor in marriage. *Communication Quarterly, 46,* 342–352.

Hong, J. S., Cho, H., & Lee, A. S. (2010). Revisiting the Virginia Tech shootings: An ecological systems analysis. *Journal of Loss and Trauma, 15, 561–575.*

hooks, b. (1992a). *Black looks: Race and representation.* Boston, MA: South End Press.

hooks, b. (1992b). Men in the feminist struggle—the necessary movement. In K. L. Hagan (Ed.), *Women respond to the men's movement* (pp. 111–118). San Francisco, CA: Harper.

Hopper, R., Knapp, M. L., & Scott, L. (1981). Couples' personal idioms: Exploring intimate talk. *Journal of Communication, 31, 23–33.*

Horan, S. M., & Booth-Butterfield, M. (2010). Investing in affection: An investigation of affection exchange theory and relational qualities. *Communication Quarterly, 58,* 394–413.

Horan, S. M., & Booth-Butterfield, M. (2011). Is it worth lying for? Physiological and emotional implications of recalling deceptive affection. *Human Communication Research, 37,* 78–106.

Horowitz, C. F. (1990). Homelessness is exaggerated. In L. Orr (Ed.), *The homeless: Opposing viewpoints* (pp. 21–27). San Diego, CA: Greenhaven Press.

Houston, M. (2004). When black women talk with white women: Why the dialogues are difficult. In A. González, M. Houston, & V. Chen (Eds.), *Our voices: Essays in culture, ethnicity, and communication* (pp. 119–125). Los Angeles: Roxbury.

http://blog.nielsen.com/nielsenwire/media_entertainment/number-of-u-s-tvhouseholds-climbs-by-one-million-for-2010-11-tv-season. Nielsen estimates number of U.S. television homes to be 114.7 million.

http://californiawatch.org/dailyreport/tracking-unmarried-same-sex-couples-using-social-maps-4233. Tracking unmarried, same-sex couples using social maps.

http://divorcerate2011.com/divorce-statistics/divorce-rate-by-age-or-religion. Divorce rate by age or religion.

http://eagleforum.org. Should parents or the village raise children.

http://goodnewstucson.wordpress.com/2010/05/05/the-real-root-cause-of-violent-crime-the-breakdown-of-the-family. The real root cause of violent crime: The breakdown of the family.

http://mormonexpression.com/blogs/2011/07/09/more-than-6-of-temple-married-mormons-get-divorced. More than 6% of temple-married Mormons get divorced.

http://ohiodailyblog.com/content/wouldn't-you-know-it%3F-catholic-bishops-involved-komen-debacle. Wouldn't you know it? Catholic bishops involved in Komen debacle.

http://parenting.blogs.nytimes.com/2011/06/02/with-more-single-fathers-a-changing-family-picture. With more single fathers, a changing family picture.

http://pewresearch.org/pubs/1802/decline-in-marriage-rise-new-families. The decline of marriage and rise of new families.

http://www.acf.hhs.gov/healthymarriage/pdf/Gender_Norms.pdf. Gender norms and the role of the extended family.

http://www.cdc.gov/nchs/data/series/sr_23/sr23_028.pdf. (2011). Marriage and cohabitation in the United States: A statistical portrait based on cycle 6 (2002) of the National Survey of Family Growth.

http://www.cdc.gov/nchs/fastats/lifeexpec.htm. Life expectancy.

http://www.census.gov/compendia/statab/cats/international_statistics.html. International statistics.

http://www.census.gov/newsroom/releases/archives/children/cb09-170.html. Nearly half of parents get full amount of child support, Census reports.

http://www.census.gov/newsroom/releases/archives/families_households/cb10-174. html. Profile America: Facts for features.

http://www.census.gov/prod/2011pubs/11statab/pop.pdf. Population.

http://www.census.gov/prod/2011pubs/p70-126.pdf. Living arrangements of children: 2009.

http://www.endhomelessness.org/section/about_homelessness/snapshot_of_homelessness. Snapshot of homelessness.

http://www.familiesandwork.org/site/newsroom/releases/pr_malemystique_110630. html. Increasing job demands and long work hours among the factors contributing to increased work-family conflict in men.

http://www.familiesandwork.org. A selection of Families and Work Institute's ahead of the curve publications.

http://www.frc.org. The problem with same-sex marriage.

http://www.gallup.com/poll/121253/extramarital-affairs-sanford-morally-taboo.aspx. Extramarital affairs, like Sanford's, morally taboo.

http://www.gallup.com/poll/147662/first-time-majority-americans-favor-legal-gay-marriage.aspx. For first time, majority of Americans favor gay marriage.

http://www.globalsecurity.org/military/world/vietnam/rvn-family.htm. The family unit.

http://www.huduser.org/publications/homeless/homelessness/ch_2e.html. Income, employment, and other income sources.

http://www.ncsl.org/issues-research/human-services/same-sex-marriage-overview.aspx. Defining marriage: Defense of marriage acts and same-sex marriage laws.

http://www.nefe.org. Financial education.

http://www.pewforum.org/Age/Religion-Among-the-Millennials.aspx. Religion among the millennials.

http://www.pewsocialtrends.org/2010/03/18/the-return-of-the-multi-generational-family-household. The return of the multi-generational household.

http://www.saafamilies.org. Welcome to the Stepfamily Association of America.

http://www.unmarried.org/statistics.html. Alternatives to marriage project.

Hughes, D. (2010). The communication of emotions and the growth of autonomy and intimacy within family therapy. *Psychotherapy in Australia, 16,* 54–65.

Hughes, P. C., & Dickson, F. C. (2005). Keeping the faith(s): Religion, communication and marital satisfaction in interfaith marriages. *Journal of Family Communication, 5,* 25–41.

Hughes, P. C., & Dickson, F. C. (2006). Relational dynamics in interfaith marriage. In L. H. Turner & R. West (Eds.), *The family communication sourcebook* (pp. 373–387). Thousand Oaks, CA: Sage.

Hummert, M. L., Nussbaum, J. F., & Wiemann, J. M. (1994). Interpersonal communication and older adulthood: An introduction. In M. L. Hummert, J. M. Wiemann, & J. F. Nussbaum (Eds.), *Interpersonal communication in older adulthood: Interdisciplinary theory and research* (pp. 1–14). Thousand Oaks, CA: Sage.

Huston, M., & Schwartz, P. (1995). The relationships of lesbians and of gay men. In J. T. Wood & S. Duck (Eds.), *Under-studied relationships: Off the beaten track* (pp. 89–121). Thousand Oaks, CA: Sage.

Huston, T. L., & Holmes, E. K. (2004). Becoming parents. In A. L. Vangelisti (Ed.), *Handbook of family communication* (pp. 105–134). Mahwah, NJ: Erlbaum.

Huston, T. L., & Vangelisti, A. L. (1991). Socioemotional behavior and satisfaction in marital relationships: A longitudinal study. *Journal of Personality and Social Psychology, 61,* 721–733.

Huston, T. L., & Vangelisti, A. L. (1995). How parenthood affects marriage. In M. A. Fitzpatrick & A. L. Vangelisti (Eds.), *Explaining family interactions* (pp. 147–176). Thousand Oaks, CA: Sage.

Imber-Black, E. (2010). The power of secrets. Retrieved from *http://www.psychology-today.com/articles/200909/the-power-secrets*.

Infante, D. A. (1995). Teaching students to understand and control verbal aggression. *Communication Education, 44*, 51–63.

Infante, D. A., & Rancer, A. S. (1996). Argumentativeness and verbal aggressiveness: A review of recent theory and research. In B. R. Burleson (Ed.), *Communication yearbook, 19* (pp. 319–351). Thousand Oaks, CA: Sage.

Infante, D. A., & Wigley, C. J. (1986). Verbal aggressiveness: An interpersonal model and measure. *Communication Monographs, 53*, 61–69.

Infante, D. A., Chandler, T. A., & Rudd, J. E. (1989). Test of an argumentative skill deficiency model of interspousal violence. *Communication Monographs, 56*, 163–177.

Infante, D. A., Myers, S. A., & Buerkel, R. A. (1994). Argument and verbal aggression in constructive and destructive family and organizational disagreements. *Western Journal of Communication, 58*, 73–84.

Infante, D. A., Rancer, A. S., & Womack, D. F. (1997). *Building communication theory.* Prospect Heights, IL: Waveland.

Ishii-Kuntz, M. (1997). Japanese American families. In M. K. DeGenova (Ed.), *Families in cultural context: Strengths and challenges in diversity* (pp. 131–153). Mountain View, CA: Mayfield.

Ivy, D. (2012). *GenderSpeak.* New York: McGraw-Hill.

Ivy, D. K., & Backlund, P. (2004). *Exploring genderspeak: Personal effectiveness in gender communication.* New York: McGraw-Hill.

James, C. C. (2010). *Half the church: Recapturing God's global vision for women.* Grand Rapids, MI: Zondervan Books.

James, N. C. (2004). When Miss America was always white. In A. González, M. Houston, & V. Chen (Eds.), *Our voices: Essays in culture, ethnicity, and communication* (pp. 61–65). Los Angeles, CA: Roxbury.

Jandt, F. (2012). *An introduction to intercultural communication: Identities in a global community.* Thousand Oaks, CA: Sage.

Jandt, F. E. (1996). *Intercultural communication.* Thousand Oaks, CA: Sage.

Jansen, B. J., Tapia, A., & Spink, A. (2010). Searching for salvation: An analysis of religious searching on the World Wide Web. *Religion, 40*, 39–52.

Janus, S., & Janus, C. (1993). The Janus report on sexual behavior.

Jayson S. (2010). Nearly 40% say marriage is becoming obsolete. Retrieved from *http://www.usatoday.com/yourlife/sex-relationships/marriage/2010-11-18-pew18_ST_N.htm*.

Jayson, S. (2010, March 10). Living together first has little effect on marriage success. *USA Today*, 7D.

Jayson, S. (2010, July 21). More young couples are having babies, then deciding to wed. *USA Today*, 6D.

Jayson, S. (2011). NOW at 45: Is feminism over the hill? Retrieved from *http://yourlife.usatoday.com/mind-soul/story/2011-10-26/As-NOW-marks-45-years-is-feminism-over-the-hill/50939774/1*.

Jencks, C. (1994). *The homeless.* Cambridge, MA: Harvard University Press.

Jeremiah, D. (2011). *I never thought I'd see the day.* Boston, MA: FaithWords.

Johansson, T. (2011). Fatherhood in transition: Paternity leave and changing masculinities. *Journal of Family Communication, 11*, 165–180.

Johnson, A. J., Craig, E. A., Haigh, M. M., Gilchrist, E. S., Lane, L. T., & Welch, N. S. (2009). Stepfamilies interacting outside the home: Barriers to stepparent/stepchild communication with educational, medical, and legal personnel. In T. J. Socha and G. H. Stamp (Eds.), *Parents and children communicating with society: Managing relationships outside of home* (pp. 305–322).

Johnson, K. L., & Roloff, M. E. (1998). Serial arguing and relational quality: Determinants and consequences of perceived resolvability. *Communication Research, 25,* 327–343.

Jones, K. (2011). A range of social and emotional problems. Retrieved from *http://www.calcatholic.com/news/newsArticle.aspx?id=d3e9b42f-fda4-47ac-bc91-adab-808d7a21.*

Jones, K. J. (2011). Increased cohabitation means more instability for children. Retrieved from *http://www.catholicnewsagency.com/news/increased-cohabitation-rates-mean-more-instability-for-children/.*

Jones, R. K., & Dreweke, J. (2011). *Countering conventional wisdom: New evidence on religion and contraception.* New York: Guttmacher Institute.

Jones, T. S. (1982). *Analysis of family metaphor: Methodological and theoretical implications.* Paper presented at the annual meeting of the Speech Communication Association, Louisville, KY.

Jonsson, P. (2000, September 21). Churches give single moms a warmer shoulder. *Christian Science Monitor, 92,* 1.

Jorgenson, J. (2001). Interpreting the intersections of work and family: Frame conflicts in women's work. *Electronic Journal of Communication/Revue Electronique de Communication, 10.*

Jorgenson, J., & Bochner, A. P. (2004). Imagining families through stories and rituals. In A. L. Vangelisti (Ed.), *Handbook of family communication* (pp. 513–538). Mahwah, NJ: Erlbaum.

Joseph, A. L., & Afifi, T. D. (2010). Military wives' stressful disclosures to their deployed husbands: The role of protective buffering. *Journal of Applied Communication Research, 38,* 412–434.

Jourard, S. (1971). *The transparent self.* New York: Van Nostrand Reinhold.

Jurkowitz, M. (2001, February 7). Sexual fare souring on TV, study finds. *The Boston Globe,* pp. A1, A20.

Kaduvettoor-Davidson, A., & Inman, A. (2011). Predictors of cultural values conflict for Asian Indian women. *Journal of Multicultural Counseling and Development, 40,* 2–10.

Kamalipour, Y. R. (1999). Introduction. In Y. R. Kamalipour (Ed.), *Images of the U.S. around the world: A multicultural perspective* (pp. xxi–xxxi). Albany, NY: State University of New York.

Kanter, R. M. (1977). *Men and women of the corporation.* New York: Basic Books.

Kantor, D., & Lehr, W. (1975/1985). *Inside the family: Toward a theory of family process.* San Francisco, CA: Jossey-Bass.

Karpel, M. (1980). Family secrets: Conceptual and ethical issues in the relational context: II. Ethical and practical considerations in therapeutic management. *Family Process, 19,* 295–306.

Kasindorf, M., & El Nasser, H. (2001, March 12). Impact of census race data debated. Retrieved from *www.usatoday.com/news/nation/census/2001-03-12-censusimpact.htm.*

Kaufman, M., & Kimmel, M. (2011). *A guy's guide to feminism.* Jackson, TN: Seal Press.

Kawamoto, W. T., & Cheshire, T. C. (1997). American Indian families. In M. K. DeGenova (Ed.), *Families in cultural context: Strengths and challenges in diversity* (pp. 15–34). Mountain View, CA: Mayfield.

Kerfoot, D., & Miller, C. (2010). Organizing entrepreneurship? Women's invisibility in self-employment. In P. Lewis & R. Simpson (Eds.), *Revealing and concealing gender: Issues of visibility in organizations* (pp. 100–123). London: Palgrave Macmillan.

Khalil, D. (2010). *From veils to thongs*. Charleston, SC: CreateSpace.

Kiesinger, C. E. (2002). My father's shoes: The therapeutic value of narrative reframing. In A. Bochner & C. Ellis (Eds.), *Ethnographically speaking: Autoethnography, literature, and aesthetics* (pp. 95–114). Walnut Creek, CA: AltaMira Press.

Kimmel, M. (1987). *Changing men: New directions in research on men and masculinity*. Newbury Park, CA: Sage.

Kimmel, M. S. (2000). *The gendered society*. Oxford: Oxford University Press.

Kimoto, D. M. (1997). Being *Hapa*: A choice for cultural empowerment. In A. Gonzalez, M. Houston, & V. Chen (Eds.), *Our voices: Essays in culture, ethnicity, and communication* (pp. 157–162). Los Angeles: Roxbury.

Kirby, E. L. (2000). Should I say as you say or do as you do? Mixed messages about work and family. *Electronic Journal of Communication/Revue Electronique de Communication, 10*.

Kirby, E. L., & Krone, K. J. (2002). "The policy exists but you can't really use it": Communication and the structuration of work-family policies. *Journal of Applied Communication Research, 30*, 50–77.

Kirby, E. L., Golden, A., Medved, C., Jorgensen, J., & Buzzanell, P. M. (2003). An organizational communication challenge to the discourse of work and family research: From problematics to empowerment. In P. Kalbfleisch (Ed.), *Communication yearbook 27* (pp. 1–44). Mahwah, NJ: Erlbaum.

Kitson, G. C., & Morgan, L. A. (1990). The multiple consequences of divorce: A decade review. *Journal of Marriage and the Family, 52*, 913–924.

Kittrels, A. (2011, February 12). Filthy is not funny: The best jokes are clean. *Philadelphia Inquirer*, 3B.

Klasen, S., & Waibel, H. (2013). *Vulnerability to poverty: Theory, measurement, and determinants*. New York: Palgrave Macmillan.

Knapp, M. L., & Vangelisti, A. L. (2000). *Interpersonal communication and human relationships*. Boston: Allyn & Bacon.

Knapp, M. L., & Vangelisti, A. L. (2009). *Interpersonal communication and human relationships*. Boston: Pearson.

Knapp, S. J. (2009). Critical theorizing: Enhancing theoretical rigor in family research. *Journal of Family Theory & Review, 1*, 133–145.

Knox, D., & Schacht, C. (2012). *Choices in relationships*. Belmont, CA: Wadsworth.

Koblinsky, S. A., & Anderson, E. A. (1999). Extending Head Start to homeless families: A university-community partnership. In T. Chibucos & R. Lerner (Eds.), *Serving children and families through community-university partnerships: Success stories* (pp. 143–147). Norwell, MA: Kluwer.

Kochman, T. (1981). *Black and white styles in conflict*. Chicago, IL: University of Chicago Press.

Koerner, A. F., & Fitzpatrick, M. A. (2002). You never leave your family in a fight: The impact of family of origin on conflict-behavior in romantic relationships. *Communication Studies, 53*, 234–251.

Kopel, D. (2000). Fatherlessness: The root cause. Retrieved from *www.nationalreview.com/comment/comment050200c/htm*.

Kozol, J. (1988). *Rachel and her children: Homeless families in America*. New York: Fawcett Columbine.

Kranstauber, H., & Kellas, J. K. (2011). "Instead of growing under her heart, I grew in it": The relationship between adoption entrance narratives and adoptees' self-concept. *Communication Quarterly, 59*, 179–199.

Krendl, K. A., Clark, G., Dawson, R., & Troiano, C. (1993). Preschoolers and VCRs in the home: A multiple methods approach. *Journal of Broadcasting & Electronic Media, 37,* 293–312.

Krendl, K. A., Troiano, C., Dawson, R., & Clark, G. (1993). OK, where's the remote?: Children, families, and remote control devices. In J. R. Walker & R. V. Bellamy (Eds.), *The remote control in the new age of television* (pp. 137–153). Westport, CT: Praeger.

Krieder, R. M. (2010). Increase in opposite-sex cohabiting couples from 2009–2010 in the annual social and economic supplement (ASEC) to the current population survey (CPS). Retrieved from *http://www.census.gov/population/www/socdemo/Inc-Opp-sex-2009-to-2010.pdf.*

Krieder, R. M., & Ellis, R. (2011). Living arrangements of children: 2009. Retrieved from *http://www.census.gov/prod/2011pubs/p70-126.pdf.*

Krieder, R. M., & Fields, J. M. (2002). Number, timing and duration of marriages and divorces: 1996. *Current Populations Reports: U.S. Department of Commerce,* 70–80.

Kristof, N. D. (1996, February 11). Who needs love? In Japan, many couples don't. *The New York Times, International Edition,* pp. 1, 12.

Kubba, S. (2011). *The Iraqi marshlands and the marsh Arabs.* Ithaca, NY: Ithaca Press.

Kuczynski, L. (Ed.). (2003). *Handbook of dynamics in parent-child relations.* Thousand Oaks, CA: Sage.

Kurdek, L. A. (2008). Differences between partners from black and white heterosexual dating couples in a path model of relationship commitment. *Journal of Social and Personal Relationships, 25,* 51–70.

Laing, R. D. (1971). *The politics of the family and other essays.* New York: Pantheon Books.

Lakoff, G., & Johnson, M. (1980). *Metaphors we live by.* Chicago, IL: University of Chicago Press.

Langellier, K. M., & Peterson, E. E. (1993). Family storytelling as a strategy of social control. In D. K. Mumby (Ed.), *Narrative and social control: Critical perspectives* (pp. 49–76). Newbury Park, CA: Sage.

Langellier, K. M., & Peterson, E. E. (2004). *Storytelling in daily life.* Philadelphia: Temple University Press.

LaRossa, R. (2004). The culture of fatherhood in the fifties: A closer look. *Journal of Family History, 29,* 47–70.

Larson, J. H., Parks, A. A., Harper, J. M., & Heath, V. A. (2001). A psychometric evaluation of the family rules from the past questionnaire. *Contemporary Family Therapy, 23,* 83–103.

Larson, J. H., Taggart-Ready, M., & Wilson, S. M. (2001). The effects of perceived dysfunctional family-of-origin rules on the dating relationships of young adults. *Contemporary Family Therapy, 23,* 489–512.

Lay, L. S. (2000, April). *Yours, mine, or ours? Money as a source of conflict and power in the family.* Paper presented at the annual meeting of the Eastern Communication Association, Pittsburgh, PA.

Leach, M., & Braithwaite, D. O. (1996). A binding tie: Supportive communication of family kinkeepers. *Journal of Applied Communication, 24,* 200–216.

Lee, C. (1996). The faintest echo of our language. In S. S. Fiffer & S. Fiffer (Eds.), *Family: American writers remember their own* (pp. 27–42). New York: Pantheon Books.

Lee, P., Hagans, K., Powers, K., & Hass, M. (2011). Developing school psychology in Vietnam. *Communique, 39,* 8–10.

Lee, S. O. (2010). *Stop it!* Charleston, SC: BookSurge Publishing.

Leeds-Hurwitz, W. (2006). Social theories: Social constructionism and symbolic interactionism. In D. O. Braithwaite & L. A. Baxter (Eds.), *Engaging theories in family communication: Multiple perspectives* (pp. 229–242). Thousand Oaks, CA: Sage.

LePoire, B. A., Haynes, J., Driscoll, J., Driver, B. N., Wheelis, T. F., Hyde, M., Prochaska, M., & Ramos, L. (1997). Attachment as a function of parental and partner approach-avoidance tendencies. *Human Communication Research, 23,* 413–441.

Lev, I. A. (2010). How queer!—The development of gender identity and sexual orientation in LGBTQ-headed families. *Family Process, 49,* 268–290.

Levine, K. (2012). A can't miss idea for a family sitcom. Retrieved from *http://kenlevine.blogspot.com/2012/04/cant-miss-idea-for-family-sitcom.html.*

Levine, T. R., & Boster, F. J. (2001). The effects of power and message variables on compliance. *Communication Monographs, 68,* 28–46.

Lewis, J. M., Wallerstein, J. S., & Johnson-Reitz, L. (2004). Communication in divorced and single-parent families. In A. L. Vangelisti (Ed.), *Handbook of family communication* (pp. 197–214). Mahwah, NJ: Erlbaum.

Liebes, T., & Livingstone, S. (1994). The structure of family and romantic ties in the soap opera: An ethnographic approach. *Communication Research, 21,* 717–741.

Lin, C., & Liu, W. T. (1993). Intergenerational relationships among Chinese immigrant families from Taiwan. In H. P. McAdoo (Ed.), *Family ethnicity: Strength in diversity* (pp. 271–286). Newbury Park, CA: Sage.

Lind, M. (1998, August 15). The beige and the black. *New York Times Magazine,* pp. 38–39.

Lindenmeyer, A., Griffiths, F., Green, E., Thompson, D., & Tsouroufli, M. (2009). Family health narratives: Midlife women's concepts of vulnerability to illness. *Health, 12,* 275–293.

Lindner, E. E. (Ed.) (2012). *Yearbook of American and Canadian churches.* Nashville, TN: Abingdon.

Lindsey, E. W., & Sanchez, C. A. (2010). Homeless families: An extreme stressor. In S. Price, C. A. Price, & P. McHenry (Eds.), *Families and change: Coping with stressful events and transitions* (pp. 333–356). Thousand Oaks, CA: Sage.

Lips, H. (1994). Power in the family. In G. Handel & G. G. Whitchurch (Eds.), *The psychosocial interior of the family* (pp. 341–362). New York: Aldine de Gruyter.

Liss, L. (1987). Family and the law. In M. B. Sussman & S. K. Steinmetz (Eds.), *Handbook of marriage and the family* (pp. 767–794). New York: Plenum Press.

Littlejohn, S. W., & Foss, K. A. (2011). *Theories of human communication.* Long-Grove, IL: Waveland Press.

Lockhart, W. H. (2000). "We are one life," but not of one gender ideology: Unity, ambiguity, and the Promise Keepers. *Sociology of Religion, 61,* 73–92.

Loehwing, M. (2010). Homelessness as the unforgiving minute of the present: The rhetorical tenses of democratic citizenship. *Quarterly Journal of Speech, 96,* 380–403.

Lovheim, M. (2004). Young people, religious identity, and the Internet. In L. L. Dawson & D. E. Cowan (Eds.), *Religion online: Finding faith on the Internet* (pp. 59–73). New York: Routledge.

Loving, T. J., Heffner, K. L., Kiecolt-Glaser, J. K., Glaser, R., & Malarkey, W. B. (2004). Stress hormone changes and marital conflict: Spouses' relative power makes a difference. *Journal of Marriage and Family, 66,* 594–611.

Lustig, M., & Koester, J. (1999). *Intercultural competence.* New York: Addison Wesley Longman.

Lustig, M., & Koester, J. (2010). *Intercultural competence.* Boston, MA: Pearson.

Maccoby, E. E., & Jacklin, C. N. (1987). Gender segregation in childhood. *Advances in Child Development and Behavior, 20,* 239–287.

MacDonald, J. F. (1992). *Blacks and white television: African Americans in television since 1948.* Chicago, IL: Nelson-Hall.

MacDonald, J. F. (2009). Blacks in TV: No-stereotypes versus stereotypes. Retrieved from *http://jfredmacdonald.com/bawtv/bawtv2.htm.*

MacWilliams, M. W. (2004). Virtual pilgrimage to Ireland's Croagh Patrick. In L. L. Dawson and D. E. Cowan (Eds.), *Religion online: Finding faith on the Internet* (pp. 223–237). New York: Routledge.

Mahdi, A. A. (1999). Trading places: Changes in gender roles within the Iranian immigrant family. Retrieved from *www.owu.edu/~aamahdi/rolechng-galy.htm.*

Maher, B. E. (2001). Divorce reform: Forming ties that bind. Retrieved from *www.frc.org/papers/insight.*

Malinowski, B. (1913). *The family among the Australian Aborigines.* London: University of London Press.

Manne, S., Ostroff, J., Sherman, M., Glassman, M., Ross, S., Goldstein, L., & Fox, K. (2003). Buffering effects for family and friend support on associations between partner unsupportive behaviors and coping among women with breast cancer. *Journal of Social and Personal Relationships, 20,* 771–792.

Marciano, T. D. (1987). Families and religion. In M. B. Sussman & S. K. Steinmetz (Eds.), *Handbook of marriage and the family* (pp. 285–316). New York: Plenum Press.

Mares, M. (1995). The aging family. In M. A. Fitzpatrick & A. L. Vangelisti (Eds.), *Explaining family interactions* (pp. 344–374). Thousand Oaks, CA: Sage.

Margolin, L. (1992). Beyond maternal blame: Physical child abuse as a phenomenon of gender. *Journal of Family Issues, 13,* 410–423.

Marriage Savers. (2004). Churches virtually eliminate divorce. Retrieved from *www.marriagesavers.org/10%20Churches.htm.*

Martin, M. M., Anderson, C. M., & Mottet, T. P. (1999). Perceived understanding and self-disclosure in the stepparent-stepchild relationship. *Journal of Psychology Interdisciplinary and Applied, 133,* 281–290.

Martin, M. M., Anderson, C. M., & Rocca, K. A. (2005). Perceptions of the adult sibling relationships. *North American Journal of Psychology, 7,* 107–117.

Martin, A. (1993). *The lesbian and gay parenting handbook.* New York: HarperCollins.

Martin, M. M., Anderson, C. M., Burant, P. A., & Weber, K. (1996). *Verbal aggression in friendships.* Paper presented at the annual meeting of the Speech Communication Association, San Diego, CA.

Martin, M. M., Anderson, C. M., Weber, K., & Burant, P. A. (1996). *Verbal aggression, sarcasm, and criticism in stepparent relationships.* Paper presented at the annual meeting of the Speech Communication Association, San Diego, CA.

Martinez, R. (2000, July 16). The next chapter: America's next great revolution in race relations is already under way. *New York Times Magazine,* pp. 11–12.

Masheter, C., & Harris, L. H. (1986). From divorce to friendship: A study of dialectic relationship development. *Journal of Social and Personal Relationships, 3,* 177–190.

Mather, M. (2010). U.S. children in single-mother families. Retrieved from *http://www.prb.org/Publications/PolicyBriefs/singlemotherfamilies.aspx.*

Matsunaga, M., & Imahori, T. T. (2009). Profiling family communication standards: A U.S.-Japan comparison. *Communication Research, 36,* 3–31.

Mattingly, C. (2010). *The paradox of hope: Journeys through a clinical borderline.* Berkeley, CA: University of California Press.

Mayerle, J. (1991). Roseanne—how did you get inside my house? A case study of a hit blue-collar situation comedy. *Journal of Popular Culture, 24,* 71–88.

Mazur, M. A., & Ebesu Hubbard, A. S. (2004). "Is there something I should know?": Topic avoidant responses in parent-adolescent communication. *Communication Reports, 17,* 27–37.

McAdoo, J. L. (1993). Decision making and marital satisfaction in African American families. In H. P. McAdoo (Ed.), *Family ethnicity: Strength in diversity* (pp. 109–119). Newbury Park, CA: Sage.

McAdoo, H.P. (2007). *Black families.* Thousand Oaks, CA: Sage.

McCubbin, H. I., Cauble, A. E., & Patterson, J. M. (1982). Introduction. In H. I. McCubbin, A. E. Cauble, & J. M. Patterson (Eds.), *Family stress, coping, and social support* (pp. xi–xvii). Springfield, IL: Thomas.

McFarland, H. N. (1991). Religion in contemporary Japanese society. *Asia Society,* 14–21.

McGoldrick, M., Gerson, R., & Shellenberger, S. (1999). *Genograms: Assessment and innovation.* New York: Norton.

McGoldrick, M. (2004). Mourning in Irish families. In F. Walsh and M. McGoldrick (Eds.), *Living beyond loss: Death in the family* (pp. 140–145). New York: Norton.

McGoldrick, M. (2011). *The genogram journey: Reconnecting with your family.* New York: Norton.

McKenry, P. C., Everett, J. E., Ramseur, H. P., & Carter, C. J. (1989). Research on black adolescents: A legacy of cultural bias. *Journal of Adolescent Research, 4,* 254–264.

McLaughlin, M. L. (1984). *Conversation: How talk is organized.* Beverly Hills, CA: Sage.

McManus, T. G., & Nussbaum, J. F. (2011). Social support expectations and strategic ambiguity in parent–young adult child divorce-related stressor conversations. *Journal of Divorce and Remarriage, 52,* 244–270.

McNay, M. (2009). Absent memory, family secrets, narrative inheritance. *Qualitative Inquiry, 15,* 1178–1188.

Mead, G. H. (1934/1956). *Mind, self, and society.* Chicago, IL: University of Chicago Press.

Meadows-Oliver, M. (2012). Mothering in public: A meta-synthesis of homeless women with their children living in shelters. *Journal for Specialists in Pediatric Nursing, 8,* 130–136.

Medved, C. E. (2004). The everyday accomplishment of work and family: Exploring practical actions in daily routines. *Communication Studies, 55,* 128–145.

Medved, C. E., & Heisler, J. (2002). A negotiated order exploration of critical student faculty interactions: Student-parents manage multiple roles. *Communication Education, 51,* 105–120.

Medved, C. E., & Kirby, E. L. (2005). Family CEOs: A feminist analysis of corporate mothering discourses. *Management Communication Quarterly, 18,* 435–478.

Memoli, M., & Barabak, M. Z. (2012). Santorum dwells on gay marriage. Retrieved from *http://articles.latimes.com/2012/jan/07/nation/la-na-campaign-20120107.*

Menaghan, E. (1982). Assessing the impact of family transitions on marital experience. In H. I. McCubbin, A. E. Cauble, & J. M. Patterson (Eds.), *Family stress, coping, and social support* (pp. 90–108). Springfield, IL: Thomas.

Menvielle, E. (2004, July). Expert speaks out: Parents struggling with their child's gender issues. *The Brown University Child and Adolescent Behavior Letter, 20,* 1, 3–4.

Merrit, B. D. (1991). Bill Cosby: TV auteur? *Journal of Popular Culture, 24,* 89–102.

Messner, M. (2000). Barbie girls vs. sea monster: Children constructing gender. *Gender & Society, 14,* 765–784.

Metts, S., & Bowers, J. (1994). Emotion in interpersonal communication. In M. L. Knapp & G. R. Miller (Eds.), *Handbook of interpersonal communication* (2nd ed., pp. 508–541). Thousand Oaks, CA: Sage.

Metts, S., & Cupach, W. R. (1989). The role of communication in human sexuality. In K. McKinney & S. Sprecher (Eds.), *Human sexuality: The societal and interpersonal context* (pp. 139–161). Norwood, NJ: Ablex.

Metts, S., & Cupach, W. R. (1995). Postdivorce relations. In M. A. Fitzpatrick & A. L. Vangelisti (Eds.), *Explaining family interactions* (pp. 232–252). Thousand Oaks, CA: Sage.

Miedzian, M. (1992). "Father hunger": Why "soup kitchen" fathers are not good enough. In K. L. Hagan (Ed.), *Women respond to the men's movement* (pp. 127–132). San Francisco: Harper.

Mikkelson, A. C., & Hesse, C. (2009). Discussions of religion and relational messages: Differences between comfortable and uncomfortable interactions. *Southern Journal of Communication, 74,* 40–56.

Mikkelson, A., Myers, S., & Hannawa, A. (2011). The differential use of relational maintenance strategies in adult sibling relationships. *Communication Studies, 62,* 258–271.

Millar, F. E., & Rogers L. E. (1976). A relational approach to interpersonal communication. In G. R. Miller (Ed.), *Explorations in interpersonal communication* (pp. 87–203). Beverly Hills, CA: Sage.

Millar, F. E., & Rogers, L. E. (1987). A relational approach to interpersonal dynamics. In M. E. Roloff & G. R. Miller (Eds.), *Interpersonal processes: New directions in communication research* (pp. 117–139). Newbury Park, CA: Sage.

Miller, A. (2000, March 20). Your room is a pigsty. *Newsweek,* 75–76.

Miller, A. E. (2011). Did soul food get too hot to handle? Retrieved from *http://www.zesterdaily.com/zester-soapbox-articles/1079-lets-stop-demonizing-fried-chicken.*

Miller, K. I., Shoemaker, M. M., Willyard, J., & Addison, P. (2008). Providing care for elderly parents: A structurational approach to family caregiver identity. *Journal of Family Communication, 8,* 19–43.

Miller, P. (2011). A critical analysis of the research on student homelessness. *Review of Educational Research, 81,* 308–337.

Millman, M. (1994). The work of love. In G. Handel & G. G. Whitchurch, *The psychosocial interior of the family* (pp. 313–324). New York: Aldine de Gruyter.

Mintz, S., & Kellogg, S. (1988). *Domestic revolutions: A social history of American family life.* New York: Free Press.

Minze, L. C., McDonald, R., Rosentraub, E. L., & Jouriles, E. N. (2010). Making sense of family conflict: Intimate partner violence and preschoolers' externalizing problems. *Journal of Family Psychology, 24,* 5–11.

Moen, P., & Schorr, A. (1987). Families and social policies. In M. Sussman & S. Steinmetz (Eds.), *Handbook of marriage and the family* (pp. 795–813). New York: Plenum Press.

Montalbano-Phelps, L. L. (2003). Discourse of survival: Building families free of unhealthy relationships. *Journal of Family Communication, 3,* 149–177.

Montgomery, B. M. (1992). Communication as the interface between couples and culture. In S. A. Deetz (Ed.), *Communication yearbook 15* (pp. 475–507). Newbury Park, CA: Sage.

Moore, M. (1992). The family as portrayed on prime-time television, 1947–1990: Structure and characteristics. *Sex Roles, 26,* 41–60.

Moore, M. R. (2008). Gendered power relations among women: A study of household decision making in black, lesbian stepfamilies. *American Sociological Review, 73,* 335–356.

Morgan, D. (2012). Catholic bishops pressured Komen over Planned Parenthood. Retrieved from *http://www.reuters.com/article/2012/03/15/us-usa-komen-catholic-idUSBRE82E12Q20120315.*

Motley, M. T. (1990). On whether one can (not) not communicate. An examination via traditional communication. *Western Journal of Speech Communication, 54,* 1–20.

Nakanishi, M., & Johnson, K. M. (1993). Implications of self-disclosure on conversational logics, perceived communication competence, and social attraction. In R. L. Wiseman & J. Koester (Eds.), *Intercultural communication competence* (pp. 204–221). Newbury Park, CA: Sage.

Nanji, A. (1993). The Muslim family in North America: Continuity and change. In H. P. McAdoo (Ed.), *Family ethnicity: Strength in diversity* (pp. 229–244). Newbury Park, CA: Sage.

Nanji, A. (2011). A changing religious landscape: Perspectives on the Muslim experience in North America. Retrieved from *http://www.iis.ac.uk/view–article. asp?ContentID=101080.*

National Association of School Psychologists. (2012). Understanding cultural issues in death. Retrieved from *http://www.nasponline.org/resources/principals/culture_death.aspx.*

National Center for Health Statistics. (2003). Faststats: Marriage and divorce. Retrieved from *www.cdc.gov/nchs/fastats/divorce.htm.*

National Center for Health Statistics. (2012). How's your state doing? Retrieved from *http://nchspressroom.wordpress.com/category/divorce-rate.*

National Child Care Information Center. (2002). Number of children in early care and education programs. Retrieved from *www.nccic.org.*

National Coalition for the Homeless. (2001). Homeless families with children. Retrieved from *www.nationalhomeless.org/families.html.*

National Coalition for the Homeless. (2002). How many people experience homelessness? Retrieved from *www.nationalhomeless.org/numbers/html.*

National Coalition for the Homeless (2011). *Student homeless challenge project.* Washington, D.C.: National Coalition for the Homeless.

National Opinion Research Center. (2001). American sexual behavior. Retrieved from *www.norc.org.*

National Stepfamily Resource Center. (2011). Selected articles. Retrieved from *http://www.stepfamilies.info/selected-articles.php.*

Nelson, H. L. (2001). *Damaged identities, narrative repair.* Ithaca, NY: Cornell University Press.

Newman, K. (2012). *The accordion family: Boomerang kids, anxious parents, and the private toll.* Boston, MA: Beacon Press.

Nicolas, G., Desilva, A., Prater, D., & Bronkoski, E. (2009). Empathic family stress as a sign of family connectedness in Haitian immigrants. *Family Process, 48,* 135–150.

Nielsen, L. (1999). Demeaning, demoralizing and disenfranchising divorced dads: A review of the literature. *Journal of Divorce & Remarriage, 31,* 139–177.

Noller, P. (1995). Parent-adolescent relationships. In M. A. Fitzpatrick & A. L. Vangelisti (Eds.), *Explaining family interactions* (pp. 77–111). Thousand Oaks, CA: Sage.

Noller, P., & Fitzpatrick, M. A. (1993). *Communication in family relationships.* Englewood Cliffs, NJ: Prentice Hall.

Noller, P., Feeney, J. A., Bonnell, D., & Callan, V. J. (1994). A longitudinal study of conflict in marriage. *Journal of Social and Personal Relationships, 11,* 233–252.

Noller, P., Feeney, J. A., Peterson, C. C., & Sheehan, G. (1995). Learning conflict patterns in the family: Links between marital, parental, and sibling relationships. In T. Socha & G. Stamp (Eds.), *Parents, children, and communication* (pp. 273–298). Mahwah, NJ: Erlbaum.

Norwood, K. (2012). Transitioning meanings? Family members' communicative struggles surrounding transgender identity. *Journal of Family Communication, 12,* 75–92.

Norwood, K. M., & Baxter, L. A. (2011). "Dear birth mother": Addressivity and meaning-making in online adoption-seeking letters. *Journal of Family Communication, 11,* 198–217.

Nussbaum, J. F. (1991). Communication, language, and the institutionalized elderly. *Aging and Society, 11,* 149–166.

Nydegger, C. N., & Mitteness, L. S. (1988). Etiquette and ritual in the family conversation. *American Behavioral Scientist, 31,* 702–716.

Ochs, E. (1989, July). Table talk: The family detective story. *USA Today,* 9A.

Ochs, E. (1997). Narrative. In T. A. van Dijk (Ed.), *Discourse as structure and process* (pp. 185–207). London: Sage.

Ochs, E., & Capps, L. (1996). Narrating the self. *Annual Review of Anthropology, 25,* 19–43.

Odun, A. (2003, October). Helping boomerang kids: How do parents deal with the blessing of children who move back home? *Better Homes and Gardens,* pp. 19–22.

Okimoto, J. D., & Stegall, P. J. (1987). *Boomerang kids: How to live with adult children who return home.* New York: Pocket.

Oliphant, A. E., & Kuczynski, L. (2011). Mothers' and fathers' perceptions of mutuality in middle childhood: The domain of intimacy. *Journal of Family Issues, 32,* 1104–1124.

Olson, D. H., & Gorall, D. M. (2003). Circumplex model of marital and family systems. In F. Walsh (Ed.), *Normal family processes* (pp. 514–547). New York: Guilford.

Olson, D. H., & Olson, A. K. (2000). *Empowering couples: Building on your strengths.* Minneapolis, MN: Life Innovations.

Olson, D. H., Sprenkle, D. H., & Russell, C. S. (1979). Circumplex model of marital and family systems: Cohesion and adaptability dimension, family types, and clinical applications. *Family Process, 18,* 3–28.

Olson, L. (2011). How to cope with the stress of unemployment. Retrieved from *http://money.usnews.com/money/blogs/outside-voices-careers/2011/10/20/how-to-cope-with-the-stress-of-unemployment.*

Olson, L. N. (2002). "As ugly and painful as it was, it was effective": Individuals' unique assessment of communication competence during aggressive conflict episodes. *Communication Studies, 53,* 171–188.

Olson, L. N. (2004). Relational control-motivated aggression: A theoretically-based typology of intimate violence. *Journal of Family Communication, 4,* 209–233.

Olson, L. N. (2009). Relational control-motivated aggression: A theoretical framework for identifying various types of violent couples. In D. D. Cahn (Ed.), *Family violence: Communication processes* (pp. 27–47). Albany, NY: SUNY Press.

Olson, L. N., & Braithwaite, D. O. (2004). "If you hit me again, I'll hit you back": Conflict management strategies of individuals experiencing aggression during conflicts. *Communication Studies, 55,* 271–285.

Olson, L. N., Wilson-Kratzer, J. M., & Symonds, S. E. (2012). *The dark side of family communication.* Cambridge, UK: Polity Press.

Overberg, P. (2009). Diversity in the USA. *USA Today, 5A.*

Owen, R. (2000). On the tube: "Will and Grace" falls into NBC's good graces. Retrieved from *http://old.post-gazette.com/tv/20000719owen2.asp.*

Owen, W. F. (1985). Thematic metaphors in relational communication: A conceptual framework. *Western Journal of Speech Communication, 49,* 1–13.

Papernow, P. (1993). *Becoming a stepfamily.* San Francisco: Jossey-Bass.

ParentFurther. (2011). What makes your "Modern Family" strong? Retrieved from *http://www.nytimes.com/2011/01.23/fashion/23THISLIFE.html?pagewanted-all.*

Pasley, K., & Ihinger-Tallman, M. (1989). Boundary ambiguity in remarriage: Does ambiguity differentiate degree of marital adjustment and integration? *Family Relations, 38,* 46–52.

Pasley, K., & Minton, C. (2001). Generative fathering after divorce and remarriage: Beyond the "disappearing dad." In T. J. Cohen (Ed.), *Men and masculinity.* Belmont, CA: Wadsworth.

Patrick, S., Sells, J. N., Giordano, F. G., & Tollerud, T. R. (2007). Intimacy, differentiation, and personality variables as predictors of marital satisfaction. *The Family Journal: Counseling and Therapy for Couples and Families, 15,* 359–367.

Patterson, V. (2012). *The vacant paradise.* Berkeley, CA: Counterpoint Press.

Pawlowski, D. R., Myers, S. A., & Rocca, K. A. (2000). Relational messages in conflict situations among siblings. *Communication Research Reports, 17,* 271–277.

Pear, R. (1996, June 1). Thousands rally in capital on children's behalf. *The New York Times,* p. 10.

Pearson, J. C. (1992). *Lasting love: What keeps couples together.* Dubuque, IA: Brown.

Pearson, J. C. (1996). Positive distortion: "The most beautiful woman in the world." In K. M. Galvin & P. Cooper (Eds.), *Making connections: Readings in relational communication* (pp. 175–181). Los Angeles: Roxbury.

Pearson, J. C., West, R., & Turner, L. H. (1995). *Gender and communication.* Madison, WI: Brown & Benchmark.

Pearlin, L. I., Mullan, J. T., Semple, S. J., & Skaff, M. M. (1990). Caregiving and the stress process: An overview of concepts and their measures. *The Gerontologist, 30,* 583–594.

Pease, B. (2009). Racialized masculinities and the health of immigrant and refugee men. In A. Broom & P. Tovey (Eds.), *Men's health: Body, identity and social context* (pp. 182–201). Chichester, England: Wiley-Blackwell.

Penington, B. A. (1997). *Pecked to death by ducks: Managing dialectical tensions in the mother-adolescent daughter relationship.* Paper presented at the annual meeting of the Communication Research Symposium, Milwaukee, WI.

Penington, B. A. (2004). The communicative management of connection and autonomy in African American and European American mother–daughter relationships. *Journal of Family Communication, 4,* 3–34.

Peplau, L. A. (1994). Men and women in love. In D. L. Sollie & L. A. Leslie (Eds.), *Gender, families, and close relationships* (pp. 19–49). Thousand Oaks, CA: Sage.

Peplau, L. A., & Beals, K. P. (2004). The family lives of lesbians and gay men. In A. L. Vangelisti (Ed.), *Handbook of family communication* (pp. 233–248). Mahwah, NJ: Erlbaum.

Perse, E. M., & Ferguson, D. A. (1993). Gender differences in remote control use. In J. R. Walker & R. V. Bellamy (Eds.), *The remote control in the new age of television* (pp. 169–186). Westport, CT: Praeger.

Perse, E. M., Pavitt, C., & Burggraf, C. S. (1990). Implicit theories of marriage and evaluation of marriage on television. *Human Communication Research, 16,* 387–408.

Peterson, K. (2010). Promise Keepers. In R. Chapman (Ed.), *Culture wars: An encyclopedia of issues, voices, and viewpoints* (pp. 130–145). Armonk, NY: M. E. Sharpe.

Peterson, K. S. (2003, September 18). Unmarried with children: For better or worse? *USA Today,* 1A, 8A.

Peterson, K. S. (2004, December 3). Divorces can break more than hearts. *USA Today,* 5D.

Peterson, R. R. (1989). *Women, work, and divorce.* Albany: SUNY Press.

Petronio, S. (2000). The boundaries of privacy: Praxis of everyday life. In S. Petronio (Ed.), *Balancing the secrets of private disclosures* (pp. 37–49). Mahwah, NJ: Erlbaum.

Petry, S. (2011). Spirituality and the family life cycle. In M. McGoldrick, B. Carter, & Nydia Garcia Preto (Eds.), *The expanded family life cycle: Individual, family, and social perspectives* (pp. 133–148). Boston, MA: Allyn & Bacon.

Pew Research Center. (2010). The return of the multi-generational household. Retrieved from *http://www.pewsocialtrends.org/2010/03/18/the-return-of-the-multi-generational-family-household/.*

Pickhardt, C. (2001). *Boomerang kids.* Naperville, IL: Sourcebooks.

Pickhardt, K. (2011). *Boomerang kids.* New York: Sourcebooks.

Pitts, V. (2004). Illness and Internet empowerment: Writing and reading breast cancer in cyberspace. *Health, 8,* 33–59.

Planalp, S. (1993). Communication, cognition, and emotion. *Communication Monographs, 60,* 3–9.

Planalp, S. (1999). *Communicating emotion: Social, moral, and cultural processes.* Paris: Cambridge University Press and the Editions de la Maison des Sciences de l'Homme.

Pollitt, K. (2009). Can this marriage be saved? Retrieved from *http://www.thenation.com/article/can-marriage-be-saved-1.*

Pollock, R. (2002). *The everything world's religions book.* Avon, MA: Adams Media.

Popenoe, D. (1999). *Life without father: Compelling new evidence that fatherhood and marriage are indispensable for the good of children and society.* Cambridge, MA: Harvard University Press.

Powell, H., & Segrin, C. (2004). The effect of family and peer communication on college students' communication with dating partners about HIV and AIDS. *Health Communication, 16,* 427–449.

Prager, K. J. (1995). *The psychology of intimacy.* New York: Guilford.

Prentice, C. M. (2008). The assimilation of in-laws: The impact of newcomers on the communication routines of families. *Journal of Applied Communication Research, 36,* 74–97.

Prescott, M. E., & LePoire, B. A. (2002). Eating disorders and mother–daughter communication: A test of inconsistent nurturing as control theory. *Journal of Family Communication, 2,* 59–78.

Price, R. (2003, January 13). A storyteller's starter kit, stocked with family memories. *New York Times,* pp. B1, B3.

Prusank, D. T. (1993). Contextualizing social control: An ethnomethodological analysis of parental accounts of discipline interactions. In N. Coupland & J. Nussbaum (Eds.), *Discourse and lifespan identity* (pp. 132–153). Newbury Park, CA: Sage.

Punyanunt-Carter, N. M. (2007). Using attachment theory to study communication motives in father-daughter relationships. *Communication Research Reports, 24,* 311–318.

Purdy, M. (2000, June 18). Men searching for road map on ever-evolving role of fathers. *The New York Times,* p. 25.

Putnam, L. L., & Wilson, C. E. (1982). Communication strategies in organizational conflicts: Reliability and validity of a measurement scale. In M. Burgoon (Ed.), *Communication yearbook 6* (pp. 629–652). Beverly Hills, CA: Sage.

Putnam, R. (2010). *American grace: How religion divides and unites us.* New York: Simon and Schuster.

Ragsdale, J. D., Brandau-Brown, F., & Bello, R. (2010). Attachment style and gender as predictors of relational repair among the remarried: Rationale for the study. *Journal of Family Communication, 10,* 158–173.

Rawlins, W. K. (1992). *Friendship matters: Communication, dialectics, and the life course.* New York: Aldine de Gruyter.

Real, M. R. (1991). Bill Cosby and recording ethnicity. In L. Vande Berg & L. A. Wenner (Eds.), *Television criticism* (pp. 58–84). White Plains, NY: Longman.

Recchia, H. E., Ross, H. S., & Vickar, M. (2010). Power and conflict resolution in sibling, parent-child, and spousal negotiations. *Journal of Family Psychology, 24,* 605–615.

Regalado, M., Sareen, H., Inkelas, M., Wissow, L. S., & Halfon, N. (2004). Parents' discipline of young children: Results from the national survey of early childhood health. *Pediatrics, 113,* 1952–1958.

Reger, J. (2012). *Everywhere and nowhere: Contemporary feminism in the United States.* New York: Oxford University Press.

Reich, N. M. (2002). Towards a rearticulation of women-as-victims: A thematic analysis of the construction of women's identities surrounding gendered violence. *Communication Quarterly, 50,* 292–311.

Reis, H. T., & Patrick, B. C. (1996). Attachment and intimacy: Component processes. In E. T. Higgins & A. Kruglanski (Eds.), *Social psychology: Handbook of basic principles* (pp. 523–563). New York: Guilford.

Reis, H. T., & Shaver, P. (1988). Intimacy as an interpersonal process. In S. W. Duck (Ed.), *Handbook of personal relationships* (pp. 367–389). Chichester, UK: Wiley.

Reiss, I. L. (1990). *An end to shame: Shaping our next sexual revolution.* Buffalo, NY: Prometheus.

Rhucharoenpornpanich, O., Chamratrithirong, A., Fongkaew, W., Miller, B. A., Cupp, P. K., Rosati, M. J., Byrnes, H. F., Atwood, K. A., & Chookhare, W. (2012). Parent-teen communication about sex in urban Thai families. *Journal of Health Communication, 4,* 380–396.

Rickabaugh, C. A. (1994). Just who is the guy, anyway? Stereotypes of the men's movement. *Sex Roles, 30,* 459–470.

Riessman, C. K. (1990). *Divorce talk: Women and men make sense of personal relationships.* New Brunswick, NJ: Rutgers University Press.

Riessman, C. K. (1992). Making sense of marital violence: One woman's narrative. In G. C. Rosenwald & R. L. Ochberg (Eds.), *Storied lives: The cultural politics of self-understanding* (pp. 231–249). New Haven, CT: Yale University Press.

Riley, G. (1992). *Divorce: An American tradition.* New York: Oxford University Press.

Risman, B. J., & Johnson-Summerford, D. (2001). Doing it fairly: A study of postgender marriages. In T. F. Cohen (Ed.), *Men and masculinity* (pp. 219–238). Belmont, CA: Wadsworth.

Roberto, A. J., Carlyle, K. E., Goddall, C. E., & Castle, J. D. (2009). The relationship between parents' verbal aggressiveness and responsiveness and young adult children's attachment style and relational satisfaction with parents. *Journal of Family Communication, 9,* 90–106.

Roberts, K. G. (2004). Texturing the narrative paradigm: Folklore and communication. *Communication Quarterly, 52,* 129–142.

Robila, M., & Krishnakumar, A. (2004). The role of children in Eastern European families. *Children and Society, 18,* 30–41.

Robinson, B. A. (2001, January 14). Native American spirituality. Retrieved from *www. religioustolerance.org/nataspir/htm.*

Rodgers, R. H. (1973). *Family interaction and transaction: The developmental approach.* Englewood Cliffs, NJ: Prentice Hall.

Rodgers, R. H., & White, J. M. (1993). Family development theory. In P. Boss, W. Doherty, R. LaRossa, W. Schumm, & S. Steinmetz (Eds.), *Sourcebook of family theories and methods: A contextual approach* (pp. 225–254). New York: Plenum Press.

Rodriguez, G. (2012). *The pregnancy project.* New York: Simon and Schuster.

Roehling, P. V., & Moen, P. (2003). Dual-earner couples. *Sloan work and family research network resources for teaching: Work and family encyclopedia.* Retrieved from *www.bc.edu/bc/org/avp/wfnetwork/rft/wfpedia/index.html.*

Rogers, L. E., & Farace, R. V. (1975). Analysis of relational communication in dyads: New measurement procedures. *Human Communication Research, 1,* 222–239.

Rogers, L. E., Castleton, A., & Lloyd, S. A. (1996). Relational control and physical aggression in satisfying marital relationships. In D. D. Cahn & S. A. Lloyd (Eds.), *Family violence from a communication perspective* (pp. 218–239). Thousand Oaks, CA: Sage.

Rohter, L. (2012). *Brazil on the rise: The story of country transformed.* New York: Palgrave Macmillan.

Roloff, M. E. (1996). The catalyst hypothesis: Conditions under which coercive communication leads to physical aggression. In D. Cahn & S. Lloyd (Eds.), *Family violence from a communication perspective* (pp. 20–36). Thousand Oaks, CA: Sage.

Roloff, M. E., & Cloven, D. (1990). The chilling effect in interpersonal relationships. In D. D. Cahn (Ed.), *Intimates in conflict* (pp. 49–76). Hillsdale, NJ: Erlbaum.

Roloff, M. E., & Johnson, D. I. (2001). Reintroducing taboo topics: Antecedents and consequences of putting topics back on the table. *Communication Studies, 52,* 37–50.

Romeo, V. (2011). *Behind the store: Stories of a first-generation Italian American childhood.* Bloomington, IN: iUniverse.

Rosen, C. (2004). The age of egocasting. Retrieved from *http://www.thenewatlantis. com/publications/the-age-of-egocasting.*

Rosen, E. J., & Weltman, S. F. (1996). Jewish families: An overview. In M. McGoldrick, J. Giordano, & J. K. Pearce (Eds.). *Ethnicity and family therapy* (pp. 113–119). New York: Guilford.

Rosenblatt, P. C. (1994). *Metaphors of family systems theory: Toward new constructions.* New York: Guilford.

Rosenfeld, L. B. (2000). Overview of the ways privacy, secrecy, and disclosure are balanced in today's society. In S. Petronio (Ed.), *Balancing the secrets of private disclosures* (pp. 3–17). Mahwah, NJ: Erlbaum.

Rowland, R. C. (1987). Narrative: Mode of discourse or paradigm? *Communication Monographs, 54,* 264–275.

Rubin, L. B. (1994). *Families on the fault line.* New York: HarperCollins.

Rukeyser, M. (1968). *The speed of darkness.* New York: Random House.

Rusbult, C. E., Drigotas, S. M., & Verette, J. (1994). The investment model: An interdependence analysis of commitment processes and relationship maintenance phenomena. In D. J. Canary & L. Stafford (Eds.), *Communication and relational maintenance* (pp. 115–139). San Diego, CA: Academic.

Russell, B. (1929). *Marriage and morals.* New York: Liveright.

Sabourin, T. C. (1996). The role of communication in verbal abuse between spouses. In D. Cahn & S. Lloyd (Eds.), *Family violence from a communication perspective* (pp. 199–217). Thousand Oaks, CA: Sage.

Sabourin, T. C. (2003). *The contemporary American family: A dialectical perspective on communication and relationships.* Thousand Oaks, CA: Sage.

Sabourin, T. C., & Stamp, G. H. (1995). Communication and the experience of dialectical tensions in family life: An examination of abusive and nonabusive families. *Communication Monographs, 62,* 213–242.

Sabourin, T. C., Infante, D. A., & Rudd, J. E. (1993). Verbal aggression in marriages: A comparison of violent, distressed but nonviolent, and nondistressed couples. *Human Communication Research, 20,* 245–267.

Saillant, C. (2000, June 25). Straining family bonds. *Los Angeles Times,* p. 1.

Samp, J. A., & Abbott, T. J. (2012). Women coping with cancer: Family communication, conflict, and support. In F. C. Dickson & L. M. Webb (Eds.), *Communication for families in crisis: Theories, research, strategies* (pp. 205–228). New York: Peter Lang.

Sanchez, Y. (1997). Face the nation: Race, immigration, and the rise of nativism in late twentieth-century America. *International Migration Review, 31,* p. 1009–1030.

Satir, V. (1972). *Peoplemaking.* Palo Alto, CA: Science & Behavior Books.

Savin-Williams, R. C., & Esterberg, K. G. (2000). Lesbian, gay, and bisexual families. In D. H. Demo, K. Allen, & M. A. Fine (Eds.), *Handbook of family diversity* (pp. 197–215). New York: Oxford University Press.

Savorelli, A. (2010). *Beyond sitcom: New directions in American television comedy.* Jefferson, NC: McFarland.

Scanzoni, J., & Polonko, K. (1980). A conceptual approach to explicit marital negotiation. *Journal of Marriage and the Family, 42,* 31–44.

Schement, J. R., & Stephenson, H. (1996). Religion and the information society. In D. Stout & J. M. Buddenbaum (Eds.), *Religion and mass media: Audiences and adaptations* (pp. 261–290). Thousand Oaks, CA: Sage.

Schmeeckle, M., & Sprecher, S. (2004). Extended family and social networks. In A. L. Vangelisti (Ed.), *Handbook of family communication* (pp. 349–375). Mahwah, NJ: Erlbaum.

Schmeeckle, M., & Sprecher, S. (2012). Extended family and social networks. In A. Vangelisti (Ed.), *Routledge handbook of family communication* (pp. 340–366). New York: Routledge.

Schmeer, K. K. (2011). The child health disadvantage of parental cohabitation. *Journal of Marriage and the Family, 73,* 181–193.

Schrodt, P., Miller, A.E., & Braithwaite, D.O. (2011). Ex-spouses' relational satisfaction as a function of coparental communication in stepfamilies. *Communication Studies, 62,* 272–290.

Schrodt, P., Soliz, J., & Braithwaite, D. O. (2008). A social relations model of everyday talk and relational satisfaction in stepfamilies. *Communication Monographs, 75,* 190–217.

Schwandt, T. A. (2000). Three epistemological stances for qualitative inquiry. In N. K. Denzin & Y. S. Lincoln (Eds.), *Handbook of qualitative research* (2nd ed., pp. 189–213). Thousand Oaks, CA: Sage.

Schwartz, M. A., & Scott, B. (2013). *Marriages and families.* Boston, MA: Pearson.

Schwartz, P. (1994). *Peer marriage: How love between equals really works.* New York: Free Press.

Scott, K. (1995). Identity and ideology in black women's talk about their talk: A report of research in progress. *Women and Language, 20,* 8–10.

Segrin, C., & Flora, J. (2005). *Family communication.* Mahwah, NJ: Erlbaum.

Semke, C. A., & Sheridan, S. M. (2011). Family-school connections in rural educational settings: A systematic review of the empirical literature. Retrieved from *www.r2ed.unl.edu.*

Seward, R. R. (1978). *The American family: A demographic history.* Beverly Hills, CA: Sage.

Sex and the Internet. (2000). Retrieved from *www.harrisinteractive.com.*

Sexuality Information and Education Council (SIECUS). (2012). Position statements. Retrieved from *www.siecus.org.*

Shade, L. R. (2004). Bending gender into the Net: Feminizing content, corporate interests, and research strategy. In P. N. Howard & S. Jones (Eds.), *Society online: The Internet in context* (pp. 57–70). Thousand Oaks, CA: Sage.

Shanok, R. S. (1994). When you share family stories. *Parents, 65,* 187.

Shaver, P. R., Hazan, C., & Bradshaw, D. (1988). Love as attachment: The integration of three behavioral systems. In R. J. Sternberg & M. L. Barnes (Eds.), *The psychology of love* (pp. 68–99). New Haven, CT: Yale University Press.

Shearman, S. M., & Dumlao, R. (2008). A cross-cultural comparison of family communication patterns and conflict between young adults and parents. *Journal of Family Communication, 8,* 186–211.

Shearman, S. M., Dumlao, R., & Kagawa, N. (2011). Cultural variations in accounts by American and Japanese young adults: Recalling a major conflict with parents. *Journal of Family Communication, 11,* 105–125.

Sheehy, G. (2010). Caregivers need government help or they'll go broke. Retrieved from *http://yourlife.usatoday.com/parenting-family/new-passages/story/2011/05/Caregivers-need-governmentn-help-or-theyll-go-broke/46729532/1.*

Sheehy, G. (2011, July 25). Middle-aged women care for everyone but themselves. *USA Today,* 4D.

Shelton, M. (2013). *Family pride: What LGBT families should know about living in isolated, unwelcoming, or hostile communities.* Boston, MA: Beacon Press.

Shewey, D. (1991, November 5). Wild in the suites: At the first international men's conference. *Voice,* 43–44.

Shields, C.M., &Warke, A. (2010). The invisible crisis: Connecting schools with homeless families. *Journal of School Leadership, 20,* 789-819.

Shimanoff, S. (1980). *Communication rules: Theory and research.* Beverly Hills, CA: Sage.

Shimkowski, J. R., & Schrodt, P. (2012). Coparental communication as a mediator of interparental conflict and young adult children's mental well-being. *Communication Monographs, 79,* 48–71.

Shotter, J. (1993). Becoming someone: Identity and belonging. In N. Coupland & J. F. Nussbaum (Eds.), *Discourse and lifespan identity* (pp. 5–27). Newbury Park, CA: Sage.

Shook, J.R. (2011). *The God debates. A 21st century guide for atheists and believers (and everyone in between).* Malden, MA: Wiley-Blackwell.

Shulz, G. (2012). *The rise of the mythopoetic men's movement: A psychosocial analysis.* New York: LAP Lambert.

Shutiva, C. (2004). Native American culture and communication through humor. In A. González, M. Houston, & V. Chen (Eds.), *Our voices: Essays in culture, ethnicity, and communication* (pp. 134–138). Los Angeles: Roxbury.

Sillars, A. L., & Weisberg, J. (1987). Conflict as a social skill. In M. E. Roloff & G. R. Miller (Eds.), *Interpersonal processes: New directions in communication research* (pp. 140–171). Newbury Park, CA: Sage.

Sillars, A. L., & Wilmot, W. W. (1989). Marital communication across the life span. In J. F. Nussbaum (Ed.), *Lifespan communication: Normative processes* (pp. 225–253). Hillsdale, NJ: Erlbaum.

Sillars, A., Canary, D. J., & Tafoya, M. (2004). Communication, conflict, and the quality of family relationships. In A. L. Vangelisti (Ed.), *Handbook of family communication* (pp. 413–446). Mahwah, NJ: Erlbaum.

Sillars, A., L. Shellen, W., McIntosh, A., & Momegranate, M. (1997). Relational characteristics of language: Elaboration and differentiation in marital conversations. *Western Journal of Communication, 61,* 403–423.

Simmons, T., & Dye, J. L. (2003). Grandparents living with grandchildren: 2000. Census 2000 brief. Retrieved from *www.census.gov/prod/2003pubs/c2kbr-31.pdf.*

Simmons, T., & O'Neill, G. (2001). Households and families: 2000. Census 2000 brief. Retrieved from *www.census.gov/prod/2001pubs/c2kbr01-8.pdf.*

Sirota, K. G. (2010). Narratives of transformation: Family discourse, autism and trajectories of hope. *Discourse & Society, 21,* 544–564.

Sloan, B. (1999). These keys . . . written personal narratives as family lore and folk object. *Library Trends, 47,* 395–413.

Sluzki, C. (1983). Process, structure, and world views: Toward an integrated view of systemic models in family therapy. *Family Process, 22,* 469–476.

Smith, D. C. (2008). Critiquing reality-based televisual black fatherhood: A critical analysis of *Run's House* and *Snoop Dogg's Father Hood. Critical Studies in Media Communication, 25,* 393–412.

Smith, D. M., & Gates, G. (2001). Same-sex unmarried partner households. Retrieved from *www.urban.org.*

Smythe, M. J. (1995). Talking bodies: Body talk at Bodyworks. *Communication Studies, 46,* 245–260.

Snyder, M., & Hombs, M. E. (1990). Homelessness is serious. In D. L. Bender & B. Leone (Eds.), *Homelessness: Opposing viewpoints* (pp. 17–20). San Diego, CA: Greenhaven.

Socha, T. (1991). *The parental guilt episode: Exploring parents' messages.* Paper presented at the annual meeting of the Speech Communication Association, Atlanta, GA.

Socha, T. (2006). Orchestrating and directing domestic potential through communication: Toward a positive reframing of "discipline." In L. H. Turner & R. West (Eds.), *The family communication sourcebook* (pp. 219–236). Thousand Oaks, CA: Sage.

Socha, T. J., & Stamp, G. H. (2009). A new frontier for family communication studies: Parent-child-societal communication. In T. J. Socha & G. H. Stamp (Eds.), *Parents and children communicating with society: Managing relationships outside of home* (pp. 1–16). New York: Routledge.

Socha, T. J., & Yingling, J. (2010). *Families communicating with children.* Cambridge, UK: Polity Press.

Socha, T., Sanchez-Hucles, J., Bromley, J., & Kelly, B. (1995). Invisible parents and children: Exploring African-American parent–child communication. In T. Socha & G. Stamp (Eds.), *Parents, children, and communication* (pp. 127–146). Mahwah, NJ: Erlbaum.

Soliz, J. (2008). Intergenerational support and the role of grandparents in postdivorce families: Retrospective accounts of young adult grandchildren. *Qualitative Research Reports in Communication, 9,* 72–80.

Soliz, J. E., Lin, M., Anderson, K., & Harwood, J. (2006). Communication in grandparent–grandchild relationships. In K. Floyd & M. T. Morman (Eds.),

Widening the family Circle: New research on family communication (pp. 65–79). Thousand Oaks, CA: Sage.

Sollie, D. L., & Leslie, L. A. (Eds.) (1994). *Gender, families, and close relationships.* Thousand Oaks, CA: Sage.

Solomon, D. H. (2008). Uncertainly reduction theory. In W. Donsbach (Ed.), *The international encyclopedia of communication* (pp. 5208–5212). Oxford, UK: Wiley-Blackwell.

Solomon, D. H., Knobloch, L. K., & Fitzpatrick, M. A. (2004). Relational power, marital schema, and decisions to withhold complaints: An investigation of the chilling effect on confrontation in marriage. *Communication Studies, 55,* 146–167.

Somerville, M. (2011). The case against same-sex marriage. Retrieved from *http://www.mercatornet.com/articles/view/the_case_against_same-sex_marriage.*

Song, Y., & Zhang, Y. B. (2012). Husbands' conflict styles in Chinese mother/daughter-in-law conflicts: Daughters-in-law's perspectives. *Journal of Family Communication, 12,* 57–74.

Sopory, P. (2008). Metaphor and intra-attitudinal structural coherence. *Communication Studies, 59,* 164–181.

Sotirin, P., Buzzanell, P.M., & Turner, L.H. (2007). Colonizing family: A feminist critique of family management texts. *Journal of Family Communication, 7,* 245–263.

Sotirin, P., Turner, L. H., & Buzzanell, P. M. (2005). *Why families are not like organizations: Family management, managerialism, and feminist re-visions.* Paper delivered at the annual meeting of the International Communication Association, May, New York.

Spanier, G. B., & Thompson, L. (1984). Relief and distress after marital separation. *Journal of Divorce, 7,* 31–49.

Speer, R. B., & Trees, A. R. (2007). The push and pull of stepfamily life: The contribution of stepchildren's autonomy and connection-seeking behaviors to role development in stepfamilies. *Communication Studies, 58,* 377–394.

Spigel, L. (2012). Family on television. Retrieved from *http://www.museum.tv/eotvsection.php?entrycode=familyontel.*

Spitzack, C., & Carter, K. (1987). Women in communication studies: A typology for revision. *Quarterly Journal of Speech, 73,* 401–423.

Spooner, S. (1982). Intimacy in adults: A developmental model for counselors and helpers. *Personnel and Guidance Journal, 60,* 168–170.

Sprecher, S. (1989). Influences on choice of a partner and on sexual decision making in the relationship. In K. McKinney & S. Sprecher (Eds.), *Human sexuality: The societal and interpersonal context* (pp. 115–138). Norwood, NJ: Ablex.

Sprecher, S., & McKinney, K. (1993). *Sexuality.* Newbury Park, CA: Sage.

Sprecher, S., & McKinney, K. (1994). Sexuality in close relationships. In A. Weber & J. Harvey (Eds.), *Perspectives in close relationships* (pp. 193–216). Boston: Allyn & Bacon.

St. George, D. (2011). Pew report shows 50-year high point for multigenerational households. *Washington Post, 5,* 6.

Stacey, J. (1994). Backward toward the postmodern family: Reflections on gender, kinship, and class in the Silicon Valley. In G. Handel & G. G. Whitchurch (Eds.), *The psychosocial interior of the family* (pp. 643–668). New York: Aldine de Gruyter.

Stacey, J., & Biblarz, T. J. (2001). (How) Does the sexual orientation of parents matter? *American Sociological Review, 66,* 159–183.

Stafford, L., & Dainton, M. (1994). The dark side of "normal" family interaction. In W. R. Cupach & B. H. Spitzberg (Eds.), *The dark side of interpersonal communication* (pp. 259–280). Hillsdale, NJ: Erlbaum.

Staggenborg, S. (2010). *Social movements.* New York: Oxford University Press.

Stamp, G. H. (1994). The appropriation of the parental role through communication during the transition to parenthood. *Communication Monographs, 61,* 89–112.

Stamp, G. H. (2004). Theories of family relationships and a family relationships theoretical model. In A. L. Vangelisti (Ed.), *Handbook of family communication* (pp. 1–30). Mahwah, NJ: Erlbaum.

Stamp, G. H., & Knapp, M. L. (1990). The construct of intent in interpersonal communication. *Quarterly Journal of Speech, 76,* 282–299.

Stamp, G. H., & Sabourin, T. (1995). Accounting for violence: An analysis of male spousal abuse narratives. *Journal of Applied Communication Research, 23,* 284–307.

Stamp, G. H., Vangelisti, A. L., & Daly, J. A. (1992). The creation of defensiveness in social interaction. *Communication Quarterly, 40,* 177–190.

Stanton, J. R. (1999). Remember we are an extended family. Retrieved from *www. theskanner.com.*

Staples, B. (2004, May 29). What adolescents miss when we let them grow up in cyberspace. *The New York Times,* p. 14.

Steen, S., & Schwartz, P. (1995). Communication, gender, and power: Homosexual couples as a case study. In M. A. Fitzpatrick & A. L. Vangelisti (Eds.), *Explaining family interactions* (pp. 310–343). Thousand Oaks, CA: Sage.

Steenland, S. (1995). Content analysis of the image of women on television. In C. M. Lont (Ed.), *Women and media: Content, careers, criticism* (pp. 179–190). Belmont, CA: Wadsworth.

Stein, S. J. (2004, October 22). A decentered religious world. *Chronicle of Higher Education, 51,* p. 4C.

Steiner, A. (2001, February). Childless . . . with children. *Utne Reader, 103,* 72–74.

Steinglass, P. (1987). A systems view of family interaction and pathology. In T. Jacob (Ed.), *Family interaction and psychotherapy* (pp. 113–130). New York: Plenum Press.

Sterk, H. M., & Turner, L. H. (1995). Gender, communication, and community. In L. H. Turner & H. M. Sterk (Eds.), *Differences that make a difference: Examining the assumptions in gender research* (pp. 213–221). Westport, CT: Bergin & Garvey.

Sternberg, R. J. (1986). A triangular theory of love. *Psychological Review, 93,* 119–135.

Stets, J. E., & Straus, M. A. (1990). Gender differences in reporting marital violence and its medical and psychological consequences. In M. A. Straus & R. J. Gelles (Eds.), *Physical violence in American families: Risk factors and adaptations to violence in 8,145 families* (pp. 151–165). New Brunswick, NJ: Transaction Books.

Stewart, C. J., Smith, C. A., & Denton, R. E. (2006). *Persuasion and social movements.* Prospect Heights, IL: Waveland Press.

Stewart, P. (2010). Stress and coping in African American families. In S. Price, C. A. Price, & P. McHenry (Eds.), *Families and change: Coping with stressful events and transitions* (pp. 311–332). Thousand Oaks, CA: Sage.

Stone, E. (2008). *Black sheep and kissing cousins: How our family stories shape us.* New York: Penguin Books.

Strom, B. (2003). Communicator virtue and its relation to marriage quality. *Journal of Family Communication, 3,* 21–40.

Strong, B., DeVault, C., & Cohen, T. F. (2010). *The marriage and family experience: Intimate relationships in a changing world.* Boston, MA: Wadsworth.

Strong, B., DeVault, C., Sayad, B. W., & Yarber, W. L. (2005). *Human sexuality: Diversity in America.* New York: McGraw-Hill.

Sugarman, S. D. (1998). Single-parent families. In M. A. Mason, A. Skolnick, & S. D. Sugarman (Eds.), *All our families* (pp. 23–39). New York: Oxford University Press.

Suggs, P. K. (1989). Predictors of association among older siblings: A black/white comparison. *American Behavioral Scientist, 33,* 70–80.

Sujah, R. (2009). Premarital sexual behaviour among unmarried college students of Gujarat, India. Retrieved from *http://www.popcouncil.org/pdfs/wp/India_HPIF/009.pdf.*

Sullivan, P. A., & Goldzwig, S. R. (1996). "Women's reality" and the untold story: *Designing Women* and the revisioning of the Thomas/Hill hearings. In P. Siegel (Ed.), *Outsiders looking in: A communication perspective on the Hill/Thomas hearings* (pp. 229–247). Cresskill, NJ: Hampton.

Swanson, A. B., & Cahn, D. D. (2009). A communication perspective on physical child abuse. In D. D. Cahn (Ed.), *Family violence: Communication processes* (pp. 135–153). Albany, NY: SUNY Press.

Talbot, M. (2001, February 4). A desire to duplicate. *New York Times Magazine,* pp. 40–45, 67–68.

Tannen, D. (1990). *You just don't understand: Women and men in conversation.* New York: Ballantine.

Tarrant, A. (2009). Constructing a social geography of grandparenthood: A new focus for intergenerationality. *Area, 42,* 190–197.

Tarrant, A. (2010). Constructing a social geography of grandparenthood: A new focus for intergenerationality. *Royal Geographical Society, 42,* 190–197.

Tavernise, S. (2011). Married couples are no longer a majority, Census finds. Retrieved from *http://www.nytimes.com/2011/05/26/us/26marry.html.*

Taylor, E. (1989). *Prime time families: Television culture in postwar America.* Berkeley, CA: University of California Press.

Taylor, H. (2003). The religious and other beliefs of Americans: 2003. Retrieved from *www.harrisinteractive.com.*

Teachman, J. D. (2000). Diversity of family structure: Economic and social influences. In D. H. Demo, K. R. Allen, & M. A. Fine (Eds.), *Handbook of family diversity* (pp. 32–58). Oxford: Oxford University Press.

Tenenbaum, H. R., & Leaper, C. (2002). Are parents' gender schemas related to their children's gender-related cognitions?: A meta-analysis. *Developmental Psychology, 38,* 615–630.

Theiss, J. (2011). Modeling Dyadic Effects in the Associations Between Relational Uncertainty, Sexual Communication, and Sexual Satisfaction for Husbands and Wives. *Communication Research, 38,* 565–584.

Thibaut, J., & Kelley, H. (1959). *The social psychology of groups.* New York: Wiley.

Thomas, C. E., Booth-Butterfield, M., & Booth-Butterfield, S. (1995). Perceptions of deception, divorce disclosure, and communication satisfaction with parents. *Western Journal of Communication, 59,* 228–245.

Thorne, B. (1992). Feminism and the family: Two decades of thought. In B. Thorne & M. Yalom (Eds.), *Rethinking the family: Some feminist questions* (pp. 1–9). Boston: Northeastern University Press.

Thornton, A., Axinn, W. G., & Hill, D. H. (1992). Reciprocal effects of religiosity, cohabitation, and marriage. *American Journal of Sociology, 98,* 628–651.

Thorson, A. R. (2012). Parental infidelity: Adult children's attributions for parents' extramarital relationships. In F.C. Dickson & L.M. Webb (Eds.), *Communication for families in crisis: Theories, research, strategies* (pp. 55–75). New York: Peter Lang.

Tierney, J. (2007, November 20). Are scientists playing God? It depends on your religion. *The New York Times,* p. 14–15.

Tinklenberg-Devega, J., & Ortega Guarkee, C. (2012). *All you want to know but didn't think you could ask: Religions, cults, and popular beliefs.* Scotland: Thomas Nelson.

Timmer, S. G., & Veroff, J. (2000). Family ties and the discontinuity of divorce in black and white newlywed couples. *Journal of Marriage and the Family, 62,* 349–362.

Todd, J. T. (2009). Warriors for Christ: Is Promise Keepers making a comeback? Retrieved from *http://www.alternet.org/belief/142000/warriors_for_christ%3A_is_ promise_keepers_making_a_comeback/?page=1.*

Tong, R. (1989). *Feminist thought: A comprehensive introduction.* Boulder, CO: Westview.

Torquati, J. C. (2002). Personal and social resources as predictors of parenting in homeless families. *Journal of Family Issues, 23,* 463–485.

Trees, A. R. (2000). Nonverbal communication and the support process: Interactional sensitivity in interactions between mothers and young adult children. *Communication Monographs, 67,* 239–261.

Trees, A. R., & Kellas, J. K. (2009). Telling tales: Enacting family relationships in joint storytelling about difficult family experiences. *Western Journal of Communication, 73,* 91–111.

Tueth, M. V. (2004). *Laughter in the living room.* New York: Peter Lang.

Turner, H. A., & Finkelhor, D. (1996). Corporal punishment as a stressor among youth. *Journal of Marriage and the Family, 58,* 155–166.

Turner, L. H. (1997). "Return to life": Communicating in families of the Holocaust. In L. A. M. Perry & P. Geist (Eds.), *Courage of conviction: Women's words, women's wisdom* (pp. 221–234). Mountain View, CA: Mayfield.

Turner, L. H. (2012). Constructing the grandmother-granddaughter relationship through communication: A review of the relevant literature. In A. Deakins, H. Sterk, & R. Lockridge (Eds.), *Mothers and daughters: Complicated connections across cultures.* New York: Rowman & Littlefield.

Turner, L. H., & West, R. (2003). Breaking through the silence: Increasing voice for diverse families in communication research. *Journal of Family Communication, 3,* 181–186.

Turner, L. H., & West, R. (2011). "Sustaining the dialogue": National culture and family communication. *Journal of Family Communication, 11,* 67–68.

U.S. Census Bureau. (1990). Marital status of the population by sex and age: 1988. In *Statistical Abstract of the United States* (pp. 41–42). Washington, D.C.: U.S. Government Printing Office.

U.S. Census Bureau. (2003). Two married parents the norm. Retrieved from *www. census.gov/Press-Release/www/2003/cb03-97.html.*

U.S. Census Bureau. (2011a). Grandparents as caregivers. Retrieved from *http://www. census.gov/newsroom/releases/archives/facts_for_features_special_editions/cb08-ff14.html.*

U.S. Census Bureau. (2011b). Older Americans month. Retrieved from *http://www.census. gov/newsroom/releases/archives/facts_for_features_special_editions/cb11-ff08.html.*

U.S. Census Bureau. (2011c). Resident population of the United States. Retrieved from *https://www.census.gov/prod/2011pubs/11statab/pop.pdf.*

U.S. Department of Health and Human Services. (2000). Report to the Congress on kinship foster care. Retrieved from *www.aspc.hhs.gov/hsp.kin-2000/index/htm.*

Uhlenberg, P., & Kirby, J. B. (1998). Grandparenthood over time: Historical and demographic trends. In M. E. Szinovacz (Ed.), *Handbook on grandparenthood* (pp. 23–39). Westport, CT: Greenwood.

Unger, D. N. S. (2010). *Men can: The changing image and reality of fatherhood in America.* Philadelphia: Temple University Press.

Urrichio, W. (2005). Television's next generation: Technology/interface culture/flow. In L. Spigel & J. Olsson (Eds.), *Television after TV: Essays on a medium in transition* (pp. 232–261). Durham, NC: Duke University Press.

Valentine, C. (2010). The role of ancestral tradition of bereavement in contemporary Japanese society. *Mortality, 15,* 275–293.

Vangelisti, A. L. (1993). Communication in the family: The influence of time, relational prototypes and irrationality. *Communication Monographs, 60,* 42–54.

Vangelisti, A. L. (1994). Family secrets: Forms, functions, and correlates. *Journal of Social and Personal Relationships, 11,* 113–136.

Vangelisti, A. L. (2004). Introduction. In A. L. Vangelisti (Ed.), *Handbook of family communication* (pp. xiii–xx). Mahwah, NJ: Erlbaum.

Vangelisti, A. L., & Banski, M. A. (1993). Couples debriefing conversations: The impact of gender, occupation, and demographic characteristics. *Family Relations, 42,* 149–157.

Veroff, J., Sutherland, L., Chadiha, L., & Ortega, R. M. (1993). Newlyweds tell their stories: A narrative method for assessing marital experiences. *Journal of Social and Personal Relationships, 10,* 437–457.

Viorst, J. (1987). *Necessary losses: The loves, illusions, dependencies, and impossible expectations that all of us have to give up in order to grow.* New York: Fawcett Gold Medal.

Vissing, Y., & Baily, W. (1996). Parent-to-child verbal aggression. In D. D. Cahn & S. A. Lloyd (Eds.), *Family violence from a communication perspective* (pp. 85–107). Thousand Oaks, CA: Sage.

Vogl-Bauer, S., Kalbfleisch, P. J., & Beatty, M. J. (1999). Perceived equity, satisfaction, and relational maintenance strategies in parent-adolescent dyads. *Journal of Youth and Adolescence, 28,* 27–50.

von Bertalanffy, L. (1968). *General system theory.* New York: George Braziller.

von Bertalanffy, L. (1975). *Perspectives on general system theory: Scientific-philosophical studies.* New York: George Braziller.

Vondra, J. I. (1990). Sociological and ecological factors. In R. T. Ammerman & M. Hersen (Eds.), *Children at risk: An evaluation of factors contributing to child abuse and neglect* (pp. 149–170). New York: Plenum Press.

Wahlroos, S. (1995). *Family communication.* Chicago, IL: Contemporary Books.

Walker, C. (1996). Can TV save the planet? Retrieved from *www.demographics.com/htm.*

Walker, J. R., & Bellamy, R. V. (2001). Remote control devices and family viewing. In J. Bryant & J. A. Bryant (Eds.), *Television and the American family* (pp. 75–90). Mahwah, NJ: Erlbaum.

Walker, R., Logan, T. K., Jordan, C. E., & Campbell, J. (2004). An integrative review of separation in the context of victimization: Consequences and implications for women. *Journal of Trauma, Violence and Abuse, 5,* 143–193.

Walkover, B. C. (1992). The family as an overwrought object of desire. In G. C. Rosenwald & R. L. Ochberg (Eds.), *Storied lives: The cultural politics of self-understanding* (pp. 178–191). New Haven, CT: Yale University Press.

Wallerstein, J. S. (1985). Children of divorce: Preliminary report of a ten-year follow-up of older children and adolescents. *Journal of the American Academy of Child Psychiatry, 24,* 545–553.

Wallerstein, J. S., Lewis, J. M., & Blakeslee, S. (2000). *The unexpected legacy of divorce.* New York: Hyperion.

Wallsten, S. S. (2000). Effects of caregiving, gender, and race on the health, mutuality, and social supports of older couples. *Journal of Aging and Health, 12,* 90–111.

Walsh, F. (2011). Families in later life: Challenges, opportunities, and resilience. In M. McGoldrick, B. Carter, & Nydia Garcia Preto (Eds.), *The expanded family life cycle: Individual, family, and social perspectives* (pp. 261–277). Boston, MA: Allyn & Bacon.

Wang, S. W., Repetti, R., & Campos, B. (2011). Job stress and family social behavior: The moderating role of neuroticism. *Journal of Occupational Health Psychology, 10,* 441–456.

Warren, C. (1995). Parent–child communication about sex. In T. Socha & G. H. Stamp (Eds.), *Parents, children, and communication* (pp. 173–202). Mahwah, NJ: Erlbaum.

Warren, J., Allen, M., Hopfer, S., & Okuyemi, K. (2010). Contextualizing single parent–preadolescent drug use talks. *Qualitative Research Reports in Communication, 11,* 29–36.

Wartella, E. (Ed.). (1997). *National television violence study.* Thousand Oaks, CA: Sage.

Watzlawick, P., Beavin, J. H., & Jackson, D. D. (1967). *Pragmatics of human communication.* New York: Norton.

Weeks, G. R. (1986). Individual-system dialectic. *American Journal of Family Therapy, 14,* 5–12.

Weigel, D. J. (2003). A communication approach to the construction of commitment in the early years of marriage: A qualitative study. *Journal of Family Communication, 3,* 1–19.

Weigel, D. J., & Ballard-Reisch, D. S. (1999). The influence of marital duration on the use of relationship maintenance behaviors. *Communication Reports, 12,* 59–70.

Weigel, D. J., & Ballard-Reisch, D. S. (2001). The impact of maintenance behaviors on marital satisfaction: A longitudinal analysis. *Journal of Family Communication, 1,* 265–279.

Weigel, D. J., & Ballard-Reisch, D. S. (2008). Relational maintenance, satisfaction, and commitment in marriages: An actor-partner analysis. *Journal of Family Communication, 8,* 212–29.

Weiner-Levy, N. (2011). Patriarchs or feminists? Relations between fathers and trailblazing daughters in Druze society. *Journal of Family Communication, 11,* 126–147.

Weitzman, L. J. (1985). *The divorce revolution: The unexpected social and economic consequences for women and children in America.* New York: Free Press.

West, R. (1996). *Confronting racist talk in elementary/secondary classrooms.* Paper presented at the annual meeting of the Speech Communication Association, San Diego, CA.

West, R., & McCall, K. (1997). *Finding empowerment in crisis: A qualitative study of the effects of rape on two women.* Paper presented at the annual meeting of the Speech Communication Association Conference, Chicago, IL.

West, R., & Turner, L. H. (1995). Communication in lesbian and gay families: Developing a descriptive base. In T. Socha & G. Stamp (Eds.), *Parents, children, and communication* (pp. 147–170). Mahwah, NJ: Erlbaum.

Westheimer, R. (1998). *Dr. Ruth talks to kids.* New York: Simon and Schuster.

Whipp, G. (2011). Modern family. *Variety,* A7.

Whitchurch, G. G. (1992). Communication in marriages and families: A review essay of family communication textbooks. *Communication Education, 41,* 337–343.

Whitchurch, G. G., & Constantine, L. L. (1993). Systems theory. In P. G. Boss, W. J. Doherty, R. LaRossa, W. R. Schumm, & S. K. Steinmetz (Eds.), *Source book of family theories and methods: A contextual approach* (pp. 325–352). New York: Plenum Press.

White, J. M. (1991). *Dynamics of family development: A theoretical perspective.* New York: Guilford.

White, J. M. (2005). *Advancing family theories.* Thousand Oaks, CA: Sage.

White, J. M., & Klein, D. M. (2002). *Family theories*. Thousand Oaks, CA: Sage.

Whitson, M., Connell, C. M., Bernard, S., & Kaufman, J. S. (in press). An examination of exposure to traumatic events and symptoms and strengths for children served in a behavioral health system of care. *Journal of Emotional and Behavioral Disorders*.

Whitson, M., Martinez, A., Ayala, C., & Kaufman, J.S. (2011). Predictors of parenting and infant outcomes for impoverished teen parents. *Journal of Family Social Work, 14*, 284–297.

Whittier, N. (2002). Persistence and transformation: Gloria Steinem, the Women's Action Alliance, and the Feminist Movement, 1971–1997. *Journal of Women's History, 13*, 1–4.

Wilcox, W. B., Chaves, M., & Franz, D. (2004). Focused on the family? Religious traditions, family discourse, and pastoral practice. *Journal for the Scientific Study of Religion, 43*, 491–504.

Wilcox, W.B. (2012). The facts of life & marriage. Retrieved from *http://www.holyspiritinteractive.net/columns/guests/wbradfordwilcox/fatsoflife.asp*.

Wilkinson, D. (1997). American families of African descent. In M. K. DeGenova (Ed.), *Families in cultural context: Strengths and challenges in diversity* (pp. 35–53). Mountain View, CA: Mayfield.

Wilkinson, H. (2000). Helen Wilkinson, social policy commentator. Retrieved from *www.news2/thls/bbc.co.uk/hi/english/st.99/helen_wilkinson/stm*.

Williams, A. (2011). Quality time, redefined. Retrieved from *http://www.nytimes.com/2011/05/01/fashion/01FAMILY.html?_r=1&adxnnl=1&pagewanted=all&adxnnlx=1336584441-k+YoT0h7z82pda1do6LX5A*.

Williams, L. E., Clinton, K. L., & Wyatt, L. (1995). The impact of racial climate on selected social behaviors: Who's dating and who's not. In C. K. Jacobson (Ed.), *American families: Issues in race and ethnicity* (pp. 325–339). New York: Garland.

Williams, R. H. (2000). Promise Keepers: A comment on religion and social movements. *Sociology of Religion, 61*, 1–10.

Willis, K. (2011). *Theories and practices of development*. New York: Routledge.

Wilmot, W., & Hocker, J. (2011). *Interpersonal conflict*, New York: McGraw-Hill.

Wilson, S. R., Norris, A. M., Shi, X., & Rack, J. J. (2010). Comparing physically abused, neglected, and nonmaltreated children during interactions with their parents: A meta-analysis of observational studies. *Communication Monographs, 77*, 540–575.

Wilson, S. R., Wilkum, K., Chernichky, S. M., MacDermid Wadsworth, S. M., & Broniarczyk, K. M. (2011). Passport toward success: Description and evaluation of a program designed to help children and families reconnect after a military deployment. *Journal of Applied Communication Research, 39*, 223–249.

Wolf, N. (1993). *Fire with fire: The new female power and how it will change the 21st century*. New York: Random House.

Wolin, S. J., & Bennett, L. A. (1984). Family rituals. *Family Process, 23*, 401–420.

Women: The most active online audience for health information. (2003, February 20). Retrieved from *www.prxy3.ursus.maine.edu*.

Wood, J. T. (1982). Communication and relational culture: Bases for the study of human relationships. *Communication Quarterly, 30*, 75–84.

Wood, J. T. (1995). *Relational communication: Continuity and change in personal relationships*. Belmont, CA: Wadsworth.

Wood, J. T. (2013). *Gendered lives*. Boston: Wadsworth/Cengage.

Wood, J. T., Dordek, E., Germany, M., & Varallo, S. M. (1994). The dialectic of difference: A thematic analysis of intimates' meanings for differences. In K. Carter & M. Presnell (Eds.), *Interpretive approaches to interpersonal communication* (pp. 115–136). New York: SUNY Press.

Worthen, M. (2010). Housewives of God. Retrieved from *http://www.nytimes.com/2010/11/14/magazine/14evangelicals-t.html?pagewanted=all.*

Wright, S. M. (2008). The use of oral narrative in North American families: Creating selves, confirming roles, and consigning traditions. In D. G. Wiseman (Ed.), *The American family* (pp. 145–160). Springfield, IL: Charles C Thomas.

www.agingcare.com. Men as caregivers.

www.barna.org/barna-update/article/13-culture/286-how-the-faith-of-african-americans-has-changed. How the faith of African Americans has changed.

www.blog.childtrends.org/2011/06/06/the-problem-with-children-watching-television. The problem with children watching television.

www.blog.nielsen.com/nielsenwire/media_entertainment/number-of-u-s-tv-housoeo-holds-climbs-by-one-million-for-2010-11-tv-season. Number of U.S. TV households climbs by one million for 2010–11 TV season.

www.bls.gov/tus/charts/LEISURE.HTM. Leisure and sports activities.

www.caregiving.org/research. General caregiving surveys.

www.childpolicy.org. Policy and program links.

www.childtrendsdatabank.org/?q=node/261. Watching television.

www.citizenlink.com. Family policy councils.

www.cnn.com/2011/OPINION/6/27/frum.gay.marriage/index.html. I was wrong about same-sex marriage.

www.divorcerate.com. Divorce rate by age or religion.

www.globalsecurity.org. The family unit.

www.huffingtonpost.com/susan-whiting/tv-were-still-watching_b_208329.html. TV: We're still watching.

www.komen.org/aboutus. About us.

www.marriagesavers.com. Welcome to Marriage Savers.

www.nccp.org. Child poverty.

www.ontheissues.org/2012/Ron_Paul_Civil_Rights.htm. Ron Paul on civil rights.

www.parentfurther.com. What makes your "modern family" strong?

www.unmarried.org/statistics.html. Alternatives to marriage project.

www.usnews.com/debate-club/should-gay-marriage-be-legal-nationwide/without-nationwide-gay-marriage-us-government-discriminates. Without nationwide gay marriage. U.S. government discriminates.

www.usinfo.state.gov/journals. Fact sheet.

www.workingmother.com/node/116542/list. 2011 Working Mother 100 best companies.

Xing, X., Wang, M., Zhang, Q., He, X., & Zhang, W. (2011). Gender differences in the reciprocal relationships between parental physical aggression and children's externalizing problem behavior in China. *Journal of Family Psychology, 25,* 699–708.

Yancey-Martin, P., & Hummer, R. A. (1995). Fraternities and rape on campus. In M. L. Andersen & P. H. Collins (Eds.), *Race, class, and gender: An anthology* (pp. 420–427). Belmont, CA: Wadsworth.

Yelsma, P. (1986). Marriage vs. cohabitation: Couples communication practices and satisfaction. *Journal of Communication, 36,* 94–107.

Yenko, J. (2011). Men and remotes. Retrieved from *http://jayne-yenko.suite101.com/men-and-remotes-a331352.*

Yerby, J. (1995). Family systems theory reconsidered: Integrating social construction theory and dialectical process. *Communication Theory, 5,* 339–365.

Young, M. A., & Kleist, D. M. (2010). The relationship process in healthy couple relationships: A grounded theory. *The Family Journal: Counseling and Therapy for Couples and Families, 18,* 338–343.

Zambrana, R. A. (2011). *Latinos in American society: Families and communities in transition.* Ithaca, NY: Cornell University Press.

Zandpour, F., & Sadri, G. (1996). Communication and personal relationships in Iran: A comparative analysis. In W. B. Gudykunst, S. Ting-Toomey, & T. Nishida (Eds.), *Communication and personal relationships across cultures* (pp. 174–196). Newbury Park, CA: Sage.

Zeiger, G. (2000, August). Old soul: How aging reveals character. *Sun, 296,* 4–9.

Zelizer, G. L. (2002, December 19). Men's absence undercuts family worship. *USA Today,* 23A.

Zhou, M. (2001). Straddling different worlds: The acculturation of Vietnamese refugee children. In R. G. Rumbaut & A. Portes (Eds.), *Ethnicities: Children of immigrants in America* (pp. 187–227). Berkeley, CA: University of California Press.

Zielinger, J. (2012). *A little f'd up: Why feminism is not a dirty word.* Jackson, TN: Seal Press.

Zimmerman, S. (1992). *Family policies and family well-being: The role of the political culture.* Newbury Park, CA: Sage.

Credits

Text and Illustrations

Photos

Name Index

Subject Index